Moral Psychology

Moral Psychology

Volume 1: The Evolution of Morality: Adaptations and Innateness

edited by Walter Sinnott-Armstrong

A Bradford Book
The MIT Press
Cambridge, Massachusetts
London, England

MIT Press books may be purchased at special quantity discounts for business or sales promotional use. For information, please e-mail special_sales@mitpress.mit.edu or write to Special Sales Department, The MIT Press, 55 Hayward Street, Cambridge, MA 02142.

This book was set in Stone Sans and Stone Serif by SNP Best-set Typesetter Ltd., Hong Kong and was printed and bound in the United States of America.

Library of Congress Cataloging-in-Publication Data

Moral psychology / edited by Walter Sinnott-Armstrong.
    v.   cm.
"A Bradford Book."
Includes bibliographical references and index.
Contents: v. 1. The evolution of morality: adaptations and innateness—v. 2. The cognitive science of morality: intuition and diversity—v. 3. The neuroscience of morality: emotion, disease, and development.
ISBN 978-0-262-19561-4 (vol. 1: hardcover : alk. paper)—ISBN 978-0-262-69354-7 (vol. 1: pbk. : alk. paper)—ISBN 978-0-262-19569-0 (vol. 2: hardcover : alk. paper)—ISBN 978-0-262-69357-8 (vol. 2: pbk. : alk. paper)—ISBN 978-0-262-19564-5 (vol. 3: hardcover : alk. paper)—ISBN 978-0-262-69355-4 (vol. 3: pbk. : alk. paper)
1. Ethics. 2. Psychology and philosophy. 3. Neurosciences. I. Sinnott-Armstrong, Walter, 1955–
BJ45.M66   2007
170—dc22   2006035509

10 9 8 7 6 5 4 3 2 1

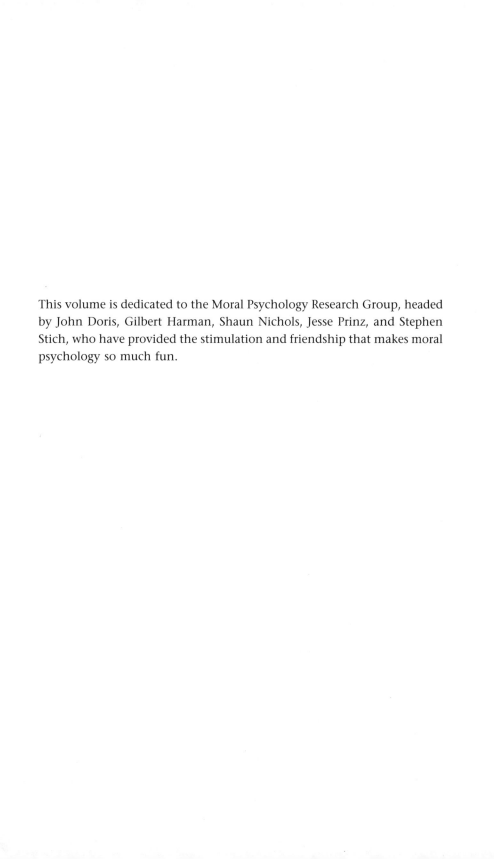

This volume is dedicated to the Moral Psychology Research Group, headed by John Doris, Gilbert Harman, Shaun Nichols, Jesse Prinz, and Stephen Stich, who have provided the stimulation and friendship that makes moral psychology so much fun.

Contents

Acknowledgments

Many people deserve my thanks for assistance as these volumes grew. For financial support of the conference that sowed the seeds for this project, I am grateful to several institutions at Dartmouth College, including the Leslie Center for the Humanities, the Dickey Center for International Understanding, the Master of Arts in Liberal Studies program, the Dean of the Faculty, the Department of Psychological and Brain Sciences, the Social Brain Science Project, the Cognitive Neuroscience Center, the Department of Philosophy, and the Institute for Applied and Professional Ethics. For help in making these essays more accessible to students, I thank Cate Birtley, Cole Entress, and Ben Shear, Dartmouth students who served as my Presidential Scholars. I also greatly appreciate the devotion and editorial skills of Kier Olsen DeVries, who worked long and hard to put the essays from these diverse authors into a single form for the publisher. Tom Stone, my editor at MIT Press, also has my gratitude for his spirited encouragement. Last but not least, I thank my family—Liz, Miranda, and Nick—for their love and patience while I spent many nights and weekends on this project.

Introduction

Walter Sinnott-Armstrong

Philosophy and science used to be close friends. Many philosophers from Aristotle to Descartes and Leibniz were leading scientists as well. Philosophers who did not do experiments still often cited contemporary science to support their philosophical views. And almost all philosophers at least tried to make their views compatible with the most recent empirical discoveries.

This friendship became strained during the twentieth century. One influence seems to have been specialization within universities. Science became so technical and labs became so large that it was practically impossible for mere mortals to do science well and also engage in philosophy. Philosophers also needed to show that they were doing something different than science in order to justify having their own departments.

Particular pressures arose within moral philosophy. G. E. Moore's (1903) diatribe against the so-called "naturalistic fallacy" set the stage for twentieth-century ethics. The main protagonists for the next sixty years—intuitionists and emotivists—were both convinced by Moore that empirical science is irrelevant to moral philosophy and to common moral beliefs. Even in the 1970s and 1980s, when a wider array of moral theories entered the scene, few moral philosophers paid much attention to developments in biology and psychology. Applied ethicists did use science to determine the facts that they needed in order to apply general moral theories to individual cases, but science was still usually seen as useless for moral theory itself.

Since the 1990s, in contrast, many philosophers have begun to mine cognitive psychology and brain science, as well as evolutionary biology, for general philosophical lessons. Philosophers have also begun to conduct their own experiments designed specifically to address philosophical issues. These collaborative projects are pursued vigorously by biologists and psychologists working with philosophers, although they have encountered stiff opposition from some more traditional philosophers. This new way of doing philosophy has reached philosophy of mind, epistemology, and philosophy of science, but it is especially strong in ethics or moral philosophy.

Although this trend continues to grow, much of this new research has been spread thinly through many journals that most philosophers rarely read. This placement limits the effect of this work. The current collection is intended to overcome this problem by bringing together some of the most innovative, insightful, and informed philosophers and psychologists working in this new way. The goal is to make it easier for anyone—philosopher, psychologist, or neuroscientist—who is considering joining this movement to discover how exciting it can be.

The first volume in this series includes recent work on the evolution of moral beliefs, attitudes, and emotions. The opening chapter is a wide-ranging survey of methodological issues.[1] Owen Flanagan, Hagop Sarkissian, and David Wong define "naturalism" (as opposed to both "supernaturalism" and "non-naturalism"), argue that moral theory should be naturalized, analyze why there is so much resistance to naturalism in ethics, and show how their version of naturalism avoids supposed fallacies, such as Moore's naturalistic fallacy. Finally, Flanagan et al. claim that normative ethics is best conceived as part of human ecology committed to pluralistic relativism, and they propose a neocompatibilist view of human agency and free will. This overall position is named "Duke naturalism," after the authors' home base.

In his comment, William Casebeer adds "three cheers for Flanagan et al." by tying their position to the demise of the analytic/synthetic distinction, to the neuroscience of executive control, and to evolved functions. Michael Ruse then points out that, because Duke naturalism depends on human nature, it avoids terrestrial relativism but allows intergalactic relativism, according to which rational beings who lack our human nature have no reason to accept the restrictions that seem natural to us as humans. The final commentator, Peter Railton, suggests that the arguments of Flanagan, Sarkissian, and Wong actually support a healthy, tolerant, pluralistic sort of moral *relationalism* which is a more intuitively plausible alternative to the ecological pluralistic *relativism* of Duke naturalists. Flanagan, Sarkissian, and Wong reply to these comments by asking whether morality by its nature must provide strong objective prescriptivity and whether relational accounts of morality can accommodate variations in fundamental moral ends.[2]

Whereas the first chapter featured philosophers commenting on evolution and psychology, the second chapter includes psychologists commenting on philosophy. Leda Cosmides and John Tooby, founders of evolutionary psychology, survey their research on how people reason about various kinds of deontic conditionals, including moral conditionals. Their empirical findings are said to be explained best by hypothesizing that people use different evolved neurocomputational systems when they reason about social exchange than when they reason about precautionary rules. This multiplicity of neural systems suggests that no single general deontic logic can respect important distinctions made in our actual deontic reasoning. If evolutionary psychologists are right, then deontic logicians (and other philosophers) cannot get all they want.[3]

Ron Mallon comments that Cosmides and Tooby's data could be explained by Richard Samuels's Library Model of Cognition without domain-specific computational mechanisms, that domain-general mechanisms and deontic logic are needed to handle cross-domain conflicts, and that deontic logics need not match computational mechanisms in order to achieve their goals. Jerry Fodor then claims that the data invoked by Cosmides and Tooby show only that content affects inferential processes, not that logical form does not affect inferential processes, but the latter claim is what Cosmides and Tooby need to support their skepticism about general deontic logic. Cosmides and Tooby reply by arguing that they do not need to deny observed effects of logical form and also that previous experiments refute both Fodor's counterhypothesis and any interpretation of the Library Model of Cognition that is incompatible with their theory.[4]

The next chapter, by Debra Lieberman, applies the general approach of evolutionary psychology to moral prohibitions and moral sentiments about incest in particular. Lieberman argues that moral sentiments regarding inbreeding by other people are by-products of adaptations designed to prevent incest by oneself, which evolved to prevent the negative fitness consequences associated with inbreeding. Lieberman cites her own studies to argue against the Standard Social Science Model and for Edward Westermarck's 1922 hypothesis that early childhood association, which typically occurs among genetic relatives, triggers the development of a sexual aversion that serves as an inbreeding avoidance mechanism. This particular example is used to raise larger issues about moral sentiments in general and why and how evolution shaped human psychology to monitor others' behaviors.

Arthur Wolf comments that Lieberman still needs accounts of what "moral" means and of how a person's aversion to sexual relations with his own kin leads to his condemning other people for taking a sexual interest in their kin, but he suggests that both accounts can be found, again, in Westermarck. Richard Joyce then argues that, even if Lieberman has established mechanisms that motivate humans to avoid incest and act against third-party incest, these mechanisms still might not affect motivation by means of distinctively moral judgments or moral sentiments, so Lieberman's position might be compatible with some antinativist views of morality.[5] In her reply, Lieberman clarifies her use of the terms "moral" and "sentiment" as well as her bottom-up method.

In chapter 4, Geoffrey Miller appeals to a very different evolutionary process, namely, sexual selection, in order to explain many aspects of human morality, especially moral virtues. In Miller's view, humans tend to choose mates with moral virtues because these moral virtues advertise both good genetic quality and good parenting abilities. To support this theory, Miller integrates recent research on mate choice, person perception, individual differences, costly signaling, and virtue ethics. He applies his theory to a wide range of moral virtues, including kindness, fidelity, magnanimity, and heroism, as well as quasi-moral traits, such as intelligence, conscientiousness, agreeableness, mental health, religiosity, and social status. Miller emphasizes that his account does not make moral virtues covertly sexual but does create problems for reflective equilibrium and other popular philosophical models of moral reflection.[6]

Catherine Driscoll criticizes Miller's sexual selection story on the grounds that moral virtues are too easy to fake and are more costly than other available ways of signaling fitness, and she provides alternative stories that might explain the same aspects of morality. Oliver Curry then argues that Miller's theory cannot account for virtues displayed in contexts other than courtship or for the traditional Christian virtues, both of which can be explained by Curry's more comprehensive conflict-resolution theory of virtue. Miller replies that moral virtues are harder to fake than Driscoll assumes, that moral virtues need not be the most efficient possible indicators of fitness to have evolved by sexual selection, and that Curry's conflict-resolution model is less a rival than a complementary costly signaling account.

The fifth chapter, by Peter Tse, focuses on the evolution of symbolic thought and its effect on human morality. In Tse's view, symbolic thought became possible when binding became a domain-general operator that could operate over many kinds of modules and link them into a common representation in a single object file. The breakdown of strict modularity permitted the emergence of abstraction, metaphorical thought, and entrainment across modules, giving birth to phenomena as diverse as dance, imaginary play, music, reminiscence, and religion. Morality also came into being because of our capacities to symbolize and to generalize to a level of categorical abstraction. Once symbolized, individual acts and things could be seen as instances of categories of events that are good or evil, acceptable or unacceptable, sanctioned or not. Tse shows how human symbolic processing gives rise to several "roots of human evil," including tokenization, sadism, rejection of the body, and culture.

Tse's commentators include a biologist and a philosopher. Michael Dietrich challenges Tse to provide more engineering details regarding neuronal and genetic mechanisms. Kathleen Wallace then questions Tse's apparent assumptions about morality, especially in his discussions of tokenization and sadism.[7] Tse replies to Dietrich that his admittedly speculative hypothesis can guide research before the engineering details are pinned down and to Wallace that his theory is descriptive, rather than prescriptive or normative, so he did not intend to address questions in moral philosophy, such as whether tokenization is good or bad.

The last two chapters turn to the related topic of innateness. On many views, if morality evolved biologically, then morality should be innate in some way. Chandra Sekhar Sripada defends a kind of innate morality, then Jesse Prinz rejects innate morality.

Sripada's chapter usefully distinguishes three models of what he calls "content nativism." Sripada argues against the Simple Innateness Model, which postulates an innate body of moral rules and principles, and also against the Principles and Parameters Model, which claims that morality is analogous to natural languages, whose basic principles are supposed to be partly innate, according to Noam Chomsky.[8] Sripada favors the Innate Biases Model, which claims that some innate structure makes the presence of some moral norms more likely without requiring or precluding any particular moral norm. Such biases might work by affecting either the emergence of moral norms[9] or the transmission of moral norms from one individual to another.[10] Sripada shows how these mechanisms can help us understand cultural change in the contents of moral norms.

In his comment, Gilbert Harman suggests that all three models might capture bases that have a significant impact on human morality, but we cannot be sure until more of the supposed moral grammar is specified. John Mikhail then defends the poverty-of-the-stimulus argument in support of the analogy between morality and language as Chomsky sees it. Sripada replies that Harman's and Mikhail's criticisms miss the mark, because they focus on capacity nativism, whereas content nativism was his topic and is best understood in terms of his Innate Biases Model.

Jesse Prinz argues for the opposite answer to the question "Is morality innate?" Prinz admits, of course, that morality depends on having particular biological predispositions, but he argues that none of these deserve to be called a "moral faculty." In his view, morality is a by-product of faculties that evolved for other purposes, including nonmoral emotions, preferences, behavioral dispositions, and perspective taking. As a result, morality is considerably more variable and versatile than nativism requires. To support these claims, Prinz discusses supposed universal moral norms,[11] universal moral domains,[12] fixed stages in moral development,[13] and precursors to morality among nonhuman animals. His wide-ranging romp touches on moral modules,[14] moral emotions,[15] the linguistic analogy,[16] and the distinction between morality and convention.[17] In the end, Prinz suggests that morality is not a hardwired mechanism but, instead, something we construct that we can change and improve upon.

In her comment, Susan Dwyer defends a faculty nativism about morality based on an analogy to language. Valerie Tiberius then discusses the relevance of moral nativism for moral philosophy in general, particularly debates about moral motivation and the justification of moral beliefs, concluding that psychologists and philosophers need to think together about how to improve morality in the way Prinz envisions. Prinz replies with new speculations about how children could learn morality from experience and new suggestions about how the nativism debate could bear on philosophical theories in ethics.

Together the chapters in this volume display how fruitful interchanges between psychologists and philosophers can be. None of these debates is close to being resolved. Indeed, almost all would admit that their basic terms need more precise and explicit reformulations and that they need much more empirical data. It is clear, nonetheless, that psychologists and philosophers have a lot to learn from each other and must work together if anyone in either field is to understand the many complex aspects of morality.

Notes

1. These methodological issues are revisited in many chapters in this collection, but especially in Joyce's closing chapter in the third volume.

2. This exchange on relativism is relevant to the chapter by Doris and Plakias in the second volume of this collection.

3. Further grounds for skepticism about the univocity of "ought" can be found in Loeb's chapter in the second volume of this collection.

4. Additional criticisms of Cosmides and Tooby's views can be found in Prinz's chapter in this volume.

5. An antinativist view is developed with reference to incest in Prinz's chapter in this volume.

6. Additional grounds for skepticism about reflective equilibrium can be found in Doris and Plakias's chapter in the second volume and in Greene's chapter in the third volume in this collection.

7. Wallace compares sadism to psychopathy in ways that can usefully be compared with the chapters by Kiehl and by Kennett and Fine in the third volume of this collection.

8. The analogy between morality and language is explored further by Prinz and his commentators in this volume and again by Hauser, Young, and Cushman and their commentators in the second volume in this collection.

9. As an example of emergence, Sripada discusses Westermarck's view of incest norms, which was covered in more depth in Lieberman's chapter in this volume.

10. Sripada takes one example of transmission from Shaun Nichols in the book that Nichols summarizes in his chapter in the second volume of this collection.

11. The supposed universality of moral norms is also criticized in the chapter by Doris and Plakias in the second volume of this collection.

12. Prinz targets the view of moral domains postulated in the chapter by Haidt and Bjorklund in the second volume of this collection.

13. Fixed stages of moral development are proposed in the chapters by Kagan and by Baird in the third volume of this collection.

14. Prinz focuses on the view of moral modules defended by Cosmides and Tooby in their chapter in this volume.

15. Moral emotions are also discussed in the chapters by Nichols and by Haidt and Bjorklund in the second volume, as well as in the chapters by Greene and by Moll et al. in the third volume of this collection.

16. The linguistic analogy is also discussed in the chapters by Sripada in this volume and by Hauser, Young, and Cushman in the second volume of this collection.

17. The moral/conventional distinction is also discussed in Nichols's chapter in the second volume of this collection.

Moral Psychology

1 | Naturalizing Ethics

Owen Flanagan, Hagop Sarkissian, and David Wong

Introduction

In this chapter we provide (1) an argument for why ethics should be naturalized, (2) an analysis of why it is not yet naturalized, (3) a defense of ethical naturalism against two fallacies—Hume and Moore's—that ethical naturalism allegedly commits, and (4) a proposal that normative ethics is best conceived as part of *human ecology* committed to *pluralistic relativism* (Flanagan, 1995, 2002; Wong, 1984, 1996, 2006b). The latter substantive view, supported by a neocompatibilist view of human agency, constitutes the essence of *Duke naturalism*. It provides a credible substantive alternative to bald or eliminativist *Australian ethical naturalism*, especially one that supports moral skepticism (Mackie), and to the more reticent *Pittsburgh naturalism*.[1]

Naturalism in the Broad Sense

Ethical naturalism is a variety of a broader philosophical naturalism, so it will be good to say what naturalism in the broad sense is. According to the *OED* the original *philosophical* meaning of the term "naturalism" dates back to the seventeenth century and meant "a view of the world, and of man's relation to it, in which only the operation of natural (as opposed to supernatural or spiritual) laws and forces is admitted or assumed."

In a recent presidential address to the American Philosophical Association, Barry Stroud writes:

Naturalism on any reading is opposed to supernaturalism. . . . By "supernaturalism" I mean the invocation of an agent or force which somehow stands outside the familiar natural world and so whose doings cannot be understood as part of it. Most metaphysical systems of the past included some such agent. A naturalist conception of the world would be opposed to all of them. (Stroud, 1996)[2]

Stroud's comment can either be about ontology (i.e., that naturalists reject agents or forces that stand outside the natural world) or about methodology (i.e., that naturalists reject the invocation of such agents or forces in their philosophical projects). These issues will be fleshed out below. For now, we can note that ethical naturalism holds a number of thin ontological commitments, and some more substantial methodological ones.

Why Ethics Isn't Naturalized

Ethical naturalism has a fair number of philosophical advocates, but most people reject it—including many in the academy. The reason has to do with the close connection in American culture (and throughout much of the rest of the world) between ethics and religion, and thus with the supernatural. Over 90% of Americans believe in a personal God who answers their prayers. Similar numbers believe in heaven (slightly fewer believe in hell). They believe that God, Yahweh, Allah is the source of moral law and he rewards (or punishes) "souls" based on how well they conform to the moral law. Most people believe in God and think that moral knowledge is knowledge of what God creates or endorses as "good," "bad," "right," and "wrong." Religious reasons are offered and accepted in America, and most of the rest of the world, as legitimate moral grounding reasons. Ethical naturalism, as a species of naturalism, rejects religious grounding reasons.

Let us call an individual a *scientific naturalist* if she does not permit the invocation of supernatural forces in understanding, explaining, and accounting for what happens in *this* world. An *ethical naturalist* (assuming this person already accepts scientific naturalism) applies the same principled restriction to describing, explaining, recommending, endorsing, prohibiting, and justifying values, norms, actions, principles, and so on.[3] In other words, the complete warrant for any norm or value must be cashed out without invoking the views or commands of a divinity.

It is an interesting and important question whether one could be a naturalist, either scientific and/or ethical, and still believe in supernatural entities or forces. A full 40% of the scientists listed in *American Men and Women in Science* not only believe in a personal God but also believe he listens to their prayers (Larson & Witham, 1997). Since (almost) all scientists are scientific naturalists at least when it comes to the domain they study in this world, the charitable interpretation is that these scientists believe that God exists in God's world, not in *this* one. If he "listens" to prayers and, especially, if he responds to them, he better utilize the laws of nature without any perceivable interference with their normal operation. So God can't (or at least doesn't) mess with f = ma, the speed of light, the nature of water, neurochemistry, economics, and so on.[4]

Call the folk view that there is a creator God (possibly one to whose bosom "we" go after we leave this world), but to whose thoughts we have no access, and who does no work in this world, has no effects on how this world operates, "folk naturalism." This view is relatively common. Indeed, it must be if we are to make sense charitably of the behavior of scientists who restrict themselves to physical explanation of physical phenomena but believe nonetheless in God.

Most people accept that science can legitimately take the folk naturalistic stance. Seamstresses, carpenters, plumbers, auto mechanics, and scientists all practice as if they are committed to folk naturalism. Scientists take official vows, as it were, when they declare themselves to be scientists in some domain of inquiry. There is no glaring inconsistency in thinking that God set up the world in such a way that scientists or auto mechanics can describe, explain, predict, and manipulate what happens in that world. The fact that there is no inconsistency does not mean it makes epistemic sense—that there are any good reasons—to believe in God.

When it comes to ethics, though, most people will balk at restricting themselves to folk naturalism. For complex reasons (though having to do in some large measure with the importance of morality), most people would like to see moral value justified in a very strong way. It would be good if moral values, beliefs, norms, and the like had something like the necessity that mathematical theorems have. One way this could work is *if* an omniscient and all-loving being makes the rules and then provides us with epistemic access to them. There are various familiar stories of how this works. Human souls exist prior to bodily implantation in the company of "The Good" and, once embodied, have the ability to remember, recollect, or intuit what is good, bad, right, and wrong (Plato; and with certain modifications G. E. Moore). God directly illuminates faithful human hearts and minds through grace (Augustine). God produces a world and mind such that his perfect nature can be deductively established, and with some additional difficulty, his will can be known (Anselm, Descartes, Alvin Plantinga).[5] God speaks to certain sages who write down his moral rules in sacred texts (the *Torah*, the *Old* and *New Testament*, the *Q'ran*), and so on. The last view—that we have epistemic access to God's will and commands through sacred texts—is the dominant view: moral values, norms, and principles have their ultimate ground or warrant in divine revelation. There are many good values expressed in these sacred texts—the Golden Rule, for example. Most naturalists will endorse the Golden Rule, but all will reject that its warrant relies on any supernatural source.

Of course, nontheistic conceptions of ethics have been nearly as prevalent in the course of human history. Confucianism, for example, does not refer to any theistic beliefs in order to justify its conception of a virtuous life. Instead, classical Confucianism appealed to notions of social harmony and emphasized the importance of a virtuous life grounded in practices of ritual propriety—that is, the importance of showing others respect by using society's ritualized forms for doing so (e.g., norms of propriety and social etiquette). Buddhism, too, does not ground its beliefs on the command of a deity or the sanctity of sacred texts but rather on the cessation of human suffering, which it believes is caused by insatiable desires based upon faulty conceptions of reality and subjectivity.

Both folk naturalism and scientific naturalism are methodological and domain restricted. Neither view *warrants* belief in any supernatural forces or entities outside this world, but both *allow* it. Naturalism in the broad sense does not prohibit there being supernatural forces or beings; it is just that such forces or beings do not—at least since she's been up and running—have causal (or any other sort of) intercourse with Mother Nature. A stronger form of naturalism says that what there is, and all there is, in this and any *actual* world is natural. Stronger still would be the claim that what there is, and all there is, in any *possible* world is natural—that it is impossible for there to be *any* world that contains supernatural beings, entities, and the like. (This view has its attractions because it has rhetorical force in telling everyday supernaturalists that one is just not going to yield them any ground. However, it epistemically overreaches.)[6]

At any rate, what seems warranted is this: there are no good epistemic reasons to believe that there are any of the entities, processes, and forces of the sort posited by any supernaturalist ontology. Call this _quietistic ontological naturalism_. The view is bold but quietistic at the same time—thus its name. The Buddha at his inaugural address claimed that no human, himself included—as enlightened as he was—was in any position to give epistemically respectable answers (possibly to even formulate epistemically respectable questions) on matters such as those that both ordinary religious folk and wooly metaphysicians are inclined to speak. The Buddha was a Wittgensteinian as far as epistemology goes: "Whereof one cannot speak, one ought to be silent." For present purposes, consider us committed to this form of naturalism. What is warranted, all things considered, is a form of ontological naturalism about *this* world, which is the only world we have reason to believe exists. Thus, for all we know, what there is—and all there is—is the natural world. Because the conception of what is "natural" is not fixed, the central concept in the motto lacks a clear and determinate meaning. Still, vague as it is, the view is not friendly to theism.[7]

Why Naturalize?

The ontological naturalism advanced in this paper opposes belief in supernatural forces. It also rejects various forms of ontological dualism, such as a sharp bifurcation of humans and the rest of the natural world, as well as mind-body dualism.

Ethical naturalism is not chiefly concerned with ontology but with the proper way of approaching moral inquiry. Ethical naturalism thus has a number of methodological commitments, only part of which consists in a rejection of supernatural forces when explaining or justifying values and principles.[8] If naturalism were only opposed to supernaturalism, then the category of ethical naturalists would be overly inclusive, and if it were only committed to being receptive to findings from the natural sciences, if its most plausible core doctrine was a kind of open-mindedness, as Barry Stroud (1996) has suggested, then it would be difficult to see how it could represent a distinctive view.

However, naturalistic ethics does have a number of substantive methodological commitments. Chief among these is the belief that moral philosophy should not employ a distinctive a priori method of yielding substantive, self-evident and foundational truths from pure conceptual analysis. The claims of ethical naturalism cannot be shielded from empirical testing. Indeed, the naturalist is committed to there being no sharp distinction between her investigation and those of relevant other disciplines (particularly between epistemology and psychology). In other words, ethical science must be continuous with other sciences.

In order to better understand what naturalistic ethics entails, it might be helpful to consider varieties of moral theory that are not supernatural yet not natural either. Some such theories are semantic and maintain that moral terms (or predicates) cannot be cashed out using non-normative terms (or predicates). More frequently, such theories affirm a metaphysical thesis which naturalists deny—namely, the existence of irreducible and non-natural moral facts or properties.[9] Other non-naturalists maintain the autonomy of the moral, that morality is essentially autonomous from other forms of inquiry—namely, from the natural sciences.

Consider, for example, morality as conceived by Immanuel Kant. In the *Groundwork*, Kant writes that a "worse service cannot be rendered morality than that an attempt be made to derive it from examples." Trying to derive ethical principles "from the disgusting mishmash" of psychological, socio-logical, or anthropological observation, from the insights about human nature that abound "in the chit-chat of daily life" and that delight "the multitude" and upon which "the empty headed regale themselves" is not the right way to do moral philosophy.[10]

What is the right way to do moral philosophy? According to Kant, we need "a completely isolated metaphysics of morals," a pure ethics unmixed with the empirical study of human nature. Once moral philosophy has derived the principles that ought to govern the wills of all rational beings, then and only then should we seek "the extremely rare merit of a truly philosophical popularity."[11]

Kantian ethics, qua philosophical theory, might not seem to be openly supernaturalistic. However, it is not naturalistic either. Kant maintains, for example, that postulating the existence of God is essential to ethics.[12] What's more, he claims that the self, the will, and the laws of freedom reside in the realm of the noumena—which is disconnected from all phenomena that could be studied by science. Kant's ethics cannot be naturalistic because we cannot give a naturalistic account of these things. For example, we cannot account for a faculty of pure practical reason that possesses moral principles not gleaned from observation and assess-ment of human practices that work differentially well to meet our aims, and which, in addition, fits with the findings of the mental sciences. There is no such faculty that meets these criteria, and thus no faculty to account for.

Kant's rationale is transcendental. Ethical naturalism is nontranscenden-tal since it rejects divine command or, in this case, since it will not locate the rationale for moral claims in the a priori dictates of a faculty of pure practical reason. Thus, ethical naturalists will need to explain the appeal of transcendental rationales and explain why they are less credible than pragmatic rationales (possibly because they are disguised forms of pragmatic rationales). Suppose, as seems plausible, that Kant intended his *grounding* of the categorical imperative in pure practical reason to both rationalize the categorical imperative and motivate us to abide by it. If one denies (as we do) that there is such a thing as pure practical reason, and if one also thinks that the categorical imperative expresses deep moral insight, then one needs to give an alternative account of how Kant came (or could have come) to express the deep insights he expressed. Likely sources include his own pietistic Lutheranism, his wise observations that many thoughtful people see a distinction between happiness and goodness, as well as emerging enlightenment ideals about human equality and respect for persons.[13]

Unless one is an eliminativist or a physicalist in the reductive sense—that is, a bald naturalist—then reasons exist, as do norms and ideals. Reasons furthermore can be causes. However, being *a reason that causes* is not the same as being *a reasonable cause*; a motivating reason is not, in virtue of being motivating, something that is reasonable to believe or invoke in justification of one's (other) thoughts or actions. The belief that "Santa Claus will deliver coal to me unless I behave myself" will motivate, but it is not the sort of thing we think a sensible adult should believe in, let alone be motivated by.

However, since beliefs that have contents that don't refer are no problem for the naturalist, the causal power and efficacy of beliefs about things that don't exist is not something that worries the naturalist either. It is largely a matter of psychological, sociological, and anthropological inquiry why different sorts of things are motivating reasons, that is, why certain reasons and not others motivate at different times and places. The role for the normative naturalist is to recommend ways of finding *good* reasons for belief and action and to indicate why it makes sense to be motivated by such reasons.[14]

Just as a naturalist cannot accept the postulate of a faculty of pure practical reason, she also cannot accept the notion (found in Kant) that humans have metaphysical freedom of the will. Descartes famously articulated the idea this way: "But the will is so free in its nature, that it can never be constrained. . . . And the whole action of the soul consists in this, that solely because it desires something, it causes a little gland to which it is closely united to move in a way requisite to produce the effect which relates to this desire." The twentieth-century philosopher Roderick Chisholm (1966) puts the point about free agency, what he calls "agent causation," this way: "[I]f we are responsible . . . then we have a prerogative which some would attribute only to God: each of us when we act, is a prime mover unmoved. In doing what we do, we cause certain things to happen, and nothing—or no one—causes us to cause those events to happen."[15] Descartes's and Chisholm's views are openly non-naturalistic. This sort of free will violates the basic laws of science, so the naturalist must offer a different analysis.

The most plausible view is "neocompatibilism" (Flanagan, 2002). Compatibilism is the view that free will is compatible with determinism. A neocompatibilist rejects the dialectic that frames the problem as one between free will and determinism because our best physics now says that there are both ontologically deterministic and indeterministic causal processes, so determinism is not the issue. Causation is. And no matter how one views things, causation is ubiquitous. So far, it does not look as if indeterministic processes at the quantum level "percolate up" to macrolevels. However, in principle, they might. If they do, some macroprocesses might not be deterministic. But it is a nonstarter to think this will help secure a place for "metaphysical freedom of the will" or "agent causation." Consider the hypothesis that there are in fact quantum-gravitational effects or processes in the microtubules of certain neuronal segments. Such random swerves do nothing to secure anything like agent causation, which involves an agent doing something as a prime mover himself unmoved.

On the other side of the dichotomy sits the concept of "free will." Descartes, in the quotation above, quantifies over will (or a faculty of will). Naturalists from Hume on have tried to tame the concept of free will. The picture that Hume and other compatibilists paint is a fairly good fit with our best contemporary science. However, to really make the compatibilist position work, one will need to read Hume et al. as resisting the posit of a distinctive faculty of will—that is, as rejecting the faculty psychology within which free will, reason, imagination, and their suite historically are situated.

What is "new"—and thus what warrants the name "neocompatibilist"—is the outright denial of any faculty that fits the description of free will. Why? Because the concept utterly fails to locate anything significant that we mean to be talking about. There is no such thing as "will" and thus no such thing as a "free will." (Here is one of the rare places where the eliminativist move is totally warranted.) There is no faculty of will in the human mind/brain. Talk of dedicated faculties can be useful when speaking of sensory and perceptual systems, but no respectable cognitive neuroscientist thinks there are distinctive faculties of will, reason, imagination, and the like.[16] If there is no such faculty as will, then there is no way for it to *be*—large, small, heavy, light, free, or unfree. As Dewey says, "what men and women have fought and died for in the name of freedom is multiple and various. But it has never been metaphysical freedom of the will." This was true when Dewey said it in 1922, and it is true 83 years later. So change the subject; there is no such thing as free will.[17]

Nevertheless, persons make choices. Typically, they do so with live options before them. If new reasons present themselves, they can change course.[18] If not, they do what they choose or intend. There is a phenomenology to these activities and processes; persons experience themselves choosing, intending, and willing. Ethics sees persons as choosing and thus works the quarry looking for veins of voluntary action that involves reasoning, deliberation, and choice. Moral practices of shaping character, of assigning praise and blame, work over the topography of voluntary, involuntary, and nonvoluntary actions, and various admixtures of these. Aristotle and Confucius saw how this worked with zero help from the fiction of "will"—"free" or otherwise.

Understanding Morality

The *genealogy of morals* asks how moral sensibilities, moral values, moral norms, and so on, originate and how they develop. There is some consensus among naturalistically oriented philosophers that some combination of cultural anthropology, the psychology of learning, and evolutionary biology will play key roles in providing a genealogy of morals. Dewey is helpful: "For practical purposes morals means customs, folkways, established collective habits. This is a commonplace of the anthropologist, though the moral theorist generally suffers from an illusion that his own place and day is, or ought to be, an exception" (Dewey, 1922, p. 55).

In the following passage from *The Descent of Man*, Darwin suggests the general form that an adequate genealogy of morals might take:

In order that primeval men, or the ape-like progenitors of man, should become social . . . they must have acquired the same instinctive feelings. . . . They would have felt uneasy when separated from their comrades, for whom they would have felt some degree of love, they would have warned each other of danger, and have given mutual aid in attack or defence. All this implies some degree of sympathy, fidelity, and courage. . . . [T]o the instinct of sympathy . . . it is primarily due that we habitually bestow both praise and blame on others, whilst we love the former and dread the latter when applied to ourselves; and this instinct no doubt was originally acquired, like all the other social instincts, through natural selection. . . . [W]ith increased experience and reason, man perceives the more remote consequences of his actions, and the self-regarding virtues, such as temperance, chastity, &c., which during earlier times are . . . utterly disregarded come to be highly esteemed or even held sacred. . . . Ultimately our moral sense or conscience becomes a highly complex sentiment—originating in the social instincts, largely guided by the approbation of our fellow-men, ruled by reason, self-interest, and in later times by deep religious feelings, and confirmed by instruction and habit. (Darwin, 1871/ 2004)[19]

Of course the genealogical story—both ontogenic and phylogenic—is even more complex than Darwin sketches. Morality evolved and developed in order to coordinate and harmonize the interests (both self- and other-regarding) of humans living in mutually dependent communities. Such communities would need to regulate conflicts of interest, divisions of labor, and hierarchy arrangements, and systems of moral norms would help make such cooperative projects beneficial. On the self-regarding side, morality evolved to shape character and specify worthwhile lives and ideals of behavior to which to strive. To understand the full story, we will need what we only have pieces of—namely, insights from evolutionary biology, animal ethology, developmental psychology, learning theory, psychiatry, cognitive neuroscience, and cultural anthropology. All these disciplines and research programs are essential to (and thus have a say in) the genealogy.

Normative ethics, on the other hand, is concerned with articulating and defending which virtues, values, norms, and principles will reliably guide favorable character development, intra- and interpersonal well-being, social coordination, and harmony. Normative ethics involves saying and justifying what is right, wrong, good, or bad. Murder and rape are wrong, honesty is the best policy, and so on. Ethical naturalists evaluate their subject matter using standards that are derived from certain human needs, desires, and purposes. Some of these might be thought of as fixed by our natures as social animals; humans need peace, security, friendship, and so on. The specific form of these needs, the ways they are best met, will have a culturally variable component. Some aims or needs are quite culturally specific and defensible. The aim(s) of morality are thus included as part of what humans need and desire.

Naturalistic Epistemology and the Problem of Normativity

In "Epistemology Naturalized," Quine (1969) suggested that epistemology be assimilated to psychology. Many have read Quine's arguments for naturalization as arguments against a normative role for epistemology. Hilary Putnam writes: "The elimination of the normative is attempted mental suicide. . . . Those who raise the slogan '*epistemology naturalized*' . . . generally *disparage* the traditional enterprises of epistemology" (Putnam, 1993, p. 229). And Jaegwon Kim writes: "If justification drops out of epistemology, knowledge itself drops out of epistemology. For our concept of knowledge is inseparably tied to that of justification ... itself a normative notion" (Kim, 1993, pp. 224–225).[20]

The alleged problem with epistemology naturalized is this: psychology is not in general concerned with *norms* of rational belief, but with the description and explanation of mental performance and mentally mediated performance and capacities. However, the best way to think of epistemology naturalized is not one in which epistemology is a "chapter of psychology" where psychology is understood merely descriptively, but rather to think of naturalized epistemology as having two components: a *descriptive-genealogical* component and a *normative* component. Furthermore, not even the descriptive-genealogical component will consist of purely psychological generalizations, for much of the information about actual epistemic practices will come from biology, cognitive neuroscience, sociology, anthropology, and history—from the human sciences broadly construed. More obviously, *normative epistemology* will not be part of psychology, for it involves the gathering together of norms of inference, belief, and knowing that lead to success in ordinary reasoning and in science. And the evolved canons of inductive and deductive logic, statistics, and probability theory most certainly do not describe actual human reasoning practices. These canons (take, e.g., principles governing representative sampling and warnings about affirming the consequent) come from abstracting successful epistemic practices from unsuccessful ones. The database is, as it were, provided by observation of humanity, but the human sciences do not (at least as standardly practiced) involve extraction of the norms. Thus, epistemology naturalized is not epistemology psychologized *simpliciter*.[21] However, since successful practice—both mental and physical—is the standard by which norms are sorted and raised or lowered in epistemic status, pragmatism reigns.[22]

The natural objection here is that all the epistemological work has been done in identifying the cognitive *aims*, and that the relevance of empirical work is just in identifying what *accomplishes* those aims. The two projects seem distinct, with neither one affecting the other. How is this "psychologizing" epistemology to any extent whatsoever? However, as we noted earlier, a naturalistic approach works back and forth between the normative and the descriptive. Our aims are various and capable of specification on many levels. Given naturalism's methodology, we can modify our cognitive aims—at least on the more specific levels—with knowledge of how our minds work.[23]

Naturalistic Ethics and the Problem of Normativity

The same worries that Putnam and Kim express over Quine's conception of naturalizing epistemology recapitulate Kant's worries over Hume's approach to naturalizing ethics. John McDowell's criticism of "bald naturalism" in favor of "second nature naturalism" is arguably a way of stating the same concern: namely, that at least some kinds of naturalism are not equipped to explain ethical normativity.[24] In any case, moral psychology, sociology, and anthropology (what Kant called the "empirical side of morals") might tell us what individuals or groups *think* ought to be done, what they *believe* is right or wrong, what they *deem* a good person, and so on. However, all the human scientific facts taken together, including that they are widely and strongly believed, could never *justify* any of these views.

But we should conceive naturalistic ethics in pretty much the same way we conceive naturalized epistemology. Naturalistic ethics will contain a *descriptive-genealogical* component that will specify certain basic capacities and propensities of *Homo sapiens*, for example, sympathy, empathy, egoism, and so on, relevant to moral life. It will explain how people come to feel, think, and act about moral matters in the way(s) they do. It will explain how and in what ways moral learning, engagement, and response involve the emotions (and which emotions). It will explain what moral disagreement consists in and why it occurs, and it will explain why people sometimes resolve disagreement by recourse to agreements to tolerate each other without, however, approving of each other's beliefs, actions, practices, and institutions. It will tell us what people are doing (or trying to do) when they make normative judgments. And finally, or as a consequence of all this, it will try to explain what goes on when people try to educate the young, improve the moral climate, propose moral theories, and so on.

Defenders of naturalistic ethics are continually asked to explain how a better picture of moral psychology *can* contribute to our understanding of ethical theory in general and normative ethics in particular. Moral psychology, cognitive science, cultural anthropology, and the other mental and social sciences can tell us perhaps how people *in fact* think and behave. Ethical theories tell us what the aims of ethics are, where to look to ground morality, and so on, while normative ethics tells us how we *ought* to feel, think, and act. It is hard to see, the objectors claim, how such factual or descriptive knowledge can contribute to the projects of helping us to understand the aims of ethics, where the sources of moral motivation lie, and how we ought to live.

First, it should be pointed out that *every* great moral philosopher has put forward certain descriptive-genealogical claims, certain theories of philo-sophical psychology which postulate basic human dispositions that help or hinder morality (e.g., reason, emotion) and the sources of moral motiva-tion. This is a ubiquitous feature of the moral tradition; *everyone* thinks that philosophical psychology (including, e.g., philosophical anthropol-ogy) has *implications* for ethics. And although most of these claims suffer from sampling problems and were proposed in a time when the human sciences did not exist to test them, they are almost all testable—indeed some have been tested (Flanagan, 1991). For example, here are four claims familiar from the history of ethics which fit the bill of testable hypotheses relevant to normative ethics: (1) He who knows the good does it, (2) if you (really) have one virtue, you have the rest, (3) morality breaks down in a roughly linear fashion with breakdowns in the strength and visibility of social constraints, and (4) in a situation of profuse abundance innate sympathy and benevolence will "receive tenfold increase" and the "cautious, jealous virtue of justice would never once have been dreamed of" (Hume 1751/1975, pp. 183–184). Presumably, how the *descriptive-genealogical* claims fare matters to the normative theories and would have mattered to their proponents.[25]

If this much is right, the question arises as to why the contemporary movement to naturalize ethics raises so many hackles. It is true that *philo-sophical psychology*—the sort that can be done from an armchair and which is an assemblage of virtually every possible view of mind—is now giving way to *scientific psychology*, which may eliminate some of the classical views of mind on empirical grounds. If this happens, then our ethical theories will be framed by better background theories about our natures. What could be wrong with this?

Hume's Objection

The standard view, again, is that nothing normative *follows* from any set of *descriptive-genealogical* generalizations. David Hume is supposed to be the father of this line of objection. Yet Hume (along with Aristotle) is often thought to be a father of ethical naturalism. Could it be that Hume was objecting to his own enterprise? In fact, Hume's "objection" is limited to one paragraph in his *Treatise of Human Nature*:

In every system of morality, which I have hitherto met with . . . the author proceeds for some time in the ordinary ways of reasoning, and establishes the being of a God, or makes observations concerning human affairs; when of a sudden I am surpriz'd to find, that instead of the usual copulations of propositions, is and is not, I meet with no proposition that is not connected with ought or ought not . . . [A]s this ought, or ought not, expresses some new relation or affirmation, 'tis necessary that shou'd be observ'd and explain'd . . . how this new relation can be a deduction from others, which are entirely different from it. (1739/1978, p. 469)

Hume is making a rather simple point here: one cannot draw normative conclusions from non-normative premises alone. But Hume found the slide from statements of mere fact to statements of value to be characteristic of "vulgar systems of morality." For him, morality was inexplicable without mentioning moral sentiments or passions.[26]

Let us return, then, to the objection in its current form—namely, that nothing normative follows from any of the empirical information we might gather from the natural, social, and human sciences. Perhaps the fear is that if the background theory is scientific, this makes ethics a science, or that if the background theory is a science, we can suddenly violate the laws of logic and derive "oughts" from "is's." However, no one has suggested these things! No important moral philosopher, naturalist or non-naturalist, has ever thought that merely gathering together all relevant descriptive truths would yield a full normative ethical theory. Morals are radically underdetermined by the merely descriptive, but so too, of course, are science and normative epistemology. All three are domains of inquiry where ampliative generalizations and underdetermined norms abound.

The smart naturalist makes no claims to establish demonstratively moral norms. Instead, he or she points to certain practices, values, virtues, and principles as reasonable based on inductive and abductive reasoning (more on this below). Indeed, anyone who thinks that Hume thought that the fallacy of claiming to move demonstratively from is's to oughts revealed that normative ethics was a nonstarter hasn't read Hume. After the famous passages in the *Treatise* about is-ought, Hume proceeds for several hundred pages to do normative moral philosophy. He simply never claims to *demonstrate* anything. Why should he? Demonstration, Aristotle taught us long ago, is for the mathematical sciences, not for ethics.

Moore's Fallacy

Regarding the challenges to naturalism based on open question arguments, the ethical naturalist has all the resources to effectively meet the challenges. Ethics naturalized need not be reductive, so there is no need to define "the good" in some unitary way such that one can ask the allegedly devastating question: "But is that which is said to be 'good,' good?"

Indeed, the force of open question arguments fizzled with discoveries about failures of synonymy across the board—with discoveries about the lack of reductive definitions for most interesting terms. Suppose "good" is taken to be a term and we think, as Moore does, that it should have a definition. If Moore thinks (as it seems he does) that a definition ought to supply necessary and sufficient conditions of application, then he is correct that if such a definition were available then it would not be "open" to "questioning." However, except for some technical terms (e.g., "even numbers" or "odd numbers") and certain scientific terms, most others do not have necessary and sufficient conditions of application. What we call "dictionary definitions" are a mix of current usage patterns and functional characterizations. This makes sense, given that most terms in natural language have some sort of prototype/exemplar/stereotype structure.[27] It is not surprising that G. E. Moore couldn't find a definition of "good." Failure to find a definition of "good" would no more prove that it names a non-natural property than the same failure to find definitions for "fuzzy" or "chair" would prove that fuzziness is a non-natural property or that chairs are non-natural objects.

Moreover, "good" is not a singular term in our language, including the moral sense of "good." Instead, it is a theoretical term in the following sense: we call different things morally good for different reasons. Moral virtues, for example, are morally good for reasons $r_1, r_2 \ldots r_n$, and so on. It takes a complex moral conception to help fix the multiple meanings of "morally good." This might be tantamount to saying that "morally good" names a heterogeneous set.

Relativism and Nihilism

This leads to some final alleged obstacles to naturalism—namely, that it typically leads to relativism, that it is deflationary and/or morally naive, or that it makes normativity a matter of power: either the power of benign but less than enlightened socialization forces or the power of those in charge of the normative order (possibly fascists, Nazis, or moral dunces).

How does naturalistic ethics avoid extreme relativism, or—even worse—nihilism? The answer is simple: *the ends of creatures constrain what is good for them*. The relativist is attuned to relations that matter, to relations that have relevance to the matter at hand. Not all kinds of food, clothing, and shelter suit us animals, us members of the species *Homo sapiens*. Nor do all interpersonal and intrapersonal practices suit us. Thus, there are substantial constraints on what might count as an adequate morality stemming from intrapersonal and interpersonal factors.[28] We are social animals with certain innate capacities and interests. Although the kinds of play, work, recreation, knowledge, communication, and friendship we seek have much to do with local socialization, the general fact that we like to play, work, recreate, know, communicate, and befriend seems to be part, as we say, of human nature.

The distinctively normative component of naturalistic ethics should explain *why* some norms (including norms governing choosing norms), values, and virtues are good or better than others. One common rationale for favoring a norm or set of norms is that it is suited to modify, suppress, transform, or amplify some characteristic or capacity belonging to our nature—either our animal nature or our nature as socially situated beings. Consider some of the core moral beliefs likely to be found across various cultures, beliefs concerning the permissibility of killing, rights to property and resources, and the need for norms of reciprocity. These beliefs might vary from culture to culture, but they all serve to regulate and promote human social life. Even prior to the powerful (natural) effects of culture, we prefer different things when it comes to shelter, play, communication, and friendship than beavers, otters, dolphins, birds, orangutans, and bonobos. Morality cannot seek to instantiate behavior that no human beings have a propensity to seek. This much constrains extreme relativism.

This seems to reduce morality to a system of *hypothetical imperatives* that hinge on our wanting to secure certain aims: "*If* you want to secure social cooperation, *then* you ought to __." It is true that naturalists cannot allow for *categorical imperatives* if they are conceived as independent of human interests and values, or categorical imperatives that are binding to all rational beings, wherever they may be. Yet while the aims of naturalistic ethics are *internal* to the motivational systems of the species *Homo sapiens*, they are *external* to any particular individual member of that species.[29] This follows from the view that there are a limited number of goods that human beings seek given their nature and potentialities, and these goods (or aims) limit what can be placed as antecedents to the hypothetical conditionals. In referring to these facts in moral discourse one is not simply pointing to preexisting propensities in any given individual but is rather referring to basic and fundamental reasons stemming from human nature that might help shape and channel the particular propensities of any given individual.

In this sense, they do have some "categorical" force.[30] Pluralistic relativism articulates and advances a theory about the constraints on "morally adequate" plural ways of life that aim at the set (or some subset) of the goods that constitute morality, broadly construed.

Nihilism is also not a problem. Humans seek value; we aspire to goods, to things that matter and interest us. Now, nihilism can be a problem for individuals when their "motivating" reasons (discussed above) are exposed as not good "grounding" or "justifying" reasons. (The loss of faith in parental wisdom and authority during adolescence is such an example.) Nihilism is also a familiar problem for theists who lose their faith, and for very depressed humans for whom things have stopped mattering. However, nihilism is not a special problem for naturalists. Animals like surviving; reflective animals like living well. Over world-historical time, reflective animals develop goals for living—welfare, happiness, love, friendship, respect, personal and interpersonal flourishing. These are not an altogether happy and consistent family of values. Still, even if there are incompatibilities involved among the ends we as animals, socialized animals, seek, the fact remains that there *are* ends we seek, and nihilism is not normally an issue—it is not usually a "live option." Nihilism is the view that *nothing* matters. Things do *matter* for us—certain things matter because of our membership in a certain biological species, and certain things in virtue of how we have evolved as social beings with a history. That is the way it is.

Ethics Naturalized: Pluralism and Human Ecology

We close with Dewey's insight that "Moral science is not something with a separate province. It is physical, biological, and historic knowledge placed in a humane context where it will illuminate and guide the activities of men" (1922, pp. 204–205). What is relevant to ethical reflection is everything we know, everything we can bring to ethical conversation that merits attention. To put a pragmatist spin on the point, we can say that moral knowledge obeys the canons of inductive and deductive logic, statistics, and probability theory in producing warranted beliefs about which traits are virtues, which are vices, and about what values, actions, norms, and principles reliably produce social coordination and human flourishing. The normative component involves the imaginative deployment of information from *any* source useful to self/social examination, forming new or improved norms and values, improving moral educational practices, training moral sensibilities, and so on. These sources include psychology, cognitive science, and all the human sciences (especially history and anthropology), as well as literature, the arts (for the arts are ways of knowing and ways of expressing insights about our nature and about matters of value and worth),[31] and ordinary conversation based on ordinary everyday observations about how individuals, groups, communities, nation states, the community of persons or sentient beings are faring. The aims relevant to this sort of pragmatic evaluation are various and capable of specification on various levels. First-order, second-order, third-order, and possibly higher-order level evaluation of norms are things natural human minds can do (or are capacities that can be developed in certain cultures). We can tinker with these aims, systematizing them where this proves useful, minding severe conflicts (e.g., between universal and particular duties), and thinking of possible ways of addressing them (e.g., through revising our norms). The pragmatist is committed to the requirement that normative judgments get filled out in conversation and debate, that his or her background criteria are open to criticism and reformulation, and that terms like "what works" and "what conduces to flourishing" are superordinate terms. Specificity is gained in more fine-grained discussion of particular issues. Even if there is no such thing as "transcendent rationality," no ultimate or non-question-begging way of establishing one's viewpoint over another, there are perfectly reasonable ways of analyzing problems and proposing solutions.

If ethics is like any science or is part of any science, it is part of *human ecology*, concerned with saying what contributes to the well-being of humans, human groups, and human individuals in particular natural and social environments. What is good depends a great deal on what is good for a particular community, but when that community interacts with other communities, then these get a say. Furthermore, what might *seem* like a good practice or ideal can, when all the information from history, anthropology, psychology, philosophy, and literature is brought in, turn out not to have been such a good idea after all. If ethics is part human ecology, the norms governing the evaluation of practices and ideals will have to be as broad as possible. To judge ideals, it will not do simply to look and see whether healthy persons and healthy communities are subserved by them in the here and now; it must also be the case that this "health" is bought without incorporating practices—slavery, racism, sexism, and the like—which we know can go unnoticed for some time but that can keep persons from flourishing and eventually poison human relations, if not in the present, at least in nearby generations.

The aims of morality are heterogeneous, not always individually or collectively or at all times optimifically satisfiable. One aim of ethics is to try to make the best of this fact in particular ecological niches, particular historical communities with their own sets of aims, practices, and so forth. Thinking of normative ethical knowledge as something to be gleaned from thinking about human good relative to particular ecological niches will make it easier for us to see that there are forces of many kinds, operating at many levels, as humans seek their good; that individual human good can compete with the good of human groups and of nonhuman systems; and finally, that only some ethical knowledge is global—most is local, and appropriately so. It might also make it seem less compelling to find ethical agreement where none is needed.

The localized and contingent nature of many of the values we hold dear is no reason for not cherishing them, no reason to deny them a constitutive role in providing meaning. There are some things to be said for contingency (besides the fact that consciousness of it can possibly undermine confidence, self-respect, and their suite). Recognition of contingency has the advantage of being historically, sociologically, anthropologically, and psychologically realistic. Realism is a form of authenticity, and authenticity has much to be said in its favor. Furthermore, recognition of contingency can engender respect for human diversity, which engenders tolerant attitudes. This has generally positive moral and political consequences. And this is all consistent with deploying our critical capacities in judging the quality and worth of alternative ways of being. Attunement to contingency, plural values, and the vast array of possible human lives and personalities opens the way for use of important and underutilized human capacities: capacities for critical reflection, for seeking deep understanding of alternative ways of being and living, and for deploying our agentic capacities to modify ourselves by engaging in identity experimentation and meaning location within the vast space of possibilities that have been and are being tried by our fellows. There are many things to be said in favor of emphasizing "consciousness of contingency."

The pluralistic relativist, the pragmatic human ecologist, has the right attitude—right for a world in which profitable communication and politics demand respect and tolerance, but in which no one expects a respectful, tolerant person or polity to lose the capacity to identify and resist evil where it exists, and right in terms of the development of our capacities of sympathetic understanding, acuity in judgment, and self-modification—and, on occasion, radical transformation.[32]

Notes

1. McDowell coined the term "bald naturalism" (McDowell, 1996) and sometimes characterizes it in a way that engenders or is akin to moral skepticism. In principle, a naturalist might be a moral skeptic, believing that there are no moral properties as ordinarily conceived and thus that moral propositions are literally false (or meaningless). There is nothing ethics is about, and so forth. See J. L. Mackie (1977). For a more recent treatment, see Joyce (2001). *Duke naturalism* is also superior to *Rutgers naturalism*, but showing this will await a subsequent paper. It is possible that *Duke naturalism* and *Michigan naturalism* can be coalesced into *Duke-Michigan naturalism*.

2. For other discussions of naturalism in philosophy, see Bouwsma (1948), Kitcher (1992), and Rosenberg (1996), as well as entries on "Naturalism" in Honderich (1995) and Audi (1999).

3. Not all scientific naturalists are ethical naturalists, but it would be a rare bird who was an ethical naturalist but not also a scientific naturalist. Typically a view that incorporates these two kinds of naturalism is *epistemically imperialistic* as far as *this* world goes.

4. There is precedent for this sort of view. The French deists thought it acceptable to posit God as creator so long as one accepted that once God got the cosmic ball rolling he removed himself from worldly affairs. This move entails that inside "the familiar natural world" all explanation and justification can be done without appeal to God's incorporeal nature, miracles, nonphysical forces, and so on. A deist, then, looks prima facie to be a type of naturalist who is not an atheist. Newton believed in God, and although he was not particularly attracted to deism, he proceeded to do physics in a fully naturalistic manner. And Darwin did biology in a fully naturalistic way both before and after he lost his faith in God because of the problem of evil—spurred by the death of a beloved child.

5. Kitcher (1992) and Stroud (1996) claim that naturalism is pretty much the only game in town. This claim has credibility to the degree that they intend some version of the idea that for the purposes of doing ontology (or for naturalized epistemology or ethics) divine agency does not need to be introduced to play an explanatory role. Stroud, for example, thinks that Plantinga is a naturalist when it comes to descriptive epistemology, but not when it comes to normative epistemology. However, there are other major contemporary philosophers whose views should also give him pause, such as W. P. Alston, Alasdair MacIntyre, and Charles Taylor. MacIntyre (1988, 1991) holds a two-level view; like Aquinas, he thinks that there are natural and supernatural justifications of norms. The natural justifications are satisfactory but the divine ones are "more" ultimate. Taylor (1989) expresses the idea that perhaps God can play a role in the justification of our ethical norms.

6. *Ontological naturalism* is the view that what there is, and all there is, is natural. Everything that exists/has existed, happens/will ever happen, is a natural phenomenon, process, or event. Every property, event, process, and thing, if it *genuinely* exists/is happening, did exist/happen, or will exist/happen, is natural. This is the right definition, but it is not especially helpful until we specify what it means to be "natural." This is surprisingly hard. Imagine a world governed by Newtonian physics and Darwin's theory, supplemented by whatever chemistry and molecular biology (etc.) go neatly with them. In this world "natural" would mean something like this: what there is and all there is, is whatever Newtonian physics and the principles of Darwinian biology say there is or can be. Furthermore, all the events in this world are explained, or explainable, by the causal laws of (or extendable from) these two theories (plus chemistry, etc.). This much would give us the familiar picture of the natural as comprised of law-governed material, and it would provide us with a story of why the physical universe contains what it does and behaves as it does, as well as how life came to be, evolved, and so on. The trouble is that contemporary physics is wilder and woolier than Newton's physics. There is quantum indeterminacy. There are particles or strings that are the same size in relation to a single proton as a single proton is in relation to known universe. There are (*if* string theory is true) at least ten spatial dimensions as well as one for time. Gravity is weak because gravitons escape from our universe into other ones through wormholes in space.

The story that our universe originated in a Big Bang thirteen or fourteen billion years ago was always somewhat mysterious. How did the singularity that banged get there? Some will say that there was "no there" then. Well, there was no "then" either because space and time as we know them only came into being when the "thing that wasn't quite there then" banged. Many sensible people have found this explanation less than satisfying. As we've said, more than 90% of Americans believe that a supernatural force, indeed a personal God, created the universe. If scientists can get away with postulating that the singularity that was not really "there then" led to there being "hereness," "thereness," "nowness," "thenness," and so on, many theists feel licensed to posit their own kind of mystery. See Craig and Sinnott-Armstrong (2004).

Contemporary physics now seriously toys with explaining away the mystery of the Big Bang in this way: our universe, which appears to be four dimensional (three space, one time), isn't. The thing that appears that way is really eleven dimensional, and it was formed—guess when?—thirteen or fourteen billion years ago when a preexisting universe wormed its way into empty space in our vicinity. How did that sneaky universe get going? Same way. It's universes all the way back, down, and so on. See, for example, Greene (2000).

7. The epistemological humility called for is not so humble that it tolerates agnosticism. The agnostic plays a familiar game, thinking it makes epistemic sense to stop with three possibilities: theism, agnosticism, and atheism. But the quietist thinks

the agnostic has been tricked into playing a fool's game. There is no reason to play the game or address the questions that force the familiar three choices. Just say "no" to talking about the supernatural and only then, apparently, will you see that nothing epistemically respectable can be said on such matters.

8. See also Putnam (2004).

9. Indeed, Pigden (1991) suggests that the belief in the nonexistence of such irreducible sui generis moral properties or facts is what unites the category of naturalists. Most naturalists maintain that if ethics provides a respectable kind of wisdom, then moral properties, values, virtues, norms, oughts, and so on must be analyzed in ways that do not involve ontologically queer properties, forces, or commitments. The kind of naturalism defended here is quietistic with regard to the existence of supernatural forces or entities. This is also true of natural moral properties. We imply no position on the question of whether there really are, or are not, moral properties in the universe in the sense debated by moral realists, anti-realists, and quasi-realists. The important thing is that moral claims can be rationally supported, not that all the constituents of such claims refer (or fail to refer) to "real" things. Furthermore, in both the realism/antirealism cases and the cognitivist/noncognitivist case, different answers might be given at the descriptive and normative levels. Mackie (1977) is an example of a philosopher who thought that ordinary people were committed to a form of realism about values but were wrong. In spite of this, Mackie saw no problem with advocating utilitarianism as the best moral theory, and in that sense was a cognitivist—a cognitivist antirealist, as it were.

10. Kant (1964).

11. Thanks (or no thanks) to Kant, the dominant conception of the intellectual division of labor makes a sharp distinction between moral philosophy and moral psychology. Moral philosophy is in the business of saying what ought to be, what is really right and wrong, good and evil, what the proper moral principles and rules are, what counts as genuine moral motivation, and what types of persons count as genuinely good. Most importantly, the job of moral philosophy is to provide philosophical justification for its "shoulds" and "oughts," for its principles and its rules.

12. Despite his commitment to the project of the enlightenment, Kant in fact believed in God—namely, the God of pietistic Lutheranism. And he believed that God was, in fact, the ultimate source of morality. Kant saw that disagreement about theological details could be circumvented so long as God had given us a faculty of pure practical reason in which and through which all conscientious persons could discover the right moral principle.

13. Kant's insights are not justified (if they are justified) by the full story of the genesis of these insights. The point, instead, is that Kant was (1) standing at a certain place in the articulation and development of certain norms in Europe, (2) was heir

to a set of critical norms for thinking about norms, and (3) deployed these norms of rationality and criticism when evaluating the practices and opinions revealed in history *and* when imaginatively extrapolating from history. His situation and his smarts enabled him to express some of the deepest moral insight ever expressed. However, although Kant was very smart, he lacked insight when it came to telling us what it was that he was consulting in displaying his deep moral insights. Hume was doing roughly the same thing, though he understood somewhat what he was doing when he engaged in espousing certain norms. Surely no one thinks that Hume's arguments against religious institutions and religious belief were based on anything like simple description of the practices of most people. He believed that religious belief and practices led, more often than not, to cruelty and intolerance. Given the fact that, in addition, such beliefs and practices are based on claims that humans lack the cognitive equipment to make with warrant, we have a two pronged argument for the adjustment of ordinary epistemic and ethical norms. For more on Kant and naturalistic ethics, see Greene in volume 3 of this collection.

14. Motivational grounds to one side, there is always the interesting question of whether, even if we judge the reasons motivating some norm(s) unwarranted, we judge the norm(s) themselves unwarranted. There is no strict implication. One is inclined to say that even if you behave well only because you believe "Santa Claus thoughts," you should still behave well even though there is no Santa Claus—albeit for non-Santa-Clausy reasons. On the other hand, it just may be the case that, across multifarious social contexts, things like "Santa Claus thoughts" motivate as well—if not better—than "Mom and Dad disapprove of __" thoughts. If this is so, we need an explanation of how beliefs in certain kinds of nonexistent objects can motivate and motivate powerfully. False beliefs that produce goods are an interesting phenomenon, but they create no special problem for the naturalist.

15. Chisholm might, however, say that the self depends on and is often affected by the body, and so is part of the natural world in this limited sense.

16. See, for example, Wegner (2002).

17. See Flanagan (2002).

18. An exception is what Dan Dennett (1984) calls "pockets of local fatalism."

19. It is worth marking the fact that when Darwin speaks of "deep religious feelings" being involved in the development of conscience, he points to an anthropological commonplace that we will try to explain. The naturalist may need to accept that humans have dispositions that easily yield religious beliefs and feelings and that these are widely utilized to produce moral motivation. This, of course, is different from saying such beliefs are warranted or true.

20. Quine does have an answer to the worry that his program eliminates the normative. Judge its adequacy for yourself: "A word now about the status, for me, of

epistemic values. Naturalization of epistemology does not jettison the normative and settle for the indiscriminate description of ongoing procedures. For me normative epistemology is a branch of engineering. It is the technology of truth-seeking, or, in a more cautiously epistemological term, prediction. Like any technology, it makes free use of whatever scientific findings may suit its purpose. It draws upon mathematics in computing standard deviation and probable error and in scouting the gambler's fallacy. It draws upon experimental psychology in exposing perceptual illusions, and upon cognitive psychology in scouting wishful thinking. It draws upon neurology and physics, in a general way, in discounting testimony from occult or parapsychological sources. There is no question here of ultimate value, as in morals; it is a matter of efficacy for an ulterior end, truth or prediction. The normative here, as elsewhere in engineering, becomes descriptive when the terminal parameter is expressed. We could say the same of morality if we could view it as aimed at reward in heaven" (Quine, 1986, pp. 664–665).

21. Alvin Goldman (1986, 1992) has produced arguably the best work in naturalized epistemology. Goldman never tries to derive normative conclusions from descriptive premises. Furthermore, he continually emphasizes the historical and social dimensions of epistemology in a way that Quine perhaps has not. See also Kornblith (1994).

22. In epistemology, pragmatic evaluation is done relative to our cognitive aims. These, to be sure, are themselves norms and, as such, are subject to the same sort of requests for rationales and warrant as all other norms.

23. If, to take one example, connectionism's right, then this must have implications for the nature of successful inquiry, and in particular what constitutes successful reasoning.

24. Although our approach is different from McDowell's, we don't think we can be charged with bald naturalism. Actually, it's unclear who he would think is an actual bald naturalist in ethics—unless he is thinking of John Mackie, possibly A. J. Ayer, and perhaps some evolutionary psychologists. We'd be interested in hearing him name names.

25. The *descriptive-genealogical* component will itself be normative in one sense: it will involve descriptions of human actions (etc.) and thus traffic in intentional description. However, it will not be normatively *ethical*.

26. See Sutherland and Hughes (2000).

27. See Casebeer (2003b) for a similar argument against Moore. Prinz (2002) has an edifying discussion of concepts and their prototype-like structure.

28. A more detailed account can be found in David Wong's (2006b) *Natural Moralities*.

29. For more on this view, see Wong (2006a, 2006b).

30. For another take on the problems of categoricity and nihilism from a naturalistic perspective, see Railton (1986). Railton believes moral imperatives apply even
to those who have no reason to follow them, because rationality is not a precondition of moral obligation. This represents one way of introducing categoricity
that is different from our own approach. Railton uses a similar tactic to evade
nihilism.

31. Richard Rorty (1991) convincingly suggests that the formulation of *general moral
principles* has proven less useful to the development of liberal institutions than has
the gradual *expansion of the imagination,* for example through the writings of individuals such as Friedrich Engels, Harriet Taylor and J. S. Mill, Harriet Beecher Stowe,
Bronislaw Malinowski, Martin Luther King, Jr., Alexis de Tocqueville, and Catherine
MacKinnon.

32. Our thanks to Walter Sinnott-Armstrong for many helpful comments on drafts
of this chapter.

Buddhism

(1)

1.1 Three Cheers for Naturalistic Ethics

William D. Casebeer

It is difficult to comment upon a chapter which so eloquently expresses many positions, arguments, and research programs with which I agree strongly, and which I have tried to articulate and advance in my own work (especially in *Natural Ethical Facts: Evolution, Connectionism, and Moral Cognition*).[1] Rather than critique Flanagan, Sarkissian, and Wong's essay as such, then, I will instead attempt to frame some of the issues they discuss in a slightly different manner and also extend arguments which they hint at in their wonderful text. My comment will thus be a "three cheers for Flanagan et al., and for San Diego naturalism!" with requisite amplifications and extensions. My three cheers are (1) a portion of the genealogical story regarding why naturalism has not been a default position in ethics is that we are still coming to grips with the collapse of the analytic/synthetic distinction, (2) a neurobiologically plausible neocompatibilism will emphasize the neural mechanisms which are important for our ability to satisfy the functional demands of our natures—a cognitive science of "critical control distinctions" is thus what is needed to extend the compatibilist research agenda, and (3) evolved functions will play an important role in providing the normative portion of Flanagan et al.'s "deductive/genealogical/normative" trio; modern history proper functions are an important candidate for the conceptual entity that will bridge facts with norms, picking out one class of natural facts as also being normative in a manner most consistent with the canons of naturalism and with our considered moral judgments. These three "cheers" would more appropriately be "generation-long conversations involving all the natural cum human sciences"; here, though, I am mercifully brief.

Flanagan and his team skillfully lay out the genetic story regarding why laypeople are sometimes reticent to be naturalists about morality. Understanding why professional academicians, especially professional philosophers, resist is more problematic, however. Often, slogan-like invocations of the naturalistic fallacy are used to justify antinaturalism about ethics.[2] Flanagan, Sarkissian, and Wong make short work of this misunderstanding of Hume, pointing out that justification in ethics will proceed *abductively*—in a pragmatic manner—not apodictically as it does in a romanticized version of pure logical reasoning. This resistance to making ethical theorizing (be it deductive, genealogical, and most especially, normative) responsive to the same methodological canons as the other natural sciences is often motivated by an underappreciation for what the collapse of the analytic/synthetic distinction entails for moral philosophy. Quine's seminal article "Two Dogmas of Empiricism" discusses in detail good reasons for thinking that the only *real* difference between dictionary and encyclopedia entries is their length; he concludes by noting the (obvious) fact that ". . . truth in general depends on both language and extra-linguistic fact."[3] But, crucially, the belief that we can therefore somehow analyze a statement into a "linguistic component" (true by definition) and a "factual component" (true because of the way the world is) is, as he famously puts it, ". . . an unempirical dogma of empiricists, a metaphysical article of faith."[4] With Quine in hand, we can insist that any a priori attempt to isolate "the good" from natural definition dodges tough questions about theory change: rather than insist that the meaning of terms like "good" precludes natural definition, why not admit that you have a *theory* of the good (rather than merely a definition of it), and let such a theory be adjudged as theories in the sciences are—by their relationship to other theories, and by their encounters with experience? Quine's arguments also had an impact on a priori truth, at least insofar as analytic statements captured a large subset of those truths that could purportedly be justified without appeal to experience. If moral truths weren't those that could be known a priori, then we must come to have knowledge of them via experience, which opens the door for a robust empirical/normative interaction. Ultimately, Quine leveled the playing field with regard to an implicit hierarchy of things known—those things that were certain and were often known with certainty (the rules of logic, the truth values of definitional sentences, moral rules) were not categorically different from those things that were contingent and usually known contingently (the deliverances of the natural sciences). On the Quinean picture, theories about all of these entities were conjoined together and made responsive to experience. As a result, areas of inquiry that were not previously thought to be amenable to empirical interpretation, such as epistemology, were ripe for naturalization as the old hierarchies collapsed . . . likewise for ethics. While it is true that shallow attempts at the naturalization of ethics (such as some pop varieties of sociobiology) have done more harm than good in the professional reception of naturalistic ethics, we should not allow past missteps to head off from the beginning a Flanagan-style conjoining of the natural and the normative. As the collapse of the analytic/synthetic distinction continues to "seep in" intellectually, the tide will turn regarding the very possibility of a naturalistic moral theory, I hope.

My second cheer is an extension of good ole compatibilism, the idea that the language of moral responsibility is compatible with the deterministic truths of the sciences. In many cognitive domains, outmoded faculty-driven notions (such as "the will") are no longer paying their way. Understanding how cognitive systems—like our brains—can be "in control," and hence responsible for action, despite the lack of this faculty is an important project for naturalistic ethics. Patricia Churchland articulates the basics of an "in control"-driven compatibilsm in chapter 5 of her excellent book *Brain-Wise: Studies in Neurophilosophy* (2002), where she argues there are real neural differences between cognitive systems that are in control of their actions and those that are not, and that these differences might allow us to salvage understandings of moral responsibility which are generally compatible with those required by traditional moral theory. As I have argued in various presentations, it is likely that a cognitive neuroscience of "critical control distinctions"—those distinctions we must draw between well-ordered and disordered cognitive systems in order to maintain attributions of responsibility—will be a necessity in the young field of neuroethics. Taking our cues from Aaron Sloman, we can think about the neural mechanisms of control by comparing and contrasting cognitive systems along multiple axes: those with short-term memory versus those with no memory, those with short-term and long-term memory versus those with only short term, those with theory of mind capacities versus those without, those that can build robust mental models versus those that can't, those that can learn from experience versus those with fixed action patterns, those that can use emotions to modulate cognitive activity versus those that can't, those with the ability to reason abductively versus those constrained more mechanically, and so on.[5] While it will be unlikely we'll draw a circle around these multiple capacities and their neural mechanisms and write "here there be '*will*,'" it is *very* likely that—in certain legal and moral contexts—we'll be able to draw circles around them and say, "this system is '*in control*' in the important senses and hence is ethically responsible for its actions." Understanding the neural systems involved in executive control, and the proper coordination of affect, emotion, and cognition, will play an important role in this process.[6]

Finally, my third cheer will be short: one fruitful avenue for connecting normative moral theory to the natural sciences is via an examination of the role that "functions" play in evolutionary biology. Some sociobiological approaches to naturalized ethics pay attention to only "distal" functions by lopsidedly concentrating on survival—our only function as evolved creatures is to reproduce. On the other hand, "capacity" conceptions of function—such as that originally offered by Larry Wright and which are ahistorical—lead to a moral relativism with little critical purchase . . . systems possess the capacities they possess, and if you'd like your eye to be a doorstop, just pluck it out and place it in front of a door. An intermediate level of analysis, modern history proper functions (where functions are fixed by recent adaptive history), best serves as the bridge to tie moral concerns to evolutionary theory.[7] The short version of the argument goes that moral statements can be fruitfully reduced to functional statements, where functions are modern history proper functions (with a tip of the hat to the pioneering work of Ruth Garrett Millikan). Some pleasant entailments of this approach are that humans have multiple functions, that these functions are evolved and hence that the study of evolutionary history matters for morality, and that functions obtain between organisms and their environments (and thus are intrinsically ecological concepts). On the whole, what emerges from this synthesis is an evolutionarily informed neo-Aristotelian naturalistic moral theory that a pragmatist such as John Dewey would be quite comfortable with.[8] As Flanagan et al. explore more fully the normative components of Duke naturalism, I hope they give consideration to a reduction of the "normative" to the "functional natural."

Three cheers for Flanagan, Sarkissian, and Wong and their well-articulated essay on naturalism in ethics. Advances in pragmatic naturalistic philosophy, the cognitive neurosciences, and ecologically sensitive evolutionary theory all promise to help cash the naturalistic checks philosophers at places such as Duke and the University of California at San Diego are writing to traditional moral theorists. I look forward to seeing how naturalistic ethics evolves as the interconnections between moral theory, the human sciences, and the more basic natural sciences multiply.

Notes

1. Casebeer (2003b). In this book, I gratefully acknowledge the intellectual inspiration provided by Flanagan's approach to moral psychology and normative moral

theory. So much of this paradigm was also "in the air" among philosophic natural-ists at the University of California at San Diego in the late 1990s and early 2000s, however, that I will—with a twinkle in my eye and a mischievous heart—call it, and paradigms which bear strong family resemblance to it, "San Diego naturalism." Welcome to the porch, ethical naturalists, ye descendents of Cornell realism, and all those frustrated with noncognitivism about morality. For my take on the con-nections between science and ethics and a similar history of naturalism, see my entry "Scientific Ethics" in 2005's *Encyclopedia of Science, Technology and Ethics*.

2. See, for example, Michael Ruse's incantation of "the naturalistic fallacy" (2004), where he baldly states "you cannot get 'ought' from 'is.'"

3. As printed in Willard Van Orman Quine (1953/1980, p. 163).

4. Ibid, p. 163.

5. For an interesting exercise in the construction of higher order cognitive concepts from more basic ones, see Braitenberg (1986).

6. For more on the neuroscience of areas related to critical control distinctions, such as anterior cingulate cortex, see articles such as Greene et al. (2004).

7. For a clear articulation of the modern history perspective on functions, see Godfrey Smith (1994).

8. See chapters 2–3 of Casebeer (2003b) or (2003a).

1.2 Response to Duke Naturalists

Michael Ruse

This is the most wonderful romp through the issues. I enjoyed it immensely. I confess I had not realized that naturalism has speciated into so many varieties. Pittsburgh naturalism, Duke naturalism, bald Australian naturalism. (Is Kim Sterelny a hairy Australian naturalist?) I have been trying to locate myself on this spectrum. I have always referred to myself as a "Darwinian naturalist." By this I mean someone who takes seriously the principles of Darwinian evolutionary theory and who tries to apply them to philosophy. Although I do not fit exactly into one of their categories, I think the authors will allow that this usage is linguistically correct. I remember once trying to explain my position to Elliott Sober, and rather snootily he replied, "Well, that is not what I mean by naturalism." I was a bit abashed but then decided that I had been long enough in the business that I could use the word as I pleased. But I think these authors do agree that a philosophical naturalist is someone who is trying to turn his or her philosophy into a natural science—not just modeling the philosophy on a natural science—and if one's favored natural science is Darwinian theory, then why not a Darwinian naturalist?[1]

If I have a criticism of these authors—and they would probably respond that in a short position piece they had room for no more—it is that, having embraced natural science, they do not let the science do more work for them. The downside to philosophical naturalism as I conceive it is that if the science is proven wrong, then you are proven wrong. Here, as a naturalist, I differ from someone like Karl Popper who would resist even God showing him wrong. The upside is that one is now part of science, and if the science is any good, then it is going to give you lots of prefabricated results, as one might say. No need to do it all yourself. It is already there on the shelf for you to use.

Turn now to naturalistic ethics. (Incidentally, I am a little puzzled by the authors' use of the pronoun "she." They seem to refer exclusively to male philosophers. Am I missing a whole literature?) Raise the issue of relativism—namely, the usual charge that if you are a naturalist, then you are stuck with many different kinds of ethical systems. Since the Nazis thought that killing Jews was okay, it was okay for them, just as it is not okay for us. Rightly, the authors scotch this one by pointing to the shared nature of human beings. But why not also use modern Darwinian thinking about social behavior? Apart from the fact that we now know that all humans have a very recent shared ancestry, perhaps 150,000 years ago out of Africa, and so would be expected to share adaptive features, sociobiologists stress that social behavior has to be social—if we are not all (or nearly all) in the game, then it will not work. Save we share the same ethics (that is, substantive ethics), it will not work. If I play the giving game and you do not, then it will break down quickly. (Remember that the Thousand Year Third Reich lasted precisely thirteen years.) It is a bit like language. I may speak the best Queen's English and you may speak in a dreadful North Carolina drawl, but if no one can understand me, then my abilities are worthless. (A similar point can be made about penis size, an exercise I will leave for other authors.)

Raise now a bigger issue, namely, that of foundations and of ethical skepticism. By this term I mean what John Mackie (1977) meant. That is, a denial that we can know foundations or even that there can be any. In other words, a metaethical claim. No one denies the existence of substantive ethics, that (for instance) you ought to love your neighbor as yourself. And let us ignore silly objections such as the ethical skeptic cannot distinguish right from wrong. The situation is like a game—for instance, cricket or baseball. There is no ultimate justification for the rules, but it is still right that in cricket you run with your bat and in baseball you do not. Rape is wrong, and charity to the poor is right.

I see our authors as so spooked by Hume that they dare not try to solve the question of justification. They raise it and talk about it and then drop it. I want to say that, as a Darwinian naturalist, you can do better than this. Take the Darwinian empirical claim that there is no necessary progress in evolution. In the words of Stephen Jay Gould: "Since dinosaurs were not moving toward markedly larger brains, and since such a prospect may lie outside the capabilities of reptilian design . . . , we must assume that consciousness would not have evolved on our planet if a cosmic catastrophe had not claimed the dinosaurs as victims. In an entirely literal sense, we owe our existence, as large and reasoning mammals, to our lucky stars" (Gould, 1989, p. 318). If this means anything, it means that there is something contingent about the content of our substantive ethics. I grant that perhaps social beings have to obey certain formal rules of reciprocation—

the sorts of things that game theorists are trying to articulate—but as Kant pointed out in his *Metaphysics of Morals*, mere formal reciprocation is not ethics. You give me a pound of potatoes, and I give you a dollar. This is not an ethical transaction. I give you a dollar because you are in need. This is an ethical transaction.

Let us agree that humans as a matter of fact think that a major moral imperative is the Love Commandment: "Love your neighbor as yourself." My point as a Darwinian is that I see no reason why rational beings, were they to evolve again or elsewhere, necessarily have to accept this. On Andromeda they might accept something else. (You can see that, although I am not a terrestrial relativist, I am an intergalactic relativist.) What else might they accept? How about what I like to call the John Foster Dulles system of morality, so-called after Eisenhower's Secretary of State at the height of the Cold War. He hated those Russians, but he knew also that they hated him, so there was a balance. What about as a major moral imperative: "Hate your neighbors but remember that they hate you so act accordingly"?

Now what does this add up to? I take it that you have already wiped out a Kantian metaethics, because it is no longer the case that rational beings, in a social situation, necessarily have to obey the Love Commandment or the Categorical Imperative or whatever. What about more realist types of metaethics—Moore's non-natural properties, Plato's Forms, God's will? It would seem now that it could be the case that we poor fools believe that we should do one thing whereas really we should do other things, and we cannot know this. And frankly, if this is not a *reductio* of what most people mean by moral realism—God wants you to hate others but you will never know this or, if you did know it, would never be able to take it seriously— I do not know what is. In other words, as a Darwinian naturalist, you ought to be an ethical skeptic.

(If you say to me, Stop! Why should the non-natural properties, the Forms, God's will, not influence your thoughts just as a moving train bearing down on you influences your thoughts, even though in both cases you are aware of these things through evolved adaptations? I respond, as a naturalist, I want to know how on earth—literally and metaphorically— these non-natural phenomena can get involved in the natural course of events? I take it that, as Humeans, both I and the Duke authors have ruled out natural phenomena as the justification of substantive ethics, even though we both agree that natural phenomena explain why we have substantive ethics. This is a major point of difference between me and my good friend Edward O. Wilson. He thinks that evolution is inherently progressive, and hence it yields value—one ought to cherish the highest product of evolution, namely, human beings. I think that this is the philosophy of a follower of Herbert Spencer, not of Charles Darwin.)

There is one final move. I take it that the Darwinian naturalist has to argue that the meaning of substantive moral claims is that one really does have obligations. Although in some sense one is a noncognitivist—one thinks that ethics is subjective—one is not an emotivist. The emotivist says that the meaning of "killing is wrong" is: "I hate killing. Boo hoo! Don't make me mad by killing." The Darwinian naturalist thinks that this is profoundly unsatisfactory, immoral even. At least, this is the reaction of this Darwinian naturalist! "Killing is wrong" means precisely that: "Killing is wrong." Killing is objectively evil. But the Darwinian naturalist speaks to this sense of objectivity, in a souped-up version of an argument put forward by John Mackie. One objectifies, to use a dreadfully ugly word. If our biology did not make us think that it has an objective referent, even though it does not, then our substantive ethics would break down. We would start to cheat, and before long everyone would be cheating and the selective advantage of substantive ethics would be lost.

Should I be saying all of this? Will our Duke authors now realize that substantive ethics is subjective and go off and rape and pillage—or mark up library books with a yellow pen—to their hearts' content? Not at all! Biology trumps philosophy. Dostoyevsky had it right in *Crime and Punishment*. Raskolnikov realized that as a human being he could not live outside the system. It was he who confessed to his crime. Hume also, as always, had it right. Philosophy leads to skepticism, but psychology puts it all right again.

Note

1. I have argued for my position in various places, most fully in my book, *Taking Darwin Seriously: A Naturalistic Approach to Philosophy*, as well as in my collection *Evolutionary Naturalism* and in one of my Gifford lectures, "Darwinian Understanding: Ethics." I have tried to relate my thinking to religion in *Can a Darwinian be a Christian? The Relationship between Science and Religion*. Other Darwinian naturalists I take to be Darwin himself, especially in the *Descent of Man*, and in the twentieth century the paleontologist George Gaylord Simpson, especially in *This View of Life*. I do not think that everyone who is interested in philosophy and a supporter of Darwin is necessarily a naturalist at heart. I would deny this title to Julian Huxley (see *Religion without Revelation*) and Edward O. Wilson (see *On Human Nature* or *Biophilia*). Among philosophers, I think that John Mackie would have been a full-blown Darwinian naturalist if he had lived long enough, and Jeffrey Murphy's too-little-known book *Evolution, Morality, and the Meaning of Life* is an exemplar.

1.3 | Naturalism Relativized?

Peter Railton

I

Critics often argue that ethical naturalism fails to capture certain central characteristics of moral practice, most notably, the categorical and motivating character of moral judgments. Ethical naturalism, critics claim, leads to a kind of "hypotheticalism"—a subjectivism or moral relativism that is untrue to the objective purport and "action-guiding force" of actual moral judgments. The Duke Naturalists—Owen Flanagan, Hagop Sarkissian, and David Wong—advance a form of ethical naturalism that does not shrink from these consequences. Rather, they seek to show that such consequences still leave us with a workable and credibly down-to-earth moral outlook. They make a good case, and I will offer in section III what I hope they will see as a friendly suggestion for strengthening it. However, as I will argue in section IV, I also believe that their positive arguments support a yet more intuitively plausible conclusion—a relational alternative to relativism.

II

Flanagan et al. depart from the common but regrettable philosophical practice of ignoring religious points of view when discussing the foundations of ethics. I wish I could follow their example, since their discussion raises a number of interesting issues about how naturalists might avoid simply begging the question against the epistemic claims of religious experience. However, space constrains me to move directly to what seems to me the main issue: the philosophical challenge to ethical naturalism that comes not from theism or supernaturalism but from ethical non-naturalism.

Flanagan et al. consider one very important ethical non-naturalist, Kant. But the features of Kant's view on which they focus their critical scrutiny—the existence of a noumenal free will, the possibility of pure practical reason, the tenability of transcendental deduction, and so on—belong to Kant, and not to ethical non-naturalism as such. Among contemporary forms of ethical non-naturalism, *expressivism* is the clearest rival to ethical naturalism, and the one least encumbered by questionable metaphysical or epistemic baggage. Indeed, as developed by Allan Gibbard (1990, 2003) and Simon Blackburn (1998), expressivism is defended using a methodology every bit as down-to-earth and naturalistic as that of Flanagan et al.

Far from shrinking from the task of explaining moral phenomena as part of the natural and social world, Gibbard and Blackburn argue that expressivism affords a *better* explanation of crucial features of moral discourse and practice than ethical naturalism, namely, (1) the nonhypothetical character of moral judgment, (2) the link between moral judgment and motivation, (3) the nonrelativistic character of moral assessment, and (4) the resistance of fundamental moral disagreement to resolution by empirical means. They account for (1)–(3) by providing a semantic theory according to which moral judgments express nonhypothetical, motivating attitudes on the part of the speaker (e.g., attitudes of norm acceptance). And they account for (4) by showing how this semantic theory leaves a conceptual gap between any merely descriptive claim and a substantive moral judgment. Those who would defend ethical naturalism must either provide a more convincing account of (1)–(4) or give compelling reasons for thinking that (1)–(4) mischaracterize the relevant phenomena. Let us, then, consider what the Duke Naturalists have to say about (1)–(4).

III

Flanagan et al. pursue an intriguing strategy. Rather than accept (1)–(3) at face value, they explicitly embrace a hypothetical conception of moral judgment in the form of (what they call) "ecological pluralistic relativism." And they account for (4) not via a traditional "is/ought" gap but by assimilating the underdetermination of the normative by the descriptive to an underdetermination *within* the descriptive: the general underdetermination of theory by evidence. In what follows, I will focus on (1)–(3), returning to (4) only at the end.

Their approach to (1) and (3) has an attractive complementarity. A somewhat "linguistic" way of characterizing it, to which I hope they would not object, would be the following. It is a common feature of ordinary speech that we use nonhypothetical, unconditional, and unqualified statements to express tacitly conditional or qualified attitudes and to make comparisons implicitly restricted to a reference class. This is possible because *context* furnishes the tacit presuppositions and scope restrictions. For example, suppose that you have just come back from an afternoon hike and I greet you:

(A) Welcome back! Help yourself to whatever's in the fridge.

Despite the unqualified permission (A) appears to extend, it is clear to both of us in this context that I have not authorized you to clean out my refrigerator to load your car and save you from doing your weekly shopping or to warm up tonight's lentil soup to soak your feet. The invitation conveyed by (A) has contextually understood conditions and qualifications that go without saying. We can, of course, make many of these conditions and qualifications explicit, and rewrite (A) as a conditional, hedged permission: *If* you are hungry and would like to eat, *then* you should feel free to serve yourself a reasonable amount of food from the fridge. Similarly, if two preschool teachers are discussing their students, and one says,

(B) Vitaly stands out because he's so tall,

the other will not think that, improbably, his colleague believes this preschooler to be taller than the average American. Rather, he'll understand that she means to convey "Vitaly stands out as considerably taller than his fellow preschoolers."

Now, consider some apparently unqualified, nonhypothetical *normative* claims, such as:

(C) Walnuts are especially good.

(D) It is forbidden to cross another person's property without permission.

Can we say what a given use of (C) or (D) means without reference to context? Suppose that (C) appears in the context of an article about new research on the health benefits of diets that include certain fats. Then we will understand the writer of (C) to be saying, "If you seek sources of beneficial fat, look particularly to walnuts." Moreover, we will understand the writer to be saying that *eating* walnuts is recommended (not, say, rubbing them against the skin) and to be addressing those who do not have a nut allergy. And so on. It would, of course, be impossibly cumbersome to attempt to articulate all the qualifications and conditions the writer assumes readers will bring to interpreting (C). In practice, there typically is little difficulty sorting this out. Thus, if I utter (C) in the course of our kitchen conversation while you are hunting for something to enliven the endive salad, you will understand me to mean, "For a tasty endive salad, add walnuts." If (C) were found instead on a fragment of newsprint lying in the street, we would be as hard put to assign it determinate content as we would be to follow the scrawled instruction, "Take the second left," found on another wayward scrap.

Consider now (D). (D) might occur in an anthropologist's fieldwork notes, a Sunday School lesson, a rule in a game, a legal brief, a moral deliberation, or as a premise in a Proudonian critique of property as theft. In each context, absent further qualification, it would ordinarily be understood as conveying a different thought. Apart from all contexts, we would have no good way of saying just what sort of prohibition, binding upon whom, is asserted or hypothesized by (D). According to a long tradition, moral judgments are unconditional and command categorically. However, from a contextual perspective, the "categorical imperative" reading of (D) as "rationally binding on all practically rational agents, without regard to contingent variation in motive or interest" is just one more way of spelling out the tacit scope limitation and modality of prohibition. On this reading, (D) does not impose an obligation on wandering toddlers or, perhaps, on the parents chasing them. It also does not apply in societies without a system of recognized private property rights or independently of locally-articulated norms of what respect for privacy and property requires. Depending on local custom, full compliance with (D) as a moral requirement might be consistent with: neighbors allowing their chickens to roam freely, unexpected visitors walking up to one's door to knock, parents entering one's dwelling without knocking, fellow villagers crossing one's land to fetch water from the river, and so forth. Yet, in each locale, one will encounter moralizing assertions of the categorical, unqualified form of (D)—context will fill in the scope and qualifications.

Flanagan et al. think there are no requirements that bind practically rational agents as such, regardless of their contingent circumstances, motives, or purposes. "We cannot account for a faculty of pure practical reason . . . [because there is] no such faculty that meets [its] criteria, and thus no faculty to account for" (p. 6). We can see this as an underspecification of context—add some circumstances, motives, and purposes, and practical requirements will follow. So they do not despair of the possibility of distinctively moral judgments of form (D). After all, they point out, even after being disabused of the idea of pure practical reason, things still *matter* to us just as much as ever, and it remains within our power to act in cooperative or uncooperative ways that make a difference to things that matter *a lot* to almost all of us. Thus:

Ethical naturalists evaluate their subject matter using standards that are derived from certain human needs, desires, and purposes. Some of these might be thought of as fixed by our natures as social animals; humans need peace, security, friendship, and so on.... Some aims or needs are ... culturally specific.... The aim(s) of morality are thus included as part of what humans need and desire. (p. 10)

Relative to a particular social and historical context, a given set of locally articulated norms of proper conduct can be *functional* with respect to meeting important human needs, desires, and purposes in a way that fosters further cooperation and coordination. In such cases, Flanagan et al. see no reason why (D) as conditioned by this context could not be understood to express a bona fide moral judgment. Call such a context a *human socio-ecological context* and call functionality in such a context (i.e., with respect to meeting important human needs, coordinating, etc.) *human socio-ecological functionality*. What would (D) be missing as a moral judgment if understood to express a prohibition functional relative to such a context?

Well, it might be argued, (D) would not be categorical, contrary to (1). It would in some sense be hypothetical upon the substantive goal of meeting (in the context) important human needs and purposes through forms of social cooperation, and so forth. Hypotheticalness *would* be a problem for their view if the contextual functionality in question were a matter of maximizing inclusive fitness or stabilizing the dominant social hierarchy (for neither of these are morally relevant as such) or if the functionality were entirely a matter of producing appreciative sensory delight (for that would be an aesthetic, not moral, context). However, human socio-ecological contexts involve elements widely accepted as morally relevant, even central. Of course, such contexts are *socio*-ecological and characteristically involve socio-historical variations in needs as well as cultural articulations of norms and attitudes, many of which will be quite local. Still, *some* relativization to social context is a feature no sensible view can deny.[1]

Flanagan et al. note, correctly, that "hypotheticalness" in the human socio-ecological sense does not mean that judgments like (D) are hypothetical upon the contingent motives of *particular* agents or that individuals can escape the scope of moral prohibitions simply by failing to *care* about whether human needs are met under conditions of reciprocity:

... while the aims of naturalistic ethics are *internal* to the motivational systems of the species *Homo sapiens*, they are *external* to any particular ... member of that species. (p. 16)

Thus they provide a naturalized version of the nonhypothetical character of moral imperatives.

Since most actual moral discussions occur in a shared social setting, and focus on what to do, or how to feel, in that setting, moral judgments will normally take a categorical *form*, such as (D). We can understand the seriousness of moral deliberation and discussion without appeal to pure categoricity: it suffices for it to be tacit "common knowledge" among members of society that moral assessment is made with respect to "basic and fundamental reasons stemming from human nature" and the conditions for meeting human needs and wants within a social setting (p. 16).

This also affords Flanagan et al. a possible response to the objection that their account fails to preserve (2), the claimed link between sincere moral judgment and motivation. What, after all, is this link? Early on, C. L. Stevenson (1937) observed that moral judgments are closer in meaning to 'We like *x*' than 'I like *x*'. Speakers do not see themselves as simply spouting off to air their feelings but as making claims that are relevant to and significant for the acts and evaluations of others. They attempt to recruit the agreement of others, to arrive at a 'We like *x*', by adducing considerations that will count for others as relevant and important. The point of such agreement is not simply to be of one mind—it is to shape how *we* will in fact act. Against such a backdrop, it would be seen as a form of insincerity (though not a self-contradiction) for me to engage in moralizing to recruit the agreement of others while being quite unwilling to play my part in the agreement reached. I would be employing without any qualification a discourse ordinarily used to work out what *we* will think and do, while having something more like what *you* will do in mind.

Thus, even though moral judgments as understood by Flanagan et al. have no *logical* connection to motivation, they nonetheless have a characteristic function that makes sense only because there is a *regular* connection between the positions we take and defend in moral discourse and deliberation, on the one hand, and our dispositions to feel and act, on the other. Without this, moral language could have no "special action-guiding force" or give rise to interpersonal expectations. Sincere moral judgment, then, does not entail but rather (in most contexts) *implicates* a pro-attitude on the part of the speaker. And this may be enough to explain the features of actual language that seem to support (2).[2]

IV

What now of (3), the nonrelativistic purport of moral judgment? Here Flanagan et al. wish to revise common sense. Their ecological approach,

they believe, encourages a healthy, tolerant, pluralistic sort of moral relativism. However, my sense is that their ecological image favors a different
conclusion: a healthy, tolerant, pluralistic sort of moral *relationalism.* When
we view nature from an *ecological* perspective, we do not take up a perspective relativized to our own species, or to any species. Rather, we seek a
species-neutral standpoint, abandoning any talk of "higher" or "lower"
species, and considering instead the variety and interdependence of species,
the relations of organisms to their respective niches, the history of competition, adaptation, and co-evolution, the role of environmental change,
the appearance and disappearance of species, etc. We might be said to be
"species pluralists" and "niche relationalists." But isn't this just relativism?—No. The characteristic mark of relativism is the insistence that evaluation is always *indexed* (tacitly if not explicitly) to particular standpoints,
societies, times, and so forth. The ecological perspective, by contrast, is a
unified perspective—non-indexed, species-neutral, and temporally extended.
We do not say, "From the mosquito's point of view, the elongated probos-
cis is a highly effective adaptation of mouth parts to available sources of
food; whereas from the human point of view, it is a *maladaptation.*" We
say, rather, it is an adaptation *tout court.*

Adaptation thus is a *constant function* relating features of organisms to
particular selectionist histories, not a variable function whose value varies
with "point of view." Crudely put, it is an objective relation in which the
fit between an organism's features and the requirements of its niche
explains how those features, once they appeared, became predominant.
An easy analogy is with *toxin*, another relational concept that is not rela-
tivistic. We do not say that atmospheric oxygen is toxic from the "point
of view" of anaerobic bacteria but not from the "point of view" of earthworms; rather, we say that atmospheric oxygen is, from any point of view,
toxic to anaerobic bacteria and not to earthworms. This idea of a unified,
relational perspective makes it clearer why the upshot of the positive case
made by Flanagan et al. should be *pluralism.* Our concept of a toxin
requires us to accept that pluralism is a genuine possibility: according as
the nature of organisms varies, what is toxic to them will differ, and there
will be no sense to the question, "Yes, but which are the *real* toxins?"

A unified, relational perspective also makes it clear why the upshot of
their positive argument is *tolerance.* Relativism has no such upshot.
Evaluation relativized to social norms—some of which will themselves be
quite intolerant—gives us no *general* standpoint from which to criticize
intolerance. On a relational view, by contrast, we can always ask whether
a given act or set of social practices, occurring as it does in a particular
socio-ecological context, is *genuinely* functional with respect to meeting

basic needs and so on. For example, we might be tempted to condemn traditional Inuit practices of seal hunting as inhumane or criticize as unfair their norms of food distribution that allocate smaller portions of the hunt to the elderly than the young. However, a human-ecological perspective might enable us to see these traditional practices as adaptations to conditions of great scarcity and understand that they did not carry the social meaning of disrespect or lack of care. We would then have a strong relational argument for a tolerant attitude toward this vanishing way of life— an argument not "from our point of view" but from what deserves the name "the objective point of view." Such tolerance and care, however, do not require us to approve of societies that fail to meet the important human needs and purposes of its members in circumstances when more functional alternatives are realistically available.

Finally, we turn to (4), the idea that moral disputes cannot be settled by empirical means alone. Here the Duke Naturalists have an easy case to make. Since they do not offer a *conceptual* reduction of moral discourse to human socio-ecological discourse, their naturalization of moral properties still leaves a conceptual gap between "is" and "ought." They can assert, modestly, that the empirical insights of psychology, ecology, and ethnography are indispensable to the moral assessment of our own lives or the ways of life of others. And that seems like the soul of good sense.

Notes

1. Don't believe that context decisively shapes the conditions of respect? In some warrior societies, eating those slain enemies who had fought bravely was a sign of respect.

2. Of course, not all moral judgments are conversational. Some are purely deliberative and never voiced. However, it will normally be the case that one engages in *practical* (as opposed to theoretical) moral deliberation when one is concerned with the moral status of one's acts. The agent thus *brings to* practical moral deliberation a motivating attitude. For further discussion, see Railton (2005).

1.4 What Is the Nature of Morality? A Response to Casebeer, Railton, and Ruse

Owen Flanagan, Hagop Sarkissian, and David Wong

It should be obvious that, within the confines of a short response, we cannot possibly answer the question that constitutes the title of our reply. Nonetheless, each of our commentators touched upon issues that bear directly on this question, so we've chosen it as a framework within which to reflect upon their many stimulating comments.

Naturalism in moral philosophy is associated with diverse views that do not make up a happy family. At the turn of the twentieth century, G. E. Moore's *Principia Ethica* outlined a (purportedly fallacious) metaethical view that came to be known as "moral naturalism." According to Moore, this particular form of naturalism is committed to the view that moral properties are natural properties and can therefore be defined as such. Definitions provide analyses in terms of necessary and sufficient conditions; that is, they are analytic. Such analytic definitions do not leave open any questions about the relationship between the definition and what is defined. However, Moore claimed, all attempts to define the moral *do* allow for such open questions. Therefore, moral naturalism is false. In addition, the term is also used to denote a claim that natural facts can vindicate, justify, or ground moral facts in a strong sense. Now, the view we outline is, by our lights, ethically naturalistic. However, we believe neither in the reducibility of the moral *to* the descriptive nor in the vindication of the moral *by* the descriptive. We do, of course, believe that moral norms, ends, and values are amenable to rational discussion. But the strong sense of vindication—the demonstrative sort that Hume correctly saw as not in the offing—is something we reject. Thus, given the multifarious uses of the term "ethical naturalism" or "moral naturalism," it is not surprising that our commentators (naturalists themselves) would hold some beliefs different than our own.

For example, Michael Ruse believes (as J. L. Mackie did) that ethics requires a strong form of rationally compelling, objective categoricity, and since this notion is now incredible, the upshot is skepticism. We, too, reject this notion of categoricity but replace it with a naturalized version that does not lead to skepticism. After all, why think that morality *would* or *should* bind rational beings, wherever they may be? On our view, this conception is an artifact of *one* particular tradition of morality, which maintains that moral judgments and imperatives must have objective categorical prescriptive force, or else they are not moral at all. There are many naturalists who maintain this feature to be a necessary (perhaps conceptual) truth about morality; without it, morality is a fiction, a myth, an error.[1] But what, precisely, is this error? Is it that our concept of morality has no referent? Or that one particular conception of morality got things wrong and should be replaced by another? Any naturalistic genealogy of morals (including values, virtues, and norms) will reveal them as resulting from contingent biological and cultural processes, and it is entirely apt to claim, as Ruse does, that none of the imperatives of morality need bind all other rational beings, wherever they may be (and whatever that might entail). Instead, we claim that the imperatives of morality pertain to our particular species, and not to any larger, more inclusive set of "rational" beings, of which we comprise some part. As an "intergalactic relativist," we believe Ruse would agree, and as a "terrestrial relativist," we believe he has no need to be a skeptic in any radical sense. In denying that morality consists in self-certifying rational a priori truths (or deductions from such truths), one need not deny that there are sensible, rational ways of endorsing ends and means. These ways would be inductive and abductive, but this should not engender skepticism in any strong sense.[2]

William Casebeer's comments concerning the implications of the collapse of the analytic/synthetic distinction are helpful here and should make any naturalist uncomfortable in thinking that any thick concept such as morality would include a feature such as "binding on all rational beings" as a necessary conceptual truth. To borrow some of his language, why not say that instead of *conceptual truths* concerning morality, we have an evolving *theory* of morality, and that the proper way to investigate and evaluate this theory is to see how it coheres with other theories in the empirical and social sciences and with our experience of morality as found in history, literature, and phenomenology? We can characterize elements or features of morality, but Quinean criticisms and the work of cognitive linguists give us reason not to expect analytic definitions for most interesting terms outside of formal sciences. Thus, it turns out that Moore was right: questions will remain open when we want to "define" morality. But that's precisely what we should expect with *synthetic* "definitions," which are more akin to characterizations that try to isolate core or essential properties of a term and so rarely claim to be exhaustive or fully reductive.

One might wonder whether, by scuttling the strong objective prescriptivity of morality and its ties with rationality, we are throwing the moral baby out with the bathwater? Not at all. We believe there is a naturalistic story that not only captures the insights of the outdated conception mentioned above but also shows why the old conception got things wrong in the first place. For example, as Peter Railton notes, in practice, moral imperatives and judgments are often exchanged in particular contexts which include tacit background assumptions and qualifications. Indeed, they can be stated categorically only if we assume such a contextual framework. Of course, we could include all the possible exceptions and qualifications within the imperatives themselves, but that would assume a small or manageable finite set of such qualifications and exceptions, as well as a way to efficiently deploy them. Both of these claims are contentious; the former would be impossibly cumbersome (to use Railton's turn of phrase), the latter cognitively onerous. Hence, as a matter of practical usage, the imperatives of morality are often *explicitly categorical*; as regards their logical status, they are *implicitly hypothetical*, contingent on features arising in their application.

It is true that moral judgments and imperatives elicit strong reactions in individuals and are felt to be particularly compelling. It is also true that moral imperatives are often stated categorically, especially to the morally immature (though it is an interesting question to what extent moral judgments and imperatives are stated categorically by mature agents in everyday discourse). These facts arising out of moral phenomenology and practice might explain how one particular conception of morality might have seemed so cogent (namely, the one that claims for it objective categorical prescriptions binding all rational beings). They do not, however, render morality a sham.

Moral imperatives and judgments can guide action and motivate individuals not because of anything internal to their syntax, semantics, or logical structure, still less because our biology makes us think that they refer to something objective (as Ruse claims),[3] but rather because of how they relate to vital human needs, desires, and interests, such as a need for safety, security, friendship, reciprocity, and a sense of belonging. This affords an understanding of their "practical clout."[4] Without these *contingent* facts about the species *Homo sapiens*, morality would be inert. Railton describes the connection between moral language and motivation as one of *regular implication*, not *logical entailment*. Without such a regular connection, "moral language could have no 'special action-guiding force' or give rise to interpersonal expectations" (p. 42). We find this way of parsing our position agreeable.

Additionally, moral language is not merely a laundry list of acceptable and deplorable actions, and moral imperatives do not simply justify certain behaviors and proscribe others. Rather, they work to encourage members of a community to adopt a certain perspective, to shape their preexisting desires and interests in such a way as to make them conducive to moral ends.[5] In this way, some moral judgments and imperatives (in particular, the most important ones) have to be external to any particular agent and are applied to particular agents regardless of their own motivations, desires, and beliefs. If they succeed in this role, it is not because of a special force they exercise on rational beings but because they relate to needs and desires most members of our species hold dear and most have an interest in promoting.[6] Moral reasons are thus often (and rightly) presented as being in the interests of those on whom they are being urged. In other words, when we examine the way moral concepts and imperatives are deployed in social lives, and when we understand the vital functional role they play in forging our desires, we can then understand the special status many have claimed for morality without having to set apart moral language as having peculiar qualities on its own.[7]

This naturalistic developmental model helps us see morality as a functional system that aims to shape multifarious and inchoate desires (both self- and other-regarding), not merely sanction or vindicate them. Morality "works" because it answers to these deep-seated-yet-contingent interests and desires of humans. Indeed, their very biological and cultural contingency allows for the fact that, as our drives are shaped by the ecological niches we construct and the selective pressure we thereby bring upon ourselves, morality—this functional mechanism for dealing with intrapersonal and interpersonal conflict—will change along with it. Natural phenomena do not justify normative ethics, but they surely feed into this justification—even while it must take place within a normative framework (not reducible to a descriptive one).

An interesting question remains. We claim that moral statements are truth apt, and that many of them will turn out to be true. What kinds of truths do these consist in? This is a complicated question, and we cannot do it full justice in this instance. Nonetheless, there are a number of factors to consider.

For example, does moral variety result from an interplay of human interests, needs, and desires with a particular socioecological context? On one view, supported by relationalists, the answer is "yes." As individuals and environments differ, their interests will too. For any particular individual, we might say that there are objective facts concerning her best interests. What are these? They are what she *would* want in "ideal epistemic conditions," that is, with full information about her relevant capacities, history, and genes, her psychological and physical constitution, and so forth. Given these considerations, it is easy to see how and why an individual's objective interests will be fitting for her and not others. On a relational view, this can be understood as standard ecological variation. Similarly, if individuals are alike in most ways and if their niches align, then they will agree on most things.

In any event, we must assume that most people have at least some tendencies towards their own good; minimally, people must want *some* good things *some* of the time. Moreover, as noted above, these wants must be amenable to the general constraints of cooperative activity. In addition to these evolutionary constraints, we have theories, traditions, putative authorities, and other resources to help us work out intrapersonal and interpersonal tensions. With the relevant information, reasoning skills, and patience, we can arrive at objective values and truths (deploying a very unobjectionable notion of truth). This is possible on a relational model.

However, what happens when things break down, when disagreement endures? How is one to determine which side is correct? Imagine two individuals in a moral dispute. The dispute need not be grave, but let's suppose that they judge it worthy of sustained discussion. Let's further suppose (to make things advantageous to an amenable outcome) that the dispute involves persons otherwise well disposed to one another, who will be curious, sincere, and willing to expose themselves to risk, all of which are generally necessary to resolving moral disputes. So investigations are made, questions are answered (hopefully in good faith), authorities are cited, reasons are exhausted, and appeals fail to gain assent. Disagreement persists. How to understand this? We believe we can understand how this can happen, and happen regularly, by looking at an important component common to moral traditions.

Take, as an example, a Confucian community, wherein the preservation of certain relationships embodied in an ideal of social harmony would be very high in determining what the true moral duties are in that community. This kind of morality can satisfy and coordinate the intrapersonal and interpersonal needs, interests, and purposes of its members. All the same, such a morality will differ substantially from that of another community, which emphasizes the rights of the individual and the preservation of individual autonomy more than social harmony. This latter type of morality can also meet the functional requirements of satisfying and coordinating the needs, interests, and purposes of its own members. However, in both cases, part of what affords their functionality is the way these moralities *rule one another out*; indeed, moralities can only work effectively by so ruling out several possible moral options, which cannot all be included without rendering morality's "action-guiding-ness" impotent. When fundamental ends are prioritized in a certain way, there will be more or less sensible or efficient ways of configuring moral codes to meet those ends. Indeed, some such configurations will be inapt. Hence, the moral truths of one community will be relative to it in the sense that other moralities and other configurations of moral codes will be ruled out for it (even while being acceptable from the standpoint of the functional requirement).[8] Considerations of morality's functional role, together with facts about human nature, constrain only so much. A great many options will remain viable, as the very ways in which moral communities evolve— by responding and adapting to technological innovation, political change, climate change, interactions with other cultures, and so forth—lead to great contingent variation.[9] In ascertaining *how* a Confucian moral community would come to have different priorities compared to a Western one, examining the particular ecological niche will tell us a great deal. However, it cannot tell us *why* these norms are correct; they are correct not in virtue of meeting the functional requirement in a niche-specific way but in how they figure in moral systems, systems that meet this functional requirement while ruling other options out. In a sense, moral truth *has* to be relative; when everything is acceptable, nothing is action-guiding.

A relational analysis is vital to understanding certain common features of moral systems, and some moral facts might be as straightforwardly relational as atmospheric oxygen's being poisonous to anaerobic bacteria.[10] Our view therefore includes relationalism as a good explanation for some similarities and variations among moral imperatives across societies. Nevertheless, even while all true moralities will fulfill the functional requirement, and even while the moral concepts of different moral traditions will overlap to a significant degree, some aspects of particular moralities, including important variations in fundamental moral ends (such as those pertaining to social harmony versus greater individual autonomy outlined above), will be true only relative to those moralities and not others. These considerations concerning the justification of practical moral judgments and particular moral codes represent, to our mind, the real sticking point between relationalism and relativism.

Finally, what of tolerance? Moral disagreement can certainly be troubling. However, even when sincere investigation and dialogue yield no single verdict owing to fundamental variation in moral ends (and imperfect means of achieving those ends), this need not have any deleterious effects. Tolerance itself can be a moral end of many traditions, as can cognate notions such as acceptance, accommodation, forgiveness, or flexibility. Among a tradition's moral resources might be heroes or saints who were able to forge cooperation, even flourishing, in the face of serious disagreement. In any case, these are contingent matters. There is no guarantee that, even given exceptionally forgiving moral systems and exceptionally sincere moral discussions, substantive *agreement* will follow. Nevertheless, solutions can be made *agreeable*. And when strategies line up, the natural upshot can be a healthy, tolerant relativism.

Both relationalists and relativists can be pluralists and recognize a wide range of true (or justified) moralities, and naturalists of these stripes can understand certain features to be common (perhaps universal) across true moralities owing to the way they relate to human nature and owing to constraints arising from the circumstances of social coordination. Which of these approaches best captures the variation of moral traditions among our species and the nature of moral truth? We ascribe to much of what relationalism holds, but we believe a relational analysis can't take us all the way, that the truths of moral systems are underdetermined by a relational analysis. Our brand of relativism can embrace this underdetermination, owing to an understanding of a characteristic component of moral systems in general and how it works to determine what is true for any moral system in particular. Relationalism cannot.

Notes

1. Prominent contemporary error theorists include Richard Joyce, Michael Ruse, and Tamler Sommers and Alex Rosenberg, all of them naturalists. J. L. Mackie, while not an obvious choice for a naturalist, is the modern patriarch for this philosophical lineage.

2. Much of engineering, for example, consists of inductive and abductive reasoning, but no one seriously doubts that there are better and worse ways to build bridges, and so forth.

3. Ruse (p. 36). More on this issue below.

4. We borrow this phrase from Richard Joyce (2006).

5. For these reasons, we deny what Ruse claims in this regard—namely, that "biology trumps philosophy" (p. 36). Ruse claims, first, that we have a "biological" tendency

to *objectify* morality or a biological tendency to understand moral statements as having objective referents; second, that without this biological tendency, "our substantive ethics would break down" (p. 36); third, that this tendency provides us with powerful dispositions towards moral ends; and fourth, that this biological tendency cannot be trumped by "philosophical knowledge" that moral statements in fact lack objective referents. In other words, evolution selected for an overpowering tendency to objectify morality, and this explains the prescriptive force of moral claims. As it stands, this account runs contrary to much of human moral development, which is accomplished through a communal process of cultivating individuals' promoral tendencies (no easy task on its own) while reworking many other, equally natural and powerful tendencies orthogonal or antagonistic to moral ends. These other tendencies, such as those towards self-preservation, personal advantage, or even reproduction, must be made compatible with (or amenable to) moral ends. If biology provided strong, trumping promoral dispositions, then coordinating means and ends would not be so notoriously difficult. We recognize this difficulty and so deny that "biology trumps" in any interesting or deep sense. Our account (outlined below) allows us to understand the "force" of moral imperatives while eschewing such speculation.

6. This, in spite of the undeniable polymorphism of psychological traits among human beings.

7. Incidentally, Railton classifies Simon Blackburn and Alan Gibbard as nonnaturalists, whereas by our lights, and given our methodological commitments, they would qualify as naturalists.

8. For more on this aspect of morality, see Wong (2006b).

9. Compare with the "Principle of Minimal Psychological Realism" (Flanagan, 1991): "Make sure when constructing a moral theory or projecting a moral idea that the character, decision processing, and behavior prescribed are possible, or are perceived to be possible, for creatures like us" (p. 32). This both describes a feature common to many moralities and prescribes a standard of evaluation. However, a great variety of moral traditions can meet this standard of psychological realizability. In other words, it does not rule out that much. The same might be said for socioecological constraints: they do provide real criteria for evaluation, but they leave much in play.

10. Railton (p. 43).

2 Can a General Deontic Logic Capture the Facts of Human Moral Reasoning? How the Mind Interprets Social Exchange Rules and Detects Cheaters

Leda Cosmides and John Tooby

I Evolutionary Psychology and Deontic Logic

The recognition that our cognitive and motivational architecture is the product of natural selection raises the possibility that our moral concepts, moral intuitions, and moral sentiments might themselves be reflections of the evolutionary process. Indeed, this conclusion seems difficult to escape, given how natural selection works.

Using what is known about the evolutionary process and the behavioral ecology of ancestral hunter-gatherers, we initiated a research program in the early 1980s aimed at discovering whether the human mind reliably develops an evolved specialization for deontic reasoning about social exchange. Social exchange—also called "reciprocity," "reciprocal altruism," or "trade," depending on the research community—is cooperation for mutual benefit between two agents. Starting with evolutionary game theory, where it is analyzed as a repeated Prisoners' Dilemma, we developed *social contract theory*: a task analysis of the computational requirements for adaptively engaging in social exchange (see Cosmides, 1985; Cosmides & Tooby, 1989). Many of these requirements were so particular to adaptive problems that arise in social exchange that they could only be implemented by a computational system whose design was functionally specialized for this function. To discover whether a system of this kind exists in the human mind, we conducted reasoning experiments that looked for evidence of the design features predicted by social contract theory.

Our question was, does the human cognitive architecture reliably develop *social contract algorithms*: a neurocomputational system whose design features are adaptively specialized for producing the specific kinds of inferences and goals necessary to create cooperative interactions that implement an evolutionarily stable strategy (ESS)? By hypothesis:

1. Social contract algorithms are activated by particular cues indicating a criss-crossing pattern of desires, access to benefits, and intention to provide benefits that characterizes situations involving social exchange.

2. Once activated, social contract algorithms represent situations via a proprietary format that represents distinctions that were adaptively important in the domain for which they evolved (e.g., *agent$_i$ benefit to agent$_j$, requirement of agent$_j$, obligations, entitlements, cheating*).

3. Social contract algorithms are equipped with functionally specialized inferential procedures that were designed to operate on these proprietary representations, generating inferences that, while not true across domains, were adaptively useful when operating within the system's proper domain of application. Some of these inferences apply rules of transformation specific to social exchange, which allow obligations to be inferred from entitlements and vice versa—a form of deontic reasoning. Others regulate the detection of cheaters. The ability to detect cheaters is necessary to implement an ESS for social exchange. Thus, the adaptive function of a cheater detection mechanism would be to search for information that could reveal who has committed a specific kind of moral violation: intentional cheating in a situation of social exchange.

We have spent almost 25 years empirically testing the predictions of social contract theory and will review some of the evidence for it. In doing so, we will focus on results that distinguish reasoning about social exchange from reasoning about conditional rules drawn from other deontic domains, especially precautionary rules. We will do this for two reasons. First, casual readers of the reasoning literature have developed the mistaken belief that results found for reasoning problems involving social exchange are found for all deontic rules. This is untrue. Second, differences in how people reason about deontic rules drawn from different domains may have implications for a project within moral philosophy: the development of a domain-general deontic logic.

I.i   Why Should Moral Philosophers Care about Human Nature?

I.i.i   Natural Selection Is an Amoral Process, yet It Can Produce Moral Intuitions   Natural selection favors designs on the basis of how well they promote their own reproduction, not on how well they promote moral behavior. If this is not obvious, consider the fate of a mutation that alters the development of a neural circuit, changing its design away from the species standard. This new circuit design implements a decision rule that produces a radically different moral choice in a particular type of situation: help rather than hurt, cooperate rather than cheat. Will this new decision rule, initially present in one or a few individuals, be eliminated from the population? Or will it be retained, increasing in frequency over the generations until it replaces the old design, eventually becoming the new "standard model" in that species?

The fate of the mutant decision rule will be jointly determined by two ethically blind processes: chance and natural selection. Chance is blind not only to ethics, but to design: it cannot retain or eliminate circuit designs based on their consequences. Natural selection, however, is not blind to design. The mutant design and the standard design produce different ethical choices; these choices produce different consequences for the choosers, which can enhance or reduce the average rate at which they produce offspring (who carry the same design). If the mutant decision rule better promotes its own reproduction (through promoting the reproduction of its bearers), it will be favored by selection. Eventually, over the generations, it will become the new species standard. The decisions it produces—ethical or otherwise—will become intuitive for that species: a spontaneous, unreflective, "common sense" response to the type of situation that selected for its design.

This is the process that, over eons, constructed human nature—that is, the reliably developing, species-typical information-processing architecture of the human mind. As a result, human nature is comprised of programs that were selected for merely because they outreproduced alternative programs in the past. There is nothing in this process to ensure the production of decision rules or moral sentiments that track the desiderata of an ethically justifiable moral system. So why should moral philosophers care about human nature?

I.i.ii Human Nature, Evolved Inferences, and Moral Philosophy Human nature is relevant to moral philosophy for many reasons (Cosmides & Tooby, 2004, 2006), but here we will be concerned with just two of them. Moral philosophers should care about human nature first and foremost because they themselves are members of the human species. If the human cognitive architecture contains programs that generate moral intuitions and inferences in humans, then it generates moral intuitions and inferences in humans who are moral philosophers. These evolved programs cause specific moral inferences to be triggered by particular situations, whether those situations are occurring in real life or merely in imagination (Boyer, 2001; Cosmides & Tooby, 2000a). Counterfactual and suppositional arguments are important tools of the moral philosopher, but counterfactual propositions are held in metarepresentations to which evolved, domain-specific inference procedures are then applied (Leslie, 1987; Cosmides & Tooby, 2000b). Counterfactuals and their downstream inferences are thereby decoupled from the encyclopedia of world knowledge stored in one's semantic memory, preventing the kind of data corruption that Leslie (1987) has called "representational abuse" (Cosmides & Tooby, 2000b). This means that deliberative reasoning is not immune from the influence of domain-specific evolved programs (see, e.g., Lieberman, Tooby, & Cosmides, 2003; Haidt, 2001, on moral dumbfounding; Gendler, 2000, 2003, on affective transmission and imaginative resistance; Tooby & Cosmides, 2001).

As a result, evolved social inferences and moral intuitions can be expected to affect the inferences and judgments that moral philosophers make, even when they are making counterfactual or suppositional arguments that engage more domain-general metarepresentational machinery. Sometimes moral sentiments in response to counterfactual arguments will be nothing more than readouts of evolved programs that were generated by an amoral process—hardly a ringing endorsement. Moral philosophers need to recognize when their judgments are based on evolved moral sentiments and inferences and need to decide how this should factor into their theories.

A more subtle problem arises when one realizes that certain concepts themselves are products of the evolutionary process and were selected for because of the way they interacted with motivational systems (Tooby, Cosmides, & Barrett, 2005). This is true of certain moral concepts, such as the deontic notions of *obligation* and *entitlement*. A single word, such as "ought," "should," "obligated," or "must," may map onto several different evolved concepts, each embedded in a different, domain-specific inferential system. "Must," for example, refers to a different underlying concept when it appears in the context of social exchange than when it appears in a precautionary rule, as we will discuss below. This has implications for certain projects in logic and moral philosophy—which brings us to the second reason philosophers should care about the evolved architecture of the human mind.

For more than half a century, philosophers have been trying to develop a deontic logic that satisfies two goals. The first goal is to capture "the logical structure of our ordinary deontic language and . . . our ordinary deontic reasonings" (Castañeda, 1981, p. 38). The second is to create a formal calculus, a syntax that applies deontic concepts such as "obligation" in a content- and context-independent manner[1] (von Wright, 1951;

Hilpinen, 1971; McNamara, 2006). Feldman (2001, p. 1011), for example, expresses the latter hope when he says that "the plausibility of any logical claim is enhanced if it can be seen to cohere with an overarching conception of the logic of obligation." In suggesting a method for evaluating candidate deontic operators, Feldman says that in deontic logic systems

> . . . some operator (usually "O") is intended to be the formal analog of "ought" in one of its ordinary language senses. *The systematic logical features of the operator are precisely determined.* We then consider the extent to which the logical features of the formal operator correspond to those we intuitively suppose belong to "ought" in ordinary discourse. (Feldman 2001, emphasis added)

This passage acknowledges that "ought" has multiple senses in ordinary language. Yet it expresses the hope that one can determine *one set of systematic logical features* of operator "O" while still finding that these features correspond to people's ordinary intuitions about what "ought" implies. Accomplishing this should be difficult if "ought" has many senses in ordinary language: it would entail either choosing one sense and ignoring the others or discovering that what at first appear to be a multiplicity of meanings and implications really collapse onto one set that applies across contexts.

The first goal—capturing ordinary reasoning about deontic concepts—implies that the construction of a deontic logic must be constrained by empirical data on language use and deontic reasoning. Psychological data are clearly relevant to that goal, so we will review our research on deontic reasoning. But that research suggests that deontic reasoning is not a unified phenomenon. If so, then the first goal may be incompatible with the second goal: constructing a deontic logic with operators such as "O" that apply across all human contexts.

Creating a domain-general deontic logic would require deontic operators and rules of inference that apply in a uniform way across every (deontic) context involving human action. This includes social, moral, legal, religious, and prudential contexts (at minimum). But what if a single lexical item, such as "ought," "obligated," or "entitled," masks a plethora of meanings that bear only a family resemblance to one another? For example, what if the *ought* embedded in social contract algorithms has a different meaning/set of implications than the *ought* embedded in a precautionary inference system—that is, what if these concepts are better thought of as *ought*$_{SC}$ and *ought*$_{Prec}$?

We suspect this is a real possibility, for two reasons. The first is empirical: deontic reasoning seems to fractionate into functionally distinct domains, as we will discuss below. The second reason is theoretical and involves how natural selection tends to engineer evolved systems.

I.i.iii Domain Specificity, Evolution, and Deontic Reasoning What counts as adaptive social behavior differs by domain. Courtship, dyadic exchange, n-person cooperation, deep engagement friendship, dominance relationships, coalitional versus individual aggression, parent-child relationships, sibling relationships, hazard management—each is associated with a different set of adaptive information-processing problems, some of which are unique to that domain (e.g., Bugental, 2000; Buss, 1994; Cosmides & Tooby, 1987, 1989; Fiddick, Cosmides, & Tooby, 2000; Fiske, 1991; Kurzban, McCabe, Smith, & Wilson, 2001; Symons, 1987; Tooby & Cosmides, 1996; Tooby, Cosmides, & Price, 2006; Trivers, 1974). In saying that two adaptive problems are different, we mean something specific: that a neurocomputational system whose design is well engineered for solving one will not be well engineered for solving another (for extended discussion, see Tooby & Cosmides, 1992). When adaptive problems differ by domain, natural selection tends to produce different neurocomputational systems as solutions to these problems, each equipped with domain-specialized design features (for some stunning examples, see Gallistel, 2000). This perspective suggests that social interaction in humans will be regulated by a number of different evolved specializations, each of which is functionally specialized for negotiating a particular domain of social life.

Social interaction across many domains involves moves and countermoves, expectations, obligations, prohibitions, and entitlements. But the nature of these can be very different depending on whether one is interacting with a mate, a sibling, a child, an exchange partner, a dear friend, a status rival, a chief/superior, a foe, or a comrade-at-arms. This means that several evolved specializations, each domain specialized and context specific, may employ some *version* of a particular deontic concept. But each version may differ from the others by virtue of the unique inferential role it plays within its particular evolved inference system.

If this picture is even remotely correct, then the project of creating a deontic logic that is both general yet empirically descriptive may be doomed. Deontic logicians insisting on domain generality would be driven to define deontic concepts in a manner so general as to be useless—a manner that does not escape the problems of domain specificity but merely hides them.

Consider, for example, the very general definition of "ought" as "A person P ought to take action A when P has a reason to take A" (or "when there is a reason to take A"; e.g., Mackie, 1977). This appears general, but it is not: all the heavy lifting is shifted onto another word, in this case, onto what, exactly, it means "to have a reason to." "Having a reason to" could refer to having a mental representation of there being (i) means sufficient to attain a physical goal, (ii) means sufficient to attain a social goal (whether moral or not; e.g., helping a neighbor, having a good marriage, attaining dominance over others), (iii) means *believed* to help attain a goal (whether efficacious or not; e.g., sacrificing a goat to appease the gods), (iv) an ethical obligation, (v) prudential advice about how to reduce risk. "Having a reason to" could also refer to (vi) the wish to be (or appear) pious, (vii) the wish to conform to the requirements of a legal system, (viii) the wish to stay out of prison, (ix) the wish to avoid ostracism or social opprobrium, (x) the (somewhat different) wish to be seen as a good community member, and so on. Moreover, whatever its content, the mental representation of that "reason" could be in a form that allows conscious awareness, reflection, and verbal report or it could be implicit in the procedures and logic of an evolved program. In either case, the domain-specificity of "ought" creeps back in, under different cover.

A more realistic—and more illuminating—philosophical goal may be to embrace the domain and context specificity of moral concepts. The meaning of these concepts could be worked out, taking into account the role each plays in an evolved inferential system, as well as other more philosophical desiderata, such as noncontradiction, consistency, and so on. The project would not be to develop a domain-general deontic logic on analogy to the domain-general alethic logics. The project would instead be to develop a series of very well-specified domain-specific deontic logics, each of which applies within certain boundaries of human action and not outside them.[2]

Truth-preserving logics are not always good descriptions of how people intuitively reason. But who cares? They are still useful for increasing knowledge, whether they are implemented by a computer system or by a human being who is reasoning deliberatively and laboriously, using pencil and paper to store intermediate inferences and conclusions. Deontic logics can also be useful, but for a different reason: they can clarify the moral dimension of human affairs. Deontic logicians are certainly aware of this:

> . . . despite the fact that we need to be cautious about making too easy a link between deontic logic and practicality, many of the notions listed are typically employed in attempting to regulate and coordinate our lives together (but also to evaluate states of affairs). For these reasons, deontic logics often directly involve topics of considerable practical significance such as morality, law, social and business organizations

(their norms, as well as their normative constitution), and security systems. (McNamara, 2006)

The prospect of improving human affairs is a heady possibility. But how useful will a deontic logic be in this regard if it fails to capture major distinctions the human mind makes when reasoning deontically?

The fact that natural selection shaped certain mechanisms for moral reasoning does not justify them, but a formal deontic calculus that deeply violates our moral intuitions is not likely to be widely understood or adopted (Boyer, 2001; Sperber, 1996). Without being widely understood and adopted, a deontic logic will not succeed in guiding ethical decisions beyond an esoteric circle of specialists.

Deontic logics have the potential to illuminate and clarify moral reasoning, but to have a real impact on human affairs, they need to satisfy both normative and descriptive goals. With these thoughts in mind, we will review what has been learned about the deontic logic that our minds deploy in situations of social exchange. To situate these findings in the larger intellectual landscape, we begin with a brief overview of how psychologists have approached the study of reasoning, focusing on a tool used extensively in our investigations, the Wason selection task.

I.ii   Traditional Conceptions of Rationality in the Study of Human Reasoning

With the cognitive revolution, psychologists began to reverse engineer the mechanisms by which the human mind reasons. The goal was to discover what representations and inferential rules these programs apply. When this enterprise began, traditional views of rationality dominated psychological research. The first hypothesis considered was that programs that cause human reasoning implement "rational algorithms": ones that embody normative, truth-preserving rules of inference derived from formal logic (especially first-order logic) or mathematics (e.g., Bayes's theorem). For example, Peter Wason, a pioneer in the study of the psychology of reasoning, explored the notion that everyday learning was a form of Popperian hypothesis testing: one projects a hypothesis, framed as a conditional rule, and then seeks falsifying instances. His four-card selection task was designed to see whether people would spontaneously and accurately look for potential violations of a conditional rule, linguistically expressed as *If P then Q* (see figure 2.1). He found, much to his surprise, that they did not. By first-order logic, *If P then Q* is violated by any instance or situation in which *P* is true and *Q* is false, so the solution to Wason's selection

Ebbinghaus disease was recently identified and is not yet well understood. So an international committee of physicians who have experience with this disease were assembled. Their goal was to characterize the symptoms, and develop surefire ways of diagnosing it.

Patients afflicted with Ebbinghaus disease have many different symptoms: nose bleeds, headaches, ringing in the ears, and others. Diagnosing it is difficult because a patient may have the disease, yet not manifest all of the symptoms. Dr. Buchner, an expert on the disease, said that the following rule holds:

"If a person has Ebbinghaus disease, then that person will be forgetful."

If   P   then   Q

Dr. Buchner may be wrong, however. You are interested in seeing whether there are any patients whose symptoms violate this rule.

The cards below represent four patients in your hospital. Each card represents one patient. One side of the card tells whether or not the patient has Ebbinghaus disease, and the other side tells whether or not that patient is forgetful.

Which of the following card(s) would you definitely need to turn over to see if any of these cases violate Dr. Buchner's rule: "If a person has Ebbinghaus disease, then that person will be forgetful." Don't turn over any more cards than are absolutely necessary.

has Ebbinghaus disease	does not have Ebbinghaus disease	is forgetful	is not forgetful
P	not-P	Q	not-Q

Figure 2.1

The Wason selection task (indicative, descriptive rule, familiar content). In a Wason task, there is always a rule of the form *If P then Q*, and four cards showing the values *P*, *not-P*, *Q*, and *not-Q* (respectively) on the side that the subject can see. By first-order logic, only the combination of *P* and *not-Q* can violate this rule, so the correct answer is to check the *P* card (to see if it has a *not-Q* on the back), the *not-Q* card (to see if it has a *P* on the back), and no others. Few subjects answer correctly, however, when the conditional rule is descriptive (indicative), even when its content is familiar; for example, only 26% of subjects answered the above problem correctly (by choosing "has Ebbinghaus disease" and "is not forgetful"). Most choose either *P* alone or *P* & *Q*. (The italicized *P*s and *Q*s are not in problems given to subjects.)

task is to choose the *P* card (to see if it says *not-Q* on the back) and to choose the *not-Q* card (to see if it has a *P* on the back). But when the conditional rule was indicative, purporting to describe some relationship in the world, only 5%–30% of people chose *P*, *not-Q*, and no other cards. Most chose *P* alone or *P* & *Q*, behavior that is consistent with a confirmation bias. Taking a semester-long course in logic did not improve students' performance (Cheng, Holyoak, Nisbett, & Oliver, 1986). Wason even found that logicians sometimes got it wrong at first, admitting in retrospect that they should have chosen *P* & *not-Q* (Wason & Johnson-Laird, 1972).

Follow-up studies eliminated many possible reasons for this poor performance. It's not that people are interpreting the rule as a biconditional and
then reasoning logically: that would lead them to choose all four cards,
which is a rare response. It's not that people require more than one violating instance to decide the rule is false: the same levels of performance
prevail when subjects are only asked to look for potential violations of the
rule, without being asked to evaluate the truth of the rule. It's not that
the indicatives tested involved an arbitrary relation between letters and
numbers. During the late 1970s and early 1980s, indicatives involving
familiar, everyday content were tested. Wason performance on indicative
conditionals remained low whether the terms were concrete and familiar,
the relation between them was concrete and familiar, or both (e.g.,
Cosmides, 1985, 1989; Griggs & Cox, 1982; Manktelow & Evans, 1979;
Wason, 1983; Yachanin & Tweney, 1982; reviewed in Cosmides, 1985).
This should be obvious from the conditional rule shown in figure 2.1.
What could be more familiar or "natural" than the notion that a disease
causes symptoms? Yet this conditional rule elicited the correct response
from only 26% of undergraduates. (Buller's, 2005, recent claim that people
do well on the Wason task when the terms or relations of an indicative
are familiar or "natural" has been known to be false for many years.)

Most interestingly, poor performance on the selection task is not because
people don't know that an instance of *P & not-Q* would violate the rule.
When people are asked whether a case of *P & not-Q* would violate the rule
(an evaluation task), they recognize that it would (Manktelow & Over,
1987). To investigate in another way the relation between knowing what
counts as a violation and searching for one, we once did a series of Wason
studies in which we first told subjects exactly what counts as a violation.
In these studies, subjects were given a conditional rule purporting (e.g.) to
describe people's transportation habits: *If a person goes into Boston, then that
person takes the subway*. The cards represented four people, and each specified where that person went on a particular day and how they got there.
The facing side of the cards read *Boston, Arlington, subway*, and *cab*. Subjects
were asked to indicate those card(s) they would need to turn over to see if
the behavior of any of these individuals violates the rule—so far, a standard
selection task. But at the top of the page, we first explained—in ever
increasing detail—what would count as violating a conditional rule of this
kind. In one condition we put it abstractly, explaining that a rule of the
form *If X happens, then Y happens* "has been broken whenever X happens
but Y does not happen. Remember this in answering the question below."
In another condition we added to this: "So, for example, the rule below

would be broken by a person who went to Boston by cab." In yet another version, we added: "So, for example, the rule below would be broken by a person who went to Boston without taking the subway—e.g., a person who went to Boston by cab." (Note that these last two mention the precise cases of *P* and *not-Q* shown on the cards.) In all cases, performance hovered around 25% correct—no different from a condition in which we said nothing about what counts as a violation. (We did a parallel series using a deontic rule that was not a social contract; results were the same, with performance averaging 18% correct.) Combined with results from evaluation tasks, this is telling: although people *recognize* what counts as violating an indicative rule, they do not *seek out* information that could tell them whether the rule has been violated, even when they are explicitly asked to do so and have all the time they wish (see also Fiddick et al., 2000, pp. 44–45, 74–75).

Why was poor performance on Wason's selection task significant? Even the simplest computer programming languages have inferential rules that operate on the syntax of If-then, of antecedents and consequents, regardless of their content. Basic rules of logic that operate on this syntax, like *modus ponens* and *modus tollens*, are useful precisely because they allow true conclusions to be derived from true premises, no matter what the content of the premises may be. That the human brain might be equipped with such rules, operating over a content-general If-then syntax, is not only reasonable, but it fits with prevailing notions that we are the "rational animal," the species where reason emerged, erasing instincts in its wake. If the human brain, like the simplest of computer languages, is equipped with logical rules of inference operating on the syntax of If-then, then why weren't more people succeeding on the Wason selection task? *Modus ponens* would lead them to choose the *P* card, *modus tollens* to choose the *not-Q* card. Moreover, the problem space for the Wason task is finite and small: regardless of which face is up, the possible values on the cards are *P & Q*, *P & not-Q*, *not-P & Q*, *not-P & not-Q*. Given that people recognize that *P & not-Q* counts as a violating instance, an exhaustive search of this small problem space should lead them to choose the only cards that could combine these two values: the *P* card and the *not-Q* card. Indeed, they do choose the *P* card, almost always, consistent with other data suggesting that the brain's neural circuitry does implement and spontaneously apply a *modus ponens* inference rule to the syntax of If-then (e.g., when one is asked to draw a conclusion from premises or to evaluate the validity of a conclusion drawn by others; Rips, 1994; Wason & Johnson-Laird, 1972). But the *not-Q* card is chosen only about 50% of the time, consistent with other research showing that *modus tollens* is not spontaneously applied as often as *modus ponens* is (Rips, 1994; Wason & Johnson-Laird, 1972). In addition, cards inconsistent with either logical rule of inference—especially the Q card—are often chosen. Why does this happen? The task is conceptually so simple, the solution could be implemented on a computer in a few lines of code.

Selection task results for indicative conditionals led many to doubt that the brain has circuitry that implements all the rules of first-order logic. That debate remains unsettled: perhaps it does, but only within a comprehension module (Sperber, Cara, & Girotto, 1995); perhaps pre-existing beliefs hijack logical analysis (Evans, 1989); perhaps the search for confirming instances is a more useful learning strategy when someone proposes *If P then Q*, given a world where there are an infinite number of properties that have no association with the presence of property *P*, and only a few properties that do.

I.ii.i Deontic Exceptions to the Pattern Poor performance on the Wason task was first noted with indicative rules that relate numbers and letters, and then with indicatives that link more familiar terms and relations, such as "If a person eats hot chili peppers, then he will drink a cold beer"—despite the familiar experience of trying to sooth a burning mouth with a cold drink, this particular rule elicited only 35% correct from Harvard undergraduates, even when *not-Q* referred to drinking hot tea (Cosmides, 1985). The failure to answer "*P & not-Q*" was so pervasive that it was initially thought to apply to all conditional rules. But during the early to mid 1980s, it became apparent that one could elicit "*P & not-Q*" responses with tasks employing a deontic conditional, that is, a conditional statement describing what a person is *obligated* or *entitled* to do in a given context. An early example was from Griggs and Cox (1982), who elicited high levels of "*P & not-Q*" responses with the drinking age problem ("If a person is drinking beer, then the person must be over 19 years old" (*N.B.* 19 was the legal drinking age at the time.)). But high performance with this rule was not initially attributed to the fact that it is deontic rather than indicative. This law was so well-known (and so famously violated) by undergraduate subjects that excellent performance was thought to reflect the familiarity of the rule and/or the fact that many subjects had personal experiences of having violated it, which they could retrieve from memory and match to the cards. That good violation detection on the Wason task could be elicited *systematically* by certain deontic rules first became apparent from our own work (Cosmides, 1985, 1989; Cosmides & Tooby, 1989) and that of Cheng and Holyoak (1985; Cheng, Holyoak, Nisbett, & Oliver, 1986). The theoretical perspectives were quite different, but the phenomena similar: *certain* deontic rules could elicit good violation on the selection task, regardless of their familiarity.

One set of results was presented in Cosmides's (1985) dissertation and then circulated like samizdat for a number of years, eliciting published commentary (e.g., Manktelow & Over, 1987) several years before appearing in journals. (The fact that the hypotheses tested were derived from theories originating in evolutionary biology was considered inflammatory at the time and was a deal breaker for many psychology journals.) We had proposed that the human mind reliably develops *social contract algorithms*: computational machinery that is functionally specialized for reasoning about social exchange (Cosmides, 1985, 1989; Cosmides & Tooby, 1989). In this work, we showed that deontic rules that fit the template of a social contract (see below) reliably elicit high levels of violation detection on the Wason task, that they do so regardless of the rule's familiarity, that the rules of inference are specific to social exchange and do not map onto rules of inference of first-order logic, and that deontic rules that do not fit the social contract template do not elicit high levels of violation detection.[3] Because social exchange involves deontic concepts, social contract algorithms embody a form of deontic logic (Sections II and III). But their logic and operations are not general to all deontic rules: They are well engineered only for interpreting and reasoning about situations involving social exchange, and their ability to detect violations is restricted to those produced by intentional cheating (Section IV).

At the end of 1985, Cheng and Holyoak published an influential paper also showing that certain deontic rules can systematically elicit high levels of violation detection. The scope of their explanation—permission schema theory—is broader than the scope of social contract theory. If it were true, the prospects for creating a deontic logic that is content general yet still respects empirical data about the fracture points of human reasoning would be more promising. In Section IV, we will discuss data that speak against their view and others like it, showing that "deontic reasoning" fractionates into a number of different domains.

e.g.

I.iii Ecological Rationality in the Study of Reasoning

The traditional view held human reasoning to be rational to the extent that it conforms to normative theories drawn from mathematics and logic. Our research on reasoning emerged from a different view, sometimes called *ecological rationality*. According to this view, the human cognitive

architecture reliably develops a number of functionally isolable computational systems, each of which is specialized for solving a different adaptive
problem (for reviews, see Barkow, Cosmides, & Tooby, 1992; Boyer, 2001;
Buss, 2005; Hirschfeld & Gelman, 1994; Pinker, 1997; Gallistel, 2000).
When activated by content from the appropriate domain, these inference
engines impose special and privileged representations during the process
of situation interpretation, define specialized goals for reasoning tailored
to their domain, and make available specialized inferential procedures that
allow certain computations to proceed automatically or "intuitively" and
with enhanced efficiency over what a more general reasoning process could
achieve given the same input (Cosmides & Tooby 1987, 2005a; Tooby &
Cosmides, 1992, 2005). The designs of these systems may not embody
content-independent norms of rationality, such as the predicate calculus
or Bayes's rule, but they are *ecologically rational* (Gigerenzer, Todd, & ABC
Research Group, 1999; Cosmides & Tooby, 1996a; Tooby & Cosmides, in
press). That is, each embodies functionally specialized design features that
reflect the task demands of the adaptive problem it evolved to solve,
including assumptions about the evolutionarily long-term ecological structure of the world. As a result, when operating within the domain for which
they evolved, these systems solve adaptive problems reliably, efficiently,
and with limited information.

The Charlie task, from Simon Baron-Cohen's (1995) research on theory
of mind, provides a good illustration of an ecologically rational inference
system. It reveals the presence of a reasoning mechanism that is useful for
inferring people's goals and desires because its structure reflects an evolutionarily long-enduring feature of the world: that people, like other animals,
often turn their eyes in the direction of objects they are interested in.

A child is shown a schematic face ("Charlie") surrounded by four different kinds of candy. Charlie's eyes are pointed, for example, toward the
Milky Way bar. The child is then asked, "Which candy does Charlie want?"
Like you and I, a normal 4-year-old will say that Charlie wants the Milky
Way (i.e., the object of Charlie's gaze). In contrast, children with autism
fail the Charlie task, producing random responses. However—and this is
important—when asked which candy Charlie is looking at, children with
autism answer correctly. That is, children with this developmental disorder
can compute eye direction correctly, *but they cannot use that information to
infer what someone wants.*

We know, spontaneously and with no mental effort, that Charlie *wants*
the candy he is *looking at.* This is so obvious to us that it hardly seems to
require an inference at all. It is just common sense. However, this "common

sense" is caused: it is produced by cognitive mechanisms. To infer a mental state (*wanting*) and its content (*Milky Way*) from information about eye direction requires a computation. There is a little inference circuit—a reasoning instinct, if you will—that produces this inference. When the circuit that does this computation is broken or fails to develop, the inference cannot be made. Those with autism fail the Charlie task because they lack this reasoning instinct.

In what sense is this reasoning instinct domain specific, content specific, and ecologically rational? It is domain specialized because it is well engineered for making inferences about agents and their mental states, not about plants, mountains, or tools—not even about aspects of agents unrelated to their mental states (not their substance, their appropriateness as projectiles, etc.). It is content specialized for several reasons. (1) It takes information about eye direction and object-of-eye-direction as input. (2) It has specialized representational formats: it represents people as having (invisible) mental states like *wanting* that cause their behavior and infers the content of these mental states (*wants*(Milky Way)). And (3) the inferential procedure activated has nothing to do with logic or mathematics: it is specific to eye gaze and mental states. What makes it ecologically rational? When operating within its proper domain (agents and mental states), it produces inferences that are likely to be true because they are based on an ecological regularity of past[4] environments: that eye direction predicts object of attention. When operating outside its proper domain (e.g., when activated by "eyes" on a butterfly's wings), the inferences it produces are useless.

To create a content-free inference system, one whose procedures operate validly across all domains, one would need to *remove* this very useful reasoning instinct precisely because it produces useful inferences in some domains but not in others. As a result, an inference system that is completely content free would be computationally weaker than a system that is replete with ecologically rational inference procedures like this one: content-general[5] and content-specific ones, all working together.

Ecologically rational inference systems like this one gain their inferential power by taking advantage of relationships that are true (or at least statistically reliable) within a particular problem domain, and they solve specific problems that arise within that domain. These problems need not be about determining what is true of the world; they may be inferences about how to behave. A snake avoidance system isn't just about whether a snake is present; it includes the inference that one should move away from the snake (see Tooby, Cosmides, & Barrett, 2005, on how selection pressures shaping motivational systems should have shaped co-adapted conceptual systems). To solve these domain-limited problems, each of these inference systems should be designed to operate over a different and limited class of content and be activated by cues associated with their proper domain (Barrett, 2005; Sperber, 1994). On this view, we should expect to find that the human cognitive architecture is densely populated with a large number of evolved, content-specific, domain-specific inference engines (or evolved mechanisms for their developmental acquisition), in addition to whatever more domain- or content-general inferential competences may exist.

We will be discussing two computational systems of this kind. One is designed for reasoning about social exchange: for detecting when a situation involves social exchange, for making appropriate inferences about what these interactions entail, and for detecting cheaters (Cosmides, 1985, 1989; Cosmides & Tooby, 1989, 1992, 2005a). The other is designed for reasoning about risk reduction in hazardous situations and is well engineered for detecting violations of precautionary rules—instances in which a person might be in danger by virtue of having failed to take appropriate precautions (Boyer & Lienard, 2006; Cosmides & Tooby, 1997; Fiddick, 1998; Fiddick et al., 2000; Leckman & Mayes, 1998, 1999; Stone, Cosmides, Tooby, Kroll, & Knight, 2002). These systems make certain inferences easy, effortless, and intuitive when one is reasoning about problems that tap their respective domains.

As a species, we have been blind to the existence of these domain-specialized inference systems—these reasoning instincts—not because we lack them but precisely because they work so well. Because they process information so effortlessly and automatically, their operation disappears unnoticed into the background. These instincts structure our thoughts so powerfully that it can be difficult to imagine how things could be otherwise. As a result, we take "normal" inferences and behavior for granted: We do not realize that "common sense" thought and behavior need to be explained at all.

This problem—we call it "instinct blindness"—can afflict anyone, including philosophers. Occasionally, we encounter philosophers who try to account for the data we discuss below by saying that social contracts (along with other deontic rules) "have" a different interpretation than indicative rules (Buller, 2005; Fodor, 2000). This is naive realism. Social contracts do not "have" an interpretation; the mind *assigns* an interpretation to them, and it does so when certain cues and conditions are contextually present (Cosmides, 1985, 1989; Cosmides & Tooby, 1992; Fiddick et al., 2000; Gigerenzer & Hug, 1992; Platt & Griggs, 1993). Social contract theory is an account of the computational procedures *by which these interpretations are assigned*: what cues are necessary and/or sufficient, which inferential transformations these procedures license, and so on. Social contract theory predicted—in advance of the empirical evidence—that people will interpret conditionals expressing social exchange differently from other conditionals (both indicative and deontic) and make different inferences about them. That prediction, now empirically validated, is one of the facts that the theory predicted and explains. Social contract theory is an attempt to replace the black box of "interpretation" with computational machinery that does the interpreting—in short, to build a cognitive science of central processes.

We hope philosophers will spill no more ink explaining to us that interpretion plays a role in reasoning about conditional rules, including social contracts. Explaining how the mind interprets conditional rules has been an important aspect of social contract theory since its inception (Cosmides, 1985; Cosmides & Tooby, 1989). Indeed, a 2000 paper of ours highlights this in the title: "No Interpretation without Representation: The Role of Domain-Specific Representations and Inferences in the Wason Selection Task" (Fiddick et al., 2000).[6] A more productive use of time would be to propose a theory of interpretation that differs from social contract theory's, yet explains reasoning performance. In attempting to do so, however, two facts must be kept in mind, which we will elaborate on below. First, many deontic rules *do not elicit good violation detection on the Wason task*. This means that no explanation that refers to interpretation can be correct if it is general to all deontic rules. Second, whether a given social contract rule elicits good violation detection depends on whether the context proposes that the violation results from intentional cheating or an innocent mistake. *Yet the interpretation of the rule is the same in both cases*: it is precisely the same rule embedded in a story that gives each of its terms and the relation between them precisely the same social contract meaning. All that differs are the proposed motivations of the potential violator. This result is important: it means that assigning a "social contract" interpretation to a conditional rule is not sufficient for eliciting good violation detection.

That said, we turn to the theory.

II Evolutionarily Stable Strategies and Social Contract Theory

Social contract theory is based on the hypothesis that the human mind was designed by evolution to reliably develop a cognitive adaptation specialized for reasoning about social exchange. To test whether a system is

ʰat evolved for a particular function, one must produce
It is an engineering standard: functional design is evi-
⸱ ⸱et of features of the phenotype that (i) combine to solve an
⸱⸳ment of a specific adaptive problem particularly well and (ii) do so in a
way unlikely to have arisen by chance alone or as a side effect of a mechanism with a different function. Hence, the first step is to demonstrate that
the system's properties solve an adaptive problem in a well-engineered way
(Dawkins, 1996; Tooby & Cosmides, 1992, 2005; Williams, 1966). But this
requires a well-specified theory of the adaptive problem in question. How
can one develop such a theory about *social* behavior?

From an evolutionary point of view, the design of programs causing
social behavior is constrained by the behavior of other agents. More precisely, it is constrained by the design of the behavior-regulating programs
in other agents and the fitness consequences that result from the social
interactions these programs cause. These constraints can be analyzed using
evolutionary game theory (Maynard Smith, 1982). The application of game
theory to the evolutionary process provides a bridge between evolutionary
biology and the cognitive sciences that is especially relevant to analyzing
social behavior.

An *evolutionarily stable strategy* (ESS) is a strategy (a decision rule) that
can persist in a population because it produces fitness outcomes greater
than or equal to alternative strategies (Maynard Smith, 1982). The rules
of reasoning and decision making that guide social exchange in humans
would not exist unless they had outcompeted alternatives, so we should
expect that they implement an ESS.[7] By using game theory and conducting
computer simulations of the evolutionary process, one can determine
which strategies for engaging in social exchange are ESSs.

During the 1960s, evolutionary biologists became very interested in
understanding how adaptations causing individuals to help others—often
at some cost to themselves—could evolve (Hamilton, 1964; Williams,
1966). To that end, they began exploring interactions that fit the repeated
Prisoners' Dilemma, using evolutionary game theory (Axelrod, 1984;
Axelrod & Hamilton, 1981; Boyd, 1988; Trivers, 1971). Simulations of the
evolutionary process showed that only certain decision rules for conferring
benefits on unrelated others were evolutionarily stable. For example,
"Always cooperate," a decision rule that distributes benefits to others
regardless of whether the recipients ever provide benefits in return, is not
evolutionarily stable—it is selected out in any environment that includes
decision rules that sometimes "cheat" (fail to reciprocate). But "Tit for tat,"
a decision rule that helps reciprocators but not cheaters, is an ESS. It can

invade a population of cheaters (e.g., individuals equipped with decision rules such as "Always defect," which accepts benefits but never provides benefits in return) and, once established, it can remain at high relative frequencies even when "cheater" designs, such as "Always defect," are introduced into the population.

These analyses showed that ability to reliably and systematically detect cheaters is a necessary condition for cooperation in the repeated Prisoners' Dilemma to be an ESS (and also in other situations; see Stevens & Stephens, 2004; Tooby & Cosmides, 1996). To see this, consider the fate of a program that, because it cannot detect cheaters, bestows benefits on others unconditionally. These unconditional helpers will increase the fitness of any nonreciprocating design they meet in the population. But when a nonreciprocating design is helped, the unconditional helper never recoups the expense of helping: the helper design incurs a net fitness cost while conferring a net fitness advantage on a design that does not help in return.[8] As a result, a population of unconditional helpers is easily invaded and eventually outcompeted by designs that accept the benefits helpers bestow without reciprocating them. Unconditional helping is not an ESS.

In contrast, program designs that cause _conditional_ helping—that help those who reciprocate the favor, but not those who fail to reciprocate—can invade a population of nonreciprocators and outcompete them. This is because they gain the benefits of cooperation whenever they interact with another reciprocating design. Moreover, a population of such designs can resist invasion by designs that do not nonreciprocate (cheater designs). Therefore, conditional helping, which requires the ability to detect cheaters, is an ESS. There is a mutual provisioning of benefits, each conditional on the other's compliance.

Engineers always start with a task analysis before considering possible design solutions. We did, too. By applying ESS analyses to the behavioral ecology of hunter-gatherers, we were able to specify tasks that an information-processing program would have to be good at solving for it to implement an evolutionarily stable form of social exchange (Cosmides, 1985, chapter 5; Cosmides & Tooby, 1989). This task analysis of the required computations, _social contract theory_, specifies what counts as good design in this domain. We will mention a few elements of the theory here.

II.i Social Contract Theory
Selection pressures favoring social exchange exist whenever one organism (the provider) can change the behavior of a target organism to the provider's advantage by making the target's receipt of that benefit _conditional_ on

the target's acting in a required manner. Thus, we define a social exchange as a situation in which, in order to be entitled to receive a *benefit* from another agent, an individual is obligated to satisfy a requirement imposed by that agent (often, but not necessarily, at some cost to himself or herself; but see Stevens & Stephens, 2004; Tooby & Cosmides, 1996). Those who are rationing access to the benefit impose the requirement because its satisfaction creates a situation that benefits them.

A *social contract* expresses this intercontingency and can be expressed in the form of a conditional rule: "If you accept a benefit from agent X, then you must satisfy X's requirement." The agent can be an individual or set of individuals (Cosmides & Tooby, 1989; Fiddick et al., 2000; Tooby, Cosmides, & Price, 2006) and the *must* is understood as involving obligation rather than logical necessity. The specific linguistic expression is not what is important—what matters is that the situation is interpreted as involving one individual offering to provide a benefit to another contingent on that person satisfying a requirement in return, either now or in the future. Intentions to initiate exchange relationships need not be explicitly stated, either: When Agent X provides a benefit to Agent Y, triggering the expectation in both that Y will at some point provide a benefit to X in return, a social exchange relationship has been initiated. Indeed, within hunter-gatherer bands, many or most reciprocity interactions are implicit. For example, in discussing her feelings about food sharing, Nisa, a !Kung San gatherer in Botswana who was extensively interviewed by Marjorie Shostak, explained:

If a person doesn't give something to me, I won't give anything to that person. If I'm sitting eating, and someone like that comes by, I say, "Uhn, uhn. I'm not going to give any of this to you. When you have food, the things you do with it make me unhappy. If you even once in a while gave me something nice, I would surely give some of this to you." (Shostak, 1981, p. 89)

Nisa's words express her expectations about social exchange, which form an implicit social contract: *If you are to get food in the future from me, then you must share food with me.* Whether we are San foragers or city dwellers, we all realize that the act of accepting a benefit from someone triggers an obligation to behave in a way that somehow benefits the provider, now or in the future.

II.i.i Interpretation by Social Contract Algorithms When the mind registers that a situation with this structure of agents, benefits to agents, and requirements obtains—that is, when the situation is interpreted as involving an implicit or explicit agreement to engage in social exchange—social contract algorithms will apply deontic concepts such as *obligation* and *entitlement*. If the conditional is stated linguistically, they will "read in" these concepts even if they are not stated in the rule. The social contract algorithms will also infer the many implications and entailments of an exchange, listed in tables 2.1 and 2.2. For example, the following two statements will be thought to entail one another:

[1] "If you accept a benefit from agent X, then you are obligated to satisfy X's requirement."

[2] "If you satisfy agent X's requirement, then you are entitled to the benefit X offered to provide."

Because concepts such as *obligation* and *entitlement* will be read in whenever the mind registers that the situation has the deep structure of an exchange, the surface, linguistic structure of the conditional need not contain any of these words. For example, if I know my teen-aged daughter wants to borrow my car, I might say:

[3] "If you borrow my car, then fill the tank with gas" (no modal operators stated).

My daughter, by virtue of having a mind equipped with social contract algorithms, will realize that this implies:

[4] "If I fill her tank with gas, then I will be entitled to borrow her car."

Her mind will supply the concept of *entitlement*, even though I never used the word or even discussed the concept (I only mentioned what I required of *her*). If she fills the tank and I then say she cannot borrow the car after all, she should feel cheated and angry—because I have deprived her of something she now feels entitled to.

Alternatively, I could have said:

[5] "If you fill the tank with gas, then you can borrow my car" (modal *can* stated; automatically interpreted by her social contract algorithms as involving entitlement rather than possibility).

My daughter would understand that this entails:

[6] "If I borrow her car, then I will be obligated to fill her tank with gas" (*obligation* read in by her social contract algorithms).

To import concepts of obligation and entitlement into social exchange in the right way, certain situational cues must be present. Information

Table 2.1

Exchanges: Inferences licensed by social contract algorithms

"If <u>you give me P</u>, then <u>I will give you Q</u>" (= "If <u>I give you Q</u>, then <u>you give me P</u>")* either expression means (entails) the following:

1. I want you to give me P,

2. My offer fulfills the cost/benefit requirements of a sincere contract (*listed in table 2.2*),

3. I realize, and I intend that you realize, that 4–9 are entailed if, and only if, you accept my offer:

4. If you give me P, then I will give you Q,

5. By virtue of my adhering to the conditions of this contract, my belief that you have given (or will give) me P will be the cause of my giving you Q,

6. If you do not give me P, I will not give you Q,

7. By virtue of my adhering to the conditions of this contract, my belief that you have not given (or will not give) me P will be the cause of my not giving you Q,

8. If you accept Q from me, then you are obligated to give me P (alternatively, If you accept Q from me, then I am entitled to receive P from you),

9. If you give me P, then I am obligated to give you Q (alternatively, If you give me P, then you are entitled to receive Q from me).

What does it mean for you to be *obligated* to do P?

a. You have agreed to do P for me under certain contractual conditions (such as 1–9), and

b. Those conditions have been met, and

c. By virtue of your not thereupon doing P, you agree that if I use some means of getting P (or its equivalent) from you that does not involve getting your voluntary consent, then I will suffer no reprisal from you. *OR: By virtue of your not thereupon giving me P, you agree that if I lower your utility by some (optimal) amount X (where X > B_{you}—your unearned gains), then I will suffer no reprisal from you.*

What does it mean for you to be *entitled* to Q?

d. I have agreed to give you Q under certain contractual conditions (such as 1–9), and

e. Those conditions have not been met, and

f. By virtue of my not thereupon giving you Q, I agree that if you use some means of getting Q (or its equivalent) from me that does not involve getting my voluntary consent, then you will suffer no reprisal from me. *OR: By virtue of my not thereupon giving you Q, I agree that if you lower my utility by some (optimal) amount X (where X > B_{me}—my unearned spoils), then you will suffer no reprisal from me.*

---

*We used a case of giving as illustration, but social exchange encompasses more than the exchange of goods. "Give" takes three arguments: two agents and the entity given. From this perspective, it is important to preserve the correct binding of agents to items of exchange, and the intercontingent nature of the giving. It is *not* relevant which agent is the subject in the if-clause and which in the then-clause. Furthermore, the entailments all hold, regardless of who fulfills their part of the contract first (i.e., tense is irrelevant, unless it is specified that order falls under the terms of the contract).

Table 2.2
Sincere social contracts: Cost/benefit relations for an exchange of goods when one party is sincere and that party believes the other party is also sincere*

	"If you give me P, then I'll give you Q"			
	Sincere Offer		Sincere Acceptance	
My offer:	*I believe:*		*You believe:*	
P	B_{me}	C_{you}	B_{me}	C_{you}
not-P	0_{me}	0_{you}	0_{me}	0_{you}
Q	C_{me}	B_{you}	C_{me}	B_{you}
not-Q	0_{me}	0_{you}	0_{me}	0_{you}
Profit Margin:	*Positive:*	*Positive:*	*Positive:*	*Positive:*
	$B_{me} > C_{me}$	$B_{you} > C_{you}$	$B_{me} > C_{me}$	$B_{you} > C_{you}$
Translation:				
My terms	"If B_{me} then C_{me}"		"If B_{me} then C_{me}"	
Your terms	"If C_{you} then B_{you}"		"If C_{you} then B_{you}"	

*Costs and benefits are relative to a baseline that each party believes would pertain in the absence of an exchange (the zero-level utility baseline). B_x = benefit to individual x; C_x = cost to individual x; 0_x = no change from x's utility at baseline. A contract has been *sincerely* offered and accepted when both parties are being truthful about their baselines and when each believes the B > C constraint holds for the other (Cosmides, 1985; Cosmides & Tooby, 1989).

about what each agent wants (and controls access to) is important: here, that my daughter wants to borrow my car and that I would like to have gas in my tank the next time I drive it (i.e., I control access to something she wants, and there is something I want that she can provide). If that is known to the agents (or to an observer), then we need not use "Ifs" and "thens" in speaking. My daughter could say:

[7] "I need to borrow your car"

and I could reply

[8] "OK, but fill the tank with gas."

The structure of entailments in table 2.1 is triggered by the situation of my agreeing ("OK") to provide a benefit contingently ("but do X"). The social contract algorithms supply all the inferences in table 2.1 and inject the appropriate concepts of obligation and entitlement, *whether they were explicitly stated or not.*

We import all this surplus structure so automatically and intuitively that there seems to be nothing to explain: that we interpret the situation in this way is just common sense. True enough—but that is what we are trying to explain. More specifically, we are trying to understand the programming structure of the computational machinery that produces this common sense. Various sets of machinery are involved. Theory-of-mind machinery computes the desires of agents based on cues such as what a person is looking at (Charlie task), moving toward, or saying (Baron-Cohen, 1995). These representations feed into mechanisms designed to detect certain (ancestral) situation types: social exchange, threat, precautions, courtship, and so forth. Social exchange situation detectors are activated when the situation is registered as having the structure of criss-crossing wants and access described above (I control access to what she wants; she can do something I want) plus an indication of agreement to exchange. The cues can be very minimal (see Fiddick et al., 2000, Experiment 1) or floridly expressed as a conditional rule with deontic operators. But if the social exchange situation detectors fire, the social contract algorithms that embody the inferences of table 2.1 will be applied. As a result, you will understand (e.g.) that [3] and [9] entail one another—indeed, express the same social contract—even though neither contains any modal operators, deontic or otherwise:

[3] "If you borrow my car, then fill the tank with gas."

[9] "If you fill the tank with gas, then borrow the car."

Here is the key point, but one must think computationally to understand it. Let's say the computational machinery of our minds contained no social contract algorithms or other domain-specific inference systems. Let's say the only inferential rules implemented by our computational machinery were those of first-order logic, and that these rules were designed, as is common in programming languages, to recognize and operate over antecedents (*P*s) and consequents (*Q*s) as explicitly stated in a conditional rule, *If P then Q*. If this were the case, our common sense would *not* tell us that [3] entails [9] and vice versa. By the rules of inference of first-order logic, sentences [3] and [9] are not logically equivalent: *If P then Q* does not imply *If Q then P*.

Now imagine that the human mind contains computational machinery that implements social contract theory in the way we have proposed. On this view, we would see [3] as implying [9] because (i) social contract algorithms supply concepts of *obligation* and *entitlement* in just the right places when situation detectors have registered that the criss-crossing pattern of access and wants applies and an agreement to provide benefits contingently has been reached, and (ii) they apply a set of inference rules *specific to the domain of social exchange* that license each as a translation of the other (No. 8 and No. 9 in table 2.1). This will happen because, when the situation detector has activated the social contract algorithms, they will map [3] onto the deep structure specified in [1], and [9] onto the deep structure specified in [2].

II.i.i.i Applying Multiple Systems What happens if there are multiple sets of computational machinery in the mind, each implementing different rules of inference? Each would have to be equipped with situation detectors, which monitor for cues indicating whether the current situation fits the input conditions for a given adaptive specialization (Barrett, 2005; Sperber, 1994). Many situations will activate only one domain-specific inference system, but some might jointly activate two of them. For example, Cheng and Holyoak (1985) used an international border-crossing rule indicating that "If you are to enter the country, then you must have been vaccinated for cholera." This is clearly a social contract for the person who very much *wants* to enter the country. But for someone who views entering the country as hazardous because cholera is endemic—and for government officials who want to stem the tide of cholera in the country—this may be interpreted as a precautionary rule, fitting the template "If you are to engage in hazardous activity H, then take precaution R." We have also suggested that a well-designed mind containing many different inference systems may implement a *principle of preemptive specificity* (Fiddick et al., 2000). According to this metaprinciple, if a situation fits the input conditions of several inference systems in a class inclusion relationship, the most domain-specific one will preempt the operation of the more domain-general ones. For example, if, in addition to social contract algorithms, the mind also contains computational machinery that implements *modus ponens* and *modus tollens*, these will not be applied to [3] and [9]. When the situation is interpreted as involving exchange, the social contract algorithms will preempt the operation of these more domain-general inference rules. This predicts, for example, that it will be difficult to apply *modus ponens* and *tollens* to [9]. This turns out to be true, as we will explain in section IV.iii.i.

II.i.i.ii Surplus Structure Is Domain Specific We have discussed the surplus structure of obligation, entitlement, and inference that social contract algorithms supply to rules like [3] and [9]. But note that none of this happens for indicative rules. We do not interpret the Ebbinghaus rule as meaning "If a person has Ebbinghaus disease, then that person is *obligated* to be forgetful," nor do we think it implies that "If a person is forgetful, then that person is *entitled* to have Ebbinghaus disease."

Like social contracts, precautionary rules are considered deontic: they specify what you *ought* to do (when engaged in hazardous activities). Precautionary rules also activate surplus structure, but it is different from that applied to social contract rules. The *must* in "If you work with toxic gases, then you must wear a gas mask" does not imply that one has *incurred an obligation* to another person by virtue of working with toxic gases. Instead it expresses advice about how to stay safe while working with toxic gases (i.e., "You must wear it or you will be in danger").

Moreover, it would be bizarre to infer from this rule that "If you wear a gas mask, then you are *entitled* to work with toxic gas." Few people view working with toxic gases as a benefit. Having put on the mask, most people would be relieved, not angry, if I said that they don't have to work with toxic gases after all. Switching the order of the clauses within the If-then structure of the rule should cause the precautionary inference system to assign the following interpretation: "If you wear a gas mask, then *it will be safe* for you to work with toxic gases" (Fiddick et al., 2000).

What about someone who really *wants* to work with toxic gases, that is, someone who views doing so as a *benefit* that I control access to and am then denying them, despite their having met my requirement? A person with these desires would be interpreting the toxic gas rule as a social contract: "If you want the benefit (of working with toxic gases), then you must satisfy my requirement." Entitlement would then be activated by the social contract algorithms, as well as anger when that entitlement is denied. That is, *not all deontic rules activate the same surplus structure.* If situation detectors map it onto the template of a social contract ([1] or [2]), *entitlement* and *obligation* will be imported in the appropriate places. But these concepts will not be imported if situation detectors map the rule onto the hazard-precaution template of a precautionary rule. In that case, words such as "must" or "ought" will be interpreted as referring to the causal requirements of safety (section IV.iv.).

II.i.ii Cheater Detection and Social Exchange Let us now turn from interpretation to cheater detection. Figure 2.2a shows a Wason selection task in which the conditional is the social contract rule about borrowing the car discussed above. In contrast to the Ebbinghaus disease rule (figure 2.1), which elicited "*P & not-Q*" responses from only 26% of undergraduates, this social contract rule elicited that response from 76% of undergraduates. This is logically correct performance. But our claim is not that social

A.

Teenagers who don't have their own cars usually end up borrowing their parents' cars. In return for the privilege of borrowing the car, the Carters have given their kids the rule,

"If you borrow my car, then you have to fill up the tank with gas."

Of course, teenagers are sometimes irresponsible. You are interested in seeing whether any of the Carter teenagers broke this rule.

The cards below represent four of the Carter teenagers. Each card represents one teenager. One side of the card tells whether or not a teenager has borrowed the parents' car on a particular day, and the other side tells whether or not that teenager filled up the tank with gas on that day.

Which of the following card(s) would you definitely need to turn over to see if any of these teenagers are breaking their parents' rule: "If you borrow my car, then you have to fill up the tank with gas." Don't turn over any more cards than are absolutely necessary.

borrowed car	did not borrow car	filled up tank with gas	did not fill up tank with gas

B.

The mind translates social contracts into representations of benefits and requirements, and it inserts concepts such as "entitled to" and "obligated to," whether they are specified or not.

How the mind "sees" the social contract above is shown in **bold italics**.

"If you borrow my car, then you have to fill up the tank with gas."

If you take the benefit, then you are obligated to satisfy the requirement.

borrowed car	did not borrow car	filled up tank with gas	did not fill up tank with gas
= accepted the benefit	*= did not accept the benefit*	*= satisfied the requirement*	*= did not satisfy the requirement*

Figure 2.2

Wason task with a social contract rule. (A) In response to this social contract problem, 76% of subjects chose *P & not-Q* ("borrowed the car" and "did not fill the tank with gas")—the cards that represent potential cheaters. Yet only 26% chose this (logically correct) answer in response to the descriptive rule in figure 2.1. Although this social contract rule involves familiar items, unfamiliar social contracts elicit the same high performance. (B) How the mind represents the social contract shown in (A). According to inferential rules specialized for social exchange (but not according to first-order logic), "If you take the benefit, then you are obligated to satisfy the requirement" implies "If you satisfy the requirement, then you are entitled to take the benefit." Consequently, the rule in (A) implies: "If you fill the tank with gas, then you may borrow the car" (see figure 2.4, switched social contracts).

contract content activates computational machinery implementing first-order logic. Our claim is that it activates social contract algorithms, which interpret the rule as explained above, and which contain a subroutine for detecting cheaters: individuals who cheat by design, not by accident. The function of the cheater detection mechanism is to direct information search in a way that will uncover potential cheaters. Searching for violations requires more than having semantic knowledge of what counts as a violation;[9] as we discussed above, people know that the combination of P and *not-Q* violates indicative rules, but they do not spontaneously *search* for information that could reveal potential violations, *even when they are explicitly asked to do so.* By extension, searching for cheaters requires more, computationally, than having a mental representation of what counts as cheating. We have therefore posited an information search routine that directs attention to anyone who has taken the benefit (have they satisfied the requirement?) and to anyone who has not satisfied the requirement (have they taken the benefit?). By coincidence, those cards map onto the logically correct response, "*P & not-Q*" for the rule as stated in figure 2.2a. Figure 2.2b shows our view of how the mind sees this problem. According to social contract theory, social contract algorithms are not mapping propositions in the conditional onto a syntax of true antecedents and false consequents; they are mapping them onto representations of an agent who has *accepted the benefit* and of an agent who has *not satisfied the requirement,* and the cheater detection mechanism is directing information search to those agents. If the cards representing those two conditions happen to correspond to P and *not-Q*, it will look like people reasoned in accordance with first-order logic. However, it is easy to create problems in which looking for cheaters will produce a response that violates first-order logic, as we will show below.

According to social contract theory, cheating does involve the violation of a conditional rule, but it is a particular *kind* of violation of a particular *kind* of conditional rule. The rule must fit the template for a *social contract* ([1] or [2]); the violation must be one in which an individual *intentionally* took what *that* individual considered to be a *benefit* and did so without satisfying the requirement.

III   The Design of Computational Machinery That Governs Reasoning about Social Exchange

Because social contract theory provides a standard of good design against which human performance can be measured, there can be a meaningful answer to the question, "Are the programs that cause reasoning about social exchange well engineered for the task?" Well-designed programs for engaging in social exchange—if such exist—should include features that execute the computational requirements specified by social contract theory and do so reliably, precisely, and economically (Williams, 1966).

From social contract theory's task analyses, we derived a set of predictions about the design features that a neurocognitive system specialized for reasoning about social exchange should have (Cosmides, 1985; Cosmides & Tooby, 1989). The following six design features (D1–D6) were among those on the list:

D1. Social exchange is cooperation for mutual *benefit.* If there is nothing in a conditional rule that can be interpreted as a rationed benefit, then interpretive procedures should not categorize that rule as a social contract. To trigger the inferences about obligations and entitlements that are appropriate to social contracts, the rule must be interpreted as restricting access to a benefit to those who have met a requirement. (This is a necessary, but not sufficient, condition; Cosmides & Tooby, 1989; Gigerenzer & Hug, 1992.)

D2. Cheating is a specific way of violating a social contract: It is taking the benefit when you are not entitled to do so. Consequently, the cognitive architecture must define the concept of *cheating* using contentful representational primitives, referring to illicitly taken *benefits.* This implies that a system designed for cheater detection will not know what to look for if the rule specifies no benefit to the potential violator.

D3. The definition of cheating also depends on which agent's point of view is taken. Perspective matters because the item, action, or state of affairs that one party views as a benefit is viewed as a requirement by the other party. The system needs to be able to compute a cost/benefit representation from the perspective of each participant and define cheating with respect to that perspective-relative representation.

D4. To be an ESS, a design for conditional helping must not be outcompeted by alternative *designs.* Accidents and innocent mistakes that result in an individual's being cheated are not markers of a design difference. Moreover, decision rules that punish accidental violations of social contracts by refusing to cooperate further with the accidental violator lose many opportunities to gain from cooperation; simulation results show such strategies get selected out in the presence of strategies that exclude only intentional cheaters (Panchanathan & Boyd, 2003). A cheater detection system should look for cheaters: individuals equipped with programs that cheat by design.[10] Hence, intentional cheating should powerfully trigger the detection system, whereas mistakes should trigger it weakly or not at all. (Mistakes that result in an individual's being cheated are relevant only insofar as they may not be true mistakes.)

D5. The hypothesis that the ability to reason about social exchange is acquired through the operation of some general-purpose learning ability necessarily predicts that good performance should be a function of experience and familiarity. In contrast, an evolved system for social exchange should be designed to recognize and reason about social exchange interactions no matter how unfamiliar the interaction may be, provided it can be mapped onto the abstract structure of a social contract. Individuals need to be able to reason about each new exchange situation as it arises, so rules that fit the template of a social contract should elicit high levels of cheater detection, even if they are unfamiliar.

D6. Inferences made about social contracts should not follow the content-free rules of first-order logic. They should follow a content-specific adaptive logic, evolutionarily tailored for the domain of social exchange, as presented in the discussion of interpretation above (Cosmides, 1985; Cosmides & Tooby, 1989).

Each of these design features has now been tested for and empirically validated. The mechanisms that govern reasoning about social exchange have many improbable properties that are well engineered for solving adaptive problems arising in this domain. Various hypotheses positing machinery designed to operate over a class of content more general than social exchange have been proposed, but none are capable of explaining the pattern of results found. Not only is the computational machinery specialized but the process for its developmental acquisition appears to be specialized as well: the developmental evidence of precocial competence and the distribution of reasoning specializations that characterize the adult state are not consistent with any domain-general proposals for their developmental acquisition (for review and discussion, see Cosmides & Tooby, 2005a).

Cosmides and Tooby (2005a) review the design evidence that supports the claim that the human mind reliably develops an adaptive specialization for reasoning about social exchange and that rules out by-product hypotheses. In this chapter, we focus on how the evidence bears on two somewhat different issues: (i) Can this evidence be explained by positing a "deontic logic machine," that is, computational machinery that implements a domain-general form of deontic logic? (ii) If not, then what are the prospects for creating a content-general deontic logic that still respects the empirical facts about deontic reasoning?

IV Conditional Reasoning and Social Exchange: Some Empirical Findings

Reciprocation is, by definition, social behavior that is conditional: You agree to deliver a benefit *conditionally* (conditional on the other person's doing what you required in return). Understanding it therefore requires conditional reasoning.

Because engaging in social exchange requires conditional reasoning, investigations of conditional reasoning can be used to test for the presence of social contract algorithms. The hypothesis that the brain contains social contract algorithms predicts a dissociation in reasoning performance by *content*: a sharply enhanced ability to reason adaptively about conditional rules when those rules specify a social exchange. The null hypothesis is that there is nothing specialized in the brain for social exchange. This hypothesis follows from the traditional assumption that reasoning is caused by content-independent processes. It predicts no enhanced conditional reasoning performance specifically triggered by social exchanges as compared to other contents.

As discussed earlier, the Wason selection task is a standard tool for investigating conditional reasoning. Because it asks subjects to look for potential violations of conditional rules, it was particularly well suited to our purposes: We were interested in cheater detection, which is a (specialized) form of violation detection. Using this task, an extensive series of experiments has now been conducted that addresses the following questions:

- Do our minds include cognitive machinery that is *specialized* for reasoning about social exchange (alongside other domain-specific mechanisms, each specialized for reasoning about a different adaptive domain involving conditional behavior)? Or,
- Is the cognitive machinery that causes good conditional reasoning general—does it operate well regardless of content?

If the human brain had cognitive machinery that causes good conditional reasoning regardless of content, then people should be good at tasks requiring conditional reasoning. For example, they should be good at detecting violations of indicative conditional rules. Yet studies with the Wason selection task showed that they are not. If our minds were equipped with reasoning procedures specialized for detecting *logical* violations of conditional rules, the correct answer (choose *P*, choose *not-Q*) would be intuitively obvious and pop out for people. But it is not.

First-order logic provides a standard of good design for content-general conditional reasoning: its inference rules were constructed by philosophers to generate true conclusions from true premises, regardless of the subject matter one is asked to reason about. When human performance is measured against this standard, there is little evidence of good design: Conditional rules with descriptive (indicative) content fail to elicit logically correct performance from 70% to 95% of people, even when the content involves familiar terms drawn from everyday life (Cosmides, 1989; Griggs & Cox, 1982; Wason, 1983; Manktelow & Evans, 1979; Sugiyama et al., 2002). Therefore, one can reject the hypothesis that the human mind is equipped with reasoning machinery that causes good violation detection on all conditional rules, regardless of their content or domain.

IV.i A Dissociation by Content (D1, D2)

People are poor at detecting violations of conditional rules when their content is descriptive. But this result does not generalize to conditional rules that express a social contract. People who ordinarily cannot detect violations of if-then rules can do so easily and accurately when that violation represents cheating in a situation of social exchange. This pattern— good violation detection for social contracts but not for descriptive rules—is a dissociation in reasoning elicited by differences in the conditional rule's *content.* It provides (initial) evidence that the mind has reasoning procedures specialized for detecting cheaters.

The high performance—76% correct—found for the borrowing car rule of figure 2.2 is not particular to that problem: it is found whenever subjects are asked to look for violations of a conditional rule that fits the social contract template—"If you take benefit B, then you must satisfy requirement R." For *standard* social contracts (ones with the benefit to the cheater in the antecedent clause), people check the individual who accepted the benefit (*P*) and the individual who did not satisfy the requirement (*not-Q*). These are the cases that represent potential cheaters (figure 2.2b). The adaptively correct answer is immediately obvious to most subjects, who commonly experience a pop-out effect. No formal training is needed. Whenever the content of a problem asks one to look for cheaters in a social exchange, subjects experience the problem as simple to solve, and their performance jumps dramatically. In general, 65% to 80% of subjects get it right, the highest performance found for a task of this kind (for reviews, see Cosmides, 1985, 1989; Cosmides & Tooby, 1992, 1997; Fiddick et al., 2000; Gigerenzer & Hug, 1992; Platt & Griggs, 1993).

The content-blind syntax of first-order logic would treat investigating the person who borrowed the car (*P*) and the person who did not fill the gas tank (*not-Q*) as logically equivalent to investigating the person with Ebbinghaus disease (*P*) and the person who is not forgetful (*not-Q*) for the Ebbinghaus problem in figure 2.1. But everywhere it has been tested (adults in the United States, United Kingdom, Germany, Italy, France, Hong Kong, Japan; schoolchildren in Quito, Ecuador; Shiwiar hunter-horticulturalists in the Ecuadorian Amazon), people do not treat social exchange problems as equivalent to other kinds of conditional reasoning problems (Cheng & Holyoak, 1985; Cosmides, 1989; Hasegawa & Hiraishi, 2000; Platt & Griggs, 1993; Sugiyama, Tooby, & Cosmides, 2002; supports D5, D6). Their minds distinguish social exchange content from other domains and reason as if they were translating their terms into representational primitives such as *benefit*, *cost*, *obligation*, *entitlement*, *intentional*, and *agent* (figure 2.2b; Cosmides & Tooby, 1992, 2005a; Fiddick et al., 2000). Reasoning problems could be sorted into indefinitely many categories based on their content or structure (including first-order logic's two content-free categories, antecedent and consequent). Yet, even in remarkably different cultures, the same mental categorization occurs. This cross-culturally recurrent dissociation by content was predicted in advance of its discovery by social contract theory's adaptationist analysis.

It is worth noting that cognitive disorders can impair logical reasoning abilities without affecting the ability to detect cheaters on social contracts. Maljkovic (1987) compared a group of patients with schizophrenia to a control group with no cognitive impairment. She found that the schizophrenic patients had deficits compared to the controls on a battery of (non-Wason) logical reasoning tasks, in a way consistent with frontal lobe dysfunction. However, the schizophrenic patients did well—indeed just as well as the control subjects—on Wason tasks where the rule was a social contract and a violation was cheating. That their social contract reasoning was intact is striking because individuals with schizophrenia typically manifest deficits on virtually any test of general intellectual functioning they are given (McKenna, Clare, & Baddeley, 1995). Maljkovic's interesting result is consistent with the view that social contract reasoning is accomplished by a dedicated system that is functionally dissociable from more general forms of logical reasoning.

IV.ii Do Unfamiliar Social Contracts Elicit Cheater Detection? (D5)

An individual needs to understand each new opportunity to exchange as it arises, so it was predicted that social exchange reasoning should operate even for unfamiliar social contract rules (D5). This distinguishes social contract theory strongly from theories that explain reasoning performance as the product of general-learning strategies plus experience: the most natural prediction for such skill-acquisition theories is that performance should be a function of familiarity.

The evidence supports social contract theory: Cheater detection occurs even when the social contract is wildly unfamiliar (figure 2.3a). For example, the rule "If a man eats cassava root, then he must have a tattoo on his face" can be made to fit the social contract template by explaining that the people involved consider eating cassava root to be a benefit (the rule then implies that having a tattoo is the requirement an individual must satisfy to be eligible for that benefit). When given this context, this outlandish, culturally alien rule elicits the same high level of cheater detection as highly familiar social exchange rules. This surprising result has been replicated for many different unfamiliar rules (Cosmides, 1985, 1989; Cosmides & Tooby, 1992; Gigerenzer & Hug, 1992; Platt & Griggs, 1993). It supports the psychological reality of the template (see [1]) posited for the representation of social exchanges (D1, D2).

IV.ii.i Not Familiarity, Not Memory Retrieval This means the dissociation by content—good performance for social contract rules but not for descriptive ones—has nothing to do with the familiarity of the rules tested. Nor does it reflect the subject's ability to retrieve real-life instances in which they had violated the rule (a hypothesis that was once considered to explain results for the drinking age law, which is a social contract). Familiarity is neither necessary nor sufficient for eliciting high performance.

First, as discussed above, familiarity does not produce high levels of performance for descriptive (indicative) rules. If familiarity fails to elicit high performance on descriptive rules, then it also fails as an explanation for high performance on social contracts. Second, the fact that unfamiliar social contracts elicit high performance shows that familiarity is not necessary for eliciting violation detection. Third (and most surprising), people are just as good at detecting cheaters on culturally unfamiliar or imaginary social contracts as they are for ones that are completely familiar: Cosmides (1985, pp. 244–250) found that performance on unfamiliar social contracts (such as the cassava root one) was just as high as performance on familiar social contracts, including the drinking age problem. This provides a challenge for any counterhypothesis resting on a general-learning skill acquisition account (most of which rely on familiarity and repetition), or on the ability to retrieve violating instances from memory.

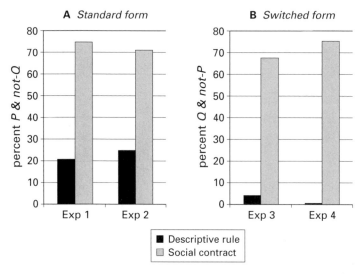

Exp 1 & 3: Social contract = social rule
Exp 2 & 4: Social contract = personal exchange

Figure 2.3
Detecting violations of unfamiliar conditional rules: Social contracts versus descriptive indicative rules. In these experiments, the same, unfamiliar rule was embedded either in a story that caused it to be interpreted as a social contract or in a story that caused it to be interpreted as a rule describing some state of the world. For social contracts, the correct answer is always to pick the *benefit accepted* card and the *requirement not satisfied* card. (A) For standard social contracts, these correspond to the logical categories P and *not-Q*. P & *not-Q* also happens to be the logically correct answer. Over 70% of subjects chose these cards for the social contracts, but fewer than 25% chose them for the matching descriptive rules. (B) For switched social contracts, the *benefit accepted* and *requirement not satisfied* cards correspond to the logical categories Q and *not-P*. This is not a logically correct response. Nevertheless, about 70% of subjects chose it for the social contracts; virtually no one chose it for the matching descriptive rule (see figure 2.4).

IV.iii Adaptive Logic, Not First-Order Logic (D3, D6)

The above shows that it is possible to construct social exchange problems that will elicit a logically correct answer. But this is not because social exchange content activates computational machinery implementing first-order logic.

First-order logic is content blind. Computational machinery implementing it—let's call this a "first-order logic machine"—would apply the same definition of violation (co-occurrence of a true antecedent with a false consequent) to all conditional rules, whether they are social contracts, threats, or descriptions of how the world works. This is because (i) first-order logic operates over propositions, regardless of their content, and (ii) it contains no procedures for importing surplus concepts such as *obligation*, *entitlement*, *agent*, *perspective*, or *intention to violate* into the rule. But the definition of cheating implied by design features D1 through D4 does not map onto this content-blind definition of violation. What counts as cheating in social exchange is so content sensitive that it is easy to create problems in which the search for cheaters will result in a logically incorrect response (and the search for logical violations will fail to detect cheaters; see figure 2.4). When given such problems, people look for cheaters, thereby giving a logically incorrect answer (Q and *not-P*). Two sets of results bear on this issue: experiments with switched social contracts and perspective change experiments.

IV.iii.i Switched Social Contracts A first-order logic machine would never infer that *If P then Q* implies *If Q then P*. In contrast, social contract algorithms should have domain-specialized deontic rules of inference according to which

[1] "If you accept a benefit from agent X, then you are obligated to satisfy X's requirement," implies

[2] "If you satisfy agent X's requirement, then you are entitled to the benefit X offered to provide"—and vice versa.

A "standard" social contract has the benefit to the potential cheater in the antecedent (*P*) clause (as in [1]); a "switched" social contract has that benefit in the consequent (*Q*) clause (as in [2]). These terms do not refer to different kinds of social contracts, only to different linguistic expressions of the same offer to exchange. For example, "If you give me your watch, I'll give you $100" and "If I give you $100, then give me your watch" are recognized by normal human minds as expressing the same offer, entailing the same entitlements and obligations for both agents.

Consider the following rule:

Standard format:

*If you take the **benefit**, then satisfy my **requirement*** (e.g., "If you borrow my car, then fill the tank")

If   P   then   Q

Switched format:

*If you satisfy my **requirement**, then take the **benefit*** (e.g., "If you fill the tank, then borrow my car")

If   P   then   Q

The cards below have information about four people. Each card represents one person. One side of a card tells whether the person accepted the benefit, and the other side of the card tells whether that person satisfied the requirement. Indicate only those card(s) you definitely need to turn over to see if any of these people have violated the rule.

	✔			✔
	Benefit accepted	Benefit not accepted	Requirement satisfied	Requirement not satisfied
Standard:	P	not-P	Q	not-Q
Switched:	Q	not-Q	P	not-P

Figure 2.4

Generic structure of a Wason task when the conditional rule is a social contract. A social contract can be translated into either social contract terms (benefits and requirements) or logical terms (Ps and Qs). Check marks indicate the correct card choices if one is looking for cheaters—these should be chosen by a cheater detection subroutine, whether the exchange was expressed in a standard or switched format. This results in a logically incorrect answer (Q & *not-P*) when the rule is expressed in the switched format, and a logically correct answer (P & *not-Q*) when the rule is expressed in the standard format. By testing switched social contracts, one can see that the reasoning procedures activated cause one to detect cheaters, not logical violations (see figure 2.3B). Note that a logically correct response to a switched social contract—where P = *requirement satisfied* and not-Q = *benefit not accepted*—would fail to detect cheaters.

Likewise, given the context of criss-crossing desires and access expressed in the car task of figure 2.2, it shouldn't matter whether the rule is expressed in standard form (as in [3]) or as a switched social contract—even one lacking explicit deontic operators, like [9] "If you fill the tank with gas, then borrow the car" (see section II.i.i). Because deontic inferences specialized for exchange will recognize them as implying the same set of obligations and entitlements, the same event will count as cheating by a teenager: borrowing the car without filling the tank.

This leads to a prediction: it should not matter whether the rule is expressed in standard ([3], [1]) or switched ([9], [2]) form. A subroutine for detecting cheaters should check teenagers who have taken the benefit (borrowed the car) and teenagers who have not satisfied the requirement that provision of this benefit was made contingent upon (didn't fill the tank).

By testing switched social contracts, we can discriminate the predictions of first-order logic from those of social contract theory. As figure 2.4 shows, the cheater-relevant cards correspond to the logical categories P and not-Q for standard social contracts. The cheater detection subroutine will therefore produce the same answer as a first-order logic machine in response to standard social contracts—not because this response is logically correct but because it will correctly detect cheaters. But for switched social contracts, a cheater detection subroutine will not produce a logically correct answer.

In the switched format, the cheater relevant cards, "borrowed the car" and "did not fill tank," correspond to the logical categories Q (true consequent) and not-P (false antecedent), respectively. Choosing them will correctly detect teenagers who are cheating, but it violates first-order logic: instances of not-P cannot violate the material conditional, whether paired with Q or not-Q. (Please note that social contracts do not imply a biconditional interpretation: filling the tank without borrowing the car may be altruistic, but it is not cheating or any other kind of violation.)

When given switched social contracts with structures like [9] or [2], subjects overwhelmingly respond by choosing Q & not-P, a logically incorrect answer that correctly detects cheaters (figure 2.3b; Cosmides, 1985, 1989; Gigerenzer & Hug, 1992; Platt & Griggs, 1993; supports D2, D6). They do this even when there are no deontic operators specified in the rule. Indeed, when subjects' choices are classified by logical category, it looks like standard and switched social contracts elicit different responses. But when their choices are classified by *social contract* category, they are invariant: for both rule formats, people choose the cards that represent an agent who took the benefit and an agent who did not meet the requirement.

The hypothesis that social contract content merely activates first-order logic is eliminated by this finding. A first-order logic machine is equipped with only one definition of violation for a conditional rule: P & not-Q. It would therefore choose those cards in response to switched social contracts like rule [9], even though this would not detect cheaters.[11] A teenager who has filled the tank (P) without borrowing the car (not-Q) may be altruistic but has not cheated.[12]

Interestingly, Gigerenzer and Hug (1992) had a handful of subjects who answered "P & not-Q" to every conditional they got. In debriefing, these individuals said they had applied formal logic to all problems—but that this had been particularly difficult for some of them. These turned out to be the switched social contracts. This kind of difficulty is expected: to apply first-order logic, they would have to suppress the spontaneous and intuitive inferences generated by their social contract algorithms (see discussion of the principle of preemptive specificity in section II.i.i.i).

IV.iii.i.i Reasoning in the Rainforest This pattern—choosing the *benefit accepted* and *requirement not met* cards on standard and switched social contracts—is not particular to people raised in advanced market economies. Sugiyama, Tooby and Cosmides (2002) adapted Wason tasks for non-literate individuals and administered them to Shiwiar hunter-horticulturalists living in a remote part of the Ecuadorian Amazon. Shiwiar subjects were given a standard social contract (like the cassava-tattoo problem), a switched social contract ("If you bring me a basket of fish, then you can borrow my motorboat"), and a descriptive problem. The Shiwiar were just as good at detecting cheaters on Wason tasks as Harvard undergraduates were. For cheater-relevant cards, the performance of Shiwiar hunter-horticulturalists was identical to that of Harvard students: *benefit accepted* and *requirement not met* were chosen by over 80% of subjects.

The Shiwiar, whose way of life involves frequent sharing, differed from Harvard students only in that they were more likely to also show interest in cheater-irrelevant cards—the ones that could reveal acts of generosity. The Shiwiar's excellence at cheater detection did not result from indiscriminate interest in all cards, however. This could be seen by comparing performance on standard and switched social contracts while controlling for logical category (e.g., P is cheater-relevant for a standard social contract (where it represents a *benefit accepted*) but cheater-irrelevant for a switched one (where it represents a *requirement satisfied*)). Controlling for logical category, Shiwiar were more than twice as likely to choose a card when it was cheater-relevant than when it was not ($p < .005$).

That there was no difference between cultures in choosing the cheater-relevant cards is expected: For social exchange to implement an ESS, the development of the cheater detection subroutine would need to be buffered against (evolutionarily normal) variations in local cultures. The only "cultural dissociation" we found was in ESS-irrelevant aspects of performance (interest in generosity).

IV.iii.i.ii Deontic Logic? Is choosing Q and *not-P* on a switched social contract consistent with content-general deontic logics? Manktelow and Over (1987) considered this question and concluded that the answer is indeterminate. Consider "If you fill the tank with gas, then you may borrow the car." Let's assume the mind contains computational machinery implementing a *domain-general* deontic logic: a deontic logic machine. Let's assume this deontic logic machine interprets this rule as having the deep structure of [2], and therefore meaning "If you fill the tank with gas, then you are *entitled* to borrow the car." Technically, no events could violate this rule: by most deontic logics, the fact that you are *entitled* to borrow the car does not mean that you are *required* to borrow the car. Thus, when subjects are asked to look for violations of the rule, the deontic logic machine should choose no cards at all. But this rarely happens.

For "Q & *not-P*" to be chosen, one needs additional assumptions. The instruction to see whether any of the *teenagers* have violated the rule would have to be a cue used by the deontic logic machine. In response to that cue, it would have to derive an *obligation* that falls on *teenagers* by virtue of the rule. To do this, the cue would have to trigger the inference that this switched social contract (with the format of [2]) implies another rule with the format of [1]. Only by that transformation could the subject tell whether the rule implies *any* obligation on the part of car-borrowing teenagers. So, even if the parents' statement had been floridly deontic, such as "If you fill the tank with gas, then you are entitled to borrow the car," the deontic logic machine would have to first derive what this implies about obligations incurred by teenagers. Without doing this, the deontic logic machine could not determine whether a violation has occurred, that is, whether an obligation has remained unfulfilled—which is necessary for choosing the "borrowed car" card (Q) and the "didn't fill tank" card (*not-P*).

Social contract algorithms are designed to make translations of precisely this kind: they are hypothesized to be sensitive to which party is the potential rule violator, to have procedures for inferring that the entitlements of that agent specified in [2] imply that that agent has the obligations specified by [1], and to search for information that could reveal whether that agent has cheated. The questions for deontic logicians are: (i) Can one build a deontic logic that does all of these things *without* it being a notational variant of social contract theory? And (ii) is it possible to build a deontic logic that does all of this *and* is general to all deontic rules, whether they are social contracts or not? We suspect the answer to both is no.

In particular, it is not clear how a deontic logic could be general to all (deontic) domains yet license the inference that

[10]   "If you satisfy requirement R, then you are entitled to E" implies

[11] "If you get E, then you are obligated to satisfy requirement R" (and vice versa).

These two rules are interesting because they are only *slightly* more domain-general statements of [2] and [1] ([10] subsumes the more domain-specific [2] as a special case; [11] similarly subsumes [1]). However, [10] and [11] cannot imply one another *across domains* without violating our moral intuitions. For example,

"If you are an American citizen, then you are entitled to be free from torture" (instance of [10])

is not usually thought to imply

"If you are free from torture, then you are *obligated* to be an American citizen" (instance of [11]).

In contrast, when the entitlement E is a benefit contingently offered *in the context of social exchange*, [2] entails [1] and vice versa. That is, the conditions under which an inference from entitlement to obligation is valid are quite domain-specific—they do not encompass all moral domains.

IV.iii.ii Perspective Change As predicted (D3), the mind's automatically deployed definition of cheating is tied to the perspective you are taking (Gigerenzer & Hug, 1992). For example, consider the following social contract:

[12] "If an employee is to get a pension, then that employee must have worked for the firm for over ten years."

This social contract rule elicits different answers depending on whether subjects are cued into the role of employer or employee. Those in the employer role look for cheating by employees, investigating cases of P and *not*-Q (employees with pensions; employees who have worked for fewer than ten years). Those in the employee role look for cheating by employers, investigating cases of *not*-P and Q (employees with no pension; employees who have worked more than ten years). *Not*-P & Q is correct if the goal is to find out whether the employer is cheating employees. But it is not *logically* correct by first-order logic, which, because it is content-blind, has no role for agents and their differing perspectives.[13]

In this social exchange, the benefit to one agent is the requirement for the other: giving pensions to employees benefits the employees but is the requirement the employer must satisfy (in exchange for the benefit to the employer of more than ten years of employee service). To capture this distinction between the perspectives of the two agents, rules of inference for social exchange must be content sensitive, defining benefits and requirements relative to the agents involved. Because the rules of first-order logic are blind to the content of the propositions over which they operate, they have no way of representing the values of an action to each agent involved.

Can a domain-general deontic logic do the trick? The answer is the same as for the switched social contracts. To determine whether the employer has cheated, the deontic logic machine would have to determine what obligation, if any, the employer owes to the employee. But rule [12] specifies no such obligation. To derive one, the deontic logic machine would need procedures that take [12] as input and derive [13] from it:

[13] "If the employee has worked for the firm for more than ten years, then the employer is obligated to give that employee a pension."

But what justifies this inference? Social contract algorithms derive this inference when they recognize that a long-working employee is a *benefit* to the employer, for which the employer is willing to give pensions. That is, [13] is derived from a representation something like this:

[14] "If the employer gets the *benefit from the employee* (of long service), then the employer is obligated to give a benefit (the pension) to that employee."

It is difficult to see how a content-blind deontic logic machine could perform this transformation as it depends on underlying representations of *benefits* to agents (and remember, the more general formulation in section IV.iii.i.ii won't work). Again, we need to ask whether there can be a version of deontic logic that is not merely a notational variant of social contract theory. Moreover, if one constructs a deontic logic that does implement the same rules as social contract algorithms, then we have to ask how it is going to achieve its content generality. How will it operate over precautionary rules, rules of etiquette, and other deontic conditionals that lack the structure of social exchange?

IV.iv   How Many Specializations for Conditional Reasoning?

Social contracts are not the only conditional rules for which natural selection should have designed specialized reasoning mechanisms (Cosmides, 1989). Indeed, good violation detection is also found for conditional rules drawn from two other domains: threats (Tooby & Cosmides, 1989) and precautionary rules. Threats are not deontic, but precautionary rules are. So we need to ask whether good performance on social contracts and precautionary rules is caused by a single neurocognitive system or by two functionally distinct ones. We also need to ask whether all deontic rules elicit good violation detection. If the answer is no, then reasoning about social exchange cannot be caused by a deontic logic machine that operates in a uniform manner on all deontic conditionals.

IV.iv.i Precautionary Rules Game theory is not needed to see that there would be a fitness advantage to machinery that makes one good at detecting when someone is in danger by virtue of having violated a precautionary rule. Precautionary rules are ones represented as fitting the template: *"If one is to engage in hazardous activity H, then one must take precaution R"* (e.g., "If you are working with toxic gases, then wear a gas mask"). Using the Wason task, it has been shown that people are very good at detecting potential violators of precautionary rules, that is, individuals who have engaged in a hazardous activity without taking the appropriate precaution (e.g., those working with toxic gases (P) and those not wearing a gas mask (*not-Q*)). Indeed, relative to descriptive rules, precautions show a spike in performance, and the magnitude of this content effect is about the same as that for detecting cheaters on social contracts (Cheng & Holyoak, 1989; Fiddick et al., 2000; Manktelow & Over, 1988, 1990; Stone et al., 2002; Ermer, Guerin, Cosmides, Tooby, & Miller, 2006).

According to hazard management theory (Fiddick et al., 2000), a system well designed for reasoning about hazards and precautions should have properties different from one for detecting cheaters, many of which have been tested for and found (Fiddick, 1998, 2004; Fiddick et al., 2000; Pereyra & Nieto, 2004; Stone et al., 2002; Ermer et al., 2006). In addition to a specialization for reasoning about social exchange, we have therefore proposed that the human brain reliably develops computational machinery specialized for managing hazards, which causes good violation detection on precautionary rules. Obsessive-compulsive disorder, with its compulsive worrying, checking, and precaution taking, may be caused by a misfiring of this precautionary system (Boyer & Lienard, 2006; Cosmides & Tooby, 1999; Leckman & Mayes, 1998, 1999).

An alternative view is that reasoning about social contracts and precautionary rules is generated by a single mechanism. Some view both social contracts and precautions as deontic rules and wonder whether there is a general system for reasoning about deontic conditionals. More specifically, Cheng and Holyoak (1985, 1989) have proposed that inferences about both types of rule are generated by a permission schema, which operates over a larger class of rules, a class that encompasses social contracts and precautions.[14] Testing permission schema theory is particularly relevant to this chapter because it proposes production rules implementing inferences that might be found in a content-general deontic logic.

Can positing a permission schema explain the full set of relevant results? Or are they more parsimoniously explained by positing two separate adaptive specializations, one for social contracts and one for precautionary rules? We are looking for a model that is as simple as possible, but no simpler.

IV.v Social Contract Algorithms or a Permission Schema? Looking for Dissociations *within* the Class of Permission Rules (D1, D2, D4)

Permission rules are a species of conditional rule. According to Cheng and Holyoak (1985, 1989), these rules are imposed by an authority to achieve a social purpose, and they specify the conditions under which an individual is permitted to take an action. Cheng and Holyoak speculate that repeated encounters with such social rules cause domain-general learning mechanisms to induce a *permission schema*, consisting of four production rules (see table 2.3). This schema generates inferences about any conditional rule that fits the following template: "If action A is to be taken, then precondition R must be satisfied."

Social contracts fit this template. In social exchange, an agent permits you to take a benefit from him or her, conditional on your having met the agent's requirement. There are, however, many situations other than social exchange in which an action is permitted conditionally. Many customs and rules of etiquette are permission rules without being social contracts (e.g., "If one is to set the table with two forks, then the salad fork should

Table 2.3
The permission schema is composed of four production rules (Cheng & Holyoak, 1985)

Rule 1: If the action is to be taken, then the precondition must be satisfied.
Rule 2: If the action is not to be taken, then the precondition need not be satisfied.
Rule 3: If the precondition is satisfied, then the action may be taken.
Rule 4: If the precondition is not satisfied, then the action must not be taken.

Social contracts and precautions fit the template of Rule 1:
Social contract: If the benefit is to be taken, then the requirement must be satisfied
Precaution: If the hazardous action is to be taken, then the precaution must be taken.

---

be on the outside"; "If you are to wear white shoes, you must do this between Memorial and Labor Days"). So are many of the baffling bureaucratic rules we are all subject to (e.g., "If you are turning in an intrauniversity memo, then it must be printed on blue paper"—we didn't make this one up!). Permission schema theory predicts uniformly high performance for the entire class of permission rules, a set that is larger, more general, and more inclusive than the set of all social contracts (see figure 2.5).

According to permission schema theory, a neurocognitive system specialized for reasoning about social exchange, with a subroutine for cheater detection, does not exist. Instead, it proposes that a permission schema causes good violation detection for all permission rules; social contracts are a subset of the class of permission rules; therefore, cheater detection occurs as a by-product of the more domain-general permission schema (Cheng & Holyoak, 1985, 1989). It is the closest the literature gets to proposing a content-general deontic logic machine.

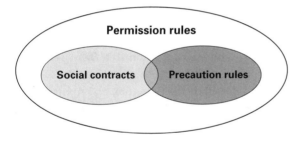

Figure 2.5
The class of permission rules is larger than, and includes, social contracts and precautionary rules. Many of the permission rules we encounter in everyday life are neither social contracts nor precautions (white area). Rules of civil society (ettiquette, customs, traditions), bureaucratic rules, corporate rules—many of these are deontic conditionals that do not regulate access to a benefit or involve a danger. Permission schema theory (see table 2.3) predicts high performance for all permission rules; however, permission rules that fall into the white area do not elicit the high levels of performance that social contracts and precaution rules do. Neuropsychological and cognitive tests show that performance on social contracts dissociates from other permission rules (white area), from precautionary rules, and from the general class of deontic rules involving subjective utilities. These dissociations would be impossible if reasoning about all deontic conditionals were caused by a single schema that is general to the domain of permission rules (e.g., a "deontic logic machine"; see text).

In contrast, social contract theory holds that the design of the reasoning system that causes cheater detection is more precise and functionally specialized than the design of the permission schema. Social contract algorithms should have design features that are lacking from the permission schema, such as responsivity to benefits and intentionality. As a result, removing benefits (D1, D2) and/or intentionality (D4) from a social contract should produce a permission rule that fails to elicit good violation detection on the Wason task.

As Sherlock Holmes might put it, we are looking for the dog that did not bark: permission rules that do *not* elicit good violation detection. That discovery would falsify permission schema theory. Social contract theory predicts functional dissociations *within* the class of permission rules, whereas permission schema theory does not.

IV.vi   No Benefits, No Social Exchange Reasoning: Testing D1 and D2
To trigger cheater detection (D2) and inference procedures specialized for interpreting social exchanges (D1), a rule needs to regulate access to benefits, not actions more generally. Does reasoning performance change when benefits are removed?

IV.vi.i   Benefits Are Necessary for Cheater Detection (D1, D2)   The function of a social exchange for each participant is to gain access to benefits that would otherwise be unavailable to them. Therefore, an important cue that a conditional rule is a social contract is the presence in it of a desired benefit under the control of an agent. *Taking a benefit* is a representational primitive within the social contract template *If you take benefit B, then you must satisfy requirement R.*

The permission schema template has representational primitives with a larger scope than that proposed for social contract algorithms. For example, *taking a benefit* is *taking an action*, but not all cases of taking actions are cases of taking benefits. As a result, all social contracts are permission rules, but not all permission rules are social contracts. Precautionary rules can also be construed as permission rules (although they need not be; see Fiddick et al., 2000, Experiment 2). They, too, have a more restricted scope: *Hazardous actions* are a subset of *actions; precautions* are a subset of *preconditions.*

Note, however, that there are permission rules that are neither social contracts nor precautionary rules (see figure 2.5). This is because there are actions an individual can take that are not *benefits* (social contract theory) and that are not *hazardous* (hazard management theory). Indeed, we encounter many rules like this in everyday life—bureaucratic rules, customs, and etiquette rules, for example, often state a procedure that is to be followed without specifying a benefit (or a danger). If the mind has a permission schema, then people should be good at detecting violations of rules that fall into the white area of figure 2.5, that is, permission rules that are neither social contracts nor precautionary. But they are not. Benefits are necessary for cheater detection.

Using the Wason task, several labs have tested permission rules that involve no benefit (and are not precautionary). As predicted by social contract theory, these do not elicit high levels of violation detection. For example, Cosmides and Tooby (1992) constructed Wason tasks in which the elders (authorities) had created laws governing the conditions under which adolescents are permitted to take certain actions. For all tasks, the law fit the template for a permission rule. The permission rules tested differed in just one respect: whether the action to be taken is a benefit or an unpleasant chore. The critical conditions compared performance on these two rules:

[15] "If one goes out at night, then one must tie a small piece of red volcanic rock around one's ankle."

[16] "If one takes out the garbage at night, then one must tie a small piece of red volcanic rock around one's ankle."

A cheater detection subroutine looks for benefits illicitly taken; without a benefit, it doesn't know what kind of violation to look for (D1, D2). When the permitted action was a benefit (getting to go out at night), 80% of subjects answered correctly; when it was an unpleasant chore (taking out the garbage), only 44% did so. This dramatic decrease in violation detection was predicted in advance by social contract theory. Moreover, it violates the central prediction of permission schema theory: that being a permission rule is sufficient to facilitate violation detection. There are now many experiments showing poor violation detection with permission rules that lack a benefit (e.g., Barrett, 1999; Cosmides, 1985, Experiments 5 and 6-C, plus all prescriptive clerical problems, referred to as "abstract" therein; Cosmides, 1989, Experiment 5; Fiddick, 2003; Griggs & Cox, 1982, Experiment 2; Griggs & Cox, 1983, Experiment 1; see discussion of deformed social contracts in Cosmides, 1985, pp. 60–64; Manktelow & Over, 1990, bingo problem; Platt & Griggs, 1993, Experiments 2 and 3).

This is another dissociation by content, but this time it is *within* the domain of permission rules—and, therefore, within the domain of deontic rules. To elicit cheater detection, a permission rule must be interpreted as restricting access *to a benefit*. It supports the psychological reality of the representational primitives posited by social contract theory, showing that the representations necessary to trigger differential reasoning are more content specific than those of the permission schema.

IV.vi.ii Benefits Trigger Social Contract Interpretations (D1)   The Wason experiments just described tested D1 and D2 in tandem. But D1—the claim that benefits are necessary for permission rules to be *interpreted* as social contracts—receives support independent of experiments testing D2 from studies of moral reasoning. Fiddick (2004) asked subjects what justifies various permission rules and when an individual should be allowed to break them. The rules were closely matched for surface content, and context was used to vary their interpretation. The permission rule that lacked a benefit (a precautionary one) elicited different judgments from permission rules that restricted access to a benefit (the social contracts). Social agreement and morality, rather than facts, were more often cited as justifying the social contract rules. But facts (about poisons and antidotes), rather than social agreement, were seen as justifying the precautionary rule. Whereas most subjects thought it was acceptable to break the social contract rules if you were not a member of the group that created them, they thought the precautionary rule should always be followed by people everywhere. Moreover, the explicit exchange rule triggered very specific inferences about the conditions under which it could be broken: those who had received a benefit could be released from their obligation to reciprocate, *but only by those who had provided the benefit to them* (i.e., the obligation could not be voided by a group leader or by a consensus of the recipients themselves).

The inferences subjects made about the rules restricting access to a benefit follow directly from the grammar of social exchange laid out in social contract theory (Cosmides, 1985; Cosmides & Tooby, 1989). These inferences were not—and should not—be applied to precautionary rules (see also Fiddick et al., 2000). According to hazard management theory, the evolved function of mechanisms for reasoning about precautionary rules is to mitigate danger. This predicts precisely what Fiddick found: that facts about hazards and precautions are what justify precautionary rules in people's minds and make them important to follow. These inferences are expected if the deep representation of a precautionary rule is "If you are to engage in hazardous situation H, then you need to take precaution R *to increase your safety.*" Words like "need," "must," or "ought" applied to the precaution do not specify an obligation to another person.

They specify a *necessary condition* for realizing a particular objective (increasing safety).

Social contracts and precautions may both be deontic, and in many cases both can be subsumed by a more general rule: "If condition C occurs, then a person *ought* to take action A." But the reasons behind that "ought" are vastly different for the two kinds of rules: safety for precautions, fulfilling an ethical obligation for social contracts. Moreover, the conditions under which this *ought* can (ethically) be ignored are different, so "ought" does not have the same moral implications in both cases. Lastly, the conditions that trigger the appropriate version of *ought* are different and content specialized. The *content* of condition C (*benefit* or *hazard*) and of action A (*provider's requirement* or *effective precaution*) need to be known to activate the domain-appropriate set of inferences.

Inferences about emotional reactions provide further evidence that social contracts and precautions activate two distinct inference systems rather than one permission schema. Fiddick (2004) asked subjects to predict which person (represented by faces with different emotional expressions) had seen someone violate a permission rule. He varied whether the permission rule provided contingent access to a benefit (i.e., was a social contract) or was precautionary. Social contract violations were thought to trigger anger, whereas precautionary violations were thought to trigger fear (Fiddick, 2004).

None of these dissociations within the realm of permission rules are predicted by permission schema theory. Moreover, because they involve different inferences and moral judgments for deontic rules drawn from different content domains, they would be difficult to explain on any content-free version of deontic logic. To be descriptively adequate, a deontic logic would have to include representational primitives like *hazardous activity*, *precaution*, *benefit*, and so on and trigger different sets of inferences when these are present. But a deontic logic with those properties would not be domain general. More likely, it would be a notational variant of the two different inferential systems proposed by social contract theory and hazard management theory.

IV.vii Intentional Violations versus Innocent Mistakes: Testing D4

Intentionality plays no role in permission schema theory. Whenever the action has been taken but the precondition has not been satisfied, the permission schema should register that a *violation* has occurred. As a result, people should be good at detecting violations of permission rules, whether the violations occurred by accident or by intention. In contrast, social contract theory predicts a mechanism that looks for *intentional* violations (D4).

Program designs that cause unconditional helping are not ESSs. Conditional helping can be an ESS because cheater detection provides a specific fitness advantage unavailable to unconditional helpers: by identifying cheaters, the conditional helper can avoid squandering costly cooperative efforts in the future on those who, by virtue of having an alternative program design, will not reciprocate. This means the evolutionary function of a cheater detection subroutine is to correctly connect an attributed disposition (to cheat) with a person (a cheater). It is not simply to recognize instances wherein an individual did not get what s/he was entitled to. That is, violations of social contracts are relevant for guiding future cooperative behavior insofar as they reveal individuals disposed to cheat—individuals who cheat by design, not by accident. Noncompliance caused by factors other than disposition, such as accidental violations and other innocent mistakes, does not reveal the disposition or design of the exchange partner. Accidents may result in someone's being cheated, but without indicating the presence of a cheater.[15] Indeed, program designs that refuse to cooperate with cooperators that may have made innocent mistakes do poorly in evolutionary simulations compared to those that forgive innocent mistakes and avoid cheaters (Panchanathan & Boyd, 2003).

Therefore, social contract theory predicts an additional level of cognitive specialization beyond looking for violations of a social contract. Accidental violations of social contracts will not fully engage the cheater detection subroutine; intentional violations will (D4).

IV.vii.i Accidents versus Intentions: A Dissociation for Social Contracts
Given the same social exchange rule, one can manipulate contextual factors to change the nature of the violation from intentional cheating to an innocent mistake. One experiment, for example, compared a condition in which the potential rule violator was inattentive but well-meaning to a condition in which she had an incentive to intentionally cheat. Varying intentionality caused a radical change in performance, from 68% correct in the intentional cheating condition to 27% correct in the innocent mistake condition (Cosmides, Barrett, & Tooby, forthcoming; supports D4). Fiddick (1998, 2004) found the same effect (as did Gigerenzer & Hug, 1992, using a different context manipulation).

In both scenarios, violating the rule would result in someone's being cheated, yet high performance occurred only when being cheated was caused by intentional cheating. Barrett (1999) conducted a series of parametric studies to find out whether the drop in performance in the innocent mistake condition was caused by the violator's lack of intentionality (D4) or by the violator's failure to benefit from her mistake (D2; see section IV.vi. on the necessity of *benefits* for eliciting cheater detection). He found that both factors independently contributed to the drop, equally and additively. Thus, the same decrease in performance occurred whether (i) violators would benefit from their innocent mistakes, or (ii) violators wanted to break the rule on purpose but would not benefit from doing so. For scenarios missing both factors (i.e., accidental violations that do not benefit the violator), performance dropped by twice as much as when just one factor was missing. That is, the more factors relevant to cheater detection were removed, the more performance dropped.

In bargaining games, experimental economists have found that subjects are twice as likely to punish defections (failures to reciprocate) when it is clear that the defector intended to cheat as when the defector is a novice who might have simply made a mistake (Hoffman, McCabe, & Smith, 1998). This provides interesting convergent evidence, using entirely different methods, for the claim that programs causing social exchange distinguish between mistakes and intentional cheating.

IV.vii.ii No Dissociation for Precautions Different results are expected for precautionary rules. Intentionality should not matter if the mechanisms that detect violations of precautionary rules were designed to look for people in danger. For example, a person who is not wearing a gas mask while working with toxic gases is in danger, whether that person forgot the gas mask at home (accidental violation) or left it home on purpose (intentional violation). That is, varying the intentionality of a violation should affect social exchange reasoning but not precautionary reasoning. Fiddick (1998, 2004) tested and confirmed this prediction: precautionary rules elicited high levels of violation detection whether the violations were accidental or intentional, but performance on social contracts was lower for accidental violations than for intentional ones. This functional distinction between precautionary and social exchange reasoning was predicted in advance based on the divergent adaptive functions proposed for these two systems.

That precautionary rules elicit no accident-intention dissociation, but social contracts do, is one more empirical fact about deontic reasoning that any domain-general deontic logic would need to somehow accommodate to be descriptively adequate. That a domain-general deontic logic would distinguish intentional from accidental violations of deontic rules is certainly reasonable—even three-year-olds make such distinctions for social contracts (Núñez & Harris, 1998). It is less clear how a deontic logic could do this for some deontic rules and not others *without distinguishing rules by their content.*

A parallel dissociation between social exchange and precautions emerged in another series of experiments: We found that the moral character of the potential rule violator affects violation detection for social contracts but not precautionary rules (Cosmides, Tooby, Montaldi, & Thrall, 1999; Cosmides, Sell, Tooby, Thrall, & Montaldi, forthcoming). Subjects first read four scenarios in which "Mary" had opportunities to cheat in situations of social exchange. In one condition she cheated all four times; in the other she refrained from doing so. When Mary had been honest in these scenarios, this prior information relaxed cheater detection on the Wason task, but only for a social exchange in which Mary was the potential cheater (not for an identical task in which another person was the potential cheater). This is consistent with the notion that an honest person would only violate a social contract by mistake. In contrast, violation detection on a precautionary rule involving Mary was high whether the prior scenarios portrayed Mary as honest or dishonest in social exchange situations.

This dissociation between social exchange and precautionary reasoning has interesting implications for what kind of inferences about Mary's moral character subjects were extracting from the scenarios we provided. They were not extracting the inference that Mary is a deontic rule follower *in general*; if they had, the "Mary is honest" condition should have relaxed violation detection on the (deontic) precautionary rule. Instead, subjects were inferring that Mary can be trusted to fulfill her obligations in a specific type of situation: those involving social exchange.

IV.vii.iii   Eliminating Permission Schema Theory   The results of sections IV.vi and IV.vii violate central predictions of permission schema theory. According to that theory, first, all permission rules should elicit high levels of violation detection, whether the permitted action is a benefit or a chore, and second, all permission rules should elicit high levels of violation detection, whether the violation was committed intentionally or accidentally. Both predictions fail. Permission rules fail to elicit high levels of violation detection when the permitted action is neutral or unpleasant (yet not hazardous). Moreover, people are bad at detecting accidental violations of permission rules that are social contracts. Taken together, these results eliminate the hypothesis that the mind contains or develops a permission schema of the kind postulated by Cheng and Holyoak (1985, 1989).

IV.vii.iv Domain-General Deontic Logics Cannot Explain the Results It is sometimes proposed that cheater detection on social contracts is caused by the application of a domain-general deontic logic (for discussion of this possibility, see Manktelow & Over, 1987). The results presented in this section eliminate this hypothesis.

All the benefit and intentionality tests described in this section involved deontic rules, but not all elicited high levels of violation detection. This creates difficulties for any explanation that relies on the application of a deontic logic that is content blind. Permission schema theory attempted to achieve content generality by using deontic versions of *must* and *may* while employing very abstract representations of *actions* and *conditions*. This is similar to the move made in some deontic logics. But it *matters* whether the action to be taken is perceived as a benefit or a chore to the agent taking it: violation detection is poor when the action is a chore (IV.vi.i). Moreover, different moral inferences are made depending on whether the action is represented as a contingently provided *benefit* or a *hazard* (IV.vi.ii). Results showing that social contracts elicit good violation detection for intentional violations but not innocent mistakes (IV.vii.i), but that this dissociation does not exist for precautionary rules (IV.vii.ii) also pose a challenge to any deontic logic that does not distinguish rules by their domain. Importantly, the accidental-intentional dissociation poses a problem for any explanation that relies solely on how the rule is interpreted.

IV.vii.iv.i Interpretation Alone Is an Insufficient Explanation That social contract rules elicit good performance merely because we understand what implications follow from them (e.g., Almor & Sloman, 1996)—is eliminated by the intention versus accident dissociation. The same social contract rule, *with the same implications*, was used in both conditions. Access to a benefit (a good high school in the area) was conditional on a student's living in Dover City—a town where people pay high taxes to support this high school ("If a student is to be assigned to Dover High School, then that student must live in Dover City"). The story context explained the tax and school quality situation. Thus, the rule and its rationale were *identical* in all conditions. All that differed was the proposed *motivation* of the potential rule violators.

If the rule's implications were understood in the intention condition, they should also have been understood in the accident condition: it was the same rule with the same rationale. Yet the accident condition failed to elicit good violation detection. Understanding the implications of a social contract may be necessary for cheater detection, but the accident results show this is not sufficient.

Social contract theory contains a theory of interpretation (specific to situations involving social exchange), but it also posits a postinterpretive process: a subroutine that looks for cheaters. The accident-intention dissociation was predicted in advance of its discovery on the basis of the ESS-based task analysis of the adaptive problems posed by cheater detection, an analysis that predicted that the postinterpretive cheater detection mechanism would not only exist but have design features specialized for distinguishing accidental from intentional violations. To explain these results, social contract specific interpretive procedures *and* a postinterpretive cheater detection mechanism must work in tandem. (Both are also needed to explain results for switched rules and perspective change; Fiddick et al., 2000, contains an extended discussion of this issue in the context of relevance theory and its reliance on logical interpretation; Sperber et al., 1995.)

It is difficult to see how the motivations of potential violators could play a role in any explanation based solely on interpretation of the implications of a conditional rule. But let's assume for the sake of argument that a deontic logic was constructed that could somehow explain why the accident/intention distinction matters for reasoning about social contracts. To account for the empirical facts, this explanation would also have to explain why the violator's motives matter for social contracts but *not* for precautionary rules. Remember that precautionary rules do not elicit a dissociation in violation detection based on accident versus intention. Any explanation of this difference between precautionary and social contract rules would have to refer to the fact that their *content* is different. And a deontic logic that distinguished the two by their content would no longer be content-free.

IV.vii.iv.ii Eliminating Fodor's Artifact Hypothesis The results of sections IV.vi and IV.vii also defeat a related claim by Fodor (2000): that "the putative cheater detection effect on the Wason task is actually a materials artifact" (p. 29). This sweeping conclusion is predicated on the (mistaken) notion that the only evidence for cheater detection comes from experiments in which the control problems are indicative (i.e., descriptive) conditionals (a curious mistake because it is refuted by experiments with *deontic* controls, which are presented in the single source Fodor cites: Cosmides & Tooby, 1992). According to Fodor (2000), the fact that people are good at detecting violations of social contracts but not indicative rules "is built into a difference between *the logic* of indicative and deontic conditionals" (emphasis added). He argues that deontic and indicative conditionals are "really about" different things and presents an argument about what "the" correct parsing (the correct interpretation) of each rule type "is." (Forgive us for seeing naive realism in this language—or, more charitably, the kind of loose talk that breeds ontological confusion.)[16]

Fodor's explanation strikes us as deeply flawed—among other things, it assumes what it seeks to explain (which he more or less acknowledges in his footnote 5). He argues that, whereas indicative conditionals are really about *P* implying *Q*, deontic conditionals are really about mandating *Q*[17] and are therefore correctly parsed as *Required: Q (in the case that P)*. For example, the car rule would be assigned the interpretation *Required: fill the tank with gas (in the case that you borrow the car)*. Because subjects can reason with the law of noncontradiction, he argues, they choose the *not-Q* card when asked to look for cases in which *required: Q* was violated. They also know to check whether the condition that triggers the requirement holds—that is, whether it is the case that *P*—so they choose the *P* card.

This account is problematic for two reasons. First, the reason given for choosing the cards is not really an explanation: it is just a redescription of the correct answer (which subjects give in response to standard social contracts). Second, it is not clear why Fodor's explanation shouldn't also apply to indicative conditionals. As Quine (1972, p. 19) points out, some logicians interpret indicative conditionals as meaning *necessarily: Q (in the case that P)*. This entirely reasonable interpretation is parallel to the logical form Fodor proposes for deontic conditionals. On this view, when given an indicative conditional and asked to look for violations, subjects will look for cases that violate *necessarily: Q*, thereby choosing the *not-Q* card (because they can reason with the law of noncontradiction). They should also choose the *P* card to check that the condition triggering the necessary presence of *Q* holds. That is, indicative conditionals should elicit high levels of "*P & not-Q*." Yet they do not.

In another passage, Fodor rejects the notion that cheater detection involves the concept of obligation (in favor of *requirement*) on the basis of (a mangled version of) the drinking age law (the high-performing version of which fits the social contract template). He says this rule cannot *obligate* one to be over 21 years old because one cannot be obligated to be other than one is.[18] Perhaps so. But the drinking age law does not obligate anyone to be 21 years old; it obligates people to *wait* until they are 21 years old before drinking beer. In social exchange, the function of providing *contingent* access to a benefit (like drinking beer) is to create a situation that benefits the agent who controls access to that benefit. In creating the drinking age law, an agent (a social group) obligates people to wait until they are old enough to behave in a responsible manner before granting access to the benefit (beer).[19] *This creates a situation that benefits the social group that made the rule*: by preventing teen-agers from drinking, it cuts down on drunk driving accidents and other negative externalities caused by drunken youths.[20] More generally, the requirement in social exchange is imposed to create a *situation* that benefits the provider. If it benefits the provider to require that a person have certain properties in order to be eligible to receive the benefit the provider is offering, so be it.

These are the problems we have with Fodor's reasoning. But instead of focusing on these issues, let us consider whether his artifact explanation can account for the cheater detection results observed. After all, there are many experiments comparing reasoning on social contracts to reasoning about other *deontic* conditionals—ones which should be assigned precisely the same interpretation *Required: Q (in the case that P).*

According to Fodor, high levels of violation detection will be found for any deontic rule that specifies what people are (conditionally) required to do because *not-Q* responses will be elicited by *Required: Q (in the case that P).* All the permission rules described in section IV.vi.i had precisely this property, all were stipulated to be rules that are in effect and, in every case, subjects were asked to reason from the rule, not about it. For example, by Fodor's account, rules [15] and [16] have precisely the same logical form: *Required: that one tie a small piece of red volcanic rock around one's ankle (in the case that P).* They differ *only in what P refers to.* In [15] it is something adolescents see as a benefit—going out at night—and in [16] it is something they see as a chore. But what *P* refers to plays no role in Fodor's account. If Fodor's artifact hypothesis were correct, both [15] and [16] should have elicited good violation detection. But [16] did not. Violation detection was poor when the deontic rule lacked a benefit, in this experiment as well as in all the others cited in section IV.vi.i.

The failure of Fodor's account is even more apparent in the accident-intention experiments (IV.vii.i). The social contract rule used was identical in all conditions, so, by Fodor's account, it would be assigned the same logical form in all conditions. Yet performance tracked the motivations of the violators: there was poor violation detection in the innocent mistake condition but good violation detection in the intentional cheating condition. Motives to violate can play no role in a "materials artifact" explanation like Fodor's. (Buller, 2005, adopted Fodor's explanation in his chapter on social exchange reasoning, similarly ignoring the data on dissociations within the domain of deontic rules. Thus, his analysis suffers from the same inability to account for the facts.)

Wason tasks involving social contracts have been compared to ones involving other types of deontic conditionals since our very first experiments in the early 1980s. The evidentiary basis for the existence of social contract algorithms, equipped with a cheater detection mechanism, has always included dissociations in performance *within* the domain of deontic rules.

IV.vii.v   Implications for Moral Reasoning?   The results of sections IV.vi and IV.vii show that it is not enough to admit that moral reasoning, social reasoning, or deontic reasoning is special. The computational machinery engaged when people reason about social exchange shows a specificity of design that is far narrower in scope. Deontic rules expressing social contracts elicit different patterns of reasoning than other deontic rules, whether precautionary or otherwise. Moreover, reasoning about social exchange is regulated by factors that have no impact on reasoning about other deontic rules, including information about the potential violator's intentions and moral character as a cooperator.

In the next section we will see that reasoning about social contracts and precautionary rules is not only functionally distinct, but it is associated with different areas of the brain.

IV.viii   A Neuropsychological Dissociation between Social Contracts and Precautions

Like social contracts, precautionary rules are conditional, are deontic, and involve subjective utilities. Moreover, people are as good at detecting violators of precautionary rules as they are at detecting cheaters on social contracts. This has led some to conclude that reasoning about social contracts and precautions is caused by a single more general mechanism (e.g., general to permissions, to deontic rules, or to deontic rules involving subjective utilities; Cheng & Holyoak, 1989; Manktelow & Over, 1988, 1990, 1991; Sperber et al., 1995). Most of these one-mechanism theories are undermined by the series of very precise, functional dissociations between social exchange reasoning and reasoning about other deontic permission rules discussed above. However, a very strong test, one that addresses *all* one-mechanism theories, would be to find a neural dissociation between social exchange and precautionary reasoning.

IV.viii.i One Mechanism or Two?

If reasoning about social contracts and precautions is caused by a single mechanism, then neurological damage to that mechanism should lower performance on both types of rule. But if reasoning about these two domains is caused by two functionally distinct mechanisms, then it is possible for social contract algorithms to be damaged while leaving precautionary mechanisms unimpaired, and vice versa.

Stone et al. (2002) developed a battery of Wason tasks that tested social contracts, precautionary rules, and descriptive rules. The social contracts and precautionary rules elicited equally high levels of violation detection from normal subjects (who scored 70% and 71% correct, respectively). For each subject, a difference score was calculated: percentage correct for precautions minus percentage correct for social contracts. For normal subjects, these difference scores were all close to zero ($M = 1.2$ percentage points, $SD = 11.5$).

This battery of Wason tasks was administered to R.M., a patient with bilateral damage to his medial orbitofrontal cortex and anterior temporal cortex, plus damage near the posterior temporal poles sufficient to disconnect both of his amygdalae. R.M.'s performance on the precaution problems was 70% correct: equivalent to that of the normal controls. In contrast, his performance on the social contract problems was only 39% correct. R.M.'s difference score (precautions minus social contracts) was 31 percentage points. This is 2.7 standard deviations larger than the average difference score of 1.2 percentage points found for control subjects ($p < .005$). In other words, R.M. had a large deficit in his social contract reasoning, alongside normal reasoning about precautionary rules.

Double dissociations are helpful in ruling out differences in task difficulty as a counterexplanation for a given dissociation (Shallice, 1988), but here the tasks were perfectly matched for difficulty. The social contracts and precautionary rules given to R.M. were logically identical, posed identical task demands, and were equally difficult for normal subjects. Moreover, because the performance of the normal controls was not at ceiling, ceiling effects could not be masking real differences in the difficulty of the two sets of problems. In this case, a single dissociation licenses inferences about the underlying mental structures. R.M.'s dissociation supports the hypothesis that reasoning about social exchange is caused by a different computational system than reasoning about precautionary rules: a two-mechanism account.

IV.viii.ii Neuroimaging and Rule Interpretation Recent functional magnetic resonance imaging studies also support the hypothesis that social contract reasoning is supported by different brain areas than precautionary reasoning (Wegener, Baare, Hede, Ramsoy, & Lund, 2004; Fiddick, Spampinato, & Grafman, 2005). We recently conducted a neuroimaging study comparing reasoning on Wason tasks involving social contracts to ones involving (i) precautionary rules and (ii) indicative rules involving social behavior (Ermer et al., 2006). Like the other studies, we found that reasoning about social exchange activates brain areas not activated by reasoning about precautionary rules, and vice versa. Unlike the other studies, however, the design of the Ermer et al. study allows one to distinguish brain activations while the rule is being read and interpreted from brain activations at the postinterpretive phase, when subjects are deciding whether a card should be turned over to detect violations. Social contracts and precautions activated different brain areas during both stages, supporting the hypothesis that the postinterpretive detection process *and* the interpretive process differ for these two, content-defined classes of deontic conditional. The results for the interpretation phase were particularly illuminating.

Baron-Cohen (1995) proposed that the theory-of-mind inference system evolved to promote strategic social interaction. Social exchange—a form of cooperation for mutual benefit—involves strategic social interaction (remember the Prisoners' Dilemma) and requires theory-of-mind inferences about the contents of other individuals' mental states, especially their *desires*, *goals*, and *intentions*. Indeed, inferences about the goals and desires of agents are necessary for situation detectors to recognize an interaction as involving social exchange (see section II.i.i). Thus, one might expect neural correlates of theory of mind to be activated when subjects are interpreting social exchange rules. That is precisely what Ermer et al. found. Anterior and posterior temporal cortex—both previously identified in the literature as neural correlates of theory-of-mind inferences—were activated when subjects interpreted social exchange rules, but not when they were interpreting precautionary rules.

Figure 2.6 shows the average signal intensity in the anterior temporal cortex for each individual social contract and precautionary problem (anterior temporal cortex was extensively damaged in R.M.). The figure shows that there is almost no overlap for these two sets of rules: signal intensities do not overlap at all for 14 of 16 problems (7 of 8 social contracts and 7 of 8 precautions). That is, the greater activation of anterior temporal cortex for social exchange rules compared to precautionary rules is systematic—it is not an artifact of one or two problems. It also shows the results are not

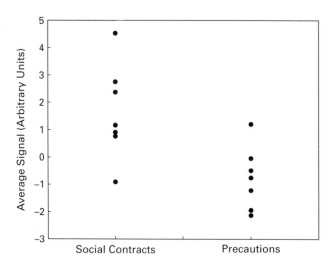

Figure 2.6
Average signal intensity in anterior temporal cortex when reasoning about social contracts and precautionary rules. Each point represents an individual reasoning problem. There is virtually no overlap in signal intensity between the social contract and precautionary rules. That this pattern of differential activation replicates across *individual problems* is expected if the activation differences reflect the underlying, content-specific representation and interpretation of social exchange versus precautionary problems.

caused by idiosyncratic, theory-irrelevant properties of individual rules. The surface content of the various social contract rules used—their particular antecedents and consequents—differed across problems; so did the surface content of the various precautionary rules used. The social exchange problems were similar to one another only by virtue of fitting the situation of social exchange described in section II.i.i and the benefit-requirement template of a standard social contract. Likewise, the precautionary rules were similar to one another only by virtue of fitting the hazard-precaution template for a precautionary rule specified in section IV.iv.i. That the pattern of differential activation replicates across *individual problems* increases our confidence that these activation differences reflect the underlying, content-specific representation and interpretation of social exchange versus precautionary problems.

These results are consistent with our task analyses of the two domains. Inferences about the content of other people's mental states—theory-of-mind inferences—are necessary for interpreting rules involving social exchange but not for interpreting precautionary rules. To interpret a rule as precautionary requires the ability to recognize facts about the world: that an activity may be hazardous and that taking a particular precaution may mitigate that hazard (sections IV.iv.i, IV.vi.ii, IV.vii.ii). No inferences about mental states are required. This result adds to the evidence that the mind distinguishes deontic rules by their content and that the interpretive process applied to social exchange rules is different from that applied to precautionary rules.

IV.viii.iii Eliminating One-Mechanism Hypotheses Every alternative explanation of cheater detection proposed so far claims that reasoning about social contracts and precautions is caused by the same neurocognitive system. R.M.'s dissociation is inconsistent with all of these one-mechanism accounts. These accounts include mental logic (Rips, 1994), mental models (Johnson-Laird & Byrne, 1991), decision theory/optimal data selection (Kirby, 1994; Oaksford & Chater, 1994), permission schema theory (Cheng & Holyoak, 1989), Fodor's deontic logic account (Fodor, 2000; Buller, 2005), relevance theory (Sperber et al., 1995), and Manktelow and Over's (1991, 1995) view implicating a system that is general to any deontic rule that involves subjective utilities. (For further evidence against relevance theory, see Fiddick et al., 2000; for further evidence against Manktelow & Over's theory, see Fiddick & Rutherford, 2006.)

Indeed, no other reasoning theory even distinguishes between precautions and social contract rules. The distinction is derived from evolutionary-functional analyses and is purely in terms of *content*. These results, together with the others discussed in section IV, indicate the presence of a very narrow, content-sensitive cognitive specialization within the human reasoning system for reasoning about social exchange.

V Conclusion

Philosophers have already expressed the wish to construct a deontic logic that captures important facts about human deontic reasoning. A fact of signal importance for the success of this project emerges from the research we have discussed: Deontic reasoning is not a unified phenomenon. Reasoning about deontic conditionals fractionates in a way implying the existence of at least two specialized systems: one for reasoning about social exchange and another for reasoning about precautionary rules. There may be others as well (Cosmides & Tooby, 2006; Tooby, Cosmides, & Price, 2006).

Deontic conditionals expressing social exchanges activate reasoning machinery that is very precisely engineered for producing an evolutionarily stable form of cooperation. When situation detectors register the presence of cues that fit the input conditions for social exchange (cues indicating what two agents want and their willingness and ability to provide these benefits to one another), they activate a domain-specialized computational system, the *social contract algorithms*. Social contract algorithms import surplus structure as they continue to interpret the situation, including any deontic conditional that has been stated, inserting very specific deontic concepts of *obligation* and *entitlement* in just the right places. Words such as "must," "may," and "ought," which can refer to very different concepts depending on context, are thus assigned an exchange-appropriate meaning. Indeed, interpretive procedures within the social contract algorithms ensure that concepts of obligation and entitlement are understood to apply, even when deontic words are missing entirely.

The social contract algorithms include a domain-appropriate set of inferential rules, which are applied spontaneously and intuitively to situations of social exchange. These license inferential transformations that are "common sense" when applied to social exchange but that violate our moral intuitions when applied to other deontic domains. They also generate very predictable moral judgments about the circumstances under which the obligations of a social contract can be lifted or ignored without blame—circumstances that do not apply to precautionary and other deontic conditionals. They include a specialized information search procedure as well—the cheater detection mechanism—that looks for information that could reveal potential cheaters, very narrowly defined. By seeing what conditions turn the cheater detection mechanism on and off, we found that its procedures define a cheater as an individual who has (i) taken the benefit the provider agreed to supply contingent on a requirement being satisfied, (ii) done so without having satisfied the provider's requirement, and (iii) taken these actions by intention rather than by accident.

Supporting the claim that reasoning about social exchange is functionally distinct from reasoning about other deontic conditionals, brain damage can impair social exchange reasoning selectively, leaving intact one's ability to reason well about deontic precautionary rules. Neuroimaging results are consistent with this finding: different patterns of brain activation are produced by reasoning about social contracts versus precautionary rules, during interpretation *and* during the violation detection process. Significantly, neural correlates of theory-of-mind are differentially activated when people interpret social exchanges compared to precautionary rules.

The behavioral data show that deontic conditionals expressing precautions activate interpretive procedures, deontic concepts, moral judgments, and violation detection procedures that differ from those activated in social exchange. Moreover, deontic conditionals that tap neither domain do not elicit the enhanced reasoning competence found for social exchange and precautionary rules. Parametric studies (Barrett, 1999; Cosmides, Barrett, & Tooby, forthcoming) and priming results (Cosmides, 1985; Cosmides & Tooby, 1997; Fiddick, 1998) suggest that those people who do reason correctly about such rules succeed when the rules contained enough input cues consistent with social exchange or precautions to weakly activate one of these specialized systems.

We should not imagine that there is a separate specialization for solving each and every adaptive problem involving deontic reasoning (Tooby, Cosmides, & Price, 2006). Nor should real differences in processing be ignored in a misguided effort to explain all reasoning performance by reference to a single mechanism. As Einstein once said, "Make everything as simple as possible, but no simpler." We think the same principle should apply to creating a deontic logic that is descriptively accurate.

A deontic calculus that is content blind would have difficulties capturing the many distinctions our minds spontaneously make between domains of deontic reasoning—we have tried to show this for each result presented. The data suggest the need for more than one deontic logic, each associated with domain-specialized inferential rules and content-defined scope boundaries (ones that respect the domain boundaries of evolved reasoning specializations); each calculus may also need some domain-specialized deontic operators to capture evolved distinctions between deontic concepts (especially insofar as one views the meaning of concepts as defined by the system of inferences in which they participate). This does not mean, however, that deontic logicians will have to create an endless series of formal calculi. There may be a kaleidoscopic array of culturally defined deontic domains (with different sets found in different cultures), but it is likely that these arose through the application of a much smaller set of evolved social inference systems (e.g., Fiske, 1991).

As Sperber (1994, 1996) has argued, an evolved mechanism's actual domain (the entire set of circumstances in which it is applied) is larger than its proper domain (the set of circumstances that selected for its evolved design). This is because an evolved system is a causal system: it will be activated whenever there are cues that fit the mechanism's input conditions. For example, other humans—agents with desires, goals, intentions, emotions, and beliefs—are the proper domain of the social contract algorithms. But people in many places are told that unseen agents—gods, ghosts, and spirits—interfere with events in pursuit of their own goals and desires. Social inference machinery is activated by these representations of agents and their desires, with predictable consequences: people propose social exchanges to their gods, promising ritual offerings, sacrifices, or reform in exchange for help (Boyer, 2001). Similarly, precautionary inferences—including ones relevant to contagion and disgust—are often applied in religious ceremonies (especially those involving dead bodies), and in certain caste systems, a path-dependent history of interaction with corpses and other polluting substances has led to the inference that certain categories of people are themselves polluted (Boyer, 2001; Fiddick, 1998, 2004; Haidt & Joseph, 2004). Failing to take the appropriate precautions when interacting with members of another caste is often considered a moral transgression, although presumably of a different kind than cheating a friend or murdering a neighbor. In the realm of political ideas, representing a citizen's relationship to government as a form of social exchange triggers the inference that paying taxes is fulfilling an obligation rather than surrendering to extortion (for more examples, see Cosmides & Tooby, 2006). That is, a small set of evolved social inference systems may give rise to a diverse array of cultural forms. In formulating domain-specific deontic logics, it may be more parsimonious to first consider the boundaries respected by the evolved architecture of the mind. As a later exercise, logicians and moral philosophers could consider metarules for adjudicating cases in which it is unclear which formal calculus should be applied.

At this point, some readers are surely thinking that the goal of capturing facts about deontic reasoning should be abandoned so as to preserve the hope of creating a single, simple deontic logic that is truly domain general. This would be unwise. First, there is the problem we raised at the beginning: the domain specificity of our deontic intuitions is likely to still be present in what is supposed to be a general deontic logic, but disguised as different kinds of "reasons" (or swept under the rug in other ways). A second problem arises when one considers the intersection of deontic logic, moral philosophy, and the epidemiology of cultural ideas, including moral ones.

By applying what is known about the evolved architecture of the human mind to various problems in cultural transmission, cognitive anthropologists are starting to understand why some ideas are contagious, spreading easily from mind to mind, whereas others are proposed and soon forgotten (Boyer, 2001; Sperber, 1996). Ideas that violate evolved intuitions can be attention grabbing (e.g., "an electron is a particle that behaves like a wave!"), but those that do not simultaneously activate an evolved system that supports rich inferences (e.g., the object mechanics inference system; Spelke, 1990; Leslie, 1994) remain the preoccupation of specialists (e.g., quantum physicists). A deontic calculus that violates too many evolved moral intuitions is likely to have a similar fate. This should concern any moral philosopher for whom outcomes matter.

Whereas some philosophers argue that an outcome is ethical if the procedure that produced it was ethical (e.g., Nozick, 1974), others are consequentialists: they argue that certain outcomes are ethically better than others and that moral choices should be based—at least in part—on how well they achieve ethical outcomes (e.g., Bentham, 1789; Rawls, 1971; Sen, 1989). Consequentialists need to be concerned with consequences: their job is not merely to define what end state is morally preferable but to elucidate methods that are likely to achieve that end state. Moral action depends, at least in part, on moral reasoning. Versions of deontic logic that capture empirical facts about deontic reasoning are likely to be intuitively compelling, easy to understand, yet precise enough to clarify moral questions in a way that can promote ethical choices. Versions that neglect these facts are less likely to be understood, accepted, or generally adopted. A consequentialist should not prefer a deontic logic merely because it is domain general. A consequentialist needs to consider whether a given deontic logic is likely to be widely adopted and used to inform the multitude of real-world decisions that shape our social world. When outcomes matter, human nature matters.

Notes

We warmly thank Walter Sinnott-Armstrong, whose insights and guidance made this chapter possible.

1. Even Castañeda (1981), whose approach sometimes distinguishes contexts, implicitly endorses this domain-general hope when he says, "a formal calculus proposed as a deontic calculus together with *its* primary interpretation is a theory about the logical structure of our ordinary deontic language and about our ordinary deontic reasonings" (38, emphasis added). "Its primary interpretation" implies a single primary interpretation, not a multiplicity of domain-specific ones. We thank Walter Sinnott-Armstrong for pointing this out.

2. A later project might be to develop a metatheory for deciding which deontic logic should apply in situations that (arguably) fall into two or more domains.

3. In this early work we referred to deontic rules as "prescriptive" (because they prescribe behavior) and indicative ones as "descriptive" (because they describe behavior or facts about the world).

4. This is a regularity in present environments as well, but the inference is obviously not induced through ontogenetic experience. First, mental states cannot be seen;

one can observe correlations between behavior and eye direction, but not between mental states and eye direction. Second, people with autism are quite capable of noticing correlations in the world, yet they do not induce this one.

5. A system can be ecologically rational yet operate over a very broad array of content. Examples would be the frequency computation system, the fast-and-frugal heuristics identified by Gigerenzer and colleagues, and the system underpinning classical conditioning, which Gallistel describes as implementing nonstationary, multivariate time-series analysis (Brase, Cosmides, & Tooby, 1998; Cosmides & Tooby, 1996a; Gigerenzer et al., 1999).

6. Surreally, this paper, which highlights interpretation in its title, is cited by Buller (2005), in the same chapter in which he claims that we do not realize that different conditional rules "have" different interpretations.

7. If the rules regulating reasoning and decision making about social exchange do not implement an ESS, it would imply that these rules are a by-product of some other adaptation that produces fitness benefits so huge that they compensate for the systematic fitness costs that result from its producing non-ESS forms of social exchange as a side effect. Given how much social exchange humans engage in, this alternative seems unlikely.

8. The same logic applies even if no cost is incurred. A design that provides benefits contingent on a benefit being provided in return will have better fitness than one that provides benefits unconditionally (Tooby & Cosmides, 1996).

9. What that "more" consists of for indicative rules is a matter of debate. Sperber, Cara, and Girotto (1995) argue that the conditional rule must first be interpreted as pragmatically implying a denial (*deny: P and not-Q*). They have a similar argument for social contracts, arguing that these are interpreted as forbidding (*forbid: P and not-Q*). Whether their argument is correct for indicatives, their extension to all deontic rules (including social contracts) is not. As we discuss in Fiddick et al. (2000), their theory does not predict that conditionals expressing trades will be interpreted as meaning *forbid: P & not-Q* (nor will most forms of social exchange). Therein we further show that their content-general interpretive procedures (employing logical equivalences) cannot explain results for switched social contracts, perspective change, or, indeed, any of the dissociations within the domain of deontic rules discussed in section IV.

10. *Programs that cheat by design* is a more general formulation of the principle, which does not require the human ability to form mental representations of intentions or to infer the presence of intentional mental states in others. An analogy to deception may be useful: birds that feign a broken wing to lure predators away from their nests are equipped with programs that are designed to deceive the predator, but the cognitive procedures involved need not include a mental representation of an *intention* to deceive.

11. First-order logic cannot solve the problem of cheater detection even if one assumes the existence of social contract algorithms that are interpreting rules and importing surplus structure into them—see Fiddick, Cosmides, and Tooby (2000) for an extended discussion of this point.

12. And one who has not filled the tank and not borrowed the car has merely decided not to take the parents up on their offer.

13. Moreover, first-order logic contains no rules of inference that allow *If P, then Q* to be translated as *If Q, then P* (i.e., no rule for translating [1] as [2]; see text) and then applying the logical definition of violation to that translation (for discussion, see Fiddick et al., 2000).

14. Cheng and Holyoak (1985) also propose an obligation schema, but permission and obligation schemas do not lead to different predictions on the kinds of rules usually tested (for discussion, see Cosmides, 1989; Rips, 1994, p. 413).

15. Mistakes can be faked, of course. Too many by a given individual should raise suspicion, as should a single mistake that results in a very large benefit. Although this prediction has not been tested yet, we would expect social contract algorithms to be sensitive to these conditions.

16. For example, is Fodor talking about properties of logic, independent of the structure of human minds? Or is he talking about properties of human minds as they interpret utterances? If it is the latter, then he is agreeing with us that the mind interprets social contracts differently from indicatives, but without providing an explanation for why this occurs. (Presumably he is not claiming that ordinary intuition is carrying out the reductio argument that he himself had difficulty constructing; see his footnote 6.)

17. Fodor doesn't appear to understand what we mean by a "social contract" (indeed the term does not appear in his piece). When I say, "If you give me your watch, then I'll give you $100" it is not to prohibit *not-Q* or to mandate Q: it is to propose a trade. For an extensive analysis of the problems with interpreting social contracts as primarily about prohibition, see Fiddick, Cosmides, and Tooby (2000, especially pp. 35–41).

18. Indeed, this "counterexample" to an implication of his reductio is what leads him to reject the proposition that *It is required that: If someone is under 18, s/he drinks coke* "isn't really about P → Q being required" (Fodor 2000, p. 31); that it is instead about Q being required (in the case that *P*).

19. Indeed, changing conceptions of what counts as "old enough to behave responsibly" are why the age was raised from 18 to 21.

20. To the extent that a subject interprets "drinking beer" as a hazardous activity, the drinking age law could be interpreted as a precautionary rule; because it has a dual interpretation, it falls into the area of intersection between social contracts and precautions on figure 2.5.

2.1 | Ought We to Abandon a Domain-General Treatment of "Ought"?

Ron Mallon

Leda Cosmides and John Tooby have some advice for moral philosophers and deontic logicians trying to understand deontic notions like *ought*: give up trying to provide a univocal, domain-general treatment. The domain-specific character of human cognition means that such a research program is probably fruitless and probably pointless. It is probably fruitless since a univocal account of the meaning of "ought" will not capture the multiple inferential patterns of deontic reasoning exhibited in different contexts (and similarly for lots of other words like "obligation," "entitlement," etc.—but let's stick with "ought"). And it is probably pointless, because even if a domain-general logic can be developed, it will fail to "capture major distinctions the human mind makes when reasoning deontically" (p. 60). As a result, it is "not likely to be widely understood and adopted," so it will "not succeed in guiding ethical decisions beyond an esoteric circle of specialists" (p. 60).

Much of this sounds pretty implausible to me, and I say why in what follows. However, I'll start by conceding lots of ground to Cosmides and Tooby. In particular, let's begin by agreeing that the mind is the product of an evolutionary process. And let us agree, at least for the moment, with many other central contentions of the school of evolutionary psychology that Cosmides and Tooby helped found. Let us agree that

1. The mind has many innate, specialized faculties, shaped by evolutionary processes for performing important tasks in our evolutionary environment.
2. At least some of these specialized faculties are cognitively central (i.e., they are not limited to cognitively peripheral functions like perception but include processes like reasoning and categorization).
3. We can use what we know about our evolutionary past and evolution itself to frame productive hypotheses about these faculties.

4. These hypotheses can and ought to be subject to subsequent empirical testing.

5. As a result of this methodology, there's now a substantial body of empirical evidence that the mind has domain-specific faculties, for example, for the analysis of social exchange.

While these theses and evolutionary psychology more generally continue to be controversial, I do not challenge these theses or an evolutionary approach to cognition in what follows. Instead, I want to raise some questions about what it would be like if these things are true. In particular, I want to address their suggestion that deontic logicians or moral philosophers ignore these facts at their peril.

Is Our Deontic Terminology Ambiguous Among Multiple Meanings?

Cosmides and Tooby focus on the project of deontic logic—the attempt to design a formal calculus whose rules of inference are more or less isomorphic to the inferential rules we implicitly employ in deontic reasoning. But their concern applies equally well to many projects in philosophy and ordinary life that implicitly or explicitly use deontic vocabulary.

In order to consider Cosmides and Tooby's argument more carefully, I begin by offering some clarificatory remarks. I take it that these clarificatory remarks go beyond what they actually say in their paper, but the remarks are meant to be friendly extensions of what I take to be presupposed there rather than an alternative reading of the background facts.

Let's assume (for the moment) that a word, "cat," is associated with a mental representation type CAT, and that both "cat" and CAT express the meaning or sense *cat*.[1] How do "cat" and CAT get their meanings? Well one common story is that "cat"—a word of natural language—inherits its meaning from the mental representation CAT it is associated with, and where a word like "bank" has two distinct meanings, there are two mental representations to go with it. How does a mental representation like CAT get its meaning then? There is much disagreement about how to answer this question, but for present purposes let us simply interpret Cosmides and Tooby as they intend: a mental representation gets its meaning, at least in part, from its inferential role. Thus they write,

what if a single lexical item, such as "ought" . . . , masks a plethora of meanings that bear only a family resemblance to one another? For example, what if the *ought* embedded in social contract algorithms has a different meaning/set of implications than the *ought* embedded in a precautionary inference system—that is, what if these concepts are better thought of as *ought*$_{SC}$ and *ought*$_{Prec}$? (p. 57)

Cosmides and Tooby believe this is so. They believe that the word "ought" (and other deontic terms as well) is associated with different mental representation types (e.g., OUGHT$_{SC}$ and OUGHT$_{PREC}$) with distinct inferential roles within distinct neurocomputational systems. These systems are activated by cues that lead them to assign interpretations to natural language utterances and "apply rules of transformation" that tell it what follows from what (p. 64).

Does "Ought" Express Different Meanings in Different Contexts?

Continuing with our concessive mood, let's concede that people do in fact follow different patterns of inference with "ought" in different domains. This indicates that *something* is computationally different about the domains, but not what. Let's use the word "faculty" to label whatever it is that results in the inferential differences among deontic domains. But exactly what is the nature of these faculties?

Cosmides and Tooby suggest that such a faculty is a distinct "neurocomputational system whose design features are adaptively specialized for producing . . . specific kinds of inferences and goals" (p. 53) and that "represent situations via a proprietary format that represents distinctions that were adaptively important in the domain for which they evolved" (p. 54) and "are equipped with functionally specialized inferential procedures that were designed to operate on these proprietary representations" (p. 54). So suppose ordinary people mentally represent

"If you borrow the car, fill it with gas."

as

IF I BORROW HER CAR, I OUGHT TO FILL IT WITH GAS.

And they move from that to

IF I FILL HER CAR WITH GAS, SHE OUGHT NOT TO MIND THAT I BORROW IT.[2]

Why do ordinary people make this inference? Cosmides and Tooby think that the inference is the result of a dedicated computational mechanism that handles social exchange problems, one that licenses inferences like this only in the domain of social exchange. However, other accounts of the faculties underlying the domain-specific inferential patterns are possible, including Richard Samuels's (1998) suggestion that domain-specific expertise may be underwritten by domain-general computational mechanisms together with domain-specific bodies of mentally represented knowledge—what he calls the "Library Model of Cognition." For example, we might posit that ordinary people have an innate "library" of mentally represented rules, such as,

IF PERSON *A* SETS A CONDITION *C* ON THE BORROWING OF *A*'S PROPERTY *P*, THEN IF PERSON *B* SATISFIES *C*, THEN *A* OUGHT NOT TO MIND THAT *B* BORROWS *P*.

The domain specificity of the inferential pattern Cosmides and Tooby identify would be explained by a domain-general inferential mechanism that operates on domain-general mental representations but exploits the domain-specific information encoded in this library.

I find Samuels's arguments that the Library Model of Cognition is a distinct and viable explanatory alternative to the dedicated neurocomputational mechanisms that Cosmides and Tooby propose to be compelling. However, it is worth noting (as Samuels does) that in terms of the larger project of evolutionary psychology, the Library Model of Cognition proposal is highly concessive. For the Library Model posits domain-specific and highly adapted bodies of encoded information, and the logic of evolution may be invoked to understand *why* we have such domain-specific knowledge in our "library," *what* domain-specific knowledge would be useful to have, and so forth.

To say the Library Model is a viable alternative is not to say that it is true, but that need not concern us here. For present purposes, the Library Model of Cognition shows that one cannot infer from the presence of distinctive inference patterns in different domains the conclusion that the computations in different domains employ proprietary mental representations or computational mechanisms. If the Library Model were correct, the mind would make use of nonproprietary mental representations and domain-general computational mechanisms and still achieve domain-specific inference patterns. For example, the same mental representation type (e.g., OUGHT) might have different inferential roles in social exchange and precautionary domains because of the presence of "libraries" of mental representations encoding information about those domains.

Why Care about Domain Generality?

The truth is that we do not know whether domain-specific inference patterns are driven by neurocomputational mechanisms with proprietary mental representations and inferential procedures or whether these inference patterns are produced by a domain-general computational mechanism operating on mental representations that interact with a domain-specific library of knowledge. And once we recognize that, it does not seem that the type identity of the token mental representations subserving different inferential patterns could really be what's at stake in designing a deontic logic.

In fact, Cosmides and Tooby might simply insist that whether or not the mental representation type is the same or different (in some syntactic sense to be specified), the domain-specific algorithms that it participates in generate such different inferential patterns that a well-designed moral vocabulary/deontic logic would do well to introduce basic terms that allow us to distinguish these inferential roles. That is, whether or not there is a mental representation type OUGHT that plays distinct roles across domains, we would do well to introduce into our moral vocabulary/deontic logic terms like "ought$_{prec}$" and "ought$_{sc}$" to capture the different inferential patterns in different domains.[3] That seems the most straightforward reading of their dilemma to the effect that we have a choice in how we proceed: we can either "develop a series of very well-specified domain-specific deontic logics, each of which applies within certain boundaries of human action and not outside them" (p. 59) or we can insist on domain generality and "be driven to define deontic concepts in manner so general as to be useless—a manner that does not escape the problems of domain specificity but merely hides them" (p. 58). Here the thought is not that our vocabulary or logical symbolism must neatly map onto our system of mental representations or inferential patterns, only that there would be important advantages if it does.

Faced with Cosmides and Tooby's proposed balkanization of deontic reasoning, we ought to pause and ask: what is the cost of pursuing the path Cosmides and Tooby choose? Is there any important role for a domain-general system of deontic reasoning? It seems that the answer is yes. Here's why. Suppose Matviyko's doctor tells him that he ought to lay off the cigarettes now because they'll eventually kill him, and his wife reminds him that he promised to finish his novel by the end of the year and get a "real job." As it happens, Matviyko knows that he cannot quit smoking and finish his novel by the end of the year.

What ought Matviyko to do? According to Cosmides and Tooby, his social exchange algorithms compute the thought that

I OUGHT$_{SC}$ TO KEEP MY PROMISE TO MY WIFE.

And this leads him to think

I OUGHT$_{SC}$ TO FINISH MY NOVEL BY THE END OF THE YEAR AND GET A REAL JOB.

And also that

I OUGHT$_{SC}$ TO CONTINUE SMOKING NOW.

Meanwhile, his precautionary rules algorithms compute that

I OUGHT$_{PREC}$ TO QUIT SMOKING NOW.

Prima facie, Matviyko's thoughts guide him to perform incompatible actions. Without some way of integrating the two sorts of OUGHT, the outputs of the two processes "talk past" each other.

Clearly people resolve such practical conflicts in some way, perhaps with a domain-general faculty of some sort, or perhaps with a domain-specific "deontic-conflict resolver." But then it seems open to us as moral theorists or deontic logicians to say that it is the operation of *this* (at least relatively) domain-general process that we are really interested in modeling.

Elsewhere, Shaun Nichols and I (Nichols & Mallon, 2006; Mallon & Nichols, forthcoming) distinguish among a number of distinct domain-specific mechanisms that may play a role in producing moral judgments about hypothetical cases, but we go on to distinguish between something being "okay" by reference to some particular criteria (e.g., okay according to a rule) and "all things considered" okay (what we call "all-in permissibility"). This capacity to decide what ought to be the case "all things considered" seems at the core of moral theory, and we require a domain-general syntax and semantics to represent it.[4]

We can now respond to Cosmides and Tooby that having a domain-general representation of the many different sorts of reasons we have for doing different things might allow us to model—in our theoretical vocabulary or our deontic logic—a process for seeing entailments or resolving conflicts between these generally conceived reasons. Matviyko, for example, realized that his reason to complete his novel by the end of the year gave him a reason not to quit smoking now while his concern for his health gave him a reason to quit smoking now, and that these reasons conflict with one another!

It seems useful to explain why and how these reasons conflict. At least Cosmides and Tooby owe a story about why that is useless. Their complaint that reasons, generally conceived, do not distinguish between the many sorts of mental representations that might be in play (p. 59) is beside the point because it presupposes that distinguishing types of mental representations is the job of moral philosophy or deontic logic. Why should that be?

Your Useless and Pointless Knowledge

Cosmides and Tooby also object that a domain-general deontic calculus is doomed to unpopularity, for "a deontic calculus that deeply violates our moral intuitions is not likely to be widely understood or adopted (Boyer, 2001; Sperber, 1996)" (p. 60), and they later write,

> By applying what is known about the evolved architecture of the human mind to various problems in cultural transmission, cognitive anthropologists are starting to understand why some ideas are contagious, spreading easily from mind to mind, whereas others are proposed and soon forgotten (Boyer, 2001; Sperber, 1996). Ideas that violate evolved intuitions can be attention grabbing (e.g., "an electron is a particle that behaves like a wave!"), but those that do not simultaneously activate an evolved system that supports rich inferences (e.g., the object mechanics inference system; Spelke, 1990; Leslie, 1994) remain the preoccupation of specialists (e.g., quantum physicists). A deontic calculus that violates too many evolved moral intuitions is likely to have a similar fate. This should concern any moral philosopher for whom outcomes matter. (pp. 116–117)

Boyer and Sperber have both argued for a central role for "psychological selection" of items in transmitted culture, leading to greater survival rates for selected cultural items. This approach, sometimes called the "epidemiology of representations," is still quite young, but it has received important experimental support (Nichols, 2002), and I'm a big fan of this work. However, Cosmides and Tooby look to me to misread the aspirations of deontic logicians and moral philosophers to practical significance and outrun the evidence considerably. I'll close my comments by saying why.

Cosmides and Tooby's argument seems to presuppose that deontic logicians hope to have their logical systems be as widely accepted as possible. But this is really odd. Are Cosmides and Tooby of the view that deontic logicians think that expressions like:

$$PEp \leftrightarrow \sim OB{\sim}p$$

$$IMp \leftrightarrow OB{\sim}p$$

will catch on among the population if only they spread the good symbol?[5] Or are we to believe, on Cosmides and Tooby's proposal, that such expressions *would* catch on if only we choose formation and transition rules that reflect domain-specific inference patterns? Both the interpretive claim and the popular success of their alternate proposal look pretty unlikely.

Of course, Cosmides and Tooby are addressing McNamara's remark that "deontic logics often directly involve topics of considerable practical significance" (2006), but it is wrong to suppose that deontic logicians are faced with a choice between abstruse obscurity or widespread mental representation of a deontic calculus. There are an enormous number of ways for a theory to have "practical significance" without the need to be widely represented in individual minds—for example, in law, in policy, and in institutional practice. Not many people understand the ins and outs of actuarial science, and fewer still understand the notation of actuarial equations, but actuarial science is a pervasive and important technology in the modern economy. Cohering with folk intuitions is simply not necessary for a theory to "matter." *Many* theories do seem to matter that have counterintuitive content, and one need not gaze into the mysterious complexities of quantum physics to find them. Even *Newtonian* physics violates the expectations of folk physics! (McCloskey, 1983a, 1983b).

One also wonders if worrying about whether one's theory is "contagious" is the sort of reason that ought to guide theorists. Indeed, if we agreed with Richard Dawkins that "we have no intuitive grasp of the immensities of time available for evolutionary change" (1996, pp. 39–40), then evolutionary psychology itself looks to be based on difficult-to-grasp conceptions of evolution over enormous time spans. Ought we then to advise Cosmides and Tooby that their modular cognitive psychology would be more likely to matter if it were framed within a more intuitive, (and popularly accepted) creationist framework?[6] Isn't this suggestion beside the point? Shouldn't the primary aim of a research tradition be to get the answer right?

In any case, examples of important cultural products that violate at least some folk intuitions show that in understanding why one cultural object succeeds and another does not, psychological selection (where that means agreement with all our domain-specific intuitions) is only one selective force among others. And *that* shows that one cannot just read the hopelessness of some intellectual project off of (even a considerably more developed) literature on the epidemiology of representations. From knowledge of some domain-specific intuitions and the fact that psychological selection causes some representations to survive more readily than others, it simply doesn't follow that we can predict of some representation type that it is unlikely to survive.

Finally, it is not clear why Cosmides and Tooby think that a domain-general deontic logic would "violate evolved moral intuitions" rather than simply failing to entail them. Suppose a domain-general deontic logic licenses inference types that obtain across domains, and the "surplus structure" Cosmides and Tooby argue for licenses additional inferences within particular domains. If so, a domain-general logical calculus might "violate" moral intuitions in the sense that it does not *entail* those intuitions (according to the transition rules of the domain-general logic), but it need not violate them in the sense that the domain-general system entails statements that contradict the deliverance of domain-specific reasoning.

Having It Both Ways

Cosmides and Tooby have been at the forefront of the effort to use evolutionary considerations to reveal the secrets of our cognitive architecture, and in this effort, they have generated a very important research program and a range of very important results. However, if what I have said is correct, when choosing our moral vocabulary or deontic calculus, we cannot and need not decide on the grounds of our knowledge of cognitive architecture alone. Moreover, even given domain-specific inferential patterns, we retain a need for representing domain-general concerns. Finally, despite my great respect for the fascinating and burgeoning literature on the epidemiology of representations, I think it is fair to say that it is not usefully applied to deciding which academic fields of inquiry have a chance to matter.

In closing, it is worth noting that nothing in what I have said suggests that we cannot identify both domain-general reasons *and* various domain-specific sorts of reasons as well. This is already implicit in the practice of moral and political philosophy, as when, for example, philosophers argue whether some reasons (viz., rights) are absolute and overriding of others (e.g., utilitarian outcomes). Cosmides and Tooby do not address this possibility, perhaps because they think any domain-general deontic logic must violate, rather than simply not entail, domain-specific judgments. But for all I can see, it ought to be possible to have our domain-specific cake and domain-generally eat it too.

Notes

I'm grateful to Walter Sinnott-Armstrong, Edouard Machery, Shaun Nichols, and Jonathan Weinberg for helpful comments on these comments.

1. As Steve Laurence and Eric Margolis (1999, pp. 5–6) have noted, psychologists, and many philosophers of psychology, use the term "concept" to mean a mental representation. Others, including many philosophers, use the word "concept" as a technical term for an abstract object—a meaning or a constituent of a proposition. Because of the chance for confusion, I simply avoid the term in what follows. I think the former use captures most of Cosmides and Tooby's practice.

2. I state these conditional thoughts differently than Cosmides and Tooby, employing "OUGHT" throughout. I do so for simplicity, and also to allow us to ask whether a single mental representation might be capable of different inferential roles in different contexts.

3. Similarly, even if there are multiple mental representation types (e.g., $OUGHT_{SC}$ and $OUGHT_{PREC}$), defenders of a domain-general logic might insist on using a single term (e.g., "ought") to symbolize both. Both suggestions amount to giving up our assumption above that each linguistic term be associated with its own mental representation.

4. At least general to the domain of deontic concerns.

5. These were taken from McNamara (2006).

6. Cf. Evans (2000) and Keleman (2004).

2.2 | Can Evolutionary Psychology Assist Logicians? A Reply to Mallon

Leda Cosmides and John Tooby

We appreciated Ron Mallon's very thoughtful and interesting response to our paper and now worry from the tone of his response that he interpreted it as being disrespectful to the project of deontic logicians. Our hope instead had been to see whether evolutionary approaches could potentially add something to their work, by bringing some pertinent results to their attention and exploring how the deontic logic enterprise might proceed in light of them.

Dueling Oughts

Mallon raises the possibility of creating a domain-general deontic logic that does not entail domain-specific inferences but that does not violate them either. We had assumed that at present the project of deontic logicians was to create an inferential system that is completely general and sufficient to generate all deontic judgments. In arguing that a domain-general deontic logic would violate inferences made by social contract algorithms or a precautionary system, what we had in mind was a deontic logic sufficient to encompass these domains and make all the inferences that social contract algorithms and precautionary mechanisms do. If, instead, the goal is modified to produce a more limited domain-general logic that complements the operation of these domain-specific systems, then Mallon may be right in arguing that this is possible.

However, we are still not clear how this more limited and complementary deontic logic would resolve conflicts that arise between the injunctions of functionally distinct "oughts," such as $OUGHT_{SC}$ and $OUGHT_{PREC}$. Let's consider Matviyko's smoking dilemma, posed by Mallon. Promises need not be social exchanges, but let's say Matviyko's agreement with his wife was one, something like, "If I (wife) support you this year, then you must finish your novel by the end of the year." As Mallon points out, people resolve dilemmas like Matviyko's every day. But are these dilemmas usually resolved by deontic reasoning? Could they, in principle, be resolved by a deontic logic? Let's consider Matviyko's options.

1. Technical fixes often work: Matviyko could satisfy both oughts with a supply of nicotine gum.
2. Matviyko's wife, deciding she cares more about his health than his promise, could release him from his obligation to finish by the end of the year. This is part of the logic of social exchange (section IV.vi.ii).
3. Matviyko could prioritize his *values*: which is more important to him, keeping his word to his wife or beginning immediately the process of improving his health? Or his decision could be regulated by computations that engage a welfare trade-off ratio (Tooby & Cosmides, 2005), a variable specifying how much of his own welfare he is willing to trade off for that of his wife.

These value judgments could be made without engaging a moral reasoning system or consulting moral principles (and evolutionary psychology has a great deal to say about how welfare trade-off ratios should regulate decisions). Alternatively, moral principles could inform and shape these value judgments: values, utilities, and value hierarchies can surely be part of moral reasoning in general. But are they part of deontic logic? How would OUGHT$_{General}$ resolve a conflict between OUGHT$_{SC}$ and OUGHT$_{PREC}$ *without* reference to values? And if values are necessary, perhaps something more than deontic logic is needed. Subjective expected utility theory integrated a calculus of utilities with the probability calculus. Perhaps moral philosophers are already working on a similar integration of values with a deontic calculus.

If not, here is another way deontic logicians may profit from considering certain aspects of evolutionary psychology. We have proposed that the human mind contains a computational system that infers and evaluates welfare trade-offs (Tooby & Cosmides, in press-b). It defines the conditions that elicit anger, guilt, affection, and other emotional/motivational systems, and interprets social interactions in terms of the welfare trade-off ratios implied by each person's actions. This raises the possibility that deontic reasoning is produced not by deontic procedures operating in isolation, but by deontic procedures supplemented by outputs from the welfare trade-off interpretive system. That is, having agreed to pick up a visiting speaker at the airport, I am obligated to do so—but not at the cost of dying. There are an infinite number of side constraints on every obligation, and these might be economically captured by a system of a few welfare trade-off variables operating in an implicit motivational/interpretive system.

Library Model of Cognition

Referring to Richard Samuels's library model, Mallon points out that domain-specific inferential results need not imply domain-specific inference procedures (which is true). He then suggests that the domain-specific pattern of results for social exchange could be produced by domain-general computational procedures operating on a library of evolved, domain-specific information about social exchange: "For example, we might posit that ordinary people have an innate 'library' of *mentally represented rules*, such as, IF PERSON *A* SETS A CONDITION *C* ON THE BORROWING OF *A*'S PROPERTY *P*, THEN IF PERSON *B* SATISFIES *C*, THEN *A* OUGHT NOT TO MIND THAT *B* BORROWS *P*" (p. 124, italics added).

But is this actually different from what we have proposed? Here are three possible interpretations.

1. *Mentally represented rules*   Mallon refers to this library entry as having "mentally represented rules," and their content is clearly about social exchange—*B*'s *borrowing* X implies that X is a *benefit* to borrower *B*, so the rule has to do with what *A* requires in exchange for providing a benefit to *B*. Thus, Mallon has proposed a library of "mentally represented rules" dealing with social exchange; social contract theory proposes a set of such rules. If what is in Mallon's library are rules of inference, then his proposal is just a different way of making the same claim that social contract theory does. After all, at some stage of processing (audition, word recognition, etc.), some relatively domain-general computational processes must interact with social contract algorithms. Our claim is just that those processes cannot, by themselves, account for the rules of transformation that people apply in interpreting and reasoning about social exchange. Domain-specialized rules are needed.

2. *Ought types and inference*   Perhaps Mallon is proposing a library with a *different* set of domain-specific rules than social contract theory proposes. For example, "Then *A* ought not to mind that *B* borrows *P*" tells us nothing about what *A* *will* mind, that is, it tells us nothing about what *A* will view as cheating. This means the rule given does not capture the reasoning patterns we have found (cheater detection; relaxing cheater detection when condition *C* was not satisfied by accident, etc.).

But let's leave that empirical matter aside: presumably Mallon thinks the library contains more mentally represented rules than this. But he then proposes that the token representation of *ought* appearing in this rule may be type-identical to an ought-token appearing in inferential rules for precautions or other domains. This, he argues, would allow for the possibility that the brain contains only one type-representation of "ought," which then acquires "different inferential roles in social exchange and precautionary domains because of the presence of 'libraries' of mental representations encoding information about those domains" (p. 124).

Mallon does not seem to object when we identify the meaning of a concept with the inferential role it plays, so on his account, the type-representation of "ought" would activate a set of domain-independent inferences and then trigger *extra* inferences depending on the inferential role it plays within each library entry in which it appears. Whether there exists a set of domain-independent *ought* inferences that are capable of meshing with these libraries is an empirical question, one which deontic logicians are well-placed to answer. But even on this account, OUGHT$_{SC}$ and OUGHT$_{PREC}$ still exist. These concepts are, precisely, the different bundles of ought-related inferences that are triggered when a library entry containing the type-representation of *ought* is activated. To be a sufficient account of deontic reasoning, the entire bundle is relevant, and each bundle should be different, even if a subset of inferences appear in each bundle.

3. *Declarative knowledge in the library*   Rather than containing rules of inference, the library entry on social exchange might be a set of inert facts, a packet of declarative knowledge that is "looked up" by domain-general procedures. (This interpretation is most consistent with the library metaphor.) Unfortunately, this version of the library model has an empirical problem: it does not explain why performance elicited by social contracts and precautions is so much higher than that elicited by other deontic rules or, indeed, by familiar indicative conditionals.

The selection task asks subjects to *search* for potential violations of a conditional. For domain-general procedures to search for violations, they must be able to look up what conditions count as a violation. And people have this knowledge, even for indicative conditionals: they have a library entry specifying that the combination of *P* and *not-Q* violates indicative rules (see section I.ii). Yet they do not spontaneously search for information that could reveal potential violations of indicative conditionals, even when they are explicitly asked to do so. In fact, they perform poorly even when we call their attention to what counts as a violation (see section I.ii). This means that *searching* for violations requires more than domain-general procedures plus a library entry specifying what counts as a violation.

It follows that having a library entry specifying what counts as cheating is not sufficient to make people good at searching for cheaters. Computationally, something more is needed. People know what counts as a violation for rules drawn from many domains, but this knowledge does not explain when they succeed and fail in their search for violations. This failure of library models was a major impetus for proposing a cheater detection mechanism, equipped with procedures that direct information search in a way likely to reveal cheaters.

Deontic Specialists (or Why Care about the Epidemiology of Representations?)

We agree with Mallon: specialists, including deontic logicians, may be pursuing valuable enterprises even when these conflict with popular belief—as Mallon points out, scientists do not abandon Darwinism for creationism just because evolved inference systems have trouble with deep time. But there is a difference between moral claims and truth claims. Truth claims, however esoteric and nonintuitive, imply facts that can be validated by empirical investigations. But what validates the truth of a moral claim? Deontic logicians do not need to answer Hume's penetrating question if their goal is to construct a deontic logic that captures the moral intuitions of a species or culture. But if they eschew this goal, concentrating instead on constructing various esoteric formalisms—ones whose conclusions conflict with one another (as well as with folk intuition)—then what? What criteria will they use to decide which of these mechanical formalisms is the right one, the one that objectively encapsulates the logic of moral obligation? Without an answer to this question, it is not clear how that particular enterprise can succeed.

There is another reason to consider the mesh between the population intended to profit from deontic discoveries and the esoteric formalisms that deontic specialists produce. Mallon argues that the public at large need not understand what specialists are thinking for their intellectual products to influence our lives, citing scientific discoveries as an example. True. But the paths by which scientific and deontic discoveries influence our lives differ in ways that are causally and morally important. Causally, I don't need to know how my car engine works (because engineers have indeed considered how to make scientific discoveries mesh with my intuitions). But I do need to understand a moral reasoning system to apply it to my decisions. The alternative is a set of deontic experts (or a computer program) making moral decisions for the rest of us. Deontic experts influence us with persuasion and sometimes through coercion (using the apparatus of the state). But in either case, the epidemiology of representations remains relevant. What happens when political and legal systems run by specialists systematically produce moral judgments or social outcomes that deeply violate evolved moral intuitions? It does not seem far-fetched to suggest that they eventually will lose public support.

So yes, deontic logicians are free to ignore the design of evolved deontic reasoning systems, but we still believe they are ill-advised to do so.

Jerry Fodor

A well-known principle of naval engagement: if you're in trouble, put out smoke. As far as I can tell, that's what Cosmides and Tooby (hereinafter C&T) are up to in the present paper.

Brief Review

Much of the substance of C&T's "massive modularity" theory of cognitive architecture is that there are distinct, specialized computational mechanisms for solving problems in each of several different cognitive domains. Each such mechanism becomes active when a problem is recognized as belonging to its proprietary domain, with the consequence that quite different computational procedures may be applied to structurally identical problems depending on domain variables. In particular, the computational treatment of problems that are similar or identical in "logical form" may be quite different depending on the "content" of the materials. "If John swims Mary walks/ John swims/ therefore Mary walks" and "If cats purr, dogs bark/cats purr/therefore dogs bark" are arguments of the same form, but if cats and dogs (or barking and purring) are in different domains, one can expect that the evaluation of these arguments may invoke quite different mental processes and hence may exhibit quite different performance profiles in experimental tasks.

C&T sought to test the hypothesis that inference is content specific in a perfectly sensible way: namely, by showing that, depending on the content of the materials, formally identical inferences exhibit different interactions with performance in the Wason selection task. Roughly, the standard Wason result is that subjects who reliably solve problems that require reasoning according to *modus ponens* reliably fail to solve problems that require reasoning according to contraposition. The experimental manipulation in the C&T experiment contrasted deontic conditionals with descriptive ones (in effect, "obligatory (if p then q)" with "if p then q").

So far so good. But notice that observed interactions of content variables with performance are germane to the domain specificity of inferential processes only if the logical form of the inferences is held constant in the materials manipulations. I argued that, as a matter of fact, this was *not* the case with respect to C&T's test materials since (according to me), descriptive and deontic conditionals ipso facto differ in their logical form. So, although it's quite possible that inferential processes are indeed sensitive to content variables *rather than* logical form, the observed results on the Wason task provide no evidence for claiming that they are.

C&T now offer replies to my suggestion; several that strike me as frivolous and one that is supposed to do the heavy lifting. I'll go through both kinds very quickly.

Frivolous Replies

I Am Accused of Naive Realism

This problem—we call it "instinct blindness"—can afflict anyone, including philosophers. Occasionally, we encounter philosophers who try to account for the data we discuss below by saying that social contracts (along with other deontic rules) "have" a different interpretation than indicative rules (Buller, 2005; Fodor, 2000). This is naive realism. Social contracts do not "have" an interpretation; the mind *assigns* an interpretation to them, and it does so when certain cues and conditions are contextually present. . . . Social contract theory is an account of the computational procedures *by which these interpretations are assigned.* . . . (pp. 68–69)

It is generally recognized, however, that "interpretation" (and the like) can be either a transitive verb (as in "John interpreted the sentence") or a nominal (as in "the interpretation of the sentence that John proposed"). "John's interpretation of the sentence" is ambiguous between the two; and sentences, contracts, and the like may have interpretations in either or both senses. Thus, one may perfectly legitimately speak of the interpretation of a sentence relative to a grammar of L, and one may equally legitimately speak of the interpretation of the sentence by L-speakers, but *it is definitely a good idea not to conflate the two.* It is widely held as an ontological/metaphysical thesis that interpretation in the first sense supervenes on interpretation in the second sense. Like practically everybody else, I'm inclined to think something of that sort (for language, though not for thought). If that makes me a naive realist, I've at least got plenty of company. Anyhow, I don't for a minute think that C&T really believe that the correct understanding of their data awaits the resolution of these very arcane metaphysical issues. "A little philosophy is a dangerous thing. . . ."

I Cite Only One of Their Articles; I Ignore Relevant Results, etc.; I Have Mangled My Account of Their Experiment; etc.

There is a laborious and exhaustive review of experiments that purport to show the domain specificity of inference in Buller (2005). Like me, Buller thinks that in many, possibly all, of them, there is an unresolved confound of content differences with logical form differences. If C&T have a substantive reply to this charge, they are curiously reticent about saying what it is. More smoke, as far as I can tell.

It is, by the way, of some interest that C&T don't refer to the one study in the literature that was explicitly directed to controlling the confound in question (Beaman, 2002). Beaman finds the effect of the deontic conditional/descriptive conditional manipulation on performance on the Wason task is very significantly reduced when the confound is removed.

I Argued Not Only that the Two Kinds of Conditionals May Differ in Logical Form, but that There's Quite Good Prima Facie Evidence that They Do

The argument is that though contraposition normally applies to formulas of the form *if p, then q*, it is invalid in the scope of the operator in formulas like "Obligatory: if you are under 21, you drink coke," which manifestly does *not* entail "if you don't drink coke, obligatory: (you are over 21)." C&T reply, "the drinking age law does not obligate anyone to be 21 years old; it obligates people to wait until they are 21 years old before drinking beer." Why on earth do they think that's germane? *Whether or not the rule entails an obligation to wait,* it patently *doesn't* entail an obligation to be over 21, which is what it *would* entail if contraposition did go through in the scope of "obligatory." So, prima facie, the logical form of "if P then Q" in the scope of "obligatory" is different from that of "if P then Q" simpliciter.

By the way, I added that, although it's nice to have this argument as evidence that the two kinds of conditionals differ in logical form, it's not crucial to the claim that an uncontrolled materials effect may be what explains their data. According to C&T, this makes my proposal question begging: ". . . it assumes what it seeks to explain (which he more or less acknowledges in his footnote 5)" (p. 107). I can't imagine what C&T have in mind.

Some Logicians Interpret Descriptive If P Then Q as Necessarily If P Then Q

That's news to me. Do such logicians really claim that no conditionals are contingent? Do any of them get tenure?

There Are Neurologically Detectable Effects of Content Variables

I should think so! Who except a dualist would deny it?

The Heavy Lifting

C&T's basic complaint is that my account of their results ignores widespread findings that there are performance effects of the content of "if P then Q" when all other relevant differences are controlled. "For example, by Fodor's account, rules [15] and [16] have precisely the same logical form. . . . They differ *only in what P refers to*. In [15] it is something adolescents see as a benefit—going out at night—and in [16] it is something they see as a chore. But what *P* refers to plays no role in Fodor's account" (p. 108).

Examples [15] and [16] in C&T are as follows:

[15] "If one goes out at night, then one must tie a small piece of red volcanic rock around one's ankle."

[16] "If one takes out the garbage at night, then one must tie a small piece of red volcanic rock around one's ankle." (p. 99)

By contrast, "A cheater detection subroutine looks for benefits illicitly taken; without a benefit, it doesn't know what kind of violation to look for. . . . When the permitted action was a benefit (getting to go out at night), 80% of subjects answered correctly; when it was an unpleasant chore (taking out the garbage), only 44% did so. This dramatic decrease in violation detection was predicted in advance by social contract theory" (p. 99).

As far as I can tell, C&T have lost their grasp of the dialectical situation. What they need—the evidence that would be relevant to whether inferential processes are domain specific—is this: *there is no effect of logical form on inferential processes when content is controlled.* But the evidence they've got is only this: *there are effects of content on inferential processes when logical form is controlled.* Somebody who thinks that typical inferential processes are domain neutral needs to deny the first claim, but there's no reason on god's green earth why he ought to deny the second. In fact, he'd be mad to do so, since materials effects on inferential tasks are a staple of texts in

Intro Cog Psy. They include, for example, effects of "aura" (does the subject independently believe the conclusion of the inference?); effects of "concreteness" ("what's 2 + 3?" as opposed to "how many little bears are three little bears plus two little bears?"); effects of "familiarity"; stereotype effects; imagability effects . . . and so forth. I did not cite these results for the same reason that I did not cite influences of the content of "p" on performance in the Wason task; namely, that they are irrelevant to the question of whether logical form per se affects performance. The most they show us is that, even if logical form does, so too do other things. It is, in short, a fallacy to argue from "if inference is content sensitive, then there is no effect of logical form on performance in the Wason task" to "if there is an effect of content on performance in the Wason task, then inference is insensitive to logical form." C&T seem to be having trouble with contraposition.

That said, it strikes me as not surprising that (all else equal) subjects are more interested in understanding the requirements for doing things that they might want to do (going out for the evening) than they are in understanding the requirements for doing things that they don't want to do (putting out the garbage). My Granny knew that (though not, I suppose, at the .05 level).

One last time: it is possible that inference is domain specific and that (as one massive modularity theorist has put it) domain-neutral logic is just something that you learn in school. However, as things stand, there are no results that make that claim seem plausible. The good news is that there's no end of data that aren't relevant to the domain specificity of inference. The bad news is that these data aren't relevant.

2.4 | When Falsification Strikes: A Reply to Fodor

Leda Cosmides and John Tooby

We thank Jerry Fodor for taking the time to write his reply. In it, fortunately, he has become clear enough that we can identify the simple factual errors on which he bases his arguments, as well as several other sources of his theoretical and experimental confusions. Once these are resolved, perhaps Fodor will be able to identify actual weaknesses in our experimental program that we could profit by addressing. Indeed, over the last two decades, we have made it a policy to test systematically against every coherent counterhypothesis to social contract theory and hazard management theory. At present, as far as we are aware, there are no remaining viable alternative theories that have not been clearly falsified by the accumulated body of results (see Cosmides & Tooby, 2005a, and this volume, for review). Obviously, testing different hypotheses requires experiments with different controls. For this reason, it is a feeble form of criticism on Fodor's part to claim that a single experiment designed to test hypothesis A, when taken in isolation, does not test against hypothesis B, when there already exist other widely known experiments that have falsified hypothesis B.

The important but uninteresting point is that every empirical test that Fodor (this volume; 2000) claims we should have made in order to establish our case has already been conducted. These tests are reported in papers that Fodor cites, as well as in papers that he does not cite. In all but a single case, he offers no argument to dispute their outcomes. He simply ignores their existence, arguing for a counterhypothesis that has been repeatedly falsified.

A more important—and more interesting—point concerns the unexamined assumptions inherent in Fodor's simple and traditional opposition of "logical form" with "content." We will turn to the problem with that opposition in due course.

Fodor's First Fundamental Error

In his reply Fodor correctly states that "C&T sought to test the hypothesis that inference is content specific in a perfectly sensible way: namely, by showing that, depending on the content of the materials, formally identical inferences exhibit different interactions with performance in the Wason selection task" (p. 137). He then, unfortunately, makes a fundamental factual error and builds his countertheory around it. Fodor goes on (emphasis added): "*The* experimental manipulation in *the* C&T experiment contrasted deontic conditionals with descriptive ones . . ." (pp. 137–138).

Even in the original article reporting social contract experiments (Cosmides, 1989), there were *nine* experiments, rather than one. These experiments contrasted social contract conditionals with a variety of deontic conditionals that were not social contracts, and not (as Fodor mistakenly believes) solely with descriptives. Fodor elaborates his fanciful view that we only contrasted "deontic conditionals with descriptive ones" (pp. 137–138), creating "an unresolved confound of content differences with logical form differences" (p. 139). He continues, "(N)otice that observed interactions of content variables with performance are germane to the domain specificity of inferential processes only if the logical form of the inferences is held constant in the materials manipulations. I argued that, as a matter of fact, this was *not* the case with respect to C&T's test materials since (according to me), descriptive and deontic conditionals ipso facto differ in their logical form" (p. 138). Fodor builds his entire case on an imaginary confound in which social contract rules (which are deontic) are only contrasted with descriptive rules (which are nondeontic). For example, Fodor (2000, p. 29) states that our interpretation of our experimental results "depends critically on assuming that deontic conditionals and their indicative controls are identical in structure."

Yet, for two decades we (and others) have systematically tested not only descriptive (indicative) control rules but control rules drawn from a large variety of theoretical categories, including a large number of conditional rules that have exactly the logical form that Fodor claims is actually responsible for the performance effect we misattribute to social contract content (i.e., deontic rules). If Fodor's substantive claim were true (i.e., that high performance derives from the logical form deontic rules have), then subjects should perform well on deontic rules as a class, and the presence of social contract content in the deontic rule should be irrelevant. Unfortunately for Fodor's theory, it has been shown on numerous occasions that being a deontic rule is not, by itself, sufficient to elicit high performance. That is, the robust and striking performance differences that subjects exhibited between deontic conditionals that are social contracts and deontic control conditionals that are not social contracts cannot be explained as the result of the non-social-contract deontic rules being descriptive rules, because (as Fodor emphasizes) deontic rules are not descriptive rules (see below, and Cosmides & Tooby, this volume, for a review of these experiments). Fodor's error could not be more basic, and it is hard to credit that he could actually have read any of the experimental findings that he cites and is attempting to construct theories about.

Fodor's Second Fundamental Error: Logical Form and Content Are Mutually Exclusive Hypotheses

Fodor is admirably clear in stating another of his major premises, which again allows us to pinpoint his confusion. He states (this volume): "As far as I can tell, C&T have lost their grasp of the dialectical situation. What they need—the evidence that would be relevant to whether inferential processes are domain specific—is this: *there is no effect of logical form on inferential processes when content is controlled.* But the evidence they've got is only this: *there are effects of content on inferential processes when logical form is controlled*" (p. 140).

This is, of course, wrong on its face. Accepting, for the moment, Fodor's simple opposition between the effects of logical form and content, there are (at least) four possibilities: logical form could have an effect, but not content; content could have an effect, but not logical form; neither might have an effect; or both could have effects. *Nothing about the claim that there exist domain-specific inferential procedures requires that there be no effects of "logical form."* These are logically independent claims. To support social contract theory, it is sufficient to show that (1) there are principled domain-specific effects, and (2) these cannot be explained as the (supposed) effects of logical form, whatever they might be. We have in fact (1) predicted and experimentally confirmed the reality of a large number of independent, previously unknown, highly specific content effects and (2) shown these effects cannot be explained as the effects of logical form (because, for one thing, logical form was held constant while the effects appear and disappear with content manipulations—exactly the tests Fodor said were "germane"). Importantly, these novel effects were predicted based on a prior principled functional analysis of what social exchange inference procedures would have to be like in order to carry out their evolved function. Indeed, we have been able to predict and to produce in a principled way distinct patterns of card choices that were "illogical" (according to the propositional calculus) that no one had ever observed before. It is simply a straightforward logical error to claim that we must also show that there are no effects of logical form.

It is possible that Fodor derives this belief from his biologically problematic views on mandatory information encapsulation in evolved specializations. If so, Fodor may think that the claim that social contract procedures are operating on representations entails the claim that other, more general logical operators cannot also operate on them. That is, if representations are "in" a social contract module, they cannot be affected by other aspects of the architecture. But nothing about an evolutionary functional perspective on neurocomputational design leads to the conclusion that all evolved computational procedures will be completely information encapsulated. In an evolutionarily well-engineered brain, circuits should be networked together whenever they (over evolutionary time) can pass useful products to each other, and such interactions do not impede efficiency. That is, information encapsulation should be only an occasional outcome and only occur when the benefits of isolation outweigh the costs. It seems unlikely that this is the case in reasoning, in which information sets are potentially relevant to each other (Cosmides & Tooby, 2000b). This suggests that various inferential operators (specialized and more general) will act on the same processing stream. No one has made any argument about why natural selection, acting in a content-structured world, would act to preserve the abstract purity of a set of general logical procedures by blocking their supplementation with additional content-sensitive problem-solving specializations. They should all be interacting in fine-grained ways in reasoning processes—a proposal that accounts for the rich, content-sensitive character of human reasoning, as well as the routine, if occasional, exhibition by mortals of inferential chains that seem to reflect the expression of more general logical operators.

Fodor Ignores the Empirical Implications of the Hypothesis That, in a Multimodular Mind, Content Is an Element of Logical Form

More interesting issues are raised by the unexamined assumptions inherent in Fodor's opposition of "logical form" with "content". He accepts it as obvious that content and logical form are different ontological kinds. However, this view is only true for domain-general logics, in which content is ignored by operators designed to act on any proposition p, regardless of content. The proposal for content-sensitive reasoning systems is far more radical than this, because it breaks down the distinction between logical form and (some) content. For domain-specialized inferential systems, *content is an element of logical form.*

In our view, the human neurocomputational architecture contains a number of functionally distinct inferential systems. Evidence suggests that some are relatively domain general and include procedures that embody certain elements of the predicate calculus, such as negation, variable binding, and *modus ponens* (Rips, 1994; Cosmides & Tooby, 1996b and this volume, sections I.ii, II.i.i.i; all further citations by section refer to Cosmides & Tooby, this volume). Yet, surprisingly, the architecture seems to lack the ability to reliably deploy many other basic logical operations. For example, the human mind seems to lack *modus tollens,* which makes following arguments involving Popperian falsification a nonroutine mental achievement for scientists as well as civilians. Thus, *contra* Fodor, we have always accepted the existence of (some) general logical procedures and consider it possible for there to be some effects of what Fodor calls (rather vaguely) "logical form" (although experiments show them to be—at most—minor in magnitude, compared to social contract effects).

Alongside these domain-general reasoning procedures are (we argue) a number of domain-specialized inferential systems. Among these is a functionally distinct system specialized for interpreting and reasoning about social exchange interactions—the *social contract algorithms*—and a system specialized for reasoning about precautions and hazards. According to social contract theory:

A. This system is equipped with domain-specialized rules of transformation and inference that operate over abstract yet contentful primitives (*agent x, benefit to agent x, cost to x, requirement of y, entitlement, obligation,* etc.). That is, it has a domain-specialized syntax, which implements and applies a domain-specialized logic of social exchange. The rules of transformation and inference implemented by the social contract algorithms differ from those of the predicate calculus in two ways.

First, they operate over abstract representations of *contentful* conceptual primitives (*benefit to x* being a particularly important one). Consider, for example, this conditional: "If a man is eating cassava root, then he must have a tattoo on his face." In predicate logic, it is irrelevant whether "eating cassava root" is a benefit or a cost to the eater, because its syntax represents this activity merely as proposition *P*. But when the mind interprets "eating cassava root" as a benefit to the eater, that representation—*benefit to agent x*—is a *syntactic* element in the logic of social exchange, an element of *logical form* with respect to the syntax of its domain-specialized internal logic. If cassava were a poison, this activity would be represented as a *cost to agent x*, so the rule would no longer have the same logical form *with respect to* the logic of social exchange. In short, what counts as content and what counts as logical form will be determined differently by the predicate calculus, by the logic of social exchange, by the logic of hazard management, and so on, according to the procedures embodied in each system.

Second, and crucially, the rules of transformation in the social exchange system license inferences that are appropriate for social exchange *but that are invalid under the predicate calculus*. Because they are specialized for exchange, they do not capture the inferences we make about indicative conditionals. Nor do they capture the inferences we make about deontic conditionals involving precautions, the inferences we make about threats, or the inferences we make about deontic conditionals that are neither social exchanges or precautions. Because they make correct inferences only within the domain of social exchange, social contract algorithms are not designed to be activated or applied outside of their proper domain.

B. Because social exchange inferences are invalid outside the domain of social exchange, they are designed to be activated only to the extent there are cues suggesting the potential presence of a social exchange situation. (Parametric investigation suggests that cues activating social contract algorithms are additive (section IV.vii.i), so that the more cues, the stronger the social contract effect.) Social contract cues are elements that indicate the presence of a situation fitting the template for a social contract: "If you take benefit B, then you must satisfy the requirement R of the agent that controls benefit B" (section II.i.). It follows directly from this that relevant cues include (1) logical operators in the conditional rule that, in context, clarify that it is a rule in which an *agent* is *requiring* something of another *agent* (e.g., *must, It is required that*, etc.), and (2) terms that, in context, are interpreted as benefits, costs, agents (etc.) congruent with the template.

Fodor puzzlingly claims that, for social contract theory to be correct, we must show that logical form has no effect. In reality, however, social contract theory straightforwardly predicts (based on A and B above) that social exchange reasoning will be sensitive not only to the presence or absence of social contract content but also to manipulations of social contract theory's version of logical form. One element of this happens to coincide with the element of general logical form that Fodor thinks is responsible for evoking striking performance effects.

Fodor thinks high levels of violation detection will be elicited by any deontic conditional because their logical form implies that these rules are really about "requiring Q," and anyone can see that cases of *not-Q* violate this requirement. That is, what Fodor has extracted from the social contract account to advance as the key element of his deontic account is a *requirement* (implicitly or explicitly made by an agent) on other agents. This is one-half of the social contract template and so is one potential cue to a social contract. All Fodor is lacking is the other half of the social contract template, which specifies that meeting the requirement allows access to the rationed benefit. *So both theories predict that adding cues about an agent making a requirement should have an effect.* Because Fodor labels this "logical form," *both theories predict that logical form* (in this delimited sense) *should have an effect* (though for different reasons). Fodor claims that this element is responsible for the entire (strong) effect on *not-Q* selections that is mis-attributed to social contract theory. In contrast, social contract theory predicts that this manipulation, by itself, should produce a weak effect on *not-Q* selections (assuming nothing else blocks a social contract interpretation), but when combined with the missing *rationed benefit* component of the template, the enhanced violation detection effect should be strong. Which claims are correct?

Experimental results closely track the predictions of social contract theory (see table 2.4.1). For example, experiments explicitly designed by Beaman (2002) to test Fodor's claims show that there are indeed effects of using requirement language—as both theories predict. However, the theories diverge sharply on their predictions about the size of the effect (among other things). Unlike Fodor's proposal, social contract theory predicts the effect will be small, because the agent-requirement cue is only one half of the social contract template. In order to provide a counterexplanation to social contract theory, Fodor's account requires the effect to be as large as the performance boosts otherwise attributed to social contract manipulations. In reality, the effect of requirement language is a mere 15 percentage point jump (hop?) in *not-Q* selections—something Fodor nonquantitatively treats as a vindication of his theory. Fodor not only ignores the fact that the magnitude of the effect of logical form is far too small to pose a challenge to social contract theory, but he completely ignores the far more striking effect of Beaman's adding back in the missing half of the social contract template: the rationed benefit component. That is, according to social contract theory, requirement language should not boost performance to the high levels typical of social contracts unless another key syntactic element is present: something that can be interpreted as a *benefit* to the agent of whom Q is required.

Table 2.4.1
Tests of Logical Form Versus Social Contract Content

Rules tested by Beaman (2002) and by Cosmides & Tooby — Logical Form (LF) of rules = indicative or deontic?	Predictions (% selecting not-Q card)		Results (% choosing:)	
	Fodor	SCT	not-Q card	P & not-Q
Beaman (2002)				
1a. *If a card has a vowel on one side, then it has an even number on the other side.* **LF = indicative**	Low	Low	25 *(odd #)*	Not reported
2a. *If a person is under 18, s(he) drinks coke in this pub.* **LF = indicative (Fodor)** **(SCT: LF = ambiguous: indicative or deontic)**	**Low**	**Med-high**	**65** *(beer)*	Not reported
1b. *It is a requirement of yours that if a card has a vowel on one side, then it has an even number on the other side.* **LF = deontic**	**High** **1b = 2b**	**Low-med**	**40** *(odd #)*	Not reported
2b. *It is a legal requirement that if a person is under 18, s(he) drinks coke in this pub.* **LF = deontic**	High **1b = 2b**	High **1b ≪ 2b**	90 *(beer)*	Not reported
Cosmides & Tooby — **LF = deontic for all**	**Predictions**		**Results** (%)	
	Fodor	*SCT*	*not-Q*	*P & not-Q*
3. *It is required that if someone is under 18, that person drinks coke.* **not-Q = drinking beer** (*Q* = drinking coke, *P* = 16 years old, *not-P* = 30 years old; N = 33)	High	High	**75.8** *(beer)*	**63.6**
4. *It is required that if someone is under 18, that person drinks coke.* **not-Q = drinking milk** (*Q* = drinking coke, *P* = 16 years old; *not-P* = 30 years old; N = 32)	**= Rule 3**	**< Rule 3**	**< Rule 3** **53.1** *(milk)*	**43.8**
5. *If a person is drinking beer, then that person must be over 18.* **not-Q = 16yrs old** (*Q* = 30 years old, *P* = drinking beer, *not-P* = drinking coke; N = 27)	**≤ Rule 3**	**> Rule 3**	**> Rule 3** **96.3** *(16yrs)*	**85.2**

The results shown in table 2.4.1 are from experiments using the Wason selection task; points where Fodor's predictions contrast with social contract theory (SCT) are in boldface. Beaman (2002) conducted a parametric test examining how adding "It is required that" before a conditional would affect not-Q selections for two rules: one with social contract content and one without. Fodor (2000) views rules [1a] and [2a] as indicative conditionals that should elicit low levels of not-Q selections, but rules [1b] and [2b] as deontic conditionals that should elicit high levels of not-Q selections. Social contract theory (SCT) also views the vowel rule [1a] as indicative, but sees rule [2a] as ambiguous as to interpretation. Beaman's subjects live in a society where alcohol consumption is a privilege reserved for adults, i.e., a rationed *benefit*. Rule [2a] is set in the context of a pub serving only whisky or coke, so most college students probably interpret it as a (weird) paraphrase of the well-known drinking age law (rule [5]), which is a (deontic) social contract. But [2a] could also be seen as indicative, describing the tastes or habits of people under 18.

Requirement language rules out indicative interpretations for both rules. SCT predicts an improvement in performance for [2b]: Anyone who was tempted to interpret [2a] as merely describing teen-agers' habits would now understand that the rule is meant to express a deontic social contract, the drinking age law. "It is a legal requirement that" *means* there are agents requiring something of other agents (part of the syntax of social exchange), and this requirement must be satisfied to be eligible for a *benefit* (another key syntactic element of social exchange). In contrast, although rule [1b] has requirement language and the instruction to look for cards that "breach your criteria" (implying someone else was supposed to follow your requirement—hence cues that an *agent* is *requiring* something of another *agent*), it has nothing interpretable as a *benefit*. Thus, SCT predicts far higher performance on the deontic social contract [2b] than on the deontic vowel problem [1b], which was found. Indeed, *not-Q* selections on the deontic vowel problem were no higher than what is usually found for *indicative* conditionals (typically, ~50% for indicatives, with ~25% choosing P, not-Q, and no other cards; see figure 2.4.1). The problems we did—rules 3–5—all involve deontic conditionals. Fodor's theory predicts [5] > [3] > [4], which is the actual observed pattern. In contrast, SCT predicts [5] > [3] > [4], see text). In contrast, SCT predicts [5] > [4] selections (or perhaps fewer for rule [5], see text).

As table 2.4.1 shows, that is precisely what Beaman (2002) found: 90% *not-Q* selections for the deontic social contract compared to 40% for the deontic vowel problem (which follows only half of the social contract theory template). These data sharply violate Fodor's key prediction: that requirement language is sufficient to elicit high levels of *not-Q* selections. As Beaman shows, holding logical form constant, the addition of the rationed benefit content caused an increase in performance, *of 40 and 50 percentage points* (rules [1a] vs. [2a] and [1b] vs. [2b], respectively), dwarfing the effect of "logical form." This social contract content effect is predicted by social contract theory but not by Fodor's deontic/indicative account, and it corresponds to an effect size (phi) of .73, more than double the effect size of .30 found for requirement language. That is, Beaman has replicated the results of our benefits experiments (section IV.vi and below) using Fodor's own preferred manipulations. Even worse for Fodor's account, the social contract *without* requirement language, [2a]—which Fodor (2000) views as indicative—outperformed by 25 percentage points the *deontic* (but non-social-contract) vowel problem, [1b], that on Fodor's account should elicit high performance. (The social contract elicited 65% vs. 40% for the non-social-contract deontic rule.) Beaman himself concludes that Fodor's variant of the Wason selection task "is insufficient to account for the 'cheater detection' effect" (in the abstract, cunningly concealed from Fodor).[1] Yet from reading Fodor's reply, readers equipped with normal pragmatics would conclude that the Beaman experiment supports Fodor's proposal that logical form manipulations (with a 15 percentage point effect) explain away social contract effects (which add an additional 50 percentage points).[2]

To prevent Fodor from improvising another post hoc explanation for Beaman's results, we conducted an additional experiment designed to test Fodor's proposal. This experiment compares two *identical* deontic rules, both of which were Fodor's (2000) flagship example of a *not-Q*-eliciting deontic conditional: "It is required that if someone is under 18, then that person drinks coke" (rules [3] and [4] in table 2.4.1). The rules are identical; all that changes is whether the *not-Q* card refers to beer or milk. This should make no difference on Fodor's theory but constitutes the addition or removal of the rationed benefit component of the social contract template and so should cause a substantial change in subject performance. When *not-Q* refers only to beer (or any kind of alcohol), then this rule is logically equivalent to "It is required that if someone is under 18, that person does not drink alcohol." Like Beaman's, our subjects see drinking alcohol as an age-related privilege, so they should interpret this rule [3] as restricting access to a *benefit*. But this interpretation should be blocked when *not-Q* refers to milk. Rule [4] is logically equivalent to "It is required that if someone is under 18, that person does not drink milk": this is certainly deontic, but it does not fit the input conditions for a social contract very well. Drinking milk is not seen as a privilege relative to drinking coke (most children think the opposite), nor should any mammal see milk drinking as a benefit reserved only for adults. We gave subjects these two problems, and the results (table 2.4.1) are clear: when *not-Q* = beer, supporting a social contract interpretation, performance was 20 percentage points higher than when *not-Q* = milk (indeed, the milk version elicited no more *not-Q* selections (53%) than indicative conditionals do; see figure 2.4.1).

And how does Fodor's flagship example compare to a version of the rule whose logical form more closely fits the syntax of social exchange? Rule [5], the drinking age law as standardly given in the literature,[3] is the contrapositive of rule [3], Fodor's flagship deontic rule. But rule [5] better fits the benefit-requirement template of a social contract: the benefit—drinking beer—is mentioned *in* the deontic rule, which says what is required if one is to be entitled to this benefit. It should outperform Fodor's rule [3] because rule [3] is more difficult to recognize as a social contract: to derive a rule fitting the benefit-requirement template, one must interpret rule [3] as implying rule [5], its contrapositive. As social contract theory predicts, the standard drinking age problem, rule [5], outperforms Fodor's flagship rule [3] by about 20 percentage points—see table 2.4.1. But this is the *opposite* of what Fodor's argument predicts.

Even worse, Fodor rejects the view that rule [3] implies its contrapositive, rule [5], because he thinks you cannot be required to be over 18.[4] Given rule [5], subjects should be puzzled; to succeed, they would have to infer that the experimenter was confused and really meant to state Fodor's rule [3]. This implies that Fodor's rule [3] should outperform our rule [5] (which it does not). Or, if subjects are surprisingly adept at deriving this *modus tollens* inference from rule [3], the two rules could elicit equivalent performance (which they do not). But there is nothing in Fodor's account that can explain what we found: *Better* performance on rule [5] than on Fodor's optimal logical form, as expressed in rule [3].

These examples provide an opportunity to understand how far we have come from Fodor's formulation of the content-logical form distinction. If the cognitive architecture contains many different inferential systems, then one cannot make the same distinction between logical form and content effects, and his distinction dissolves. Putting "it is required that"

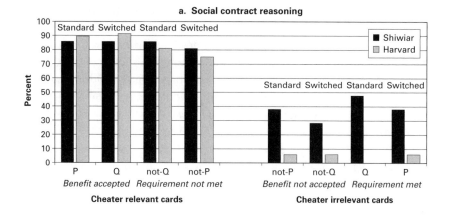

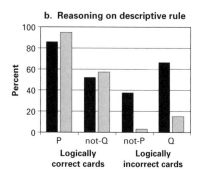

Figure 2.4.1

Panel a. The logical form of a social contract can be changed from standard to switched, yet cheater relevant cards are chosen equally often (whether subjects are Harvard students or Shiwiar—indigenous residents of the Amazon). This is a case of holding content constant, changing logical form, and showing that this does not affect the frequency with which "requirement not met" cards are selected. Panel b shows that *not*-Q is selected about 50% of the time for familiar indicative rules. This is important for evaluating whether deontic rules elicit more *not*-Q selections than indicatives; see results for Fodor's flagship rule when the *not*-Q card refers to milk rather than beer, table 2.4.1. (From Sugiyama, Tooby, & Cosmides, 2002.)

in front of a rule that would ordinarily be interpreted as an indicative conditional is not just a change in logical form; it is also a change in *content* relative to the syntax of social exchange. It implies that there is a situation with an *agent* requiring something of another *agent*—a partial but incomplete cue of social exchange. Similarly, experiments that add or subtract a rationed benefit linked to the requirement manipulates a *syntactic* element—syntactic from the point of view of the representational primitives of the social exchange system (although not syntactic within predicate or deontic logic).

In short, in evaluating the evidence, it is important to keep in mind the similarities and differences between logical form as defined by the syntax of social exchange and logical form as argued by Fodor (using his personally improvised synthesis of the predicate calculus as applied to deontic rules).[5] Because social exchange syntax is defined over contentful representations (such as *benefit to x*), it follows that reasoning will be sensitive to aspects of a problem's content that matter to this syntax. Content manipulations targeted to this syntax should change how the mind represents a given sentence, transforming its interpretation from a deontic conditional that is not a social contract to one that is (section IV.vi), and from the logical form of an indicative conditional to the representation of a deontic social contract (sections IV.ii and IV.iii.i).[6]

Précis of Other Evidence Falsifying Fodor's Proposal

When social contract theory was first formulated over two decades ago, we proposed that indicative conditionals and (deontic) social contracts are interpreted differently and processed via different "inferential routes" (Cosmides, 1985; Cosmides & Tooby, 1989). We were therefore surprised when Fodor (2000, this volume) proposed the same thing, in the belief that this claim contradicts and refutes social contract theory. However, our initial proposal went far beyond proposing different inferential routes for indicatives and deontics: we proposed that (deontic) social contracts are processed via a different inferential route than other *deontic* conditionals.

Fodor's (2000) proposal contrasts sharply with this latter claim. Empirically, his argument comes down to this: *having the logical form of a deontic conditional is sufficient to elicit the high levels of violation detection found for social contracts; this (purportedly strong) effect of being a deontic rule explains away the evidence previously and erroneously taken as support for social contract theory.*

Fodor's proposal that high levels of violation detection are produced by any deontic conditional was reasonable two decades ago, when we began our research. That is why our studies have, from the outset, included conditions that compare deontic conditionals that are social contracts to other deontic conditionals (for review, see sections IV.v–IV.viii). Fodor's proposal is far less reasonable now, when such a theory would have to address the dozens of findings that systematically falsify its key predictions. Fodor's claimed "confound" between content and logical form is absent in the tests in which deontic logical form is held constant and content is varied in ways relevant to the proposed syntax of social exchange. If Fodor's proposal were correct, all of these deontic conditionals should have elicited high levels of violation detection. But they do not. *Deontic conditionals that are not social contracts (and not hazard/precaution rules) do not elicit high levels of violation detection on the Wason task.*

Our many experiments along these lines were conducted not to flog a long dead horse—that violation detection is the result of deontic logical form. That theory is long dead, even if Fodor is now struggling to saddle up the corpse and ride triumphantly off on it. Instead, by holding deontic logical form constant and varying elements relevant to the syntax of social exchange, we were able to test (and confirm) key predictions of social contract theory.

None of these manipulations should implode performance if Fodor were right, because his proposal empirically predicts that it is the property of being a deontic conditional that elicits high levels of violation detection: (1) For deontic rules, it should not matter if P is a *benefit to agent x*, a *cost to x*, a *hazard to x*, and so forth (yet it makes a dramatic difference; sections IV.vi and IV.viii) (2) it should not matter whether the violation was intentional or accidental (yet it does; see section IV.vii). And (3) the violations people detect should be of the requirement specified by the deontic conditional they were given. They should not be looking for violations of a requirement specified by a *different* deontic rule, a rule that can be derived from the conditional given only by applying domain-specialized inference rules that are invalid outside the domain of social exchange (yet they do; see section IV.iii).

Experiments holding deontic logical form constant include the following, discussed in our paper (this volume):

• Section IV.vi: *Benefit experiments*   These varied whether P is a *benefit to x* or a *cost to x*. Violation detection dropped precipitously when the deontic rule no longer regulated access to a *benefit*—by 36 percentage points in the example discussed. This drop was predicted in advance by social contract theory: deontic rules that do not regulate access to benefits do not fit the syntax of social exchange. As discussed, Beaman (2002) found similar results: holding deontic logical form constant, 90% of subjects chose *not-Q* for the social contract versus only 40% for the non-social-contract rule.

• Section IV.vii: *Innocent mistake experiments* These held constant both logical form *and* social contract content, so, on Fodor's account, they would necessarily be assigned the same logical form and interpretation. All that was varied was whether potential violations were intentional or accidental. The function of the cheater detection system is to identify cheaters whose errors benefit themselves (and who are disposed to cheat again)— not those who commit innocent errors. As predicted, violation detection was high for intentional cheating, but not for innocent mistakes (yet these are identical rule violations, differing only in whether they could have been intentional). In contrast, the function of the precautionary system is to identify people in danger, which can happen accidentally or intentionally. As predicted, the same accident-intention manipulation did not affect performance on deontic precautionary rules at all.

• Section IV.viii: *Neural dissociation between deontic conditionals* There are two classes of high-performing deontic conditionals that have been identified so far: social contracts and precautionary rules. On Fodor's account, both would be processed via the same "inferential route." Yet brain damage can leave the ability to detect violations of deontic conditionals that are precautionary intact, while selectively impairing the ability to detect violations of deontic social contracts (Stone et al., 2002). These two classes of rule differ only in whether they fit the syntax of social exchange or the syntax of the hazard/precaution system—but Fodor's account denies that these content-specialized syntaxes exist. If all that exists is domain-general logical machinery, then when it is impaired, performance on all rule types should be degraded. It is not. Moreover, functional magnetic resonance imaging research confirms that what we consider two kinds of conditionals, and Fodor considers a single kind of conditional, are in fact treated as two distinct classes by the mind (Ermer et al., 2006). Fodor's response to this increasing body of cognitive neuroscience findings showing the mind distinguishes (along proposed evolutionary lines) classes of rules that Fodor lumps into a single class reads, in full: "Who except a dualist would deny it?" (p. 140).

• Section IV.iii.ii: *Perspective change* In these experiments, precisely the same deontic social contract—same logical form, same content—was used in both conditions; all that varied was which agent was the potential violator. Performance changed in precisely the way social contract theory predicts. For this to happen, subjects had to infer an implication of the deontic conditional that is valid for social exchange but invalid under any domain-general logic (deontic or predicate logic).

• Section IV.iii.i: *Switched social contracts*   These experiments held constant (1) social contract content, (2) the potential violator, and (3) logical form *as defined by the syntax of social exchange*. All that varied was logical form *as defined by* domain-general logics (deontic or predicate logic). This change in domain-general logical form did not influence cheater detection: subjects were just as good at looking for those who did not satisfy the requirement even when this corresponded to *not-P* (rather than *not-Q*). It did, however, cause subjects to strikingly violate the valid operations of domain-general logics, falsifying Fodor's idea that it is a general logic that is doing the work.

Fodor's Response to Experimental Falsification

What does Fodor say in his reply when confronted with the large body of empirical findings that falsify his view (identified in the paper Fodor is replying to)? Curiously, he does not respond to the great majority of them. Instead:

1. Fodor first reiterates the error in his 2000 paper, stating "The experimental manipulation in the [sic] C&T experiment contrasted deontic conditionals with descriptive ones" (pp. 137–138). It was based on this error that he claimed all of our experiments confound logical form and content and, therefore, provide no evidence for a cheater detection mechanism.

2. Fodor then contradicted this statement by acknowledging one experiment (of the many we discuss) in which deontic logical form was held constant and only social contract content was varied: a single experiment manipulating *benefit*. In his reply, Fodor began by stating that "observed interactions of content variables with performance are germane to the domain specificity of inferential processes only if the logical form of the inferences is held constant in the materials manipulations" (p. 138). So this experiment manipulating the degree of benefit should be germane: it held logical form constant ("requiring *Q*" of anyone who does *P*), varying only whether *P* was a *benefit to x* (going out at night) or a *cost to x* (taking out the garbage at night). That the former (a social contract) elicited good violation detection from 80% of subjects, compared to only 44% for the other deontic conditional, would seem to be a strong violation of Fodor's

claim that deontic logical form is the factor that elicits high levels of violation detection.

Fodor makes three contradictory responses: (1) he trance channels his grandmother, saying that she could have predicted this content effect; (2) he says that it is irrelevant to hold logical form constant and vary content (after previously admitting that this is indeed "germane"), because all that shows is a content effect, and (3) he says (erroneously) that we predict reasoning will be insensitive to logical form. Without saying why—and in direct contradiction to social contract theory as laid out in the paper to which he is replying—he states that social contract theory predicts that changes in logical form will have no effect on reasoning when (explicit) social contract content is held constant. We have already dealt with (3), but we will take the other two in turn.

Fodor's Grandmother

Those familiar with Fodor's writing know that he usually resurrects his grandmother when he wants his intuition to do the work that a good computational theory should. In this case, Fodor's improvised account is motivational: subjects "are more interested in understanding the requirements for doing things that they might want to do (going out for the evening) than they are in understanding the requirements for doing things that they don't want to do (putting out the garbage)" (p. 141). Here as elsewhere, Fodor makes no attempt to consider whether empirical predictions entailed by his ad hoc arguments are contradicted or supported by any finding outside of the inconvenient result he wishes to explain away. Unfortunately for the reputation of Fodor's grandmother, this explanation is false. That is, a large number of social-contract and non-social-contract rules have been tested in the past twenty years, and performance does not vary as a function of what *subjects* want: As social contract theory predicts, performance is just as high for dull, boring social contracts that specify requirements for doing things our subjects have no interest in, from acquiring potatoes or ostrich eggshells to procuring corn (see, e.g., Fiddick et al., 2000; Cosmides, 1989). What does govern performance is whether the rule restricts access to something that *the character in the story wants*—to something that the character considers to be a *benefit*. It does not matter whether this is something that the *subject* might want to do or finds interesting.

Fodor's motivational explanation is equally undercut by the innocent mistake experiments. Here, the social contract is precisely the same in both conditions, so *there can be no differences* in how much subjects might want to do *P* (in this case, to go to a good high school). Yet performance dropped for accidental violations, but not for intentional violations. The motivational account cannot be rescued by positing that subjects are more interested in intentional than accidental violations of deontic rules because this same manipulation has *no effect* on deontic rules that are precautionary. Motivation cannot even explain an effect of intentionality that is specific to social contracts. Fodor's grandmother would surely know that situations in which people do not get what they are entitled to are interesting, but accidental violations create this interesting situation as surely as intentional ones do. Yet performance is high only when this violation is produced by a cheater (section IV.vii; Cosmides & Tooby, 2005a, pp. 609, 618, 621).

It's "Just" a Content Effect

Fodor's next line of defense is to dismiss the idea that content effects per se can be informative about these issues, because introductory textbooks routinely admit that content affects cognition. This might be a challenge if there were an alternative theory that economically predicts the same large and diverse set of content effects on reasoning that we have found. But no such theory exists. Nevertheless, this approach can be shown to fail even in principle.

Assume, as Fodor does, that the cognitive architecture contains only one domain-general inference system, something like the predicate calculus. If this were true, it would be possible to sharply distinguish between effects of logical form and effects of content: some content might boost the application of the predicate calculus, much like (to use Fodor's example) adding teddy bears rather than integers boosts the application of the cognitive number system for preschoolers. But social contract theory is not about cheater content boosting the application of predicate logic (or any domain-general deontic logic). It proposes something far more radical: that a *logic of social exchange* inhabits the cognitive architecture, alongside other content-dependent, domain-specialized syntactic systems, and operates according to its own procedures, which sometimes sharply diverge from inferences licensed by predicate logic. This is exactly why the perspective change and switched social contract experiments are so informative: the pattern of results they elicit depends on subjects' spontaneously making inferences that are licensed by social contract algorithms, but that are *invalid* in predicate logic, and *invalid* in a general deontic logic. Any explanation about facilitating the use of predicate logic by fleshing it out in some kind of content (or about motivating subjects to use predicate logic) fails, because subjects are producing reasoning patterns strikingly at variance with predicate logic, which are consistent with the logic of social exchange.

Fodor's Final Challenge

As discussed, Fodor believes (incorrectly) that social contract theory predicts reasoning performance will be insensitive to logical form. He challenges us to pit our two views against each other by showing that varying logical form has no effect when social contract content is held constant.

However, social contract theory (and other, comparable theories about evolved specializations such as hazard management theory) predict the opposite: that inference will be sensitive to logical form (under the relevant conditions). Moreover, these theories pose deep and interesting questions about what *counts* as a difference in logical form *as defined by the architecture of the human mind.* Two deontic conditionals that Fodor interprets as "having" the logical form "it is required that (If *P* then *Q*)" should be assigned different logical forms by social contract algorithms when one fits the benefit-requirement syntax of a social contract and the other does not.

Nevertheless, social contract theory does not predict that logical form (in Fodor's sense) will have an effect regardless of any other factor. It pinpoints conditions under which the effects of logical form will appear and disappear. This makes it possible to meet Fodor's challenge.

Indeed, from our earliest experimental publications (e.g., Cosmides, 1989), we have produced a series of cases in which we did what Fodor claims is necessary. That is, we held social contract content constant, varied logical form, and showed that this has no effect on choosing the *requirement not met* card. For example, in experiments comparing standard and switched social contracts (section IV.iii.i), social contract content and social contract logical form were both held constant. What varied was logical form *as defined by predicate and deontic logics*, from "If you take the benefit, then you (must) satisfy the requirement" to "If you satisfy the requirement, then you (may) take the benefit."[7] Figure 2.4.1 shows that the percent of subjects choosing the "requirement not met" card is invariant over this change in logical form, both at Harvard and in the Ecuadorian Amazon. In a more subtle way, the perspective change experiments are also relevant: the "requirement not met" card was chosen as often for agent 1 as for agent 2, whether this corresponded to the *not-Q* card or the *not-P* card. The rule given only specified a requirement for agent 1 (e.g., employees). To detect cheating by agent 2 (the employer), a reciprocal obligation that falls on agent 2 had to be inferentially derived from the rule given, and this entails a (covert) transformation of logical form (see section IV.iii.ii for an explanation).

In sum, Fodor's alternative explanation for the performance effects triggered by manipulating social exchange variables has been falsified in a large number of independent ways. It is time that Fodor stop repeating the factual error that the primary evidence for social contract theory is a difference between reasoning on indicative and deontic conditionals and begin to grapple with the far broader and more challenging array of results testing this theory. Missing from our discussion is what is most distinctive about social contract theory and hazard management theory: that a large series of precise, surprising, and confirmed predictions about how people reason were derived in a principled way from a careful consideration of selection pressures acting on our ancestors. Readers who want to explore this larger array of findings could begin with the Cosmides and Tooby paper in this volume that sparked this exchange with Fodor. Philosophers might want to consider how the details of this dispute provide a case study of why the possible existence of content-sensitive reasoning systems in the human mind call into question (or at least bring into scrutiny) the deepest feature of traditional logics, their sharp distinction between form and content.

Notes

1. In his reply, Fodor justifies his obliviousness of the primary empirical literature that he claims to have explained by saying that Buller (2005) has reviewed it and agrees with him that there are systematic confounds between logical form and content. Fodor really needs to read these things himself, rather than—in true blind leading the blind fashion—relying on Buller's (2005) account. After all, Buller derives his 2005 account from Fodor (2000), and his "review" systematically ignores large numbers of experiments that falsified his and Fodor's view. For example, one would not know from reading Buller that there are any of the many experiments that hold deontic logical form constant, comparing deontic conditionals with and without social contract content. Bizarrely, Fodor describes us as "curiously reticient" about replying to Buller's confound charges when (among other papers) the paper Fodor is commenting on *is* a reply: we went into tedious detail on the various experiments holding logical form constant while manipulating key social contract variables. We also went into tedious detail explaining that social contract theory posits domain-specialized interpretive rules, and what they are. This was because Buller's critique posits that people make precisely the inferences that social contract theory predicts

they will—that is, these inferences are just post hoc restatements of the predictions that social contract theory makes (but without providing an alternative causal mechanism).

2. Indeed, Fodor seems confused when he talks about Beaman's results. *Fodor* is the one proposing that high levels of cheater detection reflect nothing more than a deontic/indicative manipulation, yet he says, "Beaman finds the effect of the deontic conditional/descriptive conditional manipulation on performance on the Wason task *is very significantly reduced* when the confound is removed" (italics ours; p. 139). That is, when content (vowel vs. drinking age) is held constant, the effect of Fodor's logical form variable is too small to account for social contract performance. But when logical form is held constant, Beaman found that the effect of the presence/absence of social contract content was very large in comparison.

3. It uses a "must" rather than "it is required that," but that shouldn't bother Fodor. Until Beaman (2002), no one had tested deontic social contracts using Fodor's requirement language (and no one had tested his "under 18→coke" version of the drinking age law). Thus, all the data Fodor was trying to explain in 2000—all the evidence of high-performing social contracts—used "must" or no deontic operator, yet Fodor considered that his proposal equally well accounted for results on those problems.

4. Of course, this rule does not really require you to be over 18. Pace Fodor, it requires you be over 18 *when* you drink beer *and* there is a drinking age law—something that is perfectly possible for anyone to abide by.

5. Indeed, as the linchpin of his account of Wason task results, Fodor made an appeal to intuition, claiming that the contrapositive of an indicative conditional is not parallel to the contrapositive of a deontic conditional. When we pointed out that this claim was considered debatable by logicians, Fodor resorted to ridicule—a form of argument from authority. Fodor suggested that the only philosopher who could have made such a contra-Fodorian argument was someone so hapless, he or she should never have been tenured. The proposition Fodor resists is that indicative conditionals can be seen as having a logical form parallel to that which he claims for deontic ones, that is, as asserting Q in the case that P. In other words, Fodor disputes that *if P then Q* "is commonly felt less as an affirmation of the conditional than as a conditional affirmation of the consequent." On principle, we resist arguments from authority, preferring to deal with the merits of an issue. However, for those who believe in the division of intellectual labor and want to know the relative authorities of the disputants, we point out that this quote is from a famous logic textbook by Willard Van Orman Quine (1972; see p. 19 for more explanation), who attributes the insight originally to Philip Rhinelander. Although Fodor (relying once again on his intuition) may not consider either Quine or Rhinelander his equals as logicians, we can at least testify that both got tenure—at Harvard and Stanford, respectively. In any case, Quine's interpretation is a way of capturing the

(widespread) intuition that cases of *not-P* don't really confirm $P{\to}Q$ as a whole (e.g., are black crows really evidence confirming "If x is a swan, then x is white," or are crows merely irrelevant in evaluating a conditional about swans?). It is worth pointing out that this interpretation is borne out by considering the evolution and evolved function of conditional reasoning and the functional regulation of its scope (Cosmides & Tooby, 2000b). From an adaptationist perspective, the conditional is designed to be activated by the input conditions specified in the antecedent and is simply irrelevant (computationally inactivated) when the antecedent condition is not met (in reality, or suppositionally). This would also explain why *modus ponens* is easily activated in subjects, while *modus tollens* is not spontaneously deployed: not-white is computationally not an input condition that activates the conditional, "If x is a swan, then x is white."

6. Fodor says it is not naive realism to say a sentence "has" an interpretation, because he really meant "has relative to a grammar L." But Fodor continues to presume that the mind has a single logical grammar. If there are many different grammars in the mind—different inference systems, each implementing a different syntax—then the mind will assign different logical forms to a conditional depending on whether the inferential system doing the interpreting is predicate logic, social contract algorithms, the hazard management system, a domain-general deontic logic (if such exists), and so forth. Determining which logical form a conditional "has" then becomes a matter of (theoretically guided) empirical discovery. The issue cannot be decided by a priori arguments like Fodor's, which presuppose there is only one kind of logical form. That is why a central goal of our research has been to test whether the different syntaxes of each proposed evolved logic predict which content manipulations will trigger changes in representational format and reasoning outcome—e.g., what content manipulations change a deontic rule into a social contract, and what distinguishes a social contract from a precautionary rule. *How* the mind represents different conditionals is precisely what is under investigation.

7. "Must's" and "may's" were sometimes present, and sometimes they were absent—this didn't change the results. For example, the switched social contract in the Amazon had a "may," and the switched ones in Cosmides (1989) did not—both are in figure 2.4.1.

3 | Moral Sentiments Relating to Incest: Discerning Adaptations from By-products

Debra Lieberman

Third-Party Behavior and Moral Sentiments

If an anthropologist from Mars came to study our species, surely one of the many features she would report is our seemingly endless interest in what other people do, whether it be, for example, who's forming mateships, who's cheated in a social exchange, who's formed an alliance with whom, or who's tried to deceive whom. This observation would naturally prompt many questions including: Why do we care so passionately about what others do? What is the origin of our sentiments regarding third-party behaviors,[1] that is, what is the origin of our moral sentiments?

The main goal of this chapter is to address the origin of moral sentiments within a particular domain: incest. This topic has received much attention in the social sciences, yet there is still little consensus regarding the extent to which evolved mechanisms governing inbreeding avoidance shape moral sentiments relating to incest (for a recent discussion, see Wolf & Durham, 2005). In an effort to illuminate the relationship between inbreeding avoidance and the expression of moral sentiments relating to incest, research is discussed that demonstrates how evolved psychological adaptations pattern moral sentiments in this domain (see Lieberman, Tooby, & Cosmides, 2003). Two hypotheses and supporting empirical evidence are offered: (1) moral sentiments relating to incest are, in part, *by-products* of psychological adaptations governing the development of sexual aversion toward one's own family members (Tooby, 1975), and (2) separate cognitive *adaptations* may exist to regulate the sexual behavior of one's kin due to the fitness consequences associated with close genetic relatives mating with one another (Tooby, 1977). That is, sentiments relating to inbreeding and its avoidance may be both a by-product and, separately, an adaptation. The data discussed provide support for Edward Westermarck's initial claim that the cultural prohibition regarding incest is a reflection of a biological disposition that evolved to prevent the negative fitness consequences associated with inbreeding (Westermarck, 1891/1922). Before these specific hypotheses are discussed, I begin with some brief thoughts on moral sentiments in general and why evolution is hypothesized to have shaped human psychology to monitor others' behaviors. Then, a brief history of ideas relating to incest and inbreeding is presented, setting the stage for the current discussion of the moral sentiments relating to incest.

Why Do We Care about the Behavior of Others?

From an evolutionary perspective, one reason to suspect the existence of psychological mechanisms for caring about what others do is that ancestrally, the behavior of others could have greatly affected one's own inclusive fitness (i.e., the probability of survival and reproduction of oneself and one's close genetic relatives). Indeed, the behaviors and decisions of others in the social environment could have had one of three different effects on inclusive fitness: (1) positive effects, providing the groundwork for adaptations for altruism and non-zero-sum relationships (e.g., see Cosmides & Tooby, 1997, on the evolution of adaptations for friendships and deep engagements), (2) no effect at all, or (3) negative effects (e.g., taking possession of valuable resources without permission, engaging in acts of sexual infidelity, and killing a relative, friend, or potential mate).

Consequently, in a highly social species such as our own, where individuals interacted with one another regularly over the course of the life span, a cost-effective design feature motivating an individual to decrease, if not eliminate altogether, the probability that another engaged in actions imposing large fitness costs would have conferred a selective advantage compared to design features that, for example, did not motivate the interference in behaviors negatively impacting one's inclusive fitness. Similarly, a cost-effective design feature motivating an individual to elicit fitness-enhancing behaviors from others would have gained a selective advantage over design features that were blind to the potential benefits others delivered. Whereas the former category of behaviors (i.e., those imposing fitness costs) represents acts we tend to categorize as morally repugnant, the latter category (i.e., behaviors conferring potential fitness benefits) tends to be perceived as morally virtuous and praiseworthy. The amplitude of the costs and benefits associated with particular acts is one factor among many that may influence the strength of moral disapproval or approval, respectively. In general though, the *tail ends* of the continuum of the cost-to-inclusive fitness/benefit-to-inclusive fitness ratio of third-party behaviors, which ranges from very large ratios (e.g., acts that severely jeopardize one's inclusive fitness) to zero to very small ratios (e.g., acts that have large positive effects on one's inclusive fitness), are hypothesized to define, in part, the subset of behaviors typically included in the moral domain.

According to this perspective, cognitive adaptations are hypothesized to exist to reason about others' behavior. Components of such a reasoning mechanism should include: (1) systems that monitor the actions of others (and perhaps motivate the gathering of information to assess the likely course of action of others), (2) systems that estimate the associated costs and benefits of others' actions or likely actions in accordance with the evolutionarily visible (i.e., statistically recurring) effects a particular action had on inclusive fitness, and (3) systems that use the computed cost/benefit estimates to motivate the interference (or promotion) of behaviors in a manner that led to an increase in reproductive success in ancestral environments.[2]

It is unlikely, however, that there exists one all-encompassing system for reasoning about third-party behavior, a component of the moral domain. This is because the manner in which costs and benefits are assessed may differ depending on the particular behavior at hand. For example, there are many ways other individuals could negatively impact one's fitness: one could be cheated in a social exchange, physically harmed, cuckolded (if male), or raped (if female). For each domain of behavior, different sets of information would have been required to assess whether a cost had been incurred or a benefit delivered. For example, the cues signaling a mate's sexual infidelity are likely to differ from the cues signaling a brother's sexual advance. Rather than positing a single moral reasoning system, this view suggests that assessments of others' actions and the resulting moral sentiments reflect a patchwork of different information-processing systems (e.g., emotion programs) designed to evaluate the costs and benefits of others' actions across a variety of domains that had fitness consequences throughout our species' evolutionary history.

Thus, one answer to why we care about what others do in our social environment is that their actions may carry significant fitness consequences. However, it seems we tend to care about what others do even if they are not part of our immediate social circle and the costs (or benefits) of their actions unlikely to affect us in any way. For example, we reason and have moral sentiments about a variety of third-party behaviors that, in modern society, don't seem to directly affect us. Survey of recent headlines shows much interest in and heated reaction to third-party behaviors, including assisted suicide, euthanasia, infanticide, child molestation, the marrying of one's adopted child, sexual fidelity, and abortion. Why?

One possible answer comes from considering the structure of ancestral environments and distinguishing the adaptive features of psychological systems designed to reason about third-party behavior from their by-products. Throughout much of our species' evolutionary history, we would have lived in social groups ranging in size from 25 individuals to no larger than approximately 500 people (Birdsell, 1968).[3] In such environments, it would have been likely that an individual knew everyone else and regularly encountered most members of the group over his or her lifetime. Consequently, the actions of *all members* of the group had an increased probability of truly impacting one's inclusive fitness. Thus, design features that evaluated the cost/benefit ratio of another's behaviors and motivated behavior accordingly would have functioned "properly" in ancestral environments. This suggests that our judgments of others with whom we do not interact on a regular basis in modern society may be a by-product of systems designed to deal with the social setting more typical of our hunter-gatherer ancestors.

Additionally, we may become emotionally involved in third-party actions that have no effect on us because the actions of others trip the same psychological systems that evolved to guide our own behavior. On this account, sentiments relating to some third-party behaviors may simply reflect the operation of underlying computational systems that evaluate the costs and benefits of a particular behavior on *one's own* inclusive fitness. For example, sentiments relating to third-party sibling incest may be, in part, a by-product of systems designed to assess the costs (or benefits) associated with engaging in sibling incest oneself. If so, then sentiments relating to third-party sibling incest should depend upon, among other things, whether one has an opposite-sex sibling, and, if so, the degree of certainty that he or she is indeed a sibling (see discussion below). Take another example: moral sentiments relating to sexual infidelity. One's sentiments regarding opposite-sex third-party sexual infidelities may be a product of systems designed to assess the costs of *one's own* partner's engaging in sexual infidelities.[4] This may depend on a number of factors such as age (e.g., whether one has reached puberty and adaptations for reasoning about mate choice have been activated), sex (e.g., males but not females run the risk of being cuckolded), whether one currently has or has ever had a mate, whether one has had sex before, one's own mate value, and one's mate's mate value. In general, the empirically testable hypothesis being advanced is that the evaluation of some third-party behaviors may be performed by the same systems evaluating the costs and benefits of that act *on one's own* inclusive fitness. In this way, some moral sentiments relating to third-party behavior may be *by-products* of psychological adaptations.

Summary

Due to the potential fitness consequences of others' actions in ancestral environments, psychological adaptations are hypothesized to exist that (1) monitor the behavior of others, (2) evaluate the costs and benefits associated with others' behaviors, and (3) motivate the interference or promotion of others' behaviors in accordance with the effects such decisions had on inclusive fitness over our species' evolutionary history. It is likely that the estimation of the costs and benefits of different domains of behaviors would have relied on different information (e.g., the cues signaling sexual infidelity are likely to differ from the cues used to assess whether one has been cheated in a social exchange). That is, different algorithms would have been needed to translate cues associated with different domains of social behavior into estimated fitness costs. As a result, moral sentiments are likely to be generated from a collection of specialized systems each designed to process information about a specific aspect of the social world rather than a general system that produces "the moral sense."

The adaptations that exist to regulate others' behavior in a way that positively impacted one's inclusive fitness may, *as a by-product*, take as input information regarding the actions of others with whom one does not interact and generate moral sentiments (and associated motivations) in response to these actions. This may be a result of the fact that our mind is equipped to handle ancestral environments that consisted of small social groups where the behavior of others had an increased probability of impacting one's inclusive fitness, either directly or indirectly through one's social network. Finally, it is worth acknowledging that many of these computations are hypothesized to occur outside conscious awareness. Depending on whether a particular behavior generated an estimated cost or benefit to one's inclusive fitness, different emotion systems may be triggered, activating, for example, consciously felt goals and motivations. The extent to which consciously obtained knowledge (e.g., the witnessed biological consequences of inbreeding) can penetrate and update these systems (or any other) is a good question worthy of investigation.

The Origin of Moral Sentiments Relating to Incest: A Very Brief History

The related topics of inbreeding avoidance and the incest taboo have had a long and peculiar history in the social sciences (Lieberman & Symons, 1998). Indeed, this history continues to be written, as many questions are currently being explored regarding the nature of inbreeding avoidance mechanisms in humans and the origin of cultural prohibitions and moral sentiments relating to incest. What follows is a *very* brief overview of the history of ideas relating to these topics. For a recent and more thorough discussion, please see Wolf (1995) and the chapters in Wolf and Durham (2005).

Edward Westermarck

At the end of the nineteenth century, Edward Westermarck, a Finnish social scientist, proposed an explanation for the commonplace observation that family members rarely find one another sexually appealing. Having noted the injurious effects of inbreeding in many species, Westermarck hypothesized that early childhood association, which typically occurs among genetic relatives, serves as an inbreeding avoidance mechanism by triggering the development of a sexual aversion that is expressed later during adulthood (Westermarck, 1891/1922). This has come to be known as the "Westermarck hypothesis" (WH).

In addition to proposing a specialized mechanism that functions to reduce the probability of choosing a close genetic relative as a sexual partner, Westermarck also proposed an explanation for the origin of the incest taboo. He claimed that the biological systems responsible for the development of sexual aversions between close kin were also responsible for the culturally expressed incest taboo. That is, the explicit cultural prohibitions regarding incest were hypothesized to be a *by-product* of the natural sexual disinclination that develops between near relatives. Westermarck's explanation of the incest taboo differed drastically from the reigning social learning theories of his day which privileged the cultural incest taboo as the *origin*, not consequence, of sexual avoidance behaviors (e.g., Frazer, 1910). In what has become a well-known quote, Westermarck addressed the short-comings of this alternate explanation:

> Moreover, the [social learning] theories in question imply that the home is kept free from incestuous intercourse by law, custom, or education. But even if social prohibitions might prevent unions between the nearest relatives, they could not prevent the desire for such unions. The sexual instinct can hardly be changed by prescriptions; I doubt whether all laws against homosexual intercourse, even the most

draconic, have ever been able to extinguish the peculiar desire of anybody born with homosexual tendencies. Nevertheless, our laws against incest are scarcely felt as a restraint upon individual feelings. And the simple reason for this is that in normal cases there is no desire for the acts which they forbid. Generally speaking, there is a remarkable absence of erotic feelings between persons living very closely together from childhood. Nay more, in this, as in many other cases, sexual indifference is combined with the positive feeling of aversion when the act is thought of. *This I take to be the fundamental cause of the exogamous prohibitions. Persons who have been living closely together from childhood are as a rule near relatives. Hence their aversion to sexual relations with one another displays itself in custom and law as a prohibition of intercourse between near kin.* (Westermarck, 1891/1922, pp. 192–193, italics added)

Though initially well received, the WH and Westermarck's explanation of the incest taboo gradually fell into disfavor. There were, perhaps, many reasons for this. One main reason was the widespread adoption of what has been called the "Standard Social Science Model" (SSSM) of human psychology (see Tooby & Cosmides, 1992). Whereas the WH implies the existence of *content-rich* psychological mechanisms designed by natural selection to regulate behavior in adaptive ways, according to the SSSM, the mind is akin to a *content-free* blank tape that, through processes such as enculturation and socialization, records "relevant" ambient signals from the surrounding social environment which, in turn, shape an individual's behaviors and attitudes. Applied to the domain of incest, the SSSM (which captures the social learning theories discussed by Westermarck) claims that mere exposure to incest prohibitions automatically generates feelings of sexual disinterest toward family members. The function of this taboo-generated sexual disinterest was thought to have less to do with the dangers of sexual relations *within the family* (as Westermarck proposed) than the establishment of cooperative relationships *between families* via cultural practices such as exogamy (e.g., see Frazer, 1910; Levi-Strauss, 1960; White, 1948).

Despite Westermarck's attempts to respond to his critics and explain various misunderstandings, his views were ultimately dismissed, in part, if not entirely, because they challenged the blank slate assumptions of the SSSM (see Tooby & Cosmides, 1992; Pinker, 2002). Two arguments Westermarck encountered provide a good example of how his claims were misunderstood by his critics. The first questioned the need for a taboo if sexual aversions automatically developed between close kin. The second argument focused more on the WH and noted that childhood association also generates aversions toward individuals who are genetically *unrelated* and, consequently, could not serve as a system for inbreeding avoidance. As will be discussed, each argument contains erroneous assumptions rendering them ineffective at discrediting Westermarck's explanation of inbreeding avoidance and the origin of the incest taboo.

SSSM Argument 1: If an Aversion Is Natural, Why Have a Taboo?

Critics of Westermarck pointed to the very existence of the incest taboo as evidence that his biological explanation was incorrect (e.g., see Frazer, 1910). After all, why outlaw behaviors that people would not want to otherwise commit? Quoting Frazer (1910), "It is not easy to see why any deep human instinct should need to be reinforced by law. . . . The law only forbids men to do what their instincts incline them to do; what nature itself prohibits and punishes, it would be superfluous for the law to prohibit and punish" (p. 97). Frazer's assumption, then, is that humans are instinctively incestuous and thus require laws to repress such desires. This perspective was also championed by Freud (1920/1953), who maintained that "an incestuous love choice is in fact the first and regular one" (pp. 220–221).

There are many problems with these assertions. For one, the arrow of causation is simply assumed to flow from explicit cultural taboos to internal personal preferences. Because of SSSM assumptions of how behaviors and attitudes take shape, opposite causal explanations (e.g., personal preferences can be expressed as cultural norms) are not even visible. In addition, statements such as those above assume, erroneously, that the development of a sexual aversion, because its origin is biological, is *inevitable* and would therefore develop in all individuals *regardless of circumstance*. But this is not so. There are many reasons why a biological instinct such as a sexual aversion may not be expressed, ultimately leading to patterns of variation within a population. For example, the psychological machinery governing the detection of close kin may not correctly categorize a close genetic relative as such, which would then fail to activate programs regulating sexual aversions. Kin detection isn't a foolproof procedure because genetic relatedness cannot be *directly* observed. Given the deleterious consequences of close inbreeding (Bittles, 2005), the best evolution could do was design kin-detection systems that used cues that were *highly correlated* with genetic relatedness over our species' evolutionary history to mediate the development of sexual avoidance behaviors. As a result, the classification of an individual as kin could fail due to, for example, the absence of the ecologically valid cue signaling relatedness. In this case, a strong sexual aversion would not develop, leading to an increased probability of sexual attraction. Therefore, it would not be super-fluous to have normative prohibitions against incest since the inaccuracies of kin detection could potentially create circumstances where close genetic relatives sexually desired one another.

A second reason why the presence of a taboo does not undermine Westermarck's claim is that for *some* individuals under *some* circumstances, sexual relations with a close genetic relative may have produced fitness benefits. As has been argued by Tooby (1977) and Haig (1999), there are a number of factors that determine the costs of inbreeding including the genetic load of the population, the availability of potential mates, and an individual's sex. Even with a kin-detection system that correctly catego-rized an individual as a close genetic relative, the factors just mentioned may play a role in overriding any sexual aversion that developed, especially in men, for whom the costs of inbreeding are much less than they are for women (Trivers, 1972). Consequently, within a population, it may have been the case that some individuals sexually pursued a close genetic rela-tive, creating a potential function for normative prohibitions against incest.

SSSM Argument 2: The WH Is Wrong because Childhood Association Can Produce Sexual Aversions to Nonrelatives

Westermarck also received criticism regarding the role childhood associa-tion plays as a psychological mechanism mediating inbreeding avoidance. For example, Freud wrote:

It seems to me very remarkable that Westermarck should consider that this innate aversion to sexual intercourse with those with whom one has been intimate in childhood is also the equivalent in psychical terms of the biological fact that inbreeding is detrimental to the species. A biological instinct of the kind suggested would scarcely have gone so far astray in its psychological expression that, instead of applying to blood-relatives (intercourse with whom might be injurious to repro-duction), it affected persons who were totally innocuous in this respect, merely because they shared a common home. (Freud, 1913/1950, pp. 152–153)

Freud claimed that because a sexual aversion develops between geneti-cally unrelated individuals reared together from childhood, this under-mines Westermarck's claim that childhood association serves as a biological "instinct" to avoid the costs of inbreeding. But Freud confuses two distinct levels of explanation: ultimate explanations which specify *why* a particular feature exists (e.g., the selection pressures that lead to its evo-lution and maintenance) and proximate explanations which detail *how* evolved functions are carried out in real time each generation (e.g., how information is processed and behavior regulated). Inbreeding, as Freud mentioned, is indeed harmful—it jeopardizes the health and survival of offspring (which, as a by-product, is detrimental to the species). This constitutes an ultimate level of explanation for why inbreeding avoidance mechanisms are likely to exist.

The WH is a hypothesis about the *proximate* mechanisms, that is, how inbreeding avoidance is achieved in each generation. Westermarck's hypothesis suggests that childhood coresidence serves as a *cue* to genetic relatedness. Indeed, childhood coresidence would have been one ecologically valid cue that *reliably* distinguished kin from nonkin in ancestral environments—again, reliably, not perfectly or without fail. This means that an evolved kin-detection mechanism that relies on childhood coresidence as a cue may be triggered by a genetically unrelated individual. Conversely, biological siblings not raised together from childhood may fail to categorize one another as close genetic relatives and therefore not display sexual aversions toward each other. In a similar vein, a kin-detection mechanism that relied on breast-feeding and extended care to categorize a particular female as a close genetic relative (i.e., mom) might incorrectly categorize a wet-nurse/nanny as a biological parent and incorrectly fail to categorize a true biological mother as such.[5] In general, evolution is hypothesized to have taken advantage of statistically recurring patterns to fashion kin-detection mechanisms. Since we do not possess DNA-ray vision to *directly* identify actual genetic relatives, it can only be expected that categorical errors will occur when ancestrally reliable cues no longer map onto actual genetic relatedness.

Freud's assumption that a developing "biological instinct" automatically and without fail correctly hits its adaptive target every time is simply unfounded (see discussion above). Ironically, Freud and others who pointed to Westermarck's biological instinct "gone so far astray" were actually providing insight into how kin detection operates in humans. Indeed, the fact that sexual aversions *can* develop between genetically unrelated individuals reared together from early childhood was used decades after Freud as evidence in support of the WH as a mechanism mediating inbreeding avoidance.

Westermarck Revisited

Despite the dismissal of Westermarck's claims in the first half of the twentieth century, the second half of the century witnessed the revival of Westermarck's hypothesis regarding the role childhood coresidence plays in the development of a sexual aversion. There were, perhaps, a number of reasons for this. In 1964, William Hamilton published his theory of inclusive fitness, which outlined the logic of the evolution of kin-directed altruism. Kin-directed altruism, however, requires the ability to distinguish kin from non-kin and between different types of kin (Hamilton, 1964). This prompted a number of biologists to investigate the mechanisms governing kin detection across a wide range of species (for a review of kin detection, see Holmes & Sherman, 1982; Sherman, Reeve, & Pfennig, 1997; Hepper, 1991). Among the kin-detection mechanisms found to mediate helping/nesting behavior in nonhuman animals was prior physical association (Waldman, 1987; Sherman & Holmes, 1985).

Another line of inquiry that facilitated the reemergence of the WH was the investigation of the deleterious biological consequences of inbreeding. Evidence of inbreeding depression (i.e., the reduced health and probability of survival of offspring of close genetic relatives) was found in humans (Adams & Neel, 1967; Badaruddoza, 2004; Bittles, 2005; Bittles & Makov, 1988; Bittles & Neel, 1994; Carter, 1967; Seemanova, 1971) as well as other species (see Bixler, 1992; Margulis & Altmann, 1997). This helped refuel investigations of the mechanisms mediating sexual avoidance. Similar to kin-directed altruism, inbreeding avoidance requires the existence of circuitry that discerns kin from nonkin. Recently, biologists have uncovered a handful of cues nonhuman animals use to identify kin and mediate sexual avoidance, including the matching of olfactory signatures derived from the catabolism of components of the immune system (Penn & Potts, 1998; Weisfeld et al., 2003) and prior association (Berger, Negus, & Day, 1997; Boyd & Blaustein, 1985; Kuester, Paul, & Arnemann, 1994).

In nonhuman animal studies, one technique that has been useful in investigating the WH and kin-detection mechanisms in general is cross-fostering (Mateo & Holmes, 2004). Using a species such as the mouse, where a female gives birth to multiple offspring at once, one or two offspring from a litter are swapped with one or two from another litter, creating an environment where genetically related individuals are reared alongside genetically unrelated individuals. If prior association *with a particular individual* (i.e., the WH) is the cue used to detect kin and mediate sexual avoidance, then an individual should prefer *non*littermates over littermates as sexual partners regardless of their actual genetic relatedness. If, however, some form of imprinting occurred (e.g., the olfactory signature of surrounding littermates may be imprinted upon), creating a kinship template, then not only would littermates be avoided as sexual partners but so would individuals who possessed similar olfactory signatures to those littermates, again regardless of actual genetic relatedness. In general, cross-fostering experiments allow researchers to control for many variables, thus isolating the nature of kin-detection mechanisms (e.g., Yamazaki et al., 1976; Yamazaki et al., 1988). However, this method is not employed in the investigation of kin detection in humans for a multitude of ethical reasons. Instead, researchers interested in humans have had to take advantage of historical circumstances and natural family variation to explore the cues mediating kin detection and inbreeding avoidance.

Investigating the WH in Humans

In the 1960s, a handful of researchers started to publish empirical tests of the WH in humans using populations in which cultural practices created the unusual circumstance where genetically unrelated individuals were reared together from early childhood. Two well-known "natural experiments" are the studies on the Israeli kibbutzim, where children from different families are raised together from early childhood (Shepher, 1971, 1983; Talmon, 1964), and Taiwanese minor marriages, where a young bride is adopted into her future husband's family and reared alongside her husband from early childhood (Wolf, 1995; Wolf, 2005a; Wolf & Huang, 1980). Inspecting periods of coresidence, researchers found that early childhood association led to a decreased probability of marriage in Israeli kibbutzim (Shepher, 1983) and reduced rates of fertility combined with increased rates of divorce and extramarital affairs in Taiwanese minor marriages (Wolf, 1995). All of this occurred despite the lack of sanctions preventing marriage. In fact, marriage was sometimes encouraged for coreared kibbutz members and demanded in the case of Taiwanese minor marriages.

Until recently, the few studies testing the WH have focused on exceptional populations such as Israeli kibbutzim and Taiwanese minor marriages (see also McCabe, 1983). However, a new wave of researchers has started to investigate the WH using the natural variation that occurs within and between families in which individuals reside, typically, with their actual genetic relatives (e.g., see Bevc & Silverman, 1993, 2000; Fessler & Navarrete, 2004; Lieberman, Tooby, & Cosmides, 2003, 2007; Williams & Finkelhor, 1995). Also, other cues, in addition to childhood association, are being explored, including the role of olfaction (Wedekind & Füri, 1997; Wedekind, Seebeck, Bettens, & Paepke, 1995; Weisfeld, Czilli, Phillips, Gall, & Lichtman, 2003) and physical resemblance (DeBruine, 2002). In contrast to the beginning of the previous century, it is clear that today the WH is taken as a serious hypothesis of how sexual aversions develop between close kin open to empirical investigation using multiple methods.

The Relationship between Inbreeding Avoidance and the Incest Taboo

Despite the recent advances in understanding how kin detection operates in humans as well as other species, an important question remains unanswered: To what extent do the systems governing inbreeding avoidance (e.g., mechanisms for detecting kin) also govern moral sentiments relating to third-party incest? Is there any evidence to suggest that Westermarck was correct in his claim about the origin of the incest taboo and moral sentiments relating to incest? Though evidence exists supporting the WH, it may be the case that the culturally manifested incest taboo has nothing to do with mechanisms mediating inbreeding avoidance. This, too, is an empirical question, capable of being explored using the tools of modern behavioral science. Indeed, a handful of researchers has started to investigate the relationship between evolved inbreeding avoidance mechanisms and culturally expressed attitudes regarding incest (e.g., see Fessler & Navarrete, 2004; Lieberman et al., 2003, 2007).

The remainder of this chapter will discuss the research endeavor undertaken in collaboration with John Tooby and Leda Cosmides to answer the following related sets of questions: (1) Was Westermarck correct—are moral sentiments relating to incest a reflection (i.e., a by-product) of systems guiding the development of sexual aversions toward one's own family members? Or, as suggested by traditional SSSM accounts of incest prohibitions, are our moral sentiments a result of the unbiased adoption of ambient cultural norms? (2) Did natural selection lead to the evolution of separate specialized systems for regulating the sexual behavior of others? That is, are there *adaptations* for regulating third-party incestuous behaviors? These two sets of questions are taken up separately in the remaining sections.

Moral Sentiments Relating to Incest: A By-product of Systems Designed to Deter Sexual Relations with One's Own Close Genetic Relatives?

Edward Westermarck originally proposed that the incest taboo and related moral sentiments are a cultural manifestation of a biological disinclination (Westermarck, 1891/1922). That is, sentiments relating to incest are a reflection of the activation of systems designed to prevent sexual relations *with one's own close genetic relatives*. To empirically investigate the merit of this hypothesis, it is first necessary to discuss the nature of systems for inbreeding avoidance in humans. Only then will it be possible to determine whether moral sentiments relating to incest are a function of the same factors governing the development of sexual aversions toward one's own genetic relatives. Therefore, this section begins with a discussion of why natural selection would have led to the evolution of inbreeding avoidance mechanisms and, using an adaptationist framework, the nature of the cognitive processes involved in the development of a sexual aversion toward close genetic relatives.

Selection Pressures Guiding the Evolution of Inbreeding Avoidance Mechanisms

Throughout our species' evolutionary history, the recurring presence of two selection pressures, deleterious recessive mutations (Bittles & Neel, 1994) and short-generation pathogens (Tooby, 1982), would have conferred a fitness advantage on those individuals who avoided mating with a close genetic relative and, instead, mated with someone who did not share an immediate common ancestor. Briefly, recessive mutations are typically hidden in the genome and go undetected due to the presence of a normal functioning allele inherited from the other parent. Data from a number of studies suggest that each of us possesses, on average, somewhere between two (Carter, 1967; May, 1979; Bittles & Neel, 1994) and six (Kumar, Pai, & Swaminathan, 1967; but see Roberts, 1967) lethal equivalents: alleles that, if homozygous, would cause death before an individual reached reproductive age (Morton, Crow, & Muller, 1956; Burnham, 1975).

When individuals share a recent common ancestor, there is an increased probability that they also share a similar complement of deleterious recessive mutations. This means there is an increased probability, over and above the population average, that offspring of two individuals who share a recent common ancestor will inherit two deleterious versions of the same gene. For this reason, evolution is thought to have shaped mechanisms to decrease the probability of close kin matings. To the extent that short-generation pathogens differentially affected the offspring of close genetic relatives (i.e., individuals who share a more similar internal biochemistry), pathogens constituted a second selection pressure favoring individuals who preferred to mate with nonrelatives.

The selection pressures posed by deleterious recessive mutations and short-generation pathogens would have created the adaptive problem of avoiding sexual relations with close genetic relatives. But what kinds of neural programs would have solved this adaptive problem in humans? According to one proposed model (see Lieberman et al., 2003), the following would be required; (1) programs that take in information to estimate the relatedness of other individuals in the surrounding social environment (i.e., systems for detecting kin) and (2) programs that use the computed estimates of relatedness to regulate sexual motivations according to the evolutionarily recurring costs of selecting a particular individual as a sexual partner. One program that has been proposed to motivate sexual avoidance is the emotion of disgust (Lieberman et al., 2003). However, the question remains: What information is used to estimate relatedness? That is, how do people come to know a particular individual is a close genetic relative?

Kin Detection: Cues to Siblingship

There is a problem that any genetic kinship estimator must overcome: genes were not available for direct comparison in ancestral environments. Therefore, kin detection would have had to rely on *cues* that highly correlated with patterns of underlying genetic relatedness. There are a number of cues kin-detection systems may have been designed to take as input. One potential source of information regarding kinship is linguistic and cultural input (e.g., during development you are told who counts as a close genetic relative and how to feel about them). However, these are problematic sources of input. First, kin terms can be used across genetic boundaries and blur the distinction between types of close genetic relatives and between kin and nonkin. For example, "aunt" in our culture refers to a parent's sister but also to a parent's brother's wife. Second, due to asymmetries in relatedness, individuals may not share common "interests" regarding whom to help and when. For example, a child would benefit (in terms of inclusive fitness) from helping a full sibling more than a half sibling, all other things equal. However, a female is equally related to all her own children regardless of their paternity and might therefore urge each child to, for example, "help your sister" while not linguistically differentiating between full and half siblings. Thus, kin terms might disregard or obscure genetic distinctions, making them evolutionarily *less* reliable cues to kinship (but see Jones, 2004). Last, systems for detecting kin exist in many other animal species (Hepper, 1991; Hepper & Cleland, 1999) and predate the evolution of language and culture. There is no reason to suspect that either of these recent inventions have erased or replaced such phylogenetically prior mechanisms.

So if linguistic and cultural inputs alone do not provide a stable solution, what does? Because we cannot "see" another person's genes directly, the best natural selection could do is to shape mechanisms that use cues that were reliably correlated with genetic relatedness *in the ancestral past* to compute an internal index of relatedness. To the extent that different cues reliably correlated with an individual's being a particular type of close genetic relative (e.g., mother, father, offspring, or sibling), different detection mechanisms are expected to exist. That is, there may not be a general kin-detection mechanism that relies on the same set of information for detecting *all* types of close genetic relatives. Instead, the advantages of kin selection would accrue most strongly to individuals who possessed specialized detection systems capable of narrowing in on the small subset of states that correlated with an individual's being a particular kind of kin. One category of kin that has received much attention is siblings (e.g., see Bevc & Silverman, 1993, 2000; DeBruine, 2002; Fessler & Navarrete, 2004; Lieberman, 2003; Lieberman et al., 2003; Wolf, 1995).

As already discussed, the WH proposes one potential cue to siblinghood: childhood coresidence. This cue is an evolutionarily plausible one and, on average, would have accurately categorized individuals who were indeed genetic relatives as siblings; females typically cared for (e.g., fed and protected) their own offspring throughout childhood, leading to the increased proximity of their children. Also, when hunter-gatherer bands fission into smaller units (e.g., due to size or difficult times), nuclear families (including siblings) tend to stay together as a unit (Lee & DeVore, 1968; Chagnon, 1992). Therefore, our mind may be equipped with systems that monitor for this evolutionarily reliable cue to kinship and structure kin-directed behaviors accordingly.

As mentioned above, the most well-known studies testing the WH involve children raised under (evolutionarily) unusual circumstances: the peer groups of the Israeli kibbutzim (Shepher, 1971) and the baby girls adopted into the household of their future husband in Taiwan (*sim-pua* marriage; Wolf, 1995; see discussion above). As the WH predicts, those who coresided during childhood showed little sexual interest in one another when they reached adulthood, especially when compared to individuals from the same population who had not coresided as children. As helpful as these studies have been, a number of questions remain unanswered:

1. Does coresidence duration serve as a cue to kinship for individuals who are in fact genetically related? That is, how does coresidence duration stand up as a cue in circumstances that more closely mirror those of ancestral familial environments?

2. How does coresidence duration influence *psychological* variables that guide motivations and behavior? After all, the dependent measures used

by Wolf (1995) and Shepher (1983) (e.g., marriage and fertility rates) were proxies for sexual attraction, not direct assessments of attraction and desire.

3. How does coresidence compare to other cues that may be used to identify siblings (e.g., facial similarity, olfactory cues)? In particular, is coresidence duration the best cue available for detecting both younger and older siblings for whom different cues may have been available ancestrally to assess relatedness?

From an adaptationist perspective, coresidence duration may not have been the only cue available to detect siblings. Considering the structure of ancestral environments and, independently, how natural selection might have engineered a sibling detection system, a potent and evolutionarily reliable cue for assessing the relatedness of another individual in the social environment is seeing one's mother pregnant and caring for (e.g., breast-feeding) that individual throughout childhood. Ancestrally, females gave birth to and breast-fed their own young (Boyd & Silk, 1997), providing a stable set of cues natural selection could have utilized to detect siblings. However, this information is only available to individuals already present (e.g., prior offspring of the same female). That is, only older siblings would have been able to use this information to assess the genetic relatedness of younger children in the social environment. Furthermore, this cue would not have been dependent on age and, hence, duration of coresidence. That is, regardless of whether one was 3, 13, or 23, seeing one's mother caring for an infant would have been a reliable cue in ancestral environments that the infant was a close genetic relative. However, the arrow of time prevents a newborn from seeing an older sibling being born or cared for during infancy. Consequently, coresidence duration may have been the best cue available to younger siblings for detecting potential older siblings.

It is possible to empirically investigate the role coresidence duration and other potential cues play in detecting siblings by quantitatively matching the variation in coresidence duration (or other hypothesized cue to kinship) to the variation in sexual aversions felt toward one's sibling. Using this method, John Tooby, Leda Cosmides, and I developed a database currently consisting of over 1,000 sibling pairs. In general, we have found that coresidence duration with a sibling does indeed predict levels of disgust associated with sexual behavior with that sibling (Lieberman, 2005; Lieberman et al., 2007). However, as suggested above, coresidence duration may not have served as as potent a cue for older siblings detecting potential younger siblings since more reliable cues may have been available (e.g., seeing one's mother pregnant and caring for a neonate). When younger and older siblings in our database are considered separately, we find that coresidence duration *with an older sibling* predicts sexual aversions toward that older sibling whereas coresidence duration with a younger sibling does not. This suggests that our mind evolved to take advantage of different cues to solve the adaptive problems of detecting younger and older siblings.[6] Findings from these initial studies set the stage for the empirical evaluation of Westermarck's claims regarding the origin of the incest taboo. The next section questions whether the pattern of results found in the studies on the development of sexual aversions toward one's own siblings can explain the patterns of moral sentiments relating to incest.

Are Moral Sentiments Relating to Incest a By-product of Systems Guiding One's Own Sexual Aversions? A Test of Westermarck's Proposal

Data collected in our research allow for the empirical investigation of the origin of moral sentiments relating to incest. *If Westermarck was indeed correct, then the pattern of moral opposition to third-party sibling incest should be a function of the cues our mind uses to detect older and younger siblings in same way that these cues regulate the development of a sexual aversion toward one's own siblings.*

To test this hypothesis, we developed a survey instrument and asked college undergraduates to provide information regarding coresidence duration and other childhood behaviors with each of their same- and opposite-sex siblings (Lieberman et al., 2003, 2007).[7] In addition, they were asked to rank order on a scale of moral wrongness nineteen third-party social transgressions including murder, theft, infidelity, consensual sex between different family members, and marriage between different family members. To assess moral opposition to third-party sibling incest, the ratings of the two sibling behaviors (consensual sex between a brother and sister and brother-sister marriage) were averaged and used as a dependent measure.

Our findings indicate that duration of coresidence with an opposite-sex sibling significantly predicts the degree of moral opposition reported regarding third-party sibling incest; longer periods of coresidence duration predicted stronger moral opposition to third-party sibling incest. Individuals with opposite-sex siblings who *never* lived together rated third-party sibling incest as *less* morally wrong compared to individuals who coresided with their opposite-sex siblings for any length of time. The relationship between coresidence duration and moral sentiments to third-party sibling incest was found to hold even after controlling for the number of opposite-sex siblings in the family and one's explicit beliefs about relatedness, as demonstrated by considering only individuals with step or adoptive siblings. Taken together, our data support Westermarck's claim and suggest that coresidence duration, a cue used to estimate relatedness and activate sexual aversions toward one's own siblings, also predicts the strength of moral sentiments relating to third-party sibling incest.

Alternative Hypotheses: SSSM and Cultural Transmission

There are a number of alternate hypotheses that need to be addressed to more rigorously evaluate the extent to which evolved inbreeding avoidance mechanisms mediate moral sentiments relating to incest. An alternate hypothesis we considered in our study (Lieberman et al., 2003) is that one's moral attitudes relating to incest are adopted from the surrounding social environment, either from one's parents (vertical cultural transmission) or from one's peers (horizontal cultural transmission), and thus are not a by-product of evolved adaptations. This is an explanation advanced by proponents of the SSSM, including the many critics of Westermarck (e.g., Frazer, 1910; Levi-Strauss, 1960; White, 1948). However, three lines of evidence suggest that cultural transmission cannot explain patterns of moral sentiments: (1) data regarding the cultural transmission of attitudes toward sexuality, (2) data from same- and opposite-sex siblings, and (3) data from older versus younger siblings. Each strand of evidence will be discussed in turn.

In our study, subjects were asked how restrictive or permissive their parents' attitudes were regarding sexuality. According to a cultural transmission hypothesis, the more restrictive one's parents' attitudes regarding sexuality, the more restrictive their child's attitudes should be as well. This should be reflected in the subjects' reports of moral sentiment relating to incest. However, perceived parental attitudes regarding sexuality *did not* predict subjects' moral sentiments regarding third-party sibling incest. Moreover, once ratings of parental attitudes were statistically removed, the relationship between coresidence duration and moral opposition to third-party sibling incest remained just as strong. This finding suggests that by itself, vertical cultural transmission cannot explain patterns of moral sentiments relating to incest.

What about horizontal cultural transmission? If attitudes regarding sexuality are patterned after one's peers, then one's attitudes regarding sexuality (i.e., attitudes regarding sexual restrictiveness or permissiveness) should predict variance in moral sentiments relating to incest. However, no such relationship was found (for details, see Lieberman et al., 2003).

This finding not only militates against cultural transmission hypotheses but also suggests that the systems governing one's general attitudes toward sexuality are separate from those regulating the avoidance of inbreeding.

Additional evidence that cultural transmission hypotheses fail to explain these data comes from looking at coresidence duration with the same-sex siblings. If cultural transmission is the process governing the adoption of attitudes toward incest, then one's attitudes should exist independent of the sex of one's siblings. After all, the sex of a sibling is a biological coin-flip. If this is true, then longer periods of coresidence with same- *and* opposite-sex siblings should also map onto longer periods of socialization which should lead to greater opposition to third-party sibling incest. That is, if cultural transmission hypotheses were indeed the mechanism calibrating attitudes relating to incest and if longer periods of coresidence provided greater opportunities to relay this information, then coresidence duration with any sibling should predict sentiments regardless of their sex. If, on the other hand, specialized psychological adaptations exist that govern the development of sexual aversions for the purpose of avoiding the deleterious consequences associated with inbreeding, then coresidence duration with only opposite-sex siblings should influence sexual aversions and, consequently, moral opposition. Data from our study show that coresidence duration with an opposite-sex sibling significantly predicts moral opposition to third-party sibling incest whereas coresidence duration with a same-sex sibling does not. This pattern of data speaks against cultural transmission hypotheses and supports the hypothesis that moral sentiments relating to third-party sibling incest mirror the activation of systems guiding the development of sexual aversions toward one's own opposite sex siblings.

But perhaps parents are communicating different messages to their children based on family composition. That is, it is plausible that vertical transmission of attitudes relating to incest occurs only in those families with *both* sons and daughters, environments where sibling sexual relations could potentially occur. If this is the case, then cultural transmission hypotheses would predict that the longer the coresidence duration with an opposite-sex sibling, regardless of relative age, the greater the opportunity for parents to communicate sexual prohibitions to their children, and, hence, the stronger the children's internalized attitudes regarding incest. Therefore, coresidence duration with a younger sibling should predict moral opposition to sibling incest to the same extent as coresidence duration with an older sibling. However, if moral sentiments relating to third-party sibling incest are a reflection of the activation of systems guiding one's own sexual aversions, then they should be governed by the same cues used to estimate relatedness. According to the adaptationist argument presented above, coresidence duration is a more reliable cue for detecting *older* siblings. The detection of younger siblings may rely on exposure to more potent cues such as seeing one's mother pregnant and caring for (e.g., breast-feeding) a newborn. Therefore, if moral sentiments are a by-product of adaptations governing the development of sexual aversions toward one's own siblings, then coresidence duration with an older sibling should predict moral opposition to third-party sibling incest to a stronger degree than coresidence duration with a younger sibling. This is exactly what is found. Considering individuals with only one opposite-sex sibling,[8] for those with an older sibling, coresidence duration with that older sibling significantly predicts moral sentiments relating to third-party sibling incest. In contrast, for those with a younger sibling, coresidence duration with that younger sibling does not predict moral sentiments (see also Lieberman et al., 2007). This pattern cannot be explained by different durations of coresidence for individuals with younger versus older opposite-sex siblings, as they are not significantly different from one another. Taken together, these data militate against cultural transmission hypotheses as the origin of moral sentiments. Rather, they support Westermarck's claim that moral sentiments relating to incest are a function of the same mechanisms guiding the development of a sexual aversion toward one's own close genetic relatives.

Summary

Westermarck originally suggested that cultural expressions regarding incest derive from psychological adaptations guiding inbreeding avoidance. That is, cultural prohibitions are a reflection of biological disinclinations. However, many still dispute this claim and have demanded evidence in its support (see, e.g., Durham, 2005). Evidence has arrived. The same variables shown to predict the development of a sexual aversion toward one's own sibling predict moral opposition toward third-party sibling incest. Furthermore, predictions derived from an adaptationist program, namely, the differential use of coresidence duration as a cue for detecting older siblings and the effect of coresidence duration with opposite- versus same-sex sibling (for heterosexual individuals) on moral opposition to third-party sibling incest, are supported and cannot be explained by cultural transmission hypotheses, at least not easily. The landscape of one's own sexual aversions and one's moral oppositions to incest are too similar to be coincidence and are unlikely to have arisen by chance alone. A more parsimonious explanation is that the strength of moral opposition to sibling incest is in part, if not wholly, a by-product of psychological adaptations designed to decrease the probability of close kin matings.

Moral Sentiments Relating to Incest: An Adaptation to Prevent One's Close Genetic Relatives from Mating?

Were there selection pressures that would have led to the evolution and maintenance of motivational systems for deterring (or promoting) sexual relations between third parties? That is, are there psychological *adaptations* for influencing the decisions others make with respect to mate choice? According to Williams (1966), "adaptation" is an onerous concept and should only be applied in the face of strong evidence that a system is well designed to perform a particular function. Whereas the argument presented above suggests that moral sentiments relating to sibling incest are, in part, a by-product of adaptations designed to prevent oneself from pursing a sibling as a sexual partner, it is an open question as to whether separate systems (i.e., adaptations) exist to actively regulate third-party mating decisions.

From an evolutionary perspective, the actions and decisions of close genetic relatives (as well as unrelated individuals) can greatly impact one's inclusive fitness. This holds for the decisions close genetic relatives make with respect to mate choice. Not only are instances of inbreeding potentially costly to the individuals engaging in the act (though perhaps not equally so—see Tooby, 1977, and Haig, 1999, for a discussion of inbreeding conflict), they also impose large fitness costs on close genetic relatives. Indeed, for each individual within the family, there is a cost/benefit fitness matrix that takes into account the outcome of potential incestuous unions within the family and the outcome had both family members mated outside the family. A design feature that enabled an individual to compute these costs and benefits and to interfere with (or promote) sexual unions accordingly would have out-reproduced design features that did not respond to the fitness consequences of inbreeding within the family.

To the extent that close genetic relatives could have pursued one another as a sexual partner in ancestral environments (an almost certain possibility), design features that motivated the interference of sexual unions between one's close relatives in a manner consistent with the costs and benefits associated with each particular incestuous dyad would have become more frequent in the population compared to design features that were neutral (neither motivating nor discouraging) with respect to whether family members mated with one another. That is, in addition to specialized systems for detecting close genetic relatives for the purpose of guiding one's own mating decisions, specialized systems are hypothesized to exist that assess the costs and benefits of other incestuous dyads within the family and motivate the active interference between those dyads imposing elevated costs to one's inclusive fitness (Lieberman et al., 2001). Intensity of interference should depend on a number of factors including mutation load, pathogen load, and available opportunities to secure unrelated mates (Tooby, 1977).

Empirical Investigation of Adaptations for Regulating Inbreeding Within the Family

To investigate the hypothesis that humans possess circuitry for motivating the interference of sexual relations between incestuous dyads in a manner that reflects their potential costs on inclusive fitness, John Tooby, Leda Cosmides, and I designed a study using a method borrowed from Li et al. (2002). Accordingly, subjects were asked to allocate "escape dollars" to five different incestuous dyads within the family (mother/son, father/daughter, son/daughter, brother/sister, and mate/offspring) across four different budgets (Lieberman et al., 2001). Within each budget, allocation of each escape dollar to a particular dyad reduced the probability that the incestuous union would occur (e.g., from 100% chance to 90% chance of occurring). By inspecting how subjects allocated their escape dollars, we were able to determine which dyads were most objectionable. The purpose of giving subjects four separate budgets (ranging from 7 to 19 escape dollars) was to investigate the relative order of perceived costs of all the dyads. The logic of this method is that at smaller budget sizes, subjects will allocate a larger proportion of their escape dollars to those acts they perceive to be most objectionable, thereby decreasing the probability that the most objectionable acts occur. As budget size increases, subjects have already reduced the probability that the most objectionable acts will occur and are now capable of (1) allocating their escape dollars to continue to reduce the probability that an objectionable act will occur (it requires 10 escape dollars to bring the probability an act will occur down to 0% and with a maximum of 19 escape dollars, it is only possible to do so for one act) or (2) allocating their escape dollars to those acts perceived as less objectionable. As a result of using different budget sizes, the proportion of escape dollars allocated to the most objectionable acts will decrease as budget size increases and the proportion of escape dollars allocated to the less objectionable acts will increase as budget size increases.

Our data suggest that individuals are sensitive to the different costs associated with the different incestuous dyads within the family (Lieberman et al., 2001). For example, subjects consistently found the partner-offspring dyad as most objectionable, allocating a greater proportion of escape dollars to this union at smaller budgets. This follows from a selectionist perspective since this dyad poses the greatest potential costs to one's inclusive fitness compared to the other dyads within the family. Other data, currently being examined, also support the claim that a separate cognitive system exists to monitor and regulate the sexual behavior of family members. However, much more empirical investigation is required to investigate whether this constitutes a separate cognitive adaptation or whether these results can be explained more parsimoniously as a product of other systems.

Summary

In summary, it is plausible that cognitive adaptations exist to regulate the sexual behavior of one's own family members. A system that used the computed kinship estimates that function to guide one's own sexual motivations to also assess the costs and benefits of particular unions within the family would be on its way to solving this adaptive problem. Such a system, should it exist, is hypothesized to be sensitive to a number of factors such as the local genetic load and the opportunity for mates outside the family. Again, much more work is needed to determine whether such an adaptation exists in humans.

Conclusions

It appears Westermarck was right. The evidence presented above supports the hypothesis that moral sentiments relating to incest are, in part, a by-product of psychological programs that evolved to reduce the probability of mating with one's close genetic relatives. The investigation into the structure of inbreeding avoidance mechanisms in humans has uncovered a set of ecologically valid cues that govern kin detection and sexual motivations. These same cues predict patterns of moral sentiments relating to third-party incest. Alternative hypotheses stemming from an SSSM view of human psychology (e.g., cultural transmission hypotheses) cannot explain the patterns of data discussed above without adopting some assumptions shared by evolutionary-minded researchers (e.g., specialized inbreeding avoidance mechanisms exist). Further tests of Westermarck's claim (and alternate models) regarding the origin of moral sentiments relating to incest can be performed once the cues governing kin detection between other dyads (e.g., father-offspring) have been uncovered. This will allow for a more rigorous investigation of how evolved inbreeding avoidance programs fashion moral sentiments relating to incest.

Incest is but one of a number of behaviors considered within the moral domain. It serves as a useful test case for exploring the origin of our moral sentiments across multiple domains. Specifically, the topic of incest highlights the importance of asking (at least) two distinct questions: (1) Are moral sentiments relating to third-party behavior within a particular domain a by-product of evolved systems that, for example, assess the costs and benefits of engaging in a particular behavior oneself? And (2) Do specialized cognitive adaptations exist that generate moral sentiments to regulate third-party behavior within a particular domain? In this way, it will be possible to discern evolved functions from system by-products.

Morality, traditionally a province of theologians and philosophers, has been invaded by scientists interested in understanding why we have the moral sentiments we do and why we care about the actions of others. According to the perspective discussed herein, evolution is hypothesized to have shaped our psychology to monitor third-party behavior across a number of domains that impacted our inclusive fitness (either positively or negatively) in ancestral environments. Thus, our "moral sense" may be composed of a patchwork of diverse systems, each evaluating the costs and benefits of others' actions within a particular domain. In addition, as appears to be the case with incest, our moral sense may be a function of the activation of systems naturally selected to guide our own behavior. Certainly much more work is required to determine the merit of this approach. What is clear, however, is that it is possible to dissect our moral reasoning capabilities and, domain by domain, empirically investigate the facts underlying our values.

Notes

1. I use the term "third party" to mean nonself. There is an important distinction between reactions to the behavior of others with whom one is socially engaged (i.e., second parties) and reactions to the behavior of others with whom one is not (i.e., true third parties). I have collapsed these two categories into one and labeled them "third party" since the distinction that I wanted to make was between self and other, regardless of the other's status. I apologize to the reader for any confusion. Further, I have chosen to confine my discussion of morality to adaptations for evaluating the behavior of others. Whether to include adaptations for evaluating one's own

behaviors in different social contexts as moral is an issue of categorization; see commentaries and response.

2. Note that this is one of many possible *computational* descriptions of our moral psychology. The structure of the information-processing procedures for the "moral" domain have been largely neglected, perhaps one reason why there is so much debate in this area over what words mean and what constitutes a moral judgment. All this disappears if one considers the adaptive problems the social world posed and the architecture of the information-processing procedures required for their solution including (1) the nature of the information taken as input, (2) how these inputs are represented, (3) the procedures that operate over the representations, and (4) the motivational systems that get activated or deactivated (see Marr, 1982).

3. For example, the groups of Hadza have been numbered in the fews of hundreds, ranging from over 100 to 400 individuals (Woodburn, 1968). Yanomamö village size has been estimated to range from 40 to 300 individuals (Chagnon, 1992).

4. These statements are made with heterosexual individuals in mind.

5. Is it possible that Freud was wet-nursed, leading him to categorize an unrelated female as his mother and, consequently, to not develop as strong a sexual aversion to his true biological mother? Hmmm.

6. Converging lines of evidence that coresidence duration is (1) a cue our mind uses to assess the relatedness of potential siblings and (2) a stronger cue used to estimate the relatedness of older siblings, comes from research looking at patterns of altruism, a second domain hypothesized to take estimates of relatedness as input. As mentioned above, Hamilton's theory of inclusive fitness also requires mechanisms for kin detection. One possible design of the human cognitive architecture would be to have a kin-detection system that computes estimates of relatedness and provides this information to both systems regulating sexual attraction and systems guiding altruistic effort. If this is how our mind works, then a cue to kinship (e.g., coresidence duration) should regulate patterns of sexual attraction/avoidance as well as patterns of altruism. This is exactly what has been found (Lieberman et al., 2007). While coresidence duration with a sibling predicts levels of altruism, the effect is much more pronounced when inspecting subjects and their *older* siblings. For subjects and their younger siblings, exposure to one's mother caring for a newborn was found to predict levels of altruism, even after controlling for the effects of coresidence duration.

7. See Lieberman, Tooby, and Cosmides (2003) for details. Paper is available at http://www.psych.ucsb.edu/research/cep

8. This is required methodologically since moral sentiments do not target a specific sibling, unlike, for example, questions asking about the level of disgust associated with sex with a particular sibling.

3.1 Edward Westermarck on the Meaning of "Moral"

Arthur P. Wolf

Avoiding sexual relations with one's close kin and disapproving of other people's not avoiding sexual relations with theirs are very different behaviors. Probably because he was interested in the origin of moral ideas as well as the history of human marriage, Edward Westermarck saw the difference, but most authors who have addressed "the incest problem" since he wrote have not. If they are sociologists or social anthropologists, they have offered explanations of the disapproval and assumed that most people avoid behavior that is disapproved, while if they are biologists, they have offered explanations of the avoidance and assumed that most people disapprove of behavior that is avoided.

The most attractive aspect of Lieberman's argument is that, like Westermarck, she sees that solving the incest problem requires answering at least two questions. Why do human beings usually avoid sexual relations with close kin? And why do they sanction other people who do not avoid sexual relations with their close kin? After almost a century of vituperative debate, Westermarck's answer to the first question is now widely accepted.[1] It is that "generally speaking, there is a remarkable absence of erotic feelings between persons living closely together from childhood."[2] Although we have not yet identified the proximate cause of this reaction to early association, it is generally agreed that the ultimate cause is, as Westermarck was the first to argue, the deleterious effects of inbreeding.

The second question—often not even recognized as a question—has not been answered. It could be, as Lieberman argues toward the end of her paper, that disapproval of sex *between* close kin is, like avoidance of sex *with* close kin, attributable to the dangers of inbreeding. A disposition of this kind could enhance inclusive fitness. The really difficult problem is to explain morally weighted disapproval of sex between persons who are kin to one another but not to the person voicing the disapproval. There is no obvious way of relating this to the dangers of inbreeding. My fitness is not reduced if unrelated others sleep with their brothers and sisters. It might even be enhanced if the result is that they have fewer offspring or offspring that I can easily defeat in competition for scarce resources.

Lieberman's argument is that disapproval of sex between others who are kin to one another but not my kin is "a by-product of systems designed to deter sexual relations with one's own close genetic relatives." Moral sentiments of this kind "are a reflection of the activation of systems designed to prevent sexual relations *with one's own close genetic relatives*" (p. 177). The argument is attributed to Edward Westermarck, who is quoted as claiming that the "fundamental cause of the exogamous prohibition" is the sexual aversion aroused by early association. "Persons who have been living closely together from childhood are as a rule near relatives. Hence their aversion to sexual relations with one another displays itself in custom and law as a prohibition of intercourse between near kin" (p. 171).

Lieberman presents as evidence of her hypothesis a study in which college students were asked to compare the morality of various transgressions. The study showed that students who had siblings with whom they had lived for a long time were more disapproving of incest than students with no siblings or siblings with whom they had not lived for an extended period. These results are interpreted as showing that people with a personal aversion are more likely to disapprove of incest than those without a personal aversion because the transgression is more likely to activate their incest-avoiding system.

Although there is much to be said in favor of Lieberman's argument, it lacks two things. The first—and most obvious—is a clear account of what it means to call a behavior "moral" and thus what it is that she hopes to explain. All Lieberman says is that we "tend to categorize as morally repugnant" behaviors "imposing fitness costs" (p. 166). This is inadequate for a variety of reasons. The most obvious is that people everywhere tend to categorize selfish behavior as immoral.

The second thing Lieberman's argument lacks is a clear delineation of how it is that a person's aversion to sexual relations with his own kin leads to his condemning other people for taking a sexual interest in their kin. It is not adequate to claim that condemnation of incest is "a by-product" or "a reflection" of "systems designed to deter sexual relations with one's own close genetic relatives" (p. 177). The argument requires specifying how this is accomplished.

Lieberman could have avoided both of these problems if she had read Edward Westermarck more carefully. She appears to know the work he did as a sociologist but not his work as a philosopher. In both *The Origin and*

Development of the Moral Ideas and *Ethical Relativity*, Westermarck (1932a, 1912/1932b) devoted considerable attention to what makes people see a behavior as moral or immoral.[3] "Moral disapproval is," in his view, "a form of resentment, and moral approval, a form of retributive kindly emotion." What distinguishes "these emotions from kindred nonmoral emotions—disapproval from anger and revenge, and approval from gratitude" is "disinterestedness," "apparent impartiality," and "a certain flavour of generality."[4] Westermarck did not claim that the behaviors motivated by the moral emotions are necessarily moral in any larger sense. They only become moral when people see them as moral and thus only when they appear disinterested and impartial.

Thus, for Westermarck, the problem posed by the second part of the incest problem is a matter of explaining why most people disapprove of incest and why they regard such disapproval as disinterested and impartial. The crux of his argument is suggested by the care he always takes to distinguish between "sexual indifference" and "a positive feeling of aversion."[5] The normal state of sexual feeling between persons who have been reared together is a comfortable indifference. A positive feeling of aversion is only aroused when for some reason "the act is thought of."

Although he nowhere makes this explicit, Westermarck takes "a positive feeling of aversion" to be an unpleasant, uncomfortable state. In a word, it is painful. Thus, it is to be expected that a person will disapprove of an unrelated other's having sex with a parent or a sibling. His behavior brings the possibility of such relations forcibly to mind, turns a comfortable indifference into a painful aversion, and thereby motivates disapproval. In Westermarck's view "our retributive emotions are always reactions against pain or pleasure felt by ourselves; this holds true of the moral emotions as well as of revenge and gratitude."[6]

Rooted in early experience and having a large sexual component, disapproval of incest is always emotional. It is the reason incest taboos are "characterized by a peculiar intensity and emotional quality,"[7] but it is not this that gives them their moral quality. They are moral because the disapproval is characterized by "disinterestedness"—rarely bringing social or material benefits; "apparent impartiality"—because the reaction is the same regardless of who the offender is; and "a certain flavour of generality"—because the great majority of people respond the same way. This is guaranteed by the fact that the reaction is rooted in human nature.

Thus, in Westermarck's view, the foundation of the incest taboo is what Alexander Bain called a "disinterested antipathy."[8] Incest does not cause the perpetrator's friends or neighbors injury. Their disapproval is prompted by "a sentimental aversion" that appears disinterested and impartial. These qualities of a reaction that is general, if not universal, lifts an individual response to the level of a social phenomenon. It turns simple disapproval into moral disapproval. The incest taboo is at bottom an emotionally charged reaction that becomes moral by being general and by appearing to serve no selfish interest.

This argument does not contradict anything in Lieberman's paper. It rests, as does all of Westermarck's work, on the same Darwinian foundations. It even predicts the results of the study Lieberman cites. The difference is that it is, in my view, a far more sophisticated argument. It specifies in plain language what it is that needs explaining and makes explicit the chain of causation posited.

Notes

1. See Wolf (2005b).

2. See, for example, Westermarck (1891/1922, pp. 192–193).

3. Westermarck (1912/1932b, pp. 100–107; 1932a, pp. 89–113).

4. Westermarck (1912/1932b, pp. 100–105).

5. See, for example, Westermarck (1891/1922, volume 2, pp. 192–193).

6. Westermarck (1891/1922, volume 1, p. 43).

7. Murdock (1949, pp. 287–288).

8. Bain (1880, p. 268).

Richard Joyce

Nobody knows to what extent humans have innate mechanisms pertaining to incest regulation. Debra Lieberman is certainly interested in advocating the case that we do have evolved adaptations dedicated to governing this domain of behavior, but ultimately her position is that the positive hypothesis is "plausible" and that much more empirical work remains to be done. Jesse Prinz (this volume) advocates the anti-nativist position—in relation to both morality in general and incest in particular—but he, too, settles for the conclusion that the nativist case is "incomplete" and that there is "an exciting research program waiting to be explored" (p. 405). Arguments over various general and specific forms of human psychological nativism seem to generate a peculiar amount of entrenched intellectual acerbity (not in evidence, I hasten to add, in the two papers just mentioned), and it is a useful palliative to frequently remind ourselves of the common ground shared by all reasonable advocates: that we really don't know yet.

Empirical work of the kind undertaken by Lieberman (and colleagues) is worth much more than any amount of armchair speculation. No matter how inventive and valuable such work is, however, there inevitably will be—as there should be—a body of opposition that will offer alternative models to explain the empirical data. Thus, perhaps the most useful critical response to Lieberman's paper would be to take her data and suggest a non-nativist interpretation of them. However, that is not what I intend to do in this brief commentary; rather, I will undertake a less ambitious, perhaps more pedestrian, but nevertheless equally important task: that of clarifying and paying careful critical attention to the words and phrases Lieberman uses to describe her results and conclusions. I will in particular criticize her use of the words "moral" and "sentiment." Such an enterprise will, I suppose, be rejected as being "merely a semantic argument," but semantic arguments *matter*: if one presents one's conclusions as casting light on the nature of Xs, but one is using "X" in an eccentric or restricted manner, then it may well turn out that one's conclusions do not concern Xs at all.

Lieberman chooses to frame her discussion using a rather quaint term, "moral sentiments." This phrase—seemingly more at home in an eighteenth-century treatise—appears to be undergoing a minor revival (see Slote, 2003; Nichols, 2004; Gintis, Bowles, Boyd, & Fehr, 2005), though I must confess that it is not clear to me what has been gained by substituting "sentiment" for the word it is so obviously designed to replace: "emotion." Even Edward Westermarck—some of whose views Lieberman takes her findings to corroborate—eschewed the term "sentiment" in favor of "emotion." It is true that arguments over what "emotion" denotes have become so entangled that in serious discussion one uses the word unqualified at one's own risk, yet there seems little profit in substituting a fresh term when the inevitable outcome is that the intellectual battle lines over sentiments will be drawn in exactly the same places as they were when the argument was over emotions.

The phrase "moral sentiment" (just like "moral emotion") is open to several interpretations; let me draw attention to three. Sometimes it is used as a rough synonym for "prosocial sentiment," in which case love and sympathy may be thought of as moral sentiments. Clearly, one can love someone without judging that it is morally right to love him, just as one can feel sympathy for someone without judging that one is duty-bound to care. Indeed, a creature constitutionally incapable of forming a moral concept might feel love or sympathy. Thus, if such sentiments count as "moral," it may be only in the sense that they *merit* moral praise. Alternatively, some sentiments deserve to be called "moral" in virtue of the fact that they usually (or always) *involve* the making of a moral judgment. Many theorists argue that emotions necessarily involve a cognitive element, and, it would seem, in certain cases this cognitive element involves a normative judgment. Guilt, for example, is an emotion that necessarily involves the thought that the subject has in some manner transgressed.[2] Disgust can of course have nothing to do with any moral judgment (e.g., disgust at standing in dog feces), but seems also to come in a "moralized" form (e.g., disgust at concentration camps) (see Haidt, Rozin, McCauley, & Imada, 1997; Rozin, Haidt, & McCauley, 2000).

Moral sentiments may also be characterized in a third way: by reference to their subject matter, or the domain of their prototypical elicitors. This appears to be Lieberman's route, for she uses the term "moral sentiment" to denote reactions prompted by or aimed at third-party behaviors.[3] This interpretation certainly promises to make it easier to operationalize moral sentiments, but it is nevertheless problematic. For a start, there surely exist sentiments that are directed at third parties (just as frequently as they pertain to the self) that we would not ordinarily think of as particularly *moral*: surprise, horror, and pity, for example. Conversely, there are certain sentiments usually classified as "moral" which seem very self-regarding— guilt and shame being the obvious ones. Other sentiments often classified as moral—contempt, punitive anger, moral disgust—seem to come equally in self-regarding and third-party-regarding forms, with neither having an obvious claim to being prototypical. (See Haidt, 2003, for a good discussion of moral emotions.) Lieberman's restriction of the moral realm implies the unfortunate result that a person's disgust at his own incestuous thoughts cannot count as a moral sentiment, nor can a person's disgust at his sister's sexual advances count as a moral sentiment; it is only if his disgust is directed at an incestuous union between two other persons that it can count as a moral sentiment.

It is important to bear this restriction in mind while reading Lieberman's paper, or else matters become quickly confusing. For example, one might have been tempted to see Lieberman's contrast between aversion to incest and incest-denouncing moral sentiments as a contrast between different possible mechanisms of self-regulation. There are, on the one hand, various possible self-regulatory mechanisms with *nonmoral* outputs: (1) an absence of any sexual desire towards kin (i.e., sexual indifference), (2) a positive desire to refrain from such activities (i.e., sexual aversion), (3) a negative emotional response at the thought of committing incest (self-disgust, repugnance, etc.).[4] On the other hand, one might have a *moral* resistance to one's own potential incest: (4) judging it to be forbidden, the expression of a vice, as deserving reprimand or punishment. Moral sentiments, in the second sense identified above, blur the boundary between (3) and (4), because they are to be distinguished both from nonmoral emotional opposition to incest (e.g., nonmoralized versions of anger, repugnance, fear) and from non-emotional moral condemnation of incest (e.g., agreeing that it is morally prohibited, but feeling emotionally unruffled when contemplating it). One might have expected from the title of Lieberman's paper that the discussion would focus on whether any such "moralized" emotions elicited by incest are adaptations or by-products of adaptations. But this is not her project, and her distinction between aversion and moral sentiment is not the one just canvassed. Rather, the term "aversion" seems to do the work of denoting the output of any psychological mechanism that decreases an individual's motivation to engage in incest, while "moral sentiment" is reserved for the output of any mechanism that prompts the individual to interfere with other parties' (potential) incestuous activity.

This manner of classifying matters, in my opinion, masks much that may be of interest. For a start, even when confining ourselves just to *self*-regulation with respect to incest, it would be useful to distinguish moral from nonmoral mechanisms. There is, after all, a world of difference between simply *not wanting* to have sex with someone and judging such sex to be a disgusting evil. Natural selection may have had a hand in designing either or both of these motivation-engaging mechanisms, and it would be interesting to see the matter investigated. Darwin himself considered the moral sense to be a faculty of *self*-regarding moral appraisal (i.e., the moral conscience) and claimed that it is "of all the differences between man and the lower animals ... by far the most important" (1879/2004, p. 120). Westermarck, in contrast, argued that self-directed moral evaluations are circuitously reached only "through a prior critique upon our fellow-men" (1906/1932b, volume 2, p. 123).

By the same token, it would be useful to distinguish possible moral from nonmoral negative responses to others' incestuous behavior. There is, again, a big difference between *not wanting* others to commit incest and judging any such union to be a moral abomination deserving of punishment. Even if one's opposition to others' incest manifests itself as directed anger, and even if this anger produces a retaliative reaction, there need be nothing especially moralistic about the anger or the retaliation. It is only if the anger incorporates or is accompanied by the thought that the third party has *transgressed against a norm*, and the retaliative response is motivated or justified by the thought that the punishment is *deserved*, that the opposition counts as moral. It is possible that humans have a dedicated innate mechanism that generates some form or other of nonmoral opposition to third-party incest, while the widespread human trait of moral opposition is a by-product or a cultural artifact. It is also possible that certain forms of moral opposition are also the product of another (complementary) innate mechanism. Again, it would be extremely interesting to see more empirical work aimed at resolving this matter.

It is not my intention to criticize Lieberman for failing to pursue these research questions; rather, I am just trying to tease apart these distinct research projects and get clear on the misleading terminology involved. To put my point strongly (perhaps overly so): most of Lieberman's discussion might have proceeded without the word "moral" even appearing. What she is really interested in is mechanisms that motivate humans to act against (potential) incestuous relations among third parties (are they adaptations or by-products?), and the relation these mechanisms have to any other mechanisms that motivate humans to themselves avoid incest. Whether either of these mechanisms affects motivation by generating desires, or engaging emotions, or prompting moral judgments, or some combination of the above ("moral sentiments") is not a matter that her experiments are designed to discriminate.

That Lieberman's conceptual space is coarse-grained in this respect is evidenced by the way that very different forms of "psychological opposition" (to incest) are treated as being on all fours. It is claimed that behaviors negatively affecting one's fitness are ones we tend to categorize as "morally repugnant," whereas ones that enhance fitness are considered "morally virtuous and praiseworthy." Already there are difficulties, for "moral repugnance" sounds very much like a kind of occurrent moralized emotion, whereas classifying something as "morally praiseworthy" need involve no emotion at all. In the next sentence Lieberman refers to "moral disapproval and approval"—terms that are (perhaps usefully) indeterminate. On the one hand, they are sometimes used to stand for certain moral emotions (Westermarck, e.g., insists on this usage);[5] on the other hand, someone who holds that moral judgments may be entirely cognitive and non-emotional (i.e., a psychological rationalist)[6] can, without straining language in the least, agree that moral evaluations are ways of "approving" or "disapproving." Later in the paper, Lieberman reports her 2003 study (with Tooby and Cosmides) in which subjects were asked to rank actions in terms of their "moral wrongness," and yet the experiment is taken to corroborate something about "moral sentiments." It is, again, not clear to me what is gained by introducing this loaded and problematic term; if subjects are asked questions framed explicitly in terms of "morally wrongness," then why not report the findings as concerning just their "moral *opinions*" or "moral *assessments*"? Contrary to what is claimed in the earlier article, the experiment does not "directly measure moral sentiments" (Lieberman, Tooby, & Cosmides, 2003, p. 825), unless "sentiment" is misleadingly being used in an extremely watered-down manner to mean nothing more than "moral opinion."[7]

Let me close by saying something about another word that often appears in these discussions, and, indeed, crops up in Lieberman's paper: "incest *taboo*." Westermarck's position is that the taboo against incest is a by-product of an innate aversion; he claims that humans' natural aversion to incestuous relations "displays itself in custom and law as a prohibition" (1891/1922, p. 193). Lieberman's position is sympathetic to Westermarck's, but she also speculates (on some evidential ground) that "moral sentiments" relating to family members' incest (i.e., motivational systems targeting family members' incest) are the output of a discrete adaptation. By contrast, Prinz (this volume) pushes the antinativist agenda, arguing that the evidence in support of an innate incest taboo is "less secure" than it is widely assumed to be. These seem to be three competing positions, but I would like to suggest that on a closer reading the three authors are to some extent talking past each other.

Note, to begin with, that a taboo is most naturally interpreted as a trait instantiated by *a group*; there's something very peculiar about the idea of a person's having her own personal taboos at odds with those of the population of which she is a member.[8] If this is correct, then a taboo can be innate only if we are willing to appeal to some model of multilevel selection whereby adaptations may be properties instantiated by groups rather than individuals. I hazard to suggest that those people (like Prinz) who frame the debate explicitly in terms of whether there is an "innate taboo" against incest probably do not intend to invoke any such models and, thus, should probably rephrase their terms.

What Prinz presumably has in mind is the question of whether it is a human adaptation to think of incest as morally wrong, or forbidden, or sinful (or some other morally loaded form of opposition). If everyone in a population had such an adaptation, then it is natural to think that this would manifest itself as an incest taboo (but it would still be a mistake to speak of the taboo itself being an adaptation). There are two things to note about Prinz's target question in relation to Lieberman's concerns. First, Prinz is very clear that he is discussing a *moral* form of opposition. Such opposition is related to, but nevertheless is to be distinguished from, mere *dislike* (or even hatred) of incest, and distinguished from any unmoralized emotional response (e.g., repugnance) toward incest. Second, Prinz makes no distinction between moral opposition that is self-directed and that which is other-directed. Thus, Prinz is making a distinction that Lieberman does not make, and Lieberman is making a distinction that Prinz does not make.

Westermarck is interested in the relation between the human individual's aversion to incest (which he thinks is innate) and the social taboo (which he thinks is a by-product of the former). He doesn't "moralize" the self-directed aversion; he doesn't argue that we are designed to think of sex with our own family members as *evil* or even *prohibited*; rather, we are designed just to find the prospect repellant. But, he holds, when a group of like-minded humans form a society, then this aversion that each has to the thought of having sex with his or her own family members will manifest itself as a moral prohibition within the group, as a taboo. Quite why this would occur is something of a mystery, which Arthur Wolf, in his extremely useful discussion, calls "the representation problem": "The fact that early association inhibits sexual attraction explains why most people avoid sexual relations with their parents and siblings, but it does not explain why they condemn other people for having sexual relations with *their* parent or *their* sibling" (2005b, p. 11), nor does it explain why this condemnation should have "a strongly felt moral content" (p. 12).[9] Lieberman seeks to corroborate Westermarck's "by-product hypothesis"[10] by showing that one's attitudes to third-party incest are a function of one's levels of aversion toward one's own potential incestuous relations. However, this seems to be investigating a different relation from the one Westermarck proposed. His claim was that an incest taboo as a societal trait would arise from individuals' collective self-directed aversions, not that an individual's attitudes to third-party incest would arise from an individual's self-directed aversions. The latter relation could be empirically confirmed (we could, for example, discover that the stronger an individual's aversion to her own potential incest, the stronger her dislike of others' incestuous relations) while nothing is revealed about the origin of the society's moral proscription.

The extent of disorder among these three apparently competing views is brought home when we realize that they all could be true. Suppose humans have an innate aversion to committing incest, and this aversion, when individuals join together to form a society, manifests itself (somehow) as a moral taboo. In other words, suppose Westermarck is correct. Since the innate aversion is not "moralized," and since what is moralized (the taboo) is not innate, Prinz's antinativist view of morality (and the morality of incest in particular) is consistent with Westermarck's view. Now suppose also that humans have a discrete innate mechanism designed to motivate action in response to perceived third-party incest. In other words, suppose that Lieberman is correct. This clashes with no part of Westermarck's view. Lieberman calls any such motivation-engaging responses "moral senti-ments," but I have suggested that the word "moral" here is at best optional, and at worst misguided. In any case, it is not the same sense of "moral" that Prinz employs when he denies that humans have any innate moral attitudes towards incest. Thus, it turns out that—a terminological discrep-ancy aside—Lieberman's view and Prinz's view could both be correct.

Lieberman writes, "Morality, traditionally the province of theologians and philosophers, has been invaded by scientists." The invasion is wholly to be welcomed. However, if the assorted thinkers and researchers are to avoid talking past each other, it is as well that we all pay careful critical attention to the subtleties of the language we use in attempting to describe various phenomena.

Notes

1. Certain philosophers and psychologists have offered nuanced distinctions between emotions and sentiments (and passions, affects, etc.), but it seems fair to say that these are efforts at stipulating terms of art, rather than reflections of any vernacular distinction. In any case, someone who intends to use the word "sentiment" *in contrast to* "emotion" owes the reader an explanation.

2. Cases of "survivor guilt" might be supposed to be counterexamples to this claim, but although such sufferers may know very well at a rational level that they are not responsible for the harm that befell others, they cannot shake the feeling that they have "done something wrong," and it is precisely because their experience has this phenomenology that we are inclined to call their distress "guilt." Saying that guilt necessarily involves an application of the concept *transgression* is not to say that the subject agrees *all things considered* that she has transgressed. For further discussion, see Sinnott-Armstrong (2005); Joyce (2006, chapter 3).

3. In her opening paragraph she asks, "What is the origin of our sentiments regarding third-party behaviors, that is, what is the origin of our moral sentiments?" (p. 165). The same connection is made in her 2003 paper with John Tooby and Leda Cosmides.

4. The distinction between (2) and (3) assumes that desires and emotions are distinct phenomena, which seems a safe assumption, widely upheld in both vernacular and theoretical discussions. Certainly many or perhaps all emotions implicate desires, but we usually allow that one can have a desire (e.g., to one day read *A la Recherche du Temps Perdu*) without any *emotions* being engaged in favor of the desired outcome.

5. See Westermarck (1932a, p. 63 ff).

6. See my contribution to this series (volume 3), for a characterization of different forms of moral rationalism.

7. Even here, of course, the experiment doesn't *directly* measure moral opinion but rather measures subjects' self-reports of their moral opinion.

8. This is not to say that we cannot make any sense at all of the thought of a person's having her own personal taboos. We *can* make some sense of the thought, just as we can make *some* sense of the thought of a person's having her own private language. It suffices to make the point that whatever comprehension we seem to

have of personal taboos is surely heavily derivative on our grasp of the idea a group-held taboo, to such an extent that it seems a semi-metaphorical usage.

9. Note that this problem is not the same as that identified by Prinz (this volume): that "If we naturally avoid something, we don't need a moral rule against it" (p. 379). Prinz's objection to the hypothesis that humans are innately predisposed to morally condemn incest is closely related to an objection that has been leveled many times at Westermarck's claim that the incest taboo is a by-product of an innate aversion—first by Sir James Frazer in 1910. Wolf notes that the "argument has been repeated, mantralike, by Westermarck's many critics" ever since (2005b, p. 5). But in fact Westermarck offered a perfectly cogent rejoinder in *The History of Human Marriage* (1921, volume 2, p. 203ff), which, it seems to me, serves just as convincingly against Prinz as it did against Frazer. Of course there are many instances of natural aversions for which no moral condemnation is necessary (Prinz lists some), but we can equally well think of cases where a natural aversion engages motivation only imperfectly, and where an internalized moral imperative may usefully supplement the aversion. One advantage of moral opposition is that it can be used to *justify* punishment in a way that dislike, or even emotional abhorrence, cannot. See Joyce (2006, chapter 4) for further discussion of this point.

10. This is to be distinguished from what Lieberman calls "the Westermarck hypothesis," which is the claim that childhood association is a trigger for sexual aversion. Nothing I say in this critical response bears on the Westermarck hypothesis.

Debra Lieberman

Response to Joyce

Joyce's commentary raises two issues I shall address: (1) the way I have operationalized "moral" and (2) the use of the term "sentiment" versus "emotion." In my original target paper, I equated moral sentiments with reactions to third-party behavior yet did not adequately define what I meant by "third party." By "third party," I meant the behaviors of others, that is, all nonself behavior. However, this does not distinguish between the actions of others that are directed toward oneself (e.g., another cheating you in a social exchange) and the actions of others that are not (e.g., another cheating a stranger in a social exchange). Whereas the term "third party" is typically used to describe the latter, I have used it to encompass both. I should have been more careful in my use of the term, since I do mean to include the actions of others that are directed toward oneself as well as toward others. For this reason I have updated my target article to specify what I mean by "third party." However, as Joyce correctly points out, I have not included in my working definition of "moral" reactions to one's own behavior. We do assess our own behaviors—specifically, the consequences of our actions on others (e.g., whether we have delivered a benefit to or imposed a cost on another). I am less concerned with which behaviors (self or nonself) *can* be categorized as "moral" than with the structure of our evolved adaptations for the social world. I am happy to leave the categorization process to the philosophers.

My goal in this chapter was to take a step back and pose the question of why we care about the behavior of others at all. One could imagine a species that looked like humans yet did not care one iota about how others behaved and the consequences of others' actions. A reasonable question, then, is what causal pathway(s) led to the evolution of circuitry for caring about the behavior of others? An evolutionary analysis suggests that sentiments regarding others' behaviors can be either adaptations, by-products of adaptations, or noise. The bulk of my chapter aimed to demonstrate that reactions to a specific subset of others' behavior, third-party sibling incest, are, in part, a by-product of evolved adaptations for avoiding sexual relations with one's own opposite-sex siblings. That is, the intensity of disgust and moral disapproval regarding third-party sibling sexual behavior is a reflection of the intensity of disgust generated at the thought of engaging in sexual relations with one's own sibling.

While the approval or disapproval of some third-party behaviors may be by-products of adaptations guiding our own behavior, there are likely to exist psychological *adaptations* for evaluating the behavior of others in the social environment and promoting those behaviors that conferred fitness advantages while preventing/deterring those that imposed fitness costs. As stated above, the behavior of others can affect one's fitness directly (e.g., being cuckolded, physically harmed, or cheated) or indirectly by aiding or, conversely, harming individuals in one's social network (e.g., someone might come to the aid of a family member or physically injure a close friend). The costs and benefits of others' actions range along a continuum with those behaviors at the extremes (e.g., high benefit: someone saving a family member from drowning; high cost: someone killing a family member) likely to motivate high levels of praise (positive reinforcement) or punishment (negative reinforcement) accordingly. Where one draws the line along the continuum to categorize actions as either immoral or praiseworthy may reflect, among other things, the amplitude of the costs and benefits associated with particular acts. That is, the threshold at which something becomes intuitively "morally bad" (thus motivating punishment) most likely has to do with many factors, including the costs imposed on oneself, one's family, one's network of friends and exchange partners as well as one's group. On the opposite side of the coin, the threshold at which a behavior becomes intuitively "morally right" (thus motivating reward) most likely has to do with many factors including the level of benefits conferred upon oneself, one's family, one's network of friends and exchange partners as well as one's group.

This is very much a bottom-up approach and does not start with linguistic or intuitive categories (though, of course, these can be helpful in defining the scope of inquiry). The investigation of human psychology should not necessarily hinge on our linguistic terminology. Linguistic terms, though they capture much about our psychology, can blur important distinctions (e.g., kin terms can include "genetic" and "fictive" kin, a distinction that mattered in the evolution of systems for inbreeding avoidance and kin-directed altruism). A more fruitful approach may be to start with first principles, that is, a consideration of the structure of ancestral environments, what adaptive problems may have existed, and what a well-designed system would look like to solve the specific adaptive problem at hand. Since ancestral environments consisted of individuals who could have significantly impacted one's inclusive fitness, the adaptive problem posed is how to prevent significant costs and, where possible, promote benefits. What would a system look like that evaluated others' behaviors for their likely costs and benefits and motivated an appropriate response according to the effect on individual fitness? I would argue that the description that results captures, at least in part, what is meant intuitively by "morality." Perhaps another segment includes a description of systems for evaluating the consequences of one's own behaviors on others (e.g., the benefits bestowed or the costs imposed). The main point is that an analysis of the adaptive problems and the structure of the information-processing procedures that would have solved these problems can be a useful guide for exploring social behavior.

With respect to Joyce's comment regarding the use of the term "sentiment" versus "emotion," it should be clear that the framework I am employing is more concerned about the rich description of the information-processing procedures than what they are called. Ultimately, it is all information-processing; labeling a particular feature "cognition" versus "emotion" or "emotion" versus "sentiment" is a distinction that disappears at the computational level. Thus, in this regard, the issue is entirely semantic.

Response to Wolf

In the commentary by Wolf, he states that my argument lacks two things: (1) an account of what it means to call a behavior "moral" and (2) an account of how sexual aversions toward one's own kin leads to disapproval of others for sexual interest in their own kin. Most of Wolf's first comment has already been addressed above, and I agree with him that selfish behavior is indeed categorized as immoral. My being selfish (e.g., not sharing food with you) does indeed affect you by withholding a benefit. The greater the benefit I withhold, the more immoral. Regarding Wolf's second point, he states that it is not adequate to claim that reactions to third-party incest are simply by-products of adaptations for inbreeding avoidance. He's entirely correct. I've not just claimed it to be so; I have discussed empirical evidence that it may actually be so.

What is puzzling is that though Wolf is not satisfied with my solution to how personal aversions turn into moral disapproval, he restates almost exactly the same by-product hypothesis I made in my target article. Specifically, he claims that third-party sibling incest "brings the possibility of such relations forcibly to mind, turns a comfortable indifference into a painful aversion, and thereby motivates disapproval" (p. 193). I completely agree, except I would argue it is not painful, but disgusting (my father making a sexual advance elicits an intense eeeew, not ouch!). Third-party incest trips the same mechanisms that govern sex with one's own kin, thereby activating a disgust that, instead of being directed toward one's own family member, is applied to the third-party incestuous behavior in the form of disapproval. So, it appears we agree on this but perhaps disagree on what the word "moral" means, which to me is a less interesting problem.

Final Words

In closing, despite some semantic issues my commentators address, I believe we agree on the important issue: there are a number of interesting questions that have yet to be answered regarding incest regulations, inbreeding avoidance mechanisms, and morality in general. Future investigations that take seriously a computational theory of mind and privilege first principles as starting points (i.e., a consideration of the causal processes that bring complex behaviors into existence), rather than relying solely on past formulations, will continue to make important contributions in these domains.

4 Kindness, Fidelity, and Other Sexually Selected Virtues

Geoffrey Miller

Sexual Selection for Moral Virtues

Human good turns out to be the activity of the soul exhibiting excellence.
—Aristotle (*Nichomachean Ethics*, 350 B.C.)

We feel lust for other people's bodies, but we fall in love with their mental and moral traits. Many sexually attractive facial and bodily traits evolved to reveal phenotypic condition and genetic quality, including health, fertility, and longevity (Fink & Penton-Voak, 2002; Henderson & Anglin, 2003; Langlois, Kalakanis, Rubinstein, Larson, Hallam, & Smooth, 2000). This paper explores the possibility that our distinctively human moral traits evolved through sexual selection to serve an analogous display function. The most romantically attractive mental traits—intelligence, wisdom, kindness, bravery, honesty, integrity, and fidelity—often have a moral or quasi-moral status.

Recent empirical research suggests that many of these moral traits are sexually attractive and can serve as mental fitness indicators: they reliably reveal good mental health, good brain efficiency, good genetic quality, and good capacity for sustaining cooperative sexual relationships and investing in children (e.g., Alvard & Gillespie, 2004; Hawkes & Bird, 2002). Thus, the moral virtues that we consider sexually attractive are not culturally or evolutionarily arbitrary. Rather, they evolved to advertise one's individual fitness in hard-to-fake ways that can be understood through a combination of sexual selection theory (Andersson, 1994) and costly signaling theory (Zahavi & Zahavi, 1997).

This paper develops a theory that sexual selection shaped many of our distinctively human moral virtues as reliable fitness indicators. It updates and builds upon chapter 7 ("Virtues of Good Breeding") in my book *The Mating Mind* (Miller, 2000a) and emphasizes relevant empirical and theoretical work since 2000. It tries to integrate person perception research with person-level approaches to moral philosophy, especially virtue ethics (Flanagan, 1991; Hursthouse, 1999; Pence, 1984; Stohr & Wellman, 2002) and naturalistic approaches to understanding moral intuitions (e.g., Nesse, 2001; Ridley, 1996).

The paper has twelve sections. First, it introduces the idea of sexual selection for moral virtues by considering the role of morality and romantic virtues in human courtship. Second, it emphasizes that this sexual selection model does not imply that morality is illusory, superficial, or covertly sexual. Third, it considers moral judgments of whole persons rather than isolated behavioral acts, in the general context of person perception, social attribution, and mate choice; this usefully blurs the distinction between "moral" virtues and other sexually attractive virtues such as intelligence, creativity, humor, charisma, bravery, mental health, physical health, strength, fertility, and beauty. Fourth, it reviews new "costly signaling" and "fitness indicator" models of sexual selection for "good genes" and "good parents" in relation to human altruism. Fifth, it explains how sexual selection in a socially monogamous species such as ours, with mutual mate choice, can result in minimal sex differences in the moral virtues. Sixth, it examines which specific moral virtues seem best explained by sexual selection. Seventh, it reviews evidence that the moral virtues really are sexually attractive to both sexes across many cultures. Eighth, it reviews behavior genetics evidence that the moral virtues and vices remain genetically heritable in our species, providing a continuing incentive for mate choice. Ninth, it examines moral and quasi-moral traits from the perspective of psychological research on individual differences in intelligence, personality, and psychopathology. Tenth, it considers how sexual selection may have interacted with other selection pressures (kinship, reciprocity, group selection, and equilibrium selection) to shape moral virtues. Eleventh, it identifies twenty testable empirical ways to assess whether particular moral virtues evolved through sexual selection, and it illustrates how to apply these assessments in the case of one specific virtue, sexual fidelity. Finally, this paper considers this theory's sobering implications for the practice of normative ethics by philosophers (i.e., sexually mature human males and females whose moral intuitions have been shaped by millennia of sexual selection).

Romantic Virtues and Moral Virtues

This sexual selection theory of moral virtues may appear bizarre at first to moral philosophers and moral psychologists. From Saint Augustine through

Sigmund Freud, sexuality has been viewed as morality's nemesis. It was hard to imagine that virtues might arise through mate choice when Western thought was gripped by the traditional dichotomies of body versus spirit, lust versus virtue, and sinners versus saints. Also, most philosophers after Aristotle have focused on evaluating the morality of isolated acts rather than the moral virtues of whole people. This made it hard to view ethics as a branch of person-perception or individual-differences psychology. Even within evolutionary theories of morality, moral capacities have traditionally been seen as pragmatic tools to increase individual or group survival prospects rather than as costly, conspicuous signals to increase individual reproductive prospects.

To overcome these intellectual biases, it may help to take a step back and think about moral virtues in the context of real human mate choice. Apart from physical appearance and social status, which traits most excite our romantic impulses? People often fall in love based on (unconscious) assessments of each other's generosity, kindness, honesty, courage, social sensitivity, political idealism, intellectual integrity, empathy to children, respectfulness to parents, or loyalty to friends. The most romantic personal traits are often those that have been considered praiseworthy moral virtues by the world's most influential philosophical and religious traditions from ancient Greece, Israel, Arabia, India, China, and Japan. These lovable virtues overlap almost entirely with a combination of Nietzsche's (1887/1967, 1888/1968) "pagan virtues" (e.g., leadership, bravery, strength, skill, health, fertility, beauty, tolerance, joy, humor, and grace) and the traditional "Christian virtues" (e.g., faith, hope, charity, love, kindness, fairness, equality, humility, and conscience).

Moral virtues are, among other things, personal traits that we are proud to display during courtship. Indeed, courtship in most cultures can be viewed as a ritualized test of diverse moral virtues, such as kindness in gift giving and food sharing, conscientiousness in keeping dates and promises, empathy in talking and listening, and sexual self-control. Courtship is a moral obstacle course that we set up for each other, in which we test each others' generosity, sympathy, patience, fidelity, honesty, and etiquette. For courtship to be reliable, valid, and discriminating as a moral test, it must lead to a perceivable range of moral failures (e.g., broken promises, revealed prejudices, irritabilities, infidelities, impatient sexual pressures) that reflect an underlying distribution of stable moral character traits.

In prototypical romance stories across cultures, both characters fall in love, enjoy bliss, get lazy, make some moral errors, have a moral crisis, recognize their moral failures, resolve to improve their moral character, magnanimously forgive each other, and live happily ever after. It is not romantic for characters to make and forgive purely perceptual failures (e.g., failures of depth perception or color constancy) or purely cognitive failures (e.g., base rate neglect or hindsight bias). If neither individual in a sexual relationship cares about projecting moral virtues (as in relations between prostitutes and clients, masters and slaves, or presidents and interns), then the relationship is considered superficial and unloving.

Our romantic emotions seem to amplify the subjectively perceived variance in moral character across potential lovers. When we fall in love, new lovers seem morally exemplary; when they make moral errors, they seem morally treacherous; when they make amends, they seem morally redeemed; when they divorce us, they seem morally repulsive. Borderline personality disorder (the tendency to view intimate partners in unstable, dichotomized ways, as extremely good or extremely evil—see Koenigsberg, Harvey, Mitropoulou, Schmeidler, New, et al., 2002) is just an exaggerated form of the normal human tendency to alternately overvalue and undervalue our lovers' virtues.

Conversely, moral vices are character flaws that we would be embarrassed to reveal to potential mates. These sexually embarrassing vices include not just obviously antisocial behaviors (killing, raping, lying, cheating) but also victimless addictions (sloth, gluttony, greed, envy, pride, drinking, smoking, drug taking, gambling, masturbating), failures of prosocial magnanimity (undertipping waiters, ignoring starving children, fleeing combat), and acts of symbolic meanness (kicking dogs, burning flags, cursing the gods). The common denominator in these moral vices is that they lead potential mates to hold our moral character in lower esteem, so they are less likely to breed with us. Across cultures, the leading causes of divorce (infidelity, abuse, addiction, unemployment—see Betzig, 1989) are almost all seen as serious moral failures. To many moral psychologists and philosophers, the sexual costs of moral vice may seem tangential to an evolutionary account of human morality. Yet to evolutionary biologists, a direct connection between moral vice and impaired reproductive success should be highly suggestive.

Sexually Selected Functions versus Sexual Motivations

To suggest that human moral virtues evolved through mate choice is not to suggest that morality is "really all about getting laid" at the level of individual motivation. Evolutionary functions must not be confused with proximate motivations (Richards, 2000). Just as sexual selection can produce genuinely beautiful peacock tails and genuinely creative nightingale songs, it can produce genuine psychological altruism, not just fake generosity as a seduction tactic (Miller, 2000a). Most sexually selected adaptations do not include a little copy of their adaptive function inside themselves as a secret libidinous motive. Male beards and female breasts have no doubt been shaped by mate choice (Barber, 1995), but neither beards nor breasts need to contain any subconscious sex drive to remind them that they are supposed to be attractive.

Why does this distinction between adaptive functions and subjective motives seem so clear when we think about beards and breasts but so fuzzy when we think about moral behavior? Perhaps one reason is that we have evolved a high degree of wariness about being sexually exploited. Some people are sexually predatory and consciously produce behaviors that they know will be sexually attractive just to seduce us (Mealey, 1995; Wilson, Near, & Miller, 1996). If such a person admits that their apparently moral behavior was just aimed at fornication, we rightly get upset and worry that they are a Machiavellian psychopath. Some overgeneralize this response to stigmatize any evolutionary psychologists who try to identify any repro- ductive benefits for any form of altruism.

Evaluating Moral Persons versus Moral Acts

This paper considers moral judgments and moral virtues at a level of description that is still fairly unusual in moral philosophy—the level of whole persons, not isolated behavioral acts. It argues that much of human morality emerged through the co-evolution of our moral virtues as person-ality-type dispositions, and our social-cognitive adaptations for judging those moral virtues in others. This moral-person level of description is the domain of mate choice in evolutionary psychology, person perception in social psychology, virtue ethics in moral philosophy, parole decisions in criminal justice, and voter choice of political leaders in democratic elections. By contrast, the moral-act level of description is the domain of adaptive decision making in evolutionary psychology, social attribution in social psychology, act ethics in moral psychology, and guilt-or-innocence decisions in criminal law.

On this account, we rarely made moral judgments about isolated behav- ioral acts in prehistory. Rather, we made a hierarchy of inferences—about moral personality traits (virtues or vices) from behavioral acts, and about the ethical merit of whole persons from estimates of their moral personal-ity traits. This is because we had to choose whether, when, and how to interact with a particular person as a whole package of morally valenced personality traits. They could be favorite offspring or black sheep, friend or enemy, lover or ex-lover. We could not pick and choose our social interactions trait by trait.

Also, individuals' actions were probably assessed against the background of their age, sex, health, fitness, personality, intelligence, and other individual-differences dimensions, which jointly determine our expectations about their likely moral capacities. For example, we tolerate theft by toddlers more than theft by adults. We forgive unkind words spoken during high fevers by the sick. We do not expect a keenly empathic theory of mind in the severely brain-damaged or autistic.

Further, individuals' actions were probably assessed in the context of their actual social, sexual, tribal, and/or genetic relationships to us. Different social-interaction domains called for different moral-judgment criteria, focused on different virtues. In mate choice, we may give great weight to the virtues of intelligence, kindness, fidelity, and honesty, plus a few romantic virtues such as beauty, youth, and humor. By contrast, in kin altruism, we may give higher weight to the kinship-specific virtues of genetic similarity and expected future reproductive success, while caring little about kindness, gentleness, or honesty. This is why mothers can love psychopathic sons, and why fathers can love the selfish, screaming semiclones called babies. It is mainly in the domain of social reciprocity with unrelated acquaintances that we see the sort of tit-for-tat moral accounting that corresponds to the traditional moral philosopher's emphasis on the moral evaluation of isolated behavioral acts.

The moral-person level of description is different in some key respects from the moral-act level of description. First, we generally accept as a conversational implicature that "ought implies can" when we judge moral acts (Sinnott-Armstrong, 1984), but we do not necessarily follow this implicature in judging the morality of whole persons. That is, we typically do not expect someone to follow a normative moral principle (an "ought") in a particular behavioral instance if they cannot, due to some overwhelming external or internal constraint. We don't expect quadriplegics to jump in front of trolleys to save children, or crack addicts to vote conscientiously. However, when judging the morality of whole persons in real sociosexual relationships, we are rarely so forgiving. If a potential mate has Tourette's syndrome and can't refrain from screaming "Crack-head slut!" repeatedly in public during a first date, there is unlikely to be a second date, no matter how much we understand about verbal disinhibition in neurological disorders. If a potential hunting partner had a severe head injury that renders him too clumsy to hunt effectively, we may pity him but will still exclude him from the hunt. When the fitness stakes are high, as in real sociosexual relationships, we hold people morally accountable even for faults that are not their own. If we did not, then we would be logically incapable of shunning even serial-rapist psychopaths, who, after all, must be a joint product of their genes, environment, and random developmental events (Dennett, 2003; Pinker, 2002).

Second, "morality" means something different at the person level compared to the act level. A moral act may be one that obeys some rationally defensible, universalizable, deontic or consequentialist principle. However, a moral person, from the point of view of a standard prehistoric hunter-gatherer, is someone who embodies prosocial virtues that make him or her a good mate, friend, relative, or trading partner. In economic terms, a moral person is one whose individual behavior brings "positive externalities" to their social relationships. In game-theory terms, a moral person is simply one who attaches positive utility to the welfare of others, such that they tend to play Pareto-dominant equilibria in mixed-motive games. In evolutionary terms, a moral person is one who pursues his or her ultimate genetic self-interest through psychological adaptations that embody a genuine, proximate concern for others (de Waal, 1996; Nesse, 2001). All three of these working definitions are descriptive rather than normative. They are each open to quantitative, empirical verification by measuring the net positive externalities, Pareto dominance, or proximate empathy levels manifested by individuals in real social interactions.

Costly Signaling Theory, Fitness Indicators, and Moral Virtues

Since about 1990, new theories concerning "costly signaling" have revolutionized the study of both sexual selection and human altruism (Gintis, Smith, & Bowles, 2001; McAndrew, 2002). Most animal communication is relentlessly narcissistic, advertising the signaler's own individual species, sex, age, health, fertility, social status, phenotypic condition, and/or genetic quality (Bradbury & Vehrencamp, 1998). Only rarely do animals communicate any referential information about the external world. The trouble with self-referential signals is that often, animals have incentives to lie about themselves, in order to attract more mates, solicit more parental investment, or deter predators and rivals. Why should animals ever believe any self-referential signals produced by other animals?

Costly signaling theory offers a solution: if a signal is so costly that only high-health, high-status, high-condition animals can afford to produce it, the signal can remain evolutionarily reliable (Zahavi & Zahavi, 1997).

Almost any sort of fitness-related cost will work: matter, energy, time, or risk. For example, a peacock's tail is burdensome in all four senses: its growth and maintenance requires several hundred grams of mass, many calories, much time to grow, and much risk (it is harder to escape from peacock-eating tigers). Very often, the most complex, elaborate, and puzzling signals observed in nature are the result of sexual selection through mate choice (Darwin, 1871/2004). These sexual ornaments almost always impose high costs on the bearer, guaranteeing their reliability as indicators of condition and fitness.

This paper argues that many human virtues evolved through sexual selection as costly signals, as fitness indicators. This hypothesis has been advanced by a few previous researchers (e.g., Hawkes, 1991; Tessman, 1995), and its empirical testing has been one of the most active areas of evolutionary psychology and evolutionary anthropology in the last few years. Indeed, many prosocial behaviors that were assumed to arise through kinship or reciprocity are now thought to have emerged as costly signals of individual fitness, favored by social and sexual selection.

For example, it was often assumed that risky big-game hunting evolved because the best hunters could better feed their own offspring (Lee & DeVore, 1968). However, most hunted meat from big game is distributed too widely in hunter-gatherer clans for this paternal provisioning theory to work. Rather, recent research suggests that the most successful hunters are willing to provide the prosocial "public good" of hunted meat because they attract more high-quality female mates (Alvard & Gillespie, 2004; Hawkes & Bird, 2002; Smith & Bird, 2000).

Costly signaling theory has intellectual roots in many traditions and academic fields, some of which explicitly applied it to explain human morality. In the Hasidei Ashkenaz movement of thirteenth-century German Judaism, more difficult moral acts (e.g., charity when one is poor, forgiveness when one is righteously angry) were considered more praiseworthy. In Friedrich Nietzsche's (1887/1967) *On the Genealogy of Morals*, pagan virtues were considered attractive signals of health and power. In Thorstein Veblen's *The Theory of the Leisure Class* (1899/1994), conspicuous consumption and conspicuous charity were seen as hard-to-fake signals of wealth and social status. In mid-twentieth-century economics, corporate advertising was interpreted as a costly, conspicuous signal of market power to competitors and of corporate profitability to investors, rather than just a way to entice consumer purchases (Dorfman & Steiner, 1954). In 1970s biology, Amotz Zahavi (1975) viewed many animal traits and signals as hard-to-fake indicators of animal fitness.

Our mate preferences for moral virtues may be explained by costly signaling theory. If a young woman places a single's ad stating "SHF, 26, seeks kind, generous, romantic, honest man," we can translate this in evolutionary terms as "single Hispanic female, 26, seeks a healthy male of breeding age with a minimal number of personality disorders that would impair efficient coordination and parenting in a sustained sexual relationship, and a minimal number of deleterious mutations on the thousands of genes that influence the development of brain systems for costly, conspicuous, altruistic displays of moral virtue." Of course, the single's ad itself is not the costly signal—it is cheap and easy to fake. Rather, the ad identifies some desired moral virtues that would be hard to fake consistently during a lengthy courtship.

Sexually selected costly signals typically advertise two classes of traits: good genes or good parenting abilities (Iwasa & Pomiankowski, 1999; Kokko, Brooks, McNamara, & Houston, 2002). Different moral virtues might advertise one or the other or both. Good-genes indicators advertise general "genetic quality," which probably reflects having a low "mutation load" (Eyre-Walker & Keightley, 1999; Ridley, 2001). By favoring mates with a lower-than-average number of harmful mutations, sexually reproducing organisms can increase the expected survival and reproductive prospects of their offspring—even if their mate contributes nothing as a parent after fertilization (Houle & Kondrashov, 2002). Moral virtues may function as good-genes indicators by being difficult to display impressively if one has a high mutation load that impairs the precision of body and brain development. For example, displaying a sophisticated, empathetic social intelligence requires the development of a complex theory of mind, which might be easily disrupted by a variety of mutations associated with autism, schizophrenia, mental retardation, social anxiety, and language impairments (Baron-Cohen, 2000). Thus, a conspicuously expert level of empathy may function as a sort of neurogenetic warranty.

By contrast, good-parent indicators advertise phenotypic traits that help care for offspring, such as feeding them, grooming them to remove parasites, protecting them from predators, resolving sibling rivalries, and teaching life skills through play and practice (Hoelzer, 1989; Iwasa & Pomiankowski, 1999). Thus, a conspicuously empathic personality may also function as a good-parent warranty, guaranteeing the likely patience, kindness, protectiveness, playfulness, and conscientiousness that helps children thrive.

Sexual Selection without Large Sex Differences

In most of the other 4,600+ mammalian species, sexual selection acts much more strongly on males than on females, since females do almost all of the parental care, so have incentives to be much choosier about their mates than males are (Andersson, 1994). Humans are unusual in having evolved a mating/parenting system of intensive offspring care by both mothers and fathers (Geary, 2000; Kaplan, Hill, Lancaster, & Hurtado, 2000), which favors social monogamy (at least medium-term pair-bonded relationships with expectations of sexual fidelity). This, in turn, can favor mutual mate choice by both males and females (Kokko & Johnstone, 2002; Miller, 2000a). Of course, males are not very choosy about short-term sexual partners, but become as choosy as females about committing to long-term serious relationships likely to produce children (Kenrick, Sadalla, Groth, & Trost, 1990). Thus, human mate choice is mutual, with both males and females choosing carefully when forming the long-term partnerships most likely to result in reproduction.

Sexual selection is not restricted to explaining sex differences; it can also explain sexual similarities in extravagant traits when mutual mate choice is at work (Miller, 2000a). These mutually-selected traits usually show at least some of the following criteria: (1) large differences even between closely related species (e.g., humans vs. other great apes), (2) full maturation only after puberty, (3) sexual attractiveness to both sexes, during at least some phases of mate choice, and (4) cultural embellishment through body ornamentation (for physical traits) or skill learning (for mental traits). The human morphological traits that evolved through mutual mate choice probably include long head hair, relatively hairless bodies, everted lips, and visible white scleras around the iris of the eye (Barber, 1995). The mutually selected human mental traits that show very low average sex differences include general intelligence, cognitive abilities for language, art, music, humor, and ideology, and many moral virtues (Miller, 2000a).

Thus, a sexual selection account of moral virtues absolutely does not imply that males evolve all the conspicuous virtues and females play the passive role of virtue assessment (cf. Darwin, 1871/2004). Rather, it implies that both sexes evolved the complementary adaptations for morality: moral virtues that tend to be displayed selectively in high-payoff social and sexual contexts, and person-perception mechanisms for judging the moral virtues of others.

Although this sexual selection model does not predict uniformly large sex differences across all moral virtues, it does predict some specific sex differences that cannot be explained by other models. Human males face higher variance and skew in reproductive success, so are predicted to allocate more energy, time, and risk to mating effort, including costly, dangerous, public displays of moral virtue. For example, this model naturally explains why males are overrepresented among prosocial heroes who risk their lives to save unrelated strangers (Farthing, 2005; Johnson, 1996), and why males remain overrepresented in high-risk, underpaid, altruistic professions such as the police, fire, rescue, paramedic, and other emergency services.

Which Moral Virtues Can Be Explained by Sexual Selection?

The moral virtues most readily explained by sexual selection are those most clearly manifested in sexual courtship, in long-term sexual relationships, and in child rearing. Courtship generosity is the most obvious class of sexually selected moral behaviors. It has obvious parallels to "courtship feeding" by animals, in which "nuptial gifts" are given by males to females as good-genes indicators and good-parent investments (Vahed, 1998). Human courtship generosity would include altruism, kindness, and sympathy to the sexual partner, to his or her children from previous relationships (one's stepchildren), and to his or her family members (one's in-laws). Since this sort of courtship generosity is directed at nonrelatives and is not expected to be reciprocated, it is hard to explain through kin selection or reciprocal altruism, and it qualifies as evolutionary altruism by traditional definitions.

Courtship generosity may even include much of the paternal effort that is usually assumed to arise through kin selection (where "kin" include "offspring"), since most divorced fathers cut off their paternal investment as soon as they are cut off from sexual access to mothers (Anderson, 2000; Anderson, Kaplan, & Lancaster, 1999; Hofferth & Anderson, 2003). Thus, what looks like unproblematic paternal investment by males for the sake of perpetuating one's genes in one's children may turn out to be better described as ongoing courtship generosity by males in order to maintain sexual access to the mothers of those children.

Other sexually selected moral virtues may include sexual patience, sexual fidelity, and sexual generosity. Sexual patience is the opposite of sexual harassment, sexual stalking, and sexual coercion (rape). If a potential male mate shows a virtuous degree of sexual self-restraint throughout a long courtship period, this is valuable for several reasons. It does not compromise a woman's power of mate choice, which is the foundation of sexual selection. It reliably signals that the mate is not just looking for an opportunistic short-term affair, but would value a longer term committed relationship. It also signals that the mate is not a sexually predatory psychopath, and reveals efficient frontal-lobe control over limbic impulses.

Similarly, sexual fidelity is valuable for both practical and signaling reasons. Practically, fidelity minimizes the spread of sexually transmissible pathogens, the risk of cuckoldry (a male investing in offspring that were sired by another male), and the costs of polygyny (a female losing investment in her own children if a male sires children by another female). Sexual fidelity also carries much the same signaling power as sexual patience: attractive partners who remain faithful despite credible opportunities for extra-pair copulation are revealing that they expect the long-term relationship with one another to yield higher net fitness benefits than a series of short-term flings with others. That is, they treasure, value, and love one another above all others and have the self-control to remember that even in the face of temptation. Along these lines, although males are attracted to promiscuous females as potential short-term mates (Oliver & Sedikides, 1992; Schmitt, Couden, & Baker, 2001), neither sex respects high levels of promiscuity in potential long-term mates (Marks & Fraley, 2005; Milhausen & Herold, 1999; O'Sullivan, 1995).

Sexual generosity during foreplay and copulation certainly brings proximate benefits in terms of sexual pleasure, but that begs the ultimate, evolutionary question: why does successful mutual orgasm in humans require such a high degree of attentiveness, sympathy, communication, mind-reading, and previous experience with a particular partner? Other great apes, such as chimpanzees and bonobos, of both sexes, appear to reach orgasm without such an investment of time, energy, touch, and mindfulness (Anestis, 2004; Hohmann & Fruth, 2000). Only humans seem to have transformed copulation itself into a moral test of each partner's theory of mind (and theory of body). If orgasms came easily and often to us, they would be useless for discriminating altruistic partners from selfish partners, or good-genes partners from bad-genes partners (Miller, 2000a; Thornhill, Gangestad, & Comer, 1995). Just as human females are choosier early in courtship (in deciding whether to have sex) and human males become choosier later in courtship (in deciding whether to stick around after a bit of sex), female sexual excitement is hard to achieve early in courtship, and male sexual excitement is hard to achieve after the first few years of marriage (Clement, 2002). In each case, humans have apparently evolved an orgasm-resistant brain precisely to test partners' degrees of sexual altruism—that is, their ongoing level of commitment, patience, sympathy, and creativity.

A third class of sexually selected moral virtues may include ideological extremism among young adults, who are near the peak of mating effort. Adolescents and young adults often adopt social, political, and religious views that are more extreme than any they held before puberty, and that become much less extreme in midlife after they settle down into stable monogamy and child rearing (Miller, 1996; Tilley, 2002; Visser & Krosnick, 1998). As young adults age, extreme and idiosyncratic attitudes tend to soften, increasing participation in mainstream elections, organized religions, and nonprofit charities. Conspicuous displays of ideological fervor (e.g., organizing political protests, leading revolutions) may function as reliable personality indicators. Under some oppressive regimes, they may also function as very high-risk heroic altruism indicators, especially among young males at the peak of mating effort. This may explain the moral fervor of the young Akhenaten, Buddha, St. Paul, Muhammed, Martin Luther, Thomas Jefferson, Karl Marx, Vladimir Lenin, Mao Tse-tung, Malcolm X, and Nelson Mandela—who all launched major ideological movements around age 30.

Precursors of many human moral virtues, such as empathy, fairness, and peacemaking, have been found in other great apes (de Waal, 1996, 2000; Preston & de Waal, 2002). My claim is not that sexual selection created our moral virtues from scratch in our species alone, without any primate foundation. Rather, my claim is that sexual selection amplified our standard social primate virtues into uniquely elaborated human forms.

Are the Moral Virtues Really Sexually Attractive?

The two largest cross-cultural studies of mate preferences have been coordinated by David Buss (1989) and David Schmitt (2004a, 2004b). Buss and his collaborators (1989) asked 10,047 people from 37 cultures to rate and rank order the desirability of several traits in a sexual partner. Among the top ten traits most desired by both men and women across almost all cultures were kindness, intelligence, exciting personality, adaptability, creativity, chastity, and beauty. Each of these has at least quasi-moral status in many cultures. Schmitt and collaborators (2004a, 2004b) gathered data on 17,804 people from 62 cultures and found that sexual promiscuity, infidelity, and "mate poaching" were predicted by low agreeableness, low conscientiousness, and high extraversion (Schmitt, 2004a, 2004b). Thus, three of the "Big Five" personality traits (Goldberg, 1990) carry a sexual-morality valence that would be important in mate choice. Also, 49 out of 62 cultures (79%) endorsed a normative ideal of "secure" romantic attachment, as opposed to dismissing, preoccupied, or fearful attachment (Schmitt et al., 2004c). That is, most people in 79% of sampled cultures supported a moral ideal that couples should strive for a stable, low-conflict, high-mutual-valuation relationship. Also, many studies show that single's ads across cultures often advertise and seek moral traits—especially kindness, generosity, honesty, fidelity, and capacity for commitment (e.g., Koziel & Pawlowski, 2003; Oda, 2001). Thus, morality and mate choice are tightly interwoven across human cultures.

In addition to these large-scale cross-cultural studies, research has confirmed that many particular moral virtues are sexually attractive and relationship stabilizing. These include the following:

- Kindness: emotional responsiveness to the needs of others (e.g., Jensen-Campbell, Graziano, & West, 1995; Karney & Bradbury, 1995; Li, Bailey, Kenrick, & Linsenmeier, 2002).
- Empathy: lovingness, affection, fondness, commitment, forgivingness, trust, and perspective taking (e.g., Miller & Rempel, 2004; Wieselquist, Rusbult, Foster, & Agnew, 1999).
- Niceness: emotional stability, conscientiousness, agreeableness, nonirritability, and nonviolence (Bouchard, Lussier, & Sabourin, 1999; Gottman, Coan, Carrere, & Swanson, 1998; Herold & Milhausen, 1999; Shackelford & Buss, 2000; Urbaniak & Kilman, 2003).
- Honesty (e.g., DePaulo & Kashy, 1998; Haselton, Buss, Oubaid, & Angleitner, 2005; Shackelford & Buss, 1996; Williams, 2001).
- Generosity to partner, children, and strangers (e.g., Buss & Schmitt, 1993; Goldberg, 1995).
- Capacity for self-control, self-respect, and self-disclosure (e.g., Byers & Demmons, 1999; Finkel & Campbell, 2001).
- Heroism (e.g., Farthing, 2005; Johnson, 1996; Kelly & Dunbar, 2001).

Of course, these moral-virtue preferences are typically stronger when seeking a serious long-term partner than a short-term lover (Herold & Milhausen, 1999; Scheib, 2001; Urbaniak & Kilman, 2003).

Apart from the sexual attractiveness of moral virtues, sexual competition seems to explain the evolution of many specific moral vices and antisocial behaviors. For example, most male violence, homicide, and warfare seem to reflect direct sexual competition for mates, for mating-relevant resources, and for mate-attracting social status (Daly & Wilson, 1988; Ellis, 2001; Summers, 2005). This probably explains the dramatic sex differences in aggressive risk-taking across many domains (Byrnes, Miller, & Schafer, 1999) and the high rates of violence perpetrated by young males at peak mating effort across cultures (Daly & Wilson, 2001; Wrangham & Peterson, 1996). In males, testosterone seems important in organizing and activating these intrasexual competition adaptations, including aggressiveness, sensation seeking, risk seeking, and sexual motivation (Aluja & Garcia, 2005; Harris, Rushton, Hampson, & Jackson, 1996). Thus, testosterone could be construed as an "antivirtue hormone" in some sense. Over the longer term, many forms of intimate cruelty, such as derogating, abusing, and beating sexual partners, can be seen as "mate retention tactics" (Buss & Shackelford, 1997). Thus, sexual selection seems to explain not only the attractive, prosocial virtues (mostly through intersexual mate choice) but also the antisocial vices (mostly through intrasexual competition).

An apparent inconsistency arises: does human female choice really favor niceness or dominance, lovers or fighters, dads or cads? It seems to depend on the relationship context, the male's sexual strategy, and the male's other traits. Males who are low on "sociosexuality" (interest in multiple short-term matings) tend to project a "nice guy" image that is attractive for committed long-term relationships (Simpson, Gangestad, Christensen, & Leck, 1999). Male dominance is especially attractive when combined with a prosocial demeanor (Jensen-Campbell et al., 1995). Women seeking a long-term mate are more attracted to niceness, whereas women seeking a short-term mate are more attracted to physical appearance (Urbaniak & Kilman, 2003). By contrast, women at peak fertility, midcycle, when they would gain the greatest benefits from short-term good-genes mate choice, tend to prefer dominance to niceness (Gangestad, Simpson, Cousins, Garver-Apgar, & Christensen, 2004). As in other species, adaptive female choice requires an extraordinary sensitivity to the costs versus benefits of male dominance and aggressiveness—which can increase male intrasexual competitive ability and short-term sexiness, but which also predict a male's likelihood of using sexual coercion (Cristopher, Owens, & Stecker, 1993).

Are the Moral Virtues Really Heritable?

If the moral virtues are favored as good-genes indicators, and if they are heritable, then sexual selection should favor them and increase their frequency in the population. Yet, if the virtues are driven to fixation (100% genetic prevalence) in the population, then there would no longer be any heritable variation in virtues, so the incentives for good-genes mate choice would evaporate. Thus, we might expect good-genes mate choice to cannibalize the heritability of the traits that it favors. Is this a big problem for my model?

Actually, this is a special case of what biologists call the "lek paradox": the puzzling fact that sexual ornaments remain conspicuously variable and heritable even when females choose males in large courtship-display congregations called "leks," in which good-genes sexual selection is very strong. Biologists used to worry a lot more about the lek paradox, but they think there are some pretty good solutions now. For example, sexual ornaments may remain heritable because they are enormously complex and depend on many, many genes; sexual selection is constantly removing harmful mutations that have arisen in some of these genes, but new mutations are constantly arising in other genes (Rowe & Houle, 1996; Tomkins, Radwan, Kotiaho, & Tregenza, 2004). This mutation-selection balance maintains a large number of harmful mutations at equilibrium, on average. Yet it also tends to maintain a large variance in mutation load across individuals, and this is what keeps sexual ornaments heritable—why not all peacocks have equally spectacular tails, and why not all humans are equally virtuous.

This mutation-selection resolution of the lek paradox may sound fine in theory, but is there any evidence that the moral virtues are heritable in our species? There is much more behavior genetics work on the vices than on the virtues. Over 50 studies report substantial heritability for various forms of antisocial behavior and its personality correlates, such as psychopathy, sensation seeking, and disagreeableness (e.g., Agrawal, Jacobson, Prescott, & Kendler, 2004; Eley, Lichtenstein, & Moffitt, 2003; Jang, McCrae, Angleitner, Riemann, & Livesley, 1998; Krueger, Hicks, & McGue, 2001; Rhee & Waldman, 2002; Taylor, Loney, Bobadilla, Iacono, & McGue, 2003).

The heritability of prosocial virtues has been less well studied. Moderate heritability for altruism, empathy, nurturance, and/or responsibility has been found in a few twin studies (e.g., Beatty, Heisel, Hall, Levine, & La France, 2002; Davis, Luce, & Kraus, 1994; Zahnwaxler, Emde, & Robinson, 1992). For example, Rushton (2004) recently found moderate heritability for altruism, empathy, nurturance, and responsibility in 322 twin pairs. Several other morally relevant traits are known to be heritable, including social attitudes (e.g., conservatism, authoritarianism) and religiosity (e.g., D'Onofrio, Eaves, Murrelle, Maes, & Spilka, 1999; Koenig et al., 2005; McCourt, Bouchard, Lykken, Tellegen, & Keyes, 1999; Olson, Vernon, Harris, & Jang, 2001).

The general message from behavior genetics is that virtually every reliably measurable human behavioral trait shows a heritability of about .50, plus or minus .20 (Bouchard & McGue, 2003; Plomin, DeFries, McClearn, & McGuffin, 2001). We should not be surprised that the moral virtues fit this pattern, so there are continuing evolutionary incentives for good-genes mate choice based on moral virtues displayed in courtship.

Moral and Quasi-Moral Traits in Individual-Differences Psychology

The best studied individual differences dimensions in psychology—intelligence, personality traits, and psychopathologies—all have moral or quasi-moral status when they are assessed in social and sexual interaction. That is, the most important individual-differences dimensions are morally valenced, and their morally praiseworthy extremes increase sexual attractiveness.

Cognitive Traits

Intelligence (in the sense of general cognitive ability, the g factor, or IQ) is a morally valenced concept, which is why it has been so controversial throughout a century of psychometrics. In every domain of life, smart is good, and stupid is bad. This is not just because intelligence predicts objective performance and learning ability across all important life domains that show reliable individual differences (Jensen, 1998; Deary, 2000). It is also because having higher intelligence predicts many behaviors that we consider morally virtuous, such as being emotionally sensitive to the needs of others (Schulte, Ree, & Carretta, 2004), being an effective group leader (Judge, Colbert, & Ilies, 2004), working conscientiously (Gottfredson, 1997; Kuncel, Hezlett, & Ones, 2004; Lynn & Vanhanen, 2001), staying healthy through exercise and diet (Gottfredson, 2004; Gottfredson & Deary, 2004), and staying happily married (Gottfredson, 1997; Jensen, 1998). Conversely, having lower intelligence predicts many behaviors that most people consider morally objectionable, such as murder, rape, assault, alcoholism, drug addiction, absenteeism, child abuse and neglect, passing along sexually transmissible infections, and causing fatal traffic accidents (Gordon, 1997; Gottfredson, 1997; Lubinski & Humphreys, 1997). This may be one reason why intelligence is so attractive when both men and women consider potential long-term partners (Kenrick, Sadalla, Groth, & Trost, 1990; Li et al., 2002; Miller, 2000c).

One might object that intelligence is not really a "moral virtue"; it just happens to predict a wide range of specific moral behaviors. Yet, what is a "moral virtue," if not an individual-differences dimension, a psychological construct, an attributed trait, that predicts a wide range of specific moral behaviors? Moral virtues are socially attributed traits that carry predictive information about morally relevant behaviors. If kindness is a moral virtue because it predicts specific prosocial behaviors and is valued as such, then intelligence must also be a moral virtue—besides being an academic, economic, and epistemological virtue.

Personality Traits

Each of the Big Five personality dimensions (Goldberg, 1990) seems to have a moral valence that is positively correlated with its sexual attractiveness. These traits can be remembered with the acronym "OCEAN": openness to experience, conscientiousness, extraversion, agreeableness, and neuroticism.

Openness to experience implies intelligence, curiosity, tolerance, and broad-mindedness. It predicts emotional sensitivity (Schutte et al., 1998), social tolerance (Dollinger, Leong, & Ulicni, 1996), political liberalism (McCrae, 1996), and support for universalist values—the sort that would be supported by Kant's categorical imperative (Roccas, Sagiv, Schwartz, & Knafo, 2002). People low in openness to experience tend to show unvirtuous traits such as being more prejudiced, racist, sexist, and anthropocentric, and higher on "right-wing authoritarianism" and "social dominance orientation" (Ekehammar, Akrami, Gylie, & Zakrisson, 2004; Heaven & Bucci, 2001; Van Hiel, Mervielde, & De Fruyt, 2004).

Conscientiousness implies fulfilling promises, respecting commitments, and resisting bad habits. It subsumes individual differences in industriousness, self-control, responsibility, and several other virtues (Roberts, Chernyshenko, Stark, & Goldberg, 2005). It predicts emotional maturity (McCrae et al., 1999), romantic lovability in relationships (Engel, Olson, & Patrick, 2002), team cooperation ability (Barrick, Stewart, Neubert, & Mount, 1998), and not killing people by driving safely (Arthur & Graziano, 1996). It also predicts prosocial civic and organizational engagement (Organ & Ryan, 1995; Penner, Dovidio, Piliavin, & Schroeder, 2005) and honesty, integrity, dependability, trustworthiness, and reliability at work (Sackett & Wanek, 1996). Further, conscientiousness positively predicts virtually every health-related behavior that increases longevity, including eating a healthy diet, exercising, and avoiding tobacco, excessive alcohol, addictive drugs, risky sexual behavior, risky driving, and suicide (Bogg & Roberts, 2004). Conscientiousness is also closely related to the capacity for self-control, which is a key virtue. Prefrontal brain damage, as in the famous case of Phineas Gage, tends to reduce conscientiousness and dis-inhibits impulsive antisocial behavior, so it reduces both moral virtue and long-term sexual attractiveness.

Extraversion implies gregariousness, social intelligence, self-esteem, and leadership—some Nietzschean pagan virtues. It predicts prosocial volun-teerism (Carlo et al., 2005) and happiness and optimism (Furnham & Cheng, 1999; Lucas, Diener, Grob, Suh, & Shao, 2000). However, extraver-sion is closely related to social attention seeking (Ashton, Lee, & Paunonen, 2002), so depending on whether virtue or vice attract more attention, extraversion may be associated with prosocial or antisocial behavior.

Agreeableness implies kindness, sympathy, and nonaggressiveness; it predicts benevolence and respect for moral traditions (Roccas et al., 2002), the quality and peacefulness of social relationships (Asendorpf & Wilpers, 1998), and success in jobs requiring teamwork and social interaction (Mount, Barrick, & Stewart, 1998). It is probably the most morally valenced of all the Big Five traits, with conscientiousness a close second.

Emotional stability (the opposite of neuroticism and anxiety) implies dependability, maturity, confidence, self-control, and equanimity. Its strongly predicts happiness (DeNeve & Cooper, 1998), which is sexually attractive. It also predicts marital satisfaction in many studies (e.g., Caughlin, Huston, & Houts, 2000). Emotional stability is also related to the "secure attachment" style that predicts stability, intimacy, and fidelity in sexual relationships (Allen & Baucom, 2004; Bogaert & Sadava, 2002) and that is valued across cultures (Schmitt et al., 2004c).

All of the morally positive, socially desirable ends of the Big Five dimen-sions tend to be valued in mate choice and marital satisfaction (Berry & Miller, 2001; Botwin, Buss, & Shackelford, 1997; Bouchard et al., 1999; Donnellan, Conger, & Bryant, 2004). Mate choice for the Big Five traits may reflect both good-genes and good-parent effects. All of the Big Five are moderately heritable (Plomin et al., 2001). Yet good parenting ability is also positively predicted by openness, conscientiousness, extraversion, agreeableness, and emotional stability (Kochanska, Friesenborg, Lange, & Martel, 2004; Metsapelto & Pulkkinen, 2003; Spinath & O'Connor, 2003).

Psychologists typically avoid morally evaluative labels for personality traits, to avoid mixing descriptive science with normative ethics. However, one can remain perfectly descriptive by stepping back and considering person perception as a morally evaluative function of social cognition: our social-attribution systems tend to attribute moral valences to most person-ality traits when we observe them in other people. Indeed, this is one reason for the runaway success of the Implicit Association Test in recent social cognition research: it reveals the deeply evaluative nature of implicit person perception (Greenwald et al., 2002).

Moral philosophers have lately rediscovered the old social psychology critiques of personality psychology, as in the "person versus situation" debate (Mischel, 1968) and work on the "fundamental attribution error" (Ross, 1977). Social psychology's concern was that apparently stable personality traits may not really exist, but may be projections of a biased social-attribution system. Citing this literature, Gilbert Harman (1999b, 2000b) argued that virtue ethics cannot succeed because social psychology shows there are no stable personality traits that could correspond to virtues. Unfortunately, virtue ethicists have usually responded to Harman's critique with rather weak theoretical arguments (e.g., Merritt, 2000; C. Miller, 2003) rather than by citing the now well-established reliability, validity, stability, and heritability of personality traits (Funder, 2004; Matthews, Deary, & Whiteman, 2003) across cultures and even across species (Gosling, 2001; King, Weiss, & Farmer, 2005). Also, there have been some incisive critiques of situationist research in social psychology (e.g., Andrews, 2001; Sabini, Siepmann, & Stein, 2001) that may undermine some of Harman's grounds for concern.

Psychopathology Traits

All major psychopathologies tend to increase perceived selfishness and to decrease perceived moral virtue, sexual attractiveness, and social status (McGuire, Fawzy, & Spar, 1994; Wakefield, 1999). This seems especially true for the most common and severe psychopathologies, such as psychopathy, major depression, and schizophrenia (Nesse, 2000; Shaner, Miller, & Mintz, 2004; Wilson et al., 1996). Many personality disorders, such as paranoid, narcissistic, and borderline disorders, also predict antisocial behavior (Coid, 2003). Signs of mental illness typically lead to social and sexual rejection by others—that is, to stigmatization through negative social attributions (Corrigan, 2000; Crisp, Gelder, Rix, Meltzer, & Rowlands, 2000). Serious mental illness almost always reduces reproductive success by reducing sexual attractiveness (Avila, Thaker, & Adami, 2001; Haukka, Suvisaari, & Lonnqvist, 2003). The only exception seems to prove the rule: the manic phase of bipolar disorder ("manic-depression") often leads to increased magnaminity, heroism, gift giving, and moral crusading, and also leads to new love affairs, infidelities, promiscuity, and babies (Jamison, 1993; Wilson, 1998).

Religiosity

In most hierarchical, large-scale societies throughout history, religion has provided a cultural framework for the display and evaluation of moral virtues. Yet in all societies, there are conspicuous individual differences in public religiosity (e.g., frequencies of churchgoing, tithe giving, public prayer) and in private faith. Psychology of religion research has shown that, although cultural and family environments determine specific religious affiliations, beliefs, and rituals, religiosity as an individual-differences trait shows moderate heritability that increases through adolescence to adulthood (D'Onofrio et al., 1999; Koenig et al., 2005). Religiosity also shows mild positive correlations with agreeableness, conscientiousness, and extraversion (Saroglou, 2002). It positively predicts moral conservatism, traditionalism, benevolence, and conformity, and negatively predicts hedonism, status striving, and universalism (Saroglou, Delpierre, & Dernelle, 2004). There is strong assortative mating not only for specific religious affiliation but also for religiosity (Feng & Baker, 1994; Kalmijn, 1998).

Other Psychological Traits

There are many other traits that show both sexual attractiveness and a quasi-moral status, at least in a substantial proportion of societies. These include the capacities for the following:

- Creativity (Haselton & Miller, in press; Kanazawa, 2000; Miller, 1997, 1999).
- Artistic virtuosity (Boas, 1955; Kohn & Mithen, 1999; Miller, 2001).
- Achieving social status through merit (Ellis, 2001; Pérusse, 1993).
- Acquiring wealth through merit (Conniff, 2002; Frank, 1999; Veblen, 1899/1994).

Even if some critics insist on a narrower list of "true" moral virtues, these core virtues may still be explained by this sexual selection model. Kindness, for example, would surely be on any reasonable list of the core virtues, and it appears to fit the standard pattern of sexually selected traits given mutual mate choice: reliability as a stable personality trait, validity as a good-genes and good-parent indicator, heritability, sexual attractiveness in long-term relationships, and conspicuous display in courtship. Thus, for purposes of assessing this sexual selection model, it may not matter much exactly where we draw the line between moral and nonmoral virtues.

Are These Traits Really Judged as Moral Virtues or Vices?

In what sense do these cognitive, personality, and psychopathology traits have a "quasi-moral status"? There are at least four reasons to think they do—three from social psychology and one from theology. First, most people show a "just world belief" (Lerner, 1980) that creativity, beauty, status, and wealth are merited by those who enjoy them, as both causes and consequences of moral virtue. Second, there is a powerful "halo effect" around such traits, so they are judged as boosting the likely moral virtues of judged individuals (Nisbett & Wilson, 1977). For example, defendants in criminal cases who are more physically attractive, high in occupational status, and wealthy are more likely to be acquitted or given lighter sentences by juries of their (often lower status) peers (McKelvie & Coley, 1993). Some halo effects may reflect accurate inferences about genuinely correlated traits ("true halo") rather than perceiver bias ("halo error") (Solomonson & Lance, 1997). Third, research using the Implicit Association Test shows that many dimensions judged in person perception are highly evaluative and load on a common good/bad dimension that confounds moral goodness, likeability, pleasantness, status, racial similarity, and physical attractiveness (Fazio & Olson, 2003; Greenwald et al., 2002).

Finally, the theological reason: religious people often attribute these quasi-moral traits in hypertrophied form to deities as a reason for valuing their goodness, as when they feel gratitude to a God credited with creating the world in all its beauty, out of a magnanimous generosity to mortals (Boyer, 2001; Roes & Raymond, 2003). Believers typically credit benevolent deities with supernatural levels of the quasi-moral personality traits (intelligence, conscientiousness, agreeableness, and emotional stability), as well as the standard sexually selected fitness indicators (size, strength, status, beauty, longevity). In monotheistic religions, these traits are bundled together; in polytheistic religions (e.g., ancient Egyptian, Greek, Roman, Norse, and Aztec pantheons; Hinduism, Confucianism), different supernormal traits are attributed to different deities. Contemporary comic books and fantasy films show the standard polytheistic pattern, with different supernormal quasi-moral traits attributed to different superheroes (e.g., the Marvel comics *X-Men* pantheon of Professor X, Wolverine, Cyclops, and Storm; the Tolkien pantheon of Gandalf, Aragorn, Legolas, and Frodo).

Ever since Socrates, philosophy has tried to develop precise distinctions between theoretical constructs that are often empirically correlated. Most philosophers think in terms of necessary and sufficient conditions, not in terms of factor analysis. Thus, moral philosophers may balk at such flagrantly irrational conflations of moral goodness, social reputation, eco-nomic power, and sexual attractiveness. Indeed, they may be tempted to quote a cautionary verse from Ogden Nash: "It's always tempting to impute/Unlikely virtues to the cute." But moral philosophers did not drive the genetic evolution of human virtues; ordinary folks did. If we are seeking a descriptive explanation for human morality, we should attend to the person-perception judgments that may have causally driven moral evolution in our species. Ultimately, it is an empirical psychological question whether ordinary folks judge these traits to have a moral or quasi-moral status, especially in making social and sexual judgments about others.

Virtue Ethics, Virtue Epistemology, and Virtue Aesthetics

One reason for accepting the quasi-moral status of individual-differences traits such as intelligence and physical attractiveness is the recent conver-gence between virtue ethics, virtue epistemology, and virtue aesthetics. Philosophers are once again considering the relationships between good-ness, truth, and beauty.

For example, there is clear overlap between virtue ethics and virtue epis-temology, which is the study of cognitive and intellectual virtues (DePaul & Zagzebski, 2003). Traditional epistemology focuses on evaluating the truth of particular concepts and conceptual systems through consistency and coherence criteria. By contrast, virtue epistemology tries to understand the normative properties of beliefs in terms of the normative properties of cognitive agents. For example, Aristotle named intuition, wisdom, prudence, and science as intellectual virtues. For the virtue epistemologist then, true beliefs arise out of acts of intellectual virtue—acts typical of intelligent, rational, cognitively complex agents (Zagzebski, 1996) who show impartiality, epistemic responsibility, and intellectual courage (Code, 1987; Montmarquet, 1993). In virtue epistemology as in virtue ethics, the favored level of description is the whole individual as a cognitive/moral agent, not the isolated belief or moral act. This naturally leads to an emphasis on individual differences in epistemological virtue—differences that intelligence researchers have already succeeded in measuring with unparalleled reliability and validity for over a century.

Virtue epistemology and virtue ethics also strive for a unified theory of value across moral and cognitive domains (Brady & Pritchard, 2003). For Montmarquet (1993) the key intellectual virtue of "epistemic consci-entiousness" resembles a moral personality trait more than a cognitive ability, and it seems closely related to the Big Five traits of openness and conscientiousness. Kvanvig (1992) views intellectual virtues as cognitive ideals valued by people in social groups, thus relating virtue epistemology to person-perception research. Zagzebski (1996) has gone furthest in viewing the intellectual virtues as a subset of the moral virtues. Thus, if truth, knowledge, and accuracy are epistemological virtues, perhaps they are moral virtues as well. As with moral virtues, there is a strong distinction in virtue epistemology between getting things right accidentally versus intentionally: praiseworthy beliefs are those that are due to an individual's own abilities, efforts, actions, and skills rather than dumb luck or blind chance (Greco, 2000; Lehrer, 2000). In summary, virtue epistemology would see mate choice for intelligence as mate choice for a cardinal moral virtue.

Likewise, there is an evolutionarily deep relationship between moral goodness and aesthetic beauty, as reflected in the overlap between virtue ethics and the recent revival of Darwinian aesthetics (Grammer, Fink, Moller, & Thornhill, 2003; Miller, 2001; Thornhill, 1998). This has intellectual roots in late nineteenth-century evolutionary biology, when mate choice for sexual ornaments was seen as the central evolutionary process that creates organic beauty (Darwin, 1871/2004; Grosse, 1897; Spencer, 1887). Darwinian aesthetics is a virtue aesthetics insofar as it views beauty prototypically as an agent-level property of living organisms, as they are perceived by other members of the same species.

Beauty is thus an emergent property of coevolution between a signaling system (the beauty cues displayed by some individuals) and a receiver system (the aesthetic judgment system in other individuals). It is partly in the objective genetic quality and phenotypic condition of the beautiful individual and partly in the perceptual adaptations of the beholder (Senior, 2003; Symons, 1995). Darwinian aesthetics has successfully analyzed human facial and bodily attractiveness in costly signaling terms as a set of good-genes and good-phenotype indicators (e.g., Fink & Penton-Voak, 2002; Grammer et al., 2003; Langlois et al., 2000).

Darwinian aesthetics extends well beyond an animal's physical attractiveness. Art, music, and performances produced by animals (e.g., bowerbird nests, nightingale songs, hominid hand-axes, Cindy Sherman's self-portraits) can all be viewed as part of the organism's "extended phenotype" (Borgia, 1995; Dawkins, 1982; Kohn & Mithen, 1999). Such aesthetic behavioral products may be assessed by somewhat different perceptual adaptations than physical attractiveness, but they obey the same basic principles of costly signaling theory, such as conspicuous cost and conspicuous precision (Boas, 1955; Miller, 2001).

The question remains: is there any substantive overlap between virtue ethics and virtue aesthetics, such that beauty in the Darwinian-aesthetic sense could be construed as a genuine moral virtue? There are a few examples of beauty serving as a reliable cue of altruism. First, some sexually selected beauty advertises ability and willingness to invest resources in mates and offspring—that is, to perform acts of unselfish altruism in the interests of one's family (Iwasa & Pomiankowski, 1999; Kokko, 1998). This good-parent sexual selection process favors the bright red plumage of male cardinals (Linville, Breitwisch, & Schilling, 1998), the dark chest-badges of male house sparrows (Voltura, Schwagmeyer, & Mock, 2002), and the aesthetically conspicuous resource displays of humans (Conniff, 2002; Miller, 2001). Second, some recent research confirms nineteenth-century criminologist Cesare Lombroso's view that convicted felons (i.e., individuals low in virtue) tend to be less physically attractive than average. For example, adult felons, violent juvenile delinquents, and antisocial children show increased "minor physical anomalies," craniofacial abnormalities, and neurodevelopmental abnormalities, and decreased body symmetry, "developmental stability," and overall attractiveness (e.g., Arsenault, Tremblay, Boulerice, Seguin, & Saucier, 2000; Harris, Rice, & Lalumiere, 2001; Lalumiere, Harris, & Rice, 2001). Finally, some recent philosophical work considers the intersection of aesthetics and ethics (Eaton, 1992; Levinson, 1998). For example, McGinn's (1997) "aesthetic theory of virtue" argues that virtue coincides with "beauty of the soul," and vice with ugliness of the soul.

The good, the true, and the beautiful are closely related—not because they share some conceptual overlap of necessary and sufficient conditions but because, in the real world, each tends to be disrupted by the same kinds of genetic mutations, developmental errors, and neuropsychological abnormalities. The result is that human moral virtues, cognitive abilities, and sexually attractive traits tend to positively correlate with each other across individuals.

How Sexual Selection May Have Interacted with Other Selection Pressures to Shape Human Moral Virtues

Many forms of social selection probably shaped human morality, including the following:

- Kin selection (Hamilton, 1964; Daly, Salmon, & Wilson, 1997).
- Reciprocal altruism (Trivers, 1971; Sugiyama, Tooby, & Cosmides, 2002).

- Commitment mechanisms (Frank, 1988; Nesse, 2001).
- Risk-sharing mechanisms (Boone, 1998; Sugiyama & Sugiyama, 2003).
- Social norm and punishment mechanisms (Fehr & Fischbacher, 2004; Henrich & Boyd, 2001).
- Group selection (Boehm, 1996; Wilson, Timmel, & Miller, 2004).
- Equilibrium selection among alternative evolutionary strategies (Alvard & Nolin, 2002; Boyd & Richerson, 1990).

In each case, sexual selection would tend to anticipate, sharpen, and amplify the social selection pressure to produce a more extreme, more costly, more prosocial version of the moral virtue than social selection could achieve alone. The reason is that nonsexual forms of social selection can shape morality only insofar as they confer fairly concrete survival benefits (e.g., shared food, protection from predators) on the morally virtuous. Mate choice can shape morality much more powerfully and broadly, because it demands only that moral behaviors carry some signaling value about a potential mate's good genes and/or good parenting abilities. In general, sexual selection can "supercharge" other evolutionary processes by adding just the sort of positive-feedback dynamics that tend to trigger evolutionary innovation and speciation (Crespi, 2004; Miller & Todd, 1995).

An especially interesting, powerful, and neglected interaction may be that between sexual selection and group-level equilibrium selection (not to be confused with standard group selection—see Miller, 2000a). Many evolutionary games have multiple "Nash equilibria": states where each player is maximizing their individual payoffs given the strategies already played by others. For example, male cetacean mating strategies have at least two equilibria: peacefully attracting females through long, loud songs (as in the humpback whales) or aggressively herding and raping females (as in the bottlenose dolphins—Connor, Smolker, & Richards, 1992). Some equilibria are better for everybody (they bring net positive payoffs to everyone; they are "Pareto dominant"); some equilibria are worse for everybody ("Pareto inferior") but cannot be escaped easily because individuals who deviate from the equilibrium do even worse. A virtuous bottlenose dolphin could not opt out of his species' coercion-based mating system without negating his reproductive success.

Normally, natural selection alone is not very good at escaping from such Pareto-inferior equilibria to reach Pareto-dominant equilibria (Boyd & Richerson, 1990). Sexual selection may help, by conferring reproductive benefits on individuals who deviate from selfish, antisocial equilibria

(Miller, 2000a). This sexual payoff for virtue is functionally similar to the social-reputation payoffs for virtue modeled by other researchers (e.g., Barclay, 2004; Milinski, Semmann, & Krambeck, 2002). However, standard social-reputation models create a second-order "free-rider" problem (Gintis, 2000): who will altruistically take the trouble to punish the wicked and reward the virtuous? As research from behavioral game theory (e.g., on the Ultimatum Game) shows, most humans are emotionally compelled to impose this sort of "altruistic punishment" on others who act selfishly (Fehr & Gächter, 2002); the question is why? Most explanations make somewhat vague appeals to cultural evolution or social norms (e.g., Boyd, Gintis, Bowles, & Richerson, 2003) without identifying any plausible individual fitness payoffs for punishing the wicked. By contrast, this sexual payoff model solves it by identifying selfish mate-choice incentives (e.g., good-dad and good-gene payoffs) for "rewarding" the virtuous with sexual relationships.

Most contemporary theories of moral evolution accept the importance of multilevel selection across the genetic, individual, and group levels—either implicitly or explicitly (Wilson et al., 2004). Generally, group-level selection for prosocial behavior is what "breaks the symmetry" between alternative equilibria in evolutionary games to allow the evolution of genuine empathy and altruism (Lahti & Weinstein, 2005). This model of sexual selection interacting with group-level equilibrium selection is a potent way that prosocial virtues can establish a genetic beachhead in an otherwise selfish population, long before group-level equilibrium selection can favor morally unified groups.

Predictions of the Sexual Selection Model for Moral Virtues

This sexual selection model makes a large number of testable predictions. These often take an unusual form, since costly signaling adaptations have very different phenotypic and genetic features compared to other types of adaptations. In particular, many of these predictions concern individual differences in virtues—not a common research topic in evolutionary psychology or moral philosophy, which tend to focus on species-typical moral judgments and behaviors. For more detail on the rationale behind these predictions, see Miller (2000a, 2000b, 2000c, 2001).

To test most of these predictions, it would be necessary to develop reliable, valid measurement scales that can identify stable individual differences in particular kinds of moral virtues. Such scales should ideally show the psychometric properties desired of any intelligence test or personality assessment: internal consistency reliability, parallel-forms reliability, test-retest reliability, interrater reliability, face validity, construct validity, predictive validity, concurrent validity, convergent validity, discriminant validity, and ecological validity (Anastasi & Urbina, 1997). To discriminate between rival theories concerning the evolutionary origins and adaptive functions of specific human virtues, we need to assess the adaptive design features of each putative virtue in reliable quantitative ways. This will require much more psychometrically sophisticated approaches to virtue ethics—not just asking people to give answers to a few multiple-choice "trolley problems" from moral philosophy.

Generally, sexually selected virtues as quantified in this way should show most of the following twenty features:

Genetic Features

1. Positive heritability: if virtues are good-genes indicators, they should prove genetically heritable in twin and adoption studies or using other behavior-genetic methods. If virtues are costly and evolved under sexual selection, the genes underlying virtues should become more expressed only after sexual maturity, perhaps in response to sex hormones. This should lead to higher virtue heritability in adults than in children, as has been found with intelligence (Plomin et al., 2001).

2. Negative correlations with mutation load (number of harmful genetic mutations): heritable variation in virtues should reflect variation in overall mutation load, as intelligence may do (Prokosch, Yeo, & Miller, 2005). For example, since mutation load in sperm increases dramatically as men age (Crow, 2000), younger fathers should, all else being equal, sire more virtuous children.

3. Genetic inbreeding effects: if virtues are good-genes indicators, the offspring of sibling or cousin marriages should show reduced virtue levels, due to the increased expression of harmful homozygous mutations.

4. Molecular genetic features: specific virtue-reducing alleles should be mostly of fairly recent evolutionary origin that have not yet been eliminated by sexual selection in particular breeding populations; thus, despite the heritability of virtue, it will be extremely difficult to find specific "virtue genes" that replicate across human groups (see Shaner et al., 2004).

5. Positive genetic correlations between trait and preference: if mate choice was shaping virtues over recent evolutionary history, we should expect to see a positive genetic correlation between virtues themselves and choosiness about virtues. Such genetic correlations can be assessed with standard

multivariate genetic modeling, based on the cross-trait, cross-twin correlations in identical versus fraternal twin pairs.

Phenotypic Features

6. Stable phenotypic variance: virtues should vary significantly between individuals in the species, and the differences should be fairly consistent across situations (cf. Harman, 1999b). Without variance, there is no way for mate choice to use the trait as an indicator; without stability, there is no way to generalize the trait from one situation to another.

7. Condition-dependent costs: virtues should incur a significant cost to produce, in energy, time, risk, or nutritional resources. Individuals with higher genetic fitness or better phenotypic conditions should be better able to bear these costs.

8. Positive correlation with other objective fitness indicators: variation in virtues should correlate positively with other well-established fitness indicators, such as physical health, mental health, longevity, fertility, body size, body symmetry, and intelligence (e.g., Gangestad & Thornhill, 1999; Prokosch et al., 2005).

9. Comorbidity among vices, and between vices and brain abnormalities: if different virtue deficits (vices) reflect harmful pleiotropic mutations with partly overlapping effects, then vices should show positive genetic correlations (genetic comorbidity) with each other, especially as vices become more serious and extreme. Also, if vices reflect harmful mutations that impair normal neurodevelopment, then they should be associated with various standard brain abnormalities widely observed for other fitness-reducing behavioral traits such as mental illness and mental retardation: smaller cortical volume, larger ventricles, abnormal cortical lateralization, atypical localization of processing as observed in functional magnetic resonance imaging studies, and so forth.

10. Higher trait variance in males: in species that evolved with some degree of polygyny and some frequency of extra-pair copulation, the higher male variance and skew in reproductive success should favor a risk-seeking pattern of trait expression, such that male virtue levels show higher variance than female trait values (see Archer & Mehdikhani, 2003). That is, there should be more supervirtuous males but also more virtue-deficient males.

11. Strategic investment in trait based on self-assessed talent: in species such as humans that have several different kinds of behavioral courtship displays, there are different sexual/status niches (Ellis, 2001; Weisfeld, 1999). Juveniles should assess their relative virtues and invest time and

effort in sharpening virtue-display skills preferentially in their highest virtue areas.

Social and Sexual Features

12. Perceivability: variation in virtues should be perceivable, directly or indirectly, consciously or unconsciously, by the opposite sex, in a way that could potentially influence mate choice.

13. Positive correlations with other subjectively desired traits, such as physical attractiveness, social status, charisma, and so forth; these correlations should be genuine, not just stereotyped "halo effects" (cf. Nisbett & Wilson, 1977).

14. Positively valued in mate choice: all else being equal, virtues should be favored in mate choice. Virtues as good-genes indicators may be favored more often by males in short-term relationships, and by women at peak fertility near ovulation. Virtues as good-parent indicators may be favored more often by females in long-term relationships, and by women at lower fertility in the cycle. During peak mating effort, virtues may be favored more in the opposite sex than in one's own sex, and more in potential mates of appropriate age than in younger or older individuals.

15. Conspicuous courtship display: during courtship, individuals should conspicuously (if unconsciously) display virtues to the opposite sex. This could be measured across different time scales, comparing courtship to noncourtship situations across ovulation cycle stages, relationship stages, and social contexts.

16. Young-adult peak in trait expression: for sexually selected behavioral traits, conspicuous virtue displays should peak in young adulthood, at the peak of mating effort. They should be low before puberty, should increase rapidly thereafter, and should decline gradually as individuals shift their time and energy from courtship to parenting.

17. Alternative mating strategies: individuals lacking the sexually attractive virtues should more often pursue alternative mating strategies that try to circumvent mate choice by the opposite sex, including increased use of sexual harassment and sexual coercion (Gangestad & Simpson, 2000; Thornhill & Palmer, 2000).

18. Positive assortative mating: in species with social monogamy such as ours, individuals should assortatively mate with respect to virtues, because the competitive mating market should ensure that high-virtue individuals prefer each other, leaving lower virtue individuals no choice but to settle for each other (see Todd & Miller, 1999).

19. Derogation of trait quality in sexual competitors: if virtues are valued in courtship, same-sex rivals should selectively derogate each other with respect to virtue deficits (see Buss & Dedden, 1990).

20. Gossip about trait values: in social species such as ours with collective mate choice that takes into account the views of family and friends, gossip about potential mates should focus some attention on virtues as fitness indicators, with high virtue recognized and praised.

Example: Sexual Fidelity as a Moral Virtue

For example, suppose a researcher hypothesizes that sexual fidelity evolved by sexual selection through mutual mate choice (rather than through kin selection, reciprocal altruism, or group selection). A first step might be to investigate fidelity's sociosexual features. Do surveys, interviews, and experiments show that people prefer sexually faithful mates, all else being equal? Yes: jealousy research shows that men and women across cultures react very negatively to sexual infidelity, yet are highly motivated to discover it (Buss, 2000; Shackelford & Buss, 1997). Do people verbally derogate their sexual rivals for being unfaithful, using technical moral-philosophy terms such as "bimbo," "floozy," "skank," "slut," "tart," "tramp," "trollop," "whore" (for females), or "bastard," "bum," "cad," "cheat," "creep," "dog," "knave," "lecher," "rat," "rogue," "scoundrel," "sleazeball," "slimebucket," "snake" (for males)? Do people gossip about other people's sexual infidelities, especially to friends and family? (Indeed, if there is an infidelity to gossip about, do we ever gossip about anything else?) Do people conspicuously display their likely future fidelity in courtship, for example, by making impassioned, adaptively self-deceptive declarations of infinite, eternal, exclusive love?

If the answers are generally yes, then the researcher might progress to phenotypic studies of sexual fidelity as an individual-differences dimension. Are there stable individual differences in the likelihood of fidelity versus infidelity, or is infidelity driven entirely by chance and opportunity? Research on the opposite of fidelity, the personality construct of "sociosexuality" (interest in promiscuous, short-term, or extra-pair mating), confirms there are stable individual differences in this trait dimension (Gangestad & Simpson, 2000). Is fidelity positively correlated with other desirable moral virtues and fitness-related traits, such as kindness, conscientiousness, agreeableness, mental health, longevity, and intelligence? (This question becomes complicated, since individuals of higher mate value will be sought more often for short-term, extra-pair copulations, so will be tempted by more opportunities for infidelity—Gangestad &

Simpson, 2000. Mate value and infidelity opportunities would have to be carefully statistically controlled in studies of fidelity's correlations with other moral virtues.)

The genetic studies of infidelity would be the hardest to perform, but often the most informative. Would twin and adoption studies show that the propensity to infidelity versus relationship stability is heritable? (Actually, they do already: Bailey et al., 2000; Cherkas, Oelsner, Mak, Valdes, & Spector, 2004.) Would genetic inbreeding (e.g., offspring of first-cousin matings) reduce fidelity, suggesting a role for partially recessive harmful mutations in driving infidelity? Would one find positive genetic correlations between the tendency to fidelity and the mate preference for fidelity—as might be expected if there has been sexual selection for the trait?

Clearly, the sexual selection hypothesis for moral virtues is eminently testable. However, it requires new ways of thinking about costly signaling adaptations (Miller, 2000b, 2000c). These cannot be assessed using the standard adaptationist criteria for naturally selected traits (e.g., low cost, high efficiency, high modularity, low phenotypic variance, low heritability, and reliable development across all individuals) that are more familiar to evolutionary theorists (e.g., Andrews, Gangestad, & Matthews, 2003; Tooby & Cosmides, 1992). For naturalistic moral philosophy to benefit maximally from contemporary scientific insights, it must not only increase its appreciation of sexual selection's power, but also expand its understanding of how to analyze costly signaling adaptations.

Implications for Normative Ethics

Normative ethics is supposed to help us distinguish right from wrong and good from evil. It tries to achieve a "reflective equilibrium" between (1) possible universal moral principles, (2) derived moral implications that would apply in particular situations, and (3) human moral intuitions that react to those principles, implications, and situations (Rawls, 1971; Daniels, 1996). The hope is that normative ethicists can articulate a set of universal, coherent, consistent moral principles that yield intuitively acceptable moral implications across all possible situations, and that thereby embody a rational distillation of human moral sensibility. Almost all moral philosophers accept that this is the legitimate goal of normative ethics, though debates still rage between consequentialists and deontologists, between act ethicists and virtue ethicists, and so on. However, if moral virtues arose through sexual selection, this reflective equilibrium approach to normative ethics is likely to fail for at least three reasons.

First, suppose human moral intuitions evolved as part of our person-perception system for inferring stable, morally valenced, mating-relevant personality traits from observable behaviors. If so, we are trying to do ethical alchemy: trying to refine unconscious, domain-specific, species-specific, person-perception adaptations (the base metal) into verbally articulated, domain-general, universal moral principles (the gold). This is likely to be an uphill battle. One reason it is difficult to make our moral intuitions consistent and coherent is that moral intuitions usually precede reasoned moral judgments (Haidt, 2001) and are often driven by morally judgmental emotions that figure prominently in sexual relationships, such as anger (Ellis & Malamuth, 2000), disgust (Rozin, Haidt, & McCauley, 1999), jealousy (Buss, 2000), embarrassment (Keltner & Buswell, 1997), shame (Tangney, 1999), and gratitude (McCullough, Emmons, Kilpatrick, & Larson, 2001).

Second, if our person-perception system relies on social-inference heuristics that are fast, frugal, and pragmatic, then our moral judgments will often violate procedural norms of rationality derived from logic, statistics, and rational choice theory, such as consistency, transitivity, and completeness (Gigerenzer, Todd, & ABC Research Group, 1999). There are deep decision-theoretic reasons why it may be impossible to derive a set of consistent, coherent moral preferences from the operation of such social-inference heuristics. To know whether this is a fatal objection to the reflective equilibrium approach to normative ethics, we need to learn a lot more about moral judgment heuristics in the context of person-perception research (e.g., Funder, 2004; Haselton & Funder, 2006).

Third, human moral intuitions evolved to assess people's stable moral virtues in ancestrally typical, fitness-relevant situations, and to guide ancestrally feasible forms of social response such as forming friendships or mateships, gossiping about liars, punishing cheaters, or ostracizing psychopaths. There is no reason to expect our moral intuitions to show consistent, logically defensible reactions to evolutionarily novel moral dilemmas that involve isolated, hypothetical, behavioral acts by unknown strangers who cannot be rewarded or punished through any normal social primate channels.

For example, we often seem cognitively paralyzed by many current debates in reproductive bioethics (Petrinovich, 1995). How should we feel about abortion, sperm donation, egg donation, surrogate pregnancy, human cloning, genetic testing, or genetic enhancement? Different framings of these issues will activate different, domain-specific moral intuitions (Haidt, 2001). This is precisely why rhetorical metaphors are effective in such moral debates. For example, "genetic enhancement" may seem pernicious fascism if we view it as a limited resource that will be appropriated by the powerful for their nefarious ends, or it may seem democratically liberating if we view it as a natural extension of good-genes mate choice, for those whose own suboptimal mate value precludes getting good genes from a willing partner (Miller, 2000a). Is there any neutral, rational position from which we can judge such issues, without assimilating them to one or another of our domain-specific moral intuitions? Probably not: rational decision making depends upon subjective utility functions that must be supplied either by the genetic imitation of ancestral utilities ("gut instinct") or the social imitation of peer utilities ("learning," "social norms"). Gut moral instincts will be mute or misleading guides to moral dilemmas raised by new technology, and moral conformity to peer opinion will be biased by vested political, corporate, and media interests that define the current "ethical issues" in their own interests.

These three evolutionary psychology problems resemble some philosophical problems with the reflective equilibrium method (Brandt, 1990). Basically, there is no compelling logical reason to think that our moral intuitions have any true normative credibility as guides to genuinely moral behavior, and a coherently systematized set of these subjective moral fictions will remain fictional. Of course, there may be evolutionary reasons to expect that species-typical human moral intuitions would tend to maximize inclusive fitness under ancestral conditions. However, that is quite different from claiming that they are normatively justifiable in any broader sense. For example, Peter Singer (1990, 1994) has made some compelling but counterintuitive arguments concerning animals rights, euthanasia, and infanticide; in such cases, it seems impossible to reach a reflective equilibrium between our gut moral instincts and our scientifically informed normative judgments.

In the light of these moral-psychological problems, consider two different forms of a typical normative-ethics question. Abstract form: Is it morally right to assassinate a genocidal war criminal? (Perhaps—many have praised the attempted assassination of Adolf Hitler by Colonel Claus von Stauffenberg on July 20, 1944). Personal form: Suppose there is a twenty-first-century head of state who ordered his country into a fraudulent and illegal war that resulted in thousands of needless civilian casualties, but who is almost certain to avoid accountability to the International Criminal Court in The Hague. Would it be moral to feel sexually attracted to a man who succeeded in killing the wicked head of state, with a single head shot from a Barrett M82A1 .50-caliber semi-automatic sniper rifle at 800 meters on a windy day? The personal form is much more specific about the identities of the moral judgment maker, the morally judged individual, the civilian victims, the nature of the assassination, and the fitness-relevant, sociosexual implications of the moral judgment. These details should and do matter in making adaptive mate-choice judgments about the moral virtues of snipers. A woman who knows her ordnance might admire the sniper's good-genes indicators, such as his resourcefulness (the M82A1 costs $7,775 retail), his physical condition (the rifle is 5 feet long and weighs 34 pounds), and his marksmanship (the 800-meter head shot was near the rifle's maximum effective antipersonnel range of 1,000 meters). Yet she may equally worry about his good-dad indicators: his vigilante action may reveal psychopathy, paranoid schizophrenia, bipolar disorder, impulsiveness, fame-seeking narcissism, or high-risk sensation seeking (Fein & Vossekuil, 1999; Meloy, James, Farnham, Mullen, Pathe, Darnley, & Preston, 2004). She can only tell by gathering further information about his virtues, both moral and nonmoral—which is the function of prolonged human courtship.

Note

For helpful discussions, guidance, and/or feedback on these ideas, thanks to Paul Andrews, Rosalind Arden, Helena Cronin, Oliver Curry, Dylan Evans, Steve Gangestad, Walter Sinnott-Armstrong, and Peter Todd.

4.1 Why Moral Virtues Are Probably Not Sexual Adaptations

Catherine Driscoll

For a short time he loved me sincere, he used me both kindly and civil
The honeymoon scarcely was o'er, when he turned out a quare divil!
—Trad.

Geoffrey Miller's work in evolutionary psychology is nearly unique in its emphasis on the importance of Darwin's "other theory"–sexual selection– in human evolutionary history. It's an important reminder not to neglect this possible explanation for human physiological and psychological traits and, as such, is a very interesting and useful contribution to the study of "human nature." However, I doubt that Miller's explanation for moral virtues as involving a combination of sexual selection and group selection will work.

Sexual selection theory claims that the presence or fixation in a population of some trait of organisms of one sex can sometimes be explained in terms of the sexual choices of members of the opposite sex, or by sexual competition, and not because of the contribution that trait plays in the survival of the individual that possesses it. A classic example of such a trait is the peacock's tail. The showy tail contributes nothing to the survival of the peacock; if anything, the tail is actively detrimental, since it increases the peacock's risk of being killed by predators. What the peacock's tail does do is make the peacock more attractive to peahens. Peacocks with big showy tails attract more mates than peacocks without, and hence they have more offspring with tails like their own. The biggest problem that sexual selection theory faces is that peahens, and their preferences, are also subject to natural selection. Peacocks without big showy tails are fitter than peacocks with such tails, all else being equal; only peahens' choices make the difference. Thus, peahens who make choices of mates who are otherwise fitter ought to do better than those who make choices of mates who are less fit, because good choosers have fitter offspring and thus ultimately more grandchildren than bad choosers. Therefore, sexual selection theory needs some way of explaining why peahens that like showy tails have not become selected against in favor of more sensible peahens. The suggested solution to this problem (Zahavi & Zahavi, 1997) is that costly traits like peacocks' tails act as signals of the fitness of their bearers. Choosing a fit mate is a difficult decision/problem for a peahen—she cannot determine, by ordinary observation, which peacock is the fittest. What peahens need is a reliable way of telling when peacocks are fit and when they are not. The proposal made is that complex showy traits like peacocks' tails work as indicators of the overall fitness of the peacock. By choosing good tails, the females choose mates who are fitter overall. The idea is that peacock tails can only be made by peacocks that have other sorts of good genes and hence can "afford" the fitness cost of a fancy tail. This works so long as good tails are well correlated with good genes, which means choosing good tails allows females to reliably choose good genes. This solves the problem of the evolution of mate preferences. Since there is no other way to choose highly fit mates, fancy tail preferences win over non-fancy-tail preferences.

This problem of the origin of mate preferences is one that surfaces again in Miller's work. Miller's paper does not claim that the virtues came about in *exactly* the same way as the peacock's tail—that is, because they acted as a costly signal. Instead, moral virtues are supposed to spread via a combination of sexual selection and group selection. Miller's claim is that the moral virtues spread primarily via group selection, but that getting group selection going required something to break the nonmoral equilibrium that existed in groups before morality arose. Group selection occurs when groups differ in their group-level properties rather than in the properties that belong to the individuals that make up those groups, and that because of differences in group-level properties, some groups give rise to more new groups than others. An example of a group-level property would be "composed largely of virtuous individuals"; an example of an individual-level property would be "possessed of moral virtues." Moral virtues could spread via group selection if groups with larger numbers of individuals with virtues gave rise to more new groups than groups without. This requires, however, that there be groups which are composed largely of virtuous individuals. The problem is that while moral individuals are assumed to do well in all moral groups (since, e.g., moral individuals avoid punishment that might be given to nonmoral individuals), they tend to do poorly in all nonmoral groups (since they're exploited by nonmoral individuals or are not as ruthless in pursuit of their interests as nonmoral individuals).

?

Aristotle

This means that while groups with many moral individuals would be selected for once they existed, it would be hard to get large numbers of moral individuals in groups to start with, since moral individuals are selected against when they arise. Miller is suggesting that mate preferences for moral virtues could solve this problem—mate preferences for virtues would lead to individuals with virtues having greater numbers of offspring, and this would lead to an increase in the numbers of moral individuals within groups, breaking the nonmoral equilibrium. Once the numbers are high enough, group selection for the highly moral groups could get going.

This is an interesting idea, but it creates a problem—how do mate preferences for moral individuals evolve if moral individuals were less fit than those without morals? I presume we're assuming that preferences for virtues are competing with neutral mate preferences, and both exist in these groups. However, if this is the case, then neutral preferences will evolve at the expense of preferences for virtues. If individuals with moral virtues are less fit, then their (moral) offspring are less fit, and thus the offspring of those that mate with them. Hence, individuals with moral mate preferences would get selected against within groups, just as would moral individuals themselves. So why would preferences for moral mates arise? One possibility is that moral virtues are a costly signal, like the peacock's tail. Mate preferences for moral virtues persist because by choosing moral virtues, individuals choose mates who are overall fitter. Thus, despite the fitness cost that moral virtues impose on their possessors, preferences for moral virtues could evolve. In other words, moral virtues act as costly signals or fitness indicators, just like the peacock's tail.

So could moral virtues be costly signals? The case of the peacock's tail allows us to identify six important characteristics that costly signals need to have. First, and most obviously, costly signals need to be demonstrably costly. They need to have a negative fitness effect that can only be managed by an individual with plenty of fitness "to spare." Second, they need to be employed in sexual choice—individuals actually have to use the trait that acts as a signal as a means of choosing between partners. Third, they need to be heritable, such that parents with the costly signal trait have offspring with that trait. Fourth, the costly signal trait has to correlate well with some reasonable fitness-increasing trait or traits. Fifth, the signal has to be hard to fake—that is, it mustn't be possible for individuals to routinely deceive others into thinking that they have that trait; otherwise individuals with preferences for the signal will not reliably choose better mates and that preference will be selected against. Finally, preferences for costly signals are only selected for in cases in which the information the costly signal provides cannot be more easily acquired in some other way. So how does Miller do at showing that these six things are true of moral virtues?

I think Miller's evidence for the first through fourth characteristics (i.e., costliness, use in courtship, heritability, and correlation with other fitness-increasing traits), though sometimes anecdotal, is not highly problematic. He has a tendency to construe "virtue" and "vice" rather loosely to compensate for the absence of discussion in the psychology and biology literature of the traits that *philosophers* might think of as virtues, but this is not his fault. There are much more serious problems, however, with how far the fifth and sixth characteristics of costly signals apply to moral virtues. Preferences for costly signals evolve only in a context in which the costly signal can't be faked *and* when there isn't any other reliable but less costly way for the one relying on the signal to acquire the information it conveys. This raises two problems for moral virtues as costly signals. The first is that courtship for humans usually isn't all that long a period of time, and it is in the interests of individuals without virtues to temporarily pretend to be virtuous—to be kind to the stepchildren, to be generous to the waitstaff on dates—in order to secure sexual access to the other person. It might also be possible to fake good behavior for longer periods of time by being good when observed, saying the right things, and so forth, to secure one's social and sexual relationships, while at the same time using every opportunity to exploit others and behave immorally. Both of these strategies are relatively cheap (and anecdotally widely recognized) ways of exploiting the mate preferences of other individuals without paying the cost of really being moral, and they would undermine the selection in favor of preferences for moral virtues. Hence, moral virtues don't look like reliable, unfakeable costly signals.

The second problem is that Miller has not demonstrated that moral virtues provide information about the fitness of their possessors that can't be acquired any other (cheaper) way. Miller claims that moral virtues signal a low mutation load in a person's genes. The idea is that the brain systems that produce morality are complicated and require lots of genes to build them, to the extent that even a few mutations could quickly end a person's capacity to be moral. Hence, an individual could tell that potential partners are free of mutations if they behave morally. However, Miller doesn't provide any evidence that only people with generally undamaged brains can manage moral virtues. Indeed, I might note that individuals with certain severe genetic or developmental syndromes such as Down's or Williams syndrome might be considered more virtuous in some regards than many normal individuals—they are noted for their kindness, friendliness, and sociability. However, they are often severely mentally disabled. Instead of trying to offer evidence for the general claim that moral virtues signal good genes, Miller tries to show that moral virtues are correlated with particular fitness-increasing traits such as general intelligence. This leaves him with a new problem—costly signaling isn't needed to choose mates with the traits Miller discusses. It is as easy to see if your mate is smart, for example, as to see if he or she is generous or kind—by seeing how well he or she handles language, say, or crossword puzzles, or solves more serious problems. These other abilities involve little or no fitness cost (or even a fitness benefit) to their bearer. If an individual can make judgments of a potential partner's intelligence using such abilities, why rely on whether they have moral characteristics? Choosing a mate with a costly signal trait leads an individual to have offspring with the costly signal trait and hence ultimately represents a fitness cost to that individual.

If Miller wants to show that moral virtues are a costly signal, he needs to show either that moral virtues can only be present in generally good brains or that there is a correlation between virtues and fitness-increasing traits that cannot be observed directly. However, he has not done either of these things. This strongly suggests there is a serious problem with the explanation Miller is offering. However, some of Miller's evidence is, at the very least, intuitively compelling. If moral virtues have not arisen by sexual selection, then why are we so interested in moral virtues in our partners? My worry is that there are two perfectly reasonable alternative stories that explain our preferences without purporting to explain the origin of moral virtues. The first is that our preferences for moral individuals evolved (culturally or genetically) because being moral was itself an advantage in all-moral groups in which there was punishment or other forms of exclusion for those who were nonmoral. It was important for one's children to be moral, and hence mating with moral people was fitness increasing. Hence mate preferences for moral virtues were another way for individuals in moral groups to ensure their and their children's reproductive success. In other words, once morality was established by other means, it became worthwhile to prefer moral people as sexual partners. Space prohibits me from exploring some of the suggestions for how tendencies for morality might have evolved, but there are plenty of alternatives, primarily some form of explanation involving cultural or genetic group selection (e.g., Henrich & Boyd, 1998; Sober & Wilson, 1998). The second story, and perhaps one that is even more likely, is that preferences for moral mates involve simple self-interest—no one wants to marry a nasty person, since nasty people tend to be nasty to you and hurt you and your children or make you unhappy. Mate preferences for moral individuals could simply involve the use of more ordinary general preferences for safety and well-being and, thus, wouldn't need a separate explanation in terms of sexual selection theory.

4.2 The Conflict-Resolution Theory of Virtue

Oliver Curry

There has been a long-standing debate in the history of moral thought over the nature of virtue—the enduring traits that are indicative of a good moral character. One tradition—represented by Aristotle, Cicero, Machiavelli, Nietzsche, and Hume—has celebrated the so-called "pagan" virtues of beauty, strength, courage, magnanimity, and leadership. Another tradition—represented particularly by theologians—has celebrated exactly the opposite set of traits: the so-called "Christian" virtues of humility, meekness, quietude, asceticism, and obedience (Berlin, 1997). But what are the virtues? Where do they come from? Why do they consist of these two apparently incompatible sets of traits? And why have they been considered moral?

Geoffrey Miller rightly argues that the virtues are not explained by existing evolutionary theories of morality, such as kin or reciprocal altruism. Instead, Miller argues, such traits are the product of sexual selection; specifically, they are products of mate choice for reliable signals of genetic and phenotypic quality. Thus, the virtues are analogous to the peacock's tail; they are dazzling, conspicuous displays of the qualities and character traits that members of the opposite sex look for in a mate.

However, Miller's theory leaves two kinds of virtues unaccounted for: first, virtues displayed in contexts other than courtship and, second, the traditional Christian virtues. Moreover, Miller's theory doesn't explain why some sexually attractive traits—such as beauty—have been considered moral. Nor does it provide a criterion for distinguishing sexually attractive traits that are morally virtuous, such as beauty, from sexually attractive traits that are morally neutral, such as immuno-compatibility.

I shall outline a more comprehensive evolutionary theory of virtue. This "conflict-resolution theory" argues that the virtues are adaptations for competing without coming to blows; they serve to avoid, forestall, or defuse more violent means of competing for scarce resources. This theory incorporates both the "pagan" and the "Christian" virtues. The pagan virtues are "signals of superiority." They are used to resolve conflict in two ways. First, they are used to attract mates—for here, natural selection has favored aesthetic and altruistic displays over aggression as a means of competing for mates. These are the virtues that Miller draws attention to. Second, signals of superiority are used to deter rivals. They do this as part of a "display-defer" strategy—that is, a strategy that uses, on the one hand, displays of fighting prowess and, on the other hand, ritual displays of deference to superior displays to turn otherwise bloody battles into relatively harmless contests. These displays of prowess are the second kind of pagan virtue. And this brings us to the Christian virtues. For they are the flip side of the display-defer strategy of resolving conflicts. They are "signals of submission," conspicuous displays of deference that bring conflict to an end.

Thus, the conflict-resolution theory provides a secure theoretical foundation that accounts for a broader range of virtues and that subsumes Miller's mate-choice theory. What is more, the conflict-resolution theory explains why these particular sets of traits have been seen as moral; it is because, like other aspects of morality, they constitute a successful solution to one of the recurrent problems of social life—in this case, the problem of settling disputes.

Below I briefly review the evolutionary theory of conflict resolution and look at some animal examples. I review the evidence for equivalent traits in humans. And I show how the conflict-resolution theory of virtue makes sense of various aspects of traditional moral thought.

The Virtues of the Hawk and the Virtues of the Dove

The conflict-resolution theory of virtue begins with the logic of animal conflict. Animals often come into conflict over resources such as food, territory, and mates. On the surface, such conflicts look like straightforward zero-sum games. However, in fact, there are costs involved in conflict—time, energy, and injury—that the players have a common interest in avoiding. For this reason, in the paper that first introduced evolutionary game theory, John Maynard Smith and George Price (1973) portrayed animal conflict as a nonzero-sum game—specifically, a hawk-dove game in which the worst outcome occurs if both players adopt a "hawkish" strategy of all-out aggression. Thus, conflict presents combatants with an opportunity to cooperate, in the sense of competing in less mutually destructive ways.

Over evolutionary time, natural selection has favored a number of ways of competing that involve an exchange of signals rather than an exchange of blows. These signals provide reliable information about the relative merits of the protagonists—be it genetic or phenotypic quality, or formidability—that can settle the dispute without resort to violence. It is the traits that convey this information that have been called "virtues."

The pagan virtues—beauty, strength, courage, magnanimity, and leadership—are "signals of superiority."

Consider beauty. Many animals, when competing for mates, eschew violence and instead devote their energies to spectacular aesthetic displays. Peacocks, for example, compete for mates not by fighting but by growing beautiful tails. These tails act as reliable indicators of the birds' genetic and phenotypic quality, allowing a peahen to make a judicious choice from among her eager suitors, rather than having them fight it out among themselves. In other species, bright coloration, symmetrical plumage, singing, dancing, and creativity perform a similar function (Cronin, 1991; Darwin, 1871/2004; Miller 2000a; Ridley, 1993).

Now consider strength, or "fortitude." When engaged in direct competition with other individuals—over food, territory, and mates—many animals avoid all-out war by employing a strategy that combines "hawkish" displays of prowess with "dove-ish" displays of deference to superior displays. Maynard Smith and Price showed that such a strategy is evolutionarily stable because, when combatants differ in their ability to win a fight, it pays both parties to establish who is likely to prevail by means of an exchange of signals that reliably indicate each party's fight-winning abilities rather than through a violent battle. And, once established, it pays the weaker party to bow out gracefully. This way, the stronger wins the resource he was going to win anyway, and both parties benefit by avoiding the costs of conflict.

The classic example of this "display-defer" strategy comes from a study of stag red deer competing over the control of harems (Clutton-Brock & Albon, 1979). The contest begins with a roaring match lasting several minutes. Roaring is a reliable signal of size and strength; usually, the stag with the less impressive roar will retreat. However, if the stags are too closely matched for their roars to be decisive, the contest moves to a "parallel walk" stage, where the combatants have the chance to size one another up. If this doesn't settle the dispute, then the stags lock antlers and begin a pushing contest, and the loser retreats. In other competitions in other species, hawkish displays of size, weight, age, and experience may carry the day. (For a review, see Riechert, 1998.)

Next, consider altruism. Some creatures settle disputes by means of displays that, as an added bonus, provide benefits for their audience. Male ravens, for example, compete for mates not by fighting but by performing "acts of bravery"; they undertake the risky task of checking to see whether potential carrion is in fact dead and not merely sleeping or injured. "[B]y demonstrating that they have the courage, experience, and quickness of reaction to deal with life's dangers," says Frans de Waal (1996, p. 134), "the occasional boldness of corvids serves to enhance status and impress potential mates." Similarly, male chimpanzees sometimes compete through "magnanimity"—that is, altruism directed to subordinates. They take risks in order to provide the troop with food, are generous with their own kills, and confiscate the kills of others and redistribute them. As de Waal observes, "instead of dominants standing out because of what they take, they now affirm their position by what they give" (1996, p. 144). Also, some primates compete for status through "public service" or "leadership"—that is, altruism in support of other forms of cooperation. Thus, dominant chimpanzees, stump-tailed monkeys, and gorillas all compete by intervening to end disputes among subordinates (Das, 2000; de Waal, 1996). These dominant individuals are unusual in that they intervene not in support of their families and allies but "on the basis of how best to restore peace" (de Waal, 1996, p. 129). Consequently, "the group looks for the most effective arbitrator in its midst, then throws its weight behind this individual to give him a broad base of support for guaranteeing peace and order" (de Waal, 1996, p. 130).

Thus, beauty, strength, courage, magnanimity, and leadership are all examples of traits that provide reliable information about the underlying qualities of the protagonists. They serve to attract mates or deter rivals. And, by doing so, they reduce or avoid the costs of violent conflict. In this way, evolutionary theory explains the existence, and conspicuous display, of exactly those hawkish traits that, in humans, have been called the "pagan virtues."

But what about the apparently opposite set of Christian virtues—humility, meekness, quietude, asceticism, and obedience? Conflict-resolution theory has a ready explanation for these, too. They are "signals of submission," the conspicuous displays of deference that form the flip side of the display-defer strategy of resolving conflicts. They manifest the "dove-ish" branch of the strategy—recognizing when you're beaten and signaling to your opponent that you accept defeat and intend to withdraw, thereby bringing the conflict to an end.

Not surprisingly, dove-ish cues of submission have been designed by natural selection to be the exact opposite of hawkish cues of dominance.

Indeed, cues of submission were Darwin's prime example of "the principle of antithesis" in the expression of emotions: "directly opposite state[s] of mind" lead to "the performance of movements of a directly opposite nature" (Darwin, 1872/1998, p. 55). For example, when discussing submission in dogs, Darwin observed that:

> The feeling of affection of a dog towards his master is combined with a strong sense of submission, which is akin to fear. Hence dogs not only lower their bodies and crouch a little as they approach their masters, but sometimes throw themselves on the ground with their bellies upwards. This is a movement as completely opposite as is possible to any show of resistance. . . . By this action [the dog seems] to say more plainly than by words, 'Behold, I am your slave.'[1]

In social species, where regular contests lead to the formation of hierarchies, displays of submission become swifter and more symbolic—they involve elaborate greeting rituals or "etiquette." For example, subordinate macaques give a "silent bared-teeth display" and chimpanzees "use a vocal-gestural signal of subordination consisting of repetitive pant-grunting and bowing towards the dominant."[2]

Thus, traits such as humility, meekness, quietude, asceticism, and obedience can be seen as different manifestations of submission—of the tendency to beat a strategic retreat in the face of overwhelming odds—which is an integral part of the display-defer strategy of resolving disputes. In this way, evolutionary theory explains the existence, and conspicuous display, of exactly those dove-ish traits that, in humans, have been called the "Christian virtues".

Thus, the conflict-resolution theory explains the origin of hawkish "pagan" and dove-ish "Christian" virtues. And it also explains why these traits have been considered moral. It is simply because, like other aspects of morality, the virtues solve a recurrent problem of social life, to the benefit of all those involved. Just as conventions solve coordination problems, and reciprocity solves free-rider problems, virtues solve conflict-resolution problems.

Human Adaptations for Conflict Resolution

Let's now turn to our own species. Given how widespread adaptations for conflict resolution are in nature, especially among social primates, and given that there is no reason to suppose that such traits have been erased during the course of hominid evolution, we should expect to find an equivalent set of adaptations in humans. And indeed we do.

This aspect of human nature was first described and documented by that perceptive student of the human condition, David Hume. Indeed, his account of virtue strikingly anticipates many aspects of the conflict-resolution theory that I have outlined.

David Hume compared human virtue to the hawkish displays of "excellence"—such as the peacock's tail and the nightingale's song—exhibited by other animals. He argued that "the same qualities cause pride in the animal as in the human kind; and it is on beauty, strength, swiftness or some other useful or agreeable quality that this passion is always founded" (1739/1978, pp. 376–377). Hume proceeded to argue that pride is "essential to the character of a man of honour," and that it gives rise to traits that benefit others—the "heroic" or "shining virtues" of "[c]ourage, intrepidity, ambition, love of glory, magnanimity" (1739/1978, pp. 376–377).

Hume also discussed the social utility of dove-ish traits, such as humility. He notes that differences in ability give rise to hierarchies in which "certain deferences and mutual submissions" are required "of the different ranks of men towards each other." He says, "Tis necessary, therefore, to know our rank and station in the world, . . . to feel the sentiment and passion of pride in conformity to it, and to regulate our actions accordingly."[3] Humility, or "a just sense of our weakness," then "is esteem'd virtuous, and procures the good-will of everyone" (Hume 1739/1978, p. 642).

Hume even explained why dove-ish virtues have become associated with the Christian church. He argued that humility, combined with contemplation of a "supreme being," tends to produce exaggerated submission displays. The thought of an omnipotent god, fostered by religions such as Christianity, is apt "to sink the human mind into the lowest submission and abasement, and to represent the monkish virtues of mortification, penance, humility, and passive suffering, as the only qualities which are acceptable to him" (Hume 1757/1889, p. 43). In such circumstances, says Hume, "instead of the destruction of monsters, the subduing of tyrants, the defence of our native country; whipping and fasting, cowardice and humility, abject submission and slavish obedience, are become the means of obtaining celestial honors among mankind."[4]

Hume managed to get this far without the aid of modern evolutionary theory. We now have the theoretical and empirical tools to develop a more up-to-date account of human virtue. And, already, several strands of research are providing support for the hypothesis that humans possess adaptations for conflict resolution, and they are beginning to shed light on exactly what they look like.

First, Allan Mazur and Alan Booth (1998) have documented how, in humans as in other animals, the hormone testosterone regulates participation in dominance encounters. Testosterone rises in anticipation of a challenge, thereby boosting "coordination, cognitive performance, and concentration" (Mazur & Booth, 1998). After the contest, levels of testosterone remain high in the winner—he experiences "increased assertiveness, and a display of dominant signs such as erect posture, sauntering or striding gait, and direct eye contact with others. [He] may seek out new dominance encounters and [is] bolstered to win them." The loser, meanwhile, experiences a drop in testosterone "reducing his assertiveness, diminishing his propensity to display the dominant actions associated with high status, and increasing his display of such submissive signs as stooped posture, smiling, or eye aversion. . . . Faced with a new dominance encounter, [the loser] is more likely than before to retreat or submit" (Mazur & Booth, 1998, p. 359).

Second, there is evidence that, in addition to displays of physical prowess, men signal status with displays of intelligence, aestheticism, and creativity—the human equivalent of the peacock's tail or the nightingale's song. As Geoffrey Miller (2000a) has observed, in every cultural sphere, including art, music, and literature, men are responsible for around ten times as much cultural production as women; male cultural production peaks at the same time that testosterone and mating effort peaks (i.e., during early adulthood); and displays of intelligence, wit, and creativity form an important part of human courtship.

Third, there is anthropological evidence that men compete for status by performing acts of generosity and largesse, in the form of potlatch feasts, bonanzas, and festivals. For example, Kristen Hawkes et al. (2001) argue that Hazda hunters compete for status and access to mates by means of big-game hunting, which can be seen as a form of "showing off" (Hawkes, 1991). This form of hunting generates more food than a hunter or his family can eat, and the surplus meat is not distributed in the expectation of reciprocity. Rather, the distribution of meat from the kill serves to raise the hunter's status among other men and to increase his access to mates. Hawkes reports that successful hunters are more often named as lovers and have more surviving offspring. Selection of such altruistic signals is consistent with the observation that "generosity" is universally admired in leaders (Brown 1991, pp. 137–140).

Fourth, as predicted, women find "winning" cues of dominance and status sexually attractive (Buss, 1994; Ellis, 1992; Miller, 1998). As the anthropologist Edgar Gregersen concludes from a study of almost 300 cultures: "for women the world over, male attractiveness is bound up with social status, or skills, strength, bravery, prowess, and similar qualities" (Gregersen, 1982). Not surprisingly, high-testosterone males also report more sexual partners (Townsend, 1998). The conflict-resolution theory of virtue also predicts that, in the context of male-male competition, men should attend to, be intimidated by, and defer to hawkish traits in other males. Unfortunately, perhaps because the answer seems so obvious, this prediction has yet to be rigorously tested.

Finally, humans display typical mammalian cues of submission. As the ethologist Desmond Morris observes:

Passive submission in the human animal is much the same as in other mammals. In extreme cases it takes the form of cringing, crouching, grovelling, whimpering, and attempts to protect the most vulnerable parts of the body. . . . It presents a picture of "instant defeat" and thereby avoids the damaging physical process of actually being defeated. Its success depends on the presentation of signals which are the exact opposite of the threat signals of our species. A threatening man will square up to an opponent, his body tense, his chest expanded, his face glaring, his fists clenched, his voice deep and snarling. By contrast, the submissive individual tries to make his body seem as small and limp as possible, with shoulders hunched, his face wincing, his hands spread, and his voice high and whining. (1982, p. 217)

More symbolic versions of these signals—in the form of greetings, manners, etiquette, and other marks of respect—are used to lubricate formal dominance hierarchies (Morris, 1982, pp. 217–228). And, intriguingly, the tendency to ignore cues of submission in an opponent—and hence to continue attacking a defeated foe—is one symptom of psychopathy (Blair, 1995).

Much work remains to be done to develop and test this theory of human adaptations for conflict resolution. However, it is reasonable to conclude that humans do indeed possess such adaptations. We can also be confident that further attempts "to introduce the experimental method of reasoning into moral subjects" will, as Hume envisaged, shed yet more light on the nature of the virtues.[5]

Traditional Accounts of the Virtues

The conflict-resolution account of virtue provides a rich deductive structure in which to locate, make sense of, and reconcile several previous theories of, and observations about, the virtues.

First, the conflict-resolution theory neatly reconciles the "pagan" and "Christian" accounts of virtue. In the absence of such a theory, the celebration of two diametrically opposed sets of moral virtues has been something of a scandal for moral philosophy. Surveying the debate between the pagans and the Christians, Isaiah Berlin (1997) concluded, rather gloomily, that the two sets of virtues are "incompatible" and "incommensurable"; that there is no prospect of reconciling them; and that this undermines the philosophical project of finding the single best way to live. However, as we have seen, it is a prediction of, rather than a problem for, the conflict-resolution theory of virtue that there should be two sets of traits—the virtues of the hawk and of the dove—and that these two sets should appear to be opposites. Contrary to Berlin, the theory shows that these sets of virtues are neither "incompatible" nor "incommensurable." On the contrary, they are two sides of the same coin—two aspects of the same component of human nature. They are complementary in that they work together to keep the peace, and their contribution can be measured in the common metric of cooperation.

Second, the conflict-resolution theory explains a wide range of miscellaneous observations about virtue. For example, it explains why the word "virtue" comes from the Latin for "proper to a man" (as in "virile");[6] why Aristotle argued that the most virtuous man will "offer aid readily" but "is ashamed to accept a good turn, because the former marks a man as superior, the latter as inferior" (Aristotle 1962, IV, iii, p. 246); and why Nietzsche argued that virtues reveal "processes of physiological prosperity or failure" and exhibit "the charm of rareness, inimitableness, exceptionalness, and unaverageness" (quoted in Miller 2000a, pp. 337–338). The conflict-resolution theory also accounts for "superogatory acts"—acts of benevolence, mercy, heroism, and self-sacrifice that are "beyond the call of duty"— whose explanation eluded John Rawls. The theory explains why Hume, Machiavelli, and Nietzsche criticize the Christian church for inculcating extreme "monkish" virtue—a "slave morality"—at the expense of more socially useful "heroic" virtue. And the theory explains why males and females have, traditionally, had different virtues; why the traits used to compete for paternal investment—beauty, chastity, and fidelity—are among the traditional "feminine virtues"; and why it is possible for men, but not women, to regain their "virtue" once it has been lost.

Conclusion

In recent years, evolutionary psychologists have begun to chart the evolved mechanisms responsible for moral thought and behaviour. Kin selection explains family values and the prohibition against incest; mutualism explains sympathy, friendship, and convention; and reciprocal altruism explains trust, gratitude, guilt, and punishment.[8] To this list we may now add: conflict resolution explains virtue.

The theory of conflict resolution explains why humans and other animals engage in displays of prowess and why they defer to superior displays. It explains how these hawkish and dove-ish traits help to solve a recurrent problem of cooperation—the problem of conflict resolution. And it explains why two apparently incompatible sets of traits have been celebrated as moral virtues.

Geoffrey Miller has led the way in one area of this theory. He has used evolutionary theory to derive predictions about the form and function of the signals employed in mate choice, and he has outlined a promising program of research that puts the predictions to the test. What we now need are parallel research programs in the other areas of conflict-resolution theory—answering in more detail such questions as the following: How does the psychology of dominance and submission work in humans? Which "virtues" are most effective in commanding deference and respect? To what extent are the virtues heritable? What age and sex differences do they exhibit? Which aspects of the environment are important for the development of the virtues?

Progress in this area will see a further branch of human morality demystified and its study placed on a firm scientific basis.

Notes

I should like to express my gratitude to Helena Cronin for her invaluable support and assistance at every stage of writing this commentary.

1. Darwin (1872/1998, p. 120). The same applies to submission cues in other species. As the primatologists Preuschoft and van Schaik (2000) put it: "While threat displays accentuate size and weapons and elicit yielding on the part of the recipient, displays of submission reduce apparent size, conceal weapons, and correlate with yielding on the part of the sender" (p. 85).

2. Preuschoft and van Schaik (2000, p. 93, p. 96). Established hierarchies constitute a further de-escalation of hostilities. To quote Preuschoft and van Schaik, "dominance in groups seems to function as a conflict management device, preventing escalated competition by conventionalizing means and priority of access [to scarce resources], thus allowing for peaceful coexistence of group members" (p. 90).

3. Hume (1739/1978, p. 650). "A sense of superiority in another breeds in all men an inclination to keep themselves at a distance from him, and determines them to

redouble the marks of respect and reverence, when they are oblig'd to approach him" (p. 441).

4. Hume (1757/1889, p. 43). Desmond Morris (1982) concurs:

Religious Displays . . . are submissive acts performed towards dominant individuals called gods. The acts themselves include various forms of body-lowering, such as kneeling, bowing, kowtowing, salaaming and prostration; also chanting and rituals of debasement and sacrifice; the offering of gifts to the gods and the making of symbolic gestures of allegiance. The function of all these actions is to appease the super-dominant beings and thereby obtain favours or avoid punishments. . . . Subordinates throughout the animal world subject themselves in a similar way. But the strange feature of these human submissive actions is that they are performed towards a dominant figure, or figures, who are never present in person. (p. 229)

5. "An Attempt to Introduce the Experimental Method of Reasoning into Moral Subjects" is the subtitle to Hume's *A Treatise of Human Nature*.

6. "Appelata est enim a viro virtus: viri autem propria maxime est fortitudo" ("The term virtue is from the word that signifies man; a man's chief quality is fortitude"; Cicero, 1945, I, ix, 18).

7. "It is good to do these actions but it is not one's duty or obligation. Supererogatory acts are not required, though normally they would be were it not for the loss or risk involved for the agent himself. . . . Supererogatory acts raise questions of first importance for ethical theory. For example, it seems offhand that classical utilitarian theory cannot account for them" (Rawls, 1971, p. 117).

8. For example, see Cosmides and Tooby (2005a); Lieberman, Tooby, and Cosmides (2003); Tooby and Cosmides (1996); Trivers (1971).

Geoffrey Miller

Catherine Driscoll and Oliver Curry provided thoughtful commentaries that suggest some refinements of my theory and some new directions for research. For clarity, I'll enumerate my responses.

First, my chapter relies heavily on costly signaling theory and sexual selection theory to explain moral virtues, as reliable indicators of general fitness that were favored in mate choice. Catherine Driscoll is correct that any costly signaling explanation for a trait must ideally show that the most attractive form of the trait is hard to fake, and she argues that moral virtues would have been rather easy to fake in prehistoric courtship. If this were true, my theory would not work. However, I think she underestimates what our Pleistocene ancestors could have learned about each other's moral virtues before having sex long enough to get pregnant. As I argued in *The Mating Mind*, prehistoric courtship would have occurred in a highly social context of small hunter-gatherer groups, in which everyone knows everyone pretty well—either personally or by reputation. Courtship would not have been like strangers meeting privately in a single's bar. Any budding sexual relationship would have provoked active information gathering, incisive judgment, and vociferous commentary by all interested parties, including both lovers' friends and families. This is standard procedure in all traditional cultures, from !Kung san hunter-gatherers through Jane Austen's Regency England.

Gossip, reputation damage, and social ostracism are potent deterrents—not just to free riding in reciprocal altruism but also to misbehaving in any way that undermines one's chances of mating well. Sexual gossip—especially gossip about the moral faults of would-be seducers—is especially salient, memorable, and quick to spread (Foster, 2004; West & Salovey, 2004). This is why psychopathy never evolved even a 1% prevalence in traditional societies. The sexually exploitative, seduce-and-abandon psychopaths who thrived in the last few hundred years of chaotically migratory European colonialism would have been quickly discovered, judged, and killed or ostracized in more stable, small-scale societies. This may also explain why the United States has a higher rate of psychopathy (c. 3.6%—Grant et al., 2004) than Europe (c. 0.7% in Oslo—Torgersen, Kringlen, & Cramer, 2001)—the European psychopaths emigrated and found a good mating niche (cf. Cooke & Michie, 1999; Cooke, Michie, Hart, & Clark, 2005). This may also be why American academics, suffering their share of unpunished psychopaths in faculty meetings and university administration, tend to overestimate the likely reproductive success of prehistoric psychopaths.

Second, Driscoll also makes the interesting suggestion that individuals with Down or Williams syndromes might be considered more virtuous in some respects than "normal" people, despite their severe neurogenetic disorders. This is true for a few "Christian" virtues (sociability, friendliness, empathy) in Williams syndrome (Jones, Bullugi, Lai, Chiles, Reilly, Lincoln, & Adolphs, 2000; Mervis & Klein-Tasman, 2000). Also, individuals with Down syndrome show lower aggressiveness, antisocial behavior, property destruction, attention seeking, lying, and stealing compared to age- and IQ-matched individuals with other neurodevelopmental disorders (but not compared to normal individuals) (Chapman & Hesketh, 2000). However, Down and Williams syndromes rarely lead to conspicuous "pagan" virtues such as magnaminity, heroism, altruism, conscientiousness, patience, or norm-enforcement, or to epistemological virtues such as intelligence, integrity, or wisdom. On the contrary, Down syndrome is associated with increased selfishness ("demandingness"), hyperactivity, anxiety, depression, and social withdrawal (Chapman & Hesketh, 2000; Roach, Orsmond, & Barratt, 1999). Williams syndrome tends to produce a loquacious over-gregariousness that, though more benign in the short term, taxes the patience of family and friends much as a narcissist or bore would. These are some reasons why individuals with these syndromes have trouble attracting mates.

Also, these syndromes are rare: about 1 in 500 for Down syndrome even in populations with age-delayed fertility profiles (Wald, Rodeck, Hackshaw, Walters, Chitty, & Mackinson, 2003), and 1 in 7,500 births for Williams syndrome (Stromme, Bjornstad, & Ramstad, 2002). Prehistoric hunter-gatherer tribes (with younger mothers and unsentimental attitudes toward infanticide of newborns with craniofacial abnormalities) might have encountered a sexually mature individual with one of these syndromes only once in every ten or twenty generations.

Costly signals need not be 100% reliable to evolve. If good brains and good genes show good statistical associations with moral virtues, then the latter can serve as a good indicator of the former. I have not demonstrated that all good brains show moral goodness or that all moral goodness issues forth from good brains. However, I did review substantial evidence that almost all mental health problems and intelligence-reducing neurodevelopmental disorders tend to undermine both the Christian and the pagan virtues.

Third, Driscoll's most important criticism of my costly signaling model is that the putative indicator trait (e.g., a moral virtue) must be the most efficient possible trait for an observer to assess, out of all possible traits that might advertise certain components of phenotypic or genetic quality. Such optimization reasoning is appropriate for most kinds of adaptations, but not for signaling adaptations, because signal evolution is highly stochastic and path dependent. This is why every animal species has a different set of fitness indicators and why taxonomists routinely use sexual ornaments (including genital morphology and courtship displays) to categorize animals. Sexual selection is a major source of biodiversity precisely because the demands of costly signaling vastly underspecify the precise design details of fitness indicators (Todd & Miller, 1997). Any indicator will do, as long as it is costly, complex, and hard to fake. This is a strength of costly signaling theory because it gives the theory very broad applicability, but it is a weakness because it makes almost impossible any a priori predictions about the design details of indicators in particular species. We can recognize an indicator post hoc when we see one, but we may have never been able to predict which indicators would evolve in which lineages.

Fourth, in a related point, Driscoll argues that the fitness information conveyed by moral virtues could be assessed more easily and reliably through other cues, such as verbal intelligence. True, if the set of phenotypic traits and genes advertised through moral virtues were precisely equivalent to the set of traits and genes advertised through verbal intelligence, then the virtues would be redundant signals. On the other hand, if there were no overlap between the traits and genes advertised by these two fitness indicators, one could not claim that they tap into a common construct of "fitness." The information they convey must overlap a bit, but not too much—like questions in a well-constructed personality scale or athletic events in a decathlon. This is a basic principle of psychometrics: more indicators yield more information. My challenge in this paper was to show that moral virtues do indeed tap into general fitness traits such as intelligence, mental health, and brain efficiency; apparently I went too far in making the virtues sound redundant as fitness signals. Of course, the existence of many individuals with high intelligence but low moral standards (e.g., promiscuous novelists, narcissistic professors, corrupt politicians, some lawyers and journalists) suggests that cognitive abilities do not overlap entirely with moral virtues.

Fifth, Driscoll mentions that mate preferences for moral virtues may have arisen as a side effect of other prior selection pressures for morality (e.g., favoring mates whose offspring will thrive given strong reciprocity, in-group norms, and punishment mechanisms), or as a side effect of a general preference for safety and well-being in sexual relationships (e.g., favoring mates who are nice rather than nasty partners). These offer reasonable alternative launchpads for getting mate preferences for moral virtues off the ground.

The question remains: once there is a fitness benefit for favoring sexual partners who seem like good strong reciprocators and/or nice partners, would these mate preferences not impose sexual selection on such traits? This is a generic problem with apparently parsimonious explanations of mate preferences as side effects of other preferences—such hypotheses rarely take the next step and consider the resulting sexual selection pressures. If prehistoric hominids routinely favored sexual partners who seemed likely to be nice rather than nasty, then they would have imposed sexual selection for niceness—over and above any other selection pressures that favored niceness.

Sixth, Oliver Curry develops a fascinating account of the virtues as conflict-resolution devices. It is a complementary costly signaling account: whereas I focus on intersexual selection (mate choice), Curry focuses on intrasexual rivalry (conflict, dominance, and submission). Both processes were probably important in human evolution, so both imposed selection pressures for certain kinds of moral virtues as costly signals of superiority or of submissiveness. His account is especially good at accounting for (1) the disjunction between pagan virtues (superiority signals) and Christian virtues (submissiveness signals), (2) the submissive, dove-like qualities of many religious practices, and (3) the functional and behavioral similarities between many human virtues and animal conflict-resolution signals. Both of our theories seem pretty good at explaining superogatory acts (conspicuously virtuous behavior that goes beyond the call of duty) by drawing attention to the social-signaling and reputational benefits of such acts for mate attraction and rival intimidation.

Seventh, Curry's dominance/submission focus sheds new light on some aspects of human courtship that I had not considered before. Courtship in many societies (and in many animal species) requires an extraordinarily complex, dynamic alternation between dominance signals and submission signals. A male must approach a female confidently and assertively yet show cues of deference, innocuousness, and respect for her power of mate choice. A female must test a male's fitness and resolve by resisting his current advances, yet inviting further attempts. This is not sexist stereotyping, but Animal Behavior 101. Pure dominance does not provoke sexual attraction, nor does pure submissiveness. Frequent subtle reversals of romantic power and dominance seem the most exciting. The skilled, socially intelligent, maximally virtuous lover can switch from hawk to dove and back again within one kiss. This is the basic plotline in many sexual fantasies (Leitenberg & Henning, 1995), in female-oriented romance novels (Salmon & Symons, 2004), in ritualized sex play involving bondage, domination, sadism, and masochism (Baumeister, 1997), and in copulation itself. These aspects of courtship seem to involve a sort of metadisplay of signaling prowess: male and female demonstrate their mastery of the conflict-resolution signals through continually testing each other's dominance and submissiveness. Those who are poor at such metadisplay may seem too pushy or wimpy, too ardent or cool; they may adopt alternative sexual strategies that get diagnosed as "courtship disorders" such as paraphilias (exhibitionism, frotteurism, voyeurism) or crimes (stalking, harassment, rape; Freund & Seto, 1998). Thus, mate choice may favor displays of one's ability to modulate dominance/submission signals quickly, creatively, and adaptively, as a reliable indicator of intrasexual conflict-resolution skill.

5 | Symbolic Thought and the Evolution of Human Morality

Peter Ulric Tse

How Human Symbolic Thought Came into Being

While the cognitive, perceptual, and emotional capacities of humans and apes share much in common (e.g., numeric thought: Hauser, Dehaene, Dehaene-Lambertz, & Patalano, 2002; certain substrates of language: Hauser, Chomsky, & Fitch, 2002), there is a core set of abilities that makes humans fundamentally different from apes and other animals in kind, not just in degree. There are no documented cases of other animals dancing to rhythmic sounds, intentionally producing art, or spontaneously generating and manipulating meaningful symbols. Although some animals have learned to use what appear to be symbols in a rudimentary fashion (e.g., Savage-Rumbaugh, McDonald, Sevcik, Hopkins, & Rubert, 1986; Savage-Rumbaugh, 1987; see also Kaminsky, Call, & Fischer, 2004; Pepperberg, 2002), they do not generate them spontaneously in the wild and cannot do so in the flexible, generative, and recursive manner of humans (Petitto & Seidenberg, 1979; Terrace, Petitto, Sanders, & Bever, 1979). While chimpanzees and bonobos can be trained to associate a meaning with an arbitrary sign, establishing such an association typically takes many trials (Petitto & Seidenberg, 1979). Humans still have associative learning in common with other animals, but in addition humans have one-shot learning of associations among arbitrary categories of things and events. While there are instances of one-shot associative learning in the animal world, such as the Garcia effect, where animals learn to avoid the food last eaten before becoming nauseous (even when the food could not have caused the nausea), cases such as the Garcia effect are the exception that proves the rule. One-shot learning is possible in such special cases because certain animals are hardwired to make particular kinds of one-shot associations, such as between nausea and food. In general, however, animals, unlike humans, are not hardwired for one-shot learning if the learning takes place between arbitrary classes of events. Repetition is typically necessary to learn arbitrary associations for mammals other than ourselves because this type of learning is the learning of probabilities of event co-occurrence and predictiveness. Associative learning through repetition is a far cry from the one-shot learning of a symbol's referent by a human child or the ease with which a child can change a symbol's referent at will. Such learning can occur in the absence of co-occurrence between a thing and that to which it refers, and indeed it can occur in the absence of any direct experience with a thing at all, as when a child learns the meaning of the word "ancestor" or "heaven." Indeed, the cognitive/neural changes that made one-shot learning among arbitrary events possible also made symbolic cognition possible. Our nearest animal relatives may be able to learn arbitrary associations, but they are not using symbols in the way that we humans use symbols. Beyond lacking syntax, they are not typically able to effortlessly assign or reassign an arbitrary meaning to a given symbol once an association has been learned. It is this arbitrary and flexible relationship between a symbol and its referent(s) that is the hallmark of true symbolic thought, setting it apart from mere association, and it is one that all other known animals appear to lack. While it has often been emphasized that syntax and language are what most separate us from higher apes, syntax and language are most likely more recent developments[1] that emerged long after the more fundamental ability to understand and use arbitrary symbols nonsyntactically. In short, the capacities that set humans apart in kind, not just in degree, from all other known animals include capacities and propensities for art, music, dance, analogical reasoning, abstract thought, the spontaneous generation and use of symbols, and the ability to reason abstractly about others (e.g., Povinelli & Preuss, 1995; Povinelli, Dunphy-Lelii, Reaux, & Mazza, 2002) and about events, as well as the ability to manipulate symbols recursively and syntactically. The first part of this paper explores the hypothesis that all these modes of human behavior and cognition share a common root cause.

The central claim developed here is that neuronal circuits underlying perceptual, motoric, and cognitive capacities that were functionally distinct and modularly encapsulated (Fodor, 1983) in our earlier chimp-like ancestors came to interact through a new type of attentional binding in our more recent ancestors. This paper addresses the architectural changes in information processing that permitted this breakdown of modularity,[2] without getting too deeply into any "engineering" solutions at the level of neuronal circuitry that might have realized these architectural changes. However, one or more neural/genetic changes must have occurred to account for the emergence of uniquely human modes of behavior and thought at or after the divergence of our genetic line from that which led to chimpanzees and bonobos. Because of this change, operators previously limited to operands within a given module could now operate over the operands of other modules. Cross-modular binding and entrainment are seen as the root cause underlying the birth of uniquely human modes of cognition.

The Nature of Symbols

It is not necessary to review the complexities of semiotic theory to understand that a symbol has various aspects. One is the perceived "sign," which exists as a representation that is seen, heard, touched, or otherwise experienced. For a given person, a sign can stand for one or more referents, which can be thought of as the meaning of the sign. A sign's referent(s) can belong to many different types of mental representations, which themselves need not be signs. If the mental representation is one of an object (or type of object) in the outside world, then the sign symbolizes that thing in the world. When a sign has a referent (i.e., a meaning) for a particular perceiver, it is a symbol for that perceiver. A symbol is assumed to possess two key defining properties: (1) a symbol is a mental representation that can be stored in long-term memory or held in short-term memory that can stand for one or more arbitrary stored or online representations; (2) a symbol can be flexibly remapped to an existing or new referent without a need for many trials of learning to build up an association. In other words, a symbol is arbitrary. Its meaning is not based on the likelihood or degree of co-occurrence between a sign and its referent. It is simply assigned. Several animals may have some capacity to process information in the sense of (1), but only humans, as far as we know, possess the capacity to process symbols in the sense of (2) as well. A mind capable of (1) but incapable of (2) can learn complex associations between an object or event and some referent, but it is "associational" rather than truly symbolic. Many animal minds are exquisitively sensitive to probabilities of co-occurrence. If one object or event tends to predict or accompany the occurrence of some other object or event, cognition capable of (1) can make and learn an association between these objects and events. Classical conditioning is an example of an ancient form of associational learning. In contrast, a three-year-old child can pretend that a block is a truck and then, a moment later, pretend that it is a monster. This capacity to instantly remap the referent of an object file is unique to humans and is at the heart of why our cognition can be truly symbolic. Even if it turns out that symbolic processing is not unique to humans, this would in no way alter the present theory, since the goal here is to explain the changes in cognitive architecture that led to human symbolic cognition. If dolphins, bonobos, or martians turn out to be symbolic as well, that would be nice, but it has no apparent bearing on how we became symbolic. It so happens that humans appear to be unique in our symbolic cognitive capacities, but this is not in itself all that interesting. What is interesting is understanding how our minds came to be the way they are.

Attention and Object Files

An "object file" (Kahneman, Treisman, & Gibbs, 1992) is a metaphor for attentional processes that combine multiple types of information existing over various modalities into a common bound representation of an object. An object file is an attentionally tracked "figure" (Lamy & Tsal, 2000) integrated as a temporary episodic representation in a short-term memory buffer (Kahneman, Treisman, & Gibbs, 1992; Schneider, 1999) that maintains a coherent identity even as the particular contents defining that identity change over time. While there are a variety of conceptions of what an object file is (Pylyshyn & Storm, 1988; Carey & Xu, 2001; Scholl, Pylyshyn, & Feldman, 2001), all conceptions have in common a psychological entity that keeps track of an object over time, within some space. This space need not be spatial space. It could be any space that obeys a metric. For example, one can track in musical space. One can listen to a symphony and track the oboe. Once can then listen to the same symphony again and this time track the lead violin. In both cases the sensory input is the same. What differs is the nature of the object file one constructs. Object files can only exist in the context of a memory buffer that keeps track of the bound representation. Even though the term "object file" contains the word "object," an object file need not correspond to an object in the outside world. It could just as well correspond to a thought or plan that one is keeping track of in the presence of complete sensory deprivation. Nonetheless, the prototypical example of an object file is one associated with a tracked visual object, and it is in the domain of concrete object tracking that object files may have had their origin. The contents of an object file may change, and the labels attached to that object file may change, as when one says, "It's a bird; it's a plane; it's Superman!" However, the object endures as a single object over time by virtue of having a single object file associated with it, not by virtue of having constant contents or a constant label. The contents of an object file are thought to be mid to high level. That is, there is widely thought to be a preattentive stage of representation that cannot be attended and whose contents cannot be added to an object file (Wolfe, 2003; Treisman & Gelade, 1980). Attention can only operate over automatically preprocessed representations available after the operators of early perceptual systems have transformed raw sensory input into mid-level representations. Possible object file contents can be perceptual features, such as color and texture, that may exist on feature maps (Treisman, 1992; Quinlan, 2003), mid-level structures such as surfaces (He & Nakayama, 1992), abstract identity tags (Gordon & Irwin, 1996), or higher level conceptual information (Gordon & Irwin, 2000). The contents of an object file are not static. They are also not simply dictated by the flux of bottom-up sensory input. They can be changed through the manipulations of numerous cognitive operations, such as mental rotation or attention, as when one attends to any of a number of well-known bistable figures to bring out the appearance of one figure and then another. The sensory input has not changed, but the contents of the object file have changed dramatically because of the action of a cognitive operator on sensory operands.

One of the central ideas developed here is that symbols and symbolic thought are inherently attentional in nature, because they involve (now or involved in the past) the binding of a sign with arbitrary referents, whether temporarily in working memory or more durably in long-term memory. With unintentional repetition or intentional practice, arbitrary representations can become bound together in memory. This is the relatively slow process of associative learning that humans share with other animals. With attention to joint object files, however, arbitrary representations can become bound together in memory after one instance.[3] Attentionally bound symbols and referents can be "chunked" or bound together in memory, recalled as a unit, and later processed without the need for further attention. However, at the stage of encoding, one-shot binding of symbol and referent occurs because symbols and referents occupy a common object file. Symbols are inherently attentional because binding (within a tracked object file) is just what attention is.

How Object Files Changed: Cross-Modular Binding

Whereas many nonhuman animals appear to have the capacity to monitor, select, ignore, track, and otherwise attend to objects and therefore must have analogs of human object files in their cognitive architecture, human and animal object files differ. A dog's object file of a tree, for instance, presumably contains color and shape information represented in different neural populations or maps, indexed by location, as well as other information that the dog has learned to associate with this particular tree or trees in general. A dog's object file can be multimodal, in the sense that auditory, haptic, olfactory, visual, and other information can all occupy the object file of the tree. All types of information, however, are about the tree. A dog's object file is encapsulated in the sense that it cannot contain information about irrelevant objects or events. Object file encapsulation presumably helps animals survive, because irrelevant information is not represented, permitting the animal to remain undistracted and unconfused by matters irrelevant to survival and the matter at hand.[4] Human object files, unlike animal object files, can contain *any* information which can be attended or downloaded from memory into the object file. As such, human object files can enact truly cross-modular binding. Because any representation can be downloaded into the object file of a tree, a tree can be taken to stand for "my friend Bob," "truth," or anything else. This requires tagging the tree component of the object file as real (i.e., pointing to the world) and the Bob component as not real or referential (i.e., pointing to a representation that need not be in the world). In the absence of such a tag, a person might take a tree to really be Bob. Cognitive modularity and encapsulation protect animal minds from cognitive "noise" and the obvious dangers of misrepresentation, psychosis, delusion, and hallucination.

Whereas animals seem to be capable of internally modeling events that might happen or might have happened, humans go beyond this "literal" capacity to one of imagination that can model events and objects that could never happen and could never exist in the real world. Imagination became possible when arbitrary contents and operators could be downloaded to a common object file. For example, the representation of wings could be downloaded into the object file containing the representation of tree. The operator that places one object onto another could then be accessed to create a new representation of a tree with wings. Such a construction was not possible in the more chimp-like minds of our early ancestors.

A human object file of a tree can contain everything that a dog's would, plus information that has nothing to do with this particular tree or any tree. For example, a man looking at a tree can simply decide that it stands for his wife. This is accomplished by downloading representations of his wife into the object file holding the tree information. That information can be as minimal as a label or pointer to the concept wife, or it could be much more specific to his particular wife and as elaborate as circumstances demand. Importantly, this downloading to the present object file need not take place in a conscious manner or a manner dictated by the plans or goals of a central executive. It can happen entirely automatically and unconsciously. Because of automatic cross-modular binding, he may see a tree standing next to a bush, and this may remind him of his wife and son because of their similar size relationships. He did not plan this to happen. It happened in a stimulus-driven manner because similarity in one domain automatically triggered activation on other maps encoded in terms of the same relationships, and these new activations, in this case corresponding to representations of his wife and son, were automatically downloaded to the object file containing the representations of the tree and bush, which then could function as symbols of his wife and son. He might say that the tree and bush remind him of his wife and son, but this fact became available to his conscious report after the link between disparate representations had been made. Thus, symbols, although inherently attentional in nature, because initially mediated by the attentional construct of an object file, are not necessarily volitionally constructed. It must be emphasized that symbolic thought, though inherently attentional, need not be driven by volition or intentions, although it can be. Just as a motion in the visual periphery will automatically draw one's attention, symbolic thought can be carried out in an automatic or nonvolitional mode. In particular, reminding is a consequence of the basic architecture of human symbolic cognition. A dog cannot be reminded of anything by a tree and a bush other than things that have a direct link in its experience or in the world with a tree and a bush. Animal cognition, lacking any basis for symbolism, reminding, or metaphor, is inherently literal.

Cross-Modular Binding Gave Rise to New Types of Mental Dysfunction

Human cognition, though much richer than that of a dog or chimpanzee, runs the danger of associational breakdown where everything reminds one of everything else, or stands for anything else, and also runs the danger of hallucination, where the border between what is real and self-generated breaks down. Quite simply, our minds can break down in novel ways that the minds of most animals cannot. It is possible that various types of psychosis, schizophrenia, and many other human mental disorders are the result of the malfunctioning of neuronal systems or cognitive operations which in mentally healthy individuals permit the possibility of symbolic, analogic, creative, and imaginative thought. Examining the neural and genetic bases of disorders of these types of higher cognitive processing holds great promise in revealing the genetic basis of the change(s) in neural circuitry that must have given rise to cross-modular binding.

Symbolic Thought versus Syntactic Thought

The ability to use and recognize symbols must have preceded the evolution of language, because whereas syntactic processing is necessarily symbolic, symbolic processing need not be syntactic. Language by its very nature involves the utterance and manipulation of symbols. It is therefore unlikely that language as such was the capacity that first emerged to define protohuman symbolic cognition. According to the cross-modular binding hypothesis, primitive types of dance, art, music, humor, analogy, and symbolic reasoning evolved early, followed potentially much later by the emergence of syntactic operations over symbols. Indeed, binding and the ability to form associations across previously encapsulated classes of information may have at first been relatively rudimentary capacities. The first symbols used by our ancestors may have been no more than sticks and stones used to stand for and mimic objects, animals, or people. And the human body itself could easily have served as a symbol, because pretending to be something or someone else would require placing the body and the referent in the same object file. Indeed, some recent authors suggest that early human communication took the form of mimesis rather than language (Corballis, 2002; Donald, 1991). No such use of symbols would have left material evidence in the fossil record. It would therefore be a mistake to assume that symbolic reasoning emerged with the first evidence of art in the fossil record. However, once even rudimentary symbolic reasoning was in place, selective pressure could operate on this new capacity, leading over time to the complex forms of symbol manipulation found in modern humans.

Cross-modular binding freed object files to contain information from other modules. The "primary" content of an object file corresponding to a perceived sign became a symbol when information to which the sign referred could be added to the object file. Although an initial binding between symbol and referent requires attention in the case of one-shot learning, once encoded together as a "chunk," a symbol can access its meaning directly, even in the absence of attention, because it is bound with its meaning in memory. Thus, a symbol need not invoke a joint attentional object file if it has already been "chunked" and laid down in long-term memory. That is, such prebound symbols can be processed in the absence of attention. However, even a prebound symbol must have once been an attentional construct, because only attention can bind disparate types of information within a common object file.

Cross-modular binding may also be able to account for the emergence of syntax, which presumably evolved over a long period after the emergence of primitive symbolic expression. The syntactic symbol manipulation found in language and mathematics has as its core the recursive application of rules for the manipulation of symbols (Chomsky, 1965; Hauser, Chomsky, & Fitch, 2002). Other animals apply computations recursively (e.g., to the representation of their own position when they navigate or when they carry out sequential motoric acts with their hands), but these nested computations appear to be largely modular. Hauser, Chomsky, and Fitch (2002) have recently suggested that such modular and domain-specific recursive computations may have become domain general over the course human evolution. That is, the recursion found in one module could be applied to the contents of other modules. This hypothesis is consistent with the general principles developed here. Binding across modules may have permitted computations carried out over, say, a recursive navigational map, or the body's nested sequencing movements through space, to be applied to the contents of other maps. Once recursion could be applied to symbols, symbols could be combined recursively and therefore generatively. Natural and sexual selection could then act on this capacity, resulting ultimately in our present capacity of language. The focus here, however, is to explain not the emergence of syntax and language but the emergence of the symbolic cognition that must have preceded syntactic and linguistic cognition.

Cross-Modular Neuronal Entrainment

Although this is a cognitive theory of cross-modular binding, some speculation concerning the neuronal mechanisms underlying cross-modular binding may be useful. It should be emphasized, however, that cognitive architectural changes described up until now could be correct even if the neuronal mechanism outlined here turns out not to be correct.

Until this point cross-modular binding has been talked about as cross-modular attentional binding involving symbolic referents. However, some forms of cross-modular excitation or inhibition may have happened in a bottom-up manner not requiring the imposition of symbolic referents. One of the most basic and perhaps earliest consequences of cross-modular information transfer was entrainment across previously encapsulated modular representations. That such entrainment occurs in the human mind is an important clue to the manner in which modular encapsulation broke down. One fascinating clue is that some form of dancing occurs in all human cultures. A martian who descended to earth would probably find it curious that only one species on earth undulates its body in synchrony with patterns of air pressure in the 1-Hz range. He might find it equally curious that this species does not spontaneously undulate in the presence of rhythmic pulses of odor, light, or taste. This asymmetry offers clues to the neural substrate of cross-modular binding. Dancing affords the simplest example of a novel behavior that arose because of binding across modules. After the mutation(s) in question, neurons tuned to auditory stimuli could entrain motor neurons, allowing auditory rhythms to trigger rhythmic motoric behavior. Prior to the occurrence of the gene mutation(s) that presumably caused the rewiring of neuronal circuitry that permitted cross-modular binding, even rudimentary dancing behaviors in response to auditory rhythms would have been cognitively and motorically impossible, because neurons within the auditory module would not have entrained motor neurons. Such entrainment presumably requires (cortico-cortical or corticothalamocortical) excitatory connections that presumably did not exist in the brains of our chimp-like ancestors and do not exist in the brains of other animals. The absence of such connections is the reason why no nonhuman animal dances or can dance to rhythmic sound. Although they can hear the sounds, they quite literally cannot be entrained to the beat.

Neural entrainment does not require the existence of object files that contain symbolic referents. Neural entrainment merely requires coexcitation of neuronal activity across and within modules. For example, the gesticulations that modern humans make while talking are precisely synchronized with speech (McNeill, 1985) and convey meaning that supplements language, particularly when the speaker is conveying information about space or emotions (Goldin-Meadow, McNeill, & Singleton, 1996). If modern human gesticulations are indicative of prelinguistic gesticulations, then hand, arm, and head motions may have become entrained to the emotional content and rhythm of existing vocalizations long before the evolution of spoken language or syntactic symbol manipulation or even symbolic thought (cf. Corballis, 2002; Donald, 1991).

The cross-modular binding hypothesis operates under the assumption that the neuronal encoding of events on different modules will share common spatiotemporal characteristics (such as bursting, or firing with a particular frequency or pattern) if the stimuli to which the corresponding neurons are tuned have common spatiotemporal characteristics (such as abruptly changing, slowly changing, intense, or nonintense). For example, the binding hypothesis would predict that the activation on the auditory module "wawawawa" should entrain and therefore be associated with smooth or undulating hand motions (motoric) or drawn curves (visual) in all human cultures, as opposed to the more abrupt hand motions or jagged shapes that would be associated with a sound like "tiktiktiktiktik." This would follow because auditory modulation is smooth in the former case but abrupt in the latter.

Neural entrainment and binding across modules can only occur if there are direct or indirect neuronal connections that permit entrainment to take place. One prediction that follows from the binding hypothesis is that there are corticocortical, corticothalamic, or thalamothalamic connections between neurons within different modules in humans that are not present in chimpanzees or other nonhuman apes. It is not simply that there is more connectivity in the human brain; it is of a different kind. Modules that function relatively independently in chimpanzees, because they are not directly connected, should share direct uni- or bidirectional axonal connections in humans or share indirect connectivity via another area, such as the thalamus. Diffusion tensor imaging and fiber tract tracing of the different species' cortices and thalami may be able to ascertain whether this prediction is correct.

Ramachandran and Hubbard (2001) have recently proposed that synesthesia is due to "cross-wiring" between the brain areas that subserve the percepts that synesthetes simultaneously perceive. For example, synesthetes who perceive different black numbers to have different colors may have fibers that link the area that codes for numbers and the area that codes for color. The authors point out that both areas lie near the angular gyrus. Because synesthesia runs in families and may be X-linked (Bailey & Johnson, 1997), it is possible that the presumed excess fiber proliferation or faulty pruning that underlies synesthesia is genetic. This proposal is related to the present cross-modular binding hypothesis to the extent that coactivation across maps arises from novel cross-connectivity. Whereas synesthesia would arise from novel cross-connectivity not found in most other people, binding arose from novel cross-connectivity that did not exist in earlier hominids. Once this trait arose, it was presumably selected for until it spread throughout the entire population. Thus, binding across modules is, according to the current hypothesis, a normal part of human cortical organization, and not a rare occurrence as is synesthesia. The current hypothesis is one about how the normal human brain developed, not just one about unusual, synesthetic brains. Moreover, their "cross-wiring" proposal does not offer a model of how neuronal connectivity gives rise to synesthesia. The binding hypothesis, in contrast, ascribes a specific function to cross-modular connectivity. In particular, neural entrainment across previously encapsulated modules is presumed to arise because of synchronous patterns of neuronal discharge. And cross-modular binding occurs in the general case because of operators and operands shared within a common object file. Future research will have to determine whether the genetic basis of synesthesia is related to the proposed genetic basis of the connectivity that underlies cross-modular binding in normal human brains. There is no reason to think that it is.

The Birth of Analogical Cognition

On this account, the human capacities for metaphor and analogy arose from cross-modular binding because events represented within one module could entrain and therefore spontaneously remind one of events represented by neurons within another module. The cross-modular binding hypothesis would predict that there are analogies that transcend cultures (cf. Lakoff & Johnson, 2003), because the root of those analogies is the entrainment of neurons across modules that are responding to corresponding properties of stimuli. For example, if neurons tend to respond with an abrupt burst of firing to the onset of a loud sound, they will entrain neurons that respond with an abrupt onset within, say, the visual module. Similarly, neurons that respond to more intense auditory stimuli by firing more would entrain neurons that respond correspondingly to visual input. Loudness and abruptness of sounds should therefore be considered analogous to brightness and abruptness of visual onset across all human cultures. In contrast, an abrupt and loud sound and a gradually modulating or dimming light should not seem analogous to any humans, regardless of culture. However, it is not only the spatiotemporal (e.g., intense, abrupt, grouped, or continuous) and physical (e.g., pitch, color) characteristics of stimuli that would entrain neurons tuned to corresponding characteristics within other modules. That is, neural entrainment need not be only sensorimotoric. The semantic, cognitive, and emotional characteristics of stimuli could drive cross-modular entrainment as well. Thus, one might predict that the feeling of sadness or depression would be associated with lowness or downness across all cultures, and that joy would be associated with highness and upness. The same might be said for intelligence and quickness or sharpness, on the one hand, and stupidity and dullness or slowness on the other. Countless similar examples can be given. Although such examples seem amusing, it really is an empirical question whether all cultures make such associations.

A deeper kind of analogical correspondence than sensory-sensory correspondence would have emerged as sensory modules entrained cognitive modules. For example, a tall tree among bushes might remind one of a tall person surrounded by short ones. It is this reminding-of that comprises the basis of analogical or metaphoric thought. Analogical thought is in turn a by-product of the synchronous firing, coupling, or entrainment of distal neuronal populations across modules. In order for such analogies to be automatically evoked by a given stimulus, the manner in which, say, tallness is encoded in the firing of neurons on the sensory module in question must be similar enough to the manner in which correspond- ing qualities are encoded across entrained modules that entrainment is possible. This raises the prospect that there is a shared neuronal pattern of firing for similar qualities of objects and their relationships, even when the neurons representing that similar information exist within different modules.

The emergence of binding across modules triggered not only the birth of symbolic thought by permitting arbitrary objects to stand for arbitrary referents but also triggered automatic cross-modular activations. Analogy and metaphor are now defining aspects of human cognition. Indeed, they are perhaps almost as important as the ability to express and entertain ideas using symbols. Analogy emerged for the same reason that symbolic thought emerged. After the emergence of cross-modular binding, an attended object represented within a given module could activate unat- tended information represented within other modules, which could then be added to the object file. That is, an object file could hold not only the module-appropriate features of the object but also activations, associations, or referents active within unrelated modules. For example, if an object moved abruptly, it could remind one of something else that changed abruptly, and if it moved slowly, it might arouse an entirely different set of associations. In this manner, a given event or object represented within, say, the visual or auditory module could come to be associated with arbi- trary activations within other modules.

Prior to the emergence of cross-modular binding, our ancestors attended in a "literal" fashion to information about objects carried by neuronal firing within functionally isolated modules. After genetic mutation(s) in genes presumably encoding aspects of how neurons form into specific neuronal circuitry during development, binding became cross-modular. A given attended stimulus could automatically evoke neuronal firing on unrelated modules, or within neighboring nodes within a module, which could in turn be attended or not. Thus, in addition to being capable of being reminded of something by something else superficially quite differ- ent, the human mind is inherently prone to making semantic associations as one activation triggers another in nodes connected to it within a network of semantic representations. In order to protect itself from associational breakdown, human mental architecture had to develop mechanisms to suppress meaningless associations and enhance meaningful associations by suppressing and enhancing the degree of firing of entrained neurons within unrelated modules or within connected nodes. Thus, human object files may differ from those of other animals not only in containing operands and operators from different once-encapsulated modules but also in their capacity to overcome or preempt distraction and in their capacity to track. One possibility is that certain executive circuitry evolved to play this role.

Cross-Modular Operators and the Birth of Human Aesthetics

To reiterate, in addition to permitting symbolic thought, a key consequence of the emergence of cross-modular binding was that operators could be bound with new types of operands, such that operators from one module could operate on the operands of previously encapsulated modules. That is, not only concepts and percepts but also operators could be downloaded into an object file. As already mentioned, nestable motoric operators could operate upon symbols rather than just physical actions, giving rise to the possibility of syntax. Another example would be that operators designed to decode the emotional content of vocalizations could now operate over nonvocal sounds, giving rise to the possibility of music. And basic aspects of art and human aesthetics may have emerged as a consequence of operators that became "disencapsulated" or "universalized." For example, operators that evolved to discern genetic health in a potential mate could now operate over visual scenes, which could then attain the status of eroticism or beauty, although obviously a scene cannot be a mate. According to this view, a macaque can assess the emotional content of a vocalization or the beauty (i.e., genetic health and fertility) of a potential mate's face and body but could not apply those operators to things other than vocalizations and bodies. Operators in a macaque are dedicated and domain-specific operators, whereas in humans they became domain general. A macaque or dog or cow can hear sounds but cannot experience music.

Because cognition and behavior leave no direct physical record, it is impossible to know the first consequences of cross-modular binding in our ancestors who first had the mutation(s) that led to this new form of binding. It could be that behavioral changes occurred immediately or that they built up over hundreds of generations as natural selection acted upon them. Some degree of speculation is unavoidable when hypothesizing about cognitive and behavioral changes brought about by connectivity changes in our ancestors' brains. However, we can examine types of cross-modular binding in modern human behavior for possible clues to the changes that may have occurred in our ancestors' minds and behaviors. Modern human behavior is rich with evidence of cross-modular binding, and it is this evidence that ties together numerous human behaviors that seem unrelated.

Of course, encapsulated modular operators could have evolved to great levels of complexity while still being limited to a particular class of operands. For example, it is possible that the mental operator that permitted the internal visualization of shape required for stone tool production developed in complete isolation from other mental operations. It could be that it was limited to the operand of stone. Indeed, it is surprising that no bone or antler tools are found until very late in the fossil record. However, once made domain general, this operator could be applied to very different operands than stone and perhaps could be used to generate more than tools. Once made domain general, such a capacity of three-dimensional visualization could permit visualization of forms and combinations that could not exist and thus could have played an important role in the birth of human imagination.

Cross-Modular Operators and the Birth of Abstract, Religious, and Causal Cognition

The essence of abstraction is the ability to detect patterns that are not evident in the immediate sensory input. That is, abstraction requires the representation of currently unobservable entities. Pattern extraction is common to the perceptual systems of many animals, but in nonhuman animals, pattern extraction may be modularly isolated from the other contents of cognition and, thus, domain specific. Once modularity broke down because of cross-modular binding, the computations underlying pattern extraction and recognition could be applied to data that were not perceptual in nature. An example of perceptual pattern recognition that became abstract pattern recognition in humans involves the inference[5] of causality. Other animals may be able to detect patterns of cause and effect in the flow of sensory input, because they carry out computations over sensory input that evolved specifically to solve this task. However, other animals may not be able to detect causal relations that are not evident in current sensory input. Because animals seem to be limited to causal pattern extraction from the current flow of sensory input, they may be

limited to detecting physical causal relations that arise from spatiotemporal contiguity and simultaneity. In the human lineage, however, the computations dedicated to the extraction of patterns of causal relation in the
sensory domain came to operate over the contents of other modules, permitting the extraction of patterns of causal relation that transcended spatiotemporal contiguity. For example, once causal relations could be detected
in the contents of memory, patterns of cause and effect could be recognized that transcended the here and now. One could become aware of a
time before one's life or after one's death. One could entertain the fact of
one's impending death. Simply put, whereas other animals can "connect
the dots" perceptually, they cannot do so abstractly. Humans, in contrast,
came to connect the dots to such an extent that hidden causes such as
invisible beings (e.g., gods, demons) and modes of causality (e.g., karma,
luck, the evil eye, curses, prayer, fate) were invoked to explain visible
events, such as the weather, or life and death. Religion began in our lineage
when pattern recognition operators became domain general. For example,
the operator that determines whether sensory input comprises an animate
being is an important operator for all mammals, since animals can be
predators, prey, or mates. After cross-modular binding permitted this
operator to become domain general, animacy and associated mental traits
such as volition, personality, and intentionality could be seen in many
patterns of events, even those that we now take to be patently nonanimate.
Once the human mind became symbolic, it became a "congenital animist."
Another example would be that operations that evolved for perceptual
grouping on the basis of similarity, or the segregation of figure from
ground, came to be applied to the contents of other modules with the
breakdown of the modular mind. Once patterns of similarity/difference
could be detected in information that was not perceptual, the human
mind gained the capacity to become "unglued" from the here and now,
free to connect the dots in novel ways. In fact, however, our ancestors
probably connected the dots in characteristically animalistic ways, for
example, tending to place events in a framework of causality governed
by invisible animate beings simply because we had inherited this way of
organizing events from our presymbolic ancestors, who organized events
in terms of the actions and intentions of other animals. We generalized
such tendencies to beyond the here and now. Human religiosity
emerged with symbolic thought by applying an ancient and presymbolic
way of inferring causality and perceiving patterns in the flow of events
to operands that went beyond events in the currently perceived
environment.

A theory of mind may have emerged with the capacity to think abstractly. As Povinelli et al. (2002) have written:

(A)lthough chimpanzees are excellent at exploiting the observable contingencies that exist between the facial and bodily postures of other agents on the one hand, and events in the world on the other, these animals may not construe others as possessing psychological states related to "seeing" or "attention." Humans and chimpanzees share homologous suites of psychological systems that detect and process information about both the static and dynamic aspects of social life, but humans alone may possess systems which interpret behavior in terms of abstract, unobservable mental states such as seeing and attention.

In order to represent others' invisible mental states, one must be able to detect patterns, including patterns of causality, in invisible, nonperceivable entities. Once the ability to think and perceive abstractly evolved, patterns of invisible behavior, such as thought, intention, perception, and attention in others, could be recognized and inferred. Before the emergence of abstract thought afforded by the application of computations originally dedicated to perceptual pattern recognition, no true theory of mind was possible.

Changes in the Nature of Play

The nature of play would also have changed as a consequence of cross-modular binding and the emergence of symbolic reasoning. In nonhuman mammals, play involves pretending to enact adult behaviors, such as fighting and hunting. In humans, however, play involves not only this but also pretending to be something that one is not. Because one can oneself symbolize anything, one can pretend to be, for example, an animal, another person, or an object. One can even pretend to be something that does not exist, such as an elf or an egg with wings. There are no examples of this kind of symbolic play in other mammals because no other animals think symbolically or even analogically, since both types of thought entail a breakdown in modularity. Once the body could be used as a symbol, the body could be used to communicate. Donald (1991) has suggested that our ancestors went through a stage where mimesis was the primary means of communication. Once our ancestors understood that objects could have arbitrary referents, the body itself could be exploited as a symbol to convey arbitrary referents. Thus pointing, mimesis, and pretend play may all have emerged with symbolic thought and cross-modular binding and operations.

Symbolic Thought and the Evolution of Human Morality

Symbolic Thought Gave Rise to Morality

The emergence of symbolic thought had profound consequences for human moral cognition. You might say that the birth of symbolic thought gave rise to the possibility of true morality and immorality, of good and evil. Once acts became symbolized, they could now stand for, and be instances of, abstract classes of action such as good, evil, right, or wrong. Symbolic thought permitted new dimensions of behavior, for example, the expression of territoriality over the ownership of an idea rather than just a concrete thing such as turf, a bone, or a mate. Thus, while a monkey has affection, social intelligence, likes, dislikes, fear, inhibitions, territoriality, deceit, aggression, vengefulness, and other predispositions that govern behavior, these are not morality. The more prosocial of these modes of feeling and thinking can be thought of as "preadaptations" for morality, but they are not morality. A monkey lacks moral judgment, prohibitions, norms, principles, laws, approval, disapproval, injunctions, the concept of good, the concept of wrong, virtues or vices. A monkey lacks morality because it lacks symbolic cognition. This is why animals in general are amoral rather than immoral or moral. They cannot conceive of doing the right thing or the wrong thing. This is why we do not put animals in prison when they do something we do not like or which violates our sense of what is good or right. This is why we do not reason with animals and would not even if we could communicate with them at the level of concepts. When they do something that offends us, either we stop them, or we punish them in a way that they understand, usually by doing something that they find aversive as soon as possible after the offending act, so that we can build up in their minds certain associations between certain types of behavior and certain consequences.

Moral and Immoral Acts as Instances of Symbolic Categories in Minds

An act becomes immoral for us, and we disapprove of it accordingly, because it comes to symbolize or stand for other similar acts and thereby becomes a member of the abstract category "bad," "wrong," or "evil." That is, morality is rooted in both our capacities to symbolize and to generalize to a level of categorical abstraction. A person, once symbolized, has done more than stolen a particular piece of, say, meat. He has become a thief. The piece of meat is not just a particular possession, but an instance of the class of things called "property," which has associated rights. Once taken, it is stolen property that happens to be a piece of meat. Once symbolized, individual acts and things can become instances of classes of events or classes of things that are good or evil, acceptable or unacceptable, sanctioned or not.

Consider the nonsymbolic mind of a little dog. How does he regard the bone that he is gnawing? It is his because he has it, not because it is his property or his in some other abstract or symbolic sense. He knows that other dogs want to get his bone, and he does his best to stop them. If a big dog comes along and forces his bone away from him, it is no longer his bone because he no longer has it. It is the big dog's bone because now the big dog has it. The little dog might be angry and frustrated that he lost his bone, but he cannot think "the big dog has my property" or "I own that bone regardless of who has it now." He can think "the big dog has a bone that I had, and I want that bone back."

In contrast, I can own an object regardless of who has it now. This is because I and other members of my society can place a representation of me along with a representation of the object in question in a common object file. A dog cannot do this, and as far as we know, no other animal can either. Humans are so advanced that they can jot symbols down as words, which can then create such an object file in the mind of a reader at any future time or place. Writing and other forms of data storage create the impression that ownership takes on a special kind of formal existence that would continue even if all people were killed. In fact, ownership (or any other abstract or legal concept) only exists insofar as such object files can be created in my mind or some other human mind. If I lose the ability to place a representation of myself along with a representation of my house in a common object file, do I own my house? Well, yes, in a legal sense, but certainly not in my own mind. If all people forever lose the ability to create such a joint object file, do I own the house? In this case, the answer is no. A legal/moral status, such as ownership, is not platonic. It requires the processing of symbolic minds and only exists in such minds.

The Domain of Moral and Immoral Acts Can Be Symbolic

Another effect of symbolic processing is that acts can be committed in the symbolic domain. For example, if I hate Mr. X, rather than attack him, I might slander his corporation or theory, because his corporation or theory stands for him. The ancient impulse toward territoriality can now be expressed and triggered over abstract representations such as infringement of perceived national interest or theft of intellectual property. The ancient impulse toward aggression can now be triggered by threats to abstractions such as one's nation. One can express aggression not only to individuals in the symbolic domain but toward abstractions such as social movements or ideas. One can hate slavery, or a slavish mentality, or one can love the teachings of Buddha. One can hate a mentality and yet not hate the person who is possessed of that mentality. None of this is possible for nonhuman animals.

Because the human mind is capable of virtually unlimited power and freedom in the domain of symbolic, abstract thought, there has been a tendency throughout history to devalue that which is not symbolic, in part because the nonsymbolic often limits our power and freedom. This is especially true of the body. The body, with its filth, lusts, and mortality, is rejected for its impurity and decay. It comes to symbolize impurity and death. Its urges are labeled immoral by many religions. It is viewed as that which must be conquered in order to be moral, spiritual, or pure. Many Christians view sex and masturbation as evil for this reason. A similar mind-set leads many religious men to reject women, with their monthly bleeding and violently birthing bodies, as inherently impure or even inherently immoral. Add to this rejection of the female body their own suppressed lust for such bodies, and you have a sure recipe for the neurosis, hypocrisy, and misogyny apparent in many men who assert their higher morality. Even in religions that embrace the body and its urges for pleasure and fulfillment, such as paganism, hedonism, or bacchanalianism, the body is symbolized. In these cases it comes to stand for something good, namely, life, the divine, or love. A fundamentalist Christian will typically reject people who embrace the body in this way as decadent or evil. Similarly, a person who embraces the body will view the Christian suppression of the body as wrong or evil. Who is right? The answer is that no one group has succeeded in imposing its morality upon all other people, causing untold suffering and death, although many have tried. The reason that no one has succeeded is that one's morality, like one's religion, and the God that one worships, is chosen based on what feels good, comfortable, and right. One's moral system largely follows one's taste and personality. And personalities differ.

In this regard, William James had a deep insight into human nature. In his book *Pragmatism and the Meaning of Truth* (1907/1978) he outlines a philosophy of truth built upon that of Charles Sanders Pierce, called "pragmatism." According to this view, truth is not what philosophers have traditionally thought it is. It is not the accurate correspondence between a proposition and that to which it refers in reality. It is also not coherence of meaning between a proposition and a model or theory in which that proposition sits. Rather, for ordinary people, practically speaking, truth is the cessation of doubt. James asserts that for most people, the feelings of uncertainty and doubt are unpleasant. So people search for the end of their doubts. They search for certainty. And when they have locked onto some belief that they are certain is correct, they feel comfortable, vindicated, set free, and, sometimes, divine. They feel safe and saved. This arrival at safety and certainty is what "truth" means in James's theory. Once locked into a belief system, the only threat to personal safety and comfort is the doubt of others. This accounts for the vehemence of many proselytizing zealots. They are proselytizing not for God or for the sake of the people they desire to save, though they may believe this. According to James, their vehemence and conviction comes from their need to be certain, which in turn comes from their own discomfort with doubt and dread. In contrast, James points out that there are certain types of people, often writers, artists, thinkers, explorers, or scientists, who are at home in doubt and uncertainty and who actually enjoy exploring the new possibilities associated with the unknown. Such personalities reject rigid dogmas. For them, truth is not the cessation of doubt but the discovery of what is. Whereas the former personality type might adopt an off-the-shelf fundamentalist belief system, the latter personality type will reject such dogmas and perhaps construct one of their own. Or they might not adopt one at all, since such personalities feel comfortable in admitting that they do not have all the answers.

Just as the type of truth that one embraces is rooted in one's personality dispositions, the morality that one embraces and attributes to God or the universe, or that one formalizes in an "objective" body of enduring law, is an external projection of private intuitions and desires. One starts out with these intuitions and desires and then builds up theories that justify them. It is not surprising, for example, that John Rawls, in his theory of justice, ends up with an ideal governmental and legal model that looks pretty much like American Jeffersonian democracy, because this is the intuitive endstate that he wanted to justify with his clever arguments and rationales. When he presents his theory, it seems that the conclusion emerges from the reasoning, but in fact the opposite is the case. Any moral or legal system constructed on the basis of reason alone which did not feel right would be rejected by most people, no matter how rational. Human moralities, in short, are rooted in irrational urges and clothe themselves in rational justifications from which they claim to derive in order to disguise this. The reason that we have conflicting moralities and conceptions of good and evil is that we have conflicting desires and feelings about the various domains of choice and activity that moralities seek to govern. What all human moralities have in common is that they are symbolic. Conservative Christians may symbolize the body as filthy and in need of suppression. Pagans may symbolize the body as a fount of life in need of expression and fulfillment. However, to neither group does the body symbolize nothing as it does for a dog. For a dog, its body is just its body, representing nothing. For humans, such a state may only exist in infancy before the advent of language and pretend play.

Understanding the Multiple Symbolic Roots of Human Evil

In order to talk about morality, it is necessary to talk about good and evil, because morality is fundamentally concerned with maximizing good and minimizing evil. It is doubtful whether "evil" can be defined in the abstract, in a manner free of any individual's frame of reference. Here "evil" will be operationally defined relative to a subject's mind to include that which harms or could harm that mind or that which that mind cares about. "Good" will be defined in a similar way to include that which benefits or could benefit a mind or that which that mind cares about. These definitions are not perfect. For example, one reasonably could argue that an act can only be good or evil if it is volitional or intended or at least the act of a conscious being. One could argue that only acts that have consequences are good or evil, or one could argue that thoughts and intentions, even in the absence of enactment, can be good or evil. However, no single conception can fully account for the numerous, often inconsistent ways that the terms "good" and "evil" are used. For present purposes, these definitions will suffice.

Because human acts and ideas operate over symbolic representations, we are capable of acts and ideas that no other animal could conceive of, let alone enact. No animal could conceive of killing all individuals who believe X or look like Y. We are capable of wanting to destroy all individuals of one group because those individuals are not truly individuals for us. They are symbols. They stand for something that we find abhorrent and want to eradicate. Since all individuals of this class stand for the same thing, they are variants of the same symbol. What we are doing when we view individuals as variants of the same symbol is this: we are tokenizing them. They are not individuals but tokens that stand for something evil that must be destroyed. Since we cannot eradicate a concept, such as that which they stand for, say the concept of "greed" or "woman" or "evil" or "deceit," we opt to eliminate the symbols. Thus, one symbolic root of human evil lies in tokenizing individuals and treating them as symbols, when they are in fact individuals with whom we might have shared a friendship under other circumstances.

Beyond merely stopping undesirable behaviors, the way to confront this source of human evil is to detokenize people in the minds of the people who tokenize them. This is more easily said than done, but it can be done. It requires a change of mind and heart. It seems that the human brain tends to minimize effort whenever possible by dealing with people, objects, and events at the level of tokens of preexisting categories or symbols that stand for preexisting concepts. For example, the upshot of many recent experiments involving change blindness is that people do not notice that a person has been replaced by another person unless that person switches categories, especially the categories of gender, race, and age, and unless they paid attention to the person and encoded their individual characteristics rather than just encoding them as the instance or token of a preexisting category. Great spiritual leaders of the past have warned against operating within this zombie-like state of tokenization, in part because it can lead to acts of stupidity and evil. They have emphasized the need to transform one's mind by cultivating compassion and love for individuals and by paying attention to the particularities of events.

Why does the brain tokenize? Minimization of effort is part of the explanation, but not all of it. There may be parts of the brain, such as certain nuclei of the amygdala, that are designed to operate at a level of tokenization in order to rapidly detect imminent threats. This brain structure may have a high rate of false alarms, but it exists because it is better to make a false alarm for certain kinds of threat than it is to make an incorrect rejection, which can result in being eaten or otherwise killed. Indeed, it is probable that the amygdala is hardwired to carry out certain kinds of stereotyping and certain types of stereotypical false alarms. This is why people across cultures tend to mistakenly see people or animals in their peripheral vision, when it was in fact only a human-like shape. It is also why people rarely experience a false alarm on things that could not be an imminent threat. It would be a strange mind indeed that often mistakenly saw a distant mountain range or constellation out of the corner of its eye. There are still other reasons why the brain tokenizes. We are taught to tokenize. We mimic and learn from those around us, and if they are operating at this level, we will probably learn to do so too, unless we are especially sensitive individuals. Another reason appears to be that tokenization and stereotyping allow us to ignore a great deal of irrelevant detail. As such, tokenization is probably a necessary cognitive strategy to avoid sensory and attentional overload.

Another symbolic source of human evil lies not in tokenization but in sadism. No animal could take sadistic pleasure in generating psychological torment in another mind, because this requires a theory of mind, which even chimpanzees appear to lack. As described earlier, the emergence of a theory of mind only became possible with the emergence of symbolic and abstract thought. The sadist internally models the mental state of his victim and draws pleasure from the power he exerts over his victim. Whereas a nonhuman animal could conceivably enjoy being in a dominant position, and may even gain pleasure from hurting another animal, it cannot gain pleasure from the psychological torment of its victim, because psychological torment is invisible and cannot be represented by nonsymbolic minds.

Interestingly, psychopathy, which can be thought of as a lack of conscience and empathy, may emerge in part from an inability to conceptualize the pain of another as if it were one's own. As such, psychopaths may be the opposite of sadists. Whereas a sadist savors the pain in another's body and mind that he is internally modeling in exquisite detail, the psychopath is incapable of this internal modeling, so operates as if other people do not feel pain as he sets about fulfilling his selfish goals. The end result, from the victim's point of view, may be similar, however. While a sadist is no doubt fully responsible for the pain he inflicts, a case could be made that a person who truly lacks a conscience is not morally responsible. But given our operational definition of evil, from the point of view of the victim, there is no difference.

Yet another source of human evil lies in conceptualizing oneself as not really doing the acts that one is doing or conceptualizing oneself as not responsible for the acts that one is committing. One is just obeying orders. One's acts are not the product of one's own volition. Hannah Arendt has used the term "the banality of evil" to describe this source of human evil. Since no one feels responsible or in charge, no one stands up to stop the evil. A more modern example would be a corporate president who knowingly engages in illegal logging in a tropical rainforest, because he has to feed his kids, and anyway, if he did not do it, someone else would.

It is commonly said that the root of all evil is money or, perhaps, greed or selfishness. However, other animals are greedy and selfish about things like food, territory, and sex. What is different about human greed/selfishness is that it is symbolic. Rather than merely wanting to maximize our share of territory, sex, and food, we want to maximize the multitude of things symbolically linked in our minds with these things. Whereas an animal might horde nuts, we might stuff our résumé with honors and prestige. Whereas an animal might try to increase its attractiveness to a potential mate by building a quality nest, we might attempt to accomplish the same by having the right career, or right opinions, or right friends. Whereas an animal might try to maximize its position in the social hierarchy, we are driven by a comparable urge for dominance but express it as a maximization of power, prestige, or honor. In general, human symbolic cognition operates on top of numerous desires and emotions that we share in common with our nonsymbolic primate relatives, including, for example, lust, fear, aggression, greed, deceit, social scheming, territoriality, jealousy, rage, and a desire for revenge. The potential for evil emerges in the symbolic enactment and fulfillment of these and other nonsymbolic urges.

Although there are several more sources of human evil that could be mentioned, the final one to be considered here is culture. Because humans are symbolic, they can have symbolic culture, in which information, behaviors, and attitudes are passed from generation to generation through symbolic modes of transmission. A culture itself can become a source of evil when it fosters information, behaviors, or attitudes that lead to evil intentions or actions. Although modern American capitalism has generated many goods for many people, and although there have been far worse cultures in the past, American culture is the dominant culture now, so a few words on its potential for generating evil are appropriate. There are certain aspects of American capitalism that can be characterized as harmful to individuals. There is a tendency in America to believe that markets are the best mechanism for making decisions. However, market mechanisms are only a way to decide prices. There are decisions that markets cannot make. Markets cannot decide what is good or beautiful or right, for example. Because of the emphasis on market mechanisms, these other things sometimes get short shrift as the majority of people pursue profit. Billboards, development, and resource extraction, processing, and use undermine beauty, health, and the environment. More insidious, the attitudes of market capitalism come to pervade many aspects of life that in the past would not have been regarded as a domain of buying and selling. There is a distinct danger in seeing oneself as an object to be sold. Once this mentality is in place, it is a short leap to wanting to improve the "product" by getting bodily implants or surgery or by continually trying to look better on paper. Seeing oneself or others as commodities to be easily replaced when used up is to see them as means to ends rather than individuals who are ends in themselves. Such a mentality, fostered by a culture, can lead to various immoral acts, such as using people to get ahead or knowingly polluting.

Understanding the Multiple Symbolic Roots of Human Goodness

If symbolic cognition affords humans the possibility of being and doing evil, it also affords them the possibility of being and doing good. Just as there are many ways to harm a mind or that which it cares about, there are many ways to benefit a mind or that which it cares about. Most of the ways of being or accomplishing good are the opposite of the above ways of being or accomplishing evil. One can be good by being kind, just as one can be evil by being unkind, the extreme of which is sadism. By its very nature, kindness occurs best when one is not tokenizing the recipient of one's kindness, since only then can one tailor one's kind acts to the particular needs of an individual. Indeed, only if one is attending to the changing needs of the recipient of one's goodness can one continually tailor one's actions to those changing needs. It requires internal modeling of the mind of the recipient. Kindness is therefore not even possible for animals, because they lack a theory of mind. Animals can be affectionate, but they cannot be kind.

It thus appears that doing and being good requires the cultivation of a certain kind of mentality, not just a certain kind of behavior, since good behaviors follow from the mentality and less so vice versa. This mentality is one that is kind and compassionate rather than cruel, attentive rather than inattentive, and focused on the individual rather than on the class or token. Just as evil can emerge in the symbolic realization of desires and urges that we have in common with animals typically centered on aggression, dominance, territoriality, and sex, good can emerge in the symbolic realization of other desires and urges that we also have in common with animals and which are not themselves symbolic. Among these would be urges and desires for affection, love, community, compassion, nurturing, protecting, parenting, commitment, and bonding. However, it would be simplistic to say that evil emerges from the symbolic enactment of one set of desires and good emerges from another, mutually exclusive set. In fact, good or evil can arise from the symbolic enactment of any one of these urges and desires. For example, overprotectiveness can harm the recipients of this excess of love by making them dependent and weak. A lack of aggression can lead to harm, as one fails to protect oneself or others whom one loves. Thus, affection can be expressed in an immoral way, and aggression can be expressed in a moral way. Morality should therefore not be equated with the enactment of prosocial desires. Immorality should not be confused with the enactment of destructive or "base" desires.

All evil and all good derive from the fact that our minds are symbolic. Even though being symbolic has cursed us with so much past and present

Korsgaard

evil and so much potential for more evil, being symbolic has blessed us with the ability to choose what is right and good. Our symbolic mind equips us to actively fight those possessed of evil mentalities. The only salvation from human evil lies in human goodness. No one will rescue us from our own minds. There is hope for us because human minds can be changed. Humans absorb and create culture and can be taught to act and think differently than they now do. This is especially true of children. However, you cannot force a change in mentality by threatening, coercing, or killing people. You can change behavior with violence or the threat of violence, but this lasts only as long as the threat is in place. A change in mentality, with its consequent changes in behavior, is enduring and only emerges as one symbol structure comes to replace another in a person's mind. The tried and true ways to accomplish such a shift are education, persuasion, and inculcation. Mentalities can change for the better in more than just incremental ways if the correct approach is taken. The only mind that we have complete access to is our own. It is here that there is the greatest hope of a transformation. But it takes a great deal of effort.

Notes

1. Information processing in animals has undergone several revolutions, where the type of information processed after the revolution differed in kind, not just degree, from the type that preceded it. Although there may be more, at least four revolutions stand out as apparent. (1) Reflexive information processing: The earliest information processing probably involved little more than detection of ambient chemical or electromagnetic energy. This detection triggered behaviors in an automatic, reflexive, and stereotyped fashion. A given input had a single possible output. Even after the evolution of multicellular organisms with neurons, reflex probably remained the dominant mode of information processing in animals. (2) Nonreflexive information processing: The second revolution occurred when nervous systems were able to represent more than one possible course of action in response to a given input. This mode of information processing required the development of memory buffers where possible courses of action and their consequences could be modeled, stored, and compared. This class of information processing reaches its highest complexity in the higher mammals, where complex scenarios can be played out before any action is taken. (3) Analogical and symbolic information processing: This revolution occurred when links could be made between classes of information and types of information processing that were previously modularly encapsulated. (4) Syntactic processing occurred when operations could be carried out upon symbols in a generative and nested fashion. There are examples where humans process input and

generate output in each of the four ways, whereas other animals generally lack the capacity for (3) and (4).

2. Other authors have written about the existence of domain-general mental capabilities that do not meet the criteria of modularity (i.e., fast, dedicated, mandatory, impenetrable, encapsulated; Karmiloff-Smith, 1995; Fodor, 1983, 2001; Gardner, 1993) which may emerge from the interplay of domain-specific types of modular representations and processes (Spelke, 2000). Fodor himself ends his 1983 book unable to account for slow, general-purpose reasoning and cognition in terms of his modularity hypothesis. Nonetheless, some authors, particularly champions of evolutionary psychology (e.g., Duchaine, Cosmides, & Tooby, 2001; Pinker, 1997) appear to focus primarily on the explanatory power of the modularity concept without emphasizing the prevalence of domain-general operators in human or animal cognition. Attention is an example of a domain-general operator, as is reason. The defining qualities of nonmodular processes are the exact opposite of those that define modularity. They are slow, not automatic, not dedicated, not mandatory, accessible to more than one module, and not encapsulated.

3. We say that attention binds the joint contents of the object file into a single bound representation, as if attention were a separate thing from the binding process itself. However, attention may just *be* binding. We will continue to use the word "attention" as shorthand, as if attention "does" binding, but really it might be more accurate to say that "binding takes place," rather than "attention binds."

4. Indeed, modular processing in general, which can be characterized as operand dedicated, encapsulated, parallel, and impenetrable to other modular or domain-general processes (Fodor, 1983), would help an animal survive precisely because it is rapid, and, being automatic and free from cross-talk interference from other operators or operands, less prone to error. Most types of recognition or response need to be done as rapidly as possible in a world where one can lose prey or become prey in an instant. Puzzling over the interpretation of a tiger or mistaking a shadow for a solid surface could result in death. The puzzle is not the existence of modularity in animals but the presence of relatively slow domain-general processes. There are presumably benefits to operations that amount to a slow, nonstereotyped consideration of options whose outcome is unpredictable. For example, always following the locally best option can lead to one's demise or getting stuck in a local minimum. One path may look pleasant and inviting, and another grim, but if the former leads to a tiger, and the latter to food, then the local characteristics are misleading. It is precisely this sort of internal generation and weighing of possible outcomes that likely led to the existence of domain-general operators. Rapidity and automaticity are a boon in the processing of local input, but when input must be integrated over multiple modules and over space and time, or when processing is open-ended (how long into the future should one consider before a path looks good?), then rapidity and automaticity are potentially fatal. Because domain-general

operators are potentially open-ended, they give rise to the danger of taking too long before a path of action is chosen. Building domain-general operations into a cognitive architecture also requires building in automatic resets, interrupts, and self-terminations of these open-ended processes. Such automatic resets may include forced reprioritization mechanisms such as exogenously driven attentional capture, hunger, pain, or fear, which would bring an animal "back to reality," and prevent it from getting stuck in an open-ended process.

5. There are two types of inferences that must be distinguished here. There are those that occur prior to consciousness and which are integrated into our conscious experience. Then there are those that are based upon the facts that present themselves in our conscious experience and which therefore follow consciousness in time. The former are largely generated by perceptual modular systems, such as the visual system, and are therefore automatic, rapid, and cognitively impenetrable. The latter are typically not perceptual but cognitive operations that are based upon facts. For example, when I go outside, I see that the ground is wet and infer that it must have rained. Seeing the ground as wet is an example of a preconscious or preperceptual inference. What I perceive has that inference built into it. Consciousness comes precompiled in the sense that I cannot choose not to see the ground as wet. I cannot choose to see the world as a collection of colors that have not been interpreted into materials, spatial layout, reflectances, shadow, lighting, and so forth. The world is presented to me as such by the visual module. When I infer that it must have rained, however, I am making a cognitive inference which is open-ended and slow. I can make countless inferences from the fact that the ground looks wet.

5.1   A Just-So Story for Symbolic Thought? Comment on Tse

Michael R. Dietrich

In this comment, I will consider Peter Tse's essay from the perspective of evolutionary biology. More precisely, I will focus on the nature of Tse's evolutionary claims and their justification.

During the debates over sociobiology in the 1970s, Stephen Jay Gould and Richard Lewontin characterized putative evolutionary explanations that were merely consistent with some of the principles of evolutionary biology as stories (later as just-so stories).[1] These evolutionary stories usually appealed to the power of natural selection and so were seen as an expression of adaptationism. The problem was that while these evolutionary stories may seem plausible and were often very imaginative, they were rarely justified evolutionary explanations. If evolutionary biology were reduced to a process of endless adaptationist conjectures, it would indeed be in danger of rendering itself an unfalsifiable morass. This does not mean that evolutionary storytelling has no value for evolutionary biology. As John Tooby and Leda Cosmides point out, the value of evolutionary just-so stories lies in their predictive utility, not their explanatory power. In their words, "modern selectionist theories are used to generate rich and specific prior predictions about new design features and mechanisms that no one would have thought to look [for] in the absence of these theories . . ."[2] With this history in mind, I will now turn to the evolutionary narrative offered by Tse.

In his essay on the origins of symbolic thought, Peter Tse has offered a compelling account of how cross-module binding could produce a wide range of cognitive consequences. He is clear that he does not want to get "too deeply into any 'engineering' solutions," (p. 270) and focuses much of his discussion on developing a cognitive theory that itself is presumed to not be tightly bound to any neuronal mechanisms (pp. 270, 277). Nevertheless, Tse does offer "some speculation" on genetic mutations that produced "the rewiring of neuronal circuitry that permitted cross-modular binding" (p. 278). He even offers a prediction that "there are corticocorti-cal, corticothalmic, and thalamothalmic connections between neurons within different modules in humans that are not present in chimpanzees or other nonhuman apes" (p. 279). As an evolutionary explanation, Tse's account of the origins of cross-module binding is a just-so story. It is consistent with the principles of evolution by natural selection, even if it is acknowledged as speculation. The question remains, however, is this a fruitful speculation from the perspective of evolutionary biology?

Tse recognizes that we cannot know the consequences of cross-module binding in our ancestors. In other words, we cannot know how natural selection or sexual selection acted on the initial effects of cross-module binding. Evolutionary conjectures concerning the origins of cross-module binding are, therefore, unavoidably speculative (p. 283). Yet, the presumption is that because "human behavior is rich with evidence of cross-modular binding" (p. 283), human anatomy will show evidence of cross-module binding, and that those anatomical structures will have been positively selected for for tens of thousands of years and that what we consider to be moral behavior is one of the many products of that process of selection. Note that no evidence of anatomical features is provided, and no specific connections are made been neuronal structures and their genetic foundation. Moreover, even if we accept the evolutionary story, it does not entail that morality itself was the object of natural selection, then or now. Many of the other features of this scenario could be the actual targets of selection, and morality could simply be along for the ride, so to speak. The connection between morality and evolution is another aspect of the story, but it is a conjecture. The plausibility and unifying power of the story should not be considered to justify it from a scientific point of view.

Evolutionary explanations lay in the engineering details. Indeed, recently many of these details are being worked out in studies linking brain development and evolution and in the effects of specific genes, such as FOXP2.[3] Tse's top-down theorizing may be useful and is certainly interesting, but without more work from the bottom up it will not qualify as an evolutionary explanation. Tse has provided an evolutionary conjecture. An interesting conjecture, but, without more biological detail, the cross-binding hypothesis cannot be evaluated as an evolutionary explanation. Instead Tse's paper is indicative of how much science remains to be done to link proposed "cognitive architectures" to genetically grounded, evolving biological systems.

Notes

1. Gould and Lewontin (1979).

2. John Tooby and Leda Cosmides (1997, July 7).

3. Gilbert, Dobyns, and Lahn (2005); Marcus and Fisher (2003).

Morality and the Capacity for Symbolic Cognition: Comment on Tse

Kathleen Wallace

In this comment I will briefly summarize Tse's theory of mind but otherwise take it for granted. The discussion of the empirical research and its implications for philosophy of mind and cognitive science I leave to others qualified in those areas. My focus will be on the claims made about morality.

Tse suggests that the roots of human good and evil lie in symbolic processing, which is accounted for by the breakdown of strict modularity in the mind. Cross-modular binding accounts for the emergence of abstraction and analogical, metaphorical, and symbolic thought. Moral judgment involves prohibitions, norms, principles, laws, and the concepts of good and bad. It is symbolic because it requires the ability to abstractly represent an act or object, that is, the ability (1) to conceptualize an act or object in terms of abstract categories (e.g., "theft," "property") and (2) to place an act in an abstract category of good or evil, right or wrong (Tse, p. 286). Cross-modular binding and the emergence of symbolic processing also account for the extent of possible human evil (or good) through the process of tokenization, through the capacity to represent another mind, and through the cultural operation of symbols. On tokenization, Tse says,

Because human acts and ideas operate over symbolic representations, we are capable of acts and ideas that no other animal could conceive of, let alone enact. . . . We are capable of wanting to destroy all individuals of one group because those individuals are not truly individuals for us. . . . They stand for something that we find abhorrent and want to eradicate . . . they are variants of the same symbol . . . We are tokenizing them. They are not individuals but tokens that stand for something evil that must be destroyed. (p. 290)

Tse explains sadism as rooted in the ability to have a theory of mind about another individual and suggests that the capacity to internally model the mental state of another person depends on the emergence of symbolic and abstract thought (p. 292). Culture, or the ability to communicate symbolically, also allows human beings to abstractly represent, for example, to commodify, individuals, *and* to extend that commodification across many individuals and perpetuate it across many generations (Tse, p. 293).

That morality requires the ability to symbolize and to abstractly represent objects, persons, events, and actions would not distinguish morality from many other distinctive human functionings—art and aesthetic judgment, scientific reasoning, and rule-governed play, to name a few—all of which equally involve capacities for abstraction, generalization, representation, tokenization, and modeling. For moral theorists, a claim that morality involves a capacity for abstract or symbolic thought, in at least some respect, seems relatively uncontroversial. Even emotivist moral theorists who think that moral judgments are simply expressions of emotional states could allow that their range is extendable by the possibility of symbolic cognition without giving up the claim that the judgments are, at bottom, emotional states. Particularists might object to characterizing good and bad acts in terms of abstract categories because that presumes too much generalization.[1] However, the claim that recognition of an act as theft or an object as property, as well as the recognition of "good" and "bad" as moral tags, would still seem to involve symbolic cognition, and particularists admit these concepts as necessary for moral judgment. Moreover, symbolic cognition could be invoked as part of an explanation of both a particularist's and a generalist's claims. Regarding particularism: if symbols are flexible and changeable in meaning and if moral judgments involve concepts that are symbolic in nature, then the flexibility of symbolic cognition might be part of the explanation of moral judgments that do not depend on principles.[2] Regarding universalism: if categorization and generalization depend on symbolic processing, then such cognition might be part of the explanation of how moral judgments do rely on principles. In either case, a capacity for symbolic cognition by itself does not appear to favor one or the other theory of moral judgment.

If symbolic processing is distinctive of human beings and is a necessary feature of morality, and if animals lack the cross-modular binding required for symbolic processing, then the theory would give a naturalistic explanation for the exclusion of animals from having moral duties.[3] There are some who suggest that the exclusion of animals from being moral agents is arbitrary.[4] It might be noted that Tse's claim turns not on animals versus human beings but on the possession of the capacity for symbolic cognition as a necessary condition for making moral distinctions.[5] If there were animals or any other beings that have a similar capacity, then they, too, would have to be regarded as capable of morality. However, even if animals are not capable of making moral distinctions due to the lack of a capacity for symbolic cognition, that would not entail that they couldn't or shouldn't be included in the sphere of beings for which a moral agent should have moral concern; nor would it entail that they couldn't have rights.[6]

There appears to be some slippage in Tse's account of how the capacity for symbolic cognition contributes to morality between the claim that symbolization and categorization is necessary for the possibility of moral categories at all and the claim that symbolization, particularly in the form of tokenization, is the root of immoral acts. Tse suggests that an act becomes immoral for us "because it comes to symbolize or stand for other similar acts and thereby becomes a member of the abstract category 'bad,' 'wrong,' or 'evil'" (p. 286). But good/right involves, he says, a kind and compassionate mentality that is "focused on the individual rather than on the class or token" (Tse, p. 294). The suggestion seems to be that tokenization itself is the basis for evil or a morally bad attitude towards others, whereas a morally good attitude toward or treatment of others involves treating them compassionately as individuals.[7] However, this is not entirely consistent with other features of the theory. For instance, if categorization is a necessary feature *of morality*, then a morally good act should be good insofar as it symbolizes or stands for other similar acts and thereby becomes a member of the abstract category "good" or "right."[8] Moreover, recognizing a human being as a member of a rights-bearing class would seem to be an instance of tokenization, but one which recognizes or creates a positive moral category. Presumably such "tokenization" would be involved in recognition of a duty to respect the rights of persons, even when a particular person is someone for whom one has little or no feelings of kindness or compassion. Ignoring individual characteristics (tokenization per se) by itself is not evil, for sometimes ignoring them, or at least not taking them as *the* basis for moral choice, is the morally right thing to do. Tokenization by itself is morally neutral; whether it is morally objectionable, or morally desirable, will depend on other features of the attitude, action or behavior and not just that it is an instance of tokenization.[9] If there are some *specific* types of tokenization that distinctively contribute to immoral actions, further study is needed to determine that. If there are conditions under which tokenization leads to evil behavior, a further question would be whether they count, noncircularly, as ones that constitute the evilness of tokenization.

Tse suggests that the capacity for compassion focused on an individual requires the ability to model another mind and, therefore, involves symbolic cognition. First, compassion: Tse's characterization seems to assume that it is, in and of itself, morally good, and that is, at the least, debatable. Compassion neither necessarily leads to moral behavior nor is necessarily a moral attitude. One can also feel compassion focused on an individual and yet be morally obligated to act against what compassion might recommend. For instance, in serving on a jury, one might feel compassion for the defendant yet be morally obligated to honestly render a guilty verdict. Of course, compassion may be moral and may be important to the development of moral sensitivity and judgment. But compassion per se is neither necessary nor sufficient for the moral goodness of an action or outlook, nor does it always contribute to a particular action's being moral even when it is present.

Second, "focusing on the individual": this is no more likely to be morally good than treating someone as a member of an abstract class. There may be times when it is morally preferable to regard someone as a member of an abstract class, such as "rights holder." Moreover, "focusing on the individual" could just as easily constitute morally reprehensible behavior. For example, Tse suggests that sadism involves deriving pleasure from the psychological torment of the particular victim. In modeling the mental state of a victim (Tse, p. 292), the sadist is focused on the individual.

The conjunction of compassion and focus on the individual is not necessary or sufficient for an action to be judged morally good. The juror mentioned earlier may be morally obligated to disregard her experience of such a conjunction and to act on the basis of legal principles and a duty to evaluate evidence.

In the discussion of a contrastive case to sadism, namely, psychopathy, Tse suggests that a psychopath lacks the capacity for internal modeling and thus may not be morally responsible for her or his actions, even though from the point of view of the victim, the sadist and the psychopath are equally morally objectionable (Tse, p. 292). However, if symbolic cognition is what distinguishes human cognitive capacity from that of other animals and explains why human actions and behavior are judged in moral terms, then on this account it seems odd to say that a psychopath's behavior is *evil* or *morally* objectionable and an animal's infliction of pain on a human being by mauling the human being is not. On Tse's account, each (the psychopath and the animal) would not be morally responsible because each lacks the appropriate capacity for symbolic cognition. The argument might be that other human beings who do have the appropriate capacity for symbolic cognition regard the psychopath and the animal differently and that's why the one is morally objectionable and the other isn't. But the question is, why do other human beings regard them differently? It would seem odd to say that, on the one hand, the capacity for symbolic cognition in the agent is the root of moral evil (as in the sadism case) but, on the other, the lack of symbolic cognition in the moral agent (as in the psychopathy case) is the root of moral evil (and only when that lack occurs in human beings, not in animals). What's odd here is not the idea that there could be multiple explanations for morally objectionable behavior. Rather, the same feature (lack of symbolic cognition in some respect) is invoked to simultaneously explain why a human being's behavior is morally objectionable and an animal's is not moral at all. However, the feature can't just change its reason-giving force randomly or as it suits an ad hoc explanation.

There is another problem with the notion of symbolic cognition and modeling that I would like to note.[10] By modeling, Tse seems to mean the ability to represent another being's mind. This is allegedly symbolic because representation is assumed to involve some abstraction and not just a picture, if you will, of the other being's mental state. Even so, modeling seems to be different from the symbolic cognition that involves generating flexible symbols that can alter their meaning (and that therefore involves cross-modular binding). Even if it were true that animals lacked the latter, that wouldn't entail that they lacked some capacity for modeling another being's mind (even if it turned out to be true that their ability to do so were more limited than human beings' is). Thus, an independent argument for why animals couldn't be compassionate or sadistic appears to be needed.

I have noted some problems with Tse's association of evil with tokenization and good with kindness and compassion that is focused on the individual, in particular, (1) a capacity to attribute or model complex mental states is equally present in sadistic and nonsadistic agents; (2) even if some kinds of immoral behavior involve "tokenization," so, too, do some kinds of morally good behavior: for example, recognizing a person as a "rights holder," a member of an abstract category. Unless it can be shown that some particular neurological process always and without exception yields the judgment that it is bad or that it is good, it is just not clear how moral judgments themselves could simply be derived from neurological processes such as tokenization. And, even if such invariance obtained, the description of the neurological features themselves does not contain the additional moral predicate. The moral or evaluative predicates may coincide with or supervene on the descriptive features, but their meaning is not captured by the neurological description.[11] If some particular kind of tokenization always resulted in a morally bad action, then that tokenization would be a contingently necessary part of the explanation for why a particular person acted in a morally condemnatory way. However, to say that a particular action is a particular species of tokenization does not seem to forestall the question, why is that particular species of tokenization bad? Is it bad because it causes pain or harm, or rather unjustified pain or harm? What makes the pain unjustified? Is some species of tokenization good because it causes pleasure or benefit, or rather pleasure or benefit that doesn't compromise other rights and duties? Or, does the badness or goodness depend on or invoke some other standard that has been developed through the exercise of substantive practical reason? That some action is or involves tokenization or a particular species of tokenization does not seem to be sufficient as an explanation or justification of its moral badness or goodness.

If Tse's claim is that a particular action can be understood simply as the expression of some symbolic processing, or of processing that has gone awry in a particular way, it also raises the question, are human beings responsible for their actions? Without any second-order reflection on and choice made with respect to possible actions contemplated or urges felt, it is not clear what responsibility would amount to. Guilt and innocence are a function of intentionality and choice, as well as of the nature of the action performed. In order to explain moral judgments of guilt and innocence, one would need to be able to explain the difference between the person who has sadistic urges but chooses to refrain from acting on them and the person who has such urges and chooses to act on them. It won't be sufficient to say (1) that the person who acted on them just had stronger urges or (2) that the person's symbolic processing rendered the person unable to comprehend the moral reprehensibility of his or her action. In the first case, one might say that the person was guilty because she ought to have had better control over her urges, but that would be somewhat different from saying that the particular expression of symbolic processing is bad or evil (even if one made that judgment as well). Or, if the person cannot exercise control over irresistible urges, then one might say that the person isn't guilty at all. While it is true that having sadistic urges or desires is not a good thing, it's not clear how symbolic processing per se is what makes them problematic. In the second case (some symbolic processing renders someone unable to comprehend the moral wrongness of his or her action), one might say that the person is simply incapable of morality.[12]

That would be an especially odd conclusion to come to if the crux of the theory is that symbolic processing is the basis for the possibility of moral judgment.

If morality necessarily involves symbolic cognition, then Tse's approach would seem to rule out any view which regarded morality in strictly non-cognitive terms—for example, a view which regarded "good" as simply an actual desire or "pro" response to some object, act, or person. Such views are implausible on other grounds; actual responses can be morally neutral, morally reprehensible (even when a "pro" response for or to an individual),[13] and morally commendable independently of the actual response. In other words, actual responses do not necessarily track moral categories. However, Tse comes very close to advocating just such a view:

[T]he morality that one embraces and attributes to God or the universe, or that one formalizes in an "objective" body of enduring law, is an external projection of private intuitions and desires. . . . Human moralities, in short, are rooted in irrational urges and clothe themselves in rational justifications from which they claim to derive in order to disguise this. The reason that we have conflicting moralities and conceptions of good and evil is that we have conflicting desires and feelings about the various domains of choice and activity that moralities seek to govern. What all human moralities have in common is that they are symbolic. (Tse, pp. 289–290)

Thus, the view appears to be a dispositionalist or response-dependent view of moral distinctions: symbolic processing provides for abstract representation of moral concepts, but moral distinctions are rooted in urges, feelings, and desires which depend on individual dispositions ("taste and personality") or on those in conjunction with cultural dispositions:[14]

A fundamentalist Christian will typically reject people who embrace the body in this way [as standing for life, the divine or love] as decadent or evil. Similarly, a person who embraces the body will view the Christian suppression of the body as wrong or evil. Who is right? The answer is that no one group has succeeded in imposing its morality upon all other people. . . . The reason that no one has succeeded is that one's morality, like one's religion, and the God that one worships, is chosen based on what feels good, comfortable and right. One's moral system largely follows one's taste and personality. (Tse, p. 288)

In this passage, Tse appears to be committed to the denial of independent formulation and justification of moral standards. If that is so, then, going back to the sadist, what Tse should say is not that the sadist's behavior *is* evil but rather that some (maybe even most) individuals or cultures regard it as evil; that even if most individuals regard the sadist's behavior as evil, that simply reflects the urges and feelings that most people happen to have about the sadist's behavior.

Tse defines "evil" and "good" as follows:

Here "evil" will be operationally defined relative to a subject's mind to include that which harms or could harm that mind or that which that mind cares about. "Good" will be defined in a similar way to include that which benefits or could benefit a mind or that which that mind cares about. (p. 290)

On this definition, the sadist's pleasure would be "good" relative to the sadist and "evil" relative to the victim, and presumably most others would see causing pain to another as harmful to what they cared about and thus would regard the sadist's behavior as wrong or evil. However, these are descriptive claims, not prescriptive ones about how people ought or ought not to behave. The actual dispositions and responses of individuals or even of most people could be morally arbitrary at any given time or in any given context. If a dispositionalist or response-dependent theory is meant to be a theory about ethical or moral distinctions per se, then there has to be a way of sorting out actual responses from moral responses.[15] Otherwise, we simply have the sadist who experiences the infliction of pain as something good and the nonsadist who experiences it as bad, and no basis for evaluating the legitimacy of such judgments and behaviors.

As moral psychology, the theory may have much to contribute to the understanding of moral judgment and agency. However, Tse seems to be staking out a stronger claim. When he asserts that morality just is a collection of moralities, and that there is no rational adjudication of one "morality" over another, he seems to be expressing the view that personal and cultural dispositions (made possible because of symbolic processing) produce moral distinctions and to the extent that they differ, then to that extent will moral distinctions differ. Such a view is unsatisfying to the philosopher, who is interested in justification, and, I suspect, to most ordinary people, who want to know which responses are in fact morally justified and which are not; who want to know how they ought to behave, not only how and why they and others do behave as they do.

That ethical knowledge and moral standards are guided by discovery about the nature of human capacities and dispositions seems right. However, that doesn't mean that ethical standards can be explained as simply the expression of particular psychological states and dispositions. For example, waterboarding[16] is wrong because human beings are so constituted that they experience pain, coercion, humiliation, and an undermining of the capacity to function freely and as moral agents when so treated. A moral judgment that such treatment is wrong involves the recognition that infliction of pain, humiliation, and loss of such capacity is bad, and that without sufficient justifying reasons for doing so, it is wrong to so inflict pain. It may be true that a nonsymbolic mind would not invent waterboarding. However, the infliction of pain on a victim is wrong not because the agent has the capacity for symbolic thought but because there is not a sufficient reason to justify the deliberate infliction of pain.[17] To take a contrasting case: if a physician is justified in deliberately inflicting pain on a patient, it is because presumably the reason for doing so (e.g., the hope of cure) is sufficient to justify the behavior and also because the patient has presumably consented to and is voluntarily undergoing the treatment.

Tse seems to want to allow for difference in moral judgment, to wit, his suggestion that morality is a collection of "moralities." However, that there could be legitimate difference in moral judgment does not entail that any difference is legitimate. For example, people may disagree over whether withholding medical treatment from a terminally ill patient is justified or not because they assign different weights to the value of suffering, extension of life, and so on.[18] What makes the disagreement *legitimate* is not that people have different urges and dispositions but that there are moral standards, principles, or rules that allow us to identify what differences and choices are morally legitimate.

Tse's account is helpful with respect to understanding psychological states, capacities, and dispositions that may influence the development of moral attitudes and behaviors. This account may be helpful in developing appropriate methods of moral education and persuasion. Tse raises the issue of moral education when he suggests that racist, sexist, and other discriminatory behavior might be altered by cultivating detokenization (Tse, p. 291). I have suggested some difficulties with the account of tokenization as evil. However, if there is a kind of tokenization that does operate with racist, sexist, and discriminatory behavior, then the theory may be helpful in developing methods in moral education that aim to disrupt the processes which lead to such attitudes. However, the solution may not be only to "detokenize," that is, to recognize and love persons as individuals.[19] Rather, an appropriate moral attitude may involve the cultivation of the right kind of "tokenization," for example, the capacity to recognize the equal humanity of all persons, even ones whom one doesn't and can't know or love as individuals.

Notes

1. For a more subtle and nuanced view of moral particularism than anything I shall discuss here, see Dancy (2004). Also, see Hooker and Little (2000).

2. Tse's own comments about the plurality of "moralities" would be consistent with this possibility (see below, p. 311).

3. Tse also claims that animals are not capable of the same degree of evil (or of good), of cruelty (or of kindness), of which human beings are capable.

4. See, for example, Hearne (1986).

5. At times it seems as if Tse is also claiming that it is sufficient for morality, but, as we shall see, it's not clear that that claim is supported.

6. Peter Singer and others argue for recognizing animals as having interests that are due the same moral concern as is due human beings and their interests. Tom Regan argues that animals have inherent value equal to that of human beings and therefore have rights and may not be treated merely as a resource for human needs and interests. Neither of these arguments depends on animals' having the capacity for symbolic cognition. And, both these claims are different from the claim (Hearne's) that animals themselves make moral distinctions or function as moral agents. (See, e.g., Singer, 1977; Regan, 1985a, 1985b.)

7. This interpretation might favor the particularist at least with regard to morally good acts, since they would depend on individual feelings and understandings rather than general or generalizable moral principles.

8. This interpretation might tend to favor the generalist over the particularist.

9. Tse recognizes that tokenization is by itself morally neutral when he comments that the brain may be "hardwired" to tokenize and that it may even be functionally desirable to do so from the point of view of survival (detection of dangers) and minimization of effort (Tse, p. 291).

10. Thanks to Walter Sinnott-Armstrong for raising this question and helping me to sharpen my thinking on it.

11. For a discussion of some of the issues involved here, see, for example, Blackburn (1993).

12. This is the tack that Tse takes in discussing the psychopath—although in that case, Tse suggests that the problem is that the psychopath lacks a particular type of symbolic cognition, namely, the capacity to model another mind.

13. For example, the juror, mentioned earlier, who allowed his or her compassion for the defendant (a "pro" response to the individual) to override an honest evaluation of the evidence might be morally reprehensible, particularly if the compassion

is itself a form of bias. For example, suppose the compassion is a response to a defendant with whom the juror personally identifies on the basis of sex, or skin color, or ethnicity, to the disregard of the law and the victim of the crime.

14. For philosophical discussions of dispositionalist or response-dependent views of morality, see, for example, Brower (1993); Enoch (2005); Johnston (1989). Actually, it is not clear to me whether Tse is expressing a dispositionalist view (that moral judgments are expressions of positive or negative psychological states) or a projectivist view (that moral properties are merely projections of our sentiments or urges onto the objects of those sentiments or urges). Even though he uses the term "projection" in the preceding quotation, the substance of his position seems closer to what philosophers would characterize as a dispositionalist view.

15. This is the purpose of idealization in idealized dispositionalist theories such as Lewis's. See Lewis (1989).

16. A form of torture in which the victim is strapped to a board with the feet higher than the head and is subjected to water treatments designed to simulate drowning. On November 18, 2005, ABC News reported that former CIA agents claimed the CIA had engaged in a modern form of waterboarding, along with five other "Enhanced Interrogation Techniques," against suspected members of al Qaeda. http://abcnews. go.com/WNT/Investigation/story?id=1322866 site visited 12/17/05.

17. I don't know whether the cat that plays with a mouse before killing it lacks the ability to model the mouse's experience, but if the cat is not morally responsible it is because it lacks the ability to conceptualize (symbolize) the actions as wrong and to engage in justificatory reflection about its action.

18. Reading the work of and discussions with Bernard Gert have been helpful in formulating this point. See Gert (2005a) and Gert (2005b).

19. Tse puts it as "the need to transform one's mind by cultivating compassion and love for individuals and by paying attention to the particularities of events" (p. 291).

5.3 | Reply to Dietrich and Wallace

Peter Ulric Tse

Michael Dietrich comments only on the first part of the essay, and Kathleen Wallace focuses only on the second part of the essay concerning morality. So I will address them in sequence.

Dietrich correctly points out that I am offering a hypothesis or conjecture about the changes in cognitive architecture that may have given rise to symbolic thought. I agree that a comprehensive theory will tackle the engineering details that may have realized this change in cognitive architecture, including changes in neural interconnectivity, as well as potential genetic underpinnings. However, none of this is remotely possible at this stage of the game. What we can do now is come up with hypotheses that will help guide us in our search for better facts and deeper theories, including theories that make specific predictions about changes in neural circuitry, and the genetic changes that caused those changes in neural circuitry. I intentionally avoided any discussion at this engineering level, because I have no idea what the changes in neuronal circuitry or genetics may have been that led to the proposed changes in cognitive architecture. Neither does anyone else in my field. In neuroscience, we do not even truly understand how a minicolumn works, which may be a basic unit of information-processing machinery in the cortex. We are simply not at a stage where we can describe potential changes in neural circuitry underlying object file formation.

Hypothesizing is a part of science. I state the hypothesis that there was a change in the cognitive architecture underlying object file formation such that operators and operands become free of previously modular constraints. This makes concrete predictions, which can be tested. As of now, we have only very vague ideas in neuroscience, concerning the neural underpinnings of object files. But we will find out within a decade or two, I hope. And when we do, I predict that the neural underpinnings of object file formation will look quite different in humans and other animals, even chimps. This might eventually require doing things that are currently impracticable, like running chimps as awake and behaving subjects in attentional tasks during functional magnetic resonance imaging experiments or running humans in single-unit work, but these things are not impossible in principle. Thus, I am stating an admittedly speculative hypothesis about the roots of human symbolic thought, but it is science, because it is at least in principle falsifiable, or will be, when we understand how object files are processed, represented, and instantiated in brain circuitry.

The term "just-so" story is really not applicable here. Rudyard Kipling came up with this term to refer to fanciful stories that explain outcomes with no reference to evolution or fact. For example, Kipling writes that a leopard got its spots because an Ethiopian left fingerprints all over its pelt. This criticism is an attempt to paint the present hypothesis as fanciful or groundless. Kipling would never have seriously claimed that his story about the leopard's spots was true. I am hypothesizing that the object file hypothesis describes something that is potentially true. It is falsifiable, so it is science. My hypothesis ties together numerous behavioral observations and observations about human cognition, and it aims to make a statement about what may really have happened in fact. This is not meant to be pure fiction like the leopard's spots. Maybe my ideas are wrong. Facts will eventually help us decide if there is anything to them. But this is not just meant to be a fanciful story. It is meant to be a hypothesis about what really happened in our ancestors' brains and minds that led their minds to become symbolic.

It seems to me that many of Kathleen Wallace's criticisms stem from a desire to find a conception of morality, good and evil, that is prescriptive. Wallace finds that my view "is unsatisfying to the philosopher, who is interested in justification, and, I suspect, to most ordinary people, who want to know which responses are in fact morally justified and which are not; who want to know how they ought to behave, not only how and why they and others do behave as they do" (p. 310). But I purposely defined good and evil in a specific way, precisely in order to avoid getting into how people ought to behave:

Here "evil" will be operationally defined relative to a subject's mind to include that which harms or could harm that mind or that which that mind cares about. "Good" will be defined in a similar way to include that which benefits or could benefit a mind or that which that mind cares about. (p. 290)

My claims about morality are unabashedly only about how and why people behave and think as they do, not about how people should act. I am being descriptive, not prescriptive or normative. I am saying how normative ideas such as "ought," "appropriate," or "evil" came into existence, not what people should do or not do. I defined good and evil in this way because I did not want to get into a discussion of what is universally good or evil intention or action for all minds, or universally good or evil, right or wrong, for any particular circumstance. I do not deny that such universalist prescriptive arguments can be made and that they can be useful and instructive. History is full of such universalist prescriptions, often conflicting with one another. I just do not want to address these questions here, since they will lead me too far from my central point, which is that the possibility of morality, good, and evil results from symbolic cognition. Instead, I focus on what is good or evil from the point of view of a single person, regardless of universalist prescriptions, while realizing the limitations of such a narrow definition. The obvious danger here is moral relativism, namely, that what seems good to a sadist, say torture, will comprise evil for her victim. In order to counter this danger, it is necessary to engage in universalist arguments that will prescribe what is right and wrong in general. I have nothing against such reasoning. It is just too far afield from the point of this essay.

I agree that tokenization, compassion, or focusing on the individual do not necessarily determine the goodness or badness of an act or intention. I do not mean to say that tokenization is necessarily a root of evil. I agree that it is in itself neutral and can lead to good or evil acts or intentions. My point is simply that tokenization is only possible for a symbolic mind. It can be one root of evil or good, and it only exists in symbolic minds where a token can be taken to stand for something more general than itself.

6 Nativism and Moral Psychology: Three Models of the Innate Structure That Shapes the Contents of Moral Norms

Chandra Sekhar Sripada

There is a God. . . . Promises are to be kept. . . . The obscene parts and actions are not to be exposed to publick view. . . . [even] in thine owne bosom, written by the finger of God, in such plain Characters, and so legible, that though thou knowest not a letter in any other booke, yet though maist read this.
—Richard Carpenter, *The Conscionable Christian*

Moral norms are the sinews of the social order. They delimit the bounds of proper behavior in a host of domains, providing a normative ruler by which people constantly judge all aspects of their own and others' behavior. Given the ubiquity and importance of moral norms in human social behavior, an intriguing question arises as to the ultimate source of these norms. How does the mind come to be furnished with the suite of moral rules that play such important roles in our lives?

In the last five decades, cognitive scientists have increasingly endorsed *nativist* explanations for the origin and development of a host of cognitive capacities. For example, theorists have argued that innate bodies of information and/or innate mechanisms play an important role in explaining the origin and development of our abilities to: learn and utilize a language (Chomsky, 1965, 1988), attribute intentional states to others (Leslie, 1994), explain and predict the motion of middle-sized physical objects (Spelke, 1988), classify animals and plants (Atran, 1998), and many other abilities as well (see Hirshfield & Gelman, 1994). Remarkably, however, cognitive scientists have devoted little systematic attention to addressing the question of nativism *specifically in the domain of moral norms*. In particular, there has been very little attention addressed to the question of what kinds of innate structure play a role in shaping the *contents* of moral norms. This is the question that I address in this essay.

This chapter is divided into five parts. I'll begin by clarifying what I mean by talk of "moral norms" and what it means to say that a moral norm is innate. In the next three parts of the chapter, I'll introduce three models of the innate structure that plays a role in shaping the contents of moral norms. The first model, which I call the "Simple Innateness Model," proposes that humans possess an innate body of moral rules and principles. These rules are universal among humans and arise without the need for any highly specific instruction or cultural inputs. As I'll argue, a problem for the Simple Innateness Model is that it has trouble accounting for the *variability* of moral norms across human groups. The next two models I discuss, which I call the "Principles and Parameters Model" and the "Innate Biases Model," are more complex in that they envision a role for *both* innate structure and culture in shaping the contents of moral norms. I will clarify the structure of these models and discuss arguments and evidence in favor of each. In the end, I'll argue that the Innate Biases Model provides the most plausible account of the innate structure that shapes the contents of moral norms.

In the final part of the paper, I'll explore an issue that is closely related to the question of nativism in moral psychology—the issue of *cultural change* in the contents of moral norms. There is excellent evidence that moral norms change over time. For example, in Western societies over the last 200 years, moral norms that permitted male control over women and limits to female autonomy have been displaced by moral norms that forbid these practices. How can fundamental change of this sort be reconciled with the existence of innate structure that shapes the contents of moral norms? I'll discuss this intriguing issue in the final part of the paper.

Preliminary Clarifications

I'll begin with an account of what I mean when I talk of "moral norms." As I use the term, a norm is a rule or principle that specifies actions which are required, permissible, or forbidden *independent* of any legal or social institution. Of course, some norms are *also* recognized and enforced by social institutions and laws, but the crucial point is that they needn't be. A second important feature of moral norms is that violations of norms, when they become known, typically engender *punitive attitudes* such as anger, condemnation, and blame, directed at the norm violator, and these attitudes sometimes lead to punitive behavior. These punitive attitudes are closely linked to a suite of emotions, including anger, contempt, and disgust when the violator is a third party, and guilt and shame when the violator is oneself. I believe that moral norms, as I've characterized them, are an important and theoretically useful subcategory of social rules, and that this characterization is broadly in line with other accounts, both historical and more recent (see Durkheim, 1903/1953; Parsons, 1952; Pettit, 1991; McAdams, 1997). However, it is worth emphasizing that my account of norms is *not* intended as a *conceptual analysis* or an account of what the term "moral norm" means to ordinary speakers. Nor do I offer this characterization of moral norms as a formal definition. At best it gives a rough and ready way to pick out what I believe is a theoretically interesting *natural kind* in the social sciences (Sripada, in preparation).

In considering the question of nativism about moral norms, it is useful to distinguish two related but quite distinct nativist theses, which I'll call "capacity nativism" and "content nativism." I'll illustrate the idea behind capacity nativism by considering an example. Consider the following moral norm: Don't kill any member of your own group. In order to understand this norm and utilize the norm in day-to-day interactions with others, it's plausible that a person will need to draw upon a large number of cognitive capacities. The cognitive scientist Marc Hauser has characterized a number of these "norm-associated" capacities (Hauser, 2006). For example, in order to recognize a particular behavior as an instance of killing, a person will need a "theory of action," that is, the capacity to parse agents' physical movements into sequences of actions with the appropriate assignment of causal relations between actions and their outcomes. A second cognitive capacity that plays a role in moral judgment is "theory of mind," that is, the capacity to attribute mental states such as beliefs and desires to other agents. Theory of mind might be used, for example, to determine whether an agent's actions are intended versus unintended, and these determinations in turn influence judgments about the agent's blameworthiness. Hauser identifies a number of other cognitive capacitates that are associated with moral judgment, including the capacity to distinguish living things from nonliving things and the capacity to exert self-control in the face of temptation.

Capacity nativism concerns the question of whether, and to what extent, the various capacities such as theory of action and theory of mind that are associated with moral judgment are innate. In this paper, I'll have relatively little to say about the issue of capacity nativism. Hauser reviews an extensive body of evidence that supports the view that many of the capacities that are associated with moral judgment are in fact innate. Readers interested in this topic will be well served by his discussion.

The focus of this paper is content nativism. The content of a moral norm consists of the class of actions that the norm prohibits, permits, or requires. Anthropologists have collected an extensive database that documents the manner in which moral norms exhibit both commonalities and differences in content across human groups. For example, in some human groups, it is permissible for a man to have several wives, use certain forms of violence to settle conflicts, and accumulate wealth and resources at levels significantly higher than his peers. In other groups, all of these practices are prohibited. Content nativism concerns the question of whether there is innate structure that shapes the content of moral norms, and if there is, what is the nature of this innate structure. In the next three parts of the paper, I'll discuss three models of the innate structure that shapes the contents of moral norms.

The Simple Innateness Model

Perhaps the most important reason for believing that there is innate structure that shapes the content of moral norms is the fact that moral norms exhibit a striking pattern of commonalities across human groups. Moral norms are not indefinitely variable or randomly distributed across human groups. Rather, there are certain kinds of norms that one sees again and again in almost all human societies, though in order to discern these commonalities, one has to stay at a fairly high level of generality. For example, most societies have rules that prohibit killing and physical assault (Brown, 1991). Also, most societies have rules promoting sharing, reciprocating, and helping, at least under some circumstances (Cashdan, 1989). Most societies have rules regulating sexual behavior among various members of society, and especially among adolescents (Bourguignon & Greenbaum, 1973). And most societies have at least some rules that promote egalitarianism and social equality. For example, in nearly all hunter-gatherer groups, attempts by individuals to reap a disproportionate share of resources, women, or power are disapproved of sharply (Boehm, 1999). Examples like these could be multiplied easily in domains such as social justice, kinship, marriage, and many others.

One way of explaining this pattern of commonalities is to propose that at least some moral norms are *innate*. In order to make this idea more precise, I now introduce what I hope is a helpful way of making innateness claims about moral norms a bit more precise. I believe that it is useful to think of moral norms as being stored in a mental database, which I shall refer to as the "Norms Box." Of course, in using the term "box," I don't intend to imply that there is literally a box that is spatially localized in the brain. Rather, the notion of a box is intended to capture the idea that moral norms play a distinct *functional role* in a person's psychology. I've already discussed certain features of this functional role. For example, I noted earlier that when people come to know about violations of moral norms, they reliably display punitive attitudes and a characteristic suite of emotions including anger and guilt. The box metaphor allows us to refer to the characteristic functional role associated with moral norms in a concise way.

According to the Simple Innateness Model, there are many moral rules that are innate elements of the Norms Box. Though there is a large philosophical literature debating the best interpretation of innateness claims in psychology (Cowie, 1999; Griffiths, 2002; Samuels, 2002), for the current purposes, we can consider a moral rule to be innate if various genetic and developmental factors make it the case that the moral rule reliably emerges in the Norm Box in a wide range of environmental conditions. In particular, I regard a moral rule to be innate if the development of the rule does not depend on any *specific* pattern of cultural input, such that different moral rules would emerge if different patterns of cultural input obtained.

If there were innate moral norms of this sort, then they would almost certainly be cultural universals. Barring extraordinary circumstances, we should expect to find them in all human groups. Are there any moral norm universals of this sort? This question must be handled with some care since many candidate norm universals are problematic because they verge on being *analytic*—true in virtue of meaning alone. For example, "Murder is wrong" and "Theft is wrong" don't count as legitimate universals since, roughly speaking, "murder" simply means killing someone else in a way which is not permissible, and "theft" simply means taking something from another in a way which is not permissible. For this reason, it is important, whenever possible, to frame the contents of norms in a non-normative vocabulary. While analytic principles like "Murder is wrong" and "Theft is wrong" may be universals, the *specific* rules that regulate the *circumstances* under which killing or taking an item in the possession of another person is permitted are not so nearly uniform across groups.

A careful look at the actual distributional pattern of moral norms across human groups reveals that there is much more variability than the Simple Innateness Model can accommodate. I'll use the case of incest norms to illustrate this point. A large cross-cultural survey by the anthropologist George Murdock revealed that almost all human societies have moral norms prohibiting sexual intercourse between members of the nuclear family (Murdock, 1949), and I'll call these nearly universal rules "core incest prohibitions." However, a closer look reveals that there is much underlying variability associated with incest prohibitions.

Incest prohibitions almost always extend beyond the core prohibition characterized above. In particular, incest prohibitions almost always apply to acts other than just *sexual intercourse* and they almost always extend beyond just the *nuclear family*; that is, they prohibit sexual activity with at least some members of one's non-nuclear kin. However, the details of how incest prohibitions extend beyond core incest prohibitions are, as numerous studies have revealed, tremendously variable (Murdock, 1949). For example, at one extreme are *exogamous groups*, in which marriage with *anyone* within one's own tribal unit is considered incestuous, though the offense is seldom seen as being of the same level of severity as intercourse within one's nuclear family. At another extreme, there are many groups, such as the nomadic Bedouins of the Arabian peninsula, for whom marrying one's first cousin is not only permitted, but in fact prescribed (Murdock, 1949).

I believe that, much as in the case with incest, more or less *all* putative examples of norm universals are actually associated with much underlying variability. There is solid ethnographic evidence that in domains such as social exchange (Fiske, 1991; Henrich et al., 2001), harms and violence (Robarchek & Robarchek, 1992; Keeley, 1996), hierarchy and social stratification (Boehm, 1999), marriage (Durham, 1991), sexual rules and prohibitions (Bourguignon & Greenbaum, 1973), food taboos (Simoons, 1994), and many others, moral norms differ substantially across human groups. In later sections of this paper, I'll draw on the ethnographic record in more detail in discussing a number of specific examples of between-groups differences in moral norms. The existence of these between-groups differences weighs heavily against the Simple Innateness Model.

The problem with the Simple Innateness Model is that it regards the development of the contents of the Norms Box as being largely insensitive to cultural inputs. However, the pattern of variability of moral norms across human groups suggests that culture does in fact play an important role in determining the specific moral norms that a person acquires. In the next two parts of the paper, I'll discuss two models of innate structure that are more complex than the Simple Innateness Model in that they allow an important role for culture in shaping the contents of moral norms. However, the specific mode of interaction between innate structure and culture is quite different in each of these two models.

The Principles and Parameters Model

Natural languages, that is, languages such as English, Japanese, and Swahili, and moral norms are similar in that in both domains there is a complex pattern of both commonalities and differences across human groups. Based on this observation, a number of theorists have proposed that language might provide a model for how to understand the innate structure that shapes the contents of moral norms. In this part of the paper, I'll explore this proposal in more detail.

Clarifying the Principles and Parameters Model

A remarkable feature of the language faculty is that it provides for a kind of "predesigned flexibility" during the course of language acquisition. The language faculty can be thought of as affording something like an innate "menu" of basic grammatical options. For example, one option concerns whether phrases require a subject or not. In English a subject is required; in Italian it isn't. Another option concerns the order in which the subject, verb, and object are placed in a sentence. Most human languages are subject-verb-object or subject-object-verb, while virtually no languages are object-subject-verb. There are a large number of other options as well. The linguist Noam Chomsky has dubbed this innate menu "Universal Grammar." While every child possesses the same innate menu, cultural experience serves to select various options from the menu, with different language groups selecting different options. Thus, Universal Grammar helps explain the existence of linguistic diversity. It also helps explain why this diversity is *restricted* in certain characteristic ways—these restrictions corresponding to the options provided by Universal Grammar.

There is considerable controversy over how to understand the structure of Universal Grammar, that is, the innate element that provides for a restricted range of linguistic flexibility. Chomsky originally conceptualized the task of learning a language in terms of *hypothesis testing* (Chomsky, 1965). The child frames hypotheses concerning possible grammars and attempts to confirm one of these hypotheses from linguistic experience. On this model, Universal Grammar consists of a range of *constraints* on candidate hypotheses available to the child. At various times, in this period, Chomsky *also* played with the idea that what Universal Grammar provided was an ordering of hypotheses. The acquisition device starts with the first ("simplest") one and sticks with it until it is disconfirmed, then it goes on to the next one. In principle, a system like this could operate without "constraints"—at least if it is possible to order every logically possible grammar.

More recently, however, Chomsky has explicated Universal Grammar along the lines of what he calls a "Principles and Parameters Model" (Chomsky, 1988). According to this model, the language faculty is associated with a set of parameters which can be set in various permissible ways.

For example, one putative parameter governs the ordering of phrases, that is, subject-verb-object, subject-object-verb, etc. . . . The linguistic experience that the child confronts serves to "toggle" the parameters associated with the language faculty, thus accounting for the child's mature language competence (Baker, 2001).

A number of theorists have proposed that a broadly Chomskian Principles and Parameters Model might provide a useful way to understand moral norm acquisition (Mikhail, Sorentino, & Spelke, 1998; Harman, 1999a; Dwyer, 1999; see also Stich, 1993). There are two kinds of arguments that have typically been deployed in support of the Principles and Parameters view. The first argument is that the Principles and Parameters Model provides a plausible account of the *distributional pattern* of moral norms across human groups. Earlier I noted that moral norms exhibit a complex pattern of commonalities and differences across human groups. Defenders of the Principles and Parameters Model have suggested that the best explanation for this pattern is that it arises due to the operation of universal underlying moral principles that allow for a highly restricted range of parameterized variability. For example, Gilbert Harman has argued that a Principles and Parameters Model provides a plausible explanation for the pattern of universality and variability associated with harm norms, that is, norms that forbid unjustified assault or other kinds of violence (Harman, 1999a). Harman proposes that it is a universal principle of all human moralities that one should not harm members of some protected class C, where "C" functions as a parameter that can be set in different ways. According to Harman, the specific moralities that prevail in different human groups differ with respect to how this parameter is set. Some specific moralities restrict membership in the protected class to an in-group such as a tribe or clan, while others allow a broader range of individuals to be included within the protected class.

A second argument used to support the Principles and Parameters Model is a *poverty of the stimulus argument*. According to this argument, there is a problem in explaining how some cognitive capacity is acquired because there is a gap between two features of the learning situation—the complexity of the learning target and the resources available to the learner. The existence of this gap is taken as evidence that there must be some kind innate structure that bridges the gap, thus explaining how children reliably end up acquiring the mature cognitive competence (see Cowie, 1999). In the case of language, a poverty of the stimulus argument has played an important role in supporting the Principles and Parameters Model of language learning. Defenders of the existence of innate parameters in the domain of moral norms have argued that their position is supported by an analogous poverty of the *moral stimulus* argument. In the next two sections, I criticize the preceding two arguments used to defend the Principles and Parameters Model, beginning with the poverty of the moral stimulus argument. Then I'll turn to a third argument that weighs against the Principles and Parameters Model, which I call the "argument from exceptions."

Problems with the Poverty of the Moral Stimulus Argument

Recall that a poverty of the stimulus argument asserts that there is a gap between two features of the learning situation—the complexity of the learning target and the resources available to the learner. In criticizing the poverty of the *moral* stimulus argument, it's useful to begin by briefly examining the structure of the poverty of the stimulus argument in the case of language. In the case of language, the existence of a gap between learning target and learning resources is indeed quite plausible.

The language learning task presents the child with an exceedingly complex learning target. All human grammars are built around complex hierarchical tree structures. In addition, there are a number of different kinds of *recursive rules* which govern how basic sentential categories such as noun phrases and verb phrases can be recursively assembled into sentences. While there is some controversy among theorists on the nature and structure of these recursive rules, almost all theorists agree that human grammars embody an exceedingly abstruse and sophisticated formal competence (see Pinker, 1994; Jackendoff, 2002).

In addition to the complexity of their learning target, language learners must also contend with the restricted nature of the learning resources available to them. This restriction arises because language learning is of necessity an *inductive learning task,* that is, a learning task in which the learner must identify a general rule based on *instances* of the rule. Other learning tasks that occur after a language has already been acquired (such as learning where to hunt or how to cook, etc.) can be facilitated by a powerful learning tool, *explicit verbal instruction*. But, of course, one cannot explicitly instruct the child on the correct grammatical rules. For example, a child cannot be told "When forming a question, take the first auxiliary verb from the main clause and move it to the front of the sentence." Understanding such a sentence would require a grammar, which is precisely what the child is trying to learn. Thus, the data available to the child must of necessity be instances of grammatical sentences from which the child must identify the correct grammar. Much recent work using formal models of language learning suggests that inductive learning tasks of this sort are extraordinarily difficult to solve and are, in some cases, simply unsolvable in the absence of strong constraints on one's hypothesis space or other kinds of learning restrictions (see Wexler & Culicover, 1980). Because language learning must necessarily be an inductive learning task, many theorists have viewed innate constraints on language learning as not only plausible but, in principle, unavoidable.

An important disanalogy between language learning and moral norm learning is that in the case of moral norm learning, the learning target is far simpler than in the case of language. Moral norms are not abstruse and far removed from experience in the same manner as the hierarchical tree structures and recursive rules of human grammars. Rather, moral norm learning merely requires that the child acquire a readily understandable collection of fairly concrete rules, for example, rules such as "Share your toys," "Don't hit other children," "Respect your elders," "Don't eat pork," and so on. Many of the more difficult rules, for example, "Treat each person with equal respect and dignity" or "Don't have extra-marital sexual relations" are learned much later in life (if at all), after the conceptual resources needed to understand such rules are firmly in place.

A second crucial disanalogy between language learning and moral norm learning is that while language learning must *necessarily* be an inductive learning problem, the learning of moral norms *needn't* be an inductive learning problem at all. That is, in the case of learning moral norms, the child already has language and can be *explicitly instructed* as to what are the correct moral norms to follow. Indeed, there is intriguing evidence that explicit verbal instruction does in fact play an important role in the acquisition of moral norms. The psychologist Carolyn Pope Edwards analyzed records of day-to-day norm transgressions among children from the Luo-speaking community in Southern Kenya. She found that children receive repeated, explicit verbal instruction (and also verbal commands and threats) during the course of norm acquisition and development (Edwards, 1987).

To sum up, learning moral norms differs from learning language in two respects. First, the learning target is far simpler and, second, the learning resources available to the child are incomparably greater. I conclude then that the poverty of the moral stimulus argument is implausible, and the use of this argument to support a Principles and Parameters Model in the moral domain is unpersuasive.

The Distributional Pattern of Moral Norms

Another argument that has been used in favor of the Principles and Parameters Model claims that this model provides the best explanation for the *distributional pattern* of moral norms across human groups. In this section, I'll argue that there appears to be *too much variation* in the contents of moral norms across human groups for the Principles and Parameters Model to accommodate. In particular, I'll argue that the pattern of variation in moral norms cannot be explained in terms of the operation of a few relatively rigid parameters. I'll use the case of harm norms, that is, moral norms that pertain to harm and violence, to illustrate this point.

Virtually all human groups have moral norms pertaining to harms. However, the *specific* harm norms that prevail across human groups differ from group to group. The Principles and Parameters Model claims that we can understand this variation in terms of the operation of underlying innate parameters. For example, earlier we encountered a proposal by Gilbert Harman that it is a universal principle of all human moralities that one should not harm members of some protected class C. However, according to Harman, the specific moralities that prevail in different human groups differ with respect to whom they include within this protected class.

A closer look at the ethnographic record suggests, however, that the pattern of variation in harm norms is much more complex, subtle, and variegated than the simple parameterized rule that Harman proposes. For example, as the philosopher Jesse Prinz points out, many human groups permit at least some kinds of harms to be committed against members of one's in-group, at least in some circumstances, and groups differ in complicated ways with respect to the kinds of harms that are permitted. Prinz notes, for example, that many groups allow scarification, piercing, adult circumcision, flagellation, and other harms to be inflicted on in-group members (Prinz, forthcoming). Furthermore, many societies permit at least some kinds of violence against various *subgroups* within one's in-group (see LeVine & Campbell, 1972). For example, many groups allow harms to be inflicted against women, children, and certain marginalized subgroups or castes, at least in some circumstances (Edgerton, 1992).

In addition to exhibiting variation with respect to the class of individuals forbidden from *committing* harms and the class of individuals *protected* from being harmed, moral norms also vary with respect to the *contexts* under which these norms apply. For example, many societies permit harms committed in the context of retaliation or punishment for a previous offense. However, the specific manner in which harms are permitted in the context of retaliation and punishment vary across groups. In so-called "Cultures of Honor," males place enormous value on maintaining a reputation for strength and probity. In these cultures, the use of violence for the purposes of defending one's honor is permissible, or even required, and even relatively minor offenses such as insults or verbal barbs may provoke a severe violent response (Nisbett & Cohen, 1996).

Harm norms also exhibit variation with respect to the *kinds of harm* and the *level of harm* which are permitted. In some societies, almost all harm-causing behaviors are strongly prohibited. Among the Semai, an aboriginal people of the Malaysian rainforest, almost all types of harm, including hitting and fighting, as well as more mundane behaviors such as insulting or slandering, are all impermissible, and Semai groups have among the lowest levels of harm and violence of any sort of any human societies (Robarchek & Robarchek, 1992). However, other groups permit a much wider spectrum of harm-causing behaviors. In groups such as the Yanomano of South America, the use of violence to settle conflicts or to obtain desired resources (especially women) is permitted (and indeed extremely common), and displays of fighting bravado are prized rather than condemned (Chagnon, 1992). Among the Yanomano, mortality due to intra- and intertribe conflict is extremely high, and some ethnographers have suggested that the level of mortality due to violence found among the Yanomano is not at all uncommon in simple societies (Keeley, 1996). Between the extremes represented by the Semai and the Yanomano, there appear to be a continuous range of intermediate positions (see Silverberg & Gray, 1992).

Overall, the pattern of variation in moral norms across human groups is too extensive and complex to be accounted for in terms of a set of relatively rigid parameters. Rather, I believe, the best description of the pattern of variation in moral norms is in terms of what I'll call "thematic clustering." There are certain *high-level themes* that one sees in the contents of moral norms in virtually all human groups—themes such as harms, incest, helping and sharing, social justice, and group defense. However, the *specific rules* that fall under these high-level themes exhibit enormous variability. The Principles and Parameters Model relies on a small set of discrete and relatively rigid parameters to explain moral norm variation and is thus ill equipped to explain this pattern of thematic clustering. Later in this essay, I'll explore the Innate Biases Model, which, I'll argue, offers a natural explanation for why the thematic clustering pattern obtains.

The Argument from Exceptions

There is another feature of the pattern of variation in moral norms that weighs against the Principles and Parameters Model. We can best appreciate this feature by considering how the model operates in the domain of language. According to Chomsky, the range of variation in languages across human groups is sharply constrained by innate linguistic parameters that admit of only certain highly restricted kinds of variation. Chomsky argues that the existence of these innate parameters forms the basis for *exceptionless generalizations* about the structure of human languages and also leads to specific predictions of the kinds of languages that are humanly possible and impossible. As Chomsky puts it, "The principles of universal grammar are exceptionless because they constitute the language faculty itself, a framework for any particular human language, the basis for the acquisi-tion of language" (Chomsky 1988, pp. 62–63). And indeed, linguists in the Chomskian tradition have identified a large number of specific linguistic parameters (or candidate parameters) that do indeed appear to lead to exceptionless generalizations about human languages (for a review, see Baker, 2001, and Pinker, 1994).

If moral norms are associated with innate parameters of the kind associated with language, then one would expect to find exceptionless generalizations in the case of moral norms as well. In particular, one would expect to find certain *norm universals* whose status as universals is underwritten by innate moral parameters that sharply restrict the class of moral norms that a person can acquire.

In assessing the question of whether there are in fact norm universals of this sort, it's important to make a distinction between moral norms which are *extremely common* across human groups and norms which are *exceptionless* universals. I think there are lots of moral norms which are extremely common across human groups. Indeed, I've cited many examples of such norms in the preceding parts of this paper. I emphasize again in the strongest terms that I do not doubt that such commonalities exist. However, I'm skeptical that there are any interesting rules which are, *and of biological necessity must be,* exceptionless, where their status as such is due to the fact that innate parameters preclude the child from ever acquiring alternative rules.

While there are many generalizations about the contents of the moral norms found across human groups, these generalizations *invariably* have exceptions. For example, the incest prohibition is sometimes cited as the best example of a norm which is a universal across all human groups. And while it is true that core incest prohibitions can be found in virtually all groups, even this generalization may not be exceptionless. There is good evidence that brother-sister marriage (including sexual relations) occurred with some frequency in Egypt during the Roman period, and was practiced openly and unabashedly (Hopkins, 1980). In addition, brother-sister marriage is known to have occurred in a number of royal lineages, including those of Egypt, Hawaii, and the Inca empire (see Durham, 1991).

Overall, many interesting candidates for being exceptionless norm universals turn out, on closer inspection, to admit of at least some exceptions. The ethnographic database records a wide variety of odd, bizarre, and frankly maladaptive moral norms, even in core areas such as incest, harm, and norms of social justice (Edgerton, 1992). The ethnographic data is further augmented by data from isolated communities such as utopian communities and splinter religious orders where a wide variety of odd or even "deviant" norms are instilled, sometimes for many generations (see, e.g., Foster, 1991). I believe that there is little solid evidence supporting the existence of exceptionless norm universals, and this fact weighs heavily against the Principles and Parameters Model.

The Innate Biases Model

I now turn to a third model of the innate structures that shapes the contents of moral norms, which I'll call the "Innate Biases Model." As I use the term, an "innate bias" on the contents of moral norms is some element of innate structure that serves to make the presence of some moral norms in the Norms Box *more likely* relative to the case in which the bias is absent. For example, the widespread presence of certain kinds of moral norms across human groups may be explained in terms of the fact that the innate structure of the mind is predisposed to *favor* the emergence or propagation of these norms or predisposed to *disfavor* the emergence or propagation of other competing norms. However, unlike in the case of the Principles and Parameters Model, which involved more or less impermeable parameters, an innate bias does not *require* or *preclude* the presence of any particular moral norm or set of moral norms in the Norms Box.

Two Ways That Innate Biases Might Work

Its useful to distinguish two ways in which innate biases might serve to shape the contents of moral norms. One way that innate biases may work is that they may bias the *transmission* of moral norms from one individual to another. When innate biases work this way, I'll say they act as "Sperberian biases," which I name after anthropologist Dan Sperber, who has probably done more than any one else to emphasize their importance (Sperber, 1996).

Consider a child who is *socially learning* a moral norm from a parent or some other member of the community. In any social learning process, a mental state in one person causes the formation of a type-similar mental state in another person, and we can call the latter mental state a *copy* of the former. However, since no transmission process is error free, the use of the term "copy" is at best an idealization. Sometimes copying errors are random, but there are a variety of ways in which copying processes can give rise to *systematic* errors. For example, some sorts of normative rules may be more or less "attractive" due to the way they interact with one's preferences, aversions, emotions, and other elements of one's psychology. For these same reasons, or for other reasons, some normative rules might be easier to detect (i.e., they may be more salient), easier to infer, or easier to remember, store, or recall. The transmission process will be influenced systematically by all these factors. When copying errors change less attractive rules into more attractive ones, the new rules will be more likely to be retained and transmitted, but when copying errors change more attractive rules into less attractive ones, the new rules will be more likely to be eliminated. It is these systematic processes affecting norm transmission that I call "Sperberian biases." Sperberian biases are typically *weak*. They need not play a role in every instance of transmission from a cultural parent to a child, and often they will affect very few. Nevertheless, when their effects are summed over populations and over time, they generate a fairly strong population-level force which can have the effect of changing the distribution of norms in the direction favored by the Sperberian bias.

We can illustrate the operation of Sperberian biases by considering an example. Shaun Nichols has proposed that *disgust* acts as a Sperberian bias in the cultural transmission of etiquette norms (Nichols, 2002). According to Nichols, disgust generates this bias by making certain kinds of etiquette rules more salient and more easily stored and recalled, and he marshals some intriguing evidence for these claims. Using data from sixteenth-century etiquette manuals from Northern Europe, Nichols shows that etiquette rules whose violation engenders disgust are more likely to be part of contemporary etiquette codes than rules that fail to implicate disgust. This finding suggests that the cumulative operation of disgust as a bias on the transmission of etiquette rules has had the long-term effect of shifting the distribution of etiquette rules over time in the direction favored by the bias. In the same way that disgust might engender a Sperberian bias in the case of etiquette norms, it's plausible that other cognitive structures, including various beliefs, preferences, aversions, and emotions, might engender Sperberian biases in the cultural transmission of other sorts of norms.

Sperberian biases operate on the *transmission* of moral norms. There is, in addition, a second pathway by which innate biases may shape the contents of moral norms—they may influence the *emergence* of moral norms. That is, innate biases may increase the likelihood that moral norms with certain kinds of contents are "founded" as opposed to other moral norms with contents that are not favored by the bias. When innate biases shape the contents of moral norms by this route, I'll say they act as "origination biases." In the following section, I'll illustrate how origination biases might work by considering an extended example.

The Westermarck Mechanism and Incest Prohibitions

Earlier, I noted that almost all human societies have some sort of incest prohibition or other, though the *specific* content of these prohibitions is subject to substantial variation. In this section, I'll argue that innate biases help to explain the origin and maintenance of incest prohibitions and the reason why these prohibitions are so widespread. I'll also argue that innate biases help to explain the variation across human groups in the specific content of incest prohibitions.

In 1891, the Finnish sociologist Edward Westermarck proposed that humans have an innate mechanism that generates a powerful aversion to having sex with people with whom one has had extended intimate association during one's childhood years (Westermarck, 1891/1922). The evolutionary rationale for this so-called "Westermarck mechanism" is clear. As numerous studies have revealed, inbreeding, that is, sexual union between close genetic relatives, has a number of deleterious effects on offspring, and these effects are quite significant from the perspective of evolutionary fitness (see Durham, 1991, for a review of these studies). Since the people whom one associates with in one's early childhood years tend to be close genetic relatives—for example, parents, siblings, aunts, uncles, and others—a mechanism that generates an aversion to sexual unions with these individuals would make evolutionary sense and would be favored by natural selection.

A number of theorists have since identified various kinds of evidence that are suggestive that Westermarck's hypothesis is correct. One particularly important source of evidence emerged from the study of sexual unions and marriages in the communal villages, or kibbutzim, of Israel. In the kibbutzim, it was a common practice that genetically unrelated children were raised together, in prolonged intimate association, as part of an age-graded peer group called the *kevutza*. Furthermore, kibbutzim children were not raised to think that sexual intercourse or marriage between members of the same kevutza constitutes incest. Yet the accumulated evidence suggests that sexual intercourse and marriage between members of the same *kevutza* was vanishingly rare, with several studies finding not a *single* instance of sexual intercourse or marriage among members of the same *kevutza* (Spiro, 1958; Shepher, 1983; see Durham, 1991, for a discussion). There is now an extensive literature on the Westermarck hypothesis (which I won't review here), and the hypothesis is not without its critics (see, e.g., Kaffman, 1977). However, in what follows, I assume that the Westermarck hypothesis is correct and that humans do in fact have an innate mechanism that generates an aversion to sexual union with close childhood associates.

At this point, it's important to emphasize that there is a distinction between an innate *aversion* and an innate *moral norm*. As I noted earlier, moral norms are associated with a number of distinctive features. For example, when violations of moral norms become known, people reliably exhibit punitive attitudes and behaviors as well as emotions such as anger and guilt. An aversion and a moral norm are quite distinct, so the mere fact that humans universally exhibit the Westermarck aversion, that is, the innate aversion to sexual unions with close childhood associates, does not by itself provide an explanation for why human groups tend to have moral norms that forbid incest. However, following a number of other theorists, including Westermarck himself, I propose that the existence of the Westermarck aversion might serve as an *innate bias* that favors the emergence moral norms that forbid incest.

I'll now sketch a scenario that links the presence of the Westermarck aversion with the emergence of moral norms that forbid incest. I begin by supposing that early human groups had rudimentary moral systems—that is, they had systems of moral norms enforced by informal sanctions such as ostracism and reputational sanctioning. There are a number of accounts of how such simple moral systems might have first emerged. I won't explore this extensive literature here (see Alexander, 1987; Boyd & Richerson, forthcoming). Rather, I presuppose that early humans had rudimentary moral systems of this sort, and I focus on the question of what happens after such systems originated.

Given the existence of simple moral systems, it is likely that new moral rules would periodically emerge over time (i.e., over the course of hundreds or thousands of years). There are several factors that might lead to the emergence of new moral rules. One reason is that the people in a group might face some novel ecological or social situation. For example, people in a group may discover some new technique for hunting large game that requires the cooperative effort of several hunters to bring down the animal. A new moral norm may need to be proposed in order to deal with the problem of how the meat should be divided among the hunters (or among the group). New moral norms may also emerge because a powerful or prestigious person decrees that some new moral rule ought to be followed. For example, a powerful person may have an aversion or reaction of disgust to a particular food item. This may lead the person to use his or her power and influence to found a taboo against the consumption of the offending food.

Given that new moral norms periodically emerge over time, I believe that the Westermarck aversion would serve to bias the origination of these moral norms in favor of moral norms that pertain to the content of the bias. Let us suppose that in some group, one person decides that he or she will have sex with a parent or sibling. Because of the existence of the Westermarck aversion, this action, once it becomes widely known, will immediately be salient to almost everyone in the group and will serve to elicit powerful aversive reactions. Furthermore, it's plausible that actions that elicit powerful aversive reactions on the part of almost everyone in the group are more likely than other sorts of actions to lead to the emergence of new moral norms that forbid the offending action. As Westermarck put it, "aversions that are generally felt readily lead to moral disapproval" (Westermarck 1891/1922). Of course, the tendency of innate aversions to bias the emergence of new moral norms need not be particularly strong. Even if the biasing effect of the Westermarck aversion is fairly weak, a weak bias of this sort, when its effect is cumulated over hundreds or thousands of generations, can have a powerful effect in shifting the distribution of moral norms significantly in the direction favored by the bias.

Thus far, I have emphasized the role of the Westermarck aversion in biasing the emergence of new moral norms. Thus, I have focused on the role of the aversion as an *origination bias*. However, it's plausible that the aversion will *also* act as *Sperberian bias* on the transmission of moral norms that forbid incest. Recall that Sperberian biases arise due to the fact that some cultural items are more "attractive" than others because of the way that these items interact with a person's beliefs, preferences, emotions, and other aspects of a person's psychology. It is likely that the existence of the Westermarck aversion as part of innate human psychology would enhance the "attractiveness" of a moral norm that forbids incest, thus helping to maintain the moral norm over extended stretches of time. Overall, I believe that the combined effect of the Westermarck aversion as an origination bias and as a Sperberian bias provides a plausible explanation for the widespread presence of incest prohibitions across human groups.

Recall, however, that while the existence of some prohibition or other against incest is nearly universal across human groups, the *specific content* of these incest prohibitions varies considerably across human groups. I've already argued that the Innate Biases Model explains the near universality of incest prohibitions. Now I'll argue that the model also explains the variation at the level of specific content of these prohibitions as well. The core idea of the Innate Biases Model is that certain innate structures, such as innate preferences and aversions, serve to favor the emergence and maintenance of some moral norms versus others. However, it's important to note that these innate biases typically operate at a fairly *general* level. That is, innate biases typically favor moral norms with certain *broad* thematic contents, but they leave open the potential for substantial variability with respect to the *specific* moral rule that is favored. I'll illustrate this point by returning to the case of moral norms that prohibit incest.

Recall that the key to the Innate Biases account of the origination of moral norms forbidding incest was the hypothesis that actions that elicit powerful aversive reactions on the part of almost everyone in the group are more likely than other sorts of actions to become the object of a moral norm. For example, I suggested that if someone has sexual relations with a parent or sibling, this action, if it becomes known widely, would elicit powerful aversive reactions on the part of others in the community. These reactions might then lead the members of the community to form a new moral norm against the offending action. The *specific content* of the newly formed incest prohibition, however, won't be so easy to predict. Most likely, the newly formed incest prohibition would forbid sexual intercourse between consanguineous members of the nuclear family, since these individuals are most likely to elicit the Westermarck aversion. However, depending on the familial structure and child rearing patterns of the local group, the incest prohibition may apply more widely than just to the nuclear family. For example, if in some community children tend to be raised in extended households with their maternal cousins, then the operation of the Westermarck mechanism will, at least typically, lead to the development of an aversion to sexual unions with one's maternal cousins. It's plausible that in such a community, it is more likely that a newly formed incest prohibition will forbid sexual relations between maternal cousins as part of the incest prohibition. Overall, innate biases such as the Westermarck aversion seldom determine in any precise or detailed way the content of the moral norms that they serve to favor. As a result, there will inevitably be a significant role for a number of other features, including the existing cultural context and, indeed, sheer happenstance, in determining the specific content of moral norms.

Earlier I argued that the pattern of variation in moral norms across human groups is best described *not* in terms of parameterized variation but rather in terms of what I called "thematic clustering"—moral norms cluster under certain high-level themes with much residual variation at the level of specific content. I believe that the Innate Biases Model provides a natural explanation for why this pattern of thematic clustering obtains. According to the Innate Biases Model, there are a number of biases that are an innate part of universal human psychology. The Westermarck aversion is one example of such a bias, and I will discuss other examples a bit later. These innate biases serve to favor the emergence and maintenance of certain kinds of moral norms rather than others. However, these biases operate at a fairly general level and seldom determine the specific content of moral norms. As a result, the distributional pattern of moral norms exhibits thematic clustering—most human groups have moral norms that fall under certain high-level themes, where these themes correspond to the content of various innate biases. However, at the level of specific content, moral norms exhibit tremendous, more or less continuous, variation.

Other Examples of Innate Biases

In this section I'll briefly explore a few other examples of innate biases that shape the contents of moral norms. My discussion will necessarily be brief, as limitations of space prevent a detailed exposition of these examples.

Evolutionary anthropologists Dan Fessler and Carlos Navarrete have invoked what I've called "innate biases" to explain the origin, maintenance, and cross-cultural distributional pattern of *food taboos*, that is, moral norms that prohibit the consumption of certain food items (Fessler & Navarrete, 2003). Fessler and Navarrete reviewed the distributional pattern of food taboos across 78 societies and found that *meat* is vastly more likely than other items, such as fruits, vegetables, spicy foods, and so forth, to be the object of food taboos. Fessler and Navarrete propose that the existence of innate dispositions to develop aversions to meat explains this preponderance of taboos directed against meat.

There is a large body of evidence, reviewed by Fessler and Navarrete, that supports the hypothesis that humans possess innate mechanisms that dispose them to develop aversions to meat. For example, meat accounts for a full one third of all acquired food aversions among North American subjects, triple the proportion of any other category of food, and significantly higher than one would predict given the frequency with which meat appears in subjects' diets. The emotion *disgust,* in particular, plays a prominent role in mediating meat aversions, and cross-cultural studies reveal that animals and animal products are prototypical elicitors of disgust (Rozin & Fallon, 1980; Fallon & Rozin, 1983). According to Fessler and Navarrete, mechanisms that dispose people to acquire aversions to meat are likely to have evolved because meat, as opposed to other categories of food, is associated with an extremely high potential for food-borne infection and other pathogenic consequences. In defending this evolutionary hypothesis, Fessler and Navarette cite evidence that primates, rodents, and cats, as well as perhaps other species, more readily develop aversions to meat than to other food items.

Fessler and Navarrete then construct detailed scenarios that explain how the existence of innate dispositions to develop aversions to meat serves to favor the emergence and maintenance of food taboos directed at meat. Their account parallels, in important respects, the account I constructed in the previous section of how the Westermarck aversion biases the emergence and maintenance of prohibitions against incest. As Fessler and Navarrete summarize their position:

[M]any cultural practices arise, spread and persist not only because they benefit the holders or their groups, but because they elicit or are congruent with intuitions generated by panhuman features of mind. . . . [S]ome ideas are "good to think" precisely because they interdigitate well with evolved psychological mechanisms, the outputs of which are often experienced as emotions, and this accounts for the widespread distribution of a small number of concepts across disparate cultures. (Fessler & Navarrete, 2003)

The philosopher Shaun Nichols has developed an account of the innate structure that shapes the contents of moral norms that is quite similar to the Innate Biases Model (Nichols, 2004). Nichols calls his account the "Affective Resonance Account," and he emphasizes the role of various innate *emotions* in favoring the cultural evolution of moral norms that are congruent with these emotions. One example that Nichols develops in some detail proposes that various innate emotions, feelings, and motivations helped to explain the near universality of *harm norms* across human groups. Nichols reviews an extensive body of evidence that humans possess innate emotion-linked mechanisms that are triggered when a person

witnesses the distress or suffering of another person, and these mechanisms give rise to motivations to relieve the victim's distress. Nichols then
proposes that these "distress-triggered emotions" serve to bias the cultural
evolution of moral norms that forbid violence and other kinds of harm-
causing behaviors. As evidence for this claim, Nichols systematically documents the cultural evolution of harm norms over the last 400 years in
Western Europe. He shows that Western European societies came to endorse
new moral norms that forbid cruelty to animals and restricted substantially
the use of corporal punishment. Nichols argues that at least part of the
explanation for the emergence of these new harm-mitigating moral norms
is that these norms enjoyed an advantage in cultural evolution due to the
manner in which they "resonate" with aspects of human psychology and,
in particular, with innate distress-sensitive emotions.

Cultural Change in the Contents of Moral Norms

In the final part of this paper, I'll explore an issue that is closely related to
the question of nativism in moral psychology—the issue of *cultural change*
in the contents of moral norms. Moral norms change over time, and sometimes these changes can be quite fundamental. A natural question arises
as to how fundamental change of this sort can be reconciled with the
existence of innate structure that shapes the contents of moral norms. In
this part of the paper, I'll offer an initial sketch of how the Innate Biases
Model might in fact be compatible with fundamental change in the contents of moral norms.

I'll begin by considering another case in which innate biases serve to
shape the contents of moral norms. This case is particularly interesting for
the present purposes because it illustrates the claim that the existence of
innate biases is compatible with the occurrence of substantial change in
the contents of moral norms in a direction that diverges from what innate
biases favor.

Moral Norms Pertaining to Male Entitlements over Women

The evolutionary psychologists Margo Wilson and Martin Daly have argued
that human males exhibit *sexually proprietary attitudes* toward women
(Wilson & Daly, 1992). That is, much as songbirds and lions defend ter-
ritories, human males lay claim to women as a valuable resource and
advertise (and execute) intentions to defend this resource from rivals.
Moreover, Wilson and Daly argue that the cluster of mechanisms and decision rules underlying these proprietary attitudes, including most pro-

minently male sexual jealousy, are evolved adaptations, which are innate and universal among human males.

Wilson and Daly go on to show how male sexual proprietariness manifests itself in the content of moral norms and normative practices of many societies. Examples of such norms and practices include the veiling of women, chaperoning, the practice of foot binding, genital mutilation, bride wealth systems, double standards in rules regarding adultery, and many others. The moral norms and practices Daly and Wilson discuss are quite varied, though obviously thematically connected to the idea of controlling and owning women. Thus, we find further confirmation for the claim that innate biases cause moral norms to cluster under general themes, with much variability in the specific rules that the biases favor.

What is perhaps most interesting about moral norms pertaining to male entitlements over women is that these norms appear to have changed in fundamental ways in the last 200 to 300 years. In Western societies in particular, there has been spectacular change in the moral norms that relate to male sexual proprietariness, and gender relations more broadly. While Wilson and Daly cite many striking historical examples from Western societies of moral norms and legal rules that reflect male sexual proprietariness, all these examples are *of necessity historical.* Contemporary norms in Western societies categorically reject male entitlements over women.

The preceding example suggests that the existence of innate biases is in fact compatible with fundamental change in the contents of moral norms in a direction that diverges from what innate biases favor. In the next and final section of the paper, I offer an initial sketch of how to explain fundamental change of this kind. A word of warning—the account I'll sketch is both speculative and highly incomplete. In offering this sketch, my primary goal is to suggest directions for future research.

Interaction between Innate Biases and Other Cultural Processes

Thus far in this paper, I have been considering the causal influences that arise from innate biases in shaping the contents of moral norms *in isolation.* However, it's plausible that causal influences that arise from innate biases will, at least in some cases, interact with causal influences that arise from other *cultural processes.* In some cases, causal influences arising from innate biases may be opposed by these other sources of causal influences, with the result that the biasing effect of the innate biases is negated, reoriented or countervailed. This possibility is particularly real because, as I've emphasized before, the magnitude of the biasing effect generated by innate biases typically isn't very large. Thus, it's plausible that, at least in some cases, other cultural processes may be sufficiently strong so as to negate and even countervail the effects of innate biases. In order to illustrate this possibility, let us consider a simple example.

The example I consider is adapted (*with significant changes!*) from a hypothesis put forward by evolutionary anthropologists Robert Boyd and Peter Richerson to explain the decline in fertility rates in rich, industrialized countries (Boyd & Richerson, 1985). My goal here is illustrative, so I'll stipulate many features of the case and won't attempt to defend these features with evidence. Let us suppose that humans have innate biases that favor having many children. According to the Innate Biases Model, the existence of innate biases that favor having many children would tend to favor the emergence and maintenance of moral norms that approve of this practice. However, innate biases needn't always operate unopposed.

Let us now introduce another cultural process that might serve to countervail the effects of innate biases. Let us suppose that humans have innate dispositions to imitate the beliefs, values, and practices of *prestigious* members of their community.[1] Furthermore, let us suppose that people who have fewer children need to invest less total time, money, and resources in their children and thus have much more to invest in their careers. As a consequence of this fact, those who have fewer children attain positions of prestige at higher rates than those who have more children.

In this example, prestige-biased imitation will tend to make the practice of having fewer children more common, due to the fact that having fewer children and attaining prestigious positions in society are correlated. Furthermore, it's plausible that at least some who adopt the practice of having fewer children because of prestige-biased imitation will *also* adopt a moral norm that approves of having fewer children. Thus, the moral norm that approves of having fewer children will also be favored by prestige-biased imitation.

In the preceding scenario, innate biases generate a force that favors moral norms that approve of having many children. However, prestige-based imitation generates a force that favors moral norms that approve of having fewer children. The moral norm that eventually prevails in the community will be determined by the relative strength of these two forces.

The preceding example is admittedly quite contrived and omits many important details. However, the point of the example is that innate biases are the basis for just one (important!) kind of causal influence that shapes the contents of moral norms. There are a large number of other cultural processes (including prestige-based imitation) that can give rise to causal influences that shape the contents of moral norms as well. The nature of many of these cultural processes is fairly complex and poorly understood, and I won't attempt to discuss these cultural processes in this paper (see Boyd & Richerson, 1985). However, the point that I want to emphasize is that it is the sum of causal influences arising from innate biases combined with causal influences arising from *other* cultural processes that ultimately determines the content and distribution of moral norms across human groups. And in some cases, causal influences arising from these other cultural processes may reorient, negate, or countervail causal influences arising from innate biases and generate moral norms that differ markedly from the norms that innate biases favor. An important task for future research will be to identify the nature and mode of operation of these cultural processes, thus helping to explain how fundamental change in the contents of moral norms is possible.

Conclusion

Nativism has been an important theoretical perspective in contemporary cognitive science. In this paper, I considered the question of what is the nature of the innate structure that shapes the contents of moral norms. I distinguished three models—the Simple Innateness Model, the Principles and Parameters Model and the Innate Biases Model—and discussed evidence that weighs in favor and against each. In the end, I argued that the Innate Biases Model provides the most plausible account of the innate structure that shapes the contents of moral norms. A topic that is closely related to moral norm nativism is the question of cultural change in the contents of moral norms over time. I argued that the Innate Biases Model is in fact compatible with fundamental change in the contents of moral norms. An important topic for future research will be to identify and illuminate the nature of some of the cultural processes that serve to reorient or countervail innate biases in generating change in the contents of moral norms over time.

Note

1. There is in fact compelling evidence that humans are innately disposed to this kind of *prestige-biased imitation*, but I won't review the evidence here (see Boyd & Richerson, 1985; Henrich & Gil-White, 2001).

6.1   Using a Linguistic Analogy to Study Morality

Gilbert Harman

In his elegant discussion, Sripada distinguishes three possible innate bases for aspects of morality: (1) certain specific principles might be innate, (2) a less simple "Principles and Parameters Model" might apply, and (3) innate biases might have some influence over what morality a person acquires without determining the content of that morality.[1] He argues against (1) and (2) and in favor of (3). Without disputing his case for (3), I will try to say why I think that his arguments against (1) and (2) are inconclusive and that it remains possible that all three kinds of bases have a significant impact on human morality.

Simple Innateness

In Sripada's initial formulation, the Simple Innateness Model holds that *some* moral *norms* are innate, but it is quickly reformulated as the claim that there are *many* innate *specific rules* whose content can be formulated *in a non-normative vocabulary*. He then notes that there is "much underlying variability" (p. 323) in what might seem at first to be universal norms, such as incest prohibitions.

My Comments

First, denying the claim that there are *many* such norms is compatible with the claim that there are *some*.

Second, I do not agree that either claim should be interpreted as referring to norms whose content is formulated in a *non-normative* vocabulary. For one thing, if norms are about what is right, wrong, good, bad, just, and unjust, then to that extent their content has to be formulated at least partly in normative terms, because those terms are normative.

If the idea is that it must be possible to identify in non-normative terms what is supposed to be right, wrong, good, bad, just or unjust according to a given norm, that rules out norms referring to norms, such as the principle that it is wrong to try to persuade someone to do something wrong.

Failing to consider such norms begs a question against the Simple Innateness Model, since at least one of the proposals is that a principle of double effect might be a norm of the relevant sort. In one version of this norm, its content is that *it is worse to cause harm to someone (who has not consented to this) as (part of) your means to bringing about a greater good to others than to cause such harm as a side effect of doing something that will bring about a greater good.* This content includes several moral notions: at least, *worse, harm,* and *greater good.*

Consider the widely accepted claim that there are universal linguistic principles. Linguists do not suppose that the content of such principles can be formulated without appeal to concepts from linguistics. Why should a proponent of universal moral principles be committed to supposing that the content of the relevant moral principles can be formulated in non-normative terms?

Third, Sripada suggests that "more or less *all* putative examples of norm universals are actually associated with much underlying variability" (p. 324). However, it is plausible that at least some moral norms are default norms which hold other things being equal, where social context is relevant to what counts as other things being equal. And it is not easy to distinguish the claim that different moralities have different default norms from the claim that they share the same default norms that interact differently with their different social contexts.

Fourth, certain underlying norms may be implicit in people's moral judgments without themselves being explicitly known to the people whose moralities reflect those norms, just as there are underlying linguistic principles that are not known to speakers of a given language. For example, some theorists have suggested that our moral judgments reflect an implicit acceptance of the principle of double effect. Supposing there is widespread implicit acceptance of such a principle, it would seem that ordinary people have no explicit knowledge of it, and it would appear not to be transmitted by explicit instruction. If there is no other obvious way for the principle to be learned, the hypothesis suggests itself that the principle is somehow innate and should be universal.

Principles and Parameters

The Principles and Parameters Model allows for universal moral principles containing parameters that can vary from one morality or another. So, for example, there might be a universal principle containing a parameter G forbidding harm to members of G, where different moralities have different specifications of the relevant G.

Sripada distinguishes two possible arguments for this model. First, the model might help to explain the complex pattern of commonalities and differences in various moralities. Even though all moralities may have a norm forbidding harm, moralities differ concerning to whom such harm is forbidden.

Second, the model might help to explain why all normal human beings acquire a morality in the face of a certain "poverty" in their experience. Normal human beings are born with an innate disposition to acquire a morality containing certain norms and need only learn the local values of certain parameters of the norms.

Poverty of Experience?

Sripada rejects this second consideration on two grounds. He says that a given moral system is a "far simpler" (p. 328) learning target than a language and, furthermore, that the learning resources available in learning a first morality are "incomparably greater" (p. 328) than the resources available in learning a first language, because explicit moral instruction of relevant principles is available in the moral case in a way it is not available to someone learning a first language.

My Comments

First, the poverty of experience argument might also be used in connection with the first model Sripada discusses, the Simple Innateness Model.

Second, it is unclear how "simple" a given morality is, because we do not yet have even the beginnings of an account of the structure of morality in the way that we have at least the beginnings of an account of the structure of language.

Third, whether the child has sufficient learning resources for acquiring certain moral principles may depend on whether those principles are explicitly invoked by others or are merely implicit in the judgments of others. Comparable linguistic principles are highly arcane and are not explicitly known to speakers of the language. The same might be true of relevant moral principles, if, for example, those principles are like double effect in not being something that ordinary people are aware of and able to teach to children acquiring a morality.

It might be said that the principle of double effect cannot be a moral universal since there are utilitarian moralities in which the principle is not accepted. However, just as universal grammar is compatible with the existence of artificial languages like Esperanto, or pidgins that violate principles of universal grammar, universal moral principles are compatible with artificial moralities like utilitarianism. Universal grammar is about languages children can acquire in the normal way in which children acquire a first language. Similarly, universal morality would characterize the sorts of moralities that children can acquire in the normal way in which children acquire a first morality.

Children of parents who speak a pidgin not satisfying principles of universal grammar do not acquire that pidgin but instead acquire a creole that does satisfy such principles. It is an interesting question whether a child of utilitarian parents will initially acquire a morality containing nonutilitarian principles like double effect and will have to be taught otherwise.

To be sure, it is no objection to utilitarianism that it might prove to be artificial in this respect, just as it is no objection to contemporary science that we are born accepting implicit principles that conflict with those of contemporary science.

In any event, it is unlikely that children require explicit instruction in order to acquire a first morality, any more than they require explicit instruction in order to acquire language, although interaction with others may be necessary in both cases. It is quite possible that children who interact mainly with each other "invent" moral systems satisfying universal moral constraints in much the way that deaf children brought up by hearing parents invent sign languages satisfying universal grammatical constraints.

Explaining the Pattern of Variation in Harm Norms

The other argument for the Principles and Parameters Model that Sripada discusses says that such a model might account for the complex pattern of commonalities and differences found in various moralities. He objects that there is too much variation to account for in terms of simple parameter setting. So, for example, although it may seem that moralities may all contain a constraint against harming members of a certain group G with different moralities defining G differently, in fact "the pattern of variation in harm norms is much more complex, subtle, and variegated than" (p. 329) simply specifying a relevant group and indeed "the pattern of variation in moral norms across human groups is too extensive and complex to be accounted for in terms of a set of relatively rigid parameters" and its "best description" is in terms of "thematic clustering" (p. 330).

My Comments

First, a Principle and Parameters account of the pattern of variation of harm norms will allow additional parameters or factors over and above the specification of a single group G.

Second, the prohibition of harms to those in G is presumably a default principle rather than an absolute prohibition. So, some or even all of the variation that Sripada discusses might be due to other differences in the moralities.

More generally, it seems to me that an evaluation of this particular case would require a more explicit account of even one person's morality than we currently have.

By the way, Dworkin discusses a different sort of example to which a Principles and Parameters account might be relevant.[2] Dworkin suggests that people generally accept a principle concerning the sacred value of human life as represented in the life of a human fetus, but they differ as to when the life of the fetus has such sacred value and as to how much sacred value it possesses in comparison with various other values. Whether his account is best represented as a Principles and Parameters account or in some other way is unclear.

Moral Psychology: The Linguistic Analogy

I do not know whether it will turn out to be useful to try to develop an analogy between languages and moralities or between linguistics and moral psychology. But some considerations suggest it might be.

For one thing, human morality differs in complexity from anything to be found in nonhuman animals, just as human language differs in complexity from systems of communication found in nonhuman animals. It has not proved illuminating to try to understand human language as an extension of systems of animal communication. It may similarly not be illuminating to try to understand human morality as an extension of social aspects of animal life.

As mentioned above, moral reasoning seems sensitive to complex principles of which most people are not conscious. It is unclear how such principles might be learned; one possibility is that they are built in ahead of time, perhaps in a "moral faculty."

Some theorists may believe that morality is determined by the acceptance of certain moral conventions, just as some theorists suppose that language is a matter of linguistic conventions. However, there are difficulties with such ideas, suggesting that the unit of analysis in each case is the internal state of the agent, the agent's I-language and the agent's I-morality.

The main difficulty in pursuing an analogy between linguistics and moral psychology is to come up with relevant moral principles beyond the most superficial ones. What are the principles that help to determine the outcome when the superficial principles conflict? Such principles, if there are any, might comprise a "moral grammar."

Such principles might be found in philosophical discussions of hard cases. In their important 1990 survey of research on "Moral rules: Their Content and Acquisition," Darley and Shultz refer (in part) to philosophical discussions, including J. L. Austin's "Plea for Excuses" and Hart and Honore's *Causation and the Law*.[3] Thomas Aquinas formulated a version of double effect,[4] and there has been further discussion of that principle and alternatives in connection with so-called "trolley problems," based on examples in Philippa Foot's (1967) "Problem of Abortion and the Doctrine of Double Effect." Dworkin's "interpretations" of certain moral and legal disputes also provide possible source material.

Although there has been considerable emphasis lately on empirical studies of moral judgments of many subjects, with or without the use of functional magnetic resonance imaging, this may not be the best approach. Certainly, it was not the way generative grammar developed in its early days. Linguists tried for the most part to write explicit rules that would account for their own sense of what is grammatical and what is not in some small part of their own dialect or idiolect. It soon emerged that the explicit rules of the sort being developed required certain principles or constraints that no one had previously noticed and that it was hard to see how anyone might be taught them. This suggested that the relevant constraints might be part of a universal language faculty, not needing to be learned. If so, the constraints should be found in all languages. Or perhaps they should be default principles that would be acquired in the absence of clear counterexamples. It was further thinking along these lines that led to the Principles and Parameters conception in which much of grammar is assumed to be built into a child's initial state and language acquisition involves learning how certain switches are set, determining, for example, where the heads of phrases occur in relation to their complements.

It is an interesting question to what extent a similar research strategy might be relevant to the study of morality. The most straightforward way of pursuing such a strategy would be to consider whether it is possible explicitly to characterize (part of) one's own moral sense, one's moral idiolect (or I-morality), in terms of certain rules or principles. Such a study might begin by looking at traditional casuistry and other philosophical accounts of how to think about certain sorts of moral problems. Such accounts might appeal to principles that are not generally expressed and not available to children acquiring morality, so there might be an initial puzzle as to how such principles are acquired, one possibility being that they are innate or somehow based on innate principles. However, it is very diffcult to evaluate this possibility in advance of the construction of such partial moral grammars.

Notes

1. Sripada (this volume).

2. Dworkin (1993).

3. Darley and Shultz (1990); Austin (1956); Hart and Honore (1959).

4. Aquinas (1981, II–II, Qu. 64, article 7).

6.2 The Poverty of the Moral Stimulus

John Mikhail

How does the mind come to be furnished with the moral rules by which we judge our own and others' behavior? In "Nativism and Moral Psychology," Chandra Sripada takes a fresh look at this question—a classic one in the history of ideas—from the perspective of nativist explanations in the cognitive sciences. In particular, Sripada invites us to consider whether certain familiar arguments, such as Chomsky's argument from the poverty of the stimulus, can inform our understanding of how moral knowledge is acquired.

Sripada's essay is rich and stimulating; however, his criticism of the argument from the poverty of the *moral* stimulus (Mikhail, 2000, 2002a; see also Dwyer, 1999; Harman, 2000a; Mahlmann, 1999; Mikhail, Sorrentino, & Spelke, 1998; Nichols, 2005) rests on at least two assumptions which do not withstand scrutiny. The first is that the learning target in the theory of moral cognition consists of a series of simple imperatives, such as "Share your toys" or "Don't hit other children." The second assumption, which follows from the first, is that the environmental resources available to the child are sufficient to explain how these rules are acquired.

Sripada's first assumption is the crucial one, for it is the complexity, or lack thereof, of the output of an acquisition model which determines whether the stimulus is impoverished with respect to that output. However, is Sripada's assumption plausible? Is the learning target in this domain adequately described by a handful of simple imperatives? I wish to suggest that careful analysis of the moral judgments people do in fact make casts doubt on any such claim.

Consider the problem Sripada unduly neglects: the problem of descriptive adequacy. Clearly, this problem is logically prior to the issue of moral nativism, because without a clear understanding of what is learned, one cannot formulate, let alone take a position on, one or another learning theory. As Rawls (1971) emphasizes, the problem is a difficult one, because to solve it one must identify a class of considered moral judgments and a set of principles from which they can be derived. "Considered judgments" is a theoretical term which refers to "those judgments in which our moral capacities are most likely to be displayed without distortion" (Rawls, 1971, p. 47)—a formulation which necessarily involves nontrivial assumptions about the modular architecture of the mind (Mikhail, 2000). Moreover, "derive" is meant literally in this context: the relevant pattern of explanation is deductive-nomological explanation, or explanation by the deductive subsumption under covering laws (Hempel, 1966).[1]

Regrettably, few theorists attempt to describe moral competence in this fashion, and as a result, the field has yet to establish itself as a serious science. If one approaches the problem in this manner, however, it soon becomes apparent that human moral intuitions are complex and depend on concepts and principles that go far beyond the rudimentary norms Sripada identifies. Indeed, when one squarely confronts the problem of descriptive adequacy, one recognizes that the moral competence of both adults and children exhibits many characteristics of a well-developed legal code, including abstract theories of crime, tort, contract, and agency. Since the emergence of this knowledge cannot be explained by appeals to explicit instruction, or to any known processes of imitation, internalization, socialization, and the like, there are grounds for concluding it may be innate (Dwyer, 1999; Mikhail, 2000).

To illustrate, consider some of what is known about the intuitive jurisprudence of young children. Three- and four-year-old children use intent or purpose to distinguish two acts with same result (Baird, 2001). They also distinguish "genuine" moral violations (e.g., theft, battery) from violations of social conventions (e.g., wearing pajamas to school; Smetana, 1983; Turiel, 1983). Four- and five-year-olds use a proportionality principle to determine the appropriate level of punishment for principals and accessories (Finkel, Liss, & Moran, 1997). Five-year-olds display a nuanced understanding of negligence and restitution (Shultz, Wright, & Schleifer, 1986).

One man shoots and kills his victim on the mistaken belief that he is aiming at a tree stump. A second man shoots and kills his victim on the mistaken belief that killing is not wrong. Five- and six-year-olds distinguish cases like these in conformity with the distinction between mistake of law and mistake of fact, recognizing that false factual beliefs may exculpate, but false moral beliefs do not (Chandler, Sokol, & Wainryb, 2000). Five- and six-year-olds also calibrate the level of punishment they assign to harmful acts on the basis of mitigating factors, such as provocation, necessity, and public duty (Darley, Klosson, & Zanna, 1978). Six- and seven-year-olds exhibit a keen sense of procedural fairness, reacting negatively when punishment is inflicted without affording the parties notice and the right to be heard (Gold, Darley, Hilton, & Zanna, 1984). In more complex cases of necessity, such as the trolley problems, children as young as eight permit killing one to save five, but only if the chosen means is not wrong, the bad effects are not disproportionate to the good effects, and no better alternative is available; that is, only in accord with the principle of double effect (Mikhail, 2000, 2002a).

In these cases and others like them (Mikhail, in press), to explain the observable data we must attribute unconscious knowledge and complex mental operations to the child that go well beyond anything she has been taught. Indeed, as difficult to accept as it may seem, we must assume that children possess an elaborate system of natural jurisprudence and an ability to compute mental representations of human acts in legally cognizable terms. In the case of trolley problems, for example, children must represent and evaluate these novel fact patterns in terms of properties like ends, means, side effects, and prima facie wrongs such as battery, even where the stimulus contains no evidence of these properties (Mikhail, 2002a, 2005). These concepts and the principles which underlie them are as far removed from experience as the hierarchical tree structures and recursive rules of linguistic grammars. It is implausible to think they are acquired by means of explicit verbal instruction or examples in the child's environment (Harman, 2000a; Mikhail, 2000).

Thus far I have focused mainly on the question of ontogeny, and I have defended the existence of a "Universal Moral Grammar" analogous to the linguist's notion of "Universal Grammar" (UG), that is, an innate function or morality acquisition device that maps the child's early experience into the system of principles that constitutes the mature state of her moral competence (Mikhail, 2000, 2002a, 2002b; Mikhail, Sorrentino, & Spelke, 1998). A different set of issues emerges when we consider multiple individuals and the question of moral diversity (see figure 6.2.1.). In linguistics, the poverty of the stimulus implies that some knowledge is innate, but the variety of human languages provides an upper bound on this hypothesis; what is innate must be consistent with the observed diversity of human languages. Because every child will acquire any natural language merely upon being placed in a suitable environment, UG must be rich and specific enough to get her over the learning hump but flexible enough to enable her to acquire different grammars in different linguistic contexts (Baker, 2001; Chomsky, 1986).

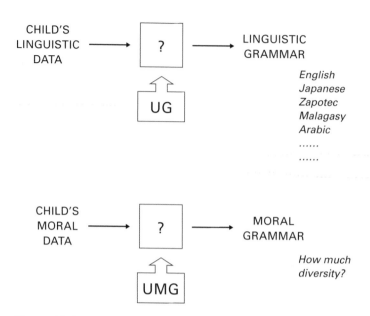

Figure 6.2.1

Acquisition models for language and morality (Mikhail, 2002a). UG, Universal Grammar; UMG, Universal Moral Grammar.

In the case of moral competence, it is unclear whether a similar tension exists between the goals of descriptive and explanatory adequacy. What we need are answers to two questions: (1) what are the properties of the rule systems or "moral grammars" people do in fact acquire, and (2) how diverse are they? Sripada suggests there may be "*too much variation in the* contents of moral norms across human groups for a Principles and Parameters Model to accommodate" (p. 329), but this claim seems untenable; even a superficial comparison of morality and language reveals that moral competence is *more* constrained than linguistic competence. The systems of linguistic intuition children in diverse cultures acquire are not only discrepant but, in the normal course of events, mutually unintelligible. A child who grows up speaking English is typically unable to locate the word boundaries of Japanese or Arabic—let alone to decide whether novel expressions in these languages are grammatical or ungrammatical. Nothing comparable exists in the moral domain, where the same event— say, a man shooting at someone he thinks is a tree stump—often triggers equivalent intuitions in persons of culturally divergent backgrounds (Mikhail, 2002b).

Furthermore, individuals frequently agree on how to analyze human actions into their main components: act, intent, motive, cause and effect, proximate and remote consequences, and other material (and immaterial) circumstances. If Sripada were correct, international human rights norms would be impossible, because the moral intuitions they embody, and their conceptual building blocks, would admit of too much variation. Yet the Universal Declaration of Human Rights, International Criminal Court, and other human rights instruments are real phenomena, which our theories must be consistent with, if not explain. Collectively, these agreements evince a degree of shared moral intuition which goes well beyond anything comparable in the case of language.

Sripada considers a moral rule to be innate if it "reliably emerges . . . in a wide range of environmental conditions," that is, "if the development of the rule does not depend on any *specific* pattern of cultural input" (p. 323). If there are innate norms in this sense, he observes, we should expect to find them in all human groups. Are there any moral universals of this sort? Sripada writes:

This question must be handled with some care since many candidate norm universals are problematic because they verge on being *analytic*—true in virtue of meaning alone. For example "Murder is wrong" and "Theft is wrong" don't count as legitimate universals since, roughly speaking, "murder" simply means killing someone else in a way which is not permissible, and "theft" simply means taking something from another in a way which is not permissible. For this reason, it is important, whenever possible, to frame the contents of norms in a non-normative vocabulary. While analytic principles like "Murder is wrong" . . . may be universals, the *specific* rules that regulate the *circumstances* under which killing . . . is permitted are not so nearly uniform across groups. (p. 323)

There are two fallacies in this passage, one concerning analyticity and the other diversity. First, Sripada is mistaken to assume that propositions like "Murder is wrong" are analytic, that is, true in virtue of meaning alone. In fact, they are synthetic: the predicate "wrongful" ("impermissible," etc.) is *not* built into the concept of murder—as Locke[2] and Hume,[3] among others, emphasized, and as any well-functioning criminal code will attest.[4] Second, the specific circumstances in which intentional killing is held to be justifiable or excusable are not as diverse as Sripada suggests. In fact, the justifications and excuses one finds in the literature on legal anthropology and comparative criminal law are remarkably similar and consist of a finite list of familiar patterns: mistake of fact, necessity, self-defense, defense of others, duress, insanity, provocation, and a handful of others. Moreover, their intersection is non-null: there are at least some acts of killing which all nations permit and at least some which all nations condemn (for extended discussion of these issues, see Mikhail, 2002b).

Finally, it is important to note that the fact that "murder is wrong" is a synthetic proposition and thus signifies something more than an empty tautology ("wrongful killing is wrong") is a property shared by other common moral and legal prohibitions. Theft, battery, rape, fraud—in each case, the *definiendum* is complex but can be explicated in a non-normative vocabulary. Each of these concepts consists of the concurrence of specific acts and mental states and of the absence of specified justifying or excusing conditions. Although not widely appreciated, the significance of this observation for the theory of moral cognition should not be underestimated. Among other things, it implies that moral judgment exhibits the poverty of the stimulus at the level of perceptual processes themselves. In each of these examples, there is "more information in [the] perceptual response than there is in the proximal stimulus that prompts the response; hence perceptual integration must somehow involve contribution of information by the perceiving organism" (Fodor, 1985, p. 2). We are thus led to inquire about the nature of this contribution. What are the precise character and scope of these prohibitions? What are the properties of the mental representations they presuppose? What is the chain of operations by which the mind converts the undifferentiated stimulus into a representation which has these properties, and to what extent is this process informationally encapsulated? Why, among logically possible alternatives, are these computations used and not others?

Questions like these do not admit of easy answers, but I believe they are the right place to start if we are to make progress in understanding the nature and origin of moral knowledge. Whether models incorporating parametric variation will ultimately play a role in this endeavor is yet to be determined. What seems clear, however, is that moral psychology must begin by isolating and describing as accurately as possible the system of moral competence that underlies the intuitive moral judgments which people do in fact make, and to do so within a mentalistic framework. Viewed from this perspective, and in light of the available evidence, Sripada's rejection of the argument from the poverty of the moral stimulus seems both premature and unfounded.

Notes

1. Rawls operationalizes the notion of a considered judgment by stipulating a set of necessary conditions moral judgments must satisfy to be a member of this class.

Among other features, considered judgments must be spontaneous, stable, impartial, intuitive, fully informed, and made with certitude. They also must not be made under duress, "when we are upset or frightened, or when we stand to gain one way or the other" (Rawls, 1971, p. 47; see also Rawls, 1950, 1951). One may question the specific criteria Rawls identifies, but his decision to limit attention to a subset of the available data in this manner should be uncontroversial. All successful sciences isolate some phenomena by ignoring others, and any serious attempt to describe the structure of a cognitive system must seek reasonable ways to reduce the complexity of that system and to identify its fundamental properties (Mikhail, 2002b). From this vantage point, Rawls's reliance on the considered judgments of an ideal moral observer appears analogous to Chomsky's use of a competence-performance distinction in the form of the grammaticality judgments of an "ideal speaker-listener" (Chomsky, 1965; see also Mikhail, 2000).

2. See Locke (1690/1991, book II, chapter 28, section 14) observing that when we consider "the complex Idea" signified by the word "Murther" and examine its particulars, we find it "to amount to a Collection of simple Ideas . . . [such as] Willing, Considering, Purposing before-hand, Malice, or wishing Ill to another; and also of Life, or Perception, and Self-Motion . . . [and] a Man, and of some Action, whereby we put an end to Perception and Motion in the Man . . . So that whencesoever we frame in our Minds the Ideas of Virtues or Vices, they consist only . . . of Collections of simple Ideas . . . [whose] Rectitude, or Obliquity, consists in the Agreement, or Disagreement, with those Patterns prescribed by some Law."

3. See Hume (1739/1978, book III, part I, section 1): "Take any action allow'd to be vicious: Wilful murder, for instance. Examine it in all its lights, and see if you can find that matter of fact, or real existence, which you call *vice*. In which-ever way you take it, you find only certain passions, motives, volitions and thoughts. There is no other matter of fact in the case. The vice entirely escapes you, as long as you consider the object. You can never find it, till you turn your reflexion into your own breast, and find a sentiment of disapprobation, which arises in you, towards this action."

4. The alternative is to have criminal trials risk faltering on whether this element has been successfully proven. Unsurprisingly, no sound criminal justice system works this way. Wrongfulness is never treated as an element of murder, but only (if at all) as a legal conclusion. The crucial issue, in other words, is one of logical priority. The law never requires an act of killing to be proven wrongful in order for it to be characterized as murder. Instead, it requires the act to be proven to be murder (or another form of criminal homicide) in order for it to be characterized as wrong (Mikhail, 2002b).

6.3 | Reply to Harman and Mikhail

Chandra Sekhar Sripada

I want to thank Gilbert Harman and John Mikhail for their thoughtful responses to my paper. In this response section, I will focus on one criticism that I view as particularly important and that forms the central thread of their critiques.

Both Harman and Mikhail take issue with my rejection of a poverty of stimulus argument in the domain of morality. I argued that one key disanalogy between language learning and moral norm learning is that in the case of moral norm learning, the learning target is far simpler than in the case of language. In particular, I argued that human grammars consist of hierarchical tree structures and recursive rules that are far removed from experience. Moral norms learning, in contrast, merely requires that the child acquire a readily understandable collection of fairly concrete rules, and I offered several examples—"Share your toys," "Don't hit other children," "Respect your elders," and "Don't eat pork."

Both Harman and Mikhail counter that I have oversimplified and thus mischaracterized the nature of the competence that is acquired by the child. They argue that the list of rather simple imperatives that I suggest misses the fact that children make subtle and sophisticated moral judgments that require complex mental operations. In their replies, they offer many examples of moral judgments that do indeed seem to embody sophisticated principles, concepts, and theories, suggesting that some kind of innate structure must be invoked to explain how young children acquire and master these judgments. I'll review some of Harman and Mikhail's examples in a moment, but before doing so, I want to raise the worry that my arguments and Harman and Mikhail's critiques are, at least in some respects, talking past each other.

In the first part of the chapter, in the section titled "Preliminary Clarifications," I drew a distinction between two kinds of nativist claims—*capacity nativism* versus *content nativism.* "Capacity nativism" refers to the question of whether, and to what extent, a number of norm-associated capacities are innate. As I wrote,

Consider the following moral norm: Don't kill any member of your own group. In order to understand this norm and utilize the norm in day-to-day interactions with others, it's plausible that a person will need to draw upon a large number of cognitive capacities. . . . For example, in order to recognize a particular behavior as an instance of killing, a person will need a "theory of action," that is, the capacity to parse agents' physical movements into sequences of actions with the appropriate assignment of causal relations between actions and their outcomes. A second cognitive capacity that plays a role in moral judgment is "theory of mind," that is, the capacity to attribute mental states such as beliefs and desires to other agents. Theory of mind might be used, for example, to determine whether an agent's actions are intended versus unintended, and these determinations in turn influence judgments about the agent's blameworthiness. (p. 321)

There are a number of other capacities that might be relevant to moral cognition besides the two listed above, including the capacity to distinguish living things from nonliving things and the capacity to exert self-control in the face of temptation. A key feature of these capacities is that while they play a role in facilitating moral judgment and moral decision making, they play a role in a host of other cognitive domains as well. For example, consider the following two scenarios: (1) a man uses a knife in order to cut a woman in order to steal her money, and (2) a child uses a knife in order to cut a lemon in order to make a glass of lemonade. Theory of mind and theory of action may play a role in understanding the intentions and actions of the agents in both of these scenarios, but the operation of these capacities is likely to be linked to moral judgment only in the former scenario and not in the latter. Thus, theory of mind, theory of action, and the other capacities listed above can be thought of as being much like the visual system in that while they may be utilized in the process of making moral judgments, they are by no means specific to the domain of moral cognition and may be utilized for a host of other functions as well.

I contrasted capacity nativism with what I called "content nativism." The content of a moral norm consists of the class of actions that the norm prohibits, permits, or requires. Anthropologists have documented a complex pattern of both commonalities and differences in the contents of moral norms across human groups in domains such as harm and violence, hierarchy, gender relations, sexual behavior, incest, and kinship and marriage, and I cited examples from many of these domains in my chapter. For example, I discussed at length the case of *harm norms*. While all societies appear to have moral norms that regulate physical violence, the content of harm norms differs across human groups in subtle and complex ways. Harm norms differ in terms of the class of individuals forbidden from *committing* harms, the class of individuals *protected* from being harmed, and the *contexts* under which these norms apply, as well as the *kinds of harm* and the *level of harm* that are permitted, and I documented this pattern of variation with anthropological evidence. The example of harm norms illustrates the central question addressed in the issue of content nativism: What kinds of innate structure best explain the complex pattern of commonalities and differences in the contents of moral norms that we observe across human groups?

I stated at the outset of my chapter that the focus of the chapter is content nativism and that I would have relatively little to say about capacity nativism. One reason for this focus is that there appears to be less disagreement about capacity nativism. As I highlighted in the opening passages of the chapter, many theorists on the contemporary scene have argued that capacities such as theory of action, theory of mind, and others are importantly innate. I and many others are quite persuaded by the arguments of these nativist theorists. Content nativism, however, is a much more controversial issue where opinions are not so uniform, thus helping justify my decision to make it the focus of the chapter.

In my view, Harman and Mikhail fail to heed the distinction between capacity nativism and content nativism, and as a result, many of their criticisms miss the mark. For example, Mikhail writes

> ... individuals frequently agree on how to analyze human actions into their main components: act, intent, motive, cause and effect, proximate and remote consequences, and other material (and immaterial) circumstances. If Sripada were correct, international human rights norms would be impossible, because the moral intuitions they embody, and their conceptual building blocks, would admit of too much variation. (p. 357)

Mikhail suggests that the capacity to parse actions into their main components, that is, the capacity for theory of action, is innate and universally shared among all humans. This fact helps explain why various kinds of moral norms, such as human rights norms, are intelligible across diverse cultures—the conceptual building blocks for these moral norms are shared in virtue of a shared capacity for theory of action. The problem with Mikhail's argument, however, is that the question of whether and to what extent theory of action is innate clearly falls under what I called the issue of "capacity nativism." Thus, even if we grant to Mikhail that theory of action is innate, which in fact I think we should, this innateness claim pertains to the issue of capacity nativism and has little direct bearing on the issue of content nativism.

Other examples cited by Mikhail fit this pattern as well:

One man shoots and kills his victim on the mistaken belief that he is aiming at a tree stump. A second man shoots and kills his victim on the mistaken belief that killing is not wrong. Five- and six-year-olds distinguish cases like these in conformity with the distinction between mistake of law and mistake of fact, recognizing that false factual beliefs may exculpate, but false moral beliefs do not (Chandler, Sokol, & Wainryb, 2000). (p. 354)

If Mikhail is right that young children make distinctions between otherwise equivalent cases based on the motivations, beliefs, and intentions of the agent, then this suggests that the capacity for theory of mind has a significant innate basis. However, here again, the nativist claim that is at issue is capacity nativism rather than content nativism.

Another example that both Harman and Mikhail pay special attention to is the doctrine of double effect. In one version of the doctrine, which Harman cites, "it is worse to cause harm to someone (who has not consented to this) as (part of) your means to bringing about a greater good to others than to cause such harm as a side effect of doing something that will bring about a greater good" (p. 346). The doctrine appears to underlie intuitions in cases such as trolley problems, and Mikhail cites evidence that children as young as eight make judgments in accordance with the doctrine.

Both Harman and Mikhail are impressed with the fact that the doctrine of double effect, as it is utilized and applied in cases such as trolley problems, contains many abstract moral concepts that are far removed from experience, thus making it difficult to understand how the doctrine could be taught. For example, Mikhail writes:

In the case of trolley problems, for example, children must represent and evaluate these novel fact patterns in terms of properties like ends, means, side effects, and prima facie wrongs such as battery, even where the stimulus contains no evidence of these properties (Mikhail, 2002a, 2005). These concepts and the principles which underlie them are as far removed from experience as the hierarchical tree structures and recursive rules of linguistic grammars. It is implausible to think they are acquired by means of explicit verbal instruction or examples in the child's environment (Harman, 2000a; Mikhail, 2000). (p. 355)

Two different innateness claims are made in the preceding passage. The first claim is that the doctrine of double effect contains many abstract concepts, and it is these constituent concepts that are innate. The second somewhat stronger innateness claim is that in addition to the constituent concepts, the *content* of the doctrine of double effect, that is, the actual proposition expressed by the doctrine, is innate as well. It is unclear whether Harman and Mikhail endorse both these claims or just the former, but I'll address them both.

With regard to the former claim, my response is that while it is true that the doctrine of double effect contains abstract concepts that are far removed from experience—concepts such as means, ends, intentional effects, side effects, and so forth—these concepts are best seen as being understood and cognized in terms of capacities such as theory of mind and theory of action. To the extent that young children master these concepts without much in the way of teaching, then this fact suggests that theory of mind and theory of action are importantly innate. Thus, here again, the example of sophisticated innate structure proposed by Harman and Mikhail pertains to the issue of capacity nativism, not content nativism.

But what about the latter claim that the actual content of the doctrine of double effect is innate? Here I am quite willing to concede this claim, which *is* a claim about content nativism, to Harman and Mikhail. However, we must be careful in understanding the significance of this concession because I feel it doesn't have the same kind of import that Harman and Mikhail assign to it. Here is why.

The chief aim of my chapter is to explore the question of what kind of innate structure explains the pattern of commonalities and differences in the contents of moral norms across human groups. In the end, I defended the Innate Biases Model, which proposes that relatively simple and often-times weak innate biases serve to favor the origination and transmission of certain moral norms across generations, thus explaining the distributional pattern of moral norms that we actually witness across human groups.

Of course, the Innate Biases Model is not intended to provide an exceptionless account of *all* the innate structure that shapes the content of *all* moral norms in *all* domains. Thus, even if it is conceded to Harman and Mikhail that the Innate Biases Model does not account for the case of the doctrine of double effect, this concession should not be seen as dispositive against the model. The fact remains that when we examine a number of moral domains centrally important to ethical and metaethical theory— harm and violence, hierarchy, social justice, gender relations, sexual behavior, incest, kinship and marriage, and many others—the Innate Biases Model stands out as providing the best general account of the distributional pattern of these norms across human groups.

7 | Is Morality Innate?

Jesse J. Prinz

[T]he Author of Nature has determin'd us to receive . . . a Moral Sense, to direct our Actions, and to give us still nobler Pleasures.
—Hutcheson (1725/1994, p. 75)

Thus declares Francis Hutcheson, expressing a view widespread during the Enlightenment and throughout the history of philosophy. According to this tradition, we are by nature moral, and our concern for good and evil is as natural to us as our capacity to feel pleasure and pain. The link between morality and human nature has been a common theme since ancient times, and, with the rise of modern empirical moral psychology, it remains equally popular today. Evolutionary ethicists, ethologists, developmental psychologists, social neuroscientists, and even some cultural anthropologists tend to agree that morality is part of the bioprogram (e.g., Cosmides & Tooby, 1992; de Waal, 1996; Haidt & Joseph, 2004; Hauser, 2006; Ruse, 1991; Sober & Wilson, 1998; Turiel, 2002). Recently, researchers have begun to look for moral modules in the brain, and they have been increasingly tempted to speculate about the moral acquisition device and innate faculty for norm acquisition akin to the celebrated language acquisition device promulgated by Chomsky (Dwyer, 1999; Mikhail, 2000; Hauser et al., in volume 2). All this talk of modules and mechanism may make some shudder, especially if they recall that eugenics emerged out of an effort to find the biological sources of evil. Yet the tendency to postulate an innate moral faculty is almost irresistible. For one thing, it makes us appear nobler as a species, and for another, it offers an explanation of the fact that people in every corner of the globe seem to have moral rules. Moral nativism is, in this respect, an optimistic doctrine—one that makes our great big world seem comfortingly smaller.

I want to combat this alluring idea. I do not deny that morality is ecumenical, but I think it is not innate—at least that the current state of evidence is unpersuasive. Morality, like all human capacities, depends on having particular biological predispositions, but none of these, I submit, deserves to be called a "moral faculty." Morality is a by-product—accidental or invented—of faculties that evolved for other purposes. As such, morality is considerably more variable than the nativism program might lead us to think, and also more versatile. It is exciting to see cognitive scientists taking such an interest in morality, but that trend carries the risk of reification. I want to argue for a messier story, but I hope that the story leads to a better understanding of how we come to care about the good. I think the nativist story oversells human decency and undersells human potential.

I will survey a lot of ground here, and, of necessity, all too quickly. With luck, a fast sweep of the landscape will suffice to sow seeds of doubt (see also Prinz, 2007, forthcoming; Nichols, 2005).

What Is Morality?

Much in our life is governed by norms: the direction we face in the elevator, the way we walk, what we wear, the volume we speak in, the way we greet people, and pretty much everything else that we do in our waking hours. Not all of these norms count as moral. My concern here is with moral norms. This is certainly not the place to fully defend an account of what distinguishes moral norms from other norms, but I will at least indicate where I stand. I think moral norms are sentimental norms: they are underwritten by various sentiments. In particular, moral norms are grounded in the moral emotions. This kind of approach has a number of supporters today (Gibbard, Blackburn, Nichols, Haidt, D'Arms, Jacobson), and, importantly, it was also the preferred view of the British moralists who did more than any other group of philosophers to promote the view that morality is innate.

The British moralists claimed that moral norms are based on approbation and disapprobation. An action is right if, under idealized conditions, we would feel approbation toward those who do it; and an action is wrong if, under idealized conditions, we would feel disapprobation. Idealized conditions include things like full knowledge and freedom from bias. The terms "approbation" and "disapprobation" are a bit antiquated, but I think they can be treated as umbrella terms for two classes of moral emotions: emotions of moral praise and emotions of moral blame. Emotions of praise include gratitude, esteem, and righteousness. Emotions of blame include other-directed-emotions, such as anger, contempt, disgust, resentment, and indignation, as well as self-directed emotions, such as guilt and shame.

To count as a moral norm, these emotions must behave in particular ways. First, a norm does not count as moral simply in virtue of eliciting *one* of the aforementioned emotions in isolation. At a minimum, moral rules involve both self-directed emotions and other-directed emotions. You might feel disgusted when you see a friend cut her finger open accidentally, but you would not feel ashamed or guilty about doing that yourself. Second, our emotions must be directed at third parties if they are to ground moral norms. Moral concern arises when we are not directly involved. Third, mature moral judgments are enforced by meta-emotions. If you do something wrong and don't feel guilty, I will be angry at you for your conduct and for your lack of remorse. I am inclined to think that meta-emotions are necessary for moralizing, but I won't rest anything on that claim here. However, I do want to suggest that these three conditions are jointly sufficient for having a moral attitude, and that the first condition is necessary. To have a moral attitude toward φ-ing, one must have a moral sentiment that disposes one to feel a self-directed emotion of blame for φ-ing, and an emotion of other-directed blame when some else φs.

I cannot adequately support the claim that moral norms are sentimental norms here, but I offer three brief lines of evidence.

First, psychologists have shown that moral judgments can be altered by eliciting emotions. For example, Wheatley and Haidt (2005) hypnotized subjects to feel a pang of disgust whenever they heard an arbitrary neutral word, such as "often." They gave these subjects stories describing various individuals and asked them to make moral assessments. Compared to a control group, the hypnotized subjects gave significantly more negative moral appraisals when the key word was in the story, and they even morally condemned individuals whom control subjects described in positive terms.

Second, emotional deficits result in moral blindness. Psychopaths suffer from a profound deficit in negative emotions, including moral emotions (Cleckley, Hare, Patrick, Blair, Kiehl). They also have a profound deficit in their understanding of moral rules. When they talk about morality, Cleckley (1941) says they simply "say the words, but they cannot understand." Blair (1995) has shown that psychopaths fail to draw a distinction between moral and conventional rules; he argues that they regard moral rules as if they were merely conventional. The prevailing interpretation of these data is that psychopaths cannot form moral judgments because they lack the emotions on which those judgments ordinarily depend.

Third, there seems to be a conceptual link between emotions and moral judgments. Someone who was fully convinced that an action would maximize happiness can still believe that that action isn't morally good. Someone who believes that an action would lead to a practical contradiction when universalized does not necessarily believe that the action is morally bad. Likewise, I submit, for every other nonsentimentalist analysis of moral judgments. (This is the kernel of truth in Moore's open question argument.) However, consider a person who feels rage at someone for performing an action and would feel guilty if she herself had performed that action. On my intuitions, such a person does thereby believe that the action is morally bad. She might revise her belief or question her belief, but one could correctly accuse her of moralizing. It is an open question whether the things we emotionally condemn are really wrong, but it is not an open question whether emotional condemnation constitutes a moral attitude.

I will presuppose the sentimentalist account of moral judgment throughout this discussion, but not every argument will depend on it. In looking for innate morality, I will be looking for evidence that we are innately disposed to make moral judgments, and I will assume that those are based on moral emotions. The hypothesis that morality is innate is not simply the hypothesis that we are innately disposed to behave in ways that are morally praiseworthy. Bees are altruistic (they die to defend their colonies), but we do not say they have a moral sense. Innate good behavior can be used as evidence for an innate moral sense, but, as we will see, the evidence is far from decisive.

What Is Innateness?

Defining innateness is itself a thorny philosophical problem. Some have argued that innateness is an incoherent concept. Others think that we can talk about genes innately coding for proteins, but not for phenotypes. I will assume that innateness is a defensible construct. Conceptually, the main idea is that a psychological phenotype P is innate if it is acquired by means of psychological mechanisms that are dedicated to P, as opposed to psychological mechanisms that evolved for some other purpose or for no purpose at all (cf. Cowie, 1999). This is only a rough characterization; I will identify cases of innateness using operational definitions.

Some innate traits are very rigid. They manifest themselves in a fixed way, and they are relatively impervious to change. A lot of insect behaviors are like this. They operate as if driven by simple, unchanging programs.

I will refer to such traits as "buggy." Humans may have some psychologically buggy traits. We feel fear when objects loom toward us, and we
experience red when presented with ripe strawberries.

Some innate traits have a range of environmentally sensitive manifestations, but the range is highly circumscribed. Consider the blue-headed
wrasse. These fish change genders under certain circumstances. When the
male leader of a harem dies, the largest female becomes male. There are two
settings (male and female), and environment selects between them. I will
call such traits "wrassey." If Chomsky is right, the human language faculty
contains wrassey rules, which he calls "parameters." For example, universal
grammar says that prepositions can either precede nouns or follow them,
and primary linguistic data then set the toggle on this switch.

Some innate traits allow much greater flexibility. Consider birdsongs.
Good mimics, like the starling, can imitate the songs of many other birds.
In this respect, their songs have an open-ended range. However, their
capacity to imitate is not a general-purpose learning system. It is evidently
evolved for the function of learning songs. The actual songs are not innate,
but they are the result of an innate song acquisition device. Some human
traits are "starlingy." Consider our capacity to abstract perceptual proto-
types from experience and use them for subsequent categorization—open-
ended but evolved for that purpose.

When we encounter traits that are buggy, wrassey, or starlingy, we can
say that they have an innate basis. In contrast there are traits that seem to
be by-products of other capacities. Skinner conditioned pigeons to play toy
pianos. Playing pianos is not an innate capacity in pigeons; instead it is
acquired using a general-purpose learning system (operant conditioning).
We too learn much using general-purpose learning systems, as when we
learn how to drive. In contrast, consider the lowly flea. Fleas do remarkable
things in flea circuses. For example, a group of fleas can play a game of
toss using a tiny ball. The trick is achieved by coating the ball in a chemical that the fleas instinctively dislike, and when one comes into contact
with the ball, it propels it away toward another flea, who then propels it
away, and so on. Fleas are not using general-purpose learning systems to
achieve this behavior; they are using systems evolved for the specific
purpose of avoiding noxious chemicals, but they are using those systems
to do something other than what they were designed for. Some human
capacities may be like flea toss. Projecting spitballs, for example, is learned
using some general-purpose mechanism, but it also capitalizes on our
capacity for spitting, which probably evolved for a specific function, not
for deployment in prankish games.

Pigeon piano and flea toss give two models for traits that are not innate: general-purpose learning and moonlighting mechanisms. We will see if morality can be understood on either model. If morality is innate, we should expect it to be buggy, wrassey, or starlingy. If morality were buggy, we might expect to find robust moral universals. If morality were wrassey, we might expect to see a fixed number of different variants on the same schematic moral rules. If morality were starlingy, we would expect that moral norm acquisition could not be explained by appeal to nonmoral learning mechanisms. If any of these nativist views were right, we might expect morality to be modular and developmentally predictable. We might also expect to see precursors of morality in other species. I will consider attempts to defend nativism in each of these ways, and I will return to bugs, fish, and birds in the concluding section.

Is Morality Innate?

Universal Rules

One might begin developing a case for moral nativism by identifying universal moral rules. If certain rules can be found in just about every culture, that could be explained by the supposition that those rules are innate. This strategy parallels arguments that have been used to support linguistic nativism. If aspects of grammar are found in all languages, then those aspects of grammar may be innate. There are two risks in arguing from universality to innateness. First, some universals (or near universals) are not innate. Most cultures have fire, weapons, religion, clothing, art, and marriage. Many also have taxes, vehicles, and schools. It is unlikely that any of these things are innate. Humans the world over face many of the same challenges, and they have the same cognitive resources. If these two are put together, the same solutions to challenges will often arise. Second, there are cases where universal traits are biologically based, but not domain specific. The sounds that are used in spoken languages are innate, insofar as our capacity to make those sounds and to perceive them categorically is biologically prepared. However, these capacities probably weren't evolved for language. Chinchillas and birds can categorically perceive human speech sounds, and rats can use acoustic information to distinguish between specific languages, such as Dutch and Japanese. To use universals to argue for innateness, a moral nativist should show (1) that there are moral universals, (2) that there are no plausible non-nativist explanations of these, and (3) that required innate machinery is specific to the domain of morality. Each of these points is difficult to establish. In this section, I will focus on a strong form of (1), according to which there are universal moral rules *with specific content*, as opposed to universal rule schema with variable content. For further discussion of this question, see Prinz (forthcoming).

What are some candidates for universal moral rules? One natural candidate is a general prohibition against harm, or at least against harming the innocent. Most people seem to have an aversive response to witnessing the suffering of others, and most people seem to avoid gratuitous acts of violence. This universal is believed by some to be innately based and to be a basic building block of human morality (Turiel, 2002; Blair, 1995).

Is there a universal prohibition against harm? The evidence is depressingly weak. Torture, war, spousal abuse, corporal punishment, belligerent games, painful initiations, and fighting are all extremely widespread. Tolerated harm is as common as its prohibition. There is also massive cultural variation in who can be harmed and when. Within our own geographic boundaries, subcultures disagree about whether capital punishment, spanking, and violent sports are permissible. Globally, every extreme can be found. In the Amazon, Yanamomo warriors engage in an endless cycle of raiding and revenge (Chagnon, 1992). Among the Ilongot of Luzon, a boy was not considered a man until he took the head of an innocent person in the next village; when he returned home, women would greet him with a chorus of cheers (Rosaldo, 1980). In the New Guinea highlands, there are many groups that engage in perpetual warfare; between twenty and thirty-five percent of recorded male deaths in these groups are due to homicide (the numbers for women are much lower; Wrangham, 2004). Throughout geography and history, cannibalism has been a common practice, most indulgently pursued by the Aztecs, who sometimes consumed tens of thousands in a single festival (Harris, 1986). Brutality is also commonplace in large-scale industrial societies. As a U.S. General recently said, "Actually, it's a lot of fun to fight. You know, it's a hell of a hoot. It's fun to shoot some people" (Schmitt, 2005).

Of course most cultures prohibit *some* harms, but there are non-nativist explanations for that. Such prohibitions are a precondition for social stability. Moreover, harming people often serves no end. We rarely have anything to gain from doing so. How would your life be improved if you could punch your neighbors regularly? Harming people only brings gains in special circumstances. Harming children who misbehave can keep them in line, harming criminals can serve as a deterrent, and harming enemies can allow us to obtain their goods. These, of course, are exactly the kinds of harms that have been tolerated by most cultures. Thus, our universal prohibition against harm amounts to the platitude "Harm when and only when the pros outweigh the cons." This is an empty mandate. It is just an instance of a general mandate to avoid gratuitous acts: "For any action A, do A when and only when pros outweigh the cons." There is no universal prohibition against harm, as such, just a prohibition against l'*acte gratuit*.

The triviality objection also counts against the tempting idea that we have a *pro tanto* reason to avoid harm. On this construal, the harm norm says, "Avoid harm unless there is an overriding reason to harm." This injunction is empty unless we can come up with a principled list of over-riding reasons. If cultures can "overrule" harm norms more or less arbi-trarily, then the *pro tanto* rule is equivalent to "Avoid harm except in those cases where it's okay not to avoid harm." One can see that this is empty by noting that one can replace the word "harm" with absolutely any verb and get a true rule. The anthropological record suggests that the range of overriding factors is open-ended. We can harm people for punishment, for beauty, for conquest, and for fun. There is little reason to think these are principled exceptions to a rule that weighs on us heavily under all other circumstances. I suspect that harm avoidance is not even a universal impulse, much less a universal moral imperative.

This cynical response to the universality claim does not do justice to the fact that we don't like to see others in distress. Doesn't vicarious distress show that we have an innate predisposition to oppose harm? Perhaps, but it's not a moral predisposition. Consider the communicative value of a conspecific's scream. The distress of others alerts us to danger. Seeing someone suffer is like seeing a snake or a bear. It's an indication that trouble is near. It's totally unsurprising, then, that we find it stressful.

In response, nativists might reply that vicarious distress promotes pro-social behavior. Blair (1995) argues that vicarious distress is part of a vio-lence inhibition mechanism. When fighting, an aggressor will withdraw when a sparing partner shows a sign of submission, including an expres-sion of distress. Here, vicarious distress directly curbs violence. Doesn't this show that vicarious distress is part of a hardwired moral capacity?

Probably not. Withdrawal of force is not a moral act. Submission triggers withdrawal because conspecific aggression probably evolved for domi-nance, not murder. Moreover, Blair's violence inhibition mechanism is highly speculative. His main evidence is that we experience vicarious dis-tress when looking at pictures of people in pain; this, I just argued, may just be a danger-avoidance response. Admittedly, we inhibit serious vio-lence when *play* fighting, but, by definition, play fighting is fighting between friendly parties. If you like the person you are roughhousing with, you are not going to draw blood or deliver a deathblow. No special violence inhibition mechanism is needed to explain that. This raises a further point. We are innately gregarious: we socialize, form attachments, and value company. Rather than presuming that we are innately disposed to avoid harm, we might say we are innately disposed to take pleasure in other people's company. Gregariousness is not, in and of itself, a moral disposition ("make friends" is not a moral injunction), but it may have implications for morality. We dislike it when our loved ones are harmed. Human friendship promotes caring, which, in turn, promotes the formation of rules that prohibit harm. Prohibitions against harm may be by-products of the general positive regard we have for each other.

I am not persuaded, therefore, that we have a violence inhibition mechanism or a biologically programmed prohibition against harm. This conclusion may sound deeply unflattering to our species, but that is not my point. As I just indicated, I think we may be biologically prone to care about each other, and I also think there are universal constraints on stable societies, which tend to promote the construction of rules against harm. More generally, it must be noted that other species (e.g., squirrels, birds, and deer) don't go around killing each other constantly, but we are not tempted to say that they have moral rules against harm. They don't need such rules, because they have no biological predispositions to aggression against conspecifics. Likewise, we may have no such predispositions, so the lack of a biologically based prohibition against violence does not mean that we are nasty and vicious. I would surmise that our default tendencies are to be pretty pleasant to each other. The difficulty is that humans, unlike squirrels, can recognize through rational reflection that violence can have positive payoffs. With that, there is considerable risk for nastiness, and that risk, not biology, drives the construction of harm norms. All this is armchair speculation, but it is enough to block any facile inference from pancultural harm norms to an innate moral rule. Harm prohibitions are not universal in form; they can be explained without innateness, through societal needs for stability; and the innate resources that contribute to harm prohibitions may not be moral in nature. In particular, harm avoidance may not be underwritten by moral sentiments.

I want to turn now to another pair of alleged moral universals: sharing and reciprocity. Human beings all over the world tend to share goods. Individuals don't hoard everything they obtain; they give it away to others. We tend to regard this as a morally commendable behavior, and failure to share is morally wrong. We also tend to reciprocate. If someone does us a good turn, we do something nice for them later. This is also moralized, and it is closely related to sharing. When we share, our acts of charity are often reciprocated, and we expect reciprocation when possible. We condemn free riders, who accept offerings from others but refuse to share.

Sharing and reciprocation are nearly universal, but they vary in significant ways across cultural boundaries. In some cultures, men eat meals before women and children, and they are not expected to share to the same degree. In most cultures, there are people who do more than their fair share and do not get adequately compensated. Among the Tasmanians, women apparently did the overwhelming majority of food collection, while men idled (Edgerton, 1992). In our own culture, the wealthy are expected to pay significant taxes, but they are certainly not expected to divide their profits. There are even apparently cultures where sharing is very rare. The Sirionó of Eastern Bolivia "constantly quarreled about food, accused one another of hoarding it, refused to share it with others, ate alone at night or in the forest and hid food from family members by, on the part of women, secreting it in their vaginas" (Edgerton, 1992, p. 13).

To assess cross-cultural differences in conceptions of fairness, a group of anthropologists recently conducted a series of studies in fifteen small-scale societies (Henrich, Boyd, Bowles, Camerer, Fehr, & Gintis, 2004). They asked members of these societies to play ultimatum games. The rules are simple. One player is given a certain amount of money and then told that she can keep some of it for herself and offer some to a second player (who is not related to the first player); if the second player does not accept the offer, neither player gets anything. The ultimatum game tests for ideals of fairness, because the player making the offer is motivated to make offers that the other player will accept. If the other player considers the initial offer unfair, she will reject it. When done in the West, players tend to offer 45% on average. I am offered $100, I will offer you $45, taking more than half but being generous. If I offered you considerably less, say $1, you would refuse to accept it out of spite, and I would lose my profit. When members of small-scale societies play the ultimatum game, everyone offers considerably more than 1%. Apparently, massively inequitable offers are rejected by most people everywhere, even when that 1% is a considerable sum. But there are still remarkable cultural differences. We tend to offer 45%. In some cultures, people offer more, and in some they offer less. Among the Machiguenga of Peru, the average sum offered was 26% and the most frequent offer was 15%, which is far below what most American subjects would consider fair. If I offered you $15 and took $85 for myself, you'd be sorely tempted to turn down the offer, and you would probably harbor a grudge. The Machiguenga have different standards, apparently. They may value sharing, but they clearly don't expect each other to share as much as we do in ultimatum games. Such findings suggest that there is not a fixed biological rule that drives us to share; the amount we share is variable.

Even so, the fact that people do share to some degree in most cultures suggests that there is a biological predisposition toward sharing—or so the nativist would argue. I am not fully convinced. Sharing also has non-nativist explanations. A person who has obtained a valued resource has strong incentives to share. Sharing helps avoid theft and it helps win friends. Sharing is a kind of insurance policy. If I give you something, you will be nice to me, and you may offer me something in the future. The nativist will be quick to respond that this reasoning presupposes reciprocity. I have no reason to think that you will share with me in the future unless people in general reciprocate acts of kindness. Mustn't reciprocity be innate? Perhaps not. There may be cultural explanations for why people reciprocate. Reciprocity promotes cooperation. If a culture has an economy that depends on cooperation, it will succeed only if reciprocity is promoted. This is true in the case of cultures that engage in heavy trade, cultures that have large-scale farms, and cultures that hunt very large game. Members of such cultures tend to offer equitable splits on the ultimatum game. The Machiguenga are foragers and horticulturalists. Their farms are small, family run, and temporary. The Machiguenga do not depend heavily on nonkin, and it is unsurprising, then, that they do not make equitable offers. Thus, there is reason to think reciprocity emerges to serve cultural subsistence practices, and the evidence from variation in ultimatum games supports that hypothesis.

Indeed, some evolutionary game theorists argue that nonkin *reciprocity* must be a cultural construction. Biologically, our behavior is driven by genes, and our genes promote only those behaviors that increase their chances of being replicated. If generosity were genetically determined, and our genes led some of us to be generous, then free riders with stingy genes would take advantage, and the generous genes would die out. If, however, generosity were driven by cultural inculcation, then all normal members of a cultural group would be equally likely to reciprocate, and the free-rider problem would be reduced. Genes alone can't make us self-sacrificing, but culture can. If this is right, then fairness and reciprocity are neither universal in form nor biologically based. I will return to this issue when I discuss animal behavior below.

Let me consider with one more example of a putatively universal moral norm: the incest taboo. Few of us feel especially inclined to have sexual relations with close kin. We are morally outraged when we hear about cases of incest, and just about every culture on record condemns incest in one form or another. There is even a genetic explanation for this universal. Inbreeding can lead to the spread of harmful recessive traits, so families that inbreed are likely to die out. Genes that promote exogamous behavior have a biological advantage. When combined with the apparent universality of incest prohibitions, we seem to have a pretty good case for moral nativism.

The evidence, however, is less secure on close examination. First of all, there is massive cultural variation in which relationships count as incestuous. In some cultures, incest is restricted to the immediate family; in others it includes cousins; in some, only blood relatives are off limits; in others sex with affinal kin is equally taboo. The case of cousins is especially illustrative. In the contemporary Judeo-Christian West, sex with a first cousin is considered revolting; sex with a second cousin is more permissible, but it still causes some people to snicker or look down their noses. The latter tendency may be a residue of the fact that the medieval Church prohibited marriage with cousins *up to seven degrees*. This was unprecedented. In the ancient world, cousin marriage was commonplace. For example, the Hebrew Bible tells us that Isaac was married to his cousin Rebecca, and Jacob was married to his two cousins, Rachel and Leah. In many contemporary cultures, cousin marriage is strongly encouraged. In one study, it was found that 57% of Pakistani couples were first cousins (Modell & Darr, 2002), and about the same rate of consanguineous marriages can be found in Saudi Arabia (El-Hamzi, Al-Swailem, Warsy, Al-Swailem, & Sulaimani, 1995). There are also cultures that tolerate sexual relations between closer relatives. The Hebrew Bible contains explicit prohibitions against immediate-family incest, but it also tells us that Abraham was married to his half-sister and that Lot's daughters seduced their father and bore his children. Greco-Roman citizens in Ptolemaic Egypt married their full siblings at very high rates, Thonga hippopotamus hunters used to have sex with their daughters, and the ancient Zoroastrians allegedly encouraged all forms of immediate-family incest (see Prinz, 2007, for review).

Hauser et al. (volume 2) have rightfully argued that we should exercise great caution in drawing conclusions from exotic cases. In their defense of moral nativism, they warn that rare exceptions cannot be used to refute the hypothesis that a particular rule is innate. I fully agree, and I don't want to place too much weight on Zoroastrian sexual proclivities. So let me divide my critique of nativism about incest taboos into two parts. The first concerns sex outside the immediate family, such as the prohibition against first-cousin incest. Violations of this rule are not exotic or unusual. Twenty percent of the world's couples are estimated to be married cousins (Bittles, 1990). There is no reason to think there is an innate taboo against sex outside of the immediate family. Now consider immediate-family incest. Here, statistics tell in favor of a universal norm. Most cultures avoid sex with immediate kin. The exceptions show that these norms can be over-ridden by culture, not that the norms are learned. However, the case against moral nativism about immediate-family incest can be fought on other grounds. If procreating with immediate family members can cause a genetic depression, then there is reason to think we would evolve a tendency to avoid incest. This concession may look like it supports the case for moral nativism, but I think it actually does the opposite. Incest avoidance may be phylogenetically ancient. It may long predate the emergence of our species and the emergence of morality. If so, we may have an innate tendency to avoid incest, but not an innate moral rule against incest. If we naturally avoid something, we don't need a moral rule against it. If we are disgusted by rotting food, we don't need to have a moral rule to prevent us from eating it; we do not feel ashamed when we accidentally eat bread with mold on it, and we would not condemn another person for doing so. To turn incest avoidance into an incest taboo, a culture must punish those who engage in incest and condition perpetrators to feel ashamed. The transition from incest avoidance to incest taboos takes cultural effort. If this story is right, then there should be a large number of societies with no explicit moral prohibition against immediate-family incest. This is exactly what the anthropological record seems to show. Thornhill (1991) found that only forty-four percent of the world's cultures, in a large diverse sample, have immediate-family incest taboos. This casts doubt on the conjecture that there is an innate *moral* rule.

It would be hasty to draw any extravagant antinativist conclusions from the discussion so far. I have not demonstrated that there are no innate universal moral rules. Instead, I have argued that some of the most obvious candidates for innate universal moral rules are either not innate, not universal, or not essentially moral. I think the considerations raised here suggest that it will be difficult to make a strong case for nativism by identifying universal moral rules. Moral nativists must rely on other evidence.

Universal Domains

I have been arguing that it is difficult to find examples of moral universals. The rules by which people abide vary across cultural boundaries. In response, the nativist might complain that I was looking for universals at too fine a grain. Perhaps specific moral precepts are variable, but broad moral categories are universal. By analogy, even if one did not find linguistic universals at the level of words, one might expect to find universals at the level of syntactic categories. If we ascend to a more abstract level of moral competence, we might find that there are moral universals after all. This is an increasingly popular view among moral nativists. It is a version of what Hauser calls "temperate nativism," and defenders include Fiske (1991), Haidt and Joseph (2004), and Shweder, Much, Mahapatra, and Park (1997). One way to think about this approach is that we have several innate moral domains, which determine the kinds of situations that are amenable to moralization. The moral domains may even contain rule schemas, whose variables get filled in by culture. For example, there might be an innate rule of the form (x) [Don't harm x, unless P]. Culture determines the scope of the quantifier (family, neighbors, all people, cows, fetuses, etc.) and the exceptions (initiation rights, revenge, deterrence, sports, etc.).

Rather than surveying all of the innate domain theories, I will focus on one recent example, which attempts to synthesize many of the others. Haidt and Joseph (2004) find that certain moral domains are mentioned more frequently than others when authors try to classify moral rules across cultures (and even across species). There are four domains that enjoy significant consensus. The first is the domain of suffering; all societies seem to have rules pertaining to the well-being of others. The schematic harm prohibition might fall into this domain, along with rules that compel us to help the needy. The second domain concerns hierarchy; here we find rules of dominance and submission, which determine the distribution of power in a society. Next comes reciprocity; this is the domain containing rules of exchange and fairness, like those discussed in the previous section. Finally, there is a domain of purity; these rules are especially prevalent in nonsecular societies, but purity rules also include some dietary taboos and sexual mores. Haidt and Joseph believe that each domain corresponds to an innate mental module, and each kind of rule is regulated by a different family of emotions. Suffering elicits sympathy and compassion; hierarchies are enforced by resentment and respect; reciprocity violations provoke anger and guilt; and purity violations instill disgust. These domains are universal, but culture can determine the specific content of rules in each.

_−D. S_

paper

What counts as an impermissible harm in one culture may be morally compulsory in another. Thus, the moral domains do not furnish us with a universal morality but rather with a universal menu of categories for moral construal. If we morally condemn some action, it is in virtue of construing it as a violation in one of these domains.

The innate moral domains theory is a significant departure from the view that we have innate moral rules. It allows for considerable moral variation. In this regard, it is a significant departure from the Enlightenment moral sense theories, according to which human beings are naturally able to perceive objective moral truths. Nevertheless, it is a form of moral nativism, and it is my task here to assess its plausibility. As with the innate rule theories, there are three questions to ask: (1) Are moral domains universal? (2) Can they be learned? And (3) are they essentially moral?

Let's begin with the question of universality. As Haidt and Joseph admit, the four moral domains are emphasized to a greater or lesser degree in different cultures. Our culture is especially preoccupied with suffering and reciprocity, whereas hierarchy and purity are more important in some parts of India. This affects how we construe moral transgression. Here is a simplified example. If someone is raped in the West, people sympathize with the victim and feel rage at the rapist. In India, there will be rage at the rapist, but there is also a tendency to think the victim has become adulterated, and that shame has been brought on her household, potentially lowering their social status. This does not refute the hypothesis that the four domains are universal, but it does suggest that they do not play the same roles across cultures. And this raises the possibility that some of the domains are not construed as _morally_ significant in every culture. In our culture, we tend to resist moralizing impurities. In other research, Haidt, Koller, and Dias (1993) show that American college students are disgusted when they hear about a man who masturbates into a chicken carcass, but they do not consider him immoral. In low-socioeconomic-status populations in Brazil, the same individual is morally condemned. Perhaps the purity domain has a moral status in those populations and not ours. On the sentimentalist theory that I am endorsing, this might be explained by saying that low-SES Brazilians have a moral sentiment toward masturbating with a chicken carcass: they find it both disgusting and shameful, and they would be inclined to blame or punish offenders. Bourgeois Americans simply find such behavior yucky. To take another case, consider the Gahuku Gama headhunters in Papua New Guinea. According to Read (1955), they do not consider it immoral to cause harm, unless that harm comes to a member of their social group. On one interpretation, they do not moralize suffering, as such, but only hierarchy and reciprocity; the Gahuku Gama think they have responsibilities to the people who depend on them and on whom they depend. The upshot is that if the four domains are universal, it does not follow that they are universally moral.

Now consider the question of learning. Are the four domains necessarily innate, or is there an alternative explanation of how they emerge? One alternative is suggested by the fact that the domains are associated with different emotions. Let's grant that the emotions mentioned by Haidt and Joseph are innate. We are innately endowed with sympathy, respect, anger, disgust, and so on. These innate emotions may be sufficient to explain how moral domains emerge over development. To illustrate, consider purity. Suppose people are naturally disgusted by a variety of things, such as pollution, rotting meat, bodily fluids, disfigurement, and certain animals. This hodgepodge is unified by the fact that they all cause disgust. The disgust response has natural elicitors, but it can be extended to other things if those things can be construed as similar to the natural elicitors. For example, we can, through construal, view spitting, oral sex, eating insects, defecation, and body modification as disgusting. Now suppose, for what-ever reason, that a particular society chooses to condemn some of these behaviors. That society will draw attention to the similarity between these behaviors and natural disgust elicitors, and it will inculcate feeling of both self- and other-directed blame for those who engage in them under certain circumstances. Once a society uses disgust to moralize certain behaviors, its members can be said to have a purity domain in their moral psychology. However, if this story is right, then the domain is a learned extension of a nonmoral emotion.

These remarks on universality and learning have both ended up in the same place. The four domains that Haidt and Joseph postulate may not be essentially moral. They may be outgrowths of universal emotions that evolved for something other than moral judgment. Each of the emotions they mention has nonmoral applications. We feel sympathy for the sick, but we do not make moral judgments about them; we feel respect for great musicians, but we do not feel morally obligated to submit to their author-ity; we feel angry at those who frustrate our goals, but we do not necessar-ily think they are morally blameworthy for doing so; and we feel disgusted by rotting food, but we would not denounce the person who finds pleasure in it. The four moral domains may be by-products of basic emotions. Negative emotions play a moral role only when they are transformed into full-blown moral sentiments. In particular, negative emotions become moral in significance only when we become disposed to feel corresponding emotions of blame toward self and others. Anger and disgust toward others take on a moral cast only when we would feel blameworthy ourselves for behaving in a similar way. In sum, I think Haidt and Joseph's four domains may be universal, but I am not convinced that they are unlearned or essentially moral. Research has not shown that all people have full-fledged moral sentiments toward behaviors in each of the four domains.

In response, the moral nativist might opt for a different strategy. Rather than looking for a family of different universal domains, nativists might look for a more fundamental divide; they might postulate a single domain of moral rules and distinguish these from nonmoral rules. On universal rule theories, some specific moral rules are universal; on universal domain theories, some general categories of moral rules are universal; on the strategy I want to consider now, the only thing that is universal is the divide between moral and nonmoral rules—it is universal that we have a morality, though the content of morality can vary in open-ended ways.

Here, I am tempted to respond by pointing out that, at this level of abstraction, the postulation of moral universals does little explanatory work. Compare Geertz: "That everywhere people mate and produce children, have some sense of mine and thine, and protect themselves in one fashion or another from rain and sun are neither false nor, from some points of view, unimportant; but they are hardly very much help in drawing a portrait of man" (1973, p. 40). If the only moral universal is the existence of morality itself, then an adequate account of human moral psychology will have to focus on culturally learned rules to gain any purchase on how we actually conduct our lives.

I do not want to let things rest with this dismissal. The claim that we have a universal disposition to create moral rules is not entirely empty. The nativist might even compare this disposition to birdsongs. Starlings may not have any specific song in common, but their tendency to sing and to acquire songs by imitation is the consequence of an innate, domain-specific faculty. Surely the fact that all cultures have moral rules is an indication of an innate moral faculty, albeit a very flexible one. Mustn't the antinativist concede this much? I think not.

To make this case, I want to consider a popular version of the proposal that morality is a human universal. Turiel (2002), Song, Smetana, and Kim (1987), Smetana (1995), and Nucci (2001) argue that, in all cultures, people distinguish between moral rules and rules that are merely conventional. For example, it's morally wrong to kick random strangers, but it is only conventionally wrong to wear pajamas to the office. Proponents of this view think that content of moral rules might be innately fixed; in particular, they think they might all be rules involving harms. In this sense, they might be regarded as defending a version of the innate domain theory according to which there is a single innate domain based on sympathy. I will not be concerned with that feature of the approach here. My main interest is the question of whether all cultures distinguish moral and conventional rules, whatever the content of those rules may be.

Defenders of the universal moral/conventional distinction test their hypothesis by operationalizing the difference between moral and conventional rules. Moral rules are said to have three defining characteristics: they are considered more serious than conventional rules, they are justified by appeal to their harmful effects on a victim, and they are regarded as objectively true, independent of what anyone happens to believe about them. Kicking a stranger is a serious offense, it is wrong because it causes pain, and it would be wrong even if the local authorities announced that it was acceptable to kick strangers. Wearing pajamas to the office is not very serious, it causes no pain, and it would be acceptable if the authorities permitted it (imagine an office slumber party or a new fashion trend).

Smetana (1995) and Turiel (1998) survey evidence that this basic division is drawn across cultures, economic classes, religions, and age groups. It seems to be universal. They think that learning may play an important role in fostering sensitivity to this distinction, but the distinction itself is unlearned. Learning awakens innate understanding of the moral domain. I will return to the issue of learning below. For now, I also want to grant that people can universally distinguish rules using the three criteria: some transgressions are serious, intrinsically harmful, and authority independent. What I want to question is whether these criteria really carve out a domain that deserves to be called "morality." I want to argue that the criteria are neither necessary nor sufficient for accommodating rules that are pretheoretically regarded as moral. My discussion is heavily influenced by Kelly and Stich (forthcoming), who offer a trenchant critique.

First, consider seriousness. Some violations of pretheoretically moral rules are serious, but others are not. It is morally wrong to eat the last cookie in the house without offering to share, but not extremely wrong. Conversely, it is seriously wrong to go to work naked, even though wearing clothing is just a societal convention. Next consider intrinsic harm. One might justify one's distaste for scarification by pointing out that it is intrinsically harmful, but this distaste reflects a personal preference, not a moral denunciation; many of us would say scarification is morally acceptable but intrinsically harmful. Conversely, some people regard certain actions as morally unacceptable, but not intrinsically harmful. For example, Haidt et al. (1993) found that some people regard it as morally wrong to wash a toilet with the national flag. Finally, consider authority independence. In many cultures people morally condemn behavior that is regarded as authority dependent. Jews, for example, sometimes say that certain dietary laws (e.g., combining dairy and meat) hold in virtue of divine command, and these laws would not hold if God had commanded different, and they do not hold for non-Jews. Smetana, Turiel, and Nucci can accommodate this case only by saying that Jews imagine God is harmed by diet violations or by saying that Jews actually regard such rules as merely conventional. Both replies are flagrantly ad hoc. Conversely, there are many rules that are authority independent but not necessarily moral: we should cultivate our talents, we should avoid eating rotten meat, and we should take advice from those who are wiser than us. There are even cases of actions that are serious, intrinsically harmful, authority independent, and, nevertheless, not immoral. Gratuitously sawing off one's own foot is an example.

In sum, the operational criteria used by Turiel, Nucci, and Smetana do not coincide perfectly with the pretheoretical understanding of the moral domain. If people are universally sensitive to these criteria, it does not follow that they universally comprehend the moral/conventional distinction. Indeed, there may be cultures where moral and conventional rules are inextricably bound. For many traditional societies, contingent social practices, including rules of diet and ornament, are construed morally. People who violate these rules are chastised and made to feel guilt or shame. The distinction is often blurry at best.

Indeed, I suspect that moral and conventional are two orthogonal dimensions. Consider a rule like "Don't harm a member of your in-group." Stated abstractly, this rule may not have any identifiable conventional component, but things change as soon as we begin to make the rule specific enough to apply in practice. We can harm in-group members in initiation rights, for example, or in sporting events. Cultural conventions determine the scope of harm prohibitions. Thus, we cannot fully specify such norms without appeal to some contingent features of culture. Consequently, we will have harm norms that are authority contingent: It is morally wrong to scar a teenager's face with a stone tool in this culture but morally acceptable in cultures where the practice of scarification is embraced. Correlatively, rules that seem to be patently conventional have a moral dimension. It's conventionally wrong to wear shoes inside in Japan, but failure to comply with this rule is a form of disrespect, and the precept that we should respect others is moral. These examples suggest that rules of conduct generally have both moral and conventional components.

The very same act can count as a moral violation or as a conventional violation depending on how it is described.

This last point is not intended as a rejection of the moral/conventional distinction. I think the distinction is real, but it is not a distinction between kinds of rules, but rather a distinction between components of rules. However, how are we to distinguish those components? I think the moral dimensions of rules ("Don't harm!" "Show respect!") are themselves culturally constructed. Thus, the distinction between moral dimensions of rules and conventional dimensions cannot be a distinction between absolute dimensions and culturally relative dimensions. Instead, I think the difference is psychological. There are dimensions of rules that we *regard* as moral, and dimensions of rules that we *regard* as merely conventional. In keeping with the account of moral judgment that I offered earlier, I would say that the moral dimensions of rules are the dimensions that are psychologically grounded in moral sentiments. On my criteria, any dimension of a rule enforced by emotions of self-blame and other blame and directed at third parties qualifies as a moral rule. When we say that a specific requirement is merely "conventional," we express our belief that we would not blame (or at least we would try not to blame) someone who failed to conform to that rule in another culture. We do not blame Westerners for wearing shoes at home when they are in the West. When we say that it is "*morally* wrong" to disrespect others, we express our belief that we would blame someone for disrespecting others. Of course, the disposition to blame people for behaving in some way may itself be a culturally inculcated value.

I have been arguing that the moral/conventional distinction is more complicated than it initially appears, but I have not rejected that distinction completely. I have admitted that certain aspects of our rules are based on emotional patterns of blame, and others are not grounded in emotion. This gives the nativist a foothold. I have admitted that there is a way to distinguish the moral and the conventional, and the nativist is now in a position to propose that the distinction that I have just been presenting is universal. Nativists can say that all cultures have rules that are grounded in moral sentiments. I certainly don't know of any exceptions to this claim, but I am unwilling to infer that this is evidence for nativism.

In responding to Haidt and Joseph, I suggested that moral rules may emerge as by-products of nonmoral emotions. If all cultures have rules grounded in moral sentiments, it does not follow that we have an innate moral domain. In all cultures, people have realized that behavior can be shaped by conditioning emotional responses. Parents penalize their children the world over to get them to behave in desirable ways. Some penalties have negative emotional consequences, as they thereby serve to foster associations between behavior and negative emotions. This may be an important first step in the emergence of moral rules. Other steps will be required as well, and I will consider them in the concluding section of this paper. The present point is that the universality of emotionally grounded rules should not be altogether surprising given the fact that we shape behavior through penalizing the young. Neither the tendency to penalize nor the resultant emotionally grounded rules qualify as evidence for an innate moral code. However, education through penalization could help to explain why emotionally grounded rules (the building blocks of morality) are found in all cultures.

Modularity

Thus far I have expressed skepticism about moral universals. If there are substantive universal moral rules or moral domains, they have yet to be identified. Moral nativists will have to look for other forms of evidence. One option is to look for moral modules in the brain. Innate faculties are often presumed to be both functionally and anatomically modular. To be functionally modular is, roughly, to process information specific to a particular domain. Modules are also sometimes said to be informationally encapsulated: they do not have access to information in other modules (Fodor, 1983; see Prinz, 2006b, for a critique of Fodorian modules). To be anatomically modular is to be located within proprietary circuits of the brain. The language faculty is often presumed to be modular in both of these senses. We process language using language-specific rules and representations, and those rules and representations are implemented in specific regions of the brain which are vulnerable to selective deficits. Functional modularity provides some support for nativist claims, because capacities acquired using general cognitive resources often make use of rules and representations that are available to other domains. Anatomical modularity provides support for nativity claims because some of the best candidates for innate modules (e.g., the sensory systems and, perhaps, language) are anatomically localizable. If moral capacities could be shown to be functionally and anatomically modular, that would help the case for moral nativism.

To explore this strategy, I will begin with some work by Cosmides and Tooby (1992). Cosmides and Tooby do not try to prove that there is a single coherent morality module. Rather, they argue that one specific aspect of moral reasoning is modular. (Presumably they think that future research will reveal that other aspects of moral reasoning are modular as well.) In particular, they say we have a module dedicated to reasoning about social exchanges, and this module contains inference rules that allow us to catch cheaters: individuals who receive benefits from others without paying the appropriate costs. To argue for functional modularity, they present subjects with a class of conditional reasoning problems called the Wason selection task. When presented with conditionals outside the moral domain, subjects perform very poorly on this task. For example, subjects might be told that, according to a women's magazine, "If a woman eats salad, then she drinks diet soda." They are then asked about which women they would need to check to confirm whether this conditional is true. Subjects realize that they need to check women who eat salads, but they often don't realize that they must also check women who don't drink diet soda. In contrast, subjects perform extremely well when they are presented with conditionals that involve cheater detection. For example, some subjects are told they need to check for violators of the rule "If you watch TV, your room has to be clean." Subjects immediately recognize that they must check people with dirty rooms and make sure that they are not watching TV. Cosmides and Tooby (1992) argue that, if people perform well on the cheater-detection task and poorly on a structurally analogous reasoning task, then cheater-detection probably recruits a specialized modular reasoning system. If there is a cheater-detection module, then that provides prima facie evidence for moral nativism.

As several critics have pointed out, there is a flaw in the argument for a cheater-detection module. To show that proprietary rules are being used for cheater detection, Cosmides and Tooby must make sure that the control task is structurally analogous. The salad/soda case must be exactly like the TV/room case, except that one involves the moral domain and the other does not. However, these cases are extremely different. In the salad/soda example, subjects are asked to determine whether a conditional is true, and in the TV/room case, they are asked to assume that the conditional is true and find violators. Put differently, one task concerns a strict regularity, and the other concerns a rule. Regularities and rules are fundamentally different. If there are violators of an alleged strict regularity, the regularity must be false; if there are violators of a rule, the rule can be true. Moreover, rule violations elicit emotions, whereas regularity violations usually do not, and we are motivated to find violators of rules, because there are negative consequences if we do not. Thus, reasoning about rules and regularities should, on any account, recruit different resources, and we should be unsurprised to find that people are better at one than the other. To show that there is a module dedicated to the moral task of detecting cheaters, Cosmides and Tooby cannot pit a regularity against a rule. They should pit nonmoral rules against moral rules. There are many rules outside the moral domain. For example, there are prudential rules, such as "If you keep your guns in the house, then unload them." Like the moral rule, this one remains true even if people don't conform to it. If subjects performed badly on prudential rules, but well on moral rules, that would be evidence for a moral module. However, this is not what Cosmides and Tooby have found. Subjects perform well on both moral and prudential conditionals. This suggests that we have a general-purpose capacity for reasoning about rules, rather than a module restricted to the moral task of cheater detection.

In response, Cosmides and Tooby proliferate modules. Rather than taking the striking similarities in moral and prudential reasoning as evidence for shared cognitive resources, they argue that there are two modules at work: one for prudential rules and one for cheater detection. To support their case, they look for dissociations in performance on these two tasks. In healthy subjects, no dissociations have been found, but Stone, Cosmides, Tooby, Kroll, and Knight (2002) have identified an individual with a brain injury who can no longer perform well on cheater-detection conditionals, even though he continues to perform well on prudential conditionals. The fact that one capacity can be impaired without impairing the other suggests that cheater detection is both functionally modular and anatomically modular—or so Stone et al. argue. However, this conclusion does not follow. The patient in question does not have a selective deficit in cheater detection nor in moral reasoning. Instead, he has a large lesion compromising both his orbitofrontal cortex and his anterior temporal cortex (including the amygdala) in both hemispheres. The result is a range of deficits in social cognition. Stone et al. do not present a full neuropsychological profile, but they mention impairments in faux pas recognition and in comprehension of psychological vocabulary. Orbitofrontal regions are also implicated in the elicitation of social emotions and in the assignment of emotional significance to social events. Given the size and location of the lesion, it is reasonable to presume that that the patient in this study has a range of general deficits in conceptualizing the social domain. These deficits are not restricted to cheater detection or moral cognition. To respond successfully on a cheater-detection task, one may have to be able to respond emotionally to social stimuli. If this patient is unable to do that, then it is unsurprising that he performs poorly on moral conditionals. The problem is not that he has a broken moral module but that he can't think well about the social domain.

The patient's general social cognition deficit could disrupt performance on the Wason task in two ways: first, he may not be able to recognize that the cheater-detection conditionals express rules, because that requires thinking about social obligations; second, even if he does comprehend that a rule is being expressed in these cases, he may not be able to elicit emotional concern about violations of that rule. In either case, the patient's abnormal conceptualization of the social domain may prevent him from inputting the cheater-detection conditionals into his general-purpose system for reasoning about rules. In other words, the patient does not provide evidence that cheater detection involves any moral modules. His behavior can be explained by postulating general systems for thinking about the social domain and general systems for thinking about rules. I conclude that Stone et al. have not adequately supported the modularity hypothesis, and, thus, their data cannot be used to support moral nativism.

Before leaving this topic, let me consider two more lines of research that might be taken as evidence for the modularity of morality. First, consider psychopaths. Psychopaths have IQ scores within the normal range, and they perform relatively well on most standard aptitude tests, but they are profoundly impaired in moral competence. As noted above, psychopaths do not distinguish between moral and conventional rules (Blair, 1995). Blair concludes that psychopaths have a selective deficit in moral competence, and he associates this deficit with abnormalities in their central nervous systems. In particular, some psychopaths have reduced cell volumes in parts of frontal cortex and the amygdala. This suggests that there is a moral module in the brain.

My response to this argument is already implicit in my discussion of psychopaths earlier in this paper. Psychopaths do not have a selective deficit. They have profound deficiencies in *all negative emotions.* This is a diagnostic symptom of psychopathy, which is easy to observe, and it has been confirmed in numerous laboratory tests. Psychopaths are less amenable than control subjects to normal fear conditioning (Birbaumer, Veit, Lotze, Erb, Hermann, Grodd, & Flor, 2005), and they have diminished startle potentiation (Patrick, 1994), little depression (Lovelace & Gannon, 1999), high pain thresholds when compared to noncriminals (Fedora & Reddon, 1993), and difficulties in recognizing facial expressions of sadness, anger, and disgust (Stevens, Charman, & Blair, 2001; Kosson, Suchy, Mayer, & Libby, 2002). Without negative emotions, psychopaths cannot undergo the kind of conditioning process that allows us to build up moral rules from basic emotions. Psychopathy is not a moral deficit but an emotional deficit with moral consequences.

The final line of research that I will consider is based on neuroimaging of healthy individuals when they engage in moral perception. Moll, de Oliveira-Souza, Bramati, and Grafman (2002) tried to identify moral circuits in the brain by comparing neuronal response to pictures of moral scenes and neuronal responses to unpleasant pictures that lack moral significance. For example, in the moral condition, subjects view pictures of physical assaults, abandoned children, and war. In the nonmoral condition, they see body lesions, dangerous animals, and body products. Moll et al. report that, when compared to the nonmoral condition, moral photographs cause increased activation in orbitofrontal cortex and medial frontal gyrus. The authors conclude that these areas play a critical role in moral appraisals. It is tempting to say that this study has identified a moral module—an area of the brain dedicated to moral cognition.

That interpretation is unwarranted. First of all, the brain structures in question are implicated in many social cognition tasks, so we do not have reason to think they are specialized for moral appraisals. Second, there is considerable overlap between the moral picture condition and the unpleasant picture condition. Both cause increased activation in limbic areas like the amygdala and insular cortex, as well as in visual areas (due presumably to increased attention to the photographs). It is reasonable to infer that negative pictures, whether moral or nonmoral, result in activation of similar emotions, as indicated by the overlapping limbic response. The main difference between the two kinds of pictures is that the moral pictures also elicit activity in brain centers associated with social cognition. This is unsurprising: seeing a child is more likely to induce a social response than seeing a body product. Thus, Moll et al. have not proven that there is a moral module. Their results support the opposite conclusion: moral stimuli recruit domain-general emotion regions and regions associated with all manner of social reasoning (as we saw in the discussion of the Wason task). The study does not reveal any regions that are distinctively moral (for a similar assessment, see Greene & Haidt, 2002).

I conclude that there is no strong evidence for a functional or anatomical module in the moral domain. Nativists must look elsewhere to support their view.

Poverty of the Stimulus

In linguistics, the best arguments for innateness take the following form: Children at age n have linguistic rule R; children at age n have not had exposure to enough linguistic data to select rule R from many other rules using domain-general learning capacities; therefore, the space of possible rules from which they select must be innately constrained by domain-specific learning capacity. Arguments of this form are called arguments from the poverty of the stimulus. The case for moral nativism would be very strong if nativists could identify poverty-of-stimulus arguments in the moral domain. I will consider two attempts to defend moral nativism along these lines (see also Nichols, 2005, for further discussion).

The first argument owes to Dwyer (1999). She has been one of the most forceful and articulate defenders of the analogy between language and morality (two other important proponents are Mikhail, 2000, and Hauser et al., in volume 2). Dwyer focuses on the moral/conventional distinction. She notes that children begin to show sensitivity to this distinction at a very young age (between two and three), yet they are not given explicit instruction. Parents do not verbally articulate the distinction between the two kinds of rules, and they penalize children for transgressions of both. In addition, there are considerable variations in parenting styles, yet children all over the world seem to end up understanding the distinction. Dwyer takes this as evidence for an innate capacity.

I think this is exactly the kind of argument that moral nativists should be constructing, but I don't think this particular instance of it succeeds. Above, I raised some general worries about the moral/conventional distinction, but I want to put those to the side. Let's assume that the distinction is real and that the operationalization offered by people like Turiel, Nucci, and Smetana captures it successfully. The question before us is whether this distinction can be acquired without an innate moral capacity. I think it can.

To begin with, we are assuming, along with researchers in this tradition, that moral and conventional rules are associated with different patterns of reasoning. Moral transgressions are regarded as more serious, more harmful, and less contingent on authorities. These reasoning patterns are exhibited by both children and adults. Therefore, children are presumably exposed to these different reasoning styles. The stimuli to which they are exposed are not impoverished. They can learn how to differentiate moral and conventional rules by imitating and internalizing the different reasoning patterns in the moral educators.

This is not idle speculation. There is ample evidence that parents adapt their styles of disciplinary intervention to the type of rule that a child violates (see Smetana, 1989, and Grusec & Goodnow, 1994, for a review). Moral rule violations are likely to be enforced using power assertion and appeals to rights, and conventional rules are likely to be enforced by reasoning and appeals to social order. Differential rule enforcement has been observed among parents of three-year-olds and is presumably operative before that age as well (Nucci & Weber, 1995). This is consistent with anecdotal evidence. I was recently at a party with four one-and-a-half-year-olds, and I made three casual observations: these children did not show remorse when they harmed each other; at such moments parents intervened with angry chastisement, social ostracism ("Sit in the corner"), and reparative demands ("Say you're sorry"); and parents never exhibited anger or punitive responses when children violated conventional norms, such as rules of etiquette. Grusec and Goodnow (1994) cite evidence that differential disciplinary styles are also used cross-culturally in Japan and India. In addition, children get socialized into moral competence by observation of adults outside of the household and from social interactions with peers. A child who violates a conventional rule may be ridiculed by peers, but she is unlikely to incur worse than that (imagine a child who wears pajamas to school one day). A child who violates a moral rule, however, is likely to incur her peers' wrath (imagine a child who starts fights). In short, different kinds of misdeeds have different ramifications, and a child is surely cognizant of this.

Dwyer might respond by conceding that children get enough feedback to know which of their own misdeeds are moral transgressions, but she might insist that they don't get enough feedback to generalize from those misdeeds to other actions that they have never experienced. Children do some bad things, but they do not commit every possible moral transgression. A child may learn from experience that it is bad to be a bully, but a child cannot learn from experience that it is bad to be an ax murderer or an embezzler. In other words, the child faces a challenging induction problem: how to generalize from a few examples of juvenile misconduct to the whole class of moral wrongs. Mustn't a child have innate moral rules to extend the category? I don't think so. Adults explicitly tell children not to harm others, and this formula can generalize to novel cases. In some moral domains, generalization from familiar cases to novel cases may be harder (hierarchy norms and sexual mores come to mind), and here, I would predict that children do a bad job at predicting adult moral values. Nativists need to come up with an example of an inductive inference that children make in spite of insufficient instruction. I am not aware of any such case.

Let me turn from the moral/conventional distinction to another argument from the poverty of the moral stimulus. To prove that morality is innate, we might look for signs of moral sensitivity in individuals who have had no moral training. There are virtually no data available on this question because it would be unethical to raise children without moral guidance. There is, however, one anecdote worth reporting. In 1799, a boy estimated to be twelve years old emerged from a forest in Saint Sernin sur Rance in France. He had apparently grown up alone in the woods without any adult supervision. The boy was given the name "Victor," after a character in a popular play, and he was placed in the care of Jean-Marc-Gaspard Itard, a young physician working in Paris. Itard tried to civilize Victor, and he wrote a book about his efforts. In one poignant episode, Itard attempted to discover whether Victor had a sense of justice. I quote at length:

(A)fter keeping Victor occupied for over two hours with our instructional procedure I was satisfied both with his obedience and his intelligence, and had only praises and rewards to lavish upon him. He doubtless expected them, to judge from the air of pleasure which spread over his whole face and bodily attitude. But what was his astonishment, instead of receiving the accustomed rewards . . . to see me suddenly . . . scatter his books and cards into all corners of the room and finally sieze upon him by the arm and drag him violently towards a dark closet which had sometimes been used as his prison at the beginning of his stay in Paris. He allowed himself to be taken along quietly until he almost reached the threshold of the door. There suddenly abandoning his usual attitude of obedience, he arched himself by his feet and hands against the door posts, and set up a most vigorous resistance against me, which delighted me . . . because, always ready to submit to punishment when it was merited, he had never before . . . refused for a single moment to submit. . . . (U)sing all my force I tried to lift him from the ground in order to drag him into the room. This last attempt excited all his fury. Outraged with indignation and red anger, he struggled in my arms with a violence which for some moments rendered my efforts fruitless; but finally, feeling himself giving way to the power of might, he fell back upon the last resource of the weak, and flew at my hand, leaving there a deep thrash of his teeth. (Itard, 1801/1962, pp. 94–95)

Itard calls this "incontestable proof that (Victor had) the feeling of justice and injustice, that eternal basis of social order" (p. 95). For our purposes, it is relevant as a possible case of a poverty-of-the-stimulus argument. Victor shows sensitivity to injustice despite having been raised (as it were) by wolves. This is an apparent example of moral competence without moral education: poverty of the stimulus.

Or is it? Itard himself might deny this interpretation. He was eager to take credit for Victor's moral education. Itard says, "On leaving the forest, our savage was so little susceptible to this sense (of justice) that for a long time it was necessary to watch him carefully in order to prevent him from indulging in his insatiable rapacity" (p. 93). Itard subjects Victor to increasingly severe punishments to prevent him from thieving. Victor's subsequent sense of justice may have been implanted through this process. Alternatively, Itard may have misdescribed his pupil's mind-set in the preceding episode. Victor had always been rewarded for doing his lessons well, and he had come to expect the reward of Itard's praises. On the occasion of this experiment, Itard replaced praises with wrath, and Victor reacted violently. This is hardly surprising. Victor was known for erratic tantrums, and he was accustomed to routine. In this case, his tantrum might have been set off by Itard's unanticipated assault. Even rats can react violently when expected reward is suddenly replaced by punishment. Rats do not need a moral sense to have a strong response under conditions of radically reversed reinforcement. For all we know, Victor had no more moral competence than a pestilent rodent.

Poverty-of-the-stimulus arguments are powerful tools in making a case for nativism. Perhaps such arguments will ultimately be found in the moral domain, but current evidence is consistent with the conclusion that children acquire moral competence through experience.

Fixed Developmental Order

Linguistic nativists sometimes argue for their cause by pointing out that language emerged in predictable ways. Children pass through similar stages in linguistic development, at similar ages, and arrive at linguistic competence around the same time. This is taken as evidence for the conclusion that language unfolds on an endogenously controlled schedule of maturation, like the secondary sex characteristics. If language were learned using general learning mechanisms, we would expect to see greater individual differences. People, after all, have different learning styles, bring different amounts of knowledge to bear, and are exposed to different experiences. One could argue for moral nativism by showing that moral development unfolds in a predictable way. One could argue that there is a fixed schedule of moral stages. Moral nativists who want to pursue this strategy might be inclined to call on the most famous theory of moral development: the theory of Lawrence Kohlberg (1984).

According to Kohlberg, there are six stages of moral development. The first two stages are "preconventional." At stage 1, children behave well out of fear of punishment, and, at stage 2, children choose behaviors that they view to be in their own best interest. The next two stages are called "conventional" because children become sensitive to the fact that certain behaviors are expected by members of their society. Stage 3 ushers in a "good boy, good girl" orientation, in which children want to be well regarded by others. At stage 4, we become preoccupied with law and order, choosing actions that conform to social norms and promote social stability. The final two stages in Kohlberg's framework are "postconventional." At stage 5, people justify the actions that they feel obligated to perform by appealing to a social contract, and, at stage 6, people attain a principled conscience; they select actions on the basis of universal principles rather than local customs. Kohlberg assumes that these stages have a kind of ontogenetic inflexibility: we pass through them in a fixed sequence. Nativists should like this picture because it parallels the stage-like progression of language, which is widely believed to be innate.

Ironically, Kohlberg does not argue that morality unfolds through a maturation process. He does not think his stages are biologically programmed. As a student of Piaget, he argues instead that social experiences cause children to reason about their current views, and this process of reflection prompts progressive improvements. Each stage is a rational successor to its predecessor. It would be a mistake to call this an *anti*nativist view, but neither is it a nativist view. Nativists cannot find a true ally in Kohlberg. Still, they might abandon his Piagetian orientation and give his levels a nativist spin.

This strategy is unpromising, because Kohlberg's theory is deeply flawed. First of all, it is a theory of how we morally reason, not a theory of how we form moral opinions. One might think our opinions are based on reasoning, but this probably isn't the case. There is evidence that moral reasoning is a post hoc process that we use to justify moral opinions that are acquired in some nonrational way (Haidt, 2001). If that's right, stage-like advances in moral reasoning may reflect a domain-general advance in rational capacities, not a change in our moral faculty. The moral opinions we have may be acquired on mother's (bended) knee and rationalized through progressively sophisticated arguments.

Second, empirical evidence has not confirmed a linear progression through Kohlberg's levels. Critics point out that people often reason at multiple levels at once, they occasionally skip stages, and they sometime move backwards through Kohlberg's sequence (Krebs, Denton, Vermeulen, Carpendale, & Bush, 1991; Puka, 1994). Evidence has also failed to establish that people advance to the highest stages in Kohlberg's scale. There was so little support for reasoning at stage 6 that Kohlberg regarded it as merely theoretical (Colby, Kohlberg, Gibbs, & Lieberman, 1983). It turns out that most adults only reliably attain stage 4 competence, and they make it to this point in their late teens or twenties; even graduate students have been shown to be stage 4 moral reasoners (Mwamwenda, 1991). This is somewhat embarrassing for the moral nativist, because cognitive capacities that are widely believed to be innate tend to emerge earlier in life. It is also noteworthy that the moral stage attained correlates with the degree of education, suggesting that moral reasoning skills are the result of training rather than maturation (Dawson, 2002).

There is also cross-cultural variation (Snarey, 1985). In small-scale village and tribal societies, people reason only at Kohlberg's third stage of development (Edwards, 1980). This does not undermine Kohlberg's theory, because he claims that environmental stimulation contributes to moral development, but it is a devastating blow to the nativist who wants to argue that Kohlberg's stages reflect the unfolding of a bioprogram. Puberty does not have radically different onset times in small-scale societies, nor does language acquisition.

There are other objections to Kohlberg (including Gilligan's, 1982, feminist critique), but this brief survey should suffice. The evidence for a fixed sequence of moral stages is underwhelming, and, to the extent such stages exist, there is little reason to think they are the result of biological maturation. Moral nativists cannot find in Kohlberg the requisite parallel to the stage-like progression in language acquisition.

Animal Precursors

I will discuss just one more class of arguments for moral nativism. Nativists often use cross-species comparisons to support their views. These comparisons can work in two ways. First, nativists can establish that other species lack some human trait, despite having similar perceptual and associative reasoning capacities. Such contrasts can show that the trait in question is not acquired through perception or conditioning, and this can be used to support the conclusion that the trait requires domain-specific learning mechanisms. Alternatively, nativists can establish that other species have a rudimentary version of some human trait, and this can be used to support the conclusion that the trait emerged through incremental biological evolution. In moral psychology, it has become increasingly popular to pursue this latter strategy. Researchers look for animal homologues of human moral traits. Most resist the temptation to say that non-human animals have a moral sense, but it is widely believed that there are precursors to human morality in the animal kingdom. I will not review the evidence here, but I want to consider a few examples that might be used in support of moral nativism (for more discussion, see de Waal, 1996; Hauser, 2001).

Let's begin, as is the custom, with rats. One might assume that these lowly creatures are oblivious to each other's welfare, but there is some reason to think that is not the case. Decades ago, Church (1959) discovered that rats would stop pressing on a lever to release food if, while doing do, they saw another rat in an adjacent chamber being shocked. Similar behaviors were subsequently observed in pigeons (Watanabe & Ono, 1986) and rhesus monkeys (Masserman, Wechkin, & Terris, 1964). Rats and pigeons resume eating after a short while, but some monkeys will endure sustained starvation to avoid seeing a conspecific in agony. Of course, vicarious distress is not necessarily altruistic. It could be, as mentioned above, that animals use the distress of others as a sign for danger. If an animal is peacefully foraging for food and it hears a conspecific cry, it will probably stop foraging and seek shelter, because the cry indicates the presence of a threat. Failure to respond in this way would be profoundly maladaptive. Consequently, these experiments do not reveal much about animals' concerns for their fellows. Even the monkeys who starved themselves may have done so because they were mortally afraid of being shocked. With vicarious distress, witnessing another creature's pain is literally painful, so the experiments essentially show that monkeys (like rats) will avoid food when they fear pain. Rats just overcome this tendency more easily.

Following up on the Church rat study, Rice and Gainer (1962) wanted to see whether rats engage in helping behavior. They hoisted one rat high up in the air, causing it to squeal and writhe. They discovered that rats on the ground would lower the suspended rat by depressing a lever rather than watching him suffer. This is an interesting result, because it shows that rats will work to avoid seeing other rats in pain. However, this behavior may be a by-product of the vicarious stress mechanisms. If rats suffer when they see the distress of their conspecifics, then it is unsurprising to find that they will work to help others. This tendency may be among the ingredients that evolved into genuinely prosocial tendencies, but there is no reason to attribute a moral sense to rats. We don't even need to suppose that rats have *concern* for each other. They just have vicarious distress.

I have already granted that humans experience vicarious distress, and I have intimated that it may play a limited role in the construction of moral rules (such as harm prohibitions). Vicarious distress may help us infer which actions are morally suspect. Blair (1995) has argued, not implausibly, that vicarious distress is a necessary precondition to the development of normal moral responses. However, it is certainly not a sufficient condition. Vicarious distress is not itself a moral attitude, and it does not prevent us from conducting and condoning acts of incredible brutality.

Let's turn from vicarious distress to fairness. Humans have a keen sense of fairness, and we resent it when we are not adequately compensated for our work. Brosnan and de Waal (2003) have argued that essentially the same tendencies exist in capuchin monkeys. They trained monkeys to exchange disks with experimenters for food reward. Some monkeys received cucumbers as the reward, and others received grapes—a much more desirable food. Some of the monkeys performing the task could see what another monkey was receiving. The crucial finding is that monkeys who received cucumbers were perfectly willing to perform the task when they did not see what other monkeys were getting, but they were significantly more likely to reject the food reward when they witnessed another monkey getting a grape for equal work. Brosnan and de Waal suggest that this reflects a nascent sense of fairness.

This interpretation has been subjected to convincing critiques. For example, Henrich (2004) argues that monkeys cannot be responding to inequity, because, by refusing to take the cucumber, they are actually increasing inequity, not reducing it. He cites evidence that humans will accept inequitable pay if they have no reason to think that rejecting that pay will have any impact on those who are receiving more. Wynne (2004) notes that cucumber-receiving monkeys also refuse rewards in a control condition in which they see grapes being placed in a pile nearby rather than seeing grapes being given to another monkey. The natural interpretation is not that monkeys have a sense of equity but rather that they will turn down mediocre rewards when something better is in view. This is simply an instance of the famous Tinklepaugh effect. Tinklepaugh (1928) showed that monkeys will turn down an otherwise desirable food reward (lettuce) when a more desirable reward has been observed (bananas). Compare a child who stops playing with a feeble toy when she spots a more exciting toy across the room. Brosnan and de Waal (2004) reply to this objection by arguing that there is a crucial difference in how their capuchins behave in the control condition with the pile of grapes and the unfairness condition where they observe another monkey receiving grapes. In the unfairness condition, the capuchins are increasingly likely to refuse cucumber compensation with each trial, whereas, in the control condition, they initially refuse cucumber compensation, but they then begin accepting cucumbers again after several trials. The authors conclude that the capuchins must be morally indignant in the unfairness condition. However, this trend can be explained without assuming the monkeys have a moral sense. As an inanimate object, the heap of grapes may become less interesting over time, and hence easier to ignore (monkey attention systems, like ours, inhibit return of attention to a previously attended location). Watching another monkey receive grapes is a more exciting stimulus;

a moving conspecific is harder to ignore. In addition, while watching another monkey eat grapes, the capuchin with the cucumbers might become increasingly aware of the fact that she could be enjoying those grapes as well. She may not be thinking, "This is unfair! I'm getting less reward for the same work," but rather, "Yum! I could be eating grapes right now." The study does not distinguish fairness from envy or mere desire.

The Brosnan and de Waal study has an ambitious aim. The authors attempt to show that monkeys make judgments about injustice. Perhaps one could find more plausible evidence for protomorality if one lowers the bar. Hauser, Chen, Chen, and Chuang (2003) present experimental evidence in support of a more modest hypothesis: monkeys reciprocate differentially. More specifically, Hauser et al. attempt to show three things: (1) monkeys will not give food to other monkeys who do not give them food; (2) monkeys will give food to other monkeys from whom they have received food; but (3) monkeys will reciprocate only if the monkeys who gave them food did not do so as a by-product of selfish actions. This last point is crucial. If monkeys merely gave food to every monkey that had given them food, the behavior might be explained as a conditioned response. If a monkey is, by chance, given food by another monkey and then, by chance, gives food in return, the first monkey's generous behavior will be positively reinforced, and that monkey will be likely to give food the next time around. In this way, patterns of reciprocal giving can emerge through conditioning. However, if monkeys reciprocate only with other monkeys who have given selflessly, then the conditioning story will lose plausibility. Selective reciprocation would be evidence that monkeys distinguish altruism from selfishness—a rudimentary moral judgment.

Hauser et al. (2003) tried to establish this with cotton-top tamarins. Two tamarins were placed in adjacent cages (Player 1 and Player 2), and they alternated trials in a reciprocation game. First, the authors established that tamarins would give food to those who gave them food selflessly. If Player 1 pulled a bar that gave Player 2 a piece of food but gave nothing to Player 1, then, on subsequent trials, Player 2 would reciprocate, by doing the same. If Player 1 never pulled the bar to give Player 2 food, then Player 2 would not reciprocate. This much might be explained by conditioning. In the crucial test, Hauser et al. set things up so that when Player 1 pulled the bar, she would get one piece of food and Player 2 would get three. When Player 2's turn came up, she would have an opportunity to reciprocate, by pulling a bar that would give her nothing in reward but would give Player 1 a piece of food. In these trials Player 2 rarely reciprocated. Hauser et al. reason as follows. Player 2 can see that Player 1 is getting food each time that Player 1 gives food to Player 2, so Player 1 is not giving away that food selflessly, and since it is a selfish act, there is no reason for Player 2 to reciprocate. Tamarins appreciate altruism. Or do they?

I think these results can be explained without assuming that monkeys have a nascent moral sense. On the conditioning account, monkeys will give food to each other if doing so has been positively reinforced in the past. In order for positive reinforcement to take place, a monkey who gives food must receive food afterwards. However, reinforcement can work only if the monkey thinks the reward is *a consequence* of her behavior. If a monkey receives a reward that would have come about no matter what, the monkey will not interpret that reward as contingent on her own behavior. This explains the experimental results. Player 2 sees that Player 1 is receiving food every time that Player 1 gives food to Player 2. Therefore, Player 2 should predict that Player 1 will pull the bar no matter what. As a result, Player 2 has no reason to think that Player 1's generosity is contingent on Player 2's response. Therefore, Player 2 will never perceive a reward to be contingent upon her own bar-pulling behavior. Thus, she will not pull the bar when it is her turn, and no reciprocation will take place. There is no need for protomorality here. The psychological mechanisms underlying these results are not much more sophisticated than the mechanisms that Skinner postulated in his behaviorist theory of animal learning.

I don't mean to suggest that nonhuman primates have no prosocial predispositions. It is well established that both monkeys and apes exchange goods and that the amount that they give to others (or allow others to take) is dependent on the amount that they have received or are likely to receive from others. Monkey and apes reciprocate (de Waal, 1996). Are we to infer from this that they have a protomorality?

I think that inference would be a mistake. First, notice an ambiguity in "protomorality." The term might refer to a disposition to behave in ways that we regard as worthy of moral praise. Any creature that engages in self-sacrificing actions might be credited with having a protomorality in this sense. Bees engage in altruistic behavior. However, "protomorality" might also mean a nascent understanding of right and wrong. On this interpretation, nonhuman animals can be said to have a protomorality only if they have psychological motives or appraisals that can qualify as homologues of the evolutionary precursors to our own moral motives and appraisals. A moral motive is a desire to do something because it's the right thing to do, and a moral appraisal is the belief that something is morally right or morally wrong. I don't think there is any reason to attribute either of these to monkeys and apes when they engage in acts of reciprocation. Like the self-sacrificing bees, some of this behavior may be thoughtless and automatic, and some of it may be driven by nonmoral motives. For example, there is now very good experimental evidence that primate food sharing correlates with harassment (Stevens, 2004). That suggests that many cases of primate "altruism" may really reflect primate fear of intimidation. This is not to deny that some primates have nobler motives. Primates share with close companions more than with strangers. However, such behavior does not entail that primates make moral judgments. We give things to our friends because we like them, not because we deem that action morally praiseworthy.

If monkeys and apes were forming moral appraisals, we would expect to find two things that have not been well demonstrated in other species. First, we would expect to find self-directed emotions of blame; apes who do not share should feel guilty about that. Second, we would expect to find third-party concern; apes would become outraged when they see two unrelated apes engage in an inequitable exchange. Apes may have both tendencies, but the evidence is scant (de Waal, 1996).

Until further evidence is in, we should resist the conclusion that apes make moral appraisals or act from moral motives. However, the nativist might object, that does not rule out the hypothesis that they make *proto-moral* appraisals. I'm not exactly sure what these would be. One possibility is that a protomoral appraisal is an appraisal comprising an other-directed emotion of blame, with no disposition to form self-blame emotions or to blame others when they mistreat unrelated third parties. I think it is misleading to call such appraisals protomoral, but that's a terminological quibble. I do concede that human moral appraisals may utilize psychological mechanisms that are homologous with the mechanisms that cause an ape to respond negatively when a conspecific, say, refuses to share. I would even concede that our biological predisposition to reciprocate furnishes us with expectations that form the foundation of our moral attitudes toward exchange. Our biological predispositions to reciprocate are fortified by culturally inculcated moral attitudes that promote self-blame and third-party concern. These concessions do suggest that we can learn something about human morality by studying other creatures. However, I emphatically deny that the psychological mechanisms in other creatures overlap sufficiently with our own to support any kind of nativist claims about morality. Moralizing does build on innate resources that we share with apes, but those resources do not qualify as moral. Hence, ape altruism does not establish that morality is innate.

Where Do Morals Come From?

The foregoing survey suggests that there is no solid evidence for an innate moral faculty. The conclusion can be summarized by revisiting the models of innateness introduced at the beginning of this discussion.

Some innate traits are buggy: they manifest themselves in the same rigid way across the species. If morality were buggy, we would expect to find universal moral rules. One might also expect to find a species-typical maturation pattern, with fixed developmental stages. We find neither. Moral rules show amazing variation across cultures, and developmental stages vary in sequence, time course, and end point.

Some innate traits are wrassey: they vary across the species and are sensitive to environmental inputs. Wrassey traits are not open-endedly varied, however. They have a few possible settings that get triggered under different circumstances. The suggestion that we have innate moral domains comes close to being a wrassey proposal. On this view, everyone cares about suffering, hierarchy, reciprocity, and purity, but the specific content of these domains, and their importance, varies across cultural environments. Notice, however, that the variation is quite open-ended. There are countless different rules pertaining to suffering, for example, and countless ways of arranging a social hierarchy. Thus, these domains do not look like the toggle switches we find in blue-headed wrasses, or in the Principles and Parameters account of the language faculty. Moreover, there is reason to think these domains may be learned.

Some innate traits are like birdsongs: there is an open-ended variety of ways that they might be expressed, but each may depend on a domain-specific learning mechanism. Arguments for the modularity of the moral domain and arguments from the poverty of the stimulus are both designed to demonstrate that there are domain-specific resources in the moral domain. I found both of these arguments wanting.

In sum, I think the evidence for moral nativism is incomplete, at best. We have, as yet, no strong reason to think that morality is innate. This conclusion is surprising because morality seems to crop up in every society, no matter how isolated and how advanced. Massive variation in religion, physical environment, and means of subsistence have no impact on the existence of morality, even if the content of morality varies widely. Capacities that are canalized in this way are often innate—often, but not always. Take the case of religion. Some people think there is an innate religion module in the human brain, but this is a minority opinion. The dominant view of religion is that it is a by-product of other human capacities: theory of mind systems, a thirst for explanation, a good memory for the exotic, emotional response to intense sensory pageantry, and so on (Boyer, 2001; Whitehouse, 1999). Religion, like morality, appears everywhere, but not because it is innate. It appears everywhere because it is a nearly inevitable consequence of other capacities.

I think the same is true for morality. In criticizing arguments for moral nativism, I indicated some of the capacities that may underlie morality. Let me mention four important psychological capacities here:

1. *Nonmoral emotions* Emotional conditioning (the main method used in moral education) may allow us to construct behavioral norms from our innate stock of emotions. If caregivers punish their children for misdeeds, by physical threat or withdrawal of love, children will feel badly about doing those things in the future. Herein lie the seeds of remorse and guilt. Vicarious distress may also be important here. If we have a nonmoral but negative emotional response to the suffering of others, moral educators can tap into this and use it to construct harm norms.

2. *Meta-emotions* In addition to our first-order emotions, we can have emotions about emotions. We can feel guilty about feeling mad or guilty about not feeling anything at all. This is doubly important for the emergence of morality. First, we sometimes judge that our first-order moral emotions are inappropriate. Consider sexual norms. A person raised to oppose homosexuality may have an inculcated, negative emotional response to homosexuals, but she may not like having that response, and she may feel guilty about it. Her second-order guilt about blaming homosexuals can play a causal role in reshaping her first-order emotions. Second, we have norms about how people should feel. A happy victimizer who causes harm without remorse is judged morally worse than a remorseful victimizer (Arsenio & Lover, 1995). By adopting rules about what people should feel, not just how they should behave, we can have greater influence on behavior.

3. *Perspective taking (theory of mind)* Nonhuman animals can be emotionally conditioned to behave in conformity with rules, but they usually do not respond negatively when third-party conspecifics violate those rules. A monkey may punish another monkey for stealing, and the punished monkey may feel bad (e.g., scared or sad or submissive) as a result, but both monkeys may be indifferent when they see another monkey stealing from a third party. Human beings tend to show third-party concern, and this may be a consequence of the fact that we are good at taking the perspective of others. When we see the victim of a transgression, we imagine being that victim, and we experience anger on her behalf.

4. *Nonmoral preferences and behavioral dispositions* In addition to our innate stock of emotions, there may be some innate social behaviors that lend themselves to moralization. Reciprocity and incest avoidance are two examples. These behaviors are not moral to begin with, I argued, because they are not innately underwritten by self-blame emotions and third-party concerns. When coupled with human emotional capacities, these behavioral tendencies take on a more moralistic character, and, perhaps, theory of mind mechanisms allow us to identify with unrelated victims of misdeeds and acquire a concern for third parties.

In addition to these four psychological mechanisms, there will also be situational factors that drive the formation of moral rules. There are some social pressures that all human beings face. In living together, we need to devise rules of conduct, and we need to transmit those rules in ways that are readily internalized. Nonhuman animals are often violent, but their potential for bad behavior may be lower than ours. Because we can reason, there is a great risk that human beings will recognize countless opportunities to take advantage of our fellows. We can recognize the value of stealing, for example, and come up with successful ways to get away with it. High intelligence may be the ultimate consequence of an evolutionary arms race, and, with it, the capacity for bad behavior greatly increases. Intelligence is the greatest asset of a free rider. To mitigate this increased risk, cultures need to develop systems of punishment and inculcate prosocial values. Cultures need to make sure that people feel badly about harming members of the in-group and taking possessions from their neighbors. Without that, there is a potential for collapse in social stability. This is a universal problem, and given our psychological capacities (for emotion, reciprocation, mental state attribution, etc.), there is also a universal solution. All cultures construct moralities. Elsewhere, I have described at length the ways in which specific cultural circumstances can shape specific moralities (Prinz, 2007). One can explain why, in certain circumstances, cannibalism, incest, polyandry, and raiding have had adaptive value. The moral systems we inherit from our communities often contain rules that are vestiges of problems that our ancestors faced. The rules are as varied as the problems, but the universal need to achieve social stability guarantees that *some* system of moral rules will be devised.

These suggestions are sketchy and speculative, but I don't mean to be presenting a model of moral development here. Rather, I want to suggest that there is an exciting research program waiting to be explored. Just as cognitive science has looked into the psychological mechanisms that lead to the emergence of religion, we can discover the mechanisms that make us moral. In both cases, those mechanisms may not be specific to the resulting domain. If I am right, then morality is not buggy, wrassey, or starlingy. It is more like pigeon piano (the result of a general-purpose conditioning mechanism) and flea toss (a new use for systems that evolved to serve other functions). Morality is a by-product of other capacities.

Sometimes cognitive scientists use such arguments to support skeptical solutions. If religion is just an accidental by-product of oversensitive theory of mind mechanisms, then perhaps we should try to get rid of it. Likewise, one might argue, if morality is just a by-product of emotional systems, then maybe we should get rid of it. This conclusion doesn't follow. As I just suggested, morality may be a solution to a social coordination problem, and, without it, we would be much worse off.

That said, the antinativist thesis does have an important ramification. The old-school moral sense theorists, like Hutcheson, often assumed there was a single human morality. There is one set of moral rules, and those are the rules we are innately designed to appreciate. Modern moral nativists are less prone to seeing morality as completely fixed, but the nativist program certainly gives rise to the impression that morality is very highly constrained. Nativists about language point out that certain grammars just don't exist, and could not. Perhaps certain moralities could not exist either, but the range of possible moralities vastly exceeds the range of possible grammars. And with that discovery, we can recognize that morality is an extremely flexible tool. If morality is something we construct, then, like other tools, it is also something we can change and improve upon. We can try to reshape moral systems to better serve our current needs and achieve greater degrees of social cohesion. The cognitive science of morality will, I think, play an important role in learning the boundaries and optimal techniques for moral change.

Note

I am indebted to Walter Sinnott-Armstrong for comments on an earlier version, to Stefan Linquist for a discussion of innateness, and to Valerie Tiberius for a commentary. All three were very helpful. I have also benefited, perhaps too late, from discussions with audience members at Dartmouth, Columbia, Rutgers, Oxford, Leeds, and at the Society for Philosophy and Psychology meeting at Wake Forest University.

7.1 How Not to Argue that Morality Isn't Innate: Comments on Prinz

Susan Dwyer

I

We must admire the ambition of Prinz's title question. But does he provide a convincing answer to it? Prinz's own view of morality as "a by-product—accidental or invented—of faculties that evolved for different purposes" (p. 368), which appears to express a negative reply, does not receive much direct argument here. Rather, Prinz's main aim is to try to show that the considerations he believes are typically presented by moral nativists are insufficient or inadequate to establish that morality is innate. He discusses, individually, how much evidential weight the (alleged) existence of (1) universal moral norms, (2) universal moral domains, (3) fixed stages in moral development, and (4) precursors to morality among nonhuman animals lend to nativist claims, and, in addition, he argues that poverty-of-the-moral-stimulus arguments are as yet unconvincing. "[C]urrent evidence," Prinz claims, "is consistent with the conclusion that children acquire moral competence through experience" (p. 395).

It is not my intention here to follow Prinz's piecemeal criticisms of moral nativism. In their attacks on linguistic nativism (see, e.g., Cowie, 1999) and now on moral nativism, empiricists typically deploy the following strategy: (1) isolate some alleged explanandum for linguistics (or moral psychology), then (2) argue that its existence and operation could be explained in empiricist terms. No serious nativist proposal will be undermined by this approach. Quite apart from its not being clear why the empiricist gets to shift the burden of proof in the first place (just why *should* empiricism be our default position?), it is important to understand that nativists are led to their position on the basis of thinking about how a related *set of capacities*, in short, an identifiable *competence*, emerges in the natural ontogenetic course of development of creatures like us. A moral nativist will not be content to rest her project on the alleged existence of a universal incest taboo alone, for example. In linguistics, arguably the field in which nativist arguments have been most successful, a major emphasis is on explaining how an *individual child* comes to be a speaker of a humanly possible language. Once one takes this focus, it is evident that it will do no good to say this or that feature of being a speaker of a natural language might have an empiricist explanation, for the individual child does it all at once (see Crain & Pietroski, 2001; Laurence & Margolis, 2001).

Hence, for present purposes I will assume that moral competence is to be understood as a set of capacities, naturally acquired in normal human social environments by all normal children. The debate between the moral nativist and the moral antinativist, then, will devolve on whether it is plausible to think that the child can mature into a creature with moral competence (so understood) on the basis of experience alone.

A great deal will hang, therefore, on what we take the relevant set of capacities to be. For my own part, the central capacities involve judgment: mature moral creatures are able to judge whether real or imagined actions are permissible, impermissible, or obligatory; they are able to judge whether and the degree to which moral agents are morally responsible for actions they perform; they are able to judge whether situations require moral responses at all.[1] Notice, also, that once we start thinking in terms of moral competence in this way, it is clear that there is something quite fishy about Prinz's guiding question, "Is morality innate?" At the very least, the question is dangerously ambiguous. One of my main aims in this comment is to indicate why this is so in a way that illuminates how the moral nativist project ought to be understood and conducted.

II

It is no secret that I contend the best hope of understanding our moral capacities rests with pursuing the so-called "linguistic analogy" in moral psychology (see Dwyer, 1999, 2006). The motivating idea here is not that morality is "like" language, whatever that might mean. Nor is it merely that morality and language appear to be two species-wide and species-specific phenomena. Rather, the big-picture reason for looking to linguistics for help in thinking about morality is that the fact of our being moral creatures—like the fact of our being speakers—is underpinned by a human normative competence, the possession of which both allows us to and makes us see the world in moral terms, while also making possible the acquisition of particular capacities that allow us to negotiate a world so conceived, in ways that are sensitive to local conditions.

The Chomskian program has always been animated by the thought that the study of language is an enormously fruitful strategy for the study of the human mind/brain itself. Our linguistic capacities are interesting in their own right, of course. However, theoretical linguistics is as much about a certain attitude to inquiry and explanation in the cognitive sciences as it is about the study of language (see Hornstein, 2004).

I belabor this point, because people are apt to ask, "If morality is innate (read: if moral nativism is true), why do people behave so badly?" But this is like asking, "If language is innate (read: if linguistic nativism is true), why do people speak and write so badly?" The linguist does not presume to address the latter question, and indeed, he will express doubt that any systematic answer can be given to it. Similarly, the moral nativist is interested in providing an account of an underlying competence. Human beings lie and cheat and harm each other for a variety of idiosyncratic reasons that cannot be the subject matter of science. And, praiseworthy or morally good behavior is not the moral nativist's primary concern. Again, to suggest otherwise would be like saying that the linguist's concern is beautiful rhetoric.[2]

A related point is this: the moral nativist does not aim to explain why humans (seem to) *care* about morality. A creature can be built to engage with a particular normative domain without caring about that domain. An innate cognitive endowment ought not be construed as evidence of an innate desire to cognize the world in the relevant ways, and certainly not as an innate desire to act in certain ways. This is again worth underscoring, for one might think that moral nativism might directly solve certain puzzles about moral motivation. (For further discussion, see Tiberius's response to Prinz, this volume.) To be sure, one wants to know precisely how moral cognition and moral motivation are related. However, the moral nativist does not and should not make promises about settling that issue.

III

To understand the awkwardness of asking whether morality is innate, we can examine the parallel question "Is language innate?" Understood as tangible, historical objects, languages like Mandarin, Urdu, and English— what linguists call "E-languages"—are not innate. Given that they are the result of a combination of economic, social, political, and cultural forces, among other things, they could not be. However, neither are the grammars of individual native speakers of these languages—what linguists refer to as I-languages—innate. For, had I grown up in Oslo, my grammar would resemble those of other native speakers of Norwegian and not those of native speakers of English. A speaker's I-language is properly taken to be a developed state of his mind/brain. More precisely, it is a steady state constituting the end point of a growth process that is itself made possible by the interaction between innate features of the human mind/brain and the environment in which particular mind/brains mature.

The term "language faculty" has been adopted to refer to these innate features. There has been considerable misunderstanding about the nature of the language faculty, which I cannot address here. Suffice it to say that one need not think of the language faculty as a module in the Fodorian sense, that is, as a dedicated piece of cognitive architecture causally responsible for speakers' linguistic behavior. Nor need one think of it as a body of explicitly or implicitly represented knowledge, consciously or unconsciously deployed by speaker-hearers. The language faculty is an abstract posit, ontologically not unlike idealized models elsewhere in science. It is not a black box in which the principles of Universal Grammar are inscribed. Rather, as Collins (2004) nicely puts it, "The language faculty is an abstractly specified computational . . . system of the mind/brain" (p. 529). It is a system that allows human speakers to associate signals with meanings. Such associations are highly constrained; indeed, what counts as legible signals and possible meanings is also constrained. And these constraints are expressed in terms of the principles of Universal Grammar. The discovery and articulation of these principles is an empirical matter.

The major argument for the existence of the language faculty, and the major mode of inquiry into the content of the principles of Universal Grammar, is the poverty-of-the-stimulus argument. I shall return to Prinz's remarks about how the poverty-of-the-stimulus argument has been deployed with respect to moral psychology below.

For now, let me repeat the basic message so far: theoretical linguistics is a *faculty* nativism. *If* one feels compelled to say that language is innate, then one must be careful to specify that what one means is that the language *faculty* is innate. E-languages, I-languages, linguistic behavior—none of these can intelligibly be said to be innate. To be a nativist about language is to assert that there is an innate faculty of the mind/brain that allows for a certain type of highly constrained cognition. We can talk about the principles that characterize the computational system as being innate, if we like. However, it is crucial not thereby to imply that the principles are represented in any explicit fashion. Correlatively, there is no reason to think that the relevant principles (once discovered) will be recognizable to speakers of a natural language as the principles that make their linguistic capacities possible.

IV

Moral nativism should also be construed as a *faculty* nativism. The empirical task for the moral nativist is the discovery and articulation of the *principles* that characterize the abstractly specified computational system of the mind/brain that makes being a moral creature possible. And, as I have argued elsewhere, there is good reason to believe that poverty-of-stimulus considerations arise for moral competence as well (Dwyer, 1999, 2006). This is one way of making it clear that moral psychology (like linguistics) is part of psychology.

I have emphasized "principles" just now in order to set up a tripartite distinction, not marked by Prinz or by the largely unnamed "nativists" he takes himself to be criticizing, between moral *principles* and moral *norms* and moral *rules*. These terms will be useful in explaining why much of Prinz's case against moral nativism fails. Moral nativism, properly construed, is not the view that moral norms or moral rules or moral domains (whatever they might be) are innate. Nor is it the view that there is a moral module, understood as a piece of causally efficacious cognitive architecture. It is the view, instead, that there is an innate moral faculty—characterizable in terms of principles.

Recall the notion of an E-language—a public, observable, tangible "thing," like Chinese or Urdu. While the individuation of E-moralities is likely to be a lot more difficult than the individuation of E-languages, we can for the moment imagine that there are such things. In particular, we might say that an E-morality is that set of publicly available, codified, moral norms operative within a given community. Such norms are highly likely to be historical products, constructed over time in light of a wide range of geographical, political, cultural, and economic factors. They will enjoy long periods of relative stability. However, their contingency predicts that they can and will change over time. Perhaps a scientifically systematic account of the emergence and development of E-moralities can be had (see, e.g., Sripada & Stich, 2006). But it's clear that it makes no sense to claim that E-moralities themselves, hence moral *norms*, are innate.

Supposing there are E-moralities, it is plausible to posit I-moralities. Consider, for example, Nisbett (2003), whose fieldwork in cultural psychology seems to suggest that there are distinctive differences in the value talk of East Asians versus Westerners, especially Americans. The moral delibera- tion of the former seems to assume a conception of persons as interdepen- dent and a collectivist conception of society, whereas that of the latter seems to assume a conception of the person as independent along with a concomitant conception of society as individualistic. If Nisbett is right, then there is evidence for the idea that individuals will converge on moral understandings that prevail in the cultural environments in which they mature. I hesitate at this juncture to say this is *just like* coming to speak Norwegian on account of growing up in Oslo. For, as I have already men- tioned, it might not be clear how to limn the contours of a distinctively Norwegian (or even Scandinavian) E-morality. And, in addition, it is not obvious that the mutual incomprehensibility that exists, say, between "conversing" speakers of Urdu and speakers of Japanese carries over to their moral deliberations.

Still, since the capacities of a mature moral creature are well entrenched and operate almost completely without effort, we must assume that its moral cognition is underpinned by some steady state of its psychology, some state of its mind/brain. Such a state might well be characterized in terms of *rules*. However, just as it would be a mistake to think of the rules that characterize a speaker's I-language as innate, it would be a mistake to think of moral rules as innate. It is no coincidence that Norwegian chil- dren's I-languages are similar: I-languages are interaction effects between the children's innate linguistic endowment and their linguistic environ- ment. Likewise, we can expect similarities between moral creatures' I- moralities. And we should think of an I-morality as an interaction effect between a child's innate endowment and the moral environment in which she matures.

This brief discussion of norms and rules suggests that Prinz is absolutely correct to emphasize the cultural contingency of moral norms and substan- tive moral rules and thus to deny that such norms and rules are innate. But, then, as I have tried to make clear, no serious moral nativist would say otherwise.

One needs to be very clear as to what one is talking about when one asserts or denies that *morality* is innate. At the very least, one needs to say whether the claim is about the E-level, the I-level, or the faculty level. My suggestion is that norms are the proper objects of inquiry if we are inter- ested in describing E-moralities; rules are the proper objects of inquiry if we are interested in characterizing I-morality; and principles are the proper objects of inquiry if we are interested in characterizing the moral faculty itself, that is, if we are interested in doing moral *psychology*.

The distinction between norms, rules, and principles also directs us to think very carefully about what a faculty moral nativist should take as data for testing her hypotheses. In linguistics, speakers' acceptability judgments play an important role in the testing and articulation of linguistic principles. To date, my thought (and that of others; see Mikhail, in press; Hauser, 2006) has been that moral creatures' permissibility judgments, evoked, for example, in trolley problem cases, can play the same role for moral nativists. I have come to doubt that we can make any inferences directly from permissibility judgments to principles. One reason for this skepticism is that the notion of permissibility seems to be conceptually a long way "downstream" from moral cognition. The concept of permissibility or, more precisely, *conceptions* of permissibility as they are deployed in the explicit judgments that moral creatures make strike me as intimately connected with prevailing norms. To put this point slightly differently, there is a lot of noise intervening between the operation of the moral faculty and the issuance of particular permissibility judgments. Still, as Cushman, Young, and Hauser (2006) have discovered, those latter judgments exhibit considerable systematicity. They appear to be constrained in interesting ways. And the thought is that those constraints are what comprise a creature's competence.

My current speculation is that moral judgment is the product of a kind of evaluation that takes place well below the level of consciousness. We may appeal to explicit codified moral norms when we are playing the game of interpersonal justification. However, we should not be misled into thinking that the cognitions that ground judgments of permissibility involve our reasoning over those codified norms.

This picture fits nicely with the phenomenon of moral dumbfounding (see Haidt, 2001). There is little reason to believe that qua nontheorists we have developed ways of talking about all that goes on in actual moral cognition. Middle school grammar teachers have ways of talking about sentence structure, and professional linguists do too, but as theoretically naive speakers, we have no readily accessible language among ourselves to talk about the violation of island constraints, say.[3] It seems to us that morality *ought* to be more articulable. However, that strikes me as symptomatic of not having taken the cognitive revolution seriously. Besides, our spoken and written language is just as, if not more, pervasive than the manifestation of our moral capacities. And we do not balk at the fact that much of what we know about our language we know tacitly.

To be sure, at this point the faculty moral nativist owes an account of the specific ways in which norms, rules, and principles might be distinguished. For example, will the distinction rest on differences between the form, the content, or the "what" of norms, rules, and principles?

Given my characterization of norms as cultural, historical products, my guess is that norms will not always be promulgated or understood as imperatives. Think, for example, of how many norms are manifest in children's stories and myths. Norms, rather, will be expressed in terms of what philosophers call "thick" ethical concepts (e.g., courage, decency, mean-spiritedness). Rules, by contrast, if they play a role in something approaching deductive moral reasoning, may well take the form of imperatives (e.g., "Do not lie," etc.).

To be frank, the form and content of the principles that I claim characterize the moral faculty remain a mystery. But what this approach predicts is that the articulation of such principles is unlikely to involve the use of terms with which moral philosophers are currently familiar. However, this is precisely what one expects in an emerging field of empirical inquiry. As to the form of principles, I think we need to think more creatively about the nature of constraints in general. Not all constraints take the form of imperatives like "No flip-flops allowed in the front bar!" In cognitive science, we can think of constraints as ways of blocking a cognitive movement; a sort of "you-can't-get-there-from-here" admonition. Consider the moral judgment that it is good to torture small babies for fun. That has the feel of something no "normal" moral creature could generate. At a really fundamental level, then, the idea is that the principles of the moral faculty are what explain why such judgments cannot be generated.

V

Prinz focuses on an earlier argument of my own (Dwyer, 1999) to the effect that there is good reason to posit something innate in order to account for the early recognition of a moral/conventional distinction in children. His main attack is to argue that the "distinction can be acquired without an innate moral capacity" (p. 392). Again, I note that the child's capacity to distinguish between different types of explicit imperatives is just one among other capacities it acquires that can fairly be thought to reflect its emerging moral competence. The truth or plausibility of faculty moral nativism does not rest solely on the idea that children could acquire *this one* capacity only if their moral cognition is innately constrained.

Prinz is certainly correct to say that *if* the moral/conventional distinction is real, then it is manifest in the reasoning behaviors of adults. Human children will then be exposed "to these different reasoning styles" (p. 392). On these grounds, Prinz asserts that "[t]he stimuli to which [children] are exposed are not impoverished" (p. 392). Moreover, he writes, children "can learn how to differentiate moral and conventional rules by imitating and internalizing the different reasoning patterns in the moral educators" (p. 392).

There are a number of points to make here. First, Prinz's general argumentative strategy comes very close to mirroring a familiar one with respect to language. Michael Dummett (1976) argues for a pair of constraints—the manifestation condition and the acquisition condition. Children must be able to acquire their language (for plainly they do); therefore, the rules of the language must be made manifest in their environment. However, this is precisely to beg the question against the nativist. The nativist can accept the following conditional: if the child is to acquire capacity C in the normal course of growing up, then she must have access to something that makes that acquisition possible. The logical space thus encompasses innate endowments *and* information available in the environment. The nativist does not deny that the environment is relevant; some things must be manifested by adults. Indeed, as I said earlier, linguists see a grammar (an I-language) as an interaction effect between Universal Grammar and the information available in the child's environment. But no one gets to exclude by fiat the contribution of an innate endowment.

Second, Prinz seems to make the following inference: adults manifest capacity C; therefore, the stimuli available to the child are not impoverished. Again, this is plainly question-begging. And no one can credibly run the same line with respect to language. Here, Jackendoff's (1994) "paradox of language acquisition" is instructive. Here is how Collins (2004) summarizes it:

The professional communities of linguists and psychologists have all the data they desire on, say, English, certainly much more than any child has ever enjoyed. They also pool their mature intellects, have equal data on many other languages, and design subtle experiments and conduct longitudinal studies over many years. Yet they still can't work out the principles, rules, and concepts that constitute competence with English which the normal child masters by the time she is five! So, it is not so much that the child's data is poor according to some absolute standard (as if such a notion makes sense); rather, if the child were relying on data, then her acquisition of language would be miraculous. The acquisition ceases to be at all miraculous if we understand the child to possess innate resources which already determine most of what is to be acquired. On this view, the child's task is so "easy" precisely because she isn't dependent on rich data, while the data inundated scientist's task is so hard precisely because he is trying to work out what the child already knows independent of data or general principles defined over it. (p. 505)

Third, the notions of imitation and internalization are nothing more than terms of wishful thinking. Imitation may approach being an explanatory notion when, for example, we have reason to believe that mirror neurons are implicated. (Needless to say, we are far from having such a reason with respect to human moral capacities.) However, to say that children internalize some set of rules is not to explain their acquisition; it is merely to restate that the rules are acquired. This has been a central failing of so-called "social-learning" accounts of morality.

Let us examine, however, the more than idle speculation Prinz presents for the claim that the moral/conventional distinction can be acquired without an innate moral capacity. To begin, Prinz cites some work about differential responses to different types of transgressions. Next he concedes that I might reply that children don't get enough information to generalize from one instance of harming, say, to all instances of harming. In this way, he interprets me as advancing the view that moral maturation involves a straightforward induction problem.

The faculty moral nativist can agree that caretakers' differential affective responses to types of behaviors their children engage in will be salient to those children. However, as I have argued elsewhere, some parents get just as hot under the collar about conventional transgressions as they do about moral transgressions. (In some middle-class households, etiquette is taken *very* seriously.) Moreover, it is likely that conventional transgressions outnumber moral transgressions, offering little opportunity for the child to observe the peculiar type of emotional reaction allegedly associated with a moral transgression. And, there is evidence that caretakers more often correct or admonish conventional transgressions than they do moral transgressions (see Nucci, 2001; Smetana, 1989). Finally, even adults have difficulty distinguishing between strong emotional reactions: is my interlocutor angry, disgusted, irritated, or disappointed with my action? It's hardly likely that very young children are any better at making finegrained discriminations between the emotionally laden responses of their caretakers.

Prinz writes, "Adults explicitly tell children not to harm others, and this formula can generalize to novel cases" (p. 393). To be frank, this strikes me as outright assertion without argument. Of course, it must be conceded that caretakers do provide explicit moral instruction. The nativist need not deny this. But she will question whether this instruction provides every child with sufficient data to acquire the capacity we are investigating.

First, it's worth noting that "You ought to keep your promises" has precisely the same form as "You ought to put the fork on the left." "I've told you before, don't do that!" is as appropriate after a hair pulling as it is after an episode of food throwing. In other words, there appears little in the positive evidence concerning rule violations generally that would cue the child as to whether a moral or a conventional rule has been transgressed. Second, there may well be a paucity of negative evidence concerning the distinction between the two types of rules. Very roughly, negative evidence is evidence the child can use to correct a false assumption she has made or which she can use (in this case) to eliminate a candidate criterion for making the discrimination.

At best, it seems that children can become aware that the adults around them exhibit some regularities, sometimes their caretakers codify those regularities by uttering "ought" statements, and their caretakers seem to care about whether those ought statements are obeyed.

Poverty-of-the-stimulus arguments get traction when we are confronted with the early acquisition of some distinctive capacities which appear to be universal across the species and which cannot be explained on the basis of the positive and negative evidence available to children everywhere. The conclusion is that the child—or, more precisely, the child's mind/brain—must contribute something to the process of acquisition.

The conclusion of such arguments in linguistics, it must be noted, operates in a domain where we have a *much richer* and *more specific* characterization of the relevant capacities (i.e., explananda). If the challenge to faculty moral nativists is to provide a better articulation of those explananda, I happily agree. My hunch is that the richer and more specific our characterization of moral capacities becomes, the less appealing empiricism will seem.

VI

Given the relative newness—at least among philosophers—of thinking seriously about morality as involving a set of capacities that are amenable to empirical investigation, it is no surprise that we currently lack a perspicuous vocabulary either for articulating or for criticizing particular positions. What I hope to have sketched here is a more systematic

[handwritten marginalia: "to rationalism + subject to emp. investigation,"]

categorization of the very different elements that are implicated when we treat morality as a dimension of human psychology.

One last point: Prinz implicitly imputes a mistaken motivation to moral nativists. One need not (indeed, should not) pursue moral nativism with the hope of making the world "comfortingly smaller" (p. 367). Positing an innate moral faculty, for example, is not necessarily in the service of promoting an optimistic view about human beings. For me, the attractions of moral nativism have very little, if anything, to do with whether humans are innately good or innately capable of being good. When the moral nativist speaks of human beings as moral creatures, she uses "moral" in a descriptive, not an evaluative, sense. The idea is that humans have an innate capacity to make moral judgments and valuations, to see the world in moral terms. What we do with those evaluations is a separate, though no less interesting question.

Notes

1. I do not mean to suggest that these capacities exhaust moral competence. I merely wish to emphasize that the capacities of interest are primarily cognitive, and certainly *not* behavioral. I say nothing here about the role that affect plays in the moral lives of creatures like us. The only kind of creatures we can be sure are moral creatures—namely, ourselves—are also affective creatures. And it is tempting to single out some emotions like guilt and shame as specifically morally emotions. Still, it seems to me to be an open empirical question precisely what relation obtains between our affective capacities and moral competence.

2. Cf. Prinz: "The hypothesis that morality is innate is not simply the hypothesis that we are innately disposed to behave in ways that are morally praiseworthy" (p. 370). I am denying that the moral nativist's hypothesis is even simply that.

3. "Island constraints" refers to restrictions on what linguistic items can be moved from where to where in, say, question formation. Consider the following pairs:

(1) A vet saw the dog that was found.
(2)* Was a vet saw the dog that found?

(3) The hiker who was lost kept walking in circles.
(4) Was the hiker who lost kept walking in circles?

In each case, the auxiliary verb "was" has been moved from within a relative clause (an island). That a restriction has been violated is evident in (2), where the result is word salad, and in (4), where the question is comprehensible but inappropriate. Naive speakers of English recognize these violations by judging that (2) and (4) are (differently) unacceptable. However, such speakers will not be able to say why (2) and (4) are unacceptable.

The Nativism Debate and Moral Philosophy: Comments on Prinz

Valerie Tiberius

In his paper for this volume, Jesse Prinz shows that the arguments in favor of moral nativism are at best inconclusive and in many cases just plain wrong. I am not going to take issue with the particular arguments within this debate; rather, my comments are about the relevance of this debate (whatever side you take) for moral philosophy. I do not mean to imply that the interest of this debate for moral philosophy is the only interest it has; of course, there is much of interest here for cognitive scientists and philosophers of mind. However, in the current spirit of interdisciplinary research, it is worth reflecting on what this debate in moral cognitive science means to one of its closely related fields.

Claims about moral innateness might be relevant to naturalistic projects in moral philosophy in at least two important ways, one having to do with motivation and the other with justification. First, nativist claims may provide a universal motive for morality, which would reduce the worry that our motivating reasons to be moral are highly contingent and non-universal. Second, nativist claims may provide a justification for universal moral truths, which would reduce worries about moral relativism, a view that is troubling to many. I take up these two topics in turn, beginning with motivation. In the last section of my comments I discuss the view about the relationship between moral cognitive science and moral philosophy that emerges from Prinz's paper.

Motivation

We might think that moral philosophers ought to be concerned about the nativism debate in virtue of a concern about moral motivation. The issue here can be appreciated independently of concerns about justification, although internalists (those who think that moral claims are inherently motivating) are likely to think that concerns about motivation lead to concerns about justification. We can distinguish this concern for now, though, at least for present purposes. The moral philosopher might worry that even if there are universal moral truths, if people have no psychological hook for them to attach to, then human beings can stray very far from what's good and right. If nativism were true, the thought is, then everyone has some motivation to be moral. If nativism is false, the possibility arises that many human beings have no motivating reason to be moral. Furthermore, the thought that we have innate psychological states that motivate us to be moral is the right kind of thought: moral philosophers who want to naturalize ethics are likely to find this story a good fit with their theories (unlike a story that relies on God's furnishing our reasons to be moral). Another way of putting the point, then, is that one compelling answer to the question "Why be moral?" is eliminated if nativism is false—hence a reason for moral philosophers to be interested in the nativism debate.

Prinz suggests that the rejection of nativism encourages the view that human motivation is "considerably more variable than the nativism program might lead us to think, and also more versatile" (p. 368). Now variability and versatility might seem worrying to a moral philosopher who thinks innate psychological states provide the motivational hook for moral principles.[1] I will argue, however, that Prinz's discussion does not really reveal that the innateness debate is relevant to moral philosophers' concerns about moral motivation.

First, Prinz's underlying assumption about the moral domain is that it is specialized and fairly narrowly circumscribed. To see this, recall the following claims from Prinz's discussion:

• "Morality, like all human capacities, depends on having particular biological predispositions, but none of these, I submit, deserves to be called a 'moral faculty'" (p. 368).
• "Doesn't vicarious distress show that we have an innate predisposition to oppose harm? Perhaps, but it's not a moral predisposition" (p. 374).
• "We are innately gregarious: we socialize, form attachments, and value company.... Gregariousness is not, in and of itself, a moral disposition ('make friends' is not a moral injunction), but it may have implications for morality" (p. 375).
• "The four moral domains may be by-products of basic emotions. Negative emotions play a moral role only when they are transformed into full-blown moral sentiments" (p. 382).

- "Moralizing does build on innate resources that we share with apes, but those resources do not qualify as moral" (p. 402).

According to Prinz, a moral motive is a desire to do something because it is right, a moral appraisal is a belief that something is morally right or wrong (p. 401), and emotions only become moral emotions when we become disposed to direct them at third parties who have no impact on us and to direct corresponding emotions toward ourselves (p. 402).[2]

Given that Prinz interprets the moral domain quite narrowly in his arguments against nativism, it isn't clear how much credence these arguments lend to the claim that moral motivation is highly adaptable or variable. Prinz admits that we have innate tendencies toward vicarious distress, gregariousness, forming social bonds, and nonmoral emotions that form the basis for full-blown moral sentiments. If this is so, and if we do have, as he says, a universal (social) problem for which morality is the answer, then variations in our motivations will only extend so far.

Conclusion 1: if morality is *not* innate in Prinz's sense, worries about moral motivation and our reasons to be moral may still not be very pressing; there may be all sorts of innate motives to which morality (given socialization) can attach.

The second thing to notice is that moral innateness as represented in Prinz's discussion doesn't seem to do much to remove worries about adaptability and motivation. Why not? First, it turns out that culture can override whatever innate tendencies we have. Prinz says this when he endorses Mark Hauser's argument that you cannot take rare cases to refute the hypothesis that a particular rule is innate: "The exceptions show that these norms can be overridden by culture, not that the norms are learned" (p. 379). Second, on many of the nativist views (the universal domain view, for example), what is innate allows for lots of adaptability anyway.

Conclusion 2: if morality *is* innate, worries about adaptability and moral motivation may be quite pressing.

The above two conclusions should make us think that the debate about moral innateness is not particularly relevant to moral philosophers' worries about moral motivation and motivating reasons. Whether moral capacities are innate or not, what is relevant is the power of education and socialization to develop, shape, and change them.

Another way of appreciating this point is to think about what naturalistic moral philosophers, like Mill and Hume, for example, could have hoped for that would have eliminated worries about moral motivation. Mill might have hoped for universal beneficence, a general love of mankind that would have furnished people with an overriding motivation to promote the greatest happiness for the greatest number without undue regard for themselves. Hume might have hoped for the dispositions to take up the general point of view and to be motivated by a feeling of sympathy that arose from taking up this perspective and crowded out all other motives. None of the nativist positions canvassed by Prinz argues for anything like this. Mill and Hume were both content with a general goodwill and/or sympathy that had to be educated and trained into a moral motive. The belief that goodwill or general sympathy were innate, which it seems Mill and Hume had, did not eliminate the need to worry about the power of society to distort these motives.

Even Aristotle and contemporary Aristotelians, many of whom rely heavily on claims about human nature, are not likely to be too concerned about the outcome of the nativism debate. Given Aristotle's emphasis on moral training, habituation, and education, Aristotelians do not need to assume that the particular dispositions that comprise the virtues are innate. — *natural virtues + intelligence*

Justification

The first thing we might wonder is what does innateness have to do with the question of justification, anyway? One obvious answer is: nothing. If we're talking about moral sentiments or emotions as moral motives, it's quite coherent to think that justification is one thing and motivation another. (Mill clearly thought just this.)

On the other hand, perhaps the idea is that innate principles or rules would be, in some way, self-justifying. This would make sense if the principle or rules in question were of the right kind. At least some obvious sources of reasonable doubt about universal principles would be removed. But the innate principles or rules proposed by nativists are not of the right kind. In some cases, as Prinz argues, they admit of too many exceptions to forestall skepticism. And in other cases, they seem not to be moral principles in the relevant sense at all. Consider the argument from the linguistic analogy. The linguistic analogy (at least Dwyer's version of it) does not purport to uncover action-guiding moral principles. Rather, according to Dwyer,

The principles the linguist articulates are intended as an abstract characterization of the structure of speakers' competence; they are not intended to provide speakers with guidance in their communicative endeavors. Neither should we look to the principles the moral psychologist uncovers for moral guidance. The moral psychologist's job is to uncover the structures and processes that make moral life possible.[3]

If it is psychological rather than moral principles that are innate, the case for nativism is not going to add to the justification of morality in a straightforward way.

I think the same point can be made about the other arguments for moral nativism. Whether the nativist's claims are about universal rules, domains, or modules of the brain, the psychological constraints putatively discovered by nativists do not answer questions about the justificatory status of moral principles or values. For example, such psychological constraints do not help us figure out which principles make the most sense, nor do they help explain why we ought to respect other people or promote their welfare. Furthermore, given the kinds of questions we have here (normative questions about justificatory reasons and what makes sense), it doesn't seem that a psychological explanation of how we make moral judgments or how we respond morally to the world could answer them. To think otherwise would be an egregious instance of the naturalistic fallacy. I do not mean to suggest that either Prinz or the nativists are committing this fallacy; my goal here has just been to rule out another way in which the debate about nativism might have been relevant to the concerns of moral philosophy.

The above point may seem too obvious to make, but there is an implication for metaethics here that is worth highlighting. Prinz confesses early on to being sympathetic to response-dependent accounts of moral norms, and he mentions a variety of cosympathizers (among whom I count myself). According to Prinz: "moral norms are sentimental norms: they are underwritten by various sentiments. In particular, moral norms are grounded in the moral emotions" (p. 368). The phrases "underwritten by" and "grounded in" hide a crucial distinction between two different kinds of response-dependent views. According to one, the expressivism favored by Blackburn and Gibbard, moral norms (or, more precisely, our judgments about them) are an *expression of* our sentiments. According to a different kind of response-dependent account, the one favored by historical sentimentalists like Hutcheson, our judgments about moral norms are *reports about* our sentiments.[4]

Expressivism does justice to the importance of the facts about our psychology to our moral life without implying that these facts determine the content of morality. For example, an expressivist can admit that we have no innate *moral* rules or domains of judgment without thinking that this implies any form of moral relativism or, in fact, anything at all about the content of moral principles, good moral judgments, or the like. The psychological explanation of our expressions does not constitute a justification for their content, and expressivism makes sense of this fact.

On the other hand, a response-dependent view that takes moral judgments to be reports about our sentiments does not maintain this desirable distinction between the descriptive and the normative. If the content of moral norms is determined by the psychological states we have, and if these psychological states vary across cultures, then moral relativism follows. But moral relativism as a substantive moral position should not follow from psychological facts about us.[5] Rather, substantive moral positions follow from *employing* moral norms in a practice of moral reasoning or conversation.

I should clarify here, lest it seem otherwise, that the argument I have just made is very much compatible with ethical naturalism. The expressivist project is a naturalistic one because it seeks to explain what we are doing when we moralize in natural psychological terms. It does not, however, conflate moralizing and explaining: what we discover in doing the latter can only have bearing on the former in virtue of the epistemological and ethical norms that make up our moral practice. According to this view, then, the question of whether there are universal moral norms or whether relativism is true is entirely independent of the nativism debate.

To return to the subject of moral justification, perhaps the point of focusing on the claim that psychological explanations are relevant to the content of moral norms is that underlying psychological mechanisms place limits on what kinds of morality we human beings are capable of and these limits at least constrain what kinds of principles or values can be justified. If certain ways of acting are psychologically impossible for us, a theory that requires such actions is indefensible.[6] (Here we come back to the issue of motivation—now in the context of motivation as a constraint on justification.)

That the psychological facts about us impose limits on the kinds of moral theories that can be justified is a sensible view. And here we do find a way in which moral cognitive science is relevant to the interests of moral philosophers. Notice, though, that insofar as the particular debate about moral nativism that Prinz describes really turns out to be about whether the capacities that have been identified should count as moral, that debate is not to the point. It seems that the best way to make progress here is to accept that what nativists are discovering are innate tendencies to reason in particular ways, patterns of emotion that form certain clusters, and other biological predispositions that we may share with animals, none of which are, in Prinz's somewhat strict sense, moral. Moral or no, these are the capacities that delimit the changes we're capable of and, therefore, constrain which moral theories might be correct.

Moral Construction

Prinz is likely to welcome the conclusion that moral cognitive science can inform moral philosophy by delineating the psychological reality within which theory must be constructed. Prinz himself emphasizes the importance of a lack of rigid constraints when he lauds the non-nativist approach for celebrating human potential:

> If morality is something we construct, then, like other tools, it is also something we can change and improve upon. We can try to reshape moral systems to better serve our current needs and achieve greater degrees of social cohesion (p. 406).

This sounds very good to me, but we should be careful not to overestimate the role of empirical psychology. Notice, first of all, that this attractive vision of morality as a tool that we use to solve coordination problems and meet our needs itself constitutes a vision of what morality is. From the moral point of view, the idea that morality is a tool to build social cohesion itself requires justification (a fact Prinz is happy to admit).

Moreover, deciding what counts as a need and what counts as desirable social cohesion is not a matter for psychologists. What is the difference between needs and wants? Are needs or desires morally interesting psychological states? Is one more important than the other? Are needs relative to culture or the same for all human beings? Are individual agents authoritative about what they need? Might we be incorrect about what our needs are, individually or as a culture? What rights and liberties are included in desirable social cohesion? What is the appropriate balance between the freedom of the individual and the good of the group? These are moral questions that have to be answered before we can think about what would constitute improvement in the moral domain.

I have argued that in thinking about how to improve morality, the crucial question for the cognitive science of morality is not whether the relevant skills are general or specific to morality; rather, the crucial questions are "What's in the toolbox?" and "How do these tools work together?" In thinking about how to improve our tools, we should be willing to marshal all of our psychological resources, whether or not they count as uniquely moral.

In this last section I have made the further point that at least as important as knowing what's in the toolbox is knowing what we're trying to build. This shows, I think, that cognitive scientists of morality would do well to work together with more traditional moral philosophers so that they don't end up showing us how to build something that doesn't do us any good. *Area exam*

Notes

1. Though Prinz himself does not see this as a cause for concern because, as we see later, he thinks this versatility is important for moral progress.

2. It is not Prinz's aim in this paper to defend this view of morality; rather, he takes it as a background assumption. It is worth noting that his conception of morality is not one that will be compelling to consequentialists and other moral philosophers who take the moral domain to encompass a wide variety of motives. For present purposes, however, we do not need to decide who is correct here.

3. Dwyer (2006).

4. This is the standard interpretation of Hutcheson, though there is a minority view according to which Hutcheson is an expressivist. For helpful discussion, see M. Gill (2006). Hobbes certainly seems to count as having a response-dependent theory of the descriptive (non-expressivist) sort. The best contemporary example of such a view comes from David Lewis (1989). There are other views that might be labeled "response dependent," but we need not be concerned with the full range here.

5. What I mean by calling moral relativism a "substantive moral position" is that moral relativism is a view about the content of moral norms that makes what is right or wrong, good or bad, relative to a subject or a culture. This seems to me not the sense of "moral relativism" that Gilbert Harman (1975) intends in his "Moral Relativism Defended."

6. This is implied by the principle of minimal psychological realism, which seems a reasonable constraint on moral theory construction. See Flanagan (1991, chapter 3, pp. 56–78).

Jesse J. Prinz

In "Is Morality Innate?" I argued that the evidence for an innate moral faculty is, at present, underwhelming. We should be open to the possibility that moral competence, like religion, tool use, and the arts, is a by-product of more general psychological resources. My case for non-nativism was far from complete. I am very fortunate to have the opportunity to respond to Susan Dwyer and Valerie Tiberius, whose thoughtful commentaries give me an opportunity to clarify and qualify my position.

Dwyer points out that I spend most of my energy raising doubts about arguments for moral nativism rather than offering positive reasons for thinking non-nativism is true. This gives the impression that I think non-nativism should be the default position, and it weakens my response to the most powerful strategy for defending moral nativism: the moral-poverty-of-the-stimulus argument. As with language, one cannot decisively refute nativism without showing that there is a viable alternative. It's not enough to show that the primary moral data are rich; I need to show that the data are rich enough to allow the acquisition of moral competence without a domain-specific learning mechanism. Tiberius pushes in another direction, one that is extremely important for fostering fruitful dialogues between those who approach ethics through cognitive science and philosophers doing metaethics and normative ethics in more traditional ways. She argues that the debate about moral nativism has no bearing on questions of whether morality is intrinsically motivating or whether moral claims are justified. If Tiberius is right, it's reasonable to ask whether traditional philosophical ethicists should care about whether morality is innate.

I will address these two issues in turn. In response to Dwyer, I will try to indicate why I think non-nativism looks so promising to me. In response to Tiberius, I will try to suggest that some outcomes of the nativism debate would have implications for philosophical theories in ethics. First, two concessions. To Dwyer, I concede that the nativism question is far from settled, and I think exchanges between nativists and non-nativists will be immensely constructive in the coming years. To Tiberius, I concede that the implications of the nativism debate for ethical theory may be modest. Hopefully, the debate is still interesting. Echoing an analogy from Dwyer, the debate about linguistic nativism is interesting even if it doesn't help us assess whether Gertrude Stein is a good poet.

Are the Primary Moral Data Impoverished?

Dwyer is a moral nativist. She believes that there is a moral faculty, which can be characterized in terms of a set of innate domain-specific principles that allow normally developing human beings to acquire moral rules and reason about morality. Along with John Rawls, John Mikhail, Gilbert Harman, and Marc Hauser, she thinks it is useful to compare the acquisition of moral competence to the acquisition of language. In a commentary on Hauser, Young, and Cushman (volume 2 in this collection), I offer some general reasons for resisting the linguistic analogy. In responding to Dwyer, I will focus on three components of the analogy that play a role in her response to me.

First, Dwyer suggests that moral judgment is driven by principles that operate below the level of consciousness (compare syntax). Indeed Dwyer confides that moral theorists have yet to identify those principles, and they may require a vocabulary unlike what we use in ordinary moral discourse. In response, I concur that evaluative reasoning often takes place outside consciousness. For example, implicit biases can affect our assessment of people in ethnic groups other than our own, and "mere exposure effects" can inflate positive attitudes toward things that are familiar. These processes presumably influence moral reasoning. However, beyond such general reasoning biases, I am not persuaded that moral reasoning is driven by principles that are inaccessible to consciousness. People can articulate moral values (killing is wrong, helping is good, etc.) and a weighted list of these values may explain most moral judgments that people make. It is plausible, in other words, that our moral judgments express *basic moral values* to which we have conscious access or extensions of those basic values that we could arrive at through conscious deliberation.

Against this supposition, Dwyer points to Haidt's (2001) discussion of moral dumbfounding. With collaborators Bjorklund and Murphy, Haidt found that many people insist that consensual sibling incest is morally wrong even if they cannot provide good arguments for that conclusion.

Dwyer implies that such people are inarticulate about their reasons for their moral appraisals because their reasons are not accessible to consciousness. An alternative interpretation is that, for these subjects, the moral disapproval of incest is a basic value. It isn't based on reasons or reasoning at all. People may, with greater or lesser success, try to come up with arguments to justify their basic values, but, from a psychological perspective, these justifications are post hoc: the value is psychologically independent of the reasons offered in its defense. On this interpretation of the data, nothing is hidden. People strongly believe that incest is categorically wrong, and their behavior in the lab can be explained on that basis. The basic values approach can explain why people are often bad at articulating reasons for moral judgments.

A second alleged analogy between morality and language involves the notion of constraints. Dwyer says that no serious moral nativist would deny the cultural contingency of moral rules; instead, serious nativists would predict that our innate moral principles constrain the space of possible rules. As her example, she suggests that no normal moral creature could generate the rule that it's good to torture small babies for fun. I tend to think, somewhat cynically, that the range of moral rules is relatively unconstrained. Unlike language, where certain grammars apparently never occur, moral variation seems to be relatively open-ended. I adamantly believe that we could teach people to value the recreational torture of small babies. Romans valued blood sports, Aztecs valued cannibalism, the Balinese value cockfights, the Phoenicians sacrificed infants, and the ancient Greeks practiced infanticide by exposure. Cruelty seems to be a common feature of human existence; torture comes all too easily. I'm sure a search of the anthropological record would uncover groups that tortured babies for fun—especially if the babies belonged to enemy groups who were defeated in battle. It's far less plausible that we'd find groups that tortured their own babies for fun, but there is no need to postulate a moral faculty to explain that. Groups that inflict harm on their young might not survive, and parents in such a group would be disinclined to give up their babies for torture. In this respect, I think there are some constraints on morality. Nonmoral preferences (such as parental instincts) and the need for group cohesion may render certain moral values unlikely. However, these constraints do not require moral nativism, and they may be weak— that is, we *could* acquire values that violate the constraints, but they would meet with resistance and fare badly in the long run. At present, I think there is no evidence for the view that morality is constrained in the way that language is.

The third point of alleged analogy between language and morality is the most important for the present discussion. As with language, Dwyer believes that moral nativism can be supported by appeal to a poverty-of-stimulus argument. She suspects that the adult moral discourse and behavior to which children are exposed does not include the information that would be required (e.g., robust statistical reliability, explicit instruction, negative data, etc.) to allow children to acquire moral competence using learning mechanisms that are not specific to the moral domain. Poverty-of-stimulus arguments usually proceed by presenting specific aspects of competence that seem difficult to acquire given the primary data. Dwyer advances a poverty-of-stimulus argument concerning the moral/conventional distinction. She believes that children could not learn to distinguish moral and conventional rules as early as they do if they were not equipped with an innate moral faculty. I am not persuaded. In my original essay, I cited empirical evidence that parents enforce moral and conventional rules in different ways, and I suggested that this might be sufficient for explaining how children acquire the distinction. Dwyer rightly points out that the mere fact that there is a difference in adult enforcement behavior does not undermine the nativist argument. The difference in adult behavior must be robust, children must be sensitive to it, and it must be sufficient to generalize in a way that locks children onto the right distinction. Here, I will elaborate on why I think adult enforcement behavior meets these requirements.

As a preliminary remark, let me reiterate that I am skeptical about the moral/conventional distinction, at least as it is characterized in the empirical literature. The distinction was introduced into the literature on moral development by a group of post-Kohlbergian psychologists (see Turiel, 1998). On their operationalization, moral rules differ from conventional rules in three ways: they are considered less contingent on authorities, they are regarded as more serious, and they are justified by appeal to such things as the suffering that would be caused if they were violated. Various authors have argued that these operationalizations do not correspond to a sharp distinction in the evaluative domain. Some conventional rules are regarded as independent of authorities; for example, Nichols (2002) has shown that this is the case for etiquette norms that regulate behavior that people find disgusting, such as spitting. Some moral norms are regarded as authority dependent; for example, Kelly et al. (in press) found that some subjects say it was okay for the Romans to enslave war captives. Some conventional rule violations are more serious than some moral rule violations: for example, cross-dressing is regarded as worse than, say, taking an aspirin from a friend's medicine cabinet without asking. And some moral rules are not justified by appeal to the suffering of others; for example, some people find it morally wrong to masturbate into a chicken carcass, even though they know that no one is harmed by such behavior (Haidt, Koller, & Dias, 1993). The standard operationalization of the moral/conventional does not align perfectly with the norms we call "moral" and "conventional." Rather, the operationalization corresponds to something like the distinction between harm norms and conventional norms that are not underwritten by strong physical disgust. The evidence that young children grasp the moral/conventional distinction is based on research that uses the standard operationalization. We should take that evidence as showing that young children distinguish harm norms and violations of affectively benign social conventions. I do not think we need to posit an innate moral faculty to explain this developmental achievement.

Let's begin with harm norms, such as "Don't hit." When children violate harm norms, three responses are most typical (Hoffman, 2000). First, there's power assertion: if Lulu hits her baby brother, her parents are likely to get very angry, and they may even take hold of Lulu in a threatening way. Second, there's love withdrawal: if little Lulu smacks Daddy's face while playing, he may say, "That's not nice; I'm not going to play with you any more." Most importantly, there's induction of empathetic distress: when Lulu hits her baby brother, and he begins to cry, they will say, "Look what you've done; you made your brother cry." Each of these methods can be quite effective. Power assertion helps Lulu see that this is a serious rule. Her parents regard hitting as *very* bad. Power assertion also leads Lulu to fear punishment when she hits, and, through imitative learning, it leads her to get angry at others who hit. Dwyer dismisses my appeal to "imitation," but there is considerable evidence that children imitate parents' emotional attitudes (e.g., Sorce et al., 1985), and there is evidence that mirror neurons translate perceived displays of emotions into corresponding emotional feelings (Goldman & Sripada, 2005). Love withdrawal is also good for conditioning Lulu's emotions. If Lulu can't play with Daddy after hitting him, she will feel sad, and she will associate the sadness with the hitting; this is just associative learning. Induction of empathy conditions Lulu to associate distress with hitting, and it teaches her a justification for the norm that hitting is wrong: hitting causes misery in others. These parental enforcement techniques result in "internalization," another term that Dwyer dislikes. For me, an internalized rule is just a rule of conduct toward which one has an emotional attitude that leads one to be motivated to act in accordance with the rule and to negatively regard others who fail to act in accordance with the rule.

Contrast all this with the enforcement of conventional rules, such as "Don't make noise in a restaurant." If Lulu violates this rule, her parents are likely to get mad. They may even take her outside and make her take a time out, but the degree of expressed anger is likely to be milder than it would be in the hitting case. Moreover, Lulu's parents probably won't try to punish her through love withdrawal (perhaps she is making noise because they are not giving her enough attention in the first place), and they won't be able to induce vicarious distress because Lulu's behavior is not visibly harming anyone. Notice, too, that the norm against making noise is restricted to specific contexts. Lulu is permitted to make noise on playgrounds but not in restaurants. Thus, Lulu learns that norms against noisemaking are contingent. The emotions underlying conventional rules are weaker than the emotions underlying moral rules (e.g., we do not fly into a rage when someone puts a fork on the wrong side of a table setting), they are more contingent (e.g., we don't care about table settings at a picnic), and they are qualitatively different (e.g., we are embarrassed by violating etiquette norms, not ashamed or guilty).

These differences in how norms are enforced are demonstrable at the youngest ages that have been tested and are probably manifested as soon as children start violating norms. Together they can account for the three dimensions of the moral/conventional distinction. First, consider seriousness. Children may learn that hitting is more serious than making noise in a restaurant because parental response to the former is more intense. Next, consider the manner of justification. Children may justify the norm that hitting is wrong by appeal to the suffering of the victim because this consequence is made salient to them through the strategy of induction of vicarious distress—a strategy totally unavailable when parents are teaching conventional norms. Finally, consider authority independence. How do children learn that it's wrong to hit regardless of what authorities say? Vicarious distress may matter here, too (Blair, 1995). In enforcing harm norms, caregivers draw children's attention to the pain caused by hitting, kicking, and biting. In so doing, they lead children to associate these behaviors with vicarious distress. Importantly, the vicarious distress would remain in place even if authorities announced that hitting, kicking, and biting were permitted. Once children become aware that certain behaviors cause harm, they begin to regard those behaviors as wrong regardless of what authorities say. Hitting, kicking, and biting seem wrong because they induce negative feelings in their victims and, vicariously, in the perpetrator. The negative feelings do not hinge on a negative attitude from a caregiver once children appreciate harm. This explanation makes the following prediction: if the victim of the hitting did not mind being hit and a child were told it's okay to hit by authorities, then a child should judge that hitting, in that instance, is okay. Boxing matches are an obvious example of this. When it comes to social conventions, there is no victim, so all the negative feeling associated with a conventional rule violation comes from the negative attitude of authorities or other onlookers—unless violating the rule causes physical disgust. Moreover, many conventional rules apply only in specific contexts, so children learn that they are contingent.

All of these points are speculative, but, on the face of it, children get exactly the kind of data they need to treat moral norms—and harm norms, in particular—in line with the three operational criteria used in the literature on the moral/conventional distinction. Thus, in response to Dwyer, my claim is not merely that parents treat moral and conventional norms differently. My claim is that the specific way that moral norms are enforced leads directly to the operational differences that have been demonstrated in studies of moral development. Indeed, those operational differences may correlate with enforcement differences better than they correlate with the pretheoretical distinction between moral and conventional rules.

Dwyer knows that I think the differences in parental enforcement are sufficient to account for children's success in distinguishing moral and conventional norms (or, as I have stressed here, harm norms and certain kinds of conventional norms). In her commentary, she offers some lines of response. First, she says that some parents get hot under the collar about conventional norms. In this reply, I have tried to identify some empirically demonstrable differences in how adults enforce harm norms and etiquette norms. I would predict that if a child's parent really treated an etiquette norm with the same regimen of enforcement as a harm norm, the child would probably come to have a moral attitude toward that etiquette norm. Second, Dwyer says that conventional transgressions outnumber moral transgressions and are corrected more often. Notice that nothing in the foregoing account appeals to the frequency of correction. I claim that it's the way in which moral norms are enforced that matters. Third, Dwyer claims that even adults have difficulty distinguishing between such emotions as anger, disgust, and disappointment, so we can't expect children to be sensitive to the subtle differences in adult emotions when they enforce rules. This claim strikes me as empirically dubious. Both adults and children are very good at distinguishing emotions (e.g., Field & Walden, 1982). Moreover, even if parents sometimes exhibit the same emotions to enforce moral and conventional norms, there are other differences that I have described here. Induction of empathy is common in the case of harm norms but often inapplicable in the case of conventional norms.

In sum, I think there is good reason to speculate that the techniques frequently used by parents in the course of moral education are well suited for teaching children that certain moral transgressions are serious, bring misery to others, and are bad regardless of what authorities say. If I am right, these enforcement techniques could lead children to distinguish moral and conventional rules without postulating an innate moral faculty.

Does Nativism Bear on Motivation and Justification?

Let me turn now to the very different issues raised by Valerie Tiberius. There is a growing methodological divide in philosophy between those who rely on empirical evidence and those who use more traditional philosophical methods, such as conceptual analysis. Ethics has been dominated by traditionalists, but, in recent years, empirically oriented philosophers have been actively contributing to this area, as this volume attests. Often the empirically oriented philosophers imply that their theories bear directly on issues that traditionalists work on. Theories developed by traditionalists are alleged to make implicit empirical assumptions that can be tested. Tiberius does not oppose this approach. She recognizes that philosophical theories must be consistent with what we discover about human psychology. However, she questions whether the nativism debate is relevant to contemporary debates in metaethics. In particular, Tiberius argues that no plausible outcome of the nativism debate can tell us whether moral judgments are intrinsically motivating or justified. I am largely sympathetic to this assessment, but I want to point out a couple of ways in which the nativism debate might bear indirectly on these enduring philosophical questions.

Let's begin with motivation. According to motivational internalists, moral judgments are intrinsically motivating; externalists deny that. I happen to think that the debate about internalism can be settled empirically if it can be settled at all (Prinz, 2006b; see the exchange between Kennett, Fine, Smith, & Roskies in volume 3). Tiberius may agree. Her main point is that *the nativism debate* does not bear on the internalism debate. The internalism debate is a debate about the nature of moral judgments, and the nativism debate is a debate about where moral judgments come from. The origin of morality does not decide the essence of morality.

I find Tiberius's arguments compelling: the nativism debate does not bear directly on the internalism debate. However, I think nativism bears *indirectly* on internalism in the following way. Let's assume that internalism is true and that certain moral principles are innate. If moral principles are innate, there are two polar possibilities and various gradations in between. One possibility is that the innate principles are immutable, and the other is that innate principles can be completely overridden through experience. Both possibilities have implications for internalism. If innate moral principles are immutable, then it would be impossible for someone to be indifferent to those principles, barring cases of psychopathology. If moral principles are innate but mutable, then anyone who lacks the innate principles has, in some respect, gone against nature. Thus, nativism seems to entail that those who are not motivated by certain moral principles—the innate ones—are unnatural.

This difference matters because debates about internalism are often tied in with debates about normativity. What sort of normative force do moral judgments have? Internalists say that moral judgments are motivating and, thus, at a minimum, have a kind of psychological normativity: they feel like imperatives to their possessors. However, one might wonder, why should we heed our feelings? Are we really obligated to do what we feel compelled to do? If nativism is right, then some of those feelings have their basis in human nature. This suggests a kind of teleological normativity. There are natural compulsions, and one might answer the normative question—Why should I be moral?—with an appeal to teleology: because it is in my nature. Teleology is normative because it implies that some forms of behavior are incorrect, in a biological sense of the word. Nativists can argue that culturally constructed moral rules that violate innate principles lack this kind of normativity. Non-nativists cannot appeal to teleology in the same way. Non-nativists might allow that some norms violate aspects of our nonmoral human nature, but they have no room for norms that are unnatural, morally speaking.

Arguably, this subtle difference in normative status has been of tremendous importance within traditional ethical theory. In Aristotelian ethics, morality is bound up with virtues, and virtues are defined, teleologically, as character traits that constitute flourishing because it is part of human nature to possess them. If Aristotle's theory is interpreted as an ethical theory—as the claim that it is morally good to flourish—then we need to think of the virtues as not merely being natural but as being naturally good. Non-nativists reject the whole idea of natural goodness and thus challenge the kind of normativity implied by the Aristotelian program. Or consider Hume. Hume agrees that some virtues are artificial, and hence not innate, but he also believes in natural virtues, and, crucially, he insists that the artificial virtues depend on the natural virtues. He thinks that the good is that toward which we have approbation, and we naturally have approbation toward certain traits, such as benevolence, in virtue of the natural sympathy we feel for (some of) those who benefit from benevolent acts. Other traits, such as female chastity, are not innate objects of approbation, but we learn to value chastity, Hume says, because if we didn't, men might be stuck raising children that aren't their own and that would bring them despair, and despair would elicit our sympathy and that would lead to disapproval. It's crucial for Hume that some of our moral attitudes are natural, and these become the foundation of his program. For Hume, the natural virtues are privileged. Finally, consider Nietzsche. He argues that Christian values are culturally constructed, and he recommends that we get rid of them. In their place, he imagines us returning to values similar to those that were dominant in ancient Rome, and Nietzsche regards these values as more natural; he says they are active rather than reactive, and he implies that they reflect human nature rather than cultural history. Thus, for Nietzsche too, there is an assumption that some values are natural and that natural values have a different normative status than values that are unnatural.

In response to all this, Tiberius might reject the idea that any value should be privileged simply in virtue of being natural. My point here is not that Aristotle, Hume, and Nietzsche were right to think that natural values are privileged. My point is that ethical theorists have traditionally been committed to such views, and thus, if one takes these theories seriously, the nativism debate has considerable relevance. Moreover, even if one resists the inference from natural to good, it must at least be appreciated that nativism introduces a distinction between natural values and unnatural values, and that has implications for moral psychology. Resolving the nativism debate cannot tell us whether moral judgments are intrinsically motivating, but it can tell us whether we are naturally motivated by certain moral values and not others. This raises questions about how we should think about people whose motivations differ from our own. Are such people defective or merely different? What should we do about them? Can cultures inculcate values that are more in line with natural morality? Should they?

In discussing motivation, I have already shifted into issues of justification, which is the second main theme in Tiberius's commentary. I have been suggesting that traditional ethical theorists have sometimes presumed that some moral values are more natural than others, and these natural values have been regarded as privileged. One might interpret these ethical theorists as supposing that natural moral values are more justified than those that are unnatural. Of course, that supposition is highly contentious. With Tiberius, I agree that an innate value may be unjustified, and a learned value may be justified. However, to promote fruitful discussion, I want to consider two ways in which the nativism debate could bear on questions of justification.

First, a nativist might be able to get some mileage out of the fact that many innate capacities are adaptations. An adaptation is a trait that has been selected, over evolutionary time, for its contribution to fitness. This could be used to argue for the conclusion that innate moral values are justified. Here's how the argument might go. First, one might argue that, if moral principles are innate, then they are probably adaptations. Then one might argue that if something is an adaptation, it was adaptive in the past and is likely to be adaptive in the present. Adaptive traits increase fitness, which means they are prudentially rational. Therefore, moral principles are likely to be prudentially rational, if innate, and hence rational (in a practical sense). Any principle that is rational in a practical sense is also justified in a practical sense (i.e., it makes sense for us to act in accordance with such principles). Thus, if moral principles are innate, they are likely to be practically justified. This inference from innateness to justification is obviously defeasible. Every step could be debated, and it relies heavily on probabilistic inferences. However, the argument illustrates a way in which innateness could bear on one kind of rationality. Conversely, if moral principles are human creations, the argument can be stopped at the start. Human creations are not adaptations, and there is no probabilistic inference from the supposition that a principle is socially constructed to the conclusion that it is adaptive (recall Nietzsche on maladaptive Christian values). In sum, the innateness debate might be a context in which one could determine whether our values owe to natural selection or human invention, and that issue has potential implications for questions about whether we are justified, in some practical sense, when we act on our moral values. In general, I think that we can make progress on the question of whether morals are good for us by inquiring into their origins. No outcome to the nativism debate directly entails that morals are justified or unjustified, but the debate may bear on questions of justification nonetheless.

There is a second potential link between innateness and justification that I want to bring out. If there are innate moral principles, then these principles are presumably universal or nearly universal (I'll ignore the possibility that moralities differ genetically across individuals, like personality traits). It's possible that culture can reshape and even override innate principles, but they can serve, at least, as a common denominator. Take two cultural groups that come into conflict because of a moral disagreement. A shared stock of innate morals might be used to settle certain disagreements. The groups might discover that their moral differences derived from the fact that some of their values are cultural constructions, while also recognizing that they are naturally furnished with some overlapping values. These overlapping values could be treated as an impartial common ground. For example, if the two cultures lived in a single nation, they might decide to use the innate morals as the basis for the legal system, which governs all citizens. There is a sense in which this would be justified. The shared values might have no special claim to truth, as compared to the conflicting values, but they might have claim to being a fair basis for adjudication, because they are not biased against either group. In evaluative domains, freedom from bias is often regarded as a kind of objectivity (the view from everywhere, one might say), and objectivity can serve as a surrogate for truth in assessing whether an evaluative claim in justified. Suppose, in contrast, that all values are social constructions. If that is the case, there may be no unbiased common ground, and moral justification will, of necessity, be parochial.

These last considerations may imply that nativism is a more desirable view than non-nativism because it provides us with a resource for resolving some moral debates. In my essay, I tried to counterbalance such advantages by pointing out that a non-nativist position may entail that morality is a tool that can be dramatically changed and improved. In the final section of her commentary, Tiberius addresses this point and argues that once we turn to the project of improving morality, we need some basis for assessing what qualifies as an improvement. This is a normative project, and Tiberius cautions against the view that empirical psychology is the best tool for guiding that project. I want to conclude by indicating how empirical psychology might be put to use in normative philosophy.

I think normative questions always have to be asked from within a system of values. We cannot step outside the values that we already possess and ask what values we should adopt. Normative questions are questions about what we value. If that is right, then psychology can be conducive to normative ends in a number of ways. First, psychology can help us get clear on what things we value. Sometimes our values are not obvious to us. For example, people are not very aware of what leads to well-being. They think that wealth and extremely positive life events are more important than frequent moderate happiness. Tiberius (2004) has reviewed psychological research showing that some of these assumptions are wrong. In order to figure out what we should do, we should use psychological research to help us determine what we really want. Second, psychology can also be used to identify inconsistencies in our values. People have double standards. For example, we cherish human dignity and tolerate brutality. One way to improve morality is to identify evaluative inconsistencies and resolve them; psychology can help in the identification process. Third, psychology can help us see places where our reasoning is unduly influenced by factors that we consider morally insignificant (e.g., geographical distance may lead us to underestimate the moral urgency of assisting the victims of catastrophes in foreign lands). Fourth, psychology can help us identify precise cross-cultural differences in values, and that can aid us in setting an agenda for developing evaluative compromises. Fifth, when we develop new policies or forms of governance that appear to be utopian improvements over what we currently have, psychology can be used to help assess whether the changes would lead to a world that conforms more successfully to our values or, on the contrary, whether the new policies would invite corruption, exploitation, and moral collapse. Sixth, if we want to persuade those whose values differ from our own, it is useful to understand the psychological basis of those values, as well as the historical factors that led to their formation. This list could be extended. My point is that psychology offers techniques that can be very useful in moral improvement. I don't mean to imply that psychology should replace traditional moral philosophy. I mean to suggest that psychology can be an integral part of the normative projects that have traditionally been insulated from the social sciences, on the grounds that the social sciences are "merely descriptive." Psychologists study social influence, racial bias, criminality, reasoning errors, jury deliberation, and the motivations of suicide terrorists. The lessons that have been learned from all this research are descriptive, but they can certainly be of use to those who are engaged in normative projects. I know Tiberius agrees with this, and I welcome her plea for greater collaboration between those who approach ethics empirically and those whose methods have been more traditional in philosophy.

References

Adams, M. S., & Neel, J. V. (1967). Children of incest. *Pediatrics, 40,* 55.

Agrawal, A., Jacobson, K. C., Prescott, C. A., & Kendler, K. S. (2004). A twin study of personality and illicit drug use and abuse/dependence. *Twin Research, 7*(1), 72–81.

Agrawal, N., Sinha, S. N., & Jensen, A. R. (1984). Effects of inbreeding on Raven Matrices. *Behavior Genetics, 14*(6), 579–585.

Alexander, R. D. (1987). *The biology of moral systems.* New York: Aldine de Gruyter.

Allen, E. S., & Baucom, D. H. (2004). Adult attachment and patterns of extradyadic involvement. *Family Processes, 43*(4), 467–488.

Almor, A., & Sloman, S. (1996). Is deontic reasoning special? *Psychological Review, 103,* 374–380.

Aluja, A., & Garcia, L. F. (2005). Sensation seeking, sexual curiosity, and testosterone in inmates. *Neuropsychobiology, 51*(1), 28–33.

Alvard, M., & Gillespie, A. (2004). Good Lamalera whale hunters accrue reproductive benefits. *Socioeconomic Aspects of Human Behavioral Ecology. Research in Economic Anthropology, 23,* 223–245.

Alvard, M., & Nolin, D. A. (2002). Rousseau's whale hunt? Coordination among big-game hunters. *Current Anthropology, 43*(4), 533–559.

Anastasi, A., & Urbina, S. (1997). *Psychological testing* (7th ed.). Upper Saddle River, NJ: Prentice Hall.

Anderson, K. G. (2000). The life histories of American stepfathers in evolutionary perspective. *Human Nature, 11,* 307–333.

Anderson, K. G., Kaplan, H., & Lancaster, J. B. (1999). Paternal care by genetic fathers and stepfathers: I. Reports from Albuquerque men. *Evolution and Human Behavior, 20,* 405–431.

Andersson, M. (1994). *Sexual selection*. Princeton, NJ: Princeton University Press.

Andrews, P. W. (2001). The psychology of social chess and the evolution of attribution mechanisms: Explaining the fundamental attribution error. *Evolution and Human Behavior, 22*, 11–29.

Andrews, P. W., Gangestad, S. W., & Matthews, D. (2003). Adaptationism: How to carry out an exaptationist program. *Behavioral and Brain Sciences, 25*(4), 489–553.

Anestis, S. F. (2004). Female genito-genital rubbing in a group of captive chimpanzees. *International Journal of Primatology, 25*(2), 477–488.

Aquinas, T. (1981). *Summa theologica* (Vols. 1–5, Fathers of the English Dominican Province, Trans.). Grand Rapids, MI: Christian Classics. (Original work written 1265–1273)

Archer, J., & Mehdikhani, M. (2003). Variability among males in sexually selected attributes. *Review of General Psychology, 7*(3), 219–236.

Arendt, H. (1994). *Eichmann in Jerusalem: A report on the banality of evil*. New York: Penguin Books.

Aristotle. (1962). *Nichomachean Ethics* (M. Oswald, Trans.). Englewood Cliffs, NJ: Prentice-Hall.

Arsenault, L., Tremblay, R. E., Boulerice, B., Seguin, J. R., & Saucier, J. F. (2000). Minor physical anomalies and family adversity as risk factors for violent delinquency in adolescence. *American Journal of Psychiatry, 157*(6), 917–923.

Arsenio, W. F., & Lover, A. (1995). Children's conceptions of sociomoral affect: Happy victimizers, mixed emotions and other expectancies. In M. Killen & D. Hart (Eds.), *Morality in everyday life: Developmental perspectives* (pp. 87–128). Cambridge: Cambridge University Press.

Arthur, W., & Graziano, W. G. (1996). The five-factor model, conscientiousness, and driving accident involvement. *Journal of Personality, 64*(3), 593–618.

Asendorpf, J. B., & Wilpers, S. (1998). Personality effects on social relationships. *Journal of Personality and Social Psychology, 74*(6), 1531–1544.

Ashton, M. C., Lee, K., & Paunonen, S. V. (2002). What is the central feature of extraversion? Social attention versus reward sensitivity. *Journal of Personality and Social Psychology, 83*(1), 245–252.

Atran, S. (1998). Folk biology and the anthropology of science: Cognitive universals and cultural particulars. *Behavioral and Brain Sciences, 21*, 547–609.

Audi, R. (Ed.). (1999). *Cambridge dictionary of philosophy* (2nd ed.). Cambridge: Cambridge University Press.

Austin, J. L. (1956). A plea for excuses. *Proceedings of the Aristotelian Society, 57,* 1–30.

Avila, M., Thaker, G., & Adami, H. (2001). Genetic epidemiology and schizophrenia: A study of reproductive fitness. *Schizophrenia Research, 47*(2–3), 233–241.

Axelrod, R. (1984). *The evolution of cooperation.* New York: Basic Books.

Axelrod, R., & Hamilton, W. D. (1981). The evolution of cooperation. *Science, 211,* 1390–1396.

Badaruddoza, B. (2004). Effect of inbreeding on Wechsler intelligence test scores among North Indian children. *Asia-Pacific Journal of Public Health, 16,* 99–103.

Bailey, J. M., Kirk, K. M., Zhu, G., Dunne, M. P., & Martin, N. G. (2000). Do individual differences in sociosexuality represent genetic or environmentally contingent strategies? Evidence from the Australian Twin Registry. *Journal of Personality and Social Psychology, 78*(3), 537–545.

Bailey, M. E. S., & Johnson, K. J. (1997). Synaesthesia: Is a genetic analysis feasible? In S. Baron-Cohen & J. E. Harrison (Eds.), *Synaesthesia* (pp. 182–207). Cambridge: Blackwell.

Bain, A. (1880). *The emotions and the will* (3rd ed.). London: Longmans, Green. (Original work published 1859)

Baird, J. A. (2001). *Motivations and morality: Do children use mental state information to evaluate identical actions differently?* Paper presented to the biennial meeting of the Society for Research in Child Development, Minneapolis, MN.

Baker, M. (2001). *The atoms of language: The mind's hidden rules of grammar.* New York: Basic Books.

Barber, N. (1995). The evolutionary psychology of physical attractiveness, sexual selection, and human morphology. *Ethology and Sociobiology, 16,* 395–424.

Barclay, P. (2004). Trustworthiness and competitive altruism can also solve the "tragedy of the commons." *Evolution and Human Behavior, 25,* 209–220.

Barkow, J., Cosmides, L., & Tooby, J. (Eds.). (1992). *The adapted mind: Evolutionary psychology and the generation of culture.* New York: Oxford University Press.

Baron-Cohen, S. (1995). *Mindblindness: An essay on autism and theory of mind.* Cambridge: MIT Press.

Baron-Cohen, S. (2000). The cognitive neuroscience of autism: Evolutionary approaches. In M. S. Gazzaniga (Ed.), *The new cognitive neurosciences* (2nd ed., pp. 1249–1257). Cambridge: MIT Press.

Barrett, H. C. (1999, June). *Guilty minds: How perceived intent, incentive, and ability to cheat influence social contract reasoning.* Paper presented at the 11th annual meeting of the Human Behavior and Evolution Society, Salt Lake City, UT.

Barrett, H. C. (2005). Enzymatic computation and cognitive modularity. *Mind and Language, 20,* 259–287.

Barrick, M. R., Stewart, G. L., Neubert, M. J., & Mount, M. K. (1998). Relating member ability and personality to work-team processes and team effectiveness. *Journal of Applied Psychology, 83*(3), 377–391.

Baumeister, R. F. (1997). The enigmatic appeal of sexual masochism: Why people desire pain, bondage, and humiliation in sex. *Journal of Social and Clinical Psychology, 16*(2), 133–150.

Baumeister, R. F., & Exline, J. J. (1999). Virtue, personality, and social relations: Self-control as the moral muscle. *Journal of Personality, 67*(6), 1165–1194.

Beaman, C. P. (2002). Why are we good at detecting cheaters? A reply to Fodor. *Cognition, 83,* 215–220.

Beatty, M. J., Heisel, A. D., Hall, A. E., Levine, T. R., & La France, B. H. (2002). What can we learn from the study of twins about genetic and environmental influences on interpersonal affiliation, aggressiveness, and social anxiety? A meta-analytic study. *Communication Monographs, 69*(1), 1–18.

Bentham, J. (1789). *An introduction to the principles of morals and legislation.* London: T. Payne.

Berger, P. J., Negus, N. C., & Day, M. (1997). Recognition of kin and avoidance of inbreeding in the montane vole, *Microtus montanus. Journal of Mammalogy, 78,* 1182–1186.

Berlin, I. (1997). *The proper study of mankind: An anthology of essays.* London: Pimlico.

Berry, D. S., & Miller, K. M. (2001). When boy meets girl: Attractiveness and the five-factor model in opposite-sex interactions. *Journal of Research in Personality, 35*(1), 62–77.

Betzig, L. (1989). Causes of conjugal dissolution: A cross-cultural study. *Current Anthropology, 30*(5), 654–676.

Bevc, I., & Silverman, I. (1993). Early proximity and intimacy between siblings and incestuous behavior: A test of the Westermarck theory. *Ethology and Sociobiology, 14,* 171–181.

Bevc, I., & Silverman, I. (2000). Early separation and sibling incest: A test of the revised Westermarck theory. *Evolution and Human Behavior, 21,* 151–161.

Birbaumer, N., Veit, R., Lotze, M., Erb, M., Hermann, C., Grodd, W., & Flor, H. (2005). Deficient fear conditioning in psychopathy: A functional magnetic resonance imaging study. *Archives of General Psychiatry, 62,* 799–805.

Birdsell, J. B. (1968). Some predictions for the Pleistocene based on equilibrium systems among recent hunter-gatherers. In R. B. Lee & I. DeVore (Eds.), *Man the hunter* (pp. 229–240). New York: Aldine de Gruyter.

Bittles, A. H. (1990). *Consanguineous marriage: Current global incidence and its relevance to demographic research* (Research Report No. 90–186). Ann Arbor: University of Michigan, Population Studies Center.

Bittles, A. H. (2005). Genetic aspects of inbreeding and incest. In A. P. Wolf & W. H. Durham (Eds.), *Inbreeding, incest, and the incest taboo* (pp. 38–60). Palo Alto, CA: Stanford University Press.

Bittles, A. H., & Makov, E. (1988). Inbreeding in human populations: An assessment of the costs. In C. G. N. Mascie-Taylor & A. J. Boyce (Eds.), *Human mating patterns* (pp. 153–167). New York: Cambridge University Press.

Bittles, A. H., & Neel, J. V. (1994). The costs of inbreeding and their implications for variations at the DNA level. *Nature Genetics, 8,* 117–121.

Bixler, R. H. (1992). Why littermates don't: The avoidance of inbreeding depression. *Annual Review of Sex Research, 3,* 291–328.

Black, D. (1998). *The social structure of right and wrong.* San Diego, CA: Academic Press.

Blackburn, S. (1993). Realism, quasi or queasy? In J. Haldane & C. Wright (Eds.), *Reality, representation and projection* (pp. 365–383). New York: Oxford University Press.

Blackburn, S. (1998). *Ruling passions: A theory of practical reasoning.* Oxford: Clarendon Press.

Blair, R. J. R. (1995). A cognitive developmental approach to morality: Investigating the psychopath. *Cognition, 57,* 1–29.

Boas, F. (1955). *Primitive art.* New York: Dover.

Boehm, C. (1996). Emergency decisions, cultural-selection mechanics, and group selection. *Current Anthropology, 37*(5), 763–778.

Boehm, C. (1999). *Hierarchy in the forest.* Cambridge: Harvard University Press.

Bogaert, A. F., & Sadava, S. (2002). Adult attachment and sexual behavior. *Personal Relationships, 9*(2), 191–204.

Bogg, T., & Roberts, B. W. (2004). Conscientiousness and health-related behaviors: A meta-analysis of the leading behavioral contributors to mortality. *Psychological Bulletin, 130*(6), 887–919.

Boone, J. L. (1998). The evolution of magnaminity: When is it better to give than to receive? *Human Nature, 9*(1), 1–21.

Borgia, G. (1995). Complex male display and female choice in the spotted bower-bird: Specialized functions for different bower decorations. *Animal Behavior, 49*, 1291–1301.

Botwin, M. D., Buss, D. M., & Shackelford, T. K. (1997). Personality and mate preferences: Five factors in mate selection and marital satisfaction. *Journal of Personality, 65*(1), 107–136.

Bouchard, G., Lussier, Y., & Sabourin, S. (1999). Personality and marital adjustment: Utility of the five-factor model of personality. *Journal of Marriage and the Family, 61*(3), 651–660.

Bouchard, T. J., & McGue, M. (2003). Genetic and environmental influences on human psychological differences. *Journal of Neurobiology, 54*(1), 4–45.

Bourguignon, E., & Greenbaum, L. (1973). *Diversity and homogeneity in world societies.* New Haven, CT: HRAF Press.

Bouwsma, O. K. (1948). Naturalism. *Journal of Philosophy, 48*, 12–21.

Boyd, R. (1988). Is the repeated prisoner's dilemma a good model of reciprocal altruism? *Ethology and Sociobiology, 9*, 211–222.

Boyd, R., Gintis, H., Bowles, S., & Richerson, P. (2003). The evolution of altruistic punishment. *Proceedings of the National Academy of Sciences, USA, 1006*, 3531–3535.

Boyd, R., & Richerson, P. (1985). *Culture and the evolutionary process.* Chicago: University of Chicago Press.

Boyd, R., & Richerson, P. J. (1990). Group selection among alternative evolutionarily stable strategies. *Journal of Theoretical Biology, 145*, 331–342.

Boyd, R., & Richerson, P. (Forthcoming). *Not only in our genes.*

Boyd, R., & Silk, J. B. (1997). *How humans evolved.* New York: Norton.

Boyd, S. K., & Blaustein, A. R. (1985). Familiarity and inbreeding avoidance in the gray-tailed vole (*Microtus canicaudus*). *Journal of Mammalogy, 66*, 348–352.

Boyer, P. (2001) *Religion explained: The evolutionary origins of religious thought.* New York: Basic Books.

Boyer, P., & Lienard, P. (2006). Why ritualized behavior? Precaution systems and action parsing in developmental, pathological, and cultural rituals. *Behavioral and Brain Sciences, 29*(6), 595–650.

Bradbury, J. W., & Vehrencamp, S. L. (1998). *Principles of animal communication.* Sunderland, MA: Sinauer.

Brady, M. S., & Pritchard, D. H. (Eds.). (2003). *Moral and epistemic virtues.* Oxford: Basil Blackwell.

Braitenberg, V. (1986). *Vehicles: Experiments in synthetic psychology.* Cambridge: MIT Press.

Brandt, R. (1990). The science of man and wide reflective equilibrium. *Ethics, 100,* 259–278.

Brase, G., Cosmides, L., & Tooby, J. (1998). Individuation, counting and statistical inference: The role of frequency and whole object representations in judgment under uncertainty. *Journal of Experimental Psychology: General, 127,* 1–19.

Brosnan, S. F., & de Waal, F. B. M. (2003). Monkeys reject unequal pay. *Nature, 425,* 297–299.

Brosnan, S. F., & de Waal, F. B. M. (2004). Brosnan and de Waal reply. *Nature, 428,* 140.

Brower, B. (1993). Dispositional ethical realism. *Ethics, 103,* 221–249.

Brown, D. (1991). *Human universals.* New York: McGraw-Hill.

Bugental, D. B. (2000). Acquisition of the algorithms of social life: A domain-based approach. *Psychological Bulletin, 26,* 187–209.

Buller, D. (2005). *Adapting minds: Evolutionary psychology and the persistent quest for human nature.* Cambridge: MIT Press.

Burnham, J. T. (1975). Incest avoidance and social evolution. *Mankind, 10,* 93–98.

Buss, D. M. (1989). Sex differences in human mate selection: Evolutionary hypotheses tested in 37 cultures. *Behavioral and Brain Sciences, 12*(1), 1–49.

Buss, D. M. (1994). *The evolution of desire: Strategies of human mating.* New York: Basic Books/HarperCollins.

Buss, D. M. (2000). *The dangerous passion.* New York: Free Press.

Buss, D. M. (Ed.). (2005). *The handbook of evolutionary psychology.* Hoboken, NJ: Wiley.

Buss, D. M., & Dedden, L. A. (1990). Derogation of competitors. *Journal of Social and Personal Relationships, 7*(3), 395–422.

Buss, D. M., & Schmitt, D. P. (1993). Sexual strategies theory: An evolutionary perspective on human mating. *Psychological Review, 100*(2), 204–232.

Buss, D. M., & Shackelford, T. K. (1997). From vigilance to violence: Mate retention tactics in married couples. *Journal of Personality and Social Psychology, 72*(2), 346–361.

Byers, E. S., & Demmons, S. (1999). Sexual satisfaction and sexual self-disclosure within dating relationships. *Journal of Sex Research, 36*(2), 180–189.

Byrnes, J. P., Miller, D. C., & Schafer, W. D. (1999). Gender differences in risk taking: A meta-analysis. *Psychological Bulletin, 125,* 367–383.

Carey, S., & Xu, F. (2001). Infants' knowledge of objects: Beyond object files and object tracking. *Cognition, 80*(1–2), 179–213.

Carlo, G., Okun, M. A., Knight, G. P., & de Guzman, M. R. T. (2005). The interplay of traits and motives on volunteering: Agreeableness, extraversion, and prosocial value motivation. *Personality and Individual Differences, 38*(6), 1293–1305.

Carruthers, P., Laurence, S., & Stich, S. (Eds.). (2007). *The innate mind: Structure and contents.* New York: Oxford University Press.

Carter, C. O. (1967). Risk of offspring of incest. *Lancet, 1,* 436.

Casebeer, W. D. (2003a). Evolutionary ethics: An argument for "new wave" Aristotelianism. *Politics and the Life Sciences, 22,* 67–70.

Casebeer, W. D. (2003b). *Natural ethical facts: Evolution, connectionism, and moral cognition.* Cambridge: MIT Press.

Casebeer, W. D. (2005). Scientific ethics. In C. Mitcham (Ed.), *Encyclopedia of science, technology, and ethics* (Vol. 4, pp. 1726–1732). Woodbridge, CT: MacMillan Reference USA.

Cashdan, E. (1989). Hunters and gatherers: Economic behavior in bands. In S. Plattner (Ed.), *Economic anthropology.* Palo Alto, CA: Stanford University Press.

Castañeda, H.-N. (1981). The paradoxes of deontic logic: The simplest solution to all of them in one fell swoop. In R. Hilpinen (Ed.), *New studies in deontic logic* (pp. 37–85). Dordrecht, the Netherlands: D. Reidel.

Caughlin, J. P., Huston, T. L., & Houts, R. M. (2000). How does personality matter in marriage? An examination of trait anxiety, interpersonal negativity, and marital satisfaction. *Journal of Personality and Social Psychology, 78*(2), 326–336.

Chagnon, N. A. (1992). *Yanomamö: The last days of Eden* (4th ed.). San Diego, CA: Harcourt Brace Javanovich.

Chandler, M., Sokol, B., & Wainryb, C. (2000). Beliefs about truth and beliefs about rightness. *Child Development, 71*(1), 91–97.

Chapman, R. S., & Hesketh, L. J. (2000). Behavioral phenotype of individuals with Down syndrome. *Mental Retardation and Developmental Disabilities Research Reviews, 6*(2), 84–95.

Cheng, P., & Holyoak, K. (1985). Pragmatic reasoning schemas. *Cognitive Psychology, 17*, 391–416.

Cheng, P., & Holyoak, K. (1989). On the natural selection of reasoning theories. *Cognition, 33*, 285–313.

Cheng, P., Holyoak, K., Nisbett, R., & Oliver, L. (1986). Pragmatic versus syntactic approaches to training deductive reasoning. *Cognitive Psychology, 18*, 293–328.

Cherkas, L. F., Oelsner, E. C., Mak, Y. T., Valdes, A., & Spector, T. D. (2004). Genetic influences on female infidelity and number of sexual partners in humans: A linkage and association study on the role of the vasopressin receptor gene (AVPR1A). *Twin Research, 7*, 649–658.

Chisholm, R. (1966). Freedom and action. In K. Lehrer (Ed.), *Freedom and determinism* (pp. 11–44). New York: Random House.

Chomsky, N. (1965). *Aspects of the theory of syntax*. Cambridge: MIT Press.

Chomsky, N. (1986). *Knowledge of language: Its nature, origin, and use*. Westport, CT: Praeger.

Chomsky, N. (1988). *Language and problems of knowledge*. Cambridge: MIT Press.

Church, R. M. (1959). Emotional reactions of rats to the pain of others. *Journal of Comparative and Physiological Psychology, 52*, 132–134.

Churchland, P. (2002). *Brain-wise: Studies in neurophilosophy*. Cambridge: MIT Press.

Cicero, M. T. (1945). *Tusculan disputations* (2nd ed., J. E. King, Trans.). Cambridge: Harvard University Press.

Cleckley, H. M. (1941). *The mask of sanity: An attempt to reinterpret the so-called psychopathic personality*. St Louis, MO: Mosby.

Clement, U. (2002). Sex in long-term relationships: A systemic approach to sexual desire problems. *Archives of Sexual Behavior, 31*(3), 241–246.

Clutton-Brock, T. H., & Albon, S. D. (1979). The roaring of red deer and the evolution of honest advertisement. *Behaviour 69*, 145–170.

Code, L. (1987). *Epistemic responsibility*. Hanover, NH: University Press of New England.

Coid, J. W. (2003). The co-morbidity of personality disorder and lifetime clinical syndromes in dangerous offenders. *Journal of Forensic Psychiatry & Psychology, 14*(2), 341–366.

Colby, A., Kohlberg, L., Gibbs, J., & Lieberman, M. (1983). A longitudinal study of moral judgment. *Monographs of the Society for Research in Child Development, 48*(1–2), 1–124.

Collins, J. (2004). Faculty disputes. *Mind and Language, 19*, 503–533.

Conniff, R. (2002). *The natural history of the rich: A field guide.* New York: Norton.

Connor, R. C., Smolker, R. A., & Richards, A. F. (1992). 2 levels of alliance formation among male bottle-nosed dolphins (*Tursiops sp.*). *Proceedings of the National Academy of Sciences, USA, 89*(3), 987–990.

Cooke, D. J., & Michie, C. (1999). Psychopathy across cultures: North America and Scotland compared. *Journal of Abnormal Psychology, 108*(1), 58–68.

Cooke, D. J., Michie, C., Hart, S. D., & Clark, D. (2005). Searching for the pan-cultural core of psychopathic personality disorder. *Personality and Individual Differences, 39*(2), 283–295.

Corballis, M. C. (2002). *From hand to mouth: The origins of language.* Princeton, NJ: Princeton University Press.

Corrigan, P. W. (2000). Mental health stigma as social attribution: Implications for research methods and attitude change. *Clinical Psychology: Science and Practice, 7*(1), 48–67.

Cosmides, L. (1985). *Deduction or Darwinian algorithms? An explanation of the "elusive" content effect on the Wason selection task.* Doctoral dissertation, Department of Psychology, Harvard University (UMI No. 86–02206).

Cosmides, L. (1989). The logic of social exchange: Has natural selection shaped how humans reason? Studies with the Wason selection task. *Cognition, 31*, 187–276.

Cosmides, L., & Tooby, J. (1987). From evolution to behavior: Evolutionary psychology as the missing link. In J. Dupre (Ed.), *The latest on the best: Essays on evolution and optimality* (pp. 277–306). Cambridge: MIT Press.

Cosmides, L., & Tooby, J. (1989). Evolutionary psychology and the generation of culture: I. Case study: A computational theory of social exchange. *Ethology and Sociobiology, 10*, 51–97.

Cosmides, L., & Tooby, J. (1992). Cognitive adaptations for social exchange. In J. Barkow, L. Cosmides, & J. Tooby (Eds.), *The adapted mind* (pp. 163–228). New York: Oxford University Press.

Cosmides, L., & Tooby, J. (1996a). Are humans good intuitive statisticians after all? Rethinking some conclusions of the literature on judgment under uncertainty. *Cognition, 58*, 1–73.

Cosmides, L., & Tooby, J. (1996b). A logical design for the mind? (Review of *The Psychology of Proof*, by L. J. Rips.) *Contemporary Psychology, 41*(5), 448–450.

Cosmides, L., & Tooby, J. (1997). Dissecting the computational architecture of social inference mechanisms. In G. R. Bock & G. Cardew (Eds.), *Characterizing human psychological adaptations (Ciba Foundation Symposium #208)* (pp. 132–156). Chichester, England: Wiley.

Cosmides, L., & Tooby, J. (1999). Towards an evolutionary taxonomy of treatable conditions. *Journal of Abnormal Psychology, 108*, 453–464.

Cosmides, L., & Tooby, J. (2000a). Evolutionary psychology and the emotions. In M. Lewis & J. M. Haviland-Jones (Eds.), *Handbook of emotions* (2nd ed., pp. 91–115). New York: Guilford Press.

Cosmides, L., & Tooby, J. (2000b). Consider the source: The evolution of adaptations for decoupling and metarepresentation. In D. Sperber (Ed.), *Metarepresentations: A multidisciplinary perspective* (pp. 53–115). New York: Oxford University Press.

Cosmides, L., & Tooby, J. (2004). Knowing thyself: The evolutionary psychology of moral reasoning and moral sentiments. In R. E. Freeman & P. Werhane (Eds.), *Business, science, and ethics.* (pp. 93–128). Charlottesville, VA: Society for Business Ethics.

Cosmides, L., & Tooby, J. (2005a). Neurocognitive adaptations designed for social exchange. In D. M. Buss (Ed.), *Evolutionary psychology handbook* (pp. 584–627). New York: Wiley.

Cosmides, L., & Tooby, J. (2005b). Social exchange: The evolutionary design of a neurocognitive system. In M. S. Gazzaniga (Ed.), *The new cognitive neurosciences, III.* (pp. 1295–1308). Cambridge: MIT Press.

Cosmides, L., & Tooby, J. (2006). Evolutionary psychology, moral heuristics, and the law. In G. Gigerenzer & C. Engel (Eds.), *Heuristics and the law* (pp. 181–212). Cambridge: MIT Press.

Cosmides, L., Tooby, J., Montaldi, A., & Thrall, N. (1999, June). *Character counts: Cheater detection is relaxed for honest individuals.* Paper presented at the Human Behavior and Evolution Society, Salt Lake City, UT.

Cosmides, L., Barrett, H. C., & Tooby, J. (Forthcoming). Social contracts elicit the detection of intentional cheaters, not innocent mistakes.

Cosmides, L., Sell, A., Tooby, J., Thrall, N., & Montaldi, A. (Forthcoming). Character counts: Domain-specific effects of character information on reasoning about social exchange and precautionary rules.

Cowie, F. (1999). *What's within? Nativism reconsidered.* New York: Oxford University Press.

Craig, W. L., & Sinnott-Armstrong, W. (2004). *God? A debate between a Christian and an atheist.* New York: Oxford University Press.

Crain, S., & Pietroski, P. M. (2001). Nature, nurture and universal grammar. *Linguistics and Philosophy, 24*, 139–186.

Crespi, B. J. (2004). Vicious circles: Positive feedback in major evolutionary and ecological transitions. *Trends in Ecology & Evolution, 19*(12), 627–633.

Crisp, A. H., Gelder, M. G., Rix, S., Meltzer, H. I., & Rowlands, O. J. (2000). Stigmatisation of people with mental illnesses. *British Journal of Psychiatry, 177*, 4–7.

Cristopher, F. S., Owens, L. A., & Stecker, H. L. (1993). Exploring the dark side of courtship: A test of a model of male premarital sexual aggressiveness. *Journal of Marriage and the Family, 55*(2), 469–479.

Cronin, H. (1991). *The ant and the peacock: Altruism and sexual selection from Darwin to today.* Cambridge: Cambridge University Press.

Crow, J. F. (2000). The origins, patterns, and implications of human spontaneous mutation. *Nature Reviews Genetics, 1*(1), 40–47.

Cushman, F., Young, L., & Hauser, M. (2006). The role of reasoning and intuition in moral judgments: Testing three principles of harm. *Psychological Science, 17*(12), 1082–1089.

D'Onofrio, B. M., Eaves, L. J., Murrelle, L., Maes, H. H., & Spilka, B. (1999). Understanding biological and social influences on religious affiliation, attitudes, and behaviors: A behavior genetic perspective. *Journal of Personality, 67*(6), 953–984.

Daly, M., & Wilson, M. (1988). *Homicide.* Hawthorne, NY: Aldine de Gruyter.

Daly, M., & Wilson, M. (2001). Risk-taking, intrasexual competition, and homicide. In J. A. French, A. C. Kamil, & D. W. Leger (Eds.), *Evolutionary psychology and motivation* (pp. 1–36). Lincoln: University of Nebraska Press.

Daly, M., Salmon, C., & Wilson, M. (1997). Kinship: The conceptual hole in psychological studies of social cognition and close relationships. In J. A. Simpson & D. T. Kenrick (Eds.), *Evolutionary social psychology* (pp. 265–298). Hillsdale, NJ: Erlbaum.

Dancy, J. (2004). *Ethics without principles.* New York: Oxford University Press.

Daniels, N. (Ed). (1996). *Justice and justification: Reflective equilibrium in theory and practice.* Cambridge: Cambridge University Press.

Darley, J., Klosson, E., & Zanna, M. (1978). Intentions and their contexts in the moral judgments of children and adults. *Child Development, 49*, 66–74.

Darley, J., & Shultz, T. R. (1990). Moral rules: Their content and acquisition. *Annual Review of Psychology, 41*, 525–556.

Darwin, C. (1998). *The expression of the emotions in man and animals* (3rd ed.). London: John Murray/HarperCollins. (Original work published 1872)

Darwin, C. (2004). *The descent of man, and selection in relation to sex.* London: Penguin Books. (Original work published 1871)

Das, M. (2000). Conflict management via third parties: Post-conflict affiliation of the aggressor. In F. Aureli & F. B. M. de Waal (Eds.), *Natural conflict resolution* (pp. 263–280). Berkeley: University of California Press.

Davis, M. H., Luce, C., & Kraus, S. J. (1994). The heritability of characteristics associated with dispositional empathy. *Journal of Personality, 62*(3), 369–391.

Dawkins, R. (1976). *The selfish gene.* Oxford: Oxford University Press.

Dawkins, R. (1982). *The extended phenotype: The gene as the unit of selection.* Oxford: W. H. Freeman.

Dawkins, R. (1996). *The blind watchmaker: Why the evidence of evolution reveals a universe without design.* New York: Norton.

Dawson, T. L. (2002). New tools, new insights: Kohlberg's moral reasoning stages revisited. *International Journal of Behavioral Development, 26,* 154–166.

Deary, I. (2000). *Looking down on human intelligence.* Oxford: Oxford University Press.

DeBruine, L. M. (2002). Facial resemblance enhances trust. *Proceedings: Biological Sciences, 269,* 1307–1312.

DeNeve, K. M., & Cooper, H. (1998). The happy personality: A meta-analysis of 137 personality traits and subjective well-being. *Psychological Bulletin, 124*(2), 197–229.

Dennett, D. C. (1984). *Elbow room: The varieties of free will worth wanting.* Cambridge: MIT Press.

Dennett, D. C. (2003). *Freedom evolves.* New York: Viking.

DePaul, M., & Zagzebski, L. (Eds.). (2003). *Intellectual virtue: Perspectives from ethics and epistemology.* Oxford: Clarendon Press.

DePaulo, B. M., & Kashy, D. A. (1998). Everyday lies in close and casual relationships. *Journal of Personality and Social Psychology, 74*(1), 63–79.

Dewey, J. (1922). *Human nature and conduct: An introduction to social psychology.* New York: Modern Library.

Dollinger, S. J., Leong, F. T. L., & Ulicni, S. K. (1996). On traits and values, with special reference to openness to experience. *Journal of Research in Personality, 30*(1), 23–41.

Donald, M. (1991). *Origins of the modern mind: Three stages in the evolution of culture and cognition.* Cambridge: Harvard University Press.

Donnellan, M. B., Conger, R. D., & Bryant, C. M. (2004). The Big Five and enduring marriages. *Journal of Research in Personality, 38*(5), 481–504.

Dorfman, R., & Steiner, P. O. (1954). Optimal advertising and optimal quality. *American Economic Review, 44,* 826–836.

Du Fort, G. G., Boothroyd, L. J., Bland, R. C., Newman, S. C., & Kakuma, R. (2002). Spouse similarity for antisocial behaviour in the general population. *Psychological Medicine, 32*(8), 1407–1416.

Duchaine, B., Cosmides, L., & Tooby, J. (2001). Evolutionary psychology and the brain. *Current Opinion in Neurobiology, 11*(2), 225–230.

Dummett, M. (1976). What is a theory of meaning? II. In G. Evans & J. McDowell (Eds.), *Truth and meaning* (pp. 67–137). Oxford: Clarendon Press.

Durham, W. H. (1991). *Coevolution.* Palo Alto, CA: Stanford University Press.

Durham, W. H. (2005). Assessing the gaps in Westermarck's theory. In A. P. Wolf & W. H. Durham (Eds.), *Inbreeding, incest, and the incest taboo* (pp. 121–138). Palo Alto, CA: Stanford University Press.

Durkheim, E. (1953). *Sociology and philosophy.* New York: Free Press. (Original work published 1903)

Dworkin, R. M. (1993). *Life's dominion.* New York: Knopf.

Dwyer, S. (1999). Moral competence. In K. Murasugi & R. Stainton (Eds.), *Philosophy and linguistics* (pp. 169–190). Boulder, CO: Westview Press.

Dwyer, S. (2006). How good is the linguistic analogy? In P. Carruthers, S. Laurence & S. Stich (Eds.), *The innate mind: Vol. 2: Culture and cognition.* New York: Oxford University Press.

Eaton, M. M. (1992). Integrating the aesthetic and the moral. *Philosophical Studies, 67,* 219–240.

Edgerton, R. B. (1992). *Sick societies: Challenging the myth of primitive harmony.* New York: Free Press.

Edwards, C. P. (1980). The development of moral reasoning in cross-cultural perspective. In R. H. Munroe & B. B. Whiting (Eds.), *Handbook of cross-cultural human development.* New York: Garland Press.

Edwards, C. P. (1987). Culture and the construction of moral values: A comparative ethnography of moral encounters in two cultural settings. In J. Kagan & S. Lamb (Eds.), *The emergence of morality in young children* (pp. 123–150). Chicago: University of Chicago Press.

Ekehammar, B., Akrami, N., Gylie, M., & Zakrisson, I. (2004). What matters most to prejudice: Big Five personality, social dominance orientation, or right-wing authoritarianism? *European Journal of Personality, 18*(6), 463–482.

El-Hamzi, M., Al-Swailem, A., Warsy, A., Al-Swailem, A., & Sulaimani, R. (1995). Consanguinity among the Saudi Arabian population. *American Journal of Medical Genetics, 32*, 623–626.

Eley, T. C., Lichtenstein, P., & Moffitt, T. E. (2003). A longitudinal behavioral genetic analysis of the etiology of aggressive and nonaggressive antisocial behavior. *Development and Psychopathology, 15*(2), 383–402.

Ellis, B. J. (1992). The evolution of sexual attraction: Evaluative mechanisms in women. In J. H. Barkow, L. Cosmides, & J. Tooby (Eds.), *The adapted mind: Evolutionary psychology and the generation of culture* (pp. 267–288). New York: Oxford University Press.

Ellis, B. J., & Malamuth, N. M. (2000). Love and anger in romantic relationships: A discrete systems model. *Journal of Personality, 68*, 525–556.

Ellis, L. (2001). The biosocial female choice theory of social stratification. *Social Biology, 48*(3–4), 298–320.

Engel, G., Olson, K. R., & Patrick, C. (2002). The personality of love: Fundamental motives and traits related to components of love. *Personality and Individual Differences, 32*(5), 839–853.

Enoch, D. (2005). Why idealize? *Ethics, 115*, 759–787.

Ermer, E., Guerin, S., Cosmides, L., Tooby, J., Miller M. (2006). Theory of mind broad and narrow: Reasoning about social exchange engages TOM areas, precautionary reasoning does not. *Social Neuroscience, 1*(3–4), 196–219.

Evans, E. M. (2000). Beyond Scopes: Why creationism is here to stay. In K. Rosengren, C. Johnson, & P. Harris (Eds.), *Imagining the impossible: Magical, scientific, and religious thinking in children* (pp. 305–331). Cambridge: Cambridge University Press.

Evans, J. St. B. T. (1989). *Bias in human reasoning: Causes and consequences.* Hillsdale, NJ: Erlbaum.

Eyre-Walker, A., & Keightley, P. D. (1999). High genomic deleterious mutation rates in hominids. *Nature, 397*, 344–346.

Fallon, A. E., & Rozin, P. (1983). The psychological bases of food rejections by humans. *Ecology of Food and Nutrition, 13*, 15–26.

Farthing, G. W. (2005). Attitudes towards heroic and nonheroic physical risk takers as mates and friends. *Evolution and Human Behavior, 26*, 171–185.

Fazio, R. H., & Olson, M. A. (2003). Implicit measures in social cognition research: Their meaning and use. *Annual Review of Psychology, 54,* 297–327.

Fedora, O., & Reddon, J. R. (1993). Psychopathic and nonpsychopathic inmates differ from normal controls in tolerance to electrical stimulation. *Journal of Clinical Psychology, 49,* 326–331.

Fehr, E., & Fischbacher, U. (2004). Social norms and human cooperation. *Trends in Cognitive Sciences, 8*(4), 185–190.

Fehr, E., & Gächter, S. (2002). Altruistic punishment in humans. *Nature, 415,* 137–140.

Feigenson, L., Carey, S., & Hauser, M. (2002). The representations underlying infants' choice of more: Object files versus analog magnitudes. *Psychological Science, 13*(2), 150–156.

Fein, R. A., & Vossekuil, B. (1999). Assassination in the United States: An operational study of recent assassins, attackers, and near-lethal approaches. *Journal of Forensic Sciences, 44*(2), 321–333.

Feldman, F. (2001). Logic and ethics. In L. C. Becker & C. B. Becker (Eds.), *Encyclopedia of ethics* (2nd ed., Vol. 2, pp. 1011–1017). New York: Routledge.

Feng, D., & Baker, L. (1994). Spouse similarity in attitudes, personality, and psychological well-being. *Behavior Genetics, 24*(4), 357–364.

Fessler, D. M. T., and Navarette, C. D. (2003). Meat is good to taboo: Dietary prescriptions as a product of the interaction of psychological mechanisms and social processes. *Journal of Cognition and Culture, 3*(1), 1–40.

Fessler, D. M. T., & Navarrete, C. D. (2004). Third-party attitudes toward sibling incest: Evidence for Westermarck's hypotheses. *Evolution and Human Behavior, 25,* 277–294.

Fiddick, L. (1998). *The deal and the danger: An evolutionary analysis of deontic reasoning.* Doctoral dissertation, Department of Psychology, University of California, Santa Barbara.

Fiddick, L. (2003). Is there a faculty of deontic reasoning? A critical re-evaluation of abstract deontic versions of the Wason selection task. In D. Over (Ed.), *Evolution and the psychology of thinking: The debate* (pp. 33–60). Hove, England: Psychology Press.

Fiddick, L. (2004). Domains of deontic reasoning: Resolving the discrepancy between the cognitive and moral reasoning literatures. *Quarterly Journal of Experimental Psychology, 57A*(4), 447–474.

Fiddick, L., Cosmides, L., & Tooby, J. (2000). No interpretation without representation: The role of domain-specific representations and inferences in the Wason selection task. *Cognition 77,* 1–79.

Fiddick, L., & Rutherford, M. (2006). Looking for loss in all the wrong places: Loss-avoidance does not explain cheater detection. *Evolution and Human Behavior, 27*(6), 417–432.

Fiddick, L., Spampinato, M.V., & Grafman, J. (2005). Social contracts and precautions activate different neurological systems: An fMRI investigation of deontic reasoning. *NeuroImage, 28,* 778–786.

Field, T., & Walden, T. (1982). Production and discrimination of facial expressions by preschool children. *Child Development, 53,* 1299–1311.

Fincham, F. D., Beach, S. R. H., & Davila, J. (2004). Forgiveness and conflict resolution in marriage. *Journal of Family Psychology, 18*(1), 72–81.

Fink, B., & Penton-Voak, I. (2002). Evolutionary psychology of facial attractiveness. *Current Directions in Psychological Science, 11*(5), 154–158.

Finkel, E. J., & Campbell, W. K. (2001). Self-control and accommodation in close relationships: An interdependence analysis. *Journal of Personality and Social Psychology, 81*(2), 263–277.

Finkel, N., Liss, M., & Moran, V. (1997). Equal or proportionate justice for accessories? Children's pearls of proportionate wisdom. *Journal of Applied Developmental Psychology, 18,* 229–244.

Fiske, A. P. (1991). *Structures of social life: The four elementary forms of human relations.* New York: Free Press.

Flanagan, O. (1991). *Varieties of moral personality: Ethics and psychological realism.* Cambridge: Harvard University Press.

Flanagan, O. (1995). Ethics naturalized: Ethics as human ecology. In L. May, M. Friedman, & A. Clark (Eds.), *Mind and morals* (pp. 19–44). Cambridge: MIT Press.

Flanagan, O. (2002). *The problem of the soul: Two visions of mind and how to reconcile them.* New York: Basic Books.

Fodor, J. (1983). *The modularity of mind.* Cambridge: MIT Press.

Fodor, J. (1985). Precis of modularity of mind. *Behavioral and Brain Sciences, 8*(1), 1–42.

Fodor, J. (2000). Why we are so good at catching cheaters. *Cognition, 75,* 29–32.

Fodor, J. (2001). *The mind doesn't work that way: The scope and limits of computational psychology.* Cambridge: MIT Press.

Foot, P. (1967). The problem of abortion and the doctrine of double effect. *Oxford Review, 5,* 5–15.

Foster, E. K. (2004). Research on gossip: Taxonomy, methods, and future directions. *Review of General Psychology, 8*(2), 78–99.

Foster, L. (1991). *Women, family, and utopia: Communal experiments of the Shakers, the Oneida community and the Mormons.* Syracuse, NY: Syracuse University Press.

Frank, R. (1988). *Passions within reason: The strategic role of the emotions.* New York: Norton.

Frank, R. (1999). *Luxury fever: Why money fails to satisfy in an era of excess.* Princeton, NJ: Princeton University Press.

Frazer, J. G. (1910). *Totemism and exogamy.* Oxford: Macmillan. (Original work published 1908)

Freud, S. (1953). *A general introduction to psychoanalysis.* New York: Pocket Books. (Original work published 1920)

Freud, S. (1950). *Totem and taboo.* New York: Norton. (Original work published 1913)

Freund, K., & Seto, M. C. (1998). Preferential rape in the theory of courtship disorder. *Archives of Sexual Behavior, 27*(5), 433–443.

Funder, D. C. (2004). *The personality puzzle* (3rd ed.). New York: Norton.

Furnham, A., & Cheng, H. (1999). Personality as a predictor of mental health and happiness in the East and West. *Personality and Individual Differences, 27*(3), 395–403.

Gallistel, C. R. (2000). The replacement of general purpose learning models with adaptively specialized learning modules. In M. S. Gazzaniga (Ed.), *The cognitive neurosciences* (2nd ed., pp. 1179–1191). Cambridge: MIT Press.

Gangestad, S. W., & Simpson, J. (2000). The evolution of human mating: Trade-offs and strategic pluralism. *Behavioral and Brain Sciences, 23,* 573–644.

Gangestad, S. W., & Thornhill, R. (1999). Individual differences in developmental precision and fluctuating asymmetry: A model and its implications. *Journal of Evolutionary Biology, 12,* 402–416.

Gangestad, S. W., Simpson, J. A., Cousins, A. J., Garver-Apgar, C. E., & Christensen, P. N. (2004). Women's preferences for male behavioral displays change across the menstrual cycle. *Psychological Science, 15,* 203–207.

Gardner, H. (1993). *Frames of mind: The theory of multiple intelligences.* New York: Basic Books.

Geary, D. C. (2000). Evolution and proximate expression of human paternal investment. *Psychological Bulletin, 126*(1), 55–77.

Geary, D. C., Vigil, J., & Byrd-Craven, J. (2004). Evolution of human mate choice. *Journal of Sex Research, 41*(1), 27–42.

Geertz, C. J. (1973). *The interpretation of cultures.* New York: Harper.

Gendler, T. (2000). The puzzle of imaginative resistance. *The Journal of Philosophy, 97(2),* 55–81.

Gendler, T. (2003). On the relation between pretense and belief. In D. M. Lopes & M. Kieran (Eds.), *Imagination, philosophy, and the arts* (pp. 125–141). New York: Routledge.

Gert, B. (2005a). Moral arrogance and moral theories. *Nous-Supplement, 15,* 368–385.

Gert, B. (2005b). *Morality: Its nature and justification* (Rev. ed.). New York: Oxford University Press.

Gibbard, A. (1990). *Wise Choices, Apt Feelings: A Theory of Normative Judgment.* Cambridge, Mass.: Harvard University Press.

Gibbard, A. (2003). *Thinking How to Live.* Cambridge, Mass.: Harvard University Press.

Gigerenzer, G. (2000). *Adaptive thinking: Rationality in the real world.* London: Oxford University Press.

Gigerenzer, G., & Hug, K. (1992). Domain specific reasoning: Social contracts, cheating, and perspective change. *Cognition, 43,* 127–171.

Gigerenzer, G., Todd, P. M., & ABC Research Group (Eds.). (1999). *Simple heuristics that make us smart.* Cambridge: MIT Press.

Gilbert, S. L., Dobyns, W. B., & Lahn, B. T. (2005). Genetic links between brain development and brain evolution. *Nature Reviews Genetics, 6,* 581–590.

Gill, M. (2006). *The British moralists on human nature and the birth of secular ethics.* New York: Cambridge University Press.

Gilligan, C. (1982). *In a different voice.* Cambridge: Harvard University Press.

Gintis, H. (2000). Strong reciprocity and human sociality. *Journal of Theoretical Biology, 206,* 169–179.

Gintis, H., Bowles, S., Boyd, R. T., & Fehr, E. (Eds.). (2005). *Moral sentiments and material interests: The foundations of cooperation in economic life.* Cambridge: MIT Press.

Gintis, H., Smith, E., & Bowles, S. (2001). Cooperation and costly signaling. *Journal of Theoretical Biology, 213,* 103–119.

Godfrey Smith, P. (1994). A modern history theory of functions. *Noûs, 28,* 344–362.

Gold, L., Darley, J., Hilton, J., & Zanna, M. (1984). Children's perceptions of procedural justice. *Child Development, 55,* 1752–1759.

Goldberg, L. R. (1990). An alternative description of personality: The Big-5 factor structure. *Journal of Personality and Social Psychology, 59*(6), 1216–1229.

Goldberg, T. L. (1995). Altruism towards panhandlers: Who gives? *Human Nature,* 6(1), 79–89.

Goldin-Meadow, S., McNeill, D., & Singleton, J. (1996). Silence is liberating: Removing the handcuffs on grammatical expression in the manual modality. *Psychological Review, 103*(1), 34–55.

Goldman, A. (1986). *Epistemology and cognition.* Cambridge: Harvard University Press.

Goldman, A. (1992). *Liaisons: Philosophy meets the cognitive and social sciences.* Cambridge: MIT Press.

Goldman, A., & Sripada, C. S. (2005). Simulationist models of face-based emotion recognition. *Cognition, 94,* 193–213.

Gonzaga, G. C., Keltner, D., Londahl, E. A., & Smith, M. D. (2001). Love and the commitment problem in romantic relations and friendship. *Journal of Personality and Social Psychology, 81*(2), 247–262.

Gordon, R. A. (1997). Everyday life as an intelligence test: Effects of intelligence and intelligence context. *Intelligence, 24*(1), 203–320.

Gordon, R. D., & Irwin, D. E. (1996). What's in an object file? Evidence from priming studies. *Perception & Psychophysics, 58*(8), 1260–1277.

Gordon, R. D., & Irwin, D. E. (2000). The role of physical and conceptual properties in preserving object continuity. *Journal of Experimental Psychology: Learning, Memory, and Cognition, 26*(1), 136–150.

Gosling, S. D. (2001). From mice to men: What can we learn about personality from animal research? *Psychological Bulletin, 127,* 45–86.

Gottfredson, L. S. (1997). Why *g* matters: The complexity of everyday life. *Intelligence,* 24(1), 79–132.

Gottfredson, L. S. (2004). Intelligence: Is it the epidemiologists' elusive "fundamental cause" of social class inequalities in health? *Journal of Personality and Social Psychology, 86*(1), 174–199.

Gottfredson, L. S., & Deary, I. J. (2004). Intelligence predicts health and longevity, but why? *Current Directions in Psychological Science, 13*(1), 1–4.

Gottman, J. M., Coan, J., Carrere, S., & Swanson, C. (1998). Predicting marital happiness and stability from newlywed interactions. *Journal of Marriage and the Family,* 60(1), 5–22.

Gould, S. J. (1989). *Wonderful life: The Burgess shale and the nature of history.* New York: Norton.

Gould, S. J., & Lewontin, R. C. (1979). The spandrels of San Marco and the Panglossian paradigm: A critique of the Adaptationist Programme. *Proceedings of the Royal Society of London, B, 205*(1161), 581–598.

Grammer, K., Fink, B., Moller, A. P., & Thornhill, R. (2003). Darwinian aesthetics: Sexual selection and the biology of beauty. *Biological Reviews, 78*(3), 385–407.

Grant, B. F., Hasin, D. S., Stinson, F. S., Dawson, D. A., Chou, S. P., Ruan, W. J., & Pickering, R. P. (2004). Prevalence, correlates, and disability of personality disorders in the United States: Results from the National Epidemiologic Survey on Alcohol and Related Conditions. *Journal of Clinical Psychiatry, 65*(7), 948–958.

Greco, J. (2000). *Putting skeptics in their place.* New York: Cambridge University Press.

Greene, B. (2000). *The elegant universe: Superstrings, hidden dimensions, and the quest for the ultimate theory.* New York: Vintage Books.

Greene, J. D., & Haidt, J. (2002). How (and where) does moral judgment work? *Trends in Cognitive Sciences, 6*, 517–523.

Greene, J. D., Nystrom, L. E., Engell, A. D., Darley, J. M., & Cohen, J. D. (2004). The neural bases of cognitive conflict and control in moral judgment. *Neuron, 44*, 389–400.

Greenwald, A. G., Banaji, M. R., Rudman, L. A., Farnham, S. D., Nosek, B. A., & Mellott, D. S. (2002). A unified theory of implicit attitudes, stereotypes, self-esteem, and self-concept. *Psychological Review, 109*(1), 3–25.

Gregersen, E. (1982). *Sexual practices: The story of human sexuality.* New York: Franklin Watts.

Griffiths, P. (2002). What is innateness? *Monist, 85*(1), 70–85.

Griggs, R., & Cox, J. (1982). The elusive thematic-materials effect in Wason's selection task. *British Journal of Psychology, 73*, 407–420.

Griggs, R., & Cox, J. (1983). The effects of problem content and negation on Wason's selection task. *Quarterly Journal of Experimental Psychology, 35A*, 519–533.

Grosse, E. (1897). *The beginnings of art.* New York: Appleton.

Grusec, J. E., & Goodnow, J. J. (1994). Impact of parental discipline methods on the child's internalization of values: A reconceptualization of current points of view. *Developmental Psychology, 30*, 4–19.

Haidt, J. (2001). The emotional dog and its rational tail: A social intuitionist approach to moral judgment. *Psychological Review, 108*(4), 814–834.

Haidt, J. (2003). The moral emotions. In R. J. Davidson, K. R. Scherer, & H. H. Goldsmith (Eds.), *Handbook of affective sciences* (pp. 852–870). Oxford: Oxford University Press.

Haidt, J., & Joseph, C. (2004, Fall). Intuitive ethics: How innately prepared intuitions generate culturally variable virtues. *Daedalus: On Human Nature, 133,* 55–66.

Haidt, J., Koller, S., & Dias, M. (1993). Affect, culture, and morality, or is it wrong to eat your dog? *Journal of Personality and Social Psychology, 65,* 613–628.

Haidt, J., Rozin, P., McCauley, C., & Imada, S. (1997). Body, psyche, and culture: The relationship of disgust to morality. *Psychology and Developing Societies, 9,* 107–131.

Haig, D. (1999). Asymmetric relations: Internal conflicts and the horror of incest. *Evolution and Human Behavior, 20,* 83–98.

Hamilton, W. D. (1964). The genetical evolution of social behaviour, I and II. *Journal of Theoretical Biology, 7,* 1–16, 17–52.

Harman, G. (1975). Moral relativism defended. *The Philosophical Review, 84*(1), 3–22.

Harman, G. (1999a). Moral philosophy and linguistics. In K. Brinkmann (Ed.), *Proceedings of the 20th World Conference of Philosophy: Vol. 1: Ethics* (pp. 107–115) Bowling Green, OH: Philosophy Documentation Center. Reprinted in Harman (2000a).

Harman, G. (1999b). Moral philosophy meets social psychology: Virtue ethics and the fundamental attribution error. *Proceedings of the Aristotelian Society, 99,* 315–331.

Harman, G. (2000a). *Explaining value and other essays in moral philosophy.* New York: Oxford University Press.

Harman, G. (2000b). The nonexistence of character traits. *Proceedings of the Aristotelian Society, 100,* 223–226.

Harris, G. T., Rice, M. E., & Lalumiere, M. (2001). Criminal violence: The roles of psychopathy, neurodevelopmental insults, and antisocial parenting. *Criminal Justice and Behavior, 28*(4), 402–426.

Harris, J. A., Rushton, J. P., Hampson, E., & Jackson, D. N. (1996). Salivary testosterone and self-report aggressive and pro-social personality characteristics in men and women. *Aggressive Behavior, 22*(5), 321–331.

Harris, M. (1986). *Good to eat: Riddles of food and culture.* New York: Simon & Schuster.

Hart, H. L. A., & Honore, A. M. (1959). *Causation and the law.* Oxford: Clarendon Press.

Hasegawa, T., & Hiraishi, K. (2000). Ontogeny of the mind from an evolutionary psychological viewpoint. In S. Watanabe (Ed.), *Comparative cognitive science of mind* (pp. 413–427). Kyoto, Japan: Minerva.

Haselton, M. G., Buss, D. M., Oubaid, V., & Angleitner, A. (2005). Sex, lies, and strategic interference: The psychology of deception between the sexes. *Personality and Social Psychology Bulletin, 31*(1), 3–23.

Haselton, M. G., & Funder, D. C. (2006). The evolution of accuracy and bias in social judgment. In M. Schaller, J. A. Simpson & D. T. Kenrick, (Eds.), *Evolution and social psychology* (pp. 15–38). New York: Psychology Press.

Haselton, M. G., & Miller, G. F. (In press). Women's fertility across the cycle increases the short-term attractiveness of creative intelligence compared to wealth. *Human Nature*.

Hatfield, E., & Sprecher, S. (1995). Men's and women's preferences in marital partners in the United States, Russia, and Japan. *Journal of Cross-Cultural Psychology, 26*(6), 728–750.

Haukka, J., Suvisaari, J., & Lonnqvist, J. (2003). Fertility of patients with schizophrenia, their siblings, and the general population: A cohort study from 1950 to 1959 in Finland. *American Journal of Psychiatry, 160*(3), 460–463.

Hauser, M. D. (2001). *Wild minds: What animals really think*. New York: Henry Holt.

Hauser, M. D. (2006). *Moral minds: How nature designed our universal sense of right and wrong*. New York: Ecco Press.

Hauser, M. D., & Carey, S. (2003). Spontaneous representations of small numbers of objects by rhesus macaques: Examinations of content and format. *Cognitive Psychology, 47*(4), 367–401.

Hauser, M. D., Chen, M. K., Chen, F., & Chuang, E. (2003). Give unto others: Genetically unrelated cotton-top tamarin monkeys preferentially give food to those who altruistically give food back. *Proceedings of the Royal Society of London, B, 270*, 2363–2370.

Hauser, M. D., Chomsky, N., & Fitch, T. (2002). The faculty of language: What is it, who has it, and how did it evolve? *Science, 298*(5598), 1569–1579.

Hauser, M. D., Cushman, F., Young, L., Kang-Xing Jin, R., & Mikhail, J. (Under review). *Cross-culturally consistent moral judgments and insufficient justifications*.

Hauser, M. D., Dehaene, S., Dehaene-Lambertz, G., & Patalano, A. L. (2002). Spontaneous number discrimination of multi-format auditory stimuli in cotton-top tamarins. *Cognition, 86*(2), B23–32.

Hawkes, K. (1991). Showing off: Tests of another hypothesis about men's foraging goals. *Ethology and Sociobiology, 12,* 29–54.

Hawkes, K., & Bird, R. B. (2002). Showing off, handicap signaling, and the evolution of men's work. *Evolutionary Anthropology, 11,* 58–67.

Hawkes, K., O'Connell, J. F., Blurton Jones, N. G. (2001). Hadza meat sharing. *Evolution and Human Behavior, 22*(2), 113–142.

He, Z. J., & Nakayama, K. (1992). Surfaces versus features in visual search. *Nature, 359*(6392), 231–233.

Hearne, V. (1986). *Adam's task: Calling animals by name.* New York: Knopf.

Heaven, P. C. L., & Bucci, S. (2001). Right-wing authoritarianism, social dominance orientation, and personality: An analysis using the IPIP measure. *European Journal of Personality, 15*(1), 49–56.

Hempel, C. (1966). *Philosophy of natural science.* Englewood Cliffs, NJ: Prentice-Hall.

Henderson, J. J. A., & Anglin, J. M. (2003). Facial attractiveness predicts longevity. *Evolution and Human Behavior, 24*(5), 351–356.

Henrich, J. (2004). Inequity aversion in Capuchins? *Nature, 428,* 139.

Henrich, J., & Boyd, R. (1998). The evolution of conformist transmission and the emergence of between-group differences. *Evolution and Human Behavior, 19,* 215–241.

Henrich, J., & Boyd, R. (2001). Why people punish defectors: Weak conformist transmission can stabilize costly enforcement of norms in cooperative dilemmas. *Journal of Theoretical Biology, 208,* 79–89.

Henrich, J., & Gil-White, F. (2001). The evolution of prestige: Freely conferred deference as a mechanism for enhancing the benefits of cultural transmission. *Evolution and Human Behavior, 22*(3), 165–196.

Henrich, J., Boyd, R., Bowles, S., Camerer, C., Fehr, E., & Gintis, H. (Eds.). (2001/2004). *Foundations of human sociality: Economic experiments and ethnographic evidence from fifteen small-scale societies.* New York: Oxford University Press.

Hepper, P. G. (1991). *Kin recognition.* Cambridge: Cambridge University Press.

Hepper, P. G., & Cleland, J. (1999). Developmental aspects of kin recognition. *Genetica, 104,* 199–205.

Herold, E. S., & Milhausen, R. R. (1999). Dating preferences of university women: An analysis of the nice guy stereotype. *Journal of Sex and Marital Therapy, 25*(4), 333–343.

Hilpinen, R. (1971). *Deontic logic: Introductory and systematic readings.* Dordrecht, The Netherlands: D. Reidel.

Hirschfeld, L. A., & Gelman, S. A. (Eds.). (1994). *Mapping the mind: Domain-specificity in cognition and culture.* New York: Cambridge University Press.

Hoelzer, G. A. (1989). The good parent process of sexual selection. *Animal Behavior, 38*(6), 1067–1078.

Hofferth, S., & Anderson, K. G. (2003). Are all dads equal? Biology vs. marriage as a basis for paternal investment. *Journal of Marriage and Family, 65,* 213–232.

Hoffman, E., McCabe, K., & Smith, V. (1998). Behavioral foundations of reciprocity: Experimental economics and evolutionary psychology. *Economic Inquiry, 36,* 335–352.

Hoffman, M. L. (2000). *Empathy and moral development: Implications for caring and justice.* Cambridge: Cambridge University Press.

Hohmann, G., & Fruth, B. (2000). Use and function of genital contacts among female bonobos. *Animal Behavior, 60*(1), 107–120.

Holmes, W. G., & Sherman, P. W. (1982). The ontogeny of kin recognition in two species of ground squirrels. *American Zoologist, 22,* 491–517.

Honderich, T. (Ed.). (1995). *The Oxford companion to philosophy.* New York: Oxford University Press.

Hooker, B., & Little, M. O. (2000). *Moral particularism.* New York: Oxford University Press.

Hopkins, K. (1980). Brother-sister marriage in Roman Egypt. *Comparative Studies in Society and History, 22,* 303–354.

Hornstein, N. (2004). Foreword to Noam Chomsky, *Rules and representations* (pp. vii–lii). New York: Columbia University Press.

Houle, D., & Kondrashov, A. S. (2002). Coevolution of costly mate choice and condition-dependent display of good genes. *Proceedings of the Royal Society of London, B, 269*(1486), 97–104.

Hume, D. (1889). *The natural history of religion.* London: Freethought. (Original work published 1757)

Hume, D. (1975). *Enquiries concerning human understanding and concerning the principles of morals.* Oxford: Oxford University Press. (Original works published 1748 and 1751).

Hume, D. (1978). *A treatise of human nature.* Oxford: Oxford University Press. (Original work published 1739)

Hursthouse, R. (1999). *On virtue ethics.* New York: Oxford University Press.

Hutcheson, F. (1994). *An inquiry concerning the original of our ideas of virtue or moral good.* In R. S. Downie (Ed.), *Philosophical writings* (pp. 67–113). London: J. M. Dent. (Original work published 1725)

Huxley, J. S. (1927). *Religion without revelation.* London: Ernest Benn.

Itard, J. M. G. (1962). *The wild boy of Aveyron* (G. Humphrey & M. Humphrey, Trans.). New York: Appleton-Century-Crofts. (Original work published 1801)

Iwasa, Y., & Pomiankowski, A. (1999). Good parent and good genes models of handicap evolution. *Journal of Theoretical Biology, 200*(1), 97–109.

Jackendoff, R. (1994). *Patterns in the mind: Language and human nature.* New York: Basic Books.

Jackendoff, R. (2002). *Foundations of language.* New York: Oxford University Press.

James, W. (1978). *Pragmatism and the meaning of truth.* Cambridge: Harvard University Press. (Original works published 1907 and 1909)

Jamison, K. R. (1993). *Touched with fire: Manic-depressive illness and the artistic temperament.* New York: Free Press.

Jang, K. L., McCrae, R. R., Angleitner, A., Riemann, R., & Livesley, W. J. (1998). Heritability of facet-level traits in a cross-cultural twin sample: Support for a hierarchical model of personality. *Journal of Personality and Social Psychology, 74*(6), 1556–1565.

Jensen, A. (1998). *The G factor: The science of mental ability.* London: Praeger.

Jensen-Campbell, L. A., Graziano, W. G., & West, S. G. (1995). Dominance, prosocial orientation, and female preferences: Do nice guys really finish last? *Journal of Personality and Social Psychology, 68,* 427–440.

Johnson, R. C. (1996). Attributes of Carnegie Medalists performing acts of heroism and of the recipients of these acts. *Ethology and Sociobiology, 17,* 355–362.

Johnson-Laird, P., & Byrne, R. (1991). *Deduction.* Hillsdale, NJ: Erlbaum.

Johnston, M. (1989). Dispositional theories of value. *Proceedings of the Aristotelian Society Supplementary, 63,* 139–174.

Jones, D. (2004). The universal psychology of kinship: Evidence from language. *Trends in Cognitive Sciences, 8,* 211–215.

Jones, W., Bullugi, U., Lai, Z., Chiles, M., Reilly, J., Lincoln, A., & Adolphs, R. (2000). Hypersociability in Williams syndrome. *Journal of Cognitive Neuroscience, 12*(S1), 30–46.

Joyce, R. (2001). *The myth of morality*. Cambridge: Cambridge University Press.

Joyce, R. (2006). *The evolution of morality*. Cambridge: MIT Press.

Judge, T. A., Colbert, A. E., & Ilies, R. (2004). Intelligence and leadership: A quantitative review and test of theoretical propositions. *Journal of Applied Psychology, 89*(3), 542–552.

Kaffman, M. (1977). Sexual standards and behavior of the kibbutz adolescent. *American Journal of Orthopsychiatry, 47*, 207–217.

Kahneman, D., Treisman, A. M., & Gibbs, B. J. (1992). The reviewing of object files: Object-specific integration of information. *Cognitive Psychology, 24*, 175–219.

Kalmijn, M. (1998). Intermarriage and homogamy: Causes, patterns, trends. *Annual Review of Sociology, 24*, 395–421.

Kaminsky, J., Call, J., & Fischer, J. (2004). Word learning in a domestic dog: Evidence for "fast mapping." *Science, 304*(5677), 1682–1683.

Kanazawa, S. (2000). Scientific discoveries as cultural displays: A further test of Miller's courtship model. *Evolution and Human Behavior, 21*, 317–321.

Kant, I. (1959). *Foundations of the metaphysics of morals* (L. W. Beck, Trans.). Indianapolis, IN: Bobbs-Merrill.

Kant, I. (1964). *The groundwork to the metaphysics of morals* (H. J. Paton, Trans.). New York: Harper & Row.

Kaplan, H., Hill, K., Lancaster, K. J., & Hurtado, A. (2000). A theory of human life history evolution: Diet, intelligence, and longevity. *Evolutionary Anthropology, 9*, 156–185.

Karmiloff-Smith, A. (1995). *Beyond modularity: A developmental perspective on cognitive science*. Cambridge: MIT Press.

Karney, B. R., & Bradbury, T. N. (1995). The longitudinal course of marital quality and stability: A review of theory, method, and research. *Psychological Bulletin, 118*(1), 3–34.

Keeley, L. (1996). *War before civilization: The myth of the peaceful savage*. New York: Oxford University Press.

Kelemen, D. (2004). Are children "intuitive theists"?: Reasoning about purpose and design in nature. *Psychological Science, 15*, 285–301.

Kelly, D., & Stich, S. (Forthcoming). Two theories about the cognitive architecture underlying morality. In P. Carruthers, S. Laurence, & S. Stich (Eds.), *The innate mind: Vol. 3. Foundations and the future*. Oxford: Oxford University Press.

Kelly, D., Stich, S., Haley, K. J., Eng, S., & Fessler, D. M. T. (In press). Harm, affect and the moral/conventional distinction. *Mind and Language.*

Kelly, S., & Dunbar, R. I. M. (2001). Who dares, wins: Heroism versus altruism in women's mate choice. *Human Nature, 12*(2), 89–105.

Keltner, D., & Buswell, B. N. (1997). Embarrassment: Its distinct form and appeasement functions. *Psychological Bulletin, 122,* 250–270.

Kenrick, D. T., Sadalla, E. K., Groth, G., & Trost, M. R. (1990). Evolution, traits, and the stages of human courtship: Qualifying the parental investment model. *Journal of Personality, 58,* 97–116.

Kim, J. (1993). *Supervenience and mind: Selected philosophical essays.* Cambridge: Cambridge University Press.

King, J. E., Weiss, A., & Farmer, K. H. (2005). A chimpanzee (*Pan troglodytes*) analogue of cross-national generalization of personality structure: Zoological parks and an African sanctuary. *Journal of Personality, 73*(2), 389–410.

Kirby, K. (1994). Probabilities and utilities of fictional outcomes in Wason's four-card selection task. *Cognition, 51,* 1–28.

Kitcher, P. (1992). The naturalists return. *Philosophical Review, 101*(1), 53–114.

Knowles, D., & Skorupski, J. (Eds.). (1993). *Virtue and taste: Essays on politics, ethics, and aesthetics.* Oxford: Blackwell.

Kochanska, G., Friesenborg, A. E., Lange, L. A., & Martel, M. M. (2004). Parents' personality and infants' temperament as contributors to their emerging relationship. *Journal of Personality and Social Psychology, 86*(5), 744–759.

Koenig, L. B., McGue, M., Krueger, R. F., & Bouchard, T. J. (2005). Genetic and environmental influences on religiousness: Findings for retrospective and current religiousness ratings. *Journal of Personality, 73*(2), 471–488.

Koenigsberg, H. W., Harvey, P. D., Mitropoulou, V., Schmeidler, J., New, A. S., Goodman, M., Silverman, J. M., Serby, M., Schopick, F., & Siever, L. J. (2002). Characterizing affective instability in borderline personality disorder. *American Journal of Psychiatry, 159*(5), 784–788.

Kohlberg, L. (1984). *The psychology of moral development: Moral stages and the life cycle.* San Francisco: Harper & Row.

Kohn, M., & Mithen, S. (1999). Handaxes: Products of sexual selection? *Antiquity, 73,* 518–526.

Kokko, H. (1998). Should advertising parental care be honest? *Proceedings of the Royal Society of London, B, 265*(1408), 1871–1878.

Kokko, H., Brooks, R., McNamara, J. M., & Houston, A. I. (2002). The sexual selection continuum. *Proceedings of the Royal Society of London, B, 269*(1498), 1331–1340.

Kokko, H., & Johnstone, R. A. (2002). Why is mutual mate choice not the norm? Operational sex ratios, sex roles, and the evolution of sexually dimorphic and monomorphic signalling. *Philosophical Transactions of the Royal Society of London, B, 357*(1419), 319–330.

Kornblith, H. (1994). *Naturalizing epistemology* (2nd ed.). Cambridge: MIT Press.

Kosson, D. S., Suchy, Y., Mayer, A. R., & Libby, J. (2002). Facial affect recognition in criminal psychopaths. *Emotion, 2*, 398–411.

Koziel, S., & Pawlowski, B. (2003). Comparison between primary and secondary mate markets: An analysis of data from lonely hearts columns. *Personality and Individual Differences, 35*(8), 1849–1857.

Krebs, D., Denton, K., Vermeulen, S. C., Carpendale, J. I., & Bush, A. (1991). The structural flexibility of moral judgment. *Journal of Personality and Social Psychology: Personality, 61*, 1012–1023.

Krueger, R. F., Hicks, B. M., & McGue, M. (2001). Altruism and antisocial behavior: Independent tendencies, unique personality correlates, distinct etiologies. *Psychological Science, 12*(5), 397–402.

Krueger, R. F., Moffitt, T. E., Caspi, A., Bleske, A., & Silva, P. A. (1998). Assortative mating for antisocial behavior: Developmental and methodological implications. *Behavior Genetics, 28*(3), 173–186.

Kuester, J., Paul, A., & Arnemann, J. (1994). Kinship, familiarity and mating avoidance in Barbary macaques, *Macaca sylvanus. Animal Behaviour, 48*, 1183–1194.

Kumar, S. R., Pai, A., & Swaminathan, M. S. (1967). Consanguineous marriages and the genetic load due to lethal genes in Kerala. *Annals of Human Genetics, 31*, 141–145.

Kumashiro, M., Finkel, E. J., & Rusbult, C. E. (2002). Self-respect and pro-relationship behavior in marital relationships. *Journal of Personality, 70*(6), 1009–1049.

Kuncel, N. R., Hezlett, S. A., & Ones, D. S. (2004). Academic performance, career potential, creativity, and job performance: Can one construct predict them all? *Journal of Personality and Social Psychology, 86*(1), 148–161.

Kurzban, R., McCabe, K., Smith, V. L., & Wilson, B. J. (2001). Incremental commitment and reciprocity in a real time public goods game. *Personality and Social Psychology Bulletin, 27*(12), 1662–1673.

Kvanvig, J. (1992). *The intellectual virtues and the life of the mind.* Savage, MD: Rowman & Littlefield.

LaFollette, H. (Ed.). (2000). *The Blackwell guide to ethical theory*. Cambridge: Blackwell.

Lahti, D. C., & Weinstein, B. S. (2005). The better angels of our nature: Group stability and the evolution of moral tension. *Evolution and Human Behavior, 26*, 47–63.

Lakoff, G., & Johnson, M. (2003). *Metaphors we live by*. Chicago: University of Chicago Press.

Lalumiere, M. L., Harris, G. T., & Rice, M. E. (2001). Psychopathy and developmental instability. *Evolution and Human Behavior, 22*(2), 75–92.

Lamy D., & Tsal, Y. (2000). Object features, object locations, and object files: Which does selective attention activate and when? *Journal of Experimental Psychology: Human Perception and Performance, 26*(4), 1387–1400.

Langlois, J. H., Kalakanis, L., Rubinstein, A. J., Larson, A., Hallam, M., & Smooth, M. (2000). Maxims or myths of beauty? A meta-analytical and theoretical review. *Psychological Bulletin, 126*(3), 390–423.

Larson, E. J., & Witham, L. (1997). Scientists are still keeping the faith. *Nature, 386*, 435–436.

Laurence, S., & Margolis, E. (1999). Concepts and cognitive science. In E. Margolis & S. Laurence (Eds.), *Concepts: Core readings* (pp. 3–81). Cambridge, Mass.: Bradford Books/MIT Press.

Laurence, S., & Margolis, E. (2001). The poverty of the stimulus argument. *The British Journal for the Philosophy of Science, 52*, 217–289.

Leckman, J., & Mayes, L. (1998). Maladies of love: An evolutionary perspective on some forms of obsessive-compulsive disorder. In D. M. Hann, L. C. Huffman, I. I. Lederhendler, & D. Meinecke (Eds.), *Advancing research on developmental plasticity: Integrating the behavioral science and neuroscience of mental health* (pp. 134–152). Rockville, MD: U.S. Department of Health and Human Services.

Leckman, J., & Mayes, L. (1999). Preoccupations and behaviors associated with romantic and parental love: Perspectives on the origin of obsessive-compulsive disorder. *Obsessive-Compulsive Disorder, 8*(3), 635–665.

Lee, R. B., & DeVore, I. (Eds.). (1968). *Man the hunter*. Chicago: Aldine de Gruyter.

Lehrer, K. (2000). Theory of knowledge (2nd ed.). Boulder: Westview Press.

Leitenberg, H., & Henning, K. (1995). Sexual fantasy. *Psychological Bulletin, 117*(3), 469–496.

Lerner, M. J. (1980). *The belief in a just world: A fundamental delusion*. New York: Plenum Press.

Leslie, A. (1987). Pretense and representation: The origins of "theory of mind." *Psychological Review, 94*, 412–426.

Leslie, A. (1994). ToMM, ToBY, and agency: Core architecture and domain specificity. In L. A. Hirchfeld & S. A. Gelman (Eds.), *Mapping the mind: Domain specificity in cognition and culture* (pp. 119–148). New York: Cambridge University Press.

LeVine, R. A., & Campbell, D. (1972). *Ethnocentrism: Theories of conflict, ethnic attitudes and group behavior.* New York: Wiley.

Levinson, J. (Ed.). (1998). *Aesthetics and ethics: Essays at the intersection.* Cambridge: Cambridge University Press.

Levi-Strauss, C. (1960). The family. In H. L. Shapiro (Ed.), *Man, culture, and society* (p. 278). New York: Oxford University Press.

Lewis, D. (1989). Dispositional theories of value. *Proceedings of the Aristotelian Society, 63*, 113–137.

Li, N. P., Bailey, J. M., Kenrick, D. T., & Linsenmeier, J. A. W. (2002). The necessities and luxuries of mate preferences: Testing the trade-offs. *Journal of Personality and Social Psychology, 82*(6), 947–955.

Lieberman, D. (2003). Mapping the cognitive architecture of systems for kin detection and inbreeding avoidance: The Westermarck hypothesis and the development of sexual aversions between siblings, 2004. Abstract in *Dissertation Abstracts International, 64*, 4110B.

Lieberman, D. (2005). *Cognitive programs for human kin detection regulate incest avoidance and altruism.* Paper presented at the annual meeting of the Human Behavior and Evolution Society, Austin, TX.

Lieberman, D., & Symons, D. (1998). Sibling incest avoidance: From Westermarck to Wolf. *The Quarterly Review of Biology, 73*, 463–466.

Lieberman, D., Tooby, J., & Cosmides, L. (2001, June). *Does it pay to interfere? An investigation of whether individuals are sensitive to the different costs associated with inbreeding within the family.* Paper presented at annual meeting of the Human Behavior and Evolution Society, London, England.

Lieberman, D., Tooby, J., & Cosmides, L. (2003). Does morality have a biological basis? An empirical test of the factors governing moral sentiments relating to incest. *Proceedings of the Royal Society of London, B, 270*(1517), 819–826.

Lieberman, D., Tooby, J., & Cosmides, L. (2007). The architecture of human kin detection. *Nature, 445*, 727–731.

Linville, S. U., Breitwisch, R., & Schilling, A. J. (1998). Plumage brightness as an indicator of parental care in northern cardinals. *Animal Behavior, 55*(1), 119–127.

Locke, J. (1991). *An essay concerning human understanding*. New York: Oxford University Press. (Original work published 1690)

Lovelace, L., & Gannon, L. (1999). Psychopathy and depression: Mutually exclusive constructs? *Journal of Behavior Therapy and Experimental Psychiatry, 30,* 169–176.

Lubinski, D., & Humphreys, L. G. (1997). Incorporating general intelligence into epidemiology and the social sciences. *Intelligence, 24*(1), 159–201.

Lucas, R. E., Diener, E., Grob, A., Suh, E. M., & Shao, L. (2000). Cross-cultural evidence for the fundamental features of extraversion. *Journal of Personality and Social Psychology, 79*(3), 452–468.

Lynn, R., & Vanhanen, T. (2001). National IQ and economic development: A study of eighty-one nations. *Mankind Quarterly, 41*(4), 415–435.

MacIntyre, A. (1988). *Whose justice? Which rationality?* Notre Dame, IN: University of Notre Dame Press.

MacIntyre, A. (1991). *Three rival versions of moral inquiry*. Notre Dame, IN: University of Notre Dame Press.

Mackie, J. L. (1977). *Ethics: Inventing right and wrong*. Harmondsworth, England: Penguin Books.

Mackie, J. L. (1978). The law of the jungle. *Philosophy, 53,* 553–573.

Mahlmann, M. (1999). *Rationalismus in der praktishen theorie: Normentheorie und praktische kampetenz (Rationalism in Practical Theory: The Theory of Norms and Practical Competence)*. Baden-Baden, Germany: Nomos Verlagsgesellschaft.

Malinowski, B. (1927). *Sex and repression in savage society*. New York: Harcourt Brace.

Maljkovic, V. (1987). *Reasoning in evolutionarily important domains and schizophrenia: Dissociation between content-dependent and content independent reasoning*. Unpublished honors thesis, Department of Psychology, Harvard University.

Mallon, R., & Nichols, S. (Forthcoming). The continued importance of moral rules.

Manktelow, K., & Evans, J. St B. T. (1979). Facilitation of reasoning by realism: Effect or non-effect? *British Journal of Psychology, 70,* 477–488.

Manktelow, K., & Over, D. (1987). Reasoning and rationality. *Mind and Language, 2,* 199–219.

Manktelow, K., & Over, D. (1988, July). *Sentences, stories, scenarios, and the selection task*. Paper presented at the First International Conference on Thinking, Plymouth, England.

Manktelow, K., & Over, D. (1990). Deontic thought and the selection task. In K. J. Gilhooly, M. T. G. Keane, R. H. Logie, & G. Erdos (Eds.), *Lines of thinking* (Vol. 1, pp. 153–164). London: Wiley.

Manktelow, K., & Over, D. (1991). Social roles and utilities in reasoning with deontic conditionals. *Cognition, 39*, 85–105.

Manktelow, K., & Over, D. (1995). Deontic reasoning. In S. E. Newstead & J. St B. T. Evans (Eds.), *Perspectives on thinking and reasoning* (pp. 91–114). Hillsdale, NJ: Erlbaum.

Marcus, G. F., & Fisher, S. E. (2003). FOXP2 in focus: What can genes tell us about speech and language? *Trends in Cognitive Science, 7*, 257–262.

Margulis, S. W., & Altmann, J. (1997). Behavioral risk factors in the reproduction of inbred and outbred oldfield mice. *Animal Behaviour, 54*, 397–408.

Marks, M. J., & Fraley, R. C. (2005). The sexual double standard: Fact or fiction? *Sex Roles, 52*(3–4), 175–186.

Marr, D. (1982). *Vision.* Cambridge: MIT Press.

Masserman, J. H., Wechkin, S., & Terris, W. (1964). "Altruistic" behavior in rhesus monkeys. *American Journal of Psychiatry, 121*, 584–585.

Mateo, J. M., & Holmes, W. G. (2004). Cross-fostering as a means to study kin recognition. *Animal Behaviour, 68*, 1451–1459.

Matthews, G., Deary, I., & Whiteman, M. (2003). *Personality traits* (2nd ed.). Cambridge: Cambridge University Press.

May, R. M. (1979). When to be incestuous. *Nature, 279*, 192–194.

Maynard Smith, J., & Price, G. R. (1973). The logic of animal conflict. *Nature, 246*, 15–18.

Maynard Smith, J. (1982). *Evolution and the Theory of Games.* Cambridge: Cambridge University Press.

Mazur, A., & Booth, A. (1998). Testosterone and dominance in men. *Behavioral and Brain Sciences, 21*, 353–397.

McAdams, R. H. (1997). The origin, development, and regulation of social norms. *Michigan Law Review, 96*, 338–427.

McAndrew, F. T. (2002). New evolutionary perspectives on altruism: Multilevel selection and costly-signaling theories. *Current Directions in Psychological Science, 11*, 79–82.

McCabe, J. (1983). FBD marriage: Further support for the Westermarck hypothesis of the incest taboo. *American Anthropologist, 85*, 50–69.

McCloskey, M. (1983a). Intuitive physics. *Scientific American, 248,* 122–129.

McCloskey, M. (1983b). Naive theories of motion. In D. Gentner & A. Stevens (Eds.), *Mental models* (pp. 299–324). Hillsdale, NJ: Erlbaum.

McCourt, K., Bouchard, T. J., Lykken, D. T., Tellegen, A., & Keyes, M. (1999). Authoritarianism revisited: Genetic and environmental influences examined in twins reared apart and together. *Personality and Individual Differences, 27*(5), 985–1014.

McCrae, R. E. (1996). Social consequences of experiential openness. *Psychological Bulletin, 120*(3), 323–337.

McCrae, R. R., Costa, P. T., Jr., de Lima, M. P., Simoes, A., Ostendordf, F., Angleitner, A., Marusic, I., Bratko, D., Caprara, G. V., Barbaranelli, C., & Chae, J.-H. (1999). Age differences in personality across the adult life span: Parallels in five cultures. *Developmental Psychology, 35*(2), 466–477.

McCullough, M. E., Emmons, R. A., Kilpatrick, S. D., & Larson, D. B. (2001). Is gratitude a moral affect? *Psychological Bulletin, 127,* 249–266.

McDowell, J. (1996). *Mind and world.* Cambridge: Harvard University Press.

McGinn, C. (1997). *Ethics, evil, and fiction.* Oxford: Oxford University Press.

McGuire, M. T., Fawzy, F. I., & Spar, J. E. (1994). Altruism and mental disorders. *Ethology and Sociobiology, 15,* 299–321.

McKelvie, S. J., & Coley, J. (1993). Effects of crime seriousness and offender facial attractiveness on recommended treatment. *Social Behaviour and Personality, 21,* 265–277.

McKenna, P., Clare, L., & Baddeley, A. (1995). Schizophrenia. In A. D. Baddeley, B. A. Wilson, & F. N. Watts (Eds.), *Handbook of memory disorders* (pp. 271–292). New York: Wiley.

McNamara, P. (2006). Deontic logic. In E. N. Zalta (Ed.), *Stanford encyclopedia of philosophy.* The Metaphysics Research Lab, Center for the Study of Language and Information, Stanford University. Retrieved from http://plato.stanford.edu/entries/logic-deontic/

McNeill, D. (1985). So you think gestures are non-verbal? *Psychological Review, 92,* 350–371.

Mealey, L. (1995). The sociobiology of sociopathy: An integrated evolutionary model. *Behavioral and Brain Sciences, 18,* 523–541.

Meloy, J. R., James, D. V., Farnham, F. R., Mullen, P. E., Pathe, M., Darnley, B., & Preston, L. (2004). A research review of public figure threats, approaches, attacks, and assassinations in the United States. *Journal of Forensic Sciences, 49*(5), 1086–1093.

Merritt, M. (2000). Virtue ethics and situationist personality psychology. *Ethical Theory and Moral Practice, 3*(4), 365–383.

Mervis, C. B., & Klein-Tasman, B. P. (2000). Williams syndrome: Cognition, personality, and adaptive behavior. *Mental Retardation and Developmental Disabilities Research Reviews, 6*(2), 148–158.

Metsapelto, R. L., & Pulkkinen, L. (2003). Personality traits and parenting: Neuroticism, extraversion, and openness to experience as discriminative factors. *European Journal of Personality, 17*(1), 59–78.

Mikhail, J. (2000). Rawls' linguistic analogy: A study of the "generative grammar" model of moral theory described by John Rawls in "A Theory of Justice." Doctoral dissertation, Cornell University.

Mikhail, J. (2002a). *Aspects of the theory of moral cognition: Investigating intuitive knowledge of the prohibition of intentional battery and the principle of double effect* (Georgetown University Law Center Public Law & Legal Theory Working Paper No. 762385). Retrieved from http://ssrn.com/abstract=762385

Mikhail, J. (2002b). Law, science, and morality: A review of Richard Posner's "The Problematics of Moral and Legal Theory." *Stanford Law Review, 54,* 1057–1127.

Mikhail, J. (2005). Moral heuristics or moral competence? Reflections on Sunstein. *Behavioral and Brain Sciences, 28,* 557–558.

Mikhail, J. (In press). *Rawls' linguistic analogy.* Cambridge: Cambridge University Press.

Mikhail, J., Sorrentino, C., & Spelke, E. (1998). Toward a universal moral grammar. In M. A. Gernsbacher & S. J. Derry (Eds.), *Proceedings, Twentieth Annual Conference of the Cognitive Science Society* (p. 1250). Mahwah, NJ: Erlbaum.

Milhausen, R. R., & Herold, E. S. (1999). Does the sexual double standard still exist? Perceptions of university women. *Journal of Sex Research, 36*(4), 361–368.

Milinski, M., Semmann, D., & Krambeck, H. J. (2002). Reputation helps solve the "tragedy of the commons." *Nature, 415,* 424–426.

Miller, C. (2003). Social psychology and virtue ethics. *Journal of Ethics, 7*(4), 365–392.

Miller, G. F. (1996). Political peacocks. *Demos Quarterly, 10,* 9–11.

Miller, G. F. (1997). Protean primates: The evolution of adaptive unpredictability in competition and courtship. In A. Whiten & R. W. Byrne (Eds.), *Machiavellian intelligence*: Vol. 2. *Extensions and evaluations* (pp. 312–340). Cambridge: Cambridge University Press.

Miller, G. F. (1998). How mate choice shaped human nature: A review of sexual selection and human evolution. In C. Crawford & D. Krebs (Eds.), *Handbook of evolutionary psychology: Ideas, issues, and applications* (pp. 87–129). Mahwah, NJ: Erlbaum.

Miller, G. F. (1999). Sexual selection for cultural displays. In R. Dunbar, C. Knight, & C. Power (Eds.), *The evolution of culture* (pp. 71–91). Edinburgh, Scotland: Edinburgh University Press.

Miller, G. F. (2000a). *The mating mind: How sexual choice shaped the evolution of human nature.* New York: Doubleday/London: William Heinemann.

Miller, G. F. (2000b). Mental traits as fitness indicators: Expanding evolutionary psychology's adaptationism. In D. LeCroy & P. Moller (Eds.), *Annals of the New York Academy of Sciences: Vol. 907. Evolutionary perspectives on human reproductive behavior* (pp. 62–74). New York: New York Academy of Sciences.

Miller, G. F. (2000c). Sexual selection for indicators of intelligence. In G. R. Bock, J. A. Goode, & K. Webb (Eds.), *The nature of intelligence* (pp. 260–275). New York: Wiley.

Miller, G. F. (2001). Aesthetic fitness: How sexual selection shaped artistic virtuosity as a fitness indicator and aesthetic preferences as mate choice criteria. *Bulletin of Psychology and the Arts, 2*(1), 20–25.

Miller, G. F., & Todd, P. M. (1995). The role of mate choice in biocomputation: Sexual selection as a process of search, optimization, and diversification. In W. Banzhaf & F. H. Eeckman (Eds.), *Evolution and biocomputation: Computational models of evolution* (pp. 169–204). Berlin, Germany: Springer-Verlag.

Miller, G. F., & Todd, P. M. (1998). Mate choice turns cognitive. *Trends in Cognitive Sciences, 2*(5), 190–198.

Miller, P. J. E., & Rempel, J. K. (2004). Trust and partner-enhancing attributions in close relationships. *Personality and Social Psychology Bulletin, 30*(6), 695–705.

Mischel, W. (1968). *Personality and assessment.* New York: Wiley.

Modell, B., & Darr, A. (2002). Genetic counselling and customary consanguineous marriage. *Nature Reviews Genetics, 3,* 225–229.

Moll, J., de Oliveira-Souza, R., Bramati, I., & Grafman, J. (2002). Functional networks in emotional moral and nonmoral social judgments. *NeuroImage, 16,* 696–703.

Montmarquet, J. (1993). *Epistemic virtue and doxastic responsibility.* Lanham, MD: Rowman & Littlefield.

Moore, G. E. (1903). *Principia Ethica.* Cambridge: Cambridge University Press.

Morris, D. (1982). *The pocket guide to manwatching*. London: Triad.

Morton, N. E., Crow, J. F., & Muller, H. J. (1956). An estimate of mutational damage in man from data on consanguineous marriages. *Proceedings of the National Academy of Sciences, 42*, 855–863.

Mount, M. K., Barrick, M. R., & Stewart, G. L. (1998). Five-factor model of personality and performance in jobs involving interpersonal interactions. *Human Performance, 11*(2–3), 145–165.

Murdock, G. P. (1949). *Social structure*. New York: Free Press.

Murphy, J. (1982). *Evolution, morality, and the meaning of life*. Totowa, NJ: Rowman & Littlefield.

Mwamwenda, T. S. (1991). Graduate students' moral reasoning. *Psychological Reports, 68*, 1368–1370.

Nesse, R. M. (2000). Is depression an adaptation? *Archives of General Psychiatry, 57*, 14–20.

Nesse, R. M. (Ed.). (2001). *Evolution and the capacity for commitment*. New York: Russell Sage Foundation.

Nichols, S. (2002). On the genealogy of norms: A case for the role of emotion in cultural evolution. *Philosophy of Science, 69*, 234–255.

Nichols, S. (2004). *Sentimental rules: On the natural foundations of moral judgment*. Oxford: Oxford University Press.

Nichols, S. (2005). Innateness and moral psychology. In P. Carruthers, S. Laurence, & S. Stich (Eds.), *The innate mind: Structure and contents* (pp. 353–370). Oxford: Oxford University Press.

Nichols, S., & Mallon, R. (2006). Moral dilemmas and moral rules. *Cognition, 100*, 530–542.

Nietzsche, F. (1967). *On the genealogy of morals* (W. Kaufmann & R. J. Hollingdale, Trans.). New York: Vintage. (Original work published 1887)

Nietzsche, F. (1968). *The will to power* (W. Kaufmann & R. J. Hollingdale, Trans.). New York: Vintage. (Original work published 1888)

Nisbett, R. E. (2003). *The geography of thought: How Asians and Westerners think differently . . . and why*. New York: Free Press.

Nisbett, R. E., & Cohen, D. (1996). *Culture of Honor: The Psychology of Violence in the South*. Boulder: Westview Press.

Nisbett, R. E., & Wilson, T. D. (1977). The halo effect: Evidence for unconscious alteration of judgment. *Journal of Personality and Social Psychology, 35*, 250–256.

Norton, R. E. (1995). *The beautiful soul: Aesthetic morality in the eighteenth century.* Ithaca, NY: Cornell University Press.

Nozick, R. (1974). *Anarchy, State, and Utopia.* New York: Basic Books.

Nucci, L. P. (2001). *Education in the moral domain.* Cambridge: Cambridge University Press.

Nucci, L. P., & Weber, E. (1995). Social interactions in the home and the development of young children's conceptions of the personal. *Child Development, 66,* 1438–1452.

Núñez, M., & Harris, P. (1998). Psychological and deontic concepts: Separate domains or intimate connections? *Mind and Language, 13,* 153–170.

O'Sullivan, L. F. (1995). Less is more: The effects of sexual experience on judgments of men's and women's personality characteristics and relationship desirability. *Sex Roles, 33*(3–4), 159–181.

Oaksford, M., & Chater, N. (1994). A rational analysis of the selection task as optimal data selection. *Psychological Review, 101,* 608–631.

Oda, R. (2001). Sexually dimorphic mate preference in Japan: An analysis of lonely hearts advertisements. *Human Nature, 12*(3), 191–206.

Oliver, M. B., & Sedikides, C. (1992). Effects of sexual permissiveness on desirability of partner as a function of low and high commitment to relationship. *Social Psychology Quarterly, 55*(3), 321–333.

Olson, J. M., Vernon, P. A., Harris, J. A., & Jang, K. L. (2001). The heritability of attitudes: A study of twins. *Journal of Personality and Social Psychology, 80*(6), 845–860.

Organ, D. W., & Ryan, K. (1995). A meta-analytic review of attitudinal and dispositional predictors of organizational citizenship behavior. *Personnel Psychology, 48*(4), 775–802.

Panchanathan, K., & Boyd, R. (2003). A tale of two defectors: The importance of standing in the evolution of indirect reciprocity. *Journal of Theoretical Biology, 224,* 115–126.

Parsons, T. (1952). *The social system.* New York: Free Press.

Patrick, C. J. (1994). Emotion and psychopathy: Startling new insights. *Psychophysiology, 31,* 319–330.

Pence, G. E. (1984). Recent work on virtues. *American Philosophical Quarterly, 21,* 281–297.

Penn, D., & Potts, W. K. (1998). MHC-disassortative mating preferences reversed by cross-fostering. *Proceedings of the Royal Society of London, B, 265,* 1299–1306.

Penner, L. A., Dovidio, J. F., Piliavin, J. A., & Schroeder, D. A. (2005). Prosocial behavior: Multilevel perspectives. *Annual Review of Psychology, 56*, 365–392.

Pepperberg, I. M. (2002). In search of King Solomon's ring: Cognitive and communicative studies of Grey parrots (*Psittacus erithacus*). *Brain, Behavior and Evolution, 59*(1–2), 54–67.

Pereyra, L., & Nieto, J. (2004). La especificidad del razonamiento sobre situaciones de peligro [Reasoning specializations for situations involving hazards and precautions]. *Revista Mexicana de Psicología, 21*(2), 167–177.

Pérusse, D. (1993). Cultural and reproductive success in industrial societies: Testing the relationship at the proximate and ultimate levels. *Behavioral and Brain Sciences, 16*, 267–322.

Pettit, P. (1991). Virtus normativa: Rational choice perspectives. *Ethics, 100*(4), 725–755.

Petitto, L. A., & Seidenberg, M. S. (1979). On the evidence for linguistic abilities in signing apes. *Brain and Language, 8*(2), 162–183.

Petrinovich, L. (1995). *Human evolution, reproduction, and morality.* New York: Plenum Press.

Pigden, C. R. (1991). Naturalism. In P. Singer (Ed.), *A companion to ethics* (pp. 421–431). London: Blackwell Reference.

Pinker, S. (1994). *The language instinct.* New York: HarperCollins.

Pinker, S. (1997). *How the mind works.* New York: Norton.

Pinker, S. (2002). *The blank slate: The modern denial of human nature.* New York: Penguin/Putnam.

Platt, R., & Griggs, R. (1993). Darwinian algorithms and the Wason selection task: A factorial analysis of social contract selection task problems. *Cognition, 48*, 163–192.

Plomin, R., DeFries, J. C., McClearn, G. E., & McGuffin, P. (2001). *Behavioral genetics* (4th ed.). New York: Worth.

Povinelli, D. J., Dunphy-Lelii, S., Reaux, J. E., & Mazza, M. P. (2002). Psychological diversity in chimpanzees and humans: New longitudinal assessments of chimpanzees' understanding of attention. *Brain Behavioral Evolution, 59*(1–2), 33–53.

Povinelli, D.J., & Preuss, T. M. (1995). Theory of mind: Evolutionary history of a cognitive specialization. *Trends in Neurosciences, 18*(9), 418–424.

Preston, S. B., & de Waal, F. B. M. (2002). Empathy: Its ultimate and proximate bases. *Behavioral and Brain Sciences, 25*(1), 1–20.

Preuschoft, S., & van Schaik, C. P. (2000). Dominance and communication: Conflict management in various social settings. In F. Aureli & F. B. M. de Waal (Eds.), *Natural conflict resolution* (pp. 77–105). Berkeley: University of California Press.

Prinz, J. J. (2002). *Furnishing the mind: Concepts and their perceptual basis*. Cambridge: MIT Press.

Prinz, J. J. (2006a). The emotional basis of moral judgments. *Philosophical Explorations, 9*, 29–43.

Prinz, J. J. (2006b). Is the mind really modular? In R. Stainton (Ed.), *Contemporary debates in cognitive science.* (pp. 22–36). Oxford: Blackwell.

Prinz, J. J. (2007). *The emotional construction of morals.* Oxford: Oxford University Press.

Prinz, J. J. (Forthcoming). Against moral nativism. In M. Bishop & D. Murphy (Eds.), *Stich and his critics*. Oxford: Blackwell.

Prokosch, M., Yeo, R., & Miller, G. F. (2005). Intelligence tests with higher *g*-loadings show higher correlations with body symmetry: Evidence for a general fitness factor mediated by developmental stability. *Intelligence, 33*, 203–213.

Puka, B. (Ed.). (1994). *Moral development. A compendium: Vol. 4. The great justice debate: Kohlberg criticism*. New York: Garland.

Putnam, H. (1993). Why reason can't be naturalized. In his *Philosophical papers: Vol. 3. Realism and reason* (pp. 229–247). Cambridge: Cambridge University Press.

Putnam, H. (2004). *Ethics without ontology*. Cambridge: Harvard University Press.

Pylyshyn, Z. W., & Storm, R. W. (1988). Tracking multiple independent targets: Evidence for a parallel tracking mechanism. *Spatial Vision, 3*(3), 179–197.

Quine, W. V. O. (1969). Epistemology naturalized. In his *Ontological relativity and other essays* (pp. 69–90). New York: Columbia University Press.

Quine, W. V. O. (1972). *Methods of logic* (3rd ed.). New York: Holt, Rinehart & Winston.

Quine, W. V. O. (1980). Two dogmas of empiricism. In his *From a logical point of view: Nine logico-philosophical essays* (2nd ed., rev.) (pp. 20–46). Cambridge: Harvard University Press. (Original work published 1953)

Quine, W. V. O. (1986). Reply to Morton White. In L. E. Hahn & P. A. Schilpp (Eds.), *The philosophy of WVO Quine* (pp. 663–665). La Salle, IL: Open Court.

Quinlan, P. T. (2003). Visual feature integration theory: Past, present, and future. *Psychological Bulletin, 29*(5), 643–673.

Railton, P. (1986). Moral realism. *Philosophical Review, 95*(2), 163–207.

Railton, P. (2005). Moral factualism. In J. Dreier (Ed.), *Contemporary debates in moral theory* (pp. 201–219). Oxford: Blackwell.

Ramachandran, V. S., & Hubbard, E. M. (2001). Psychophysical investigations into the neural basis of synaesthesia. *Proceedings of the Royal Society of London, B, 268*(1470), 979–983.

Rawls, J. (1950). *A study in the grounds of ethical knowledge: Considered with reference to judgments on the moral worth of character.* Doctoral Dissertation, Princeton University.

Rawls, J. (1951). Outline of a decision procedure for ethics. *Philosophical Review, 60,* 177–197.

Rawls, J. (1971). *A theory of justice.* Cambridge: Belnap Press of Harvard University Press.

Read, K. E. (1955). Morality and the concept of the person among the Gahuku-Gama. *Oceania, 25,* 233–282.

Regan, T. (1985a). The case for animal rights. In P. Singer (Ed.), *In defense of animals* (pp. 13–26). Oxford: Blackwell.

Regan, T. (1985b). *The case for animal rights.* Berkeley: University of California Press.

Rhee, S. H., & Waldman, I. D. (2002). Genetic and environmental influences on antisocial behavior: A meta-analysis of twin and adoption studies. *Psychological Bulletin, 128*(3), 490–529.

Rice, G. E., Jr., & Gainer, P. (1962). "Altruism" in the albino rat. *Journal of Comparative and Physiological Psychology, 55,* 123–125.

Richards, J. R. (2000). *Human nature after Darwin: A philosophical introduction.* London: Routledge.

Ridley, M. (1993). *The red queen: Sex and the evolution of human nature.* London: Viking.

Ridley, M. (1996). *The origins of virtue.* New York: Penguin.

Ridley, M. (2001). *The cooperative gene: How Mendel's demon explains the evolution of complex beings.* New York: Free Press.

Riechert, S. E. (1998). Game theory and animal contests. In L. A. Dugatkin & H. K. Reeve (Eds.), *Game theory and animal behavior* (pp. 64–93). Oxford: Oxford University Press.

Rips, L. (1994). *The psychology of proof.* Cambridge, MA: MIT Press.

Roach, M.A., Orsmond, G. I., & Barratt, M. S. (1999). Mothers and fathers of children with Down syndrome: Parental stress and involvement in childcare. *American Journal on Mental Retardation, 104*(5), 422–436.

Robarchek, C. A., & Robarchek, C. J. (1992). Cultures of war and peace: A comparative study of Waorani and Semai. In J. Silverberg & P. Gray (Eds.), *Aggression and peacefulness in humans and other primates* (pp. 189–213). New York: Oxford University Press.

Roberts, B. W., Chernyshenko, O. S., Stark, S., & Goldberg, L. R. (2005). The structure of conscientiousness: An empirical investigation based on seven major personality questionnaires. *Personnel Psychology, 59*(1), 103–139.

Roberts, D. F. (1967). Incest, inbreeding and mental abilities. *British Medical Journal, 4*(575), 336–337.

Roccas, S., Sagiv, L., Schwartz, S. H., & Knafo, A. (2002). The Big Five personality factors and personal values. *Personality and Social Psychology Bulletin, 28*(6), 789–801.

Roes, F. L., & Raymond, M. (2003). Belief in moralizing gods. *Evolution and Human Behavior, 24*, 126–135.

Rorty, R. (1991). On ethnocentrism. *Philosophical Papers* (Vol. 1). Cambridge: Cambridge University Press.

Rosaldo, M. Z. (1980). *Knowledge and passion: Ilongot notions of self and social life.* Cambridge: Cambridge University Press.

Rosenberg, A. (1996). A field guide to recent species of naturalism. *British Journal of the Philosophy of Science, 47*, 1–29.

Ross, L. (1977). The intuitive psychologist and his shortcomings: Distortions in the attribution process. In L. Berkowitz (Ed.), *Advances in experimental social psychology* (Vol. 10, pp. 174–214). New York: Academic Press.

Rowe, L., & Houle, D. (1996). The lek paradox and the capture of genetic variance by condition dependent traits. *Proceedings of the Royal Society of London, B, 263*, 1415–1421.

Rozin, P., & Fallon, A. E. (1980). Psychological categorization of foods and nonfoods: A preliminary taxonomy of food rejections. *Appetite, 1*, 193–201.

Rozin, P., Haidt, J., & McCauley, C. R. (1999). Disgust: The body and soul emotion. In T. Dalgleish & M. Power (Eds.), *Handbook of cognition and emotion* (pp. 429–445). New York: Wiley.

Rozin, P., Haidt, J., & McCauley, C. R. (2000). Disgust. In M. Lewis & J. M. Haviland-Jones (Eds.), *Handbook of emotions* (2nd ed., pp. 637–653). New York: Guilford Press.

Ruse, M. (1986). *Taking Darwin seriously: A naturalistic approach to philosophy*. Oxford: Blackwell.

Ruse, M. (1991). The significance of evolution. In P. Singer (Ed.), *A companion to ethics* (pp. 500–510). Oxford: Blackwell.

Ruse, M. (1994). *Evolutionary naturalism: Selected essays*. London: Routledge.

Ruse, M. (1998). *Taking Darwin seriously: A naturalistic approach to philosophy* (2nd ed.) Buffalo, NY: Prometheus.

Ruse, M. (2001). *Can a Darwinian be a Christian? The relationship between science and religion*. Cambridge: Cambridge University Press.

Ruse, M. (2004). Review of natural ethical facts: Evolution, connectivism, and moral cognition by William D. Casebeer. *Evolutionary Psychology, 2*, 89–91.

Rushton, J. P. (2004). Genetic and environmental contributions to prosocial attitudes: A twin study of social responsibility. *Proceedings of the Royal Society of London, B, 271*(1557), 2583–2585.

Sabini, J., Siepmann, M., & Stein, J. (2001). The really fundamental attribution error in social psychological research. *Psychological Inquiry, 12*(1), 1–15.

Sackett, P. R., & Wanek, J. E. (1996). New developments in the use of measures of honesty, integrity, conscientiousness, dependability, trustworthiness, and reliability for personnel selection. *Personnel Psychology, 49*(4), 787–829.

Salmon, C., & Symons, D. (2004). Slash fiction and human mating psychology. *Journal of Sex Research, 41*(1), 94–100.

Samuels, R. (1998). Evolutionary psychology and the massive modularity hypothesis. *British Journal of Philosophy of Science, 49*, 575–602.

Samuels, R. (2002). Nativism in cognitive science. *Mind and Language, 17*, 233–265.

Saroglou, V. (2002). Religion and the five factors of personality: A meta-analytic review. *Personality and Individual Differences, 32*(1), 15–25.

Saroglou, V., Delpierre, V., & Dernelle, R. (2004). Values and religiosity: A meta-analysis of studies using Schwartz's model. *Personality and Individual Differences, 37*(4), 721–734.

Savage-Rumbaugh, S. (1987). Communication, symbolic communication, and language: Reply to Seidenberg and Petitto. *Journal of Experimental Psychology: General, 116*(3), 288–292.

Savage-Rumbaugh, S., McDonald, K., Sevcik, R. A., Hopkins, W. D., & Rubert, E. J. (1986). Spontaneous symbol acquisition and communicative use by pygmy chimpanzees (*Pan paniscus*). *Journal of Experimental Psychology: General, 115*(3), 211–235.

Scheib, J. E. (2001). Context-specific mate choice criteria: Women's trade-offs in the contexts of long-term and extra-pair mateships. *Personal Relationships, 8*(4), 371–389.

Schmitt, D. P. (2004a). The Big Five related to risky sexual behaviour across 10 world regions: Differential personality associations of sexual promiscuity and relationship infidelity. *European Journal of Personality, 18*, 301–319.

Schmitt, D. P. (2004b). Patterns and universals of mate poaching across 53 nations: The effects of sex, culture, and personality on romantically attracting another person's partner. *Journal of Personality and Social Psychology, 86*(4), 560–584.

Schmitt, D. P., & 130 co-authors. (2004c). Patterns and universals of adult romantic attachment across 62 cultural regions: Are models of self and other pancultural constructs? *Journal of Cross-Cultural Psychology, 35*(4), 367–402.

Schmitt, D. P., Couden, A., & Baker, M. (2001). The effects of sex and temporal context on feelings of romantic desire: An experimental evaluation of sexual strategies theory. *Personality and Social Psychology Bulletin, 27*(7), 833–847.

Schmitt, E. (2005, February 4). General is scolded for saying, "It's fun to shoot some people." *New York Times.*

Schneider, W. X. (1999). Visual-spatial working memory, attention, and scene representation: A neuro-cognitive theory. *Psychological Research, 62*(2–3), 220–236.

Scholl, B. J., Pylyshyn, Z. W., & Feldman, J. (2001). What is a visual object? Evidence from target merging in multiple object tracking. *Cognition, 80*(1–2), 159–177.

Schulte, M. J., Ree, M. J., & Carretta, T. R. (2004). Emotional intelligence: Not much more than *g* and personality. *Personality and Individual Differences, 37*(5), 1059–1068.

Schutte, N. S., Malouff, J. M., Hall, L. E., Haggerty, D. J., Cooper, J. T., Golden, C. J., & Dornheim, L. (1998). Development and validation of a measure of emotional intelligence. *Personality and Individual Differences, 25*(2), 167–177.

Seemanova, E. (1971). A study of children of incestuous matings. *Human Heredity, 21*, 108–128.

Sen, A. (1989). *On ethics and economics.* Oxford: Blackwell.

Senior, C. (2003). Beauty in the brain of the beholder. *Neuron, 38*(4), 525–528.

Shackelford, T. K., & Buss, D. M. (1996). Betrayal in mateships, friendships, and coalitions. *Personality and Social Psychology Bulletin, 22*(11), 1151–1164.

Shackelford, T. K., & Buss, D. M. (1997). Cues to infidelity. *Personality and Social Psychology Bulletin, 23*, 1034–1045.

Shackelford, T. K., & Buss, D. M. (2000). Marital satisfaction and spousal cost-infliction. *Personality and Individual Differences, 28*(5), 917–928.

Shallice, T. (1988). *From neuropsychology to mental structure.* Cambridge: Cambridge University Press.

Shaner, A., Miller, G. F., & Mintz, J. (2004). Schizophrenia as one extreme of a sexually selected fitness indicator. *Schizophrenia Research, 70*(1), 101–109.

Shepher, J. (1971). Mate selection among second-generation kibbutz adolescents: Incest avoidance and negative imprinting. *Archives of Sexual Behavior, 1*(1), 293–307.

Shepher, J. (1983). *Incest: A biosocial view.* New York: Academic Press.

Sherman, P. W., & Holmes, W. G. (1985). Kin recognition: Issues and evidence. In B. Hölldobler & M. Lindauer (Eds.), *Experimental behavioral ecology and sociobiology* (pp. 437–460). Stuggart, Germany: Gustav Fischer-Verlag.

Sherman, P. W., Reeve, H. K., & Pfennig, D. W. (1997). Recognition systems. In J. R. Krebs & N. B. Davies (Eds.), *Behavioral ecology: An evolutionary approach* (pp. 69–96). Oxford: Blackwell Scientific.

Shostak, M. (1981). *Nisa: The life and words of a !Kung woman.* Cambridge: Harvard University Press.

Shultz, T., Wright, K., & Schleifer, M. (1986). Assignment of moral responsibility and punishment. *Child Development, 57*, 177–184.

Shweder, R. A., Much, N. C., Mahapatra, M., & Park, L. (1997). The "Big Three" of morality (autonomy, community, divinity), and the "Big Three" explanations of suffering. In P. Rozin & A. Brandt (Eds.), *Morality and health* (pp. 119–169). New York: Routledge.

Silverberg J., & Gray, P. (1992). *Aggression and peacefulness in humans and other primates.* New York: Oxford University Press.

Simoons, F. (1994). *Eat not this flesh: Food avoidances from prehistory to the present.* Madison: University of Wisconsin Press.

Simpson, G. G. (1964). *This view of life.* New York: Harcourt, Brace, & World.

Simpson, J. A., Gangestad, S. W., Christensen, P. N., & Leck, K. (1999). Fluctuating asymmetry, sociosexuality, and intrasexual competitive tactics. *Journal of Personality and Social Psychology, 76*(1), 159–172.

Singer, P. (1977). *Animal liberation.* New York: Avon Books.

Singer, P. (1990). *Animal liberation* (2nd ed.). New York: Random House.

Singer, P. (1994). *Rethinking life and death: The collapse of our traditional ethics.* New York: St. Martin's Press.

Singer, W., & Gray, C. M. (1995). Visual feature integration and the temporal correlation hypothesis. *Annual Review of Neuroscience, 18,* 555–586.

Sinnott-Armstrong, W. (1984). "Ought" conversationally implies "can." *Philosophical Review, 93*(2), 249–261.

Sinnott-Armstrong, W. (2005). You ought to be ashamed of yourself (when you violate an imperfect moral obligation). *Philosophical Issues, 15,* 193–208.

Slote, M. (2003). *Morals from motives.* New York: Oxford University Press.

Smetana, J. G. (1981). Preschool children's conceptions of moral and social rules. *Child Development, 52,* 1333–1336.

Smetana, J. G. (1983). Social cognitive development: Domain distinctions and coordinations. *Developmental Review, 3*(2), 131–147.

Smetana, J. G. (1989). Toddlers' social interactions in the context of moral and conventional transgressions in the home. *Developmental Psychology, 25,* 499–508.

Smetana, J. G. (1995). Morality in context: Abstractions, ambiguities and applications. In R. Vasta (Ed.), *Annals of child development* (Vol. 10, pp. 83–130). London: Jessica Kingsley.

Smith, E. A., & Bird, R. B. (2000). Turtle hunting and tombstone opening: Public generosity as costly signaling. *Evolution and Human Behavior, 21,* 245–261.

Snarey, J. R. (1985). Cross-cultural universality of social-moral development: A critical review of Kohlbergian research. *Psychological Bulletin, 97,* 202–232.

Sober, E., & Wilson, D. S. (1998). *Unto others: The evolution and psychology of unselfish behavior.* Cambridge: Harvard University Press.

Solomonson, A. L., & Lance, C. E. (1997). Examination of the relationship between true halo and halo error in performance ratings. *Journal of Applied Psychology, 82*(5), 665–674.

Song, M., Smetana, J., & Kim, S. Y. (1987). Korean children's conceptions of moral and conventional transgressions. *Developmental Psychology, 23,* 577–582.

Sorce, J. F., Emde, R. N., Campos, J. J., & Klinnert, M. D. (1985). Maternal emotional signaling: Its effect on the visual cliff behavior of 1-year-olds. *Developmental Psychology, 21,* 195–200.

Spelke, E. S. (1988). The origins of physical knowledge. In L. Weiskrantz (Ed.), *Thought without language* (pp. 168–184). Oxford: Clarendon Press.

Spelke, E. S. (1990). Principles of object perception. *Cognitive Science, 14,* 29–56.

Spelke, E. S. (2000). Core knowledge. *American Psychologist, 55*(11), 1233–1243.

Spencer, H. (1887). *The factors of organic evolution.* London: Williams & Norgate.

Sperber, D. (1994). The modularity of thought and the epidemiology of representations. In L. Hirschfeld & S. Gelman (Eds.), *Mapping the mind: Domain-specificity in cognition and culture* (pp. 39–67). New York: Cambridge University Press.

Sperber, D. (1996). *Explaining culture: A naturalistic approach.* Oxford: Blackwell.

Sperber, D., Cara, F., & Girotto, V. (1995). Relevance theory explains the selection task. *Cognition, 57,* 31–95.

Spinath, F. M., & O'Connor, T. G. (2003). A behavioral genetic study of the overlap between personality and parenting. *Journal of Personality, 71*(5), 785–808.

Spiro, M. (1958). *Children of the kibbutz.* Cambridge: Harvard University Press.

Sripada, C. S. (In preparation). *Carving the social world at its joints: Conventions and moral norms as natural kinds.*

Sripada, C., & Stich, S. (2006). A framework for the psychology of norms. In P. Carruthers, S. Laurence, & S. Stich (Eds.), *Innateness and the structure of the mind* (Vol. 2). New York: Oxford University Press.

Sripada, C. S., Stich, S. P., Kelly, D., & Doris, J. (In preparation). *Norms: Psychology, evolution and philosophy.*

Stevens, D., Charman, T., & Blair, R. J. R. (2001). Recognition of emotion in facial expressions and vocal tones in children with psychopathic tendencies. *The Journal of Genetic Psychology, 762*(2), 201–211.

Stevens J. R. (2004). The selfish nature of generosity: Harassment and food sharing in primates. *Proceedings of the Royal Society of London, B, 271,* 451–456.

Stevens, J. R., & Stephens, D. (2004). The economic basis of cooperation: Trade-offs between selfishness and generosity. *Behavioral Ecology, 15*(2), 255–261.

Stevenson, C. L. (1937). The emotive meaning of ethical terms. *Mind, 46,* 14–31.

Stich, S. P. (1993). Moral philosophy and mental representation. In M. Hechter, L. Nadel, & R. Michod (Eds.), *The origin of values* (pp. 215–228). Hawthorne, NY: Aldine de Gruyter.

Stohr, K., & Wellman, C. H. (2002). Recent work on virtue ethics. *American Philosophical Quarterly, 39*(1), 49–72.

Stone, V., Cosmides, L., Tooby, J., Kroll, N., & Knight, R. (2002). Selective impairment of reasoning about social exchange in a patient with bilateral limbic system damage. *Proceedings of the National Academy of Sciences, 99*(17), 11531–11536.

Stromme, P., Bjornstad, P. G., & Ramstad, K. (2002). Prevalence estimation of Williams syndrome. *Journal of Child Neurology, 17*(4), 269–271.

Stroud, B. (1996). The charm of naturalism. *Proceedings and Addresses of the American Philosophical Society, 70*, 43–55.

Sugiyama, L. S., & Sugiyama, M. S. (2003). Social roles, prestige, and health risk: Social niche specialization as a risk-buffering strategy. *Human Nature 14*(2), 165–190.

Sugiyama, L. S., Tooby, J., & Cosmides, L. (2002). Cross-cultural evidence of cognitive adaptations for social exchange among the Shiwiar of Ecuadorian Amazonia. *Proceedings of the National Academy of Sciences, 99*(17), 11537–11542.

Summers, K. (2005). The evolutionary ecology of despotism. *Evolution and Human Behavior, 26*, 106–135.

Sutherland, K., & Hughes, J. (2000). Is Darwin right? *Journal of Consciousness Studies, 7*(7), 63–86.

Symons, D. (1987). If we're all Darwinians, what's the fuss about? In C. B. Crawford, M. F. Smith, & D. L. Krebs (Eds.), *Sociobiology and psychology* (pp. 121–146). Hillsdale, NJ: Erlbaum.

Symons, D. (1995). Beauty is in the adaptations of the beholder: The evolutionary psychology of human female sexual attractiveness. In P. R. Abrahamson & S. D. Pinker (Eds.), *Sexual nature/sexual culture* (pp. 80–118). Chicago: University of Chicago Press.

Talmon, G. Y. (1964). Mate selection in collective settlements. *American Sociological Review, 29*, 408–491.

Tangney, J. P. (1999). The self-conscious emotions: Shame, guilt, embarrassment, and pride. In T. Dalgleish & M. Power (Eds.), *Handbook of cognition and emotion* (pp. 541–568). New York: Wiley.

Taylor, C. (1989). *Sources of the self.* Cambridge: Cambridge University Press.

Taylor, J., Loney, B. R., Bobadilla, L., Iacono, W. G., & McGue, M. (2003). Genetic and environmental influences on psychopathy trait dimensions in a community sample of male twins. *Journal of Abnormal Child Psychology, 31*(6), 633–645.

Teachman, B. A., & Brownell, K. D. (2001). Implicit anti-fat bias among health professionals: Is anyone immune? *International Journal of Obesity, 25*(10), 1525–1531.

Terrace, H. S., Petitto L. A., Sanders R. J., & Bever, T. G. (1979). Can an ape create a sentence? *Science, 206*(4421), 891–902.

Tessman, I. (1995). Human altruism as a courtship display. *Oikos, 74*(1), 157–158.

Thornhill, N. W. (1991). An evolutionary analysis of rules regulating human inbreeding and marriage. *Behavioral and Brain Sciences, 14,* 247–293.

Thornhill, R. (1998). Darwinian aesthetics. In C. Crawford & D. Krebs (Eds.), *Handbook of evolutionary psychology* (pp. 543–572). Mahwah, NJ: Erlbaum.

Thornhill, R., Gangestad, S. W., & Comer, R. (1995). Human female orgasm and mate fluctuating asymmetry. *Animal Behavior, 50*(6), 1601–1615.

Thornhill, R., & Palmer, C. T. (2000). *The natural history of rape: Biological bases of sexual coercion.* Cambridge, Mass.: MIT Press.

Tiberius, V. (2004). Cultural differences and philosophical accounts of well-being. *Journal of Happiness Studies, 5,* 293–314.

Tilley, J. (2002). Is youth a better predictor of sociopolitical values than is nationality? *Annals of the American Academy of Political and Social Science, 580,* 226–256.

Tinklepaugh, O. L. (1928). The self-mutilation of a male Macacus rhesus monkey. *Journal of Mammalogy, 9,* 293–300.

Todd, P. M., & Miller, G. F. (1997). Biodiversity through sexual selection. In C. G. Langton & K. Shimohara (Eds.), *Artificial life: Vol. V. Proceedings of the Fifth International Workshop on the Synthesis and Simulation of Living Systems* (pp. 289–299). Cambridge: MIT Press/Bradford Books.

Todd, P. M., & Miller, G. F. (1999). From pride and prejudice to persuasion: Satisficing in mate search. In G. Gigerenzer & P. M. Todd. (Eds.), *Simple heuristics that make us smart* (pp. 286–308). New York: Oxford University Press.

Tomkins, J. L., Radwan, J., Kotiaho, J. S., & Tregenza, T. (2004). Genic capture and resolving the lek paradox. *Trends in Ecology & Evolution, 19*(6), 323–328.

Tooby, J. (1975). The evolutionary psychology of incest avoidance and its impact on culture. *Proceedings of the Institute for Evolutionary Studies, 75*(1), 1–91.

Tooby, J. (1977). Factors governing optimal inbreeding. *Proceedings of the Institute for Evolutionary Studies, 77*(1), 1–54.

Tooby, J. (1982). Pathogens, polymorphism, and the evolution of sex. *Journal of Theoretical Biology, 97,* 557–576.

Tooby, J., & Cosmides, L. (1989, August). *The logic of threat.* Paper presented at the Human Behavior and Evolution Society, Evanston, IL.

Tooby, J., & Cosmides, L. (1992). The psychological foundations of culture. In J. H. Barkow, L. Cosmides, & J. Tooby (Eds.), *The adapted mind: Evolutionary psychology and the generation of culture* (pp. 19–136). New York: Oxford University Press.

Tooby, J., & Cosmides, L. (1996). Friendship and the Banker's Paradox: Other pathways to the evolution of adaptations for altruism. In W. G. Runciman, J. Maynard Smith, & R. I. M. Dunbar (Eds.), *Proceedings of the British Academy: Vol. 88. Evolution of social behaviour patterns in primates and man* (pp. 119–143). London: British Academy/Oxford University Press.

Tooby, J., & Cosmides, L. (1997, July 7). Letters to the Editor on Stephen Jay Gould's "Darwinian Fundamentalism" (June 12, 1997) and "Evolution: The Pleasures of Pluralism" (June 26, 1997). *The New York Review of Books.*

Tooby, J., & Cosmides, L. (2001). Does beauty build adapted minds? Toward an evolutionary theory of aesthetics, fiction and the arts. *SubStance, Issue 94/95, 30*(1), 6–27.

Tooby, J., & Cosmides, L. (2005). Conceptual foundations of evolutionary psychology. In D. M. Buss (Ed.), *The handbook of evolutionary psychology* (pp. 5–67). Hoboken, NJ: Wiley.

Tooby, J., & Cosmides, L. (In press-a). Ecological rationality in a multimodular mind. In J. Tooby & L. Cosmides (Eds.), *Evolutionary psychology: Foundational papers.* Cambridge: MIT Press.

Tooby, J., & Cosmides, L. (In press-b). The evolutionary psychology of the emotions and their relationship to internal regulatory variables. In M. Lewis & U. M. Haviland (Eds.), *Handbook of emotions, 3rd Edition.* NY: Guilford.

Tooby, J., Cosmides, L., & Barrett, H. C. (2005). Resolving the debate on innate ideas: Learnability constraints and the evolved interpenetration of motivational and conceptual functions. In P. Carruthers, S. Laurence, & S. Stich (Eds.), *The innate mind: Structure and contents* (pp. 305–337). New York: Oxford University Press.

Tooby, J., Cosmides, L., & Price, M. (2006). Cognitive adaptations for n-person exchange: The evolutionary roots of organizational behavior. *Managerial and Decision Economics, 27*, 103–129.

Torgersen, S., Kringlen, E., & Cramer, V. (2001). The prevalence of personality disorders in a community sample. *Archives of General Psychiatry, 58*(6), 590–596.

Townsend, J. M. (1998). Dominance, sexual activity, and sexual emotions. *Behavioral and Brain Sciences, 21*, 386.

Treisman, A. (1992). Perceiving and re-perceiving objects. *American Journal of Psychology, 47*(7), 862–875.

Treisman, A., & Gelade, G. (1980) A feature-integration theory of attention. *Cognitive Psychology, 12,* 97–136.

Trivers, R. L. (1971). The evolution of reciprocal altruism. *Quarterly Review of Biology, 46,* 35–57.

Trivers, R. L. (1972). Parental investment and sexual selection. In M. B. Campbell (Ed.), *Sexual selection and the descent of man* (pp. 136–179). Chicago: Aldine.

Trivers, R. L. (1974). Parent-offspring conflict. *American Zoologist, 14,* 249–264.

Turiel, E. (1983). *The development of social knowledge: Morality and convention.* New York: Cambridge University Press.

Turiel, E. (1998). The development of morality. In N. Eisenberg (Ed.), *Handbook of child psychology: Vol. 3. Social, emotional, and personality development* (pp. 863–932). New York: Wiley.

Turiel, E. (2002). *The culture of morality: Social development, context, and conflict.* Cambridge: Cambridge University Press.

Urbaniak, G. C., & Kilman, P. R. (2003). Physical attractiveness and the "nice guy paradox": Do nice guys really finish last? *Sex Roles, 49*(9–10), 413–426.

Vahed, K. (1998). The function of nuptial feeding in insects: Review of empirical studies. *Biological Reviews, 73*(1), 43–78.

Van Hiel, A., Mervielde, I., & De Fruyt, F. (2004). The relationship between maladaptive personality and right wing ideology. *Personality and Individual Differences, 36*(2), 405–417.

Veblen, T. (1994). *The theory of the leisure class.* Mineola, NY: Dover. (Original work published 1899)

Visser, P. S., & Krosnick, J. A. (1998). Development of attitude strength over the life cycle: Surge and decline. *Journal of Personality and Social Psychology, 75*(6), 1389–1410.

Voltura, K. M., Schwagmeyer, P. L., & Mock, D. W. (2002). Parental feeding rates in the house sparrow, *Passer domesticus*: Are larger-badged males better fathers? *Ethology, 108*(11), 1011–1022.

de Waal, F. B. M. (1996). *Good natured: The origins of right and wrong in humans and other animals.* Cambridge: Harvard University Press.

de Waal, F. B. M. (2000). Primates: A natural heritage of conflict resolution. *Science, 289*(5479), 586–590.

Wakefield, J. C. (1999). Evolutionary versus prototype analysis of the concept of disorder. *Journal of Abnormal Psychology, 108,* 374–399.

Wald, N. J., Rodeck, C., Hackshaw, A. K., Walters, J., Chitty, L., & Mackinson, A. M. (2003). First and second trimester antenatal screening for Down's syndrome: The results of the Serum, Urine and Ultrasound Screening Study (SURUSS). *Journal of Medical Screening, 10*(2), 56–104.

Waldman, B. (1987). Mechanisms of kin recognition. *Journal of Theoretical Biology, 128,* 159–185.

Wason, P. (1966). Reasoning. In B. M. Foss (Ed.), *New horizons in psychology* (pp. 135–151). Harmondsworth, England: Penguin.

Wason, P. (1983). Realism and rationality in the selection task. In J. St. B. T. Evans (Ed.), *Thinking and reasoning: Psychological approaches* (pp. 44–75). London: Routledge.

Wason, P., & Johnson-Laird, P. (1972). *The psychology of reasoning: Structure and content.* Cambridge: Harvard University Press.

Watanabe, S., & Ono, K. (1986). An experimental analysis of "empathic" response: Effects of pain reactions of pigeon upon other pigeon's operant behavior, *Behavioural Processes, 13,* 269–277.

Wedekind, C., & Furi, S. (1997). Body odour preferences in men and women: Do they aim for specific MHC combinations or simply heterozygosity? *Proceedings of the Royal Society of London, B, 264,* 1471–1479.

Wedekind, C., Seebeck, T., Bettens, F., & Paepke, A. (1995). MHC-dependent mate preferences in humans. *Proceedings of the Royal Society of London, B, 260,* 245–249.

Wegener, J., Baare, W., Hede, A., Ramsoy, T., & Lund, T. (2004, October). *Social relative to non-social reasoning activates regions within anterior prefrontal cortex and temporal cortex.* Paper presented at Abstracts of the Society for Neuroscience, San Diego, CA.

Wegner, D. M. (2002). *The illusion of conscious will.* Cambridge: MIT Press.

Weisfeld, G. E. (1999). *Evolutionary principles of human adolescence.* New York: Basic Books.

Weisfeld, G. E., Czilli, T., Phillips, K., Gall, J. A., & Lichtman, C. M. (2003). Possible olfaction-based mechanisms in human kin recognition and inbreeding avoidance. *Journal of Experimental Child Psychology, 85,* 279–295.

West, S. R., & Salovey, P. (2004). A social comparison account of gossip. *Review of General Psychology, 8*(2), 122–137.

Westermarck, E. (1922). *History of human marriage* (Vol. 2). New York: Allerton. (Original work published 1891)

Westermarck, E. (1932a). *Ethical relativity*. London: Kegan Paul, Trench, Trubner.

Westermarck, E. (1932b). *The origin and development of the moral ideas*. London: Macmillan. (Original work published 1906 and 1912)

Wexler, K., & Culicover, P. (1980). *Formal principles of language acquisition*. Cambridge: MIT Press.

Whalley, L. J., & Deary, I. J. (2001). Longitudinal cohort study of childhood IQ and survival up to age 76. *British Medical Journal, 322*(7290), 819–822.

Wheatley, T., & Haidt, J. (2005). Hypnotically induced disgust makes moral judgments more severe. *Psychological Science, 16*, 780–784.

White, L. (1948). The definition and prohibition of incest. *American Anthropologist, 50*, 417.

Whitehouse, H. (1999). *Arguments and icons*. Oxford: Oxford University Press.

Wieselquist, J., Rusbult, C. E., Foster, C. A., & Agnew, C. R. (1999). Commitment, pro-relationship behavior, and trust in close relationships. *Journal of Personality and Social Psychology, 77*(5), 942–966.

Williams, G. C. (1966). *Adaptation and natural selection*. Princeton, NJ: Princeton University Press.

Williams, L. M., & Finkelhor, D. (1995). Paternal caregiving and incest: Test of a biosocial model. *American Journal of Orthopsychiatry, 65*, 101–113.

Williams, S. S. (2001). Sexual lying among college students in close and casual relationships. *Journal of Applied Social Psychology, 31*(11), 2322–2338.

Wilson, D. R. (1998). Evolutionary epidemiology and manic depression. *British Journal of Medical Psychiatry, 71*, 367–395.

Wilson, D. S., Near, D., & Miller, R. R. (1996). Machiavellianism: A synthesis of the evolutionary and psychological literatures. *Psychological Bulletin, 119*(2), 285–299.

Wilson, D. S., Timmel, J. J., & Miller, R. R. (2004). Cognitive cooperation: When the going gets tough, think as a group. *Human Nature, 15*(3), 225–250.

Wilson, E. O. (1978). *On human nature*. Cambridge: Cambridge University Press.

Wilson, E. O. (1984). *Biophilia*. Cambridge: Harvard University Press.

Wilson M., & Daly, M. (1992). The man who mistook his wife for chattel. In J. Barkow, L. Cosmides, & J. Tooby (Eds.), *The adapted mind: Evolutionary psychology and the generation of culture* (pp. 289–322). New York: Oxford University Press.

Wolf, A. P. (1995). *Sexual attraction and childhood association: A Chinese brief for Edward Westermarck*. Palo Alto, CA: Stanford University Press.

Wolf, A. P. (2005a). Explaining the Westermarck effect. In A. P. Wolf & W. H. Durham (Eds.), *Inbreeding, incest, and the incest taboo* (pp. 76–92). Palo Alto, CA: Stanford University Press.

Wolf, A. P. (2005b). Introduction. In A. P. Wolf & W. H. Durham (Eds.), *Inbreeding, incest, and the incest taboo* (pp. 1–23). Palo Alto, CA: Stanford University Press.

Wolf, A. P., & Durham, W. H. (2005). *Inbreeding, incest, and the incest taboo.* Palo Alto, CA: Stanford University Press.

Wolf, A. P., & Huang, C. (1980). *Marriage and adoption in China 1845–1945.* Palo Alto, CA: Stanford University Press.

Wolfe, J. M. (2003). Moving towards solutions to some enduring controversies in visual search. *Trends in Cognitive Sciences, 7*(2), 70–76.

Wong, D. B. (1984). *Moral relativity.* Berkeley: University of California Press.

Wong, D. B. (1996). Pluralistic relativism. *Midwest Studies in Philosophy, 20,* 378–400.

Wong, D. B. (2006a). Moral reasons: Internal and external. *Philosophy and Phenomenological Research 72.*

Wong, D. B. (2006b). *Natural moralities.* New York: Oxford University Press.

Woodburn, J. (1968). An introduction to Hadza ecology. In R. B. Lee & I. Devore (Eds.), *Man the hunter* (pp. 49–55). New York: Aldine de Gruyter.

Wrangham, R. (2004). Killer species. *Daedalus, 133,* 25–35.

Wrangham, R., & Peterson, D. (1996). *Demonic males: Apes and the origins of human violence.* New York: Houghton Mifflin.

von Wright, G. H. (1951). Deontic logic. *Mind 60,* 1–15.

Wynne, C. D. L. (2004) Fair refusal by capuchin monkeys. *Nature, 428,* 140.

Yachanin, S., & Tweney, R. (1982). The effect of thematic content on cognitive strategies in the four-card selection task. *Bulletin of the Psychonomic Society, 19,* 87–90.

Yamazaki, K., Boyse, E. A., Mike, V., Thaler, H. T., Mathieson, B. J., Abbott, J., Boyse, J., Zayas, Z. A., & Thomas, L. (1976). Control of mating preferences in mice by genes in the major histocompatibility complex. *Journal of Experimental Medicine, 144,* 1324–1335.

Yamazaki, K., Beauchamp, G. K., Kupniewski, D., Bard, J., Thomas, L., & Boyse, E. A. (1988). Familial imprinting determines H-2 selective mating preferences. *Science, 240,* 1331–1332.

Zagzebski, L. (1996). *Virtues of the mind*. Cambridge: Cambridge University Press.

Zahavi, A. (1975). Mate selection: A selection for a handicap. *Journal of Theoretical Biology, 53*, 205–214.

Zahavi, A., & Zahavi, A. (1997). *The handicap principle: A missing piece of Darwin's puzzle*. New York: Oxford University Press.

Zahnwaxler, C., Emde, R. N., & Robinson, J. L. (1992). The development of empathy in twins. *Developmental Psychology, 28*(6), 1038–1047.

Contributors

William D. Casebeer
Air Force Academy

Leda Cosmides
University of California, Santa Barbara

Oliver Curry
London School of Economics

Michael Dietrich
Dartmouth College

Catherine Driscoll
North Carolina State University

Susan Dwyer
University of Maryland, Baltimore County

Owen Flanagan
Duke University

Jerry Fodor
Rutgers University

Gilbert Harman
Princeton University

Richard Joyce
Australian National University and the University of Sydney

Debra Lieberman
University of Hawaii

Ron Mallon
University of Utah

John Mikhail
Georgetown University Law Center

Geoffrey Miller
University of New Mexico

Jesse J. Prinz
University of North Carolina at Chapel Hill

Peter Railton
University of Michigan

Michael Ruse
Florida State University

Hagop Sarkissian
Duke University

Walter Sinnott-Armstrong
Dartmouth College

Chandra Sekhar Sripada
University of Michigan

Valerie Tiberius
University of Minnesota

John Tooby
University of California, Santa Barbara

Peter Ulric Tse
Dartmouth College

Kathleen Wallace
Hofstra University

Arthur P. Wolf
Stanford University

David Wong
Duke University

Index to Volume 1

Note: Figures are indicated by "f"; tables are indicated by "t," and footnotes by "*n.*"

Index to Volume 2

Figures are indicated by "f"; tables are indicated by "t," and footnotes by "*n*."

Index to Volume 3

Figures are indicated by "f"; tables are indicated by "t," and footnotes by "n."